Struggle and Survival in the
Modern Middle East

Struggle and Survival in the Modern Middle East

Second Edition

EDITED BY

Edmund Burke, III and David N. Yaghoubian

UNIVERSITY OF CALIFORNIA PRESS

Berkeley   Los Angeles   London

University of California Press, one of the most distinguished university presses in the United States, enriches lives around the world by advancing scholarship in the humanities, social sciences, and natural sciences. Its activities are supported by the UC Press Foundation and by philanthropic contributions from individuals and institutions. For more information, visit www.ucpress.edu.

University of California Press
Berkeley and Los Angeles, California

University of California Press, Ltd.
London, England

Library of Congress Cataloging-in-Publication Data

Struggle and survival in the modern Middle East / [edited by] Edmund Burke III and David N. Yaghoubian.— 2nd ed.
    p.   cm.
Includes bibliographical references and index.
ISBN 978-0-520-24661-4 (pbk. : alk. paper)
    1. Middle East—Biography.   I. Burke, Edmund, 1940–   II. Yaghoubian, David N. (Nejde), 1967–

CT1866.S77 2006
920.056—dc22

2005005762

Manufactured in the United States of America
16   15   14   13   12   11   10   09
11   10   9   8   7   6   5   4   3

This book is printed on New Leaf EcoBook 60, containing 60% post-consumer waste, processed chlorine free; 30% de-inked recycled fiber, elemental chlorine free; and 10% FSC-certified virgin fiber, totally chlorine free. EcoBook 60 is acid-free and meets the minimum requirements of ANSI/ASTM D5634–01 *(Permanence of Paper).*

CONTENTS

PREFACE

The present book draws its inspiration from David G. Sweet and Gary B. Nash's collection of biographies of ordinary men and women from colonial Latin America and the United States, *Struggle and Survival in the Colonial Americas* (Berkeley: University of California Press, 1981). In an era of increasing specialization, Sweet and Nash provide a human dimension to the colonial history of the Americas, offering vivid glimpses into the lived lives of real people, rather than the sterile abstractions of strict historical analysis. Their book illuminates how non-elite people managed their lives, often in the face of extreme hardship and oppression.

We believe that a similar approach has great potential for opening up the history of the modern Middle East. This book is a collaborative effort of twenty-seven individuals, for the most part unknown to one another. Through the lives of ordinary Middle Eastern men and women, it presents Middle Eastern history as it might appear when viewed from the bottom up. In the process, it exposes the discrepancy between the abstractions that are used to characterize Middle Eastern history as it is taught and written— modernization, imperialism, and nationalism—and how events were actually experienced by most people.

When we sat down to write the introduction, we were quite unprepared for the power with which this message emerged from a reading of the stories included in the volume. Official sources and the dominance of political and institutional history have masked the range of variation in views. Taken together, the biographies suggest some ways that Middle Eastern history may be rewritten to take full account of the perspectives of most Middle Easterners.

That the book exists at all is a minor miracle. This diverse collection of biographies was drawn together with no financial backing (save small grants from the University of California, Santa Cruz, Faculty Research Committee and Division of Humanities for the first edition) and no commitment from anyone but the authors. Because our disciplines are after larger, more prestigious quarry than the biographies of ordinary people, every contribution is therefore precious.

The second edition of this book has a new section, "Contemporary Lives," consisting of six new biographies. We are grateful to the new contributors, whose willingness to give this work priority often came at the expense of their other responsibilities. We hope they find in the finished book some recompense for their labor. Many individuals have contributed to the successful completion of this edition. Individuals who read one or more essays include Joel Beinin, Hugh Roberts, and Daniel Schroeter. Special thanks go to Mary Wilson, whose selfless editorial suggestions and critical advice were much appreciated. Patricia Sanders edited the entire manuscript with unfailing good humor and efficiency. Her high standards and critical judgment helped make it a better work. We also wish to thank Lynne Withey of the University of California Press, whose strong encouragement has been crucial.

Transliteration is always a problem when one is dealing with Middle Eastern languages. Because this book is addressed to a wide audience, a simplified system of transliteration from Arabic, Persian, and Turkish has been adopted. Diacritical marks and the Arabic letters hamza and ayn have usually been omitted. Standard Arabic terms used in variant versions in different countries have generally been spelled in their modified Arabic forms (e.g., Sharia, *ulama*). Geographical and proper names and terms peculiar to particular regions have been included in the form to which people reading the regional literatures are accustomed. A glossary at the back of the book provides complete transliterations and definitions of key terms.

Each chapter includes a brief editorial introduction to contextualize the story and suggest some connections between it and other selections. Readers are encouraged to develop their own connections between the selections as well.

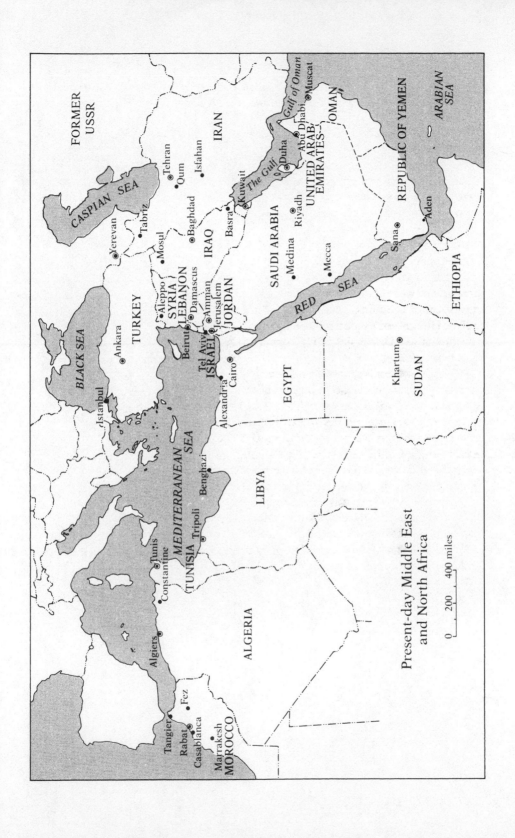

Present-day Middle East
and North Africa

0   200   400 miles

Chapter 1

Middle Eastern Societies and Ordinary People's Lives

Rethinking Middle Eastern History

Edmund Burke, III and David N. Yaghoubian

Despite a great deal of useful research on the histories of modern Middle Eastern societies, we know little of the lives of ordinary Middle Eastern men and women. Instead, we see the Middle East over the shoulders of diplomats, military officers, entrepreneurs, and bureaucrats. This essentially elite perspective has focused on the "big story": the coming to modernity of Middle Eastern states and societies, and the operation of large-scale historical forces. In the process, the perspectives of those who were on the receiving end of these changes have generally been neglected.

As a result, we tend to see the fate of the Middle East, or of Islamic societies, as determined by one or another impersonal historical force whose operation was decisive. For some authors, this force is religion; for others, capitalism, imperialism, oriental despotism, or economic dependency. These views, despite their often contradictory explanations of the mainsprings of change, have portrayed Middle Easterners as marionettes in a historical drama not of their devising, rather than as flesh-and-blood individuals with some capacity to affect their own life chances. Deprived of agency, they have become what Eric Wolf calls "peoples without history."[1]

Often unexamined, these determinisms still govern the way most of us think about the Middle East. However, they fail to take account of the complex historical processes, structural forms, and cultural patterns that have shaped the context within which individuals have lived. Instead, they provide us with a kind of just-so story (or rather a series of often conflicting just-so stories). By privileging particular groups' understanding of the past, such views have skewed our sense of how that past actually came about, and have simultaneously delegitimized the self-understanding of other groups.

Politics, however, was not always or invariably the determining factor in most people's lives, and the ups and downs of the economic roller coaster affected different people in different ways. No one schema can make sense of the quite varied historical experiences covered in this book: those of Middle Easterners from Morocco to Afghanistan, and from the middle of the nineteenth century to the present.

Instead of starting from broad generalizations about Islam or the Ottoman state, or from stereotypes about the Arab mind or Islam, a rereading of the history of the Middle East should put the experiences of ordinary men and women at its center. This new kind of history would begin with the notion that different ecologies, ways of life, and ethnic, class, and gender situations shaped individual possibilities of action. The biographies of ordinary Middle Eastern men and women in this book provide a series of vantage points from which to undertake such a rereading. (Below, we reflect on the nature of such a rereading, based on the contributions in this book.)

This book focuses on the biographies of ordinary people rather than on the lives of officials, military officers, and intellectuals. By "ordinary people" we mean the "peoples without history"—which includes non-elite men and most women (for example, tribal elite women), namely, those whose experiences have generally been left out of the history books. This is not to say that the individuals whose lives are chronicled here are ordinary. The very fact that enough information exists about them to make possible a brief biography makes them, by definition, extraordinary. As we will soon see, some of those whose lives are chronicled here were of humble origins and later moved up in the social pecking order, or became well known locally for one or another reason. Others started and remained artisans, peasants, and tribespeople and might have remained unknown but for a chance event—the opening of an official file, an encounter with an anthropologist, the desire of a descendant to explore the family tree.

A question that may arise concerns the extent to which the biographies included in this volume can be seen as typical of Middle Easterners. Despite an energetic effort to cast the net as widely as possible, not all groups are represented within these pages. Given the ethnic, linguistic, and religious diversity of the region, a comprehensive inclusiveness—a kind of Noah's Ark principle of coverage—is quite impossible. Rather, the not entirely random selection of biographies provides a set of core samples aimed at helping us understand the transformations that Middle Eastern societies have undergone since the beginning of the nineteenth century. They spotlight the dynamism of Middle Eastern men and women, as well as their attachment to old ways of doing things. At a time when the Middle East is often harshly caricatured in Western society, these portraits of ordinary men and women and their struggles and attempts to survive in a context of great uncertainty and risk serve to assert our common humanity. The sheer variety of so broad a historical and geographical sample also suggests the need to rethink much of the conventional wisdom about Middle Eastern society. In this sense, we hope that the present volume is not an end but a beginning.

To provide a framework for readers lacking a knowledge of the histories of particular Middle Eastern societies, this book is organized chronologically. Other arrangements (geographical or regional or by gender, class, or way of life) can, however, be imagined, and the reader is encouraged to develop his or her own alternative thematic or regional focus. (For example, one might wish to group the biographies of peasants, North Africans, women, or minorities.) To promote alternative foci, each chapter is preceded by a brief introduction by the editors. The chapter introductions have two purposes: to provide a historical, political, and methodological context for the essay in question, and to suggest connections with some of the other selections.

Given the uneven impact of change between and within modern Middle Eastern societies from Morocco to Afghanistan, the chronological structure of the book should be taken as a set of floating benchmarks, not a fixed Procrustean scheme. Its purpose is to draw attention to what is similar in the historical experiences of the different societies of the area, not to argue for a particular, unilinear sequence of causality. The specific pace of change varied from place to place and mattered crucially both for ordinary people and for the particular outcomes in particular places. The arrangement of the chapters in this volume has been shaped by these considerations.

Middle Eastern men and women responded to often difficult circumstances in different ways. Struggle was one dimension of their individual stories: defiance of the guild master, the cruel government official, the "system" in all its manifestations. Such efforts were by their very nature uncommon, for those in power possessed not only superior force but also (even under colonialism) a measure of cultural hegemony—what Eugene Genovese in another context has referred to as "invisible shackles of the mind."[2] Some of the individuals we will encounter in these pages were nonetheless heroes of a sort. But (as we will see) even anticolonial resistance was not an unalloyed impulse. Rather, it could, and did, often mask the settling of old scores, the chance for quick gain. (To study the roots of nationalism through the lives of ordinary people is to encounter the density and confusion of micropolitics, where moral choices were not always clear and options not unlimited.) Moreover, seen in one way a strategy of resistance might seem heroic, when from another optic it could seem quixotic. When we look at the successive strategies of an individual's entire life, coherence is hard to find.

More common was the tenacious and often courageous effort of common folk to hang in there, to survive against all odds. Rascals and scoundrels might prove better survivors for a time, but the operation of the wheel of fortune did not permit many to escape from misfortune for long.

The possibilities for individual action derived in part from the social cards an individual was dealt at birth (gender, class, and ethnicity foremost among them). But they were also determined by personal character and chance. Struggle and survival, then, are not exclusive, mutually contradictory categories, but dimensions within a field of power in which the terms are constantly shifting over time.

Part 1, titled "Precolonial Lives," contains biographies of individuals whose lives were largely untouched by the shadow of the West. Most, but not all, of them lived in the period from 1850 to World War I. Their existence was shaped by the structures of the old society: artisan guilds, kinship groups, ethnic communities. Although already in the throes of change when the nineteenth century began, as several examples show, these structures proved remarkably resilient. They also provided considerable resources for resistance and accommodation to change.

Part 2, "Colonial Lives," contains essays about persons whose lives were primarily shaped by the experiences of nationalism and colonialism.[3] Because the chronology of European rule differed from country to country within the region as a whole,[4] this section includes individuals who lived in the nineteenth as well as the twentieth century. The colonial encounter was complex and affected people differently depending upon their specific situations. Some were able to trade upon their skills and connections to advance their personal and family fortunes. Others, less favorably situated, found the going rough. Navigating in the constantly shifting political and economic tides presented tricky problems to all.

In Part 3, "Postcolonial Lives," we encounter Middle Easterners who came to maturity after World War II. Shaped by the harsher realities of nationalist and Islamic movements, the boom-and-bust cycles of the world oil market, wars, civil strife, and foreign occupation, individuals who came to maturity in this period had substantially different experiences than their parents and grandparents. Taken together, they give us a portrait, incomplete it is true, of some of the ways people have tried to cope with the dizzying transformations of the postwar era.

Part 4, "Contemporary Lives," introduces us to individuals whose lives have been shaped by recent events, including the 1990–91 Gulf War, which begins our period, and the recent U.S. interventions in Afghanistan and Iraq, which conclude it. The phase of history that began with the events of September 11, 2001, of course, is not over. So our periodization therefore can only be regarded as an interim marking of historical terrain that is largely uncharted. The attack on the Twin Towers and the Pentagon did not spring from a historical void but had deep roots in the postwar legacy of U.S. involvement in the region and the manifest incompetencies of Middle Eastern leaders. Thus, the events of 9/11 are to be understood not as a beginning but as a rising to the surface of trends already visible in the previous period. Similarly, the events of 9/11 are not in any sense to be understood as an end point to what had preceded. The forces of economic globalization, demographic increase, and political repression that we have already observed in the postcolonial period continue unabated. In this context, pious hopes for democratization appear implausible, or destabilizing if fulfilled. One thing we can say is that the lives of Americans and Middle Easterners, already interlinked by migration and trade, will be increasingly interwoven for the foreseeable future, whether for good or ill. The biographies in part 4 make us wonder whether the issue is "Why do they hate us?" or instead "What have we done to so enrage them?" It is vitally important for Americans to understand the human context in which Middle Easterners struggle to survive.

SOCIAL BIOGRAPHY AND SOCIAL THEORY

In a sense, this volume brings the field of Middle Eastern history full circle. Biography gave an early impetus to the writing of Islamic history, largely because of the central place in Islamic piety and scholarship occupied by the figure of Muhammad. The need for information about his life, seen by Muslims as a model of correct behavior, spawned a host of biographies. The most famous, Ibn Ishaq's *Sirat rasul Allah* (c. 809 C.E.), quickly acquired canonical status. For information about Muhammad, Muslims looked not only to the Quran but also to the living memory of the community. Eventually, these traditions, called *hadith* reports, were collected and written down. Over time, the Quran and *hadith* reports came to form the basis of Islamic law, the Sharia.[5]

The need to distinguish reliable *hadith* reports from pious legend provided a second impulse to the writing of biography. This took the form of a new genre of Islamic scholarship known as *tabaqat*, which contained biographies of the first generations of Muslims that focused on their ethical character and, hence, reliability as transmitters of *hadith* reports.[6] Later, *tabaqat* came to include not just the lives of the early companions of the Prophet but also of Islamic scholars (*ulama*), Sufi mystics, and notables (*ayan*) of particular cities. The *tabaqat* literature is voluminous, and more continues to be produced to this day. While *tabaqat* writings lack much that we would recognize as biography (including a sense of individual psychology), their focus on the person provides a valuable source for social history, especially for prosopography (group biography).[7] Of course, biography provided only one of the sources for Islamic history writing. Other sources included pre-Islamic Arabian tribal sagas and imperial chronicles (the best-known example of which is the monumental *History* of Tabari).[8]

In the West, biography is a well-established genre, though until recently a disfavored one in historical writing. Because it is a primary site for exploring the connections of social and cultural processes, biography has grown in importance if anything in recent times. Some exemplary histories that utilize biography in this way include Natalie Davis's *The Return of Martin Guerre,* Carlo Ginzburg's *The Cheese and the Worms,* and Jonathan Spence's *The Death of Woman Wang.*[9]

There has been a resurgence of interest in biography in the social sciences as well, notably in anthropology and sociology. In anthropology, where the relationship of the anthropologist to his or her indigenous collaborator has been a constant incitement to "read" the culture through the life of the informant, the genre has been well established since Franz Boas.[10] Recently, anthropologists have begun to acknowledge the role of their informants in their work, and to recognize that anthropological knowledge by its nature is a joint product reflecting the field situation.[11] In sociology, too, biography may now once again be coming to the fore, against the background of the statistical modeling that has become increasingly typical in that discipline. This move represents a renewal of an earlier tradition embodied in such classics as Eliott Liebow's *Tally's Corner.*[12]

Because social theories tend to be partial rather than totalizing (focusing, for example, on political or economic behavior), while real lives sprawl in their sheer exuberance across conventional categories, the patterns of individual lives elude even the best theories. The biographical approach holds out the promise of reinvigorating the relationship between social theory and empirical research. The credibility of biographies comes from the concrete details they convey about a particular life and how it was lived. The more accounts of lives we have, the better we will be able to assess their typicality and to understand individual survival strategies. It is because biography can provide fundamental insights into social and cultural processes that it was privileged by Wilhelm Dilthey and his followers.[13]

We use the term *social biography* to refer to the use of biography to explore the complex ways in which individuals navigate amidst social structures, processes, and cultural interactions. Social biography can be distinguished from literary biography, which tends to center upon the inner world or psychology of the subject and its relationship to the dynamics of the life of the individual.[14] Social biographies, especially when deployed as part of a broader research strategy, can test and refine social theories, as well as provide an alternative vantage point from which to think about the historical processes by which societies have been continually transformed.

Since World War II, growing epistemological self-consciousness has made us aware of the ways in which language structures the ways that we think about the world. Much of the heightened awareness focuses on the act of writing in the production of social scientific knowledge.[15] Literary and scientific activities are not as distinct as previously thought. Both are primarily interpretive and focus on the analysis and the production of texts (whether literary or social). Cultural interpretation and social scientific knowledge in general are inextricably connected to the specific rhetorical envelope in which they are conveyed.[16] Put more directly, there is no easily discoverable distinction between literature and social science. The facts are not separable from their literary embodiment. Rather, their very "factness" derives from the way in which they are related.

What are the implications of these reflections for the biographies in this volume? First, we must recognize that the essays in this volume are *stories*. They seek to make sense of the life of a single individual or related individuals. As stories (some more self-conscious than others) they *represent* to us the experience of people whose culture differs from our own. This they do on the basis of information gathered from historical documents, or from the fading memories of family members and anthropological informants, or from both together. Like all good stories, their narratives are designed to lead the reader to have a degree of empathy and understanding for the main characters. Their manner of doing so, however, varies considerably.

To recognize that biographies are manifestly literary products as well as products of the historical/sociological imagination is not to discount their truth value, but only to qualify it. Like all other exercises in the human sciences, social biographies are constrained by the ways language struggles to mediate between that which is observed and that which is experienced, knowing that the gap is not fully bridgeable because the "factness" of what is seen is always potentially debatable, contingent, and partial. The point is not that anything goes, but that history has only the sense we give to it, and that sense necessarily changes along with the world we live in.[17]

While we have acquired a vast amount of knowledge about the Middle East and its diverse peoples, that knowledge tends not to be reflected in the stereotypical images of the region current in the West. Each major political development in the Middle East is confidently analyzed by self-proclaimed experts as demonstrating the existence of a supposedly perennial "Muslim fanaticism," the unchanging nature of the "Arab mind," or the pulse of the "Arab street." The contrast between the knowledge that has been accumulated and the persistent racist nonsense about Middle Eastern people is striking.

Since the appearance of Edward Said's *Orientalism*,[18] we have become aware of the ways in which Western representations of Middle Eastern culture have been intertwined with the fact of European dominance of the area. Orientalism was a discipline that studied Asian civilizations through an examination of their allegedly characteristic cultural products (the Quran or other texts). By privileging certain texts as the sole authoritative sources of religious and cultural norms and neglecting others that qualify or contradict them, orientalists claimed to provide an explanation for Muslim behavior valid for all times and places.

The intersecting series of more or less connected cultural stereotypes about Islam and Middle Easterners can be called the colonial gospel. In it, Middle Easterners are represented as congenitally fatalistic, fanatical, cowardly, treacherous, despotic, sexually repressed, and patriarchal (among other things).[19] The colonial gospel constitutes an ever-present reservoir of stereotypes of the Middle Eastern "other" that purports to explain why "they" differ from "us."[20] Indeed, it undergirds the political language of the post-9/11 era, based upon the supposed existence of a "clash of civilizations," to which the biographies in this volume provide the most eloquent response.

Biographies of Middle Easterners have helped to disseminate these popular images. They play an important role in shaping Daniel Lerner's *Passing of Traditional Societies,* a classic of 1950s modernization theory in which the stereotypical biographies of the Grocer and the Chief serve as a central organizing motif.[21] Another example is Richard Critchfield's widely read *Shahhat: An Egyptian,*[22] which through the portrait of an allegedly typical peasant seeks to represent all Egyptian peasants. Shahhat, the subject of this study, is a quarrelsome, superstitious youth whose personality traits nicely conform to standard Western cultural stereotypes about shiftless Egyptian peasants. A recent critical review has suggested that there are particular reasons to distrust this work.[23] Whatever the circumstances of its preparation, what interests me about Critchfield's account in the present context is the way in which it recycles the colonial image of Egyptians.

Because the complexities of the area are so daunting, it is tempting to read Middle Eastern society through the lives of a few individuals. A homogenized and essentialist Middle East enables us to avoid engaging the historical and cultural specificities of the various groups and peoples who live there. Cultural stereotypes, by contrast, enable us to attain a misleading mastery. When those stereotypes also reinforce our sense of cultural superiority, they may well appear irresistible. There is, therefore, reason for reflection—reading the society through the lives of a few supposedly typical individuals is ultimately a quixotic venture.

How then to avoid falling into this trap? It is important to be wary of explanations that invoke allegedly innate psychological traits, such as "the Arab mind," "the fatalism of the Egyptian peasant," and the like, in place of a more historically grounded examination. While for some it may seem satisfying to view the turbulent politics of the Middle East as deriving from "tribes with flags,"[24] it is well to question such essentialist metaphors closely if we would seek a deeper understanding. More successful works, such as Roy Mottahedeh's portrait of an Iranian *mullah* in *The Mantle of the Prophet* or Erika Friedl's *Women of Deh Koh,*[25] locate their subjects in particular sociological and cultural, as well as historical, contexts, and do not invoke broad psychological or cultural traits in explanation. They are social biographies in their commitment to change and complexity, as well as to the individuality of their subjects.[26]

By their sheer variety, the twenty-four lives presented in this book constitute a potent antidote to the homogenizing and essentialist impulse. While different themes can be traced in these biographies, no one of them applies to all cases. The absolute diversity of the lives works to undermine the "verities" of the colonial vulgate. The very number of lives is an incitement to thought, for one is compelled to consider the particular factors that appear to have been significant in shaping the individual lives recounted here and to locate them in a complex and historical context. Different sources, authorial viewpoints, and connections to the subject also work to undermine efforts to extract a particular theme or lesson about Arabs, Muslims, or Middle Easterners that can apply to all experiences.

So many different cases provide the opportunity to ask some interesting questions about the impact of change and how particular groups and individuals responded. How much were women or tribespeople or villagers (to select a few examples) influenced by the particular social and cultural environments in which they existed? How important were family and patron/client connections in providing access to crucial resources? How did the modernization of society affect the life chances of particular individuals? How important was individual personality or historical conjuncture?

The biographies included here allow us to refine our understanding of how particular groups were affected by large-scale historical processes like Ottoman modernization, European colonialism, and nationalism. In this way, we can begin to develop a new understanding of the history of the region keyed to gender, ethnicity, religion, class, ecology, and way of life. In the remainder of this chapter, we explore how the history of the Middle East might be rethought from the vantage point of the ordinary people whose lives are described in this book.

MIDDLE EASTERN HISTORY
AND THE EXPERIENCE OF ORDINARY PEOPLE

Precolonial Lives

The lives of the men and women we encounter in part 1 were shaped by the urban and agrarian structures of the Ottoman Empire and the Iranian and Moroccan monarchies. Their identities derived from their family, occupation, and religion (for some, tribal affiliation was also important) rather than from their nationality or class position. Most nineteenth-century Middle Easterners expected to contend with adversity and cyclical change. But few could have imagined the extent to which their world would be altered by far-reaching forces of social change persisting over time.

Essentially, the changes they confronted were of three sorts: (1) the Ottoman *tanzimat* reforms, (2) the incorporation of the Middle East into the world economy, and (3) the growing power of the West. Each type of change had consequences that affected not just the state but also the society and individuals, opening options for some and closing them off for others. In the process, old social groups and old ways of doing things were supplemented and eventually supplanted by new classes and new ways of behaving.

Since we sometimes tend to forget that many of the chief features of the contemporary Middle East are of recent origin, it is important to add that these changes affected different groups at different rates, and some regions more than others. Until 1880, neither nationalism nor Western power, both of which were significantly to mark the region in the twentieth century, was as yet a dominant factor outside of the Balkan provinces of the Ottoman Empire. This is not to suggest that premodern Middle Eastern society was static and unchanging, as has sometimes been proposed. Nor were the old structures so oppressive as to exclude even relatively poor and powerless individuals from the possibility of some modest social mobility.

The main sources of disruption of people's lives during the nineteenth century were the *tanzimat* reforms and the incorporation of the Middle East into the world economy. Everyday life was gradually remade in response to the outcomes of the struggles around the expanding role of the state, which was the most visible source of change to contemporaries. The encroachment of the *tanzimat* reforms upon the traditional liberties of urban quarters and villages provoked opposition, migration, and accommodation. While some sought to ride the waves of change, others tried to ride them out in the interstices of the society.

By following the differential impact of the *tanzimat* reforms on different groups in Ottoman society, it is possible to gain a different perspective on them. On the level of the elite, the attempt by nineteenth-century Ottoman reformers to build a modern army, a modern bureaucracy, and a modern system of education was opposed by powerful vested interests. Most important were the janissaries, court officials, and *ulama* of the old regime. For the janissaries, the *tanzimat* reforms were a calamity. They were brutally eliminated in a series of purges. Court officials and *ulama* who opposed the reforms were marginalized, but supporters prospered.[27]

The impact of the *tanzimat* reforms on local and provincial elites similarly cut both ways. On the one hand, the creation of local and provincial administrative councils, mixed courts, and other new organizations provided unprecedented access to power and patronage resources. On the other hand, by abolishing some of the special privileges and exemptions that had benefited the elite, the reforms brought ruin to some.[28]

We have few accounts of the impact of the *tanzimat* on non-elites. But what we know about the experience of ordinary people indicates that it was

similarly mixed. Military conscription, forced labor, and a more efficient fiscal administration encroached upon the traditional liberties of populations
whose survival in the best of times was precarious, while the trickle down of
new jobs in the bureaucracy was inadequate and the jobs mostly menial.
Some peasants and villagers, threatened with ruin, sought refuge in flight
or became bandits.[29] What the reforms meant in practice to a poor
Lebanese peasant can be seen in the life of Assaf Khater, recounted in this
section.

The transformation from subject to citizen experienced by Middle Easterners is another theme of the *tanzimat* era. For the non-Muslim populations it was a transition fraught with peril. Since the minorities benefited
from the semiautonomous status accorded them as "peoples of the Book,"
or *dhimma* under Islamic law, by which they were accorded religious tolera-
tion and protection in return for their cooperation, they had a considerable
stake in the existing system. Under the *millet* system, by which the Ottomans
regulated the affairs of their non-Muslim subjects, local religious communities enjoyed freedom of worship and control over their local affairs, subject to certain conditions. By abolishing these privileges, the *tanzimat*
reforms thus posed a significant challenge to the non-Muslim elites.[30]

The situation of non-Muslim elites was complicated by the fact that in the
course of the period many of them acquired special privileges and exemptions as a result of their employment by European businesses or governments. These extraterritorial privileges, called *barat*, had originally been
granted by the Ottoman government to official representatives of European
states as part of capitulatory agreements. They carried exemption from
local taxes, justice, military service, and civic obligations. Similar arrangements existed in independent states like Afghanistan, Iran, and Morocco.

In the nineteenth century such privileges were often extended to the
local employees (and their families) of European officials and businessmen
in the Ottoman Empire. Many elite Moroccan Jews held analogous extraterritorial privileges granted by the Moroccan government. Similar arrangements existed in Iran. From the point of view of the state, the system
resulted in a significant loss to the state treasury and threatened the success
of the reform program. Because it unfairly loaded the dice against Muslim
merchants and businessmen, the capitulation system constituted a flash
point of popular Muslim indignation as well.[31]

Another theme of Ottoman modernization was reform of the educational
system. The development of an efficient and modern cadre of administrative
agents, as well as a modern officer corps for the army, required modern
schools, books, and ideas to succeed. Secular ideas began to spread throughout the society, aided by the development of the press and of a modern education system. In the process, the authority of the local clergy (Muslim,
Christian, and Jewish alike) was undermined.[32] We are relatively well

informed on how this process played itself out in the Ottoman Empire at the level of the elite, but know far less about how it worked for ordinary people.

The incorporation of the Middle East into the emerging world economy is a second major source of change in the period. The increasingly closer mesh between the economies of the area and the international economy caused the erosion of many of the basic structures of the old regime—guilds, Sufi orders and other religious groupings, quarter- and village-based communities. These, however, continued to exist and to provide a semblance of order and meaning in the lives of the people. At the same time, new opportunities stimulated the development of new activities. By the end of the period, increased rural security and better communication stimulated commercial agriculture throughout the region. In the cities, the old artisan guild structures, once a mainstay of the urban economy, were significantly affected.

Three contrasting studies focus on individuals whose lives were profoundly shaped by the structures of the guild system. Deli Mehmet, a member of the Cairo slave dealers' guild, exposed the guild to public ridicule by his flagrant abuse of the regulations of the organization. Shemsigul, the Circassian slave woman whom he raped and made pregnant, brought suit in the Sharia court. Her story, told by Ehud Toledano, throws an interesting light on a neglected corner of Egyptian history: the Ottoman elite household and the slave trade that helped to sustain it. The abolition of slavery in the Ottoman Empire at the end of the nineteenth century brought an end to the Ottoman elite household. Sherry Vatter's contribution, a collective biography of the journeyman weavers of Damascus, focuses on the response of journeymen weavers to the nineteenth-century changes that buffeted the Syrian textile handicraft industry. She argues that while the importation of cheap British cottons had an important effect on local textile producers in Damascus, the expansion of the market in the nineteenth century enabled some sectors to ride out the mid-century crisis.

Another image of the perdurance of guild structures is provided by Nels Johnson's portrait of Ahmad, a pearl diver in the now defunct Persian Gulf pearling industry. (Although Ahmad's life falls mostly in the present century, given the different rhythms of Kuwaiti history it is more usefully studied in part 1 than alongside the lives of those who are his literal contemporaries.) Ahmad's experience suggests that the guild system continued to structure people's existence in the Persian Gulf fisheries after it had lost most of its relevance in economically more dynamic areas. It also serves to remind us of how recent is the impact of the oil boom on the area. The fragile ecology of the Gulf has now been drastically affected by the development of the Gulf region and by the 1991 war.

Nineteenth-century Ottomans, even fairly farsighted ones, had little doubt that the empire would survive for some time, despite its manifest weaknesses. European rule (which was to pose a fundamental cultural challenge to all Middle Easterners) lay on the horizon, not yet fully actualized. (Of course, exception must be made here for the Maghrib, most of which slipped under French rule in the nineteenth century.) Over time, European political domination gradually altered the context within which culture and society existed, and with it the way most people led their lives.

Similarly, despite our present-day sense that Middle Eastern nationalisms are basic to the area, until the defeat and breakup of the Ottoman Empire in World War I, nationalism was not a major force among the Muslim populations outside of the Balkans. Only after the defeat of the Ottoman Empire in World War I did nationalism become a major political force among Turks and Arabs. By 1880, the nationalist "traditions" that were later to reshape the cultural and political landscape of the region were still being "invented."[33]

Since North Africa was the first portion of the Middle East to be subjected to European conquest, it is there that we must look for the first stirrings of anticolonial resistance. In this prenationalist age, resistance inevitably drew upon deeply rooted cultural and political forms, especially that of *jihad*. Yet despite the received pieties of official nationalist discourse, according to which opposition was general, the realities of the European threat were differently assessed by different people at different times. Given the overwhelming superiority of European arms, the decision to take up weapons was neither simple nor automatic. The portrait of Mohand N'Hamoucha, a Moroccan Berber tribesman, underscores the complex process by which some individuals were led to become involved in resistance.

To understand how Mohand N'Hamoucha became a local leader of opposition to French imperialism, one must consider first the ambiguous situation of his tribe, the Aith Ndhir, between the government-dominated central plain and the Middle Atlas Mountains, home to large pastoralist tribal groups. While some of his kinsmen were drawn into urban networks at Fez and Meknes and were subsequently exposed to French intimidation and blandishments, Mohand and his friends took the road to resistance. How and why they did so is the subject of Edmund Burke's contribution. Mohand's story helps distance us from the pieties of the official history, according to which there was widespread popular support for anticolonial resistance. As perceptions of the European threat and possible options changed, individuals were led to reassess their situations constantly.

The final essay in this section is Julie Oehler's account of the dramatic role played by Bibi Maryam, an elite woman of the Bakhtiyari tribal confederacy in southwestern Iran during World War I. In some ways, the situation of the Bakhtiyari resembles that of the Aith Ndhir, trapped between a would-be modernizing state and European power. But the dynamics of history in early-twentieth-century Iran diverged from those in Morocco in important ways and shaped a different context for action. Most crucially, the hierarchical structures of the Bakhtiyari, and thus of elite women's scope for political action, were quite different from the much more diffuse and egalitarian organization of the Aith Ndhir. Oehler's contribution also illuminates the public role of women in the Middle East and is usefully placed alongside Julia Clancy-Smith's chapter in the following section.

The Colonial Experience

World War I and its aftermath constituted a watershed of unprecedented significance that led to far-reaching political changes throughout the area. According to the conventional narrative, the politics of the Middle East from 1918 until 1967 revolved around the struggle of nationalism and imperialism. For the most part, the history of this period has been viewed primarily from the perspective of the elite. Part 2 of this volume brings together biographies of individuals who lived through this era. As a group, they provide the basis for an alternative reading of the history of the period.

Changes in the world of politics are the most obvious. With the collapse of the Ottoman Empire and the abolition of the caliphate (1924) and sultanate (1925), basic cultural assumptions about identity and the nature of the state were transformed. The old elites and social groups, already weakened by the nineteenth-century changes, declined rapidly, while new ones, tied to new economic and political forces, emerged. Simultaneously, personal identity became increasingly based upon linguistically defined nationality instead of upon membership in a religious community under the Ottoman sultan/padishah. The resultant rise of nationalisms constituted an unparalleled mental revolution for many.

While one world was vanishing, another was establishing itself. After 1918, European colonial empires, which had already embraced all of Arab Africa, were extended to Arab Asia as well. Even the weak Iranian and Afghan states were made to accept sharp limitations on their sovereignty. Only Turkey managed to elude this particular fate, and then only after Ataturk had defeated the Greeks, British, and French. European rule not only changed the nature of the emerging political struggle within each country, it affected to varying degrees the lives of all.

The men and women whose biographies are included in part 2 of this book are a varied group. One of the things they have in common is the fact that they were all profoundly marked by the experience of colonialism—that complex of racist attitudes, policies, and politics predicated upon notions of European superiority and virtue—which shaped the societies of the region for two generations. Thus, their experiences and expectations were significantly different from those of their parents and grandparents. As European dominance pervaded society, life was irrevocably transformed, even for peasants and tribespeople. The degree to which particular groups were affected varied, of course.

In the conventional account, colonialism is portrayed as a victimless crime that brought far more benefits than disadvantages to the area. As a consequence, we know a great deal more about colonial policymakers and the policies they implemented than we do about the ways in which colonial rule was experienced by Middle Eastern men and women.[34]

After the establishment of European rule, the folly of *jihad* and other traditional forms of armed resistance gradually became evident. European occupation drastically reduced the available options for individuals. The case of Algeria helped set the mold for what was to follow. While some elite families emigrated to other parts of the Ottoman Empire following the French takeover in 1830, most remained behind. Tacit cooperation with the French colonial authorities alternated with petty acts of resistance (such as feigning laziness, or minor acts of theft and sabotage).[35]

The experience of colonialism as it emerges in the biographies included here ran the gamut from heroism to opportunism. Julia Clancy-Smith provides a portrait of an Algerian popular Islamic saintly lineage in the mid-nineteenth century. Her essay focuses on the stratagems employed by Zaynab, the eldest daughter of a popular Sufi leader, or marabout, who succeeded her father as head of the Sufi *zawiya*, and her struggles against the French authorities on the one hand and family rivals on the other.

For non-Muslims, the period was one of narrowing options. Some were able to survive and even thrive. Others found themselves gradually marginalized in the new circumstances of the post-Ottoman Middle East. Hagob Hagobian, whose portrait is written by David Yaghoubian, is one of the first sort. Hagobian was an Armenian Christian born in eastern Anatolia, whose life began with the tragic death of his parents in the massacres of Armenians during World War I. Raised in an orphanage in northwestern Iran, he became a long-distance truck driver on the route from Tehran to the Gulf. Later in his life he migrated to California.

The narrowing personal options of the post-1918 Middle East can also be seen in Sami Zubaida's account of the life of Dr. Naji, an Iraqi Jewish provincial physician. Like many other Iraqi middle-class Jews, he was a nationalist opponent of the corrupt monarchy that ruled Iraq for Britain in the interwar period. During his career as an employee of the Iraqi Ministry of Health, he moved from one provincial post to another. His devotion to his profession eventually collided with decreasing possibilities for professional advancement and the sterner politics of the post-1948 period. As a result, he too took the path of exile.

No subject in the modern history of the Middle East has received greater attention from scholars than nationalism. The conventional account stresses the ways in which in response to heroic leaders the masses mobilized to overthrow Western rule. The obvious contradiction between the reality of ethnic diversity and the nationalist assumption of ethnic unity in Middle Eastern states is simply elided in most accounts. While we know quite a bit about nationalism as an ideology and a political movement, we are much less well informed about how it became the language of politics.[36] The role of nationalism as an ideology in serving the interests of indigenous elites in maintaining their dominance is generally not examined. It is here that the study of ordinary people's lives can contribute a great deal.

As presented in the literature, the triumph of nationalism seems foreordained and in no way problematic. Yet the terrible simplifications of the nationalist ideologues ran against the grain of the old social forms, personal attachments, and ways of thinking. By asking us to re-imagine the specific context in which nationalisms emerged, the biographies provide us with the materials of a more complex and culturally sensitive understanding of this elusive phenomenon. The rise of nationalism, these biographies suggest, needs to be situated not only in the context of Arab nationalist ideology but also in that of local politics and the specific options available to individuals.

This theme clearly emerges in Abdullah Schleifer's biography of Izz al-Din al-Qassam. Schleifer shows that Palestinian popular resistance to British and Zionist domination of mandatory Palestine arose from multiple roots. These included Islamic reformism, Sufism, and late Ottoman pan-Islam, as well as urban-based secular nationalism. Philip Khoury's portrait of Abu Ali al-Kilawi shows us an old-style neighborhood enforcer, or *qabaday*, rooted in quarter-based youth gangs, whose ideology derived from Islamic notions of chivalry and the cult of masculine physical prowess. With the changes in Damascene society, the old patronage networks grew less important and new political forms gradually emerged. Eventually, Abu Ali and those like him were replaced by a new style of resolutely modern nationalist organizers. M'hamed Ali, a Tunisian labor leader and early nationalist, is a third figure whose biography is especially revealing of the way nationalism came to the area. In his case, involvement in labor organizing followed service in the Ottoman army during World War I and exile in Berlin in the last years of World War I. Through him, we get a sense of the complex relations between the chief nationalist party, the Néo-Destour, the chief Tunisian labor union, the Confederation Général du Travail Tunisien, and the various groups on the colonial left. It is a theme that can be found elsewhere in the region.

While the major story of the period is one of the transformation of the political world, the social and cultural worlds were no less affected. Artisan shops were gradually supplemented by factories and industrial enterprises. Smokestacks increasingly rivaled minarets along the new urban skyline, and new forms of communication such as the telegraph and telephone, railroads, trucks, and airplanes displaced human and animal transport. (The old forms did not so much disappear as coexist with the new.)

As part of a trend already established by the nineteenth-century Ottoman *tanzimat* reformers, governments, whether colonial or indigenous, became insulated from the people by bureaucracies modeled on modern lines. The cityscape was transformed by masses of rural migrants who erected shanty-towns around the old *qasba* and invaded the core of the old cities. Simultaneously, the elite gradually relocated to expensive villas constructed in the suburbs. The social gulf between elites and the masses widened and was bridged only by nationalism.

Despite these dramatic changes, important continuities remained. Kinship and family patterns proved remarkably resilient, even as large numbers of rural folk migrated to the cities. The extended family survived because it provided alternative possibilities for coping with new situations: finding schools and jobs, arranging marriages, sharing scarce resources.[37] Similarly, ethnic and religious communities developed unforeseen staying power in the face of the rising tide of nationalism. In part, this was due to the deliberate policies of European colonial rulers, who played divide-and-rule games the better to establish their dominance. Thus, Berbers, Kurds, Alawis, Druze, Armenians, Jews, and other rural (often tribal) minorities were accorded varying degrees of privilege. So, too, non-Muslim groups were often the beneficiaries of favorable treatment. But ethnic communities prospered also because they continued to meet the spiritual, cultural, and material needs of large numbers of people. Nor, for all of that, did colonial efforts to foster discord necessarily succeed. Part of the success of secular nationalism derived from its ability to invent a national community in which cultural difference was authorized or at least tolerated.

Many social continuities between old and new remained as well. Artisan guild structures not only survived but were extended into new trades. (Consider, for example, the case of Hagob Hagobian, who proudly wore the badge of the long-distance truck drivers' guild.) Long-established forms of male and female sociability based in homes, *hammams,* and cafés helped to maintain sexual segregation and to provide many women and men with emotional support and networks for coping. (Note the importance of cafés in the lives of many of the men whose biographies appear in this volume.)[38]

A final theme that might be noted here is the impact of World War II. Because of the wartime role of the Middle East in Allied strategic planning, Iranians were mobilized by the Allies in support of the Russian front, while the Middle East Supply Center was located in Cairo. Hagob Hagobian's life was dramatically affected by the Allied mobilization, while the changes wrought by the war so undermined the world of Dr. Naji, the Iraqi Jewish physician whose life is presented by Sami Zubaida, that he eventually had to

leave Iraq for Britain, where he lives today. World War II was a major defining period in the life of the group of the Egyptian bedouin woman Migdim,
profiled by Lila Abu-Lughod in the next section. Migdim remembers how
things used to be before the bedouin were sedentarized by the government.
Her reminiscences afford us a privileged glimpse of some of the stratagems
for survival employed by a proud and independent woman. They also give
us a sense of her ironic and earthy sense of humor.

Postcolonial Lives

The period from 1945 to 1990 was one of extraordinary change. Hopes were
raised periodically, only to be dashed by some new turn of the historical
wheel. The biographies that comprise this section are a sobering reminder
of the human costs of much of this change—as well as the ability of people
to survive even under the most appalling conditions.

The most dramatic transformation between the end of World War II and
the 1990–91 Gulf War lay in the political arena: namely, the final act of the
colonial drama—the triumph of nationalist movements and the emergence
of independent states. Yet independence did not bring solutions to the many
problems of the societies of the region. Instead, the blighted dream of
nationalism increasingly provided the focus of political debate. As regimes
lost legitimacy due to their inability to resolve the problems of independence, opposition movements sprang up first on the secular left (inspired by
the Algerian FLN and the Palestinian commandos) and later on the Islamist
right (where the Islamic revolution in Iran was the major catalyst).

Global superpower rivalries deriving from the Cold War, Western support for Israel, and Western dependence on Middle Eastern oil all combined to skew internal debate, foreclose options, and dampen dissent even
as they weakened the legitimacy of states in the area. By the late 1970s, the
splintering of the coalitions that had sustained the nationalist movements
led to a loss of confidence in the capacity of the providential state to deliver
the goods of modernity. Also in the 1970s, the boom-and-bust cycles of the
oil economy led to the erosion of the living standard of the many and to the
scandalous enrichment of the few. Civil conflict in Afghanistan, Lebanon,
and the Sudan, and the bloody Iran-Iraq war, established the limits of the
political stalemate throughout the region. The attractiveness of Islamic
alternative solutions to many people must be understood in this context.

The rupture of the nationalist consensus and the differential impact of
economic change make it a challenge to find a common thread among the
biographies in this section. Some individuals became political militants;
others remained quiescent. Some experienced real gains in their living
standard after independence, while for others (notably tribal peoples) the
ambitious plans of modernizing regimes meant the destruction of a tradi-

tional way of life. Finally, although the increased integration of the region into the world economy facilitated large-scale labor migration (a benefit to some), the globalization of politics has led to a rash of civil wars and an upsurge in violence (especially of regimes toward domestic opponents).

The effort to find continuities founders for other reasons as well. In the transformation of the Middle East since 1800, two global historical trends, prior to and analytically distinguishable from the phenomenon of European imperialism, loom large: the expansion of the role of the state, and the integration of the Middle East into the world economy. Under colonialism, the third major force for change, centralization and economic change appeared as consequences of imperialism. The specifically Western cultural auspices under which the transformation to modernity occurred thus masked its global character. Nationalists denounced colonial abuses. Yet their ambitions to modernize and develop their societies differed little from those pursued by the imperialists. Because the nationalists assumed that states were independent actors, instead of inextricably bound into the world economy and international political systems, they were bound not only to provoke dissent but also to fail.

The post–World War II era was affected by two additional conjunctural factors. The first was the Cold War. Fear of Soviet expansionism led the United States and its allies to seek to establish alliance schemes like the Baghdad Pact (1955). It also led Western policymakers to view nationalist leaders such as Nasser, Ben Bella, and Qasim as potential Communist agents. This fundamental misreading had serious consequences. Because Western leaders never understood the indigenous roots of nationalism, they were propelled into a series of military adventures (Suez, Algeria, Iran, Lebanon, Afghanistan) that by the 1980s had drastically eroded whatever moral capital they retained. European and American interests in Middle Eastern oil and the Suez Canal in the postwar era further intensified the tendency toward interventionism.

To this must be added the Arab sense of injury stemming from the establishment of Israel. For Jews, Israel represented a haven from oppression, the fulfillment of age-old dreams, and the possibility of forging a new Jewish people outside the heritage of European racism and the Hitlerian genocide. For the Palestinian people, however, it meant the loss of their homeland. Middle Eastern peoples did not for the most part share in European anti-Semitism, and they perceived the Zionist project as a form of colonialism. In Israel, the contradictions of European history encountered those of Middle Eastern history. The roots of current Middle Eastern bitterness and distrust of the West are to be located in this tangled history.

For most people, World War II marked the point of rupture with the colonial period. The war not only inflicted suffering and death upon Middle Easterners (especially North Africans, many of whom found themselves caught in the crossfire), it also raised questions about the continued viability of the colonial empires. Whereas World War I was followed by the dismantling of the Ottoman Empire and the establishment of the colonial mandates in the Arab East, the aftermath of World War II led to the emergence of independent states throughout the region.

The rise of national states led by charismatic nationalist leaders like Gamal Abdel Nasser, Ahmed Ben Bella, and Habib Bourguiba (respectively, the heads of Egypt, Algeria, and Tunisia in the 1960s) was the most important source of change in the period. Ambitious programs of national development and more prosaic efforts on the part of newly independent governments to reward their followers led to a vast expansion of state bureaucracies. They also led to a steady extension of the involvement of the state in people's lives, with both positive and negative consequences.

What the increased role of the state meant for most people depended upon their access to government bureaucrats who might intervene on their behalf, and on their vulnerability to government policies. Both Gulab, the Afghan schoolteacher whose story is presented by Ashraf Ghani, and Haddou, the Moroccan migrant worker whose life is limned by David McMurray, benefited from the favorable decisions of government bureaucrats. Gulab became a schoolteacher, while Haddou obtained a coveted government authorization to work in Europe.

In contrast, government reforms confronted tribal peoples like Migdim or Rostam, the Iranian Qashqa'i rebel whom Lois Beck discusses in her contribution, with impossible choices. To go along with government plans and assimilate would cut them off irrevocably from their tribal roots, while opposition would be pitilessly crushed. Migdim and her bedouin group decided to submit. Rostam, on the other hand, found himself drawn into radical opposition to the Shah's forced modernization efforts. The differences between Rostam's and Migdim's responses to modernization define the options of tribal peoples throughout the region. Thus, the bedouin of Arabia, Syria, Iraq, and Jordan and the pastoralist Berbers of North Africa have tended to follow the route of sedentarization, while groups like the Kurds and the Baluch have been more divided in their responses. (In part, as well, these variations can be glossed as reflections of the different relative power positions of tribes and states in the different societies.)[39]

The differential responses of ordinary people to the political appeals of governments and oppositions in the 1945–90 period are a revealing sign of the limits of charisma. Attempts at political mobilization served chiefly to raise popular expectations and frustration. The lives of activists like Gulab, the Afghan teacher, were transformed by their political choices. Gulab's biography is the story of the political education of a provincial youth. Plunged into the seething cauldron of student politics in Kabul, Gulab was hard-pressed to choose between different groups, each of which proclaimed it had the solution to what they saw as a backward country's problems. The sharp social divisions in prerevolutionary Afghanistan—between wealth and poverty, urban and rural, and between Persian-speakers and speakers of Pashtu—only made the political footing more slippery. Eventually, Gulab found himself trapped between Left and Right, Marxists and Islamic fundamentalists. Through his dilemma we come to understand the social choices Afghans were forced to make following the overthrow of Taraki in 1978.

Since 1973, when the population of the Middle East was 85 to 90 percent rural and agricultural and mostly nonliterate, the pace of social change has quickened dramatically throughout the region. By 1990, the majority of the population of the region were urban, nonagricultural, and literate (although the percentages vary with each country). Despite sharp rises in oil revenues, population increases swamped the ability of the states outside the Persian Gulf to provide even rudimentary services. The unprecedented movement from the countryside to the cities and the simultaneous huge increase in the percentage of the population under the age of twenty-five (more than 60 percent in some countries) blighted dreams of development. The difficulties of negotiating the transition from a predominantly rural and agricultural society to a predominantly urbanized one were bound to have political consequences. The wonder is that (till now at least) they have not been greater.

These contradictions are largely responsible for the increased violence of the last decade, including the Lebanese and Afghan civil wars, the Iranian revolution, and the Iran-Iraq war. As confidence in secular nationalism has waned, political interest in Islam has grown rapidly.[40] Given this context, the survival of most of the regimes must be rated one of the biggest surprises of all. With the exception of Afghanistan, Lebanon, Iran, and Iraq, the same regimes (and often the same leaders) that were in power in 1973 are still in place in 2004.

The Lebanese and Afghan civil wars both resulted from failed leftist efforts to transform their respective societies into modern secular states. Nominally a democracy, Lebanon was stalemated by class and ethnic divisions. The presence of 300,000 Palestinian refugees and the existence of a PLO quasi-government constituted another flash point of tension. When a left-wing coalition (including the PLO) sought to introduce major reforms in 1975, right-wing Maronites, supported first by Syria and subsequently by Israel, intervened, setting off a conflict unprecedented in its complexity and savagery. The struggle took on an international dimension when the different Lebanese factions acquired foreign backers.[41]

In 1973 the monarchy of Afghanistan was displaced by a coup that brought to power the government of Muhammad Daud. When the left-leaning Daud was in turn ousted by a faction of the Afghan Communist Party under Muhammad Taraki in 1978, the society exploded. While Communist Party factions battled for power, tribal and Islamic religious leaders sought to organize resistance. The conflict swiftly became an international one, although in this case along orthodox Cold War lines. The Soviet Union backed the government, while the United States, Pakistan, Saudi Arabia, and Iran supported different factions among the *mujahidin*.

Ashraf Ghani's biography of Gulab sheds light on the hopes and expectations of the Afghan intelligentsia in the period of rising tension and conflict that immediately preceded the outbreak of the civil war. Through it we come to appreciate the ways in which families found themselves torn and lifelong friends became bitterly estranged. The stakes for both sides were high: the chance for a modern secular state on the one hand, the preservation of deeply rooted customs and religious values on the other.

Of the political earthquakes that reshaped the political landscape of the postcolonial Middle East, the most important is assuredly the Iranian revolution. Media stereotypes about the Islamic revolution, while providing the smug with a sense of superiority, were more notable for their vulgar otherizing than their ability to provide a coherent explanation of events. A more complex understanding of the stakes for ordinary Iranians is provided by the biographies included in this volume.

The quasi-autobiographical portrait of Mehdi Abedi (cowritten with Michael Fischer) describes what it was like to grow up in an Iranian village in the Shah's Iran. From it we acquire a sense of the firmly entrenched popular traditions of Shiite Islam, and their capacity to instill a love of religious learning in young men like Abedi. Abedi's personal odyssey was to lead him deep into the political factions of provincial Iran and then to the struggles between the Islamists and Marxists in Tehran and on college campuses in the United States. Abedi managed to avoid being drawn into the violence of politics, and although, like Gulab, he debated activists, he retained an independent spirit.[42]

Mehdi Abedi's biography contrasts with that of the Qashqa'i tribal rebel Rostam, Hagob Hagobian, and Khanom Gohary, the other Iranians whose portraits are drawn here. The three portraits permit us to see the quite different individual strategies pursued by Iranians in the conditions of rapid change and political repression that pertained in the 1970s.

The final two chapters of part 3 underscore the costs of the changes that the region has undergone in the contemporary period. Joost Hiltermann's biography of Abu Jamal, a Palestinian urban villager, provides a sharply etched study of life under the *intifada* in Arab Jerusalem, while David McMurray's evocative portrait of Haddou, a Moroccan migrant worker in Germany, gives us a sense of the dreams, as well as the harsh realities, that govern the lives of North Africans who work in Europe.

Contemporary Lives

For contemporary Middle Easterners, the years from 1990 to 2004 have offered the mixed blessings and frustrations of rapid change within considerable continuity. As in the immediate postcolonial period, hopes have been raised—and in some instances met—while still others have been crushed as regional and global developments have collided with the randomness of individual circumstance, class, gender, ethnicity, timing, and luck. The essays presented in this section serve to personalize the experiences of a diverse group of ordinary individuals in the contemporary Middle East. They underscore the complex and layered challenges many Middle Easterners confront in their daily lives and highlight the unique skills, tactics, and coping mechanisms individuals employ as they struggle to survive.

The most profound changes of the period since 1990 have been political in nature. Following the end of the Cold War and the demise of the Soviet Union, the unchallenged ascendancy of the United States as the dominant global economic and military power has upended preexisting regional security alliances and durably altered the international playing field. Within the Middle East and North African region, political stagnation has generally been the norm. The period concludes in 2004 with the same authoritarian regimes, oligarchies, and often individuals still in power in key states like Egypt, Saudi Arabia, Libya, Syria, Jordan, and Kuwait.

Looked at a different way, the structural readjustment of the world economy has continued to powerfully transform the lives of ordinary people. The result, together with the continued sharp population increase noted in the previous period, has been to render obsolete state-led development plans. If we would understand the despair of individuals like Nasir, Ghada, and Nadia profiled in this section, we need to consider the economic dashing of hopes as a result of poor government economic policies, population increase, and economic globalization. Under the circumstances, any government would have been hard-pressed to do better. Many, unfortunately, did worse. Economic collapse and political repression account for much of the legitimacy gap experienced by governments throughout the region. That some states in the Third World have done worse does not make the situation any more bearable for Middle Easterners.

Since 1990, the political landscape throughout the region has been powerfully shaped by the consequences of war. Yet, initially, things seemed headed in a different direction. The end of the eight-year Iran-Iraq war in 1988 brought some relief to civilian populations, while the withdrawal of Soviet troops from Afghanistan in 1992 appeared initially to favor the return of peace in that tormented land. However, Saddam Hussein's invasion of Kuwait and the subsequent outbreak of the first Gulf War of 1990–91 durably changed the political context. With the backing of the U.N., the United States assembled a coalition including forces from many

Arab states for a joint military strike to expel Iraqi military forces from Kuwait. Many Kuwaitis and Iraqis were killed and wounded in the war that followed (how many Iraqis, we will never know), leading to the expulsion of Yemenis, Palestinians, and other Arabs who had been working in Kuwait, Saudi Arabia, and Gulf states to their countries of origin. (The biographies of Talal Rizk and Ghada included in the chapters in part 4 provide us with portraits of individuals whose lives were profoundly affected by the Gulf War). The end of the war found U.S. troops stationed in Kuwait, Saudi Arabia, and the Gulf Arab states.

As the events of 9/11 would reveal, the U.S. presence proved to be a major focus of opposition, not just in the Kingdom of Saudi Arabia but throughout the Muslim world. The unresolved conclusion of the war, which left Saddam Hussein in power in Iraq, was to prove a major incitement for further U.S. interventions in Iraq and in the region as a whole. The U.S. branding of Iran and Iraq as "rogue nations" provided a pretext for unprecedented U.S. arms sales in the Middle East. Concurrently, the first Bush administration sought in 1992 to put pressure on Israel's then Likud-dominated leadership to halt settlement activity and begin peace negotiations with Arab states, which resulted a year later in the Oslo Accords. These developments at first led many to anticipate a new world order in which peace and development would return to the region. Instead, the Oslo Accords were allowed to languish, and failed to culminate in the expected Israeli-Palestinian "final status" talks on such thorny issues as the right of return for Palestinian refugees, control over Jerusalem, and Israeli settlements in the occupied West Bank and Gaza Strip.

The life of Ghada, a Palestinian woman whose biography is related by Celia Rothenberg, was directly affected by both the Gulf War and the persistence of the Israeli occupation of Palestinian lands. Born in Kuwait, where her father was working due to the economic conditions in the occupied West Bank, Ghada and her family were visiting relatives in their West Bank village of Artas in August 1990 when Iraqi troops invaded Kuwait. Following the war, Ghada had few options. As her family sought to cope with its downward-spiraling fortunes, she found herself compelled in 1992 to accept an arranged marriage to a cousin in Artas. Ghada's plan to escape this situation was simple enough, but her motivations were complex. Rothenberg helps us understand the multiple meanings of Ghada's act of defiance and resistance. As we become aware of her situation, we come to understand how international political events, the daily oppression of the Israeli occupation, the implications of divorce, and the economic and social opportunities that existed for Palestinian village women in the West Bank all fed into her decision.

Another portrait takes up the post-Oslo context from a diametrically opposed perspective. Tamara Neuman's portrait of June Leavitt, a resident of the Ultra-Orthodox Jewish settlement at Kiryat Arba (near Hebron) allows us to view the Israeli-Palestinian conflict from the perspective of a settler. One of the most intractable obstacles to a final peace agreement has been (and remains) the fate of the Jewish settlements in the occupied West Bank, Gaza Strip, and East Jerusalem. Since the June 1967 war, over 140 settlements (as well as scores of outposts) have been established. With a population of some 450,000, the settlers and their supporters have come to wield enormous power in the Knesset, the Israeli legislative assembly. Leavitt and her husband Frank were born and raised in the United States. In 1979, they immigrated to the occupied territories, with their children, from Crown Heights, Brooklyn. The family's various moves since then, from settlements in Egyptian Sinai, to the Gaza Strip, and ultimately to the Ultra-Orthodox West Bank settlement of Kiryat Arba, have kept them at the center of the conflict and the intense controversy surrounding Jewish settlement and the ongoing occupation.

It's worth noting that until the mid-1980s most settlers in the occupied territories of Gaza, the West Bank, and East Jerusalem were ideologically inspired by the Gush Emunim, a right-wing political movement that originated in 1968. Gush Emunim offered religious and nationalist justifications and material incentives for Jewish settlement on Palestinian land. The arrival of thousands of Jewish immigrants from the former Soviet Union in the late 1980s and early 1990s broadened the base of the settler movement. Attracted by Israeli government housing subsidies (underwritten in part by U.S. aid to Israel), large numbers of prospective settlers were motivated more for material than ideological reasons. Nonetheless, the political tone has continued to be set by the ideologically motivated settlers in the occupied territories. This is why Neuman's portrait of June Leavitt remains so important for us to consider.

The larger context for understanding the lives of Ghada and June is to be sought in the recent history of Israel and Palestine. Although the September 1993 signing of the Declaration of Principles (known widely as the Oslo Accord) and the Rabin-Arafat "handshake" on the White House lawn were indeed photogenic, the accord's vague wording led to different interpretations of its demands and timetable. As a result, Israeli troop withdrawals were stalled while settlement-building in the West Bank continued at an unprecedented pace. Meanwhile, rejectionists on both sides did their best to derail the already faltering peace process. The February 1994 massacre of twenty-nine Muslim worshipers at the Ibrahimi Mosque in Hebron (also known as the Tomb of the Patriarchs) by Baruch Goldstein, a doctor from the nearby Jewish settlement of Kiryat Arba, was answered forty days later with the first Palestinian suicide bombing, which claimed eight Israeli lives in Afula. A dynamic was engaged in which rejectionists were able to subvert the hopeful atmosphere engendered by the Oslo Accord. The

November 1995 assassination of Prime Minister Yitzahk Rabin by Yigal Amir, a Jewish religious student, marked the political limits of Israeli engagement. In this context, Palestinian militants continued their violent opposition to the occupation, directing attacks at Jewish settlers in the West Bank and Gaza as well as suicide bombing against civilians in Israel proper. With the United States unwilling or unable to break the deadlock, events have continued in the same vicious circle to the present time (2004).

One of the success stories of the Arab world in the 1970s was Algeria, which became independent in 1962 after a protracted anticolonial struggle. With its socialist land-reform program, extensive energy resources, and progressive foreign policy, Algeria provided an influential model to other Third World states. Nonetheless, despite record oil exports, Algeria was badly affected by the economic downturn of the 1980s. It was in this context that the ruling coalition was plunged into bitter political strife. Things came to a head following the cancellation of the second round of the nation's first multiparty elections in January 1992. When it became clear that the Islamic Salvation Front (known by its acronym, the FIS) had won, Algeria's FLN leadership declared the elections void, deposed the president, dissolved parliament, and banned the FIS. In the weeks that followed, violent demonstrations provoked a harsh government crackdown, the arrest of thousands, and the imposition of a one-year state of emergency. Algeria was plunged into a civil war that pitted the FIS and its allies against the backers of the regime, including the army and its allies. Massacres and atrocities followed one another over the years that followed. Journalists and intellectuals soon found themselves the targets of both sides, and hundreds of them were killed. The emergent conflict between Islamic radicals and militarized regimes in the 1990s is not unique to Algeria, of course, but has spread throughout the region. The Algerian case, being less familiar to Americans, provides a point from which to observe the human consequences of this struggle.

Baya Gacecmi is an Algerian woman journalist who lives and works in Algiers. Her portrait of Nadia (a pseudonym) introduces us to a poor peasant woman who had the misfortune of marrying a young villager who had become a member of the local Armed Islamic Groups (GIA). As Nadia's husband and his gang terrorized the surrounding countryside, the authorities sought to gain control of the situation and the villagers found themselves tugged first in one direction, then in the other. Algeria's collapse in the 1990s had an enormous human cost. The portrait of Nadia provides a window into just how high this cost has been. Gacemi's account provides a good sense of the brutal and senseless character of the struggle. But it fails to discuss an important aspect, namely the extent to which the Algerian state itself was implicated in some of the largest massacres. For analogies we must look to Argentina's "dirty war" of the 1970s, or the bitter struggle of the drug cartels, leftist guerilla groups, and right-wing private armies in Colombia in the 1980s and 1990s. Within the region, one thinks of Egypt in the 1990s, Lebanon in the 1980s, Afghanistan since 1979, and, more recently, Saudi Arabia.

The roots of Islamism in the Middle East and the Muslim world are a subject of much controversy. As the portraits of Nadia and, in a different way, Nasir (the young Egyptian man whose biography is sketched by Fanny Colonna) make clear, it is crucial to understand these roots as complex, deriving from both local and global contexts and experiences. Thus, the situation of Egypt in the 1980s and 1990s paralleled that of Algeria in many ways. In this period, the socialist legacy of Gamal Abdel Nasser was eroded by the rapid pace of economic globalization that ensued, along with the continued rapid increase of the population. Following the Egyptian renunciation of its alliance with the Soviet Union in 1973 under Anwar Sadat, Egypt set out on a political path of a rapid opening of the economy to the world market together with a repression of the Left. As in Algeria, Afghanistan, and, somewhat later on, Saudi Arabia, this led the government to seek an alliance with the Muslim religious parties.

What the U.S. public largely fails to understand is that the dynamics of Islamism are not just shaped by the political environment or even opposition to U.S. policies in the region, but derive from the strong desire of Middle Eastern men and women to preserve a moral world in the face of economic chaos and political repression. They are thus to be situated in the larger context of the reassertion of religious values around the world. These forces clearly shape the choices of Nasir, a young man from Aswan in Upper Egypt. But they do so in ways that cut against the grain of our expectations. His biography is interesting for a number of reasons. For one thing, Nasir's choices lead him away from Islamic insurrection and toward more personal goals.

Nasir's life is interesting to us as well because it opens to our inspection the world of Egyptian provincial university graduates, who find themselves thwarted at every turn in their efforts to find their place in the world. Not only are the skills of young men like Nasir uncompetitive in the world market, there are not enough jobs of any kind to go around. In addition, they have little chance of finding adequate housing and little or no chance of coming up with a dowry which will enable them to marry and to settle down. Nasir's dilemma is that of an entire generation of Middle Eastern men and women.

The biography of Talal Rizk, a Syrian employed in Saudi Arabia, helps us to see the broader resonance of some of the themes that have shaped Nasir's life. Nonetheless, it is important to understand that Talal's opportunities are different. Not only is Talal a Druse, a member of a non-Muslim minority, he comes from a relatively affluent urban family background and speaks several languages. Talal's more cosmopolitan background (he is a graduate of the American University of Beirut) has enabled him to marry a fellow student of Chilean heritage and to find relatively well-paid work in Saudi Arabia. Despite a history of political involvement on the political left while a student, Talal had become relatively unengaged politically at the time his portrait was sketched by Michael Provence.

A consideration of the lives of Talal and Nasir also makes it possible to compare their situations to those of Nadia and Ghada (discussed above). How do the differing contexts of women's and men's lives in the contemporary Middle East shape different possibilities of individual action? The biographies in this part allow us to ask: How do both men and women cope with similar societal, political, and economic realities?

The portrait of Khanom Gohary, a working-class woman residing in a poor neighborhood in Tehran, adds further materials to inspire such reflections. Mrs. Gohary's life provides us with a perspective on the lives of ordinary Iranian women. Contrary to media presentations of Iranian women's lives, based primarily upon the experience of elite women often living outside of Iran, Gohary's strong character, individuality, and courage have helped her triumph over many obstacles to build a life of meaning for herself and to help other poor Iranian women. As a female health caseworker in the urban slums of Tehran, she is far from unique. Through Gohary's biography we discover that despite the misogynist policies of the Islamic Republic, contemporary Iran has been strongly attached to family planning and willing to endorse unconventional measures for the purpose, including abortion and contraception. Iranian women struggle in an environment where the cards are heavily stacked against them. Nonetheless, taking advantage of shrewd alliances and available political openings, they have been able to achieve remarkable things. Theirs is far from the world of gender apartheid sketched by Western feminists.

The future of Iran remains at the moment (2004) undecided. Since the death of Ayatollah Khomeini in 1989, battles between moderate reformists and conservatives have been waged over the interrelated issues of candidate vetting by the Guardian Council, the respective powers of the Supreme Leader, *majles* (parliament), and the president, and the extent to which politics and the economy should be the providence of the *ulama*. During the first presidential term of Muhammad Khatami (1997–2001), a group of reformist *majles* deputies appeared for the moment to gain the upper hand. But since the events of 9/11 and the military intervention of the United States in Afghanistan and Iraq, the political context has tended to favor the hard-liners. How this will affect the lives of people such as Khanom Gohary we can only speculate. But at least two things are certain. One is that the political forces in Iran, as well as in the region as a whole, are too powerful and too deeply rooted to be easily changed by external intervention. The second is that no one's life will be improved by warfare.

NOTES

1. Eric Wolf, *Europe and the People without History* (Berkeley: University of California Press, 1997).

2. Eugene Genovese, *Roll, Jordan, Roll* (New York: Vintage Books, 1976).

3. Strictly speaking, the term *colonialism* implies settlers, and applies only to the Maghrib and Palestine. In this book, we use the term to refer to incorporation into a European colonial empire. What mattered to individuals were the ways Western rule altered how their societies were run.

4. European rule came gradually to the area. Some countries (Afghanistan, Iran, Saudi Arabia, and Yemen are some examples) were never officially incorporated into a colonial empire, though all came under Western hegemony in varying degrees. Prior to World War I the order of acquisition was as follows: Algeria (France, 1830), Aden (Britain, 1839), South Arabia (Britain, 1879), Tunisia (France, 1881), Egypt (Britain, 1882), Libya (Italy, 1911), and Morocco (France and Spain, 1912). As part of the World War I peace settlement, the British and French acquired mandates from the League of Nations over Iraq, Jordan, Lebanon, Palestine, and Syria. Kuwait became a formal British dependency at this time as well.

5. See P. M. Holt and Bernard Lewis, eds., *Historians of the Middle East* (Oxford: Oxford University Press, 1964).

6. On the genre of *tabaqat*, see R. Stephen Humphrys, *Islamic History: A Framework for Inquiry* (Minneapolis: Bibliotheca Islamica, 1988).

7. For an example, see Richard Bulliet, *The Patricians of Nishapur* (Cambridge, Mass.: Harvard University Press, 1972).

8. *The History of al-Tabari* (*Tarikh al-rusul wa'l-muluk*), translated from the Arabic in 37 vols. (New York: State University of New York Press, 1981–).

9. Natalie Davis, *The Return of Martin Guerre* (Cambridge, Mass.: Harvard University Press, 1983); Carlo Ginzburg, *The Cheese and the Worms: The Cosmos of a Sixteenth-Century Miller* (Baltimore: Johns Hopkins University Press, 1980); Jonathan Spence, *The Death of Woman Wang* (New York: Viking, 1978).

10. For a recent survey, see L. L. Langness and Gelya Frank, *Lives: An Anthropological Approach to Biography* (Novato, Calif.: Chandler and Sharp, 1987).

11. Several recent works treat this theme. See George E. Marcus and Michael M. J. Fischer, eds., *Anthropology as Cultural Critique* (Chicago: University of Chicago Press, 1986); James Clifford and George E. Marcus, eds., *Writing Culture: The Poetics and Politics of Ethnography* (Berkeley: University of California Press, 1986); and James Clifford, *The Predicament of Culture* (Cambridge, Mass.: Harvard University Press, 1988). In this volume, the joint article of Michael Fischer and Mehdi Abedi is an example of this new genre.

12. Eliott Liebow, *Tally's Corner* (Boston: Little, Brown, 1967). For an example of the new tendency, see the work of the French sociologist Daniel Bertaux, *Destins personnels et structures de classe: Pour une critique de l'anthropometrie politique* (Paris: P.U.F.,

1977). Also D. Bertaux, ed., *Biography and Society: The Life History Approach in the Social Sciences* (Beverly Hills: Sage, 1981); and the journal *Life Stories/Récits de vie.*

13. Wilhelm Dilthey, *Pattern and Meaning in History* (New York: Harper, 1961).

14. See also Dale Eickelman, *Knowledge and Power in Morocco: The Education of a Twentieth-Century Notable* (Princeton: Princeton University Press, 1985), who refers to "biography as social document."

15. On this subject, see Clifford Geertz, *Local Knowledge* (New York: Basic Books, 1983), and *Le mal de voir*, Cahiers Jussieu, no. 2 (Paris: Collection 10/18, 1976). See also the works mentioned in n. 10 above.

16. For an overview, see Peter Schottler, "Historians and Discourse Analysis," *History Workshop Journal* 27 (1989): 37–65. For more on "deconstruction" see Jacques Derrida, *Of Grammatology* (Baltimore: Johns Hopkins University Press, 1976); Sande Cohen, *Historical Culture: On the Recoding of an Academic Discipline* (Berkeley: University of California Press, 1986); Christopher Norris, *Deconstruction: Theory and Practice* (London: Methuen, 1982).

17. For an introduction to these issues, see Peter Novick, *That Noble Dream: The "Objectivity Question" and the American Historical Profession* (Cambridge: Cambridge University Press, 1988). Also Joan Scott, "History in Crisis? The Others' Side of the Story," *American Historical Review* 94 (1989): 680–92; and more generally Michel Foucault, *The Archeology of Knowledge* (New York: Harper, 1972).

18. Edward Said, *Orientalism* (New York: Vintage Books, 1978).

19. For an analysis of media stereotypes, see Edward Said, *Covering Islam* (New York: Vintage Books, 1997).

20. How this works out in the case of French orientalism is discussed in Edmund Burke III, "The French Tradition of the Sociology of Islam," in *Islamic Studies: A Tradition and Its Problems,* ed. Malcolm Kerr (Santa Monica: Undena University Press, 1980), 73–88. See also Edmund Burke III and David Prochaska, eds., *After the Colonial Turn: Orientalism, History, and Theory* (Lincoln: University of Nebraska Press, 2005).

21. Daniel Lerner, *The Passing of Traditional Societies: Modernizing the Middle East* (Glencoe, Ill.: Free Press, 1958).

22. Richard Critchfield, *Shahhat: An Egyptian* (Syracuse: Syracuse University Press, 1978).

23. Tim Mitchell, "The Invention and Reinvention of the Egyptian Peasant," *IJMES* 22 (1990): 129–50.

24. The title of a book by Charles Glass, *Tribes with Flags: A Dangerous Passage through the Chaos of the Middle East* (New York: Atlantic Monthly Press, 1990).

25. Roy Mottahedeh, *The Mantle of the Prophet: Religion and Politics in Iran* (New York: Pantheon, 2002); and Erika Friedl, *The Women of Deh Koh: Lives in an Iranian Village* (Washington, D.C.: Smithsonian Institution Press, 1989).

26. For some others, see Nayra Atiya, *Khul Khaal: Five Egyptian Women Tell Their Stories* (Syracuse: Syracuse University Press, 1982); Vincent Crappanzano, *Tuhami, Portrait of a Moroccan* (Chicago: University of Chicago Press, 1980); Eickelman, *Knowledge and Power in Morocco;* Martin Lings, *A Sufi Saint in the Modern World* (London: Allen and Unwin, 1971); John Waterbury, *North for the Trade* (Berkeley: University of California Press, 1972).

27. On the officials, see Carter Findlay, *Ottoman Civil Officialdom: A Social History* (Princeton: Princeton University Press, 1989). On the ulama, see the chapters by Richard Chambers and Richard Repp in *Scholars, Saints, and Sufis,* ed. Nikki Keddie (Berkeley: University of California Press, 1973).

28. Albert Hourani, "Ottoman Reform and the Politics of Notables," in *The Beginnings of Modernization in the Middle East,* ed. William Polk and Richard Chambers (Chicago: University of Chicago Press, 1968), 41–68, and the other articles in this volume.

29. Yashar Kemal's *Memed My Hawk* (New York: Pantheon, 1961) chronicles one such personal itinerary.

30. Benjamin Braude and Bernard Lewis, eds., *Christians and Jews in the Ottoman Empire,* 2 vols. (New York: Holmes and Meier, 1982).

31. On the system of extraterritoriality, see Stanford J. Shaw and Ezel K. Shaw, *History of the Ottoman Empire and Modern Turkey,* vol. 2 (Cambridge: Cambridge University Press, 1977). Also M. E. Yapp, *The Making of the Modern Near East, 1792–1923* (London: Longman, 1987).

32. Niyazi Berkes, *The Rise of Secularism in Turkey* (Montreal: McGill University Press, 1966); and Bernard Lewis, *The Emergence of Modern Turkey* (Oxford: Oxford University Press, 2001). For the non-Muslim groups, see the relevant chapters in Braude and Lewis, *Christians and Jews in the Ottoman Empire.*

33. E. J. Hobsbawm and Terence Ranger, eds., *The Invention of Tradition* (Cambridge: Cambridge University Press, 1983).

34. For representative studies, see Robert Fernea, *Shaykh and Effendi: Changing Patterns of Authority among the El Shabana of Southern Iraq* (Cambridge, Mass.: Harvard University Press, 1970); Lerner, *The Passing of Traditional Societies;* S. H. Longrigg, *Syria and Lebanon under French Mandate* (Oxford: Oxford University Press, 1956); Daniel Rivet, *Lyautey et l'institution du protectorat français au Maroc, 1912–1925,* 3 vols. (Paris: Harmattan, 1988); Robert Tignor, Modernization and British Colonial Rule in Egypt, 1882–1914 (Princeton: Princeton University Press, 1966). On the experience of colonialism see among others Jacques Berque, *French North Africa: The Maghrib between Two Wars* (New York: Praeger, 1962); and Timothy Mitchell, *Colonizing Egypt* (Cambridge: Cambridge University Press, 1988).

35. Pierre Bourdieu, *The Algerians* (Boston: Beacon Press, 1962). On peasant behavior more generally, see James Scott, *Weapons of the Weak: Everyday Forms of Peasant Resistance* (New Haven: Yale University Press, 1985).

36. See Albert Hourani, *Arabic Thought in the Liberal Age* (Cambridge: Cambridge University Press, 1983).

37. Samih Farsoun, "Family Structure and Society in Modern Lebanon," in *Peoples and Cultures of the Middle East,* ed. Louise Sweet (New York: Natural History Press, 1970).

38. Ralph Hattox, *Coffee and Coffee Houses: The Origins of a Social Beverage in the Medieval Near East* (Seattle: University of Washington Press, 1985).

39. Philip Khoury and Joseph Kostiner, eds., *Tribes and State Formation in the Middle East* (Berkeley: University of California Press, 1990).

40. See the preface to the second edition of Fatima Mernissi's *Beyond the Veil* (Bloomington: Indiana University Press, 1987) for this suggestion.

41. On the Lebanese civil war, see Kamal Salibi, *Crossroads to Civil War: Lebanon, 1958–1976* (Delmar, N.Y.: Caravan Books, 1976). Also Jonathan Randal, *Going All the Way* (New York: Viking Press, 1983).

42. For the full tale, see Mehdi Abedi and Michael Fischer, *Debating Muslims: Cultural Dialogues in Tradition and Postmodernity* (Madison: University of Wisconsin Press, 1990).

PART ONE

Precolonial Lives

Chapter 2

Assaf: A Peasant of Mount Lebanon

Akram F. Khater and Antoine F. Khater

Lebanon in the nineteenth century was part of the Ottoman Empire. It was administratively divided into several districts, the core of which was Mount Lebanon, the historic homeland of the Christian Maronite population. (It was not until the establishment of the French Mandate after World War I that Lebanon acquired its present borders.) Other important religious and linguistic ethnic groups existed: chiefly Druze (a heterodox Muslim sect), Sunni Muslims, Orthodox Christians, and in the south and east, Shii Muslims as well. Lesser numbers of Catholic Christians, Armenian Christians, and others could also be found.

The incorporation of the Middle East into the world economy had rather dramatic consequences for Lebanon. For centuries, Lebanese silk had been prized in Europe; starting in the 1840s, demand for silk thread by French manufacturers rose rapidly. Silk production increased sharply, then collapsed in 1877 and 1888 as the result of mechanization, silkworm disease, and problems with quality control. The booms and collapses seriously weakened the Maronite grip of the quasi-feudal elite on the rural populations. It also permitted the Ottoman government and foreign capitalists to develop their power further.

By 1860, when Assaf Khater was born in Lehfed, a small village in Mount Lebanon, the recession of the silk industry was pronounced. Its effects were further heightened by rapid population growth. Unable to make a go of it on his tiny plot of land, Assaf was led to seek his livelihood outside of the village. So big a step was not taken lightly, for attachment to the land was strong among Lebanese peasants.

Like many of his compatriots in these years, Assaf eventually took ship for South America, where he hoped to make his fortune as a trader. (The Arab trader, or "Turco," played an important role in the opening up of the South American interior in the nineteenth century.) Although Assaf's life resembles that of countless other Lebanese migrants of the period, it was not without some surprising twists—most notably the departure of Assaf's wife for Uruguay soon after his return to Lehfed.

The experience of the Lebanese can usefully be compared with that of the Greeks and Italians, other Mediterranean migrants to the New World. The biography of Assaf contrasts in interesting ways with the lives of the North African migrants profiled in this volume: M'hamed Ali, a Tunisian who worked in Germany in 1919, and Haddou, a Moroccan who worked in Germany during the 1980s. —Eds.

Assaf Khater was born in 1860 in Lehfed, a small village in Mount Lebanon. His parents were peasants who descended from a long line of peasants who had inhabited the village for at least the past two hundred years. If his parents had been asked to predict their son's future, they would have answered confidently that it would resemble that of any other peasant. At best, Assaf might dream of a return to a mystical past, where work was the basis of equality and where people lived off their honest work without landlords, taxes, or invading armies. But 1860 and the years that followed brought about changes that set Assaf and many peasants of his generation apart from their parents and on a track that led them away slowly but surely from peasant life and dreams. This essay is about those new dreams and the new life.

Lehfed, with its 840 inhabitants and some 120 stone cottages, was a large village by contemporary standards. It is located about sixty miles northeast of Beirut, where it rests in one of the rare plains in the steep and rugged Lebanese coastal mountain range. From the north, it is protected by a high cliff, called the *shir* in Arabic, which rises straight up for about 600 feet. By the southern part of the village rises a series of hills at a slightly gentler slope, and toward the back of the village, at its eastern end, a road meanders through the oak- and pine-covered hills, connecting Lehfed to other villages. Finally, to the west the village opens on a plain overlooking the Mediterranean. Its 3,300-foot elevation made it a historic haven from religious persecution for the Maronite community. Paradoxically, and with an irony that suffused the lives of Lebanese peasants, the village's altitude forced its inhabitants to deal with the outside world more than they might have wished. For at that elevation, and with what little soil covered the stony surface of the mountain, very few crops could be grown. Wheat, lentils, and beans were imported from Syria, and most of the livestock was supplied by the Arab bedouin tribes who migrated to the mountain pastures during the summer. Since the sixteenth century, Lehfed, like many villages in the surrounding mountains, depended on trading the major cash crop—silk—for the agricultural and animal products it needed to survive.

The village was made up of three separate sections that divided the inhabitants geographically as well as socially. At the northeastern end of the village, on the highest hill, lived the rich peasants; on the opposite, southwestern, lower ledge resided the less wealthy families; and in the small stretch of valley in between, called Saqi Rishma'ya, were the houses of those peasants who had the least amount of land. The Khater family's two-room cottage was in this area. Its walls were made of stone cut from the rock, and the roof was made up of mud and thatch that had to be packed down by a stone roller after heavy rain and shoveled after every snowstorm. One of the rooms served as a kitchen and workroom. In the other, whose ceiling was charred by years of burning dried olive pits for warmth in the winter nights, the family ate, visited, and slept. The few animals—a couple of goats, some chickens, and a rooster—lived outside in a stone shack. It was in this house that Assaf was born and raised.

From the age of five and until he was ten, Assaf attended the village's school during the late fall and winter. There, he and most of the boys in the village received a rudimentary education. In those times, the girls could barely step outside the house, let alone receive a public education. Except on extremely stormy days, Assaf walked up the small hill to the 250-year-old church where classes were held. It was not much of an education, especially since the Maronite priest who conducted the classes was barely literate himself and spent more time chastising the children than teaching them. This lackadaisical schooling did not give Assaf much reason to continue after he finished his elementary education, for it held no promise of any benefits or use for a peasant boy. Even if he had intended to go on with his education, it would have been difficult because the nearest high school was thirty miles away at Aintoura. Anyway, his family could not pay for ten-year-old Assaf's education, nor could they afford to lose his labor.

So Assaf joined his family in tilling the one acre of land that they owned. David Urquhart, a European traveler who visited Mount Lebanon in the 1850s, could have been describing the terraces in that acre when he said, "Everywhere man has planted the land, in Mount Lebanon he has made it." Aside from "making the land," the family secured its livelihood from it. A small part of the acre was occupied by a plot where the family grew tomatoes, onions, garlic, lettuce, zucchini, and some herbs, and by another plot where they grew some wheat. There was also one olive tree, which barely gave the family enough olives each year for pressing olive oil and for eating. But most of the land was occupied by about thirty mulberry trees, which were crucial for raising silkworms. It was this crop that provided the Khaters with a product for bartering, and later with the cash desperately needed by the family of seven.

Raising silkworms was extremely time consuming and labor intensive. For the Khater family, as for the 60 percent of Maronite peasants who were engaged in sericulture, the whole process started in the middle of April. Around that time, the silkworm eggs were brought down from their storage at colder, higher elevations in the Maronite monasteries. The eggs had to be kept at a certain temperature for the first few weeks until they hatched. Once the worms had hatched, Assaf's mother, brothers, and sisters had alternately to feed and fast them. The family was kept busy all day long during late spring and summer, picking leaves, cutting them into small pieces, and feeding them to the worms.

When the worms began to weave their cocoons, the pace of the work eased up for a couple of weeks. That time was occupied with tending to other chores that had been neglected. Finally, before the metamorphosed worms had a chance to break free, the family collected the cocoons and took them to the village *makhnaq* (literally, choker), where they were placed in a smoke-filled, closed room. After boiling the cocoons in limewater to remove the glue that held them together, they stretched the thread (which could extend up to 500 feet) and laid it out to dry on the rooftop. Next, the silk thread was spun and reeled by Assaf's mother and sisters on an old wooden spinning wheel that gave the silk an uneven look. Most of the silk was bartered to a traveling merchant who would take it to Damascus, where he sold it to the textile shops. In a good year, some silk thread would be left over to weave a scarf for the dowry of one of the girls.

By the time Assaf was old enough to partake in that work—around the late 1860s—things had changed. Now the silk merchants were based in Beirut, and it was they who provided the silkworm eggs to the peasants on loan, using the land as collateral. Also, by the 1860s these merchants had become the representatives of major French silk importers and had more money available for loans. While it became easier for Assaf's family to get a loan, it was now imperative that the eggs matured into a profitable cash crop in order for the Khaters to repay the egg loan and its 20 percent interest, and keep their land. The Beirut silk merchants who bought the cocoons from peasants like the Khaters took them to the new mechanized silk factories. These factories, the first of which was built around 1862, took over the jobs of preparing the cocoons and reeling the silk, which was then shipped to Marseilles.

Also around this time Assaf's family began to sell their silkworms for Turkish *qurush* (piasters) instead of bartering them for wheat or lentils. The price of silkworms fluctuated depending on the demand in France, the competition from Japan and China, and the quality of silk raised. In good years, like 1867, a price of forty to forty-four piasters for one *oke* (1.28 grams) was not unheard of, and it was better than anything the villagers could have gotten from the traveling merchant. In bad years, like 1873, the price of silk plummeted to twelve piasters per *oke*, and the family had to go deeper into debt in order to survive the winter. The constant price fluctuations were not the only thing that caused the family to go into debt. Increased income raised expectations of a better standard of living. Assaf and his family were no longer satisfied with the simple amenities of the old life. Textiles from Damascus were less in demand. By 1870, English cotton cloth was all the rage and everyone strove to have a suit made out of the fancied material. Yemeni coffee, which the Khater family had previously consumed only on special occasions, was replaced in the 1870s by regular consumption of more expensive Brazilian coffee. The family seemed to be always trying to match up its income with its ever-growing expenses, and never quite making it.

In order to supplement the family income from silk and subsistence farming, the young boys had to work outside the home. At the age of fourteen Assaf joined the older boys, who worked the land of a wealthier neighbor. Work outside the home took even peasant girls out of their traditional context. One of Assaf's nieces went to work as a reeler in a nearby silk factory in order to pay off the debt of her family. Since she had never worked in a factory or on a French reeling machine, she had to be trained by the French women supervisors who were brought there by the European owners of the factory. Thus, she was exposed to French ways of behaving and thinking. Naturally curious, she gathered whatever glimpses and ideas from these French women that the language barrier did not block. Together with her experience as a factory girl, this contact transported her beyond the village into a larger world, and she carried this vision back to her family and village community.

Assaf consequently grew up in an environment very different from his father's. The horizons of the village, while never hermetically sealed, were definitely expanding by the 1870s. Steamboats linked Beirut to Europe, and from there to the rest of the world. A railroad was built to link Beirut with Damascus, and roads were built into the mountains. Letters from emigrants, who began to leave for different parts of the New World in the early 1860s, arrived with descriptions of lands that held incredible wealth and of strange ways of living. French and American missionaries also arrived, bringing with them an education not only of the bookish kind but also about different life-styles and different worlds. Travelers from Europe came through more often, recording their impressions of "The Lebanon," while their mannerisms and habits were recorded equally by the locals.

Then there were the stories of peasants striking it rich in the silk trade and building immense houses of five rooms and a veranda—stories that were common lore by the time that Assaf was fifteen. By the age of eighteen, he had heard many letters from emigrants being read around the *ayn* (spring) in the village square, right underneath the large old walnut tree. He had heard of Naim, who had gone to Nayurk (New York) and struck enough gold to send his father fifty *ithmaliyi* (golden Turkish sovereigns), a fortune that would buy a small farm in those days and leave some to spare. He also could not have failed to see the blush of riches on the roof of Abu Latif's old house as the mud brick was replaced with imported Italian red tile. By the time Assaf was eighteen, the old Lebanon was already much changed and new opportunities beckoned.

Yet, as late as the 1850s, the way up was blocked. The *shaykhs* (landlords of the Mountain under the *iqta* system) were quick to enforce their control over the livelihood and life-style of the peasantry. So great was their influence that Assaf's father had to receive permission from Shaykh Butrus al-Khazin, who controlled the area, before getting married. By the 1860s, peasants were legally free and no such permission was required for marriage. Nor, for that matter, was marriage as socially prescribed as it used to be. A "bag of gold" could, in the 1880s, replace the required lineage as a prerequisite for marriage; hence the expression "she married gold," which became popular in the 1880s.

The changing economic tides in Lebanon that affected Assaf's family were paralleled by significant political changes. The old political system, in which villagers were governed by a *shaykh* as the local representative of the feudal *amir*, came under severe pressure in the 1850s. In the past, the *shaykh* had been the largest landowner in the village, and most villagers had worked as sharecroppers on his lands. With the assistance of his henchmen (*qabadayat*), he had administered local justice and imposed various quasi-feudal obligations on "his" peasants (including requiring gifts of honey, olives, olive oil, and chickens on particular occasions).

This peculiarly Lebanese variety of feudalism came to an end in the 1858–61 revolution. Initially a revolt of peasants and lower clergy against the higher Maronite clergy and feudal lords in the Kisrawan district, the uprising soon engulfed other Maronite villages. In a later phase, the struggle degenerated into a bitter sectarian battle between Maronites and Druze, before French and Ottoman troops restored order. The old political system was overthrown. In its place a new order guaranteed by the European states was set up, and the rule of the *amirs* was ended in the Maronite districts of Mount Lebanon. One by-product of the settlement of 1861, of special importance to peasants like Assaf, was that individual liberties were recognized, including the rights of peasants to move freely and of merchants to buy and sell unfettered by the old feudal rules.

Thus, by the time Assaf was born many of the restraints that had kept peasants from leaving the land had been loosened. As a result, Assaf and his family were more exposed to the opportunities and pitfalls of a market economy. As we have seen, this change had tangible effects on the structure of the family, its economic needs and desires. When Assaf was old enough to contemplate the prospects of his future, it was obvious to him that peasant life as it had been was no longer viable.

As Assaf was the youngest of three brothers, and thus had little hope of inheriting any land, his prospects were in fact bleaker than those of many other young peasant men. This was especially so because the population had doubled since the 1820s, while the amount of arable land had remained more or less the same. Finally, silk, the only cash crop that could be raised in Lehfed, was no longer as profitable as it had been in the 1860s and 1870s because of foreign competition and backward techniques of production. By the 1880s, Lebanese silk production was in free-fall, and by 1930 it was definitely defunct. As early as 1910, Lebanese farmers had begun to uproot their mulberry trees and plant orange and lemon trees, the latest in cash crops. In 1878 Assaf had to choose: either he would remain in the village eking out a hard living from the rocky land or he would have to move elsewhere in search of a better life. With the encouragement of his father, he opted for the latter route.

Assaf's first steps outside the village took him only as far as Baabda, the seat of the Ottoman government in Mount Lebanon. There, in 1878, he enlisted in the gendarmes, the Ottoman internal security force established in 1864. Despite the short distance he traveled, Assaf's trip was momentous. After all, a famous local proverb praised the bravery of Naimi's husband for going "to Damascus [a 100-mile trip] and coming back all by himself." So to go to Beirut (a fifty-mile trip) was in itself an act of bravery on Assaf's part. For a peasant with deeply ingrained suspicions of the government, Assaf's decision was mentally an even more substantial journey. A more cautious alternative would have been for him to become a Maronite monk, but that would have meant a celibate and circumscribed life of some schooling and church service. For a man who was to marry twice and have his last child at age fifty-two, celibacy would not seem to have been a very appealing concept. So into the gendarmes he went.

After a few weeks of training in the barracks of Baabda, Assaf was assigned to the gendarme post in Jounieh. Part of his job was to maintain public security in Jounieh and the surrounding villages and to protect peasants traveling the back roads from brigandage. But in reality the gendarmes were there to assert the authority of the government against the landlords and their *shabab*. Assaf's job also included providing protection for the government tax collectors from the peasants in the surrounding villages.

When Assaf first joined the gendarmes, he had hoped that his new job would open up avenues for advancement. But after twelve years of service, he had not advanced beyond the position of corporal. The novelty of the uniform and police life soon wore off. The respectability that he had hoped would come with the uniform was not forthcoming, for most peasants still regarded the government and its agents with deep suspicion. Thus, being a gendarme was not rewarding either psychologically or financially, and it was even less so socially. Yet for lack of a better choice Assaf stuck with it.

On one of his few visits to his village, in 1884, Assaf was approached by his father about marrying one of his cousins, Saydé. Assaf was then twenty-four, while Saydé was in her late teens. Assaf did not know Saydé well at all and had seen her only when she accompanied her mother to visit his mother. At first he resisted the idea, but his father was very insistent because he wanted to make sure that his son married someone from the village. Assaf's uncle was equally anxious to see his daughter married to one of her paternal cousins, so he added a small plot of land to her dowry to sweeten the deal. By the end of June the two cousins were married and living temporarily with Assaf's family. Assaf himself could not stay very long after the wedding, for he had to report for duty in Jounieh. Since he could not afford to have his wife live in Jounieh with him, and since it was unthinkable for her to live in a strange town with her husband gone on duty most of the time, Assaf had to leave Saydé behind. Within a year of their marriage, their first son was born, who was named Selim.

From the start, times were hard for the young couple. Not only did the long physical separation inhibit the development of normal married life, but also their financial situation was difficult. Saydé worked hard on the plot of land that she owned as part of her dowry, and she also helped Assaf's mother with her work in the house in order to make ends meet. Assaf's salary of a few hundred piasters per year was not by itself sufficient to support them; even with Saydé's work, it barely kept them out of debt. It was quite obvious, especially after their daughter Nessim was born, that the dreams of wealth and a better life that they had were not going to come true while Assaf worked as a gendarme. His stint in the gendarmes exposed him to the cosmopolitan life of Beirut, its new bourgeois manners, European clothes, and the French language. He could also see steamships cruising in and out of the port of Beirut—constructed in 1860 to facilitate silk exports to France—and streams of emigrants boarding them to make the crossing to what they anticipated was a better life. The twelve years Assaf spent in the gendarmes only made him less inclined to be a peasant and more interested in seeking other ways of making a living.

Upon the birth of his third child (named Jirjis after his grandfather), in 1890, Assaf decided to emigrate. But first he needed some money. He could either borrow, using his land as collateral, or sell the land. The second alternative was unrealistic. Despite his rejection of peasant life, ownership of land still conferred social status and economic well-being in his eyes. What he wanted was more land, not to farm himself, but to rent to a sharecropper; thereby, he could enjoy the higher social status of a landowner. So Assaf mortgaged the land, sold one of Saydé's gold bracelets, and gathered their joint savings of ten Turkish gold sovereigns for his trip. With many goodbyes and a few words to Saydé informing her that she was now responsible for their sons and the honor of their daughter, Assaf left his village for the second time to seek his fortune. With four of the gold sovereigns he was able to buy passage on a steamboat heading to Marseilles in late June.

Four days after leaving Mount Lebanon, Assaf arrived in Marseilles. Unlike most peasants who emigrated in this period, he had no relatives or acquaintances in the *mahjar* (land of emigration). Hence, he did not have any definite ideas about where his travels should take him. On the ship from Beirut he became friends with other Lebanese peasants who were going to

Uruguay, so he decided to join them. Together they set about trying to find a way to cross the Atlantic, and within a couple of days they had boarded a freighter in Marseilles heading to Uruguay. The month-long Atlantic crossing was a nightmare. He and his companions lived in the hold of the ship and were fed stale bread and brackish water. Used to feeling the ground beneath his feet, Assaf was terrified and bewildered by the way the ship's motion upset his balance. In the overcrowded conditions and stench and filth of the hold, disease spread easily. A few people even died during the voyage. That hellish experience left Assaf weak and ill upon his arrival in Montevideo, the capital of Uruguay. Luckily for him, the small local Lebanese community was quite helpful to new immigrants. He was taken into the house of the Sakaf family, who had originally emigrated there in 1880 from Zahlé, a town in the Biqaa Valley of Lebanon.

After a week of recuperating from his arduous trip, Assaf began to look for work. Since he had come to Uruguay with the intention of returning to Lebanon, Assaf had no desire to acquire land or to work as a farmer. In a place where industry was almost nonexistent, only one avenue of work was left for him: commerce. Traditionally, this was the first line of work that new immigrants engaged in. Assaf filled his beaten-up old leather valise with the few items that he had brought from Lehfed, wooden crosses and worry beads made from olive pits, together with whatever he purchased or got on loan from already established Lebanese residents of Montevideo. Thus, Assaf started his career as a peddler.

Although he knew neither Spanish nor any of the indigenous Indian languages, Assaf put together enough words to make up a vocabulary for merchandising. What he lacked in linguistic abilities he made up for with his clothes, which immediately marked him as an emigrant from the Holy Land and attracted customers. After a year, he was comfortable enough with the trade, the language, and the country to venture into inland areas away from the capital. He spent several months at a time traveling the backcountry, bringing anything from lipstick to fans to the farmers (who were mostly of Italian extraction) and to the Indian peasants. Over the following two years, Assaf traveled enough miles on foot and by boat to save money to purchase a small shop in Montevideo and to retire from at least the walking part of his newfound trade. After opening the shop, Assaf remained in Uruguay for eight years, until 1898.

Few Lebanese emigrants became wealthy, but like many others Assaf prospered enough to live comfortably and to send small amounts of money back to Lebanon, money that was invested in plots of land in Lehfed. The years of emotional and physical separation did not reward his family back in Lebanon with material comforts; if anything, times were more difficult for Saydé, who had to care for and feed the three children almost by herself. Assaf's income from the gendarmerie had stopped, and his trip had consumed most of the savings of the family. Moreover, Saydé's relationship with her in-laws was not very good. As a married woman living alone with her children, she inevitably set tongues wagging in the village about her morals, and this only added to the pressures with which she had to contend because of the absence of her husband. Although she did not starve to death, Saydé was hardly a happy woman during those eight years of separation.

Nor was she overjoyed when Assaf returned in 1898. It was difficult to pick up the pieces of a flimsy relationship that had been based for the past eight years on rare and short letters. The breakdown of their relationship was also accelerated by Assaf's changed behavior. While he did return to the village (unlike other emigrants who could not even face going back to the "old country" life-style), he could not fully bring himself to be integrated into the traditional village life. His desire to display the wealth he accumulated in Uruguay by spending large sums of money in the village's coffee shop did not sit well with Saydé. Things between them deteriorated slowly but surely, and his relations with his children fared no better. The oldest boy, Selim, was especially resentful of his father for leaving them for such a long time. The other two children did not even recognize him when he first came back, nor did they grow closer to him in the following years.

In 1900, two years after his return, matters got so bad between the married couple that Saydé took Selim and Nessim and left for Uruguay. Jirjis, the youngest boy, stayed with his father in Lehfed. This event was as shocking to the village as Assaf's sister going to work in the silk factory had been in the 1860s. Women rarely left their husbands to travel thousands of miles away, even if accompanied by a fifteen-year-old boy. Nor, for that matter, did most men allow their wife and children to leave them, let alone allow their wife to take over their business in the *mahjar*. In this particular case, the traditional social patriarchal controls had obviously been seriously weakened.

The Atlantic crossing was difficult for Saydé, who was pregnant and suffered from tuberculosis. A year and a half after reaching Uruguay, she succumbed to her illness and died, leaving Selim, then age sixteen, as the head of the family, which now included a baby boy, Khater, who was born upon their arrival in Montevideo. By 1902, when Selim started running the shop, the situation of the Lebanese immigrants had shifted from that of exotic newcomers to that of pariahs in the eyes of the indigenous population. Their practical monopoly of the market, as well as their competition with the native merchants invoked feelings of antagonism. While tensions and conflict generally remained beneath the surface, in a few cases bad feelings led to violence. Selim's was one of those cases. His youth and inexperience translated into rash behavior that got him into constant trouble. Like the Syrian protagonist in Gabriel Garcia Marquez's novel *Chronicle of a Death Foretold,* Selim had an affair with the wife of an Uruguayan merchant. Business, honor, and nationalist feelings came together in a fight that broke out between the two merchants and later developed into a big street brawl. Selim lost the fight and was humiliated publicly. As he could not bear such a dishonor, the next day he went to the house of his enemy and shot him dead. Thus he landed in an Uruguayan prison at the age of eighteen, while his sister, Nessim, who was only sixteen at the time, was left to care for the house, the business, and five-year-old Khater.

The Sakaf family—who had helped Assaf get started—took the small family in and sent for Assaf to come and deal with the situation. In 1905, Assaf got on a boat and traveled to Uruguay for the second time. Once there, he expended much time and money in getting his son out of prison. He succeeded in doing so but lost most of the money he had made in his previous, eight-year stay. Not wishing to remain in Uruguay nor to leave his second wife—whom he had married after Saydé died—and family alone in Lebanon, Assaf hurried back to the village in Lebanon. But he did so with the promised financial support of Selim, who remained in Uruguay with Nessim and Khater.

Upon his return to Lebanon, Assaf set about finishing work on his house and expanding his holdings. By 1914, he had purchased 100,000 square meters of land in Lehfed and another 2,000 square meters in Jubayl (ancient Byblos). After adding two new rooms and a veranda to the old house, Assaf looked for a different kind of investment. He bought a flour mill in Jubayl that would provide him with a more regular and immediate source of income in addition to what he received from the sale of apples that he grew on half of his land. His efforts to break his complete dependence on the land reflected the general mood of the peasant population of Mount Lebanon, who had learned after the crash of the silk market to diversify its sources of income. The lesson came in handy for Assaf during World War I, when Lebanon was plunged into economic hard times, and Selim reneged on his agreement with his father. Hunger and deprivation swept Mount Lebanon as the Allies tightened their blockade of all Ottoman lands including Lebanon. The basic necessities of life—such as flour, oil, and meat—disappeared first from the cities and towns and later from the villages. By 1919, about fifty thousand Lebanese had perished from the ensuing famine, and many towns were depopulated. Lehfed also suffered from shortages, and many tried to cross the mountains into Syria in order to buy sacks of flour and bring them back to Lebanon. Prices skyrocketed, and life became dear. Assaf did not venture over the mountains, but he was forced to sell his mill in Jubayl in order to feed his family and survive the war.

Assaf died in the cold winter of 1933. When he passed away, he was what social scientists would call a rich peasant: a man who owned quite a bit of property and who employed others to plough and sow his land. He had started moving away from the peasant life when he first joined the gendarmes, and when he left for Uruguay in 1890 he definitely set himself and his two families on a trek out of poverty into material comfort. The political, social, and economic changes that Mount Lebanon was undergoing obviously shaped the boundaries within which Assaf operated. The dramatic changes that replaced the old quasi-feudal *shaykhs* with the new silk bourgeoisie also brought down some of the obstacles that had previously kept the peasants bound to their land. At the same time these changes made life off the land even more untenable than before the watershed year of 1860; thus, many of the peasants had to move off their land and onto the roads, towns, and cities of Lebanon and the world. Assaf, among other peasants who emigrated from Lebanon, pushed the boundaries to the limit and maneuvered his way to achieving the material goals he wanted for himself and his family. In the process he was slowly and subjectively transformed from a peasant into a member of a new, amorphous class that was still too raw to be defined in any set terms. All that can be said with any certainty about Assaf, and the men and women like him, is that he dreamt of, and toiled for, a better life. He succeeded to an extent, others did better, and still others failed. For Assaf, and for Lebanon as a whole, success meant the coexistence of traditional "Eastern" social relations with new relations based on "Western" materialism, juggling ways of life that sometimes flowed almost effortlessly, and at other times came crashing down with a loud bang.

A NOTE ON SOURCES

The basic sources for this essay include the Khater family papers and personal reminiscences. Also helpful were recent works on the social and economic history of Lebanon. These include notably Dominique Chevallier, *La société du mont Liban à l'époque de la révolution industrielle en Europe* (Paris: Librairie Orientaliste Paul Geuthner, 1971); Akram Khater, *Inventing Home: Emigration, Gender, and the Making of a Lebanese Middle Class* (Berkeley: University of California Press, 2002); Toufic Touma, *Paysans et institutions féodales chez les Druses et les Maronites du Liban du XVIIIe à 1914 (Beirut: Librairie Orientale, 1971); and Boutros Labaki,* Introduction à l'histoire économique du Liban: Soie et commerce extérieur en fin de période ottomane (Beirut: Université Libanaise, 1984). The authors would like to dedicate this essay to those Lebanese whose dreams, aspirations, and homes were destroyed by the war and violence of 1975–90.

SUGGESTIONS FOR FURTHER READING

For a basic history of Lebanon, see Kamal Salibi, *The Making of Modern Lebanon,* and his *House of Many Mansions: The History of Lebanon Reconsidered* (London: I. B. Tauris, 1988). Roger Owen's *Middle East in the World Economy, 1800–1914* (London: Methuen, 1981) surveys the basic economic context.

For the nineteenth-century social and political background, see John Spagnolo, *France and Ottoman Lebanon: 1861–1914* (London: Ithaca Press, 1977). On the Kisrawan peasant revolt, see Y. Porath, "The Peasant Revolt of 1858–61 in Kisrawan," *Asian and African Studies* 2 (1966): 77–157; and Samir Khalaf, *Persistence and Change in 19th Century Lebanon* (Beirut: AUB Press, 1979). On the silk industry, Boutros Labaki, *La soie dans l' économie libanaise*, 2 vols. (Paris, 1974). On the growth of Beirut, see Leila Fawaz, *Merchants and Migrants in Nineteenth-Century Beirut* (Cambridge, Mass.: Harvard University Press, 1983). On emigration, see Elie Safa, *L'émigration libanaise* (Beirut, 1976); and the articles of Afif Tannous, notably his "Emigration: A Force of Social Change in an Arab Village," *Rural Sociology* 7 (1942).

Chapter 3

Shemsigul: A Circassian Slave in Mid-Nineteenth-Century Cairo

Ehud R. Toledano

High up on the list of Western stereotypes about Middle Eastern societies is the slave woman in the harem. The very existence of such a figure of powerlessness and degradation is a continual challenge to Western cultural values (whether patriarchal or feminist). Accordingly, to be presented with a historically existing slave woman and to seek to understand the world in which she lived and functioned is to undertake an unusual exercise in crosscultural time travel. And that is what the reader is called upon to do with Ehud Toledano's portrait of Shemsigual, a Circassian slave woman of mid-nineteenth-century Egypt. (The Circassians were a tribally organized people of the Caucasus who lived under Ottoman rule.)

By a kind of miracle, the police archives of Egypt contain documentation of a lengthy legal case brought by one Shemsigul, a Circassian woman who was purchased in an Istanbul slave market c. 1850 and brought to Cairo by Deli Mehmet, a slave dealer. The documentation contained in this file is all that is known about Shemsigul: but what is there constitutes a precious window into the lives of a whole category of women, slaves in the elite households of the Ottoman Egyptian establishment.

Toledano's contribution consists of a translation of the text of the legal inquest by the Egyptian authorities into Shemsigul's case, together with his reflections on the case in the context of what is known generally about the history of slavery and the history of women in nineteenth-century Egypt as well as what is known specifically about the slave trade in Circassian women to elite Ottoman Egyptian households.

In Greek and Roman times, the joint household staffed by female slaves and retainers (known as the *gynaeceum*) was characteristic of elite families in the Mediterranean basin, where it constituted an important locus of women's work and sociability. The *gynaeceum* was also known in the Byzantine and Persian empires prior to the coming of Islam, as were the associated cultural practices of the seclusion and veiling of elite women. The institution of slavery was also well known in the ancient world.

Under Islam both the elite household and slavery (especially domestic slavery) flourished, both hedged about by culturally accepted and religiously grounded edicts that tempered to a degree their practice. Shemsigul's story comes to our attention because she was able to avail herself of the possibility for legal redress and was able successfully to bring the slave dealer who raped her and made her pregnant to justice.

In Toledano's reconstruction, the case of Shemsigul is surprising in more than one way. For example, his portrait of the slave dealers' guild, while replete with a Simon Legree figure in the person of the villainous Deli Mehmet, is one of a professional organization that was very conscious of its reputation. Shemsigul herself, far from being a downtrodden wretch, comes across in the documents as a woman with a healthy sense of her own worth and a remarkable ability to utilize the system to her advantage.

There remains much that we do not know: How common was this sort of case? To what extent did Shemsigul fall into or take advantage of rivalries between Deli Mehmet and the other slave dealers? What became of her thereafter? Toledano's biography, because it provides us with the text of the court documents, complete with gaps and silences, can be read in more than one way, which only adds to its interest.

Little is known about nineteenth-century Middle Eastern women's lives, and what little we do know is doubly suspect. Until recently, most of our knowledge came from European observers, whose cultural presuppositions and prejudices often intruded. Moreover, almost all of the individual named women we do know about are twentieth-century elite figures. Things have begun to change, however, as a new generation of scholars has begun to write the history of Middle Eastern women, utilizing new questions and new sources. The results are bound to overturn most existing stereotypes.

For portraits of other Middle Eastern women, see the contributions in this volume by Lila Abu-Lughod, Julia Clancy-Smith, Baya Gacemi, Homa Hoodfar, Julie Oehler, Tamara Neuman, and Celia Rothenberg. —Eds.

On 30 June 1854, a young Circassian woman named Shemsigul appeared before police investigators in Cairo and presented testimony about her life over the previous two years. For both its historical significance and its human interest, the record of that testimony is a unique document. There, in the old pages of a police register at the Egyptian National Archives, in Ottoman Turkish, unravels a troubled chapter of a woman's life that began in a Circassian village in the Caucasus, continued in Istanbul, and ended in Ottoman Cairo. Through Shemsigul's testimony, we learn much about the Ottoman-Egyptian elite harem and about the possibilities for legal redress available to women in Egypt.

Shemsigul was born in the late 1830s or early 1840s in the Caucasus, which was then under Ottoman control. Slavery was still common among the tribal federations of Circassia, where a special class of agricultural slaves had existed for centuries. This was one of the few areas in the Ottoman Empire where agricultural slavery was practiced. Otherwise, free labor, local forms of serfdom, and small-scale leasing by cultivators prevailed in agriculture throughout the empire. Slave labor as practiced in the antebellum American South was virtually unknown to the Ottomans. However, for short periods of time and on a smaller scale, black slaves were used in cotton and sugar plantations in Egypt during parts of the nineteenth century.

The extreme poverty of Circassian slave families and the dire conditions among free members of the lower classes forced them to sell their young children to slave dealers, who carried them off to Istanbul and other urban centers. Parents who did so also believed that they were thus improving the chances of their offspring to attain better living conditions and an entry into the Ottoman elite. This traffic filled the ranks of Ottoman harems, a central institution of the urban governing elite. In the nineteenth century, the large majority of slaves imported from the Caucasus were young girls in their early teens. Many slave girls were subsequently socialized into the Ottoman elite. As we consider how they ultimately fared, we should weigh the loss of family and legal freedom (for those who had not been born slaves) against the possibility that they might thereby have gained access to a better life.

Born into a poor Circassian family, Shemsigul was brought to Istanbul by a relative or a slave dealer, who offered her for sale in the Ottoman capital, where the slave dealer Deli Mehmet purchased her. Deli Mehmet was based in Cairo and operated on the Mediterranean and Red Sea routes, as well as on the long-distance route to India. As we shall explain later, the Egypt that Shemsigul came to in 1852 was a tranquil and prosperous country, at peace with its neighbors and its Ottoman sovereign, the sultan, and recovering from a heroic and traumatic period that had ended in the early 1840s. It was also a society in which domestic slavery was widely known. In those years, there were between 10,000 and 15,000 slaves in Cairo alone, out of a population of about 275,000. About 5,000 slaves used to enter Egypt every year, most of whom were black women destined for menial work in Egyptian households. Shemsigul belonged to the relatively small number of white women who served in the Ottoman-Egyptian elite harems.

The portion of Shemsigul's life about which we have information begins when she came into the possession of Deli Mehmet, when she was in her mid- to late teens. It covers a little more than two years, 1852–54; the account of these years is found in the police records of the Egyptian National Archives. The events contained therein took place in Istanbul, on a boat crossing the Mediterranean, in Cairo, and in Tanta, a market town in Egypt. The specificity and high quality of the documented chapter are rare in the historical record of individuals belonging to non-elite groups in the Ottoman Middle East. In order to reconstruct the undocumented chapters with reasonable confidence, we have to rely on what we know from other cases. We begin with the full text of Shemsigul's testimony, as given to police interrogators at the end of June, 1854.

Questions: When did you come to Cairo? Who was the person who brought you? Where did you stay when you arrived? To whom were you given by the person who had brought you here?

Shemsigul: I came here two years ago. The person who brought me from Istanbul is the slave dealer Deli Mehmet. When I arrived, I was sold to the palace of Mehmet Ali Pasha [son of Mehmet Ali Pasha, governor general of Egypt, 1805–48].

Questions: Was the person who brought you over to Mehmet Ali Pasha's palace Deli Mehmet? How long did you stay there? Where did you go afterwards?

Shemsigul: The person who sold me to Mehmet Ali Pasha is Deli Mehmet. I stayed there for about five months. Afterward, the aforementioned [Deli Mehmet] took me from the palace. I [then] went to the house of Mustafa [another slave dealer].

Question: Since Deli Mehmet had sold you to the household of Mehmet Ali Pasha, and since you stayed there for five months, why did he take you from there and why did you go to Mustafa's house?

Shemsigul: After I had stayed at Mehmet Ali Pasha's palace for five months, it was suspected that I was pregnant. A midwife was brought in to examine me, and she verified that I was indeed pregnant. So they summoned Deli Mehmet and returned me to him. He then took me and brought me to the house of Mustafa.

Question: By whom did you become pregnant?

Shemsigul: I became pregnant by Deli Mehmet.

Questions: You state that you became pregnant by Deli Mehmet. Where, then, did he have sexual relations with you? And, since you became pregnant, how come he sold you [this being illegal]?

Shemsigul: In the boat, on the way here, he forced me to have sexual relations with him; he continued to sleep with me until he sold me. Before the sale, I told him: "Now you want to sell me, but I have missed my period, and I think that I am pregnant by you." When I asked him later what would happen, he did not listen, but went away, brought back some medicines, and made me drink them [to induce an abortion]. Finally, he sold me to the palace.

Question: Your answer is [now] well understood. When they said at the palace that you were pregnant, they returned you, and you went to Mustafa's house. But now, you need to explain how many days you stayed there and what was the state of your pregnancy.

Shemsigul: When I left the palace, I went to the house of Mustafa and stayed there for about ten days. While I was there, Deli Mehmet's wife came to the house and cursed me, as she also did Mustafa. Finally, when she wanted to hit me, Mustafa's wife prevented her from so doing. When Mustafa saw the woman's rudeness, he sent me to the house of Deli Mehmet. As I got there, Deli Mehmet's wife brought in a private midwife and demanded that she would perform an abortion on me.

At that, the midwife said: "This [woman's] pregnancy is well advanced, and now there is a big child in her stomach [which] cannot be aborted." Having said that, she left, but the woman [Deli Mehmet's wife] insisted, saying: "I shall put an end to this pregnancy." Later, her husband, Deli Mehmet, came. She said to him: "Let us beat this slave and end her pregnancy," [to which] Deli Mehmet stated: "I am not going to beat [her]." But the woman would not stop. She fetched a clothespress, hit me with it several times on my stomach and back, and [then] beat me with a mincing rod.

At that point, one of the neighbors, a peasant woman, came to the house. When she saw the cruelty with which I was being treated by Deli Mehmet's wife, she pitied me and went to the house of Selim Bey. As she told [them] about the beating and the pain inflicted upon me, the wife of the said dignitary heard the peasant woman, got up, and came in person to the house of the said Deli Mehmet. When she saw my suffering, she had mercy on me and said to Deli Mehmet's wife: "I shall take her and perform the abortion." She then took me to her house, but left my condition as it was. When[ever] Deli Mehmet's wife would come and ask [about the pregnancy], they [the people at Selim Bey's house] would lie to her, saying: "We are giving her medicine [to induce an abortion]." I stayed there in that way for about three months.

When the child was expected to come into the world, Deli Mehmet's wife came and stood at the bedside. As he was born, she took the child to another room and passed him through her shirt to mark that she was adopting him. To me she said that he died. Later, she went to her house, brought in a wet nurse for the child, and gave [the baby] to her [care]. One day, Selim Bey's wife brought the baby [home] secretly and showed him to me.

After twenty days, I went to the house of Deli Mehmet and stayed there for about twenty days, but they did not show me my baby. Finally, they gave me in trust to Timur (another slave dealer) in order to be sold at the Tanta fair, so I went with him to Tanta [the Tanta fair was the largest in Egypt, attracting in the first half of the nineteenth century from 100,000 to 150,000 visitors]. A few buyers came and looked me over, but did not buy. Ultimately, I returned from Tanta and stayed at the house of Timur.

Deli Mehmet took me there and gave me to [name not clear], where I stayed for three months and about ten days. Later, he returned from India and brought me to the house of the agent of

Yegen Ibrahim Pasha [to be inspected for sale by] an Indian who was going back to India. Since an agreement was not reached with the Indian, and Deli Mehmet wanted to go to the Hijaz, he took me again to the house of Mustafa the slave dealer, on the condition that he sell me to a foreigner [someone not living in Egypt]. He himself went to the Hijaz, and I stayed at Mustafa's house.

Because Mustafa had become aware of Deli Mehmet's position [regarding my having borne him a child], he did not show me to any buyers. When Deli Mehmet returned from the Hijaz, he took me [from Mustafa's house] and sold me to Timur. I stayed there [at Timur's house] for about two and a half months.

Questions: Did you, at any stage from the beginning [of the story], inform the slave dealer Timur, or anyone else, that you had been pregnant and that you were badly beaten? If you did not, why?

Shemsigul: As a slave, I was afraid to say anything about my suffering, so I did not tell Timur [or anyone else].

This testimony is revealing in more than one way. Not only do we learn about the world of the slave dealers in the Ottoman Empire and the life of the Ottoman-Egyptian elite harem; most significantly, we learn about the life of a female slave in a Muslim society in the 1850s. In the process, we are afforded a precious glimpse of a corner of Egyptian society about which we otherwise have little documentation. Shemsigul's story brings out not only her sufferings as a slave woman but also her determination and resilience. From the Egyptian police records it is possible to understand at least a part of Shemsigul's life, and thus of the situation of poor slave women more generally.

Before exploring in greater detail this corner of the social history of Egypt, it is important briefly to situate Shemsigul's story in the context of nineteenth-century Egyptian history. In those years, Egypt was recovering from the forced-march modernization policies pursued by Mehmet Ali Pasha, who had ruled Egypt with an iron fist from 1805 to 1848. The Ottoman Empire was then—despite all its internal difficulties—the strongest and largest Muslim power in the world, and Egypt was one of the wealthiest and most important provinces of the empire. Under Mehmet Ali Pasha, Egypt experienced a period of military and economic expansion. In order to realize his desire for independence, Mehmet Ali launched an ambitious, Western-oriented reform program that exhausted the country's human and material resources. When Mehmet Ali's ambitions threatened the integrity of the Ottoman Empire in 1840–41, his forces were pushed back from Syria, and his regional empire was dismantled as a result of European military and diplomatic intervention. After his death in 1848, his family, invested with the hereditary government of Egypt, pursued his reforms, but on a smaller scale and at a slower pace.

Thus, the middle decades of the century during the reigns of Abbas (1848–54) and Sait (1854–63) Pashas were a period of economic and administrative contraction. With the exception of Egypt's participation in the Crimean War (1853–56) on the Ottoman side, it was a peaceful and prosperous period. It was to this Egypt that Shemsigul came in 1852 as a young slave woman and in which she spent her adult life. We must now turn to a consideration of the slave dealers' network and the people that brought her over, sold and resold her, and affected her life to a great extent.

Until its abolition at the end of the nineteenth century, the institution of slavery was an integral part of Egyptian society. Most of the slaves in Egypt at the time were black women serving as domestics, engaged in menial jobs in urban households. A small number of black male slaves worked as attendants in better families or as assistants to artisans, shopkeepers, and merchants. Male slave labor was occasionally used on large cash-crop estates, but slaves never rivaled the Egyptian free cultivators (the *fellahin*) as a work force. During times of increased agricultural activity, such as the cotton boom of the 1860s, the use of slave labor rose significantly. White female slaves, like Shemsigul, were a minority among slaves in Egypt at the time. Some of them served as domestics, but others entered the harems and were socialized into the Ottoman-Egyptian elite.

The harem system was one of the cornerstones of Ottoman-Egyptian elite life. The harem was the most private part of the Muslim household, where the women and children lived. It reflected the values of a sexually segregated society, in which women's accessibility to men who were not members of their family was restricted. Accordingly, the harem was separated from the public section, where male guests were entertained. The master's mother, or his first (and often only) wife, managed the life of the harem, attended by female slaves and free domestics. The concubines also lived in the harem. An active social network linked harems of similar status through mutual visits and occasional outdoor excursions. Especially large and wealthy harems employed black eunuchs of slave status to guard the women and supervise their contacts with the outside, male world. The prototype of the whole system was the Ottoman imperial household, which the other households attempted to emulate on a smaller scale, according to their means.

Life in the harem was often romanticized in contemporary travel accounts by European women. To many Western men, the mystery of the harem was a rich source of fantasy. For the women who actually spent their lives there, reality was, of course, far more mixed and complicated. The women who came into the harem as slaves, many of them Circassians like Shemsigul, were taught and trained to be "ladies," with all the domestic and social roles attached to that position. As they grew up, they would be paired with the men of the family, either as concubines or as legal wives. If they bore children, the children were legally free, the mother's sale became illegal, and she would gain her freedom upon her owner's death.

However, harem slaves' freedom of choice was rather limited, as was that of women in general in an essentially male-dominated environment. In the case of harem slaves, there was not infrequently the difficulty of resisting sexual harassment from male members of the family. It was to such a life that Shemsigul, the main character of our story, was destined when Deli Mehmet purchased her in Istanbul and brought her to Cairo. There, she was sold into a prominent Ottoman-Egyptian household, that of the son of Mehmet Ali Pasha, former governor general of Egypt.

Most of the white female slaves living in Ottoman-Egyptian elite harems were imported from Istanbul by slave dealers, who used to cross the Mediterranean with small groups of slaves several times a year. This was a very profitable trade, and successful dealers conducted long-distance business also with India, the Hijaz, and East African ports. The dealers themselves were of various ethnic origins, but those who traversed the Ottoman world on a regular basis usually spoke Ottoman Turkish and were at home in Ottoman culture. Slave dealers in the various urban centers of the empire were organized in guilds. Guilds were professional associations linking practitioners under the leadership of an elder (the *shaykh*). Each guild had a strict code of ethics that was binding on the membership. In the Ottoman Empire, guilds were not free associations expressing the interests of their members. Rather, they operated under government supervision and formed a major element in the state system of urban control.

Dealers in white and black slaves were organized in separate guilds. Because it catered to an elite clientele and its business was more lucrative, the guild of the dealers in white slaves commanded greater social respect. It was, in fact, listed among the prestigious merchant guilds of the Cairo bazaar. The slave dealers were, of course, bound by the Islamic laws governing the institution of slavery, and the code of their guild reflected that. Thus, master-slave relations (and, for that matter, dealer-slave relations), concubinage, childbearing in slavery, and other matters were considered part of the intimate domain of the family. They were regulated by Islamic courts and enforced by the Ottoman state. As part of that system, the guild *shaykh* acted to ensure that members complied with the law-derived ethical code of the slave dealers' guild. Obviously, both the law and guild practice expressed Ottoman-Egyptian elite values and perceptions, which favored freeborn Muslim men. The story of Shemsigul demonstrates exactly how these mechanisms operated.

From a legal perspective, the slave dealer Deli Mehmet was the owner of Shemsigul and, as such, was allowed to have sexual relations with her. The law did not require the slave's consent, thereby allowing rape in case of the woman's resistance. The dealer was aware, of course, that when the slave lost her virginity, her market value automatically declined. Moreover, if the slave became pregnant, as indeed happened to Shemsigul, the law forbade her sale. Long-distance slave dealers spent a great deal of their time on the road, away from their families and in the company of young female slaves with whom they were legally allowed to have sex. This often led to the situation described in Shemsigul's testimony, especially if the slave dealer intended to form a long-term concubinage relationship with a specific slave. Male slaves, too, were exposed to sexual harassment, abuse, and rape by dealers and masters, although the Sharia strictly prohibited homosexual relations. Custom, however, was more lenient.

Although we have no information about whether Deli Mehmet or Shemsigul attempted to avoid pregnancy, it is clear that methods of contraception were known and practiced at the time. It is likely that sex partners, whether married or not, applied such methods in order to avoid unwanted pregnancies. Earlier and contemporary Islamic law books even discuss various methods of contraception. Thus, for example, coitus interruptus was condoned by the greatest Muslim jurist of the time. As we shall see, legal discussions of contraception and abortions reflect a male perspective that treats the well-being of the woman, if at all, as secondary. This is especially true in the case of female slaves.

Thus, some legal authorities required the consent of both sex partners to the use of contraceptive measures, which seems to have been ignored when a female slave was involved. Other doctors of law mentioned the need for a reason to avoid pregnancy, procreation being strongly favored as a rule. Others considered contraception to be legitimate in the event of anticipated hazard to the fetus, such as might result from a long-distance journey or from danger to the would-be child, especially if the birth was expected to occur in a non-Muslim territory. If the husband intended to divorce his wife at some point in the future, attempts to avoid pregnancy were also legitimate.

From the legal perspective, once Shemsigul suspected she was pregnant, her legal standing changed. Deli Mehmet's legal freedom of action was restricted, while Shemsigul's position was strengthened. As mentioned above, Islamic law stipulated that an owner, here the dealer, could not offer for sale a pregnant slave carrying his child. Accordingly, if Shemsigul gave birth, the child would be free and she would automatically be manumitted upon the death of Deli Mehmet. However, social reality did not always follow the law, as happened in this case. The new situation constituted a real threat to the status of Deli Mehmet's wife, especially if she had no children of her own, or if she had only daughters. If Shemsigul's child was a boy, the threat would be greater still, given the cultural preference for boys. Additional children would normally reduce the share of the wife's children in the father's inheritance. Thus, beyond jealousy and hurt, there were material reasons for the violent reaction of Deli Mehmet's wife to Shemsigul's pregnancy.

Shemsigul's concerns and considerations are more complex; they led her to struggle against the attempts to abort her fetus. It is certainly possible that she simply wanted to have the baby, not realizing that this would tie her to Deli Mehmet for the rest of his life. On the other hand, she might have come to see him as a lesser evil, fearing that new masters might bring new and unforetold calamities. It is also possible that she did not realize that, as she was no longer a virgin, the chances that buyers would be interested in her for marriage or concubinage leading to marriage were slim. That meant that she would rank low on the social ladder of any harem and have a more difficult life. In any event, the revelation of her pregnancy provoked the brutal physical attacks on her by Deli Mehmet and his wife. This brings us to the social and legal issue of abortion in mid-nineteenth-century Egyptian society.

Abortion was well known in premodern Islamic societies, and Ottoman Egypt was not an exception. From its inception, Islamic law dealt with abortions, but, again, mostly from a male perspective. Jurists tended to allow abortions during the first four months, or 120 days, of pregnancy. They believed that before the end of that period the fetus did not possess a human soul. The dissenting view maintained that there was life in the womb from the moment of conception and abortion was not permitted at all. In such a position, there was no room for the wishes or well-being of the pregnant woman. Some of those who consented to abortion in the early months of pregnancy required that a sufficient reason be produced for allowing it. If, for example, a woman was believed to be unable to breast-feed the child after birth, and if the man lacked the means to hire a wet nurse, this constituted a legally acceptable cause for abortion for some authorities. However, it seems that the consent of the father was, generally, not required for abortion.

Shemsigul's story shows the importance of midwives in the women's world of the time. Midwives performed a major gynecological and social role during pregnancy, birth, and early maternity. In this story, we note that a midwife was called to the palace to verify Shemsigul's pregnancy, and that another midwife was later asked by Deli Mehmet's wife to perform an abortion on Shemsigul and refused because the operation would have endangered her. Until the early 1830s, midwives in Egypt acquired their knowledge through apprenticeship and experience. Mehmet Ali Pasha introduced modernized health services, which included women's medicine as well. A school for women doctors and midwives was established in Cairo in 1829, and the first class consisted of thirteen black slaves since the idea was not readily embraced by the population and candidates were hard to recruit. It is clear from Shemsigul's story that midwives also played a role in police investigations of crimes against women.

We must now return to our story. The next witness summoned by the police on the same day, 30 June 1854, was Ali Efendi, head of the slave dealers' guild. The point to note in his testimony is the position and authority of the guild *shaykh*. In a way, this was what we might today call a preliminary hearing. The *shaykh* was empowered not only to listen to the parties but also to take action to redress grievances. The following is what he told his interrogators about the procedure he had followed.

Questions: How was the slave named Shemsigul—who had become pregnant by Deli Mehmet and bore him a child—sold to Timur? What offense was committed [thereby]? You must also make clear to the said slave where her child is.

Ali Efendi: On the morning of the third day of Bayram [a Muslim high holiday], Timur sent the slave named Shemsigul to my house. Later, he himself came and said: "The slave I had sent you is a slave who must be freed after her master's death [because she had borne him a child] and [therefore] her sale is illegal [according to Islamic law]. [But] having no previous knowledge of that, I bought her from Deli Mehmet and took a promissory note [in return]. [Thus,] there is now a [legal] dispute between us." [So] I sent for the said Deli Mehmet and had him brought in.

When I explained to him Timur's statement, he denied [all], claiming that the said slave [Shemsigul] had not been pregnant, nor was she entitled to the legal status of "mother of her master's child" [the child is considered free, and the mother, as mentioned above, cannot be resold and becomes free upon the master's death].

So I called in the said slave and asked her about the whole matter. According to her report, she had become pregnant by the said Deli Mehmet and borne him a child. She [also] reported her suffering in this regard [from Deli Mehmet and his wife].

Nevertheless, Deli Mehmet denied everything. It was suggested to him to take an oath to that effect, at which he declared: "I swear [to it]."

The slave was then asked: "Do you have proof or witnesses that you were pregnant?" She stated: "Mustafa and his wife know that I was pregnant, and Selim Bey's wife and the servants of that household know that I gave birth."

It was then again inquired of Deli Mehmet: "Will you accept [the consequences] if the said Mustafa testified that the slave was indeed pregnant and gave birth?" Deli Mehmet replied: "[If so,] I shall manumit her."

Based on this declaration, the said Mustafa was summoned and interrogated about the matter. He corroborated the slave's assertion. As it became clear from Mustafa's testimony that [Shemsigul] had borne Deli Mehmet a child, I took the promissory note from Deli Mehmet, returned it to Timur, and detained the slave at my place [pending police investigation and likely manumission].

We now come to the main culprit, Deli Mehmet. His tactics changed several times, only exacerbating his credibility problem. At first he denied all; then he stated that he did not remember Shemsigul or the circumstances of her importation and sale; then he claimed that in Istanbul he had had a concubine named Shemsigul and that she had borne him a son who died a few months later, and that she, too, had died since. Finally, he admitted that he had brought Shemsigul from Istanbul and sold her to the household of Mehmet Ali Pasha for sixty purses (about three hundred Egyptian pounds), and later to Timur for only half that amount.

Afterward, in Deli Mehmet's words,

> Shemsigul stayed at the palace [of Mehmet Ali Pasha] for about two months. Since the said slave was not on friendly terms with the harem ladies of the said Pasha, I was summoned to the palace, given back Shemsigul, and told to provide another white slave in her place. I took Shemsigul and, since she had misbehaved and claimed that she was pregnant, I asked her whom was she pregnant by. She replied that she had alleged to have been pregnant only to get herself out of the Pasha's house. Until the question of her pregnancy could be verified, I left her in trust at Mustafa's house, [where] she stayed for about a month. [It turned out that] she was not pregnant, and when she menstruated, the said Mustafa notified me. So, I removed her from there, and she spent some time at our house.

At one point, Deli Mehmet stated that if Mustafa confirmed Shemsigul's version, he would have nothing further to say on the matter. He then appealed to the mercy of the police, without, however, accepting responsibility for the offense attributed to him.

At another stage of the interrogation, Deli Mehmet was asked to produce the papers issued to him in Istanbul for traveling by steamer to Egypt. The police expected that, according to practice, the document would contain the names and sex of his family members and the number, type, and sex of the slaves he was transporting. But, perhaps not surprisingly, Deli Mehmet failed to locate the certificate among his documents at home. At that, a fellow traveler and slave dealer, Uzun Ali, was summoned to report that Deli Mehmet had on board approximately thirteen white female slaves and two white male slaves. The witness had not seen among them any female slave with a child. That testimony undermined Deli Mehmet's story about the "other" Shemsigul, the concubine he claimed to have brought with him from Istanbul with a child. The credibility of the witnesses and the compatibility of their testimonies led to one, clear conclusion, which police investigators did not fail to realize.

Thus, on 11 July 1854 the police department concluded its investigation of the Shemsigul affair. In the report submitted to the administrative court, the police accepted Shemsigul's story and rejected Deli Mehmet's version. Mustafa's testimony was pivotal in forming the view of the investigators, who believed they had established the basic facts of what had happened. Their report concluded:

> The police department informed [Deli Mehmet] that he must abandon his deceptive assertions and tell the truth. When asked "How do you answer [not]?" he here [at police headquarters] affirmed: "I have no answers but those which I had [already] given."

On the following day, the report was forwarded to the administrative court, and a week later the court gave its decision. Although I could not locate the actual ruling in the Egyptian archives, we know from the police records that after the court ruling had been studied by the police the matter was referred to the grand *mufti* of Egypt. In such cases, a legal opinion was usually solicited from the *mufti*. The probable outcome of a case such as Shemsigul's was that the slave would be manumitted and the slave dealer punished, according to circumstances. To enforce manumission, an Islamic court ruling was desirable, for which purpose, too, the case was probably referred to the grand *mufti*. It is also likely that Deli Mehmet received some punishment in addition to the loss of a valuable slave. It was rare for the court to rule against a police recommendation, especially after elaborate investigation backed by a lengthy report, as in this case.

How did this story reach the police and court? The circumstances are fairly clear, though the motives of the characters involved are not. Some two and a half months after the slave dealer Timur had bought Shemsigul, an unidentified man informed him that a while back she had borne Deli Mehmet a son. When Timur asked her about it, she confirmed the story. Realizing the legal situation, he immediately went to the *shaykh* of the slave dealers' guild. It was this official, after internal investigation, who turned the whole matter over to the police. At this point, we must consider Deli Mehmet's claim during the investigation that the whole affair was instigated by his competitors in order to hurt his business.

It is impossible to know what the motive of the unidentified man who provided Timur with the incriminating information was, but malice should not be precluded. Timur had to protect himself from possible litigation, so it is not difficult to see why he went to the head of the guild. The *shaykh* might have been able to resolve the matter inside the guild but chose not to. He might have wanted to show the authorities that he was loyal and honest or to enhance his own standing within the guild. It is also possible that he might have had it in for Deli Mehmet and seized the opportunity. We should note, however, that the risk of harboring the culprit and concealing the information from the police was considerable, given the fact that a number of people already knew about the situation. Shemsigul herself must have been made aware of Deli Mehmet's precarious position and could have used the story at one point or another to pull him down.

What happened to Shemsigul afterward must be left to the imagination. In some ways, her manumission would make her less secure and more vulnerable to harsh economic and social realities. This is not to say that there was no element of oppression in harem life. Female slaves in an Ottoman-Egyptian elite harem were restricted in their freedom of movement, association, and choice of partners. In the power relations with the adult male members of the family, slave women did not have the upper hand, though they could sometimes negotiate a highly influential position within the household. While concubinage was hardly an ideal arrangement for women like Shemsigul, it was socially respectable, and if a child was born, also legally binding on the man. However, especially for women, but for men too, freedom had its own disadvantages, limited choices, deprivation, and oppression.

The act of manumission did not usually entail severance of master-slave relations. Rather, the mutual dependence would continue under patronage without bondage and the slave would remain attached to the manumitter's household. Manumitted slaves, male or female, often remained within the family compound and were expected to render such services as were required of them. This they provided in exchange for the social and economic protection an elite household afforded. Patronage ties were often maintained even if the slave left the master's house, frequently in order to get married. Shemsigul was probably manumitted by court order with Deli Mehmet's reluctant acquiescence. Obviously, she could not expect any assistance from him. If she could not secure alternative patronage immediately upon manumission, she stood the danger of falling out of society's accepted frameworks for an unmarried woman, which could bring upon her want and destitution.

Shemsigul probably sought patronage from the house of Selim Bey, whose wife had offered her protection during the last phase of pregnancy and in whose house she gave birth. The women's world would then take her in and prevent her from drifting toward the margins of society. If she could secure patronage, she would probably live in the compound, perform services, and gradually negotiate her position in that milieu. It would be the patron's responsibility then to marry her off well and see to it that she settled down properly.

We shall probably never know how the story of Shemsigul ended. What happened to her depended on circumstance, but also on her resourcefulness. We do know that she was courageous enough to state her case and stick to it despite the pressures that were undoubtedly put on her. We also know that during her pregnancy, when she was most vulnerable and virtually defenseless, most women with whom she came into contact showed her compassion. And, not least important, although as a woman and a slave she belonged to a doubly oppressed social group, Shemsigul did ultimately receive justice in the courts. Given these propitious circumstances, there are grounds for cautious optimism that Shemsigul's story ended well.

A NOTE ON SOURCES

The police investigation report on which this article is based is found in the Egyptian National Archives in Cairo. The report, numbered 13, covers pages 44–54 in Register L/2/67/4. An earlier, and quite different, version of this paper appeared in *Slavery and Abolition* 2, no. 1 (May 1981): 53–67. It did not contain the translated excerpts from the text that are cited above.

SUGGESTIONS FOR FURTHER READING

The Islamic legal concept of slavery is summarized in R. Brunschvig, s.v. "'Abd," *Encyclopaedia of Islam,* 2nd ed. (Leiden: Brill, 1960), 1:26–31. Slavery in nineteenth-century Egypt is discussed in Gabriel Baer, "Slavery and Its Abolition," contained in his *Studies in the Social History of Modern Egypt* (Chicago: University of Chicago Press, 1969), 161–89. On the Ottoman slave trade, see Ehud R. Toledano, *The Ottoman Slave Trade and Its Suppression, 1840–1890* (Princeton, N.J.: Princeton University Press, 1982).

For insights regarding the family life of the Ottoman-Egyptian elite, see Emine Foat Tugay, *Three Centuries: Family Chronicles of Turkey and Egypt* (London: Oxford University Press, 1963). Accounts of Ottoman harem life by European women include Malik-Khanum, *Thirty Years in the Harem* (New York: Harper, 1972); Demetra Brown, *Haremlik* (Boston: Houghton Mifflin, 1909); Lucy Garnett, *The Women of Turkey and Their Folk-Lore* (London: D. Nutt, 1891); Garnett, *Home Life in Turkey* (New York: Macmillan, 1909); and Grace Ellison, *An Englishwoman in a Turkish Harem* (London: Methuen, 1915).

One place to begin reading about nineteenth-century Egypt is Edward Lane's classic, *An Account of the Manners and Customs of the Modern Egyptians* (1860; reprint, New York: Dutton, 1966). Concise and useful accounts of the political history are still P. J. Vatikiotis, *The History of Egypt* (London: Weidenfeld and Nicolson, 1980); and P. M. Holt, *Egypt and the Fertile Crescent, 1516–1922* (Ithaca, N.Y.: Cornell University Press, 1966).

A good introduction to Egyptian social history is Gabriel Baer, *Social History of Modern Egypt;* and Baer, *Fellah and Townsman in the Middle East* (London: F. Cass, 1982). Women's history is treated by Judith E. Tucker, *Women in Nineteenth-Century Egypt* (Cairo: American University in Cairo Press,

1986), although the chapter on slavery leaves much to be desired. Cairo's urban history can be found in Janet Abu-Lughod, *Cairo: 1001 Years of the City Victorious* (Princeton, N.J.: Princeton University Press, 1971).

The bureaucracy and administrative reforms in nineteenth-century Egypt are dealt with in F. Robert Hunter, *Egypt under the Khedives, 1805–1897: From Household Government to Modern Bureaucracy* (Pittsburgh: University of Pittsburgh Press, 1985). See also Ehud R. Toledano, "Muhammad Ali," *Encyclopaedia of Islam* (Leiden: Brill, 1990) (with bibliography), on the early part of the century; and Toledano, *State and Society in Mid-Nineteenth-Century Egypt* (Cambridge: Cambridge University Press, 1990).

On economic history, see Roger Owen's two books: *Cotton and the Egyptian Economy, 1820–1914: A Study in Trade and Development* (Oxford: Oxford University Press, 1969); and *The Middle East in the World Economy, 1800–1914* (London: Methuen, 1981).

Chapter 4

Journeymen Textile Weavers in Nineteenth-Century Damascus: A Collective Biography

Sherry Vatter

It is not easy to reconstruct the lives of ordinary nineteenth-century Middle Eastern men and women. Not only are the sources cruelly lacking, for the most part we do not even know the names of ordinary people. This is, of course, especially true of rural society, where peasants and tribespeople, deeply suspicious of the state and its agents, kept largely to themselves. But even in the cities, where our sources are relatively more complete, it is rare that we know even the names of individual workers and artisans (though the elite of merchants and *ulama* are better known).

Given the state of the field, Sherry Vatter's portrait of journeymen weavers in Damascus in the middle of the nineteenth century is a considerable feat of the historical imagination. Because of the absence of sources, Vatter's collective biography (or prosopography, as it is sometimes called) is focused not on a single individual but on the social category of journeyman weavers as a whole. While the weavers remain anonymous, from her account we learn a great deal about the specific conditions under which they labored. We also gain a heightened appreciation of the possibilities and limitations of artisan life in Damascus, including insight into the impact of the Ottoman reform program and of changing economic conditions. Because of the importance of the textile sector in the urban economy of Damascus (it was the major employer and paid a big share of wages and taxes), the life of journeymen weavers is of general significance for understanding the impact of change upon society as a whole.

Beginning in the 1840s, the importation of growing quantities of European finished textile goods (especially cheap Manchester cottons) drastically undercut local production throughout the region. This was especially true in Syria and Lebanon, traditional centers of textile production. As Vatter's contribution shows, the impact of these changes depended a lot on the sector of the market for which one produced. Thus, producers of expensive luxury cloth managed to retain their markets reasonably well, while producers of inexpensive cloth suffered intensely. Although the overall Syrian (and Ottoman) market expanded considerably during the century as a result of increased communications and rural security, and some did quite well, the producers of poor-quality cloth never really recovered.

Similar differences emerge if we examine the parallel fates of spinners and weavers. Some weavers did well, but many others were driven out of business by European imports. Nevertheless, as a whole the craft survived. Spinners, on the other hand, were particularly hard hit by the importation of machine-wound thread and were virtually eliminated as a category. Since most spinners were female, the loss of income must have had a considerable impact on family budgets as well as on the life chances of large numbers of women. Little is known about this as yet. (See, however, the essay of Akram Khater and Antoine Khater for the Lebanon case.)

Even within the weavers' guild, there were important differences in income, working conditions, and status. As Vatter shows, merchants controlled operations to their own benefit, and masters, journeymen, and casual employees had varying fates depending upon their specific connections to the work process. Contrary to received opinion, indigenous traditions of protest were not absent. Vatter documents how, under pressure from greedy master craftsmen in the 1870s, Damascene journeymen became involved in a wave of strikes and sabotage that persisted into the twentieth century. Struggling to survive, journeymen weavers sought successfully to protect their livelihood for over a generation. —Eds.

Ahmad paused just inside the door of the dimly lit workshop. His friend Ali sat with his back to the door, interlacing the burgundy and blue silk mounted on the loom in front of him with a strand of red cotton thread.

Ahmad watched the shuttle make a full circuit, from the right side of the loom, behind Ali's body, to the left, and to the right once again, before announcing himself.

"Peace be upon you, Ali. Well done."

"God keep you. Welcome," responded Ali, as he secured the shuttle and turned toward his visitor.

"Have you heard the news?" Ahmad queried.

"What news?"

"Wages have been cut."

"What? Not possible!"

"But yes. The masters will pay thirteen piasters per piece instead of sixteen."

"Where did you hear this?"

"In the market. Everyone is talking about it."

In the center of a small ground-floor room charcoal burned in a brazier, taking the chill out of the damp February air that intruded from the adjoining courtyard. Three young men huddled around it, giving vent to their indignation.

"Look at ups. Sharing a room, and barely managing to survive at that."

"What kind of future do we have?"

"An unbearable one!"

"They should be ashamed."

In a neighborhood coffee shop, a cluster of men passed the evening around a table, sharing a *nargila* (water pipe) and sipping tea. In subdued tones they earnestly addressed the topic of the day.

"Shall we be martyrs to their greed?"

"Will we let them profit at our expense?"

"What shall we do?"

Conversations similar to these certainly were heard in Damascus in early January 1879, just before some three thousand journeymen weavers went on strike, in protest of a wage cut, against the master weavers who employed them. They brought all activity in the city's weaving workshops to a standstill. It remained so for four weeks. Militants ensured that all weavers honored the work stoppage, by intimidating potential strikebreakers with threats and by cutting threads mounted on looms. The strikers won a resounding victory. Masters reinstated the old pay rates and journeymen returned to work.

The journeymen weavers in this provincial Ottoman capital had engaged in a recognizably modern form of labor struggle. Their militant, collective, and disciplined confrontation of employers was characteristic of actions by industrial wageworkers against employers where capitalist relations prevailed. This style of industrial politics was new to Damascus. Up to the 1870s journeymen appear to have addressed grievances as individuals, one or two confronting the master who employed them. Conflicts were not resolved in a militant or collective manner, but quickly, quietly, and out of public view.

How did a group of Middle Eastern workers come to engage in a form of struggle associated with capitalist Europe and America? Were they imitating foreigners, or did their behavior have indigenous roots? If the latter, did they find models of action already available, or did they need to invent them? These questions are best addressed from the perspective of the individual journeymen who conceived of striking and participated in strike actions.

Unfortunately, we are not yet in a position to write life histories of specific journeymen weavers. Even individuals at the forefront of change, those who first articulated a new vision of the journeyman's relationship with masters and strike leaders, remain unidentified. However, a reconstruction of the conditions under which the average Damascene journeyman weaver lived and worked between 1820 and 1880, a collective biography, if you will, promises to shed light on how thousands of individual journeymen came to engage in new forms of struggle.

Damascus had long been famed as a textile-manufacturing center. At the turn of the nineteenth century, this reputation rested upon luxury fabrics—silks, wools, and, above all, silk-cotton combinations made by interweaving silk and cotton thread, the most important of which was known as *alaja*. These fabrics were characterized by irregular, tie-dyed stripes running through a solid background. The silk thread mounted on the loom, the warp, was tie-dyed in one of a dozen or more two-toned patterns—red and yellow, blue and white, among others. The tinted cotton thread interwoven with it, the weft, was allowed to show through, contributing to the final effect.

Damascus's stature as a major textile-manufacturing center was not immediately apparent to the first-time visitor. Minarets rather than smoke-stacks defined the city's skyline. Its industry was not powered by steam but by people. At its heart were some five thousand handweavers working on pre-Jacquard looms: Christians, Shii, and Sunni Muslims, some master craftsmen, but mostly journeymen. All were men. Though women partici-pated in the formal textile sector in nineteenth-century Damascus, the com-mercial weaving of luxury fabrics was a male profession.

The typical Damascene weaver was a Sunni Muslim journeyman em-ployed weaving *alaja*. He labored in a small, dingy, second-story room, cramped together with three other weavers—two journeymen and a master craftsman—their looms, and two apprentices who assisted the weavers and ran errands for them. This workshop, like hundreds of others in the city, was located in a small *khan,* a building given over to diverse commercial and industrial purposes. Very likely, two saddlebag makers cut and sewed in a workshop across the landing, and a second group of weavers worked next door. Downstairs, several donkeys were stabled, a Baghdad merchant ware-housed Persian and Iraqi carpets, a felt merchant stored wool that his employees unloaded from the backs of donkeys and rebundled in the unkept courtyard at the heart of the *khan.* A large wooden gate stood open, allowing easy access between the courtyard and the narrow, bustling com-mercial thoroughfare beyond.

When fully employed, the journeyman weaver worked a ten-hour day, six days a week. He would be in front of his loom plying the shuttle back and forth not long after sunrise and would depart for home at sunset. On aver-age, he could expect to weave four to five pieces of *alaja* per week, complete a length of seventeen pieces every four weeks, and take a half-day break while the finished cloth was removed and the loom restrung with silk for a new one.

The pace of work was not set by clocks or bells but by the weaver himself. Work would be interrupted for mid-morning prayers, occasional forays to the market, and visits with friends who stopped by. Some days the journey-man ate a lunch of bread and cheese and took a nap on a rug rolled out in one corner of the workshop before resuming work in mid-afternoon. On others he went home for a more elaborate meal and rest.

The weaver did not work a fixed number of hours or follow the same routine year-round. As the month of Shawwal and the departure of the annual pilgrimage caravan to Mecca drew near, he would expect to work into the night seven days a week. This heavy workload anticipated the tens of thousands of pilgrims who descended annually upon Damascus, eager to purchase its fabrics. The weaver's opportunities tended to dwindle after the pilgrimage; he might go several weeks between jobs before conditions improved and full employment returned. Exports to North Africa, eastern Europe, and within the Ottoman Empire ensured a modicum of employment year-round.

Levels of employment fluctuated from year to year, depending upon export demand but above all upon how many people traveled with the Damascus pilgrimage caravan. In years when a member of the Ottoman royal family planned to make the pilgrimage, greater numbers than usual would be expected, and the weaver would find more work than usual. In others, when the trip through the desert between Damascus and the Arabian peninsula appeared hazardous, the weaver might be underemployed much of the year. Such was the case when the pilgrimage departed during the dry summer months, or when bedouin raids along the caravan route had been frequent. Political conditions might adversely affect the size of the caravan, as they did for much of the 1810s when the Wahhabis turned back or imposed heavy duties upon caravans reaching Mecca, and in the 1830s when the Egyptian occupation of Syria made Ottoman pilgrims reluctant to undertake the *hajj*.

The journeyman was not self-employed. He was a wageworker employed by a master craftsman. The latter engaged him on a piecework basis to weave a specified piece of cloth and paid him upon its completion. The journeyman depended upon the master for work space, materials ready for weaving (cotton and silk dyed appropriately and the silk mounted on the loom), and even the loom upon which he worked. If the journeyman roughly fits the profile of a modern wageworker, the master was not a typical capitalist employer.

The master was a workshop proprietor, but he worked alongside his employees. Moreover, his scale of operation was modest. Generally, he managed a single workshop and employed two or three journeymen and one or two apprentices. Some masters owned workshops, but most rented theirs from a private landowner or *waqf* endowment on an indefinitely renewable basis. Renters were not propertyless. They owned looms and other equipment as well as the right to weave in the workshop. This right was restricted to specified commercial spaces and was bought and sold independently of the building in which a workshop was housed. Its purchase was deemed a prerequisite for operating a weaving establishment. Though the master weaver owned property, he was not a textile producer.

The textile merchant controlled the overall production process. He determined what would be woven and how much, provided the raw materials, and covered the expenses of production. The merchant did not own a factory but subcontracted work to a series of artisanal specialists who worked at home or in workshops throughout the city. Each in turn received materials, oversaw one stage in the manufacturing process, and was paid for his or her contribution. Masters, journeymen, loom mounters, spinners, and other workers involved in making textiles all depended upon the merchant economically. Only masters dealt directly with merchants, however. They engaged and supervised journeymen and paid them from funds provided by the merchant.

Production involved an elaborate division of labor. Before reaching the master weaver as dyed silk and cotton thread, cotton had been spun into yarn and dyed, and silk cocoons had been graded and unwound, twisted into thread, measured into skeins, tied with fabric to establish a pattern, and dyed one or more times. Before the weaver could begin his work, the silk had first to be mounted on the loom. For this purpose, the master engaged two loom mounters. After the journeyman wove the cloth, the master turned it over to another subcontractor, who starched and pounded it to bring out its color and luster.

The journeyman, at the bottom of this distribution pyramid, had good reason to feel dissatisfied with his lot. He had little control over pay rates and the distribution of work. In slow periods the master might opt to keep the greater portion of work for himself or his relatives. The exploitative nature of the master-journeyman relationship was clearly visible. The master covered his expenses and made his living at the expense of the journeyman; he retained for himself a portion of the fee the merchant paid for the journeyman's work. The latter had reason to be dissatisfied not only with the master for whom he worked but with all master weavers.

Masters and journeymen belonged to a common professional organization, the craft corporation or "guild" (*sinf;* pl. *asnaf*) of weavers. The affairs of the weaving community—production standards, output, training of weavers, settlement of disputes—were regulated under its auspices. The guild provided weavers with a collective means of dealing with outsiders, negotiating subcontracting rates with merchants, and articulating grievances to the state.

The weavers' guild was not, however, a democratic institution. A small group of masters, the elite of the weaving community, monopolized power and exercised control over the journeyman's life in ways that the latter did not always find agreeable. Masters limited how many journeymen were promoted to their ranks. Since only masters were entitled to operate workshops, employ journeymen, and take on apprentices, they determined whether the journeyman became a self-employed small businessman or remained a wage employee for the duration of his career. The Ottoman state's use of guild structures to control and tax the urban population gave rise to other grievances. The authorities did not deal with weavers individually but as a group, through the head of the guild, the *shaykh*. This allowed the *shaykh*, in consultation with a few master craftsmen, not only to distribute the tax burden among guild members but also to place a disproportionate part of it on the journeymen.

If the guild structure embodied inequalities that fueled the journeyman's discontent with the masters, it also provided a counterweight. Its existence gave substance to the notion of collective identity and common interests. The rhetoric of craft solidarity and rituals buttressed the journeyman's feeling of solidarity with masters and downplayed differences. Ceremonies of initiation, for example, imbued potentially divisive issues with nondivisive meanings. By presenting unequal positions as sequential stages in a career, the professional hierarchy appeared to hold the promise of advancement rather than to be an obstacle to it. Thus, the weavers' guild played a role in maintaining the journeyman's identification with the master who employed him and served to minimize conflicts between them.

The journeyman's perception of himself as a member of a corporate group united by common interests was not entirely illusory. It had a basis in social reality. As a rule, masters used their power to ensure that the textile industry remained competitive and that weavers had jobs. To this end, they enforced production standards, protested increased financial burdens slapped on the industry by the state, and attempted to limit the number of weavers trained to compete for available work. Rarely did the guild masters flagrantly abuse their authority. Although bias against journeymen weavers in disputes and in the allocation of tax burden was pervasive, it was also well calibrated and subtle.

Even though the master profited at his expense, the journeyman made an adequate living. Paid eight to ten piasters per piece of *alaja*, weaving four to five pieces a week, the journeyman could expect to earn forty piasters a week in the 1820s and 1830s. In the Damascene context, this was satisfactory, since bread, the staple of the workman's diet, was not expensive, and most journeymen weavers lived in inherited housing or paid low rents. Overall, the earnings of journeymen weavers compared favorably with those of other textile workers, such as silk-thread twisters and loom mounters. Though their earnings were slightly less than those of the best-paid skilled workers, like shoemakers, blacksmiths, and carpenters, they were substantially more than those of unskilled laborers and domestic servants.

The artisanal character of the weaving profession made the master-journeyman relationship a personal and multifaceted one, not simply one of exploiter and exploited. Although at times he might see his master as harsh or even unjust, the journeyman identified with him and might be linked to him by feelings of affection and gratitude. The master was an employer but also a coworker. The fact that he left the journeyman to set his own pace of work, giving the journeyman some control over his work environment, put them on somewhat of an equal footing. Further, the master embodied the journeyman's hopes for the future. Since the master had moved up through the ranks from apprentice to journeyman to master, the journeyman might hope to do the same. These positive bonds between journeyman and master were reinforced by their relations beyond the workplace in the local neighborhood, where masters and journeymen jointly attended weddings, funerals, and other significant occasions and took up collections for weavers in need.

The complex structure of this relationship gave the journeyman good reason to acquiesce in less than satisfactory conditions—militant confrontations might jeopardize his social relationships and economic future. He depended upon the master for employment and would one day need his goodwill to be accepted into the ranks of master weavers and set up a shop of his own. Thus, although the journeyman occasionally chafed at his powerlessness and exploitation, he tended to regard the master's exercise of power as legitimate and even beneficial. Disagreements between master and journeyman were expressed individually and resolved through the intervention of guild authorities.

The above portrait, true for most of the eighteenth century, was no longer accurate by the 1830s. In the late eighteenth and the early nineteenth century, the market for Damascene and other Ottoman textiles expanded rapidly, aided by the withdrawal of French competition and a burgeoning rural market. The number of weavers proliferated throughout the region. In Damascus, janissaries, textile merchants, and other non-weavers rushed to open workshops. Because of the boom conditions, these new shops, operating outside of the official guild structures, seem to have been tolerated. The unregulated expansion of the industry was to prove a liability, however. It meant that during downswings more weavers were un- or underemployed. By the 1830s, normal fluctuations in market demand had eaten away at the journeyman's standard of living. Instead of owning his own loom, he now rented it from the master. This development undermined one of the most powerful bonds tying the journeyman to the master, his aspirations for the future. In theory, a journeyman could escape this unequal and exploitative relationship by setting up his own shop. By the 1830s, his prospects for doing so were poor. He was a wageworker who owned neither workplace, materials, nor tools of production. It was unlikely he would ever accumulate sufficient capital to rent a workshop, purchase a loom, or set up a business of his own.

The eroding position of the journeyman weaver was signaled by the fact that a declining number elected to pay for initiation into the craft corporation. As a result, a new category of skilled weavers began to emerge, trained within the corporate system, working in workshops run by master weavers, and in principle subject to decisions taken by the craft corporation but not formally entered in its rolls as journeymen.

Most of these "unofficial" journeymen failed to register because they could not afford the fees. They were not part of an organized movement, nor did they openly defy their masters. Their very existence, however, was troubling. It showed that some journeymen did not view the guild hierarchy as serving their interests or worth the cost of membership. Over time, this was to drive a wedge between masters and craftsmen. Though most journeymen continued to opt for initiation, the sense of belonging to a community of journeymen and master weavers was crumbling.

In the 1840s journeymen weavers and the industry as a whole faced a qualitatively new challenge. *Moréas, printanières,* and other cotton fabrics that aped the patterns of the city's silk-cotton combinations but sold for a fraction of the price flooded Syrian and Eastern Mediterranean markets. Swiss *moréas,* for example, sold for 1.3 to 2 piasters per meter as against 8 to 9.75 for Damascene *alaja.* Sales of the latter plummeted, as consumers rushed to buy the cheaper imports.

Moréas were not the first European imports to do well at the expense of Syrian textile products. The value of European textiles imported into the region had already jumped dramatically, from less than a million francs annually in the 1810s to fifteen million in 1841. Most, however, were relatively inexpensive cottons—chiefly British-made longcloths, grey domestics, muslins, and nankeens—which did not compete directly with Damascus's silk-cotton fabrics. Imports made gains chiefly at the expense of good-quality cottons rather than the luxury fabrics, upon which the livelihoods of most of this city's weavers depended. The number of looms in use, for example, remained roughly constant into the early 1840s. Growing demand for less expensive fabrics, reflected in increased purchases of cottons, pressured producers of luxury fabrics to hold down prices in spite of rising costs of raw silk and cotton. The merchants achieved this by substituting British machine-produced cotton yarn for the more expensive and higher-quality domestic hand-spun yarn. Thus while the position of Damascene *alaja* weavers remained stable for the time being, large numbers of Syrian women spinners were thrown out of work.

By the mid-1840s it was the weaver's turn to experience economic dislocation. With the influx of *moréas,* employment opportunities contracted, and the number of silk looms in use fell precipitously from five thousand in 1839 to one thousand in 1845, leveling off at two thousand by 1848–50.

Faced with ruin, the master weavers moved to close down the new nonguild workshops in hopes of securing the remaining work for themselves.

A case from 1842 illustrates this effort. In that year, the master weavers of Damascus sought to enforce their monopoly over weaving by getting the local authorities to close down the weaving workshop run by a merchant interloper named Mishaqa. Mishaqa, a British protégé, used the backing of the British consul to defy the order successfully. (Protégés were exempted from local taxes, laws, and civic obligations as part of the treaty rights granted Europeans and their local agents by the Ottoman government.)

The failure of the corporate leadership to eliminate unauthorized competition not only reveals the growing intervention of the West in Ottoman affairs but also demonstrates the declining effectiveness of guild structures. Even without European intervention, "illegal" workshops continued to operate in Damascus. Master weavers, despite the weight of corporate authority, were unable to close them down. Runaway shops had become too numerous and too much a part of the fabric of textile production to be easily done away with. By the 1840s, the inability of guild members to enforce their exclusive control over jobs had become an industrywide phenomenon. For example, in 1847 loom mounters attempted, also unsuccessfully, to prevent newcomers who had taken up their profession twelve years earlier from exercising it or teaching it to their children.

By the 1850s, the local textile industry entered a boom period and conflict over enforcement of guild privileges diminished. The number of weavers employed in Damascus crept upward, from 2,000 in 1848–50 to 2,800 in 1856, reaching 3,500 by early 1860. By the mid-1860s, the number had reached 5,000 and production matched 1820 levels once more.

Four main factors contributed to the recovery of the 1850s. The first was the expansion of rural markets. In response to rising demand for agricultural products and higher agricultural prices, peasants increased production. They used a part of their greater cash incomes to expand purchases of textiles, both European and Damascene, thus boosting textile production and employment in Damascus. This trend intensified during the Crimean War (1854–57) and the American Civil War (1861–65), which heightened European demand for grain and cotton, respectively. A second factor was changing consumer preferences. In the 1840s the popularity of European imports was due to both their novelty and their low prices. The imports were of inferior quality, being made of lighter-weight, less durable cotton. By the mid-1850s many Syrians resumed purchases of better-quality local products.

Thirdly, competitive pricing by Damascene merchants aided the comeback. Between 1836 and 1860 the price of the least expensive and most widely marketed *alaja* remained basically unchanged. In the 1830s the price had been eighty-five piasters a piece. In 1856 it was eighty; in 1861 it was eighty-five, and a quarter-century later in 1879 it cost only ninety. Since the piaster lost two-thirds of its value over this fifty-year period, the ten-piaster monetary increase represents a dramatic fall in real terms.

Finally, the development of new products that responded to the demand for lower prices and shifts in taste also contributed to the recovery. Two cotton fabrics developed in Damascus in the late 1850s, *dima* and *mabrum*, were particularly successful. *Dima* was a cotton version of *alaja*, comparable to *moréas* but of better quality and only slightly more expensive—2.43 to 2.55 piasters per meter as against 1.3 to 2 piasters. Credit for developing a commercially viable version of this fabric goes to Hasan al-Khanji, a master weaver who worked with the backing of a textile promoter, Abu al-Jayd al-Asfar. The technical problems of producing a competitive version of *mabrum*, a coarser cotton, the equivalent of British shirting, were also worked out in this period. When in the early 1860s these and similar fabrics proved successful, other merchants entered production and many master weavers shifted their workshops from silk-cotton to cotton weaving.

Production statistics attest to the role these fabrics played in the recovery. During the 1830s, 5,000 of the total 5,500 looms in use were employed in the making of silks, and only 500 for cottons. In 1860, most of the 3,500 in operation were still mounted with silk. However, by 1869, the number of silk looms had dropped to 1,600, those used for weaving *dima* had jumped to 2,000, and an additional, unspecified number were employed in the making of *mabrum*. By 1879, only 1,200 of a total 7,000 active looms were used for production of silk-cottons, as against 2,500 for *dima*, and 3,000 for *mabrum*.

By the late 1860s, therefore, the typical Damascene journeyman weaver produced *dima*, not *alaja*. In spite of the shift to cottons, he still worked on a hand loom for a piecework wage, weaving tie-dyed yarn with undyed cotton. Capitalists still decided what would be produced, provided raw materials to be worked, and paid masters to engage and supervise journeymen. Even the fabric patterns of *dima* and *alaja* were essentially the same.

Despite appearances, much had changed. The journeyman weaver's standard of living had fallen dramatically between 1820 and 1860. Stable prices for Damascene fabrics had been maintained by freezing the journeyman's wages at 8–10 piasters per piece. Over the same period, the cost of living had increased sharply. The journeyman paid 0.3 piasters for a kilo of wheat in the 1820s, 0.9 piasters per kilo in 1856–57, and between 3.2 and 5 piasters by 1862.

Journeymen might grumble about inadequate wages, but they refrained from demanding higher pay because they viewed their falling real incomes as part of industrywide sacrifices necessary to preserve their jobs. Both merchants' and master craftsmen's profits had fallen along with their wages, and tax farmers had gone along with this spirit of sacrifice and cut tax rates.

Instead, journeymen weavers identified grain speculators as the chief cul-
prits and complained that the government had not done enough to restrain
them. They called on local Ottoman authorities to set maximum prices for
bread.

By the late 1860s, the crisis appeared to be in the past. With the industry
out of acute danger, tax farmers doubled duties on fabrics and merchants
risked a price rise in an effort to restore profit margins. They increased the
price of the least expensive *alaja* from eighty to eighty-five piasters. This confidence proved justified, at least in the short run. The number of weavers
continued to climb, reaching a peak of seven thousand by 1879, before leveling off to five thousand, where it stayed until World War I. The merchant
passed on some of his profits to the master weaver, who in turn passed on a
portion to the journeyman in the form of a higher piecework rate.

Yet many journeymen were dissatisfied with the raise. The increase came
nowhere near covering the losses they had sustained over the previous half-
century. While the piecework rate had risen from 8–10 piasters to 16 for a
piece of *alaja* between 1820 and 1878, the cost of living had tripled. To survive, the journeyman reduced his consumption of wheat and substituted
cheaper and less desirable grains. Rising housing costs forced the unmarried journeyman to share rooms and delay marriage. Falling real wages and
the rising cost of urban real estate had broader import to the journeyman
than his immediate standard of living. Both mitigated against a journeyman
whose father was not already a master accumulating sufficient capital to set
up his own workshop. His prospects for the future were at stake. These were
not the journeyman's only complaints. He had expected to benefit from
renewed prosperity.

Indeed, in view of his sacrifices endured for the sake of the industry's survival, he felt as entitled to recoup losses as any other group. Yet his gains
were minor compared with those of others. The lion's share of the profits
went to the merchants.

The journeyman had to contend with another adverse development in
this period. This was the tendency of large merchants to bypass the guild
structures altogether and to set up large workshops that they ran themselves. These employed more journeymen weavers in one place than did the
old-style workshops, a dozen or more rather than three or four, with one
master at good wages to supervise them. In this fashion, the merchant could
dispense with the two or three additional master-subcontractors who would
have been employed under the old system.

Because the new "factory" system allowed the merchant to benefit from
economies of scale, it proved profitable. However, it was less satisfactory to
the journeyman weaver, who found himself locked into the position of a
wage employee with no possibility of becoming a master himself. Merchant-
owned and operated workshops made the guild increasingly irrelevant to

the production process. Merchant capitalists replaced master weavers as the arbitrators of workplace conditions.

In these circumstances, it would have been logical for the journeyman to identify the merchant as the source of his problems. Instead, the master weaver became the target of his anger. Master weavers increased the portion of the merchant's payment that they kept for themselves and decreased that paid to the journeyman. Since masters worked alongside journeymen, this profiteering was the more visible, and the more deeply resented. The craft elite's self-serving behavior outside the workplace was a further source of complaint. For example, when taxes increased in the mid-nineteenth century, the masters placed the burden of the new impositions disproportionately upon the journeymen, thus discrediting themselves as the journeymen's protectors.

The journeyman's dismal appraisal of his prospects for self-employment and a decent standard of living, as well as his perception of the master as unable and unwilling to look out for his interests, undermined the rationale for identifying with the master and for overlooking the unequal and exploitative aspects of their relationship. As a result, the journeyman gradually came to view his interests as separate from and antagonistic to those of the master. He felt betrayed—that the master had failed to honor obligations at the heart of artisanal ideology. The journeyman's antagonism toward the master intensified and found collective, public expression in the strikes by Damascus journeymen against master weavers over wage rates.

This new state of affairs was graphically illustrated by events in Damascus at the start of 1879. In January a number of master weavers increased their percentage of what the merchant paid for piecework. They had instituted such increases previously but had timed them to correspond with an increase in fees received from the merchant. This permitted masters to improve their position while leaving the journeyman's piecework rate intact or even raising it. On this occasion, however, no such increase was forthcoming; they lowered the journeyman's wage from sixteen to thirteen piasters.

The journeymen responded with indignation. They maintained that they would have accepted the cut if it had been instituted in order to lower the market price of fabrics. Such a move promised to make Damascene fabrics more competitive and would translate into more work for them. But since the masters merely sought their own gain, it was not accepted. The journeymen's anger was fueled by the unilaterally self-serving nature of the masters' action, a flagrant violation of the masters' historic obligation to protect the journeymen's interests as well as their own. It is noteworthy that the journeymen's novel behavior did not reflect the eclipse of communal solidarity but was spurred on by a perceived betrayal of it.

The journeymen's outrage found expression in a citywide work stoppage enforced by activists. The latter cut silk threads mounted on the looms not only of masters who had announced cuts but also of those who had not, "owing to suspicions of collusion between master and workman." After four weeks, with three thousand journeymen weavers on strike, the masters agreed to rescind the cuts. Such strikes were not a flash-in-the-pan development. Common by the 1870s, they were still part of the Damascus landscape after 1900. Journeymen were not always as successful as in 1879, as their failure to prevent cutbacks in 1902 demonstrates, but with each successive strike, their alienation from and antagonism toward the master came into sharper focus.

The persistence of labor militancy might seem to foreshadow the emergence of a mass labor movement, all the more so since the strikers did not meet with the repression that marked nineteenth-century labor struggles in Europe and the United States. The Ottoman ruling class, still dependent upon agricultural and commercial rents, did not perceive its vital interests to be riding on the outcome of industrial struggles. Government authorities and other outsiders did not intervene, leaving masters and journeymen alone to sort out their differences. Unsupported, masters were in a position of rough equality with journeymen.

In spite of favorable political conditions, a mass movement of journeymen weavers did not materialize. Strikes by journeymen weavers petered out after World War I. The French postwar mandate government, not journeymen, was responsible for establishing a union of hand-loom weavers, and it included masters as well as journeymen. In the long run, a decline in the number of handweavers brought an end to their militancy. The competition of factory-produced textiles, both imported and domestic, and changes in taste and life-styles reduced demand for hand-produced fabrics. The number of employed hand-loom weavers fell from five thousand before World War I to the handful who still work in Damascus today. As the handicraft textile sector became economically inconsequential, the journeymen's bargaining power eroded. They found themselves in the same boat as their employers—struggling to survive.

How do we situate the journeymen weavers' experience in Syrian history? It is clear that their novel behavior and the consciousness it implied were not imports but products of Damascene society brought into play by external pressures. Responses by merchants and masters to a head-on confrontation with European competition provoked journeymen to innovate. The conflicts of interest that emerged were rooted in the indigenous industrial structure that subsumed artisanal production within a commercial capitalist nexus.

On no account should the journeymen weavers be treated simply as victims. They did not passively endure change but actively participated in defining its shape. Nor would it be accurate to view their response to the challenge of Western capitalism as a quaint episode removed from the mainstream of Syrian history. We can hypothesize a connection between the journeymen's disciplined collective action and post–World War I labor unrest by factory workers, massive popular resistance to the French occupation during the 1930s, and the political successes of Communists and Arab nationalists whose platforms addressed the question of class in the 1940s and 1950s.

While the import of the journeymen weavers' experience for the broader shape of Syrian history remains to be specified, there is little doubt that handweavers, pushed from the dying handicraft industry into other jobs in other sectors, took a new consciousness and models for political expression with them and used them to help move Damascene society toward its future.

A NOTE ON SOURCES

This portrait of journeymen weavers was taken piecemeal from Iliya Qudsi, "Notice sur les corporations de Damas," *Actes du XIème Congrès des orientalistes*, pt. 2 (Leiden, 1885): 7–34; *Qamus al-Sinaat al-Shamiyya*, vol. 1 by Muhammad Said al-Qasimi; vol. 2 by Jamil al-Din al-Qasimi and Khalil al-Azm; both vols. edited by Zafir al-Qasimi (Paris: Mouton & Co., 1960); Numan Qasatli, *Al-Rawda al-Ghana fi Dimashq al Fayha*, 2nd ed. (Beirut: Maktabat al-Saih, 1982); John Bowring, *Report on the Commercial Statistics of Syria* (London: William Clowes & Sons, 1840); Dominique Chevallier, "Un exemple de résistance technique de l'artisanat syrien aux XIXe et XXe siècles," *Syria* 30 (1962): 300–24; as well as from unpublished primary sources in the British diplomatic archives housed at the Public Record Office (Kew), especially FO 371 (1878–79), vol. 70, pt. 2, Damascus, "Report by Vice-Consul Jago on the Trade and Commerce of Damascus for the Year 1879"; and from French diplomatic documents held at the Quai d'Orsay, notably "Requête des ouvriers ourdisseurs catholiques à Monsieur le Consul de France," 16 October 1846, encl. in Tippel to Guizot (35), 29 December 1846, Damascus.

More generally, see my doctoral dissertation, "A City Divided: Damascus, 1830–1860" (University of California at Los Angeles, 1992).

SUGGESTIONS FOR FURTHER READING

Published works dealing with Damascus's handweavers prior to the twentieth century are few, those in English almost nonexistent. Relevant secondary sources in English are, for the most part, unpublished dissertations. For the structure of the industry in Damascus and Lebanon, see R. Joseph, "The Material Origins of the Lebanese Conflict of 1860" (Bachelor of Letters thesis, Oxford, Magdalen College, 1977). For an overview of the textile industry and artisanal workers, see Muhammad Said Kalla, "The Role of Foreign

Trade in the Economic Development of Syria, 1831–1914" (Ph.D. diss., American University, 1969); and Abdul-Karim Rafeq, "The Impact of Europe on a Traditional Economy: The Case of Damascus, 1840–1870," in *Economie et société dans l'Empire Ottoman (fin du XVIII–début du XXe siècle)*, Colloques internationaux du CNRS, no. 601, 419–32. For industrial techniques, see Dominique Chevallier, "Techniques et société en Syrie: Le filage de la soie et du coton à Alep et à Damas," in *Villes et travail en Syrie du XIXe au XXe siècle* (Paris: G. P. Maisonneuve & Larose, 1982), 121–40.

Two general economic histories of the Middle East contain important information on the textile industry in the nineteenth and twentieth centuries: Charles Issawi, ed., *The Economic History of the Middle East, 1800–1914* (Chicago: University of Chicago Press, 1966); and Roger Owen, *The Middle East in the World Economy, 1800–1914* (London: Methuen, 1981). For a recent case study, see Donald Quataert, "Machine Breaking and the Changing Carpet Industry of Western Anatolia, 1860–1908," *Journal of Social History* 9 (1986): 473–89.

On Syrian textile workers in the twentieth century, see Elizabeth Longuenesse, "Etat et syndicalisme en Syrie: Discours et practiques," *Sou'al* 8 (1988): 97–130; Elizabeth Picard, "Une crise syrienne en 1965: Les syndicats ouvriers face au nouveau régime ba'thiste," *Sou'al* 8 (1988): 81–95. For handicraft weavers in twentieth-century Turkey, see Gunseli Burek, *Women Carpet Weavers in Rural Turkey: Patterns of Employment, Earnings, and Status*, Women, Work and Development Series, no. 15 (Geneva: International Labour Office, 1987).

For the experience of Egyptian textile workers in the twentieth century, see Joel Beinin, "Islam, Marxism, and the Shubra al-Khayma Textile Workers: Muslim Brothers and Communists in the Egyptian Trade Union Movement," in *Islam, Politics, and Social Movements*, ed. Edmund Burke, III, and Ira M. Lapidus (Berkeley: University of California Press, 1988), 207–27; and Ellis Goldberg, *Tinker, Tailor, and Textile Worker: Class and Politics in Egypt, 1930–1952* (Berkeley: University of California Press, 1986).

Chapter 5

Ahmad: A Kuwaiti Pearl Diver

Nels Johnson

So rapid has been the transformation of the economy of the Gulf region (and, alas, of its ecology as well) that it is difficult to recall that just a generation ago many people gained their livelihood from fishing the region's waters. Ahmad, a Kuwaiti pearl diver, interviewed by anthropologist Nels Johnson in 1973 was one such individual.

Johnson's account conjures up visions of a world in which Arab dhows brought the spices of China, India, Southeast Asia, and East Africa to Middle Eastern markets. Later, Chinese porcelains and Indian cottons, along with coffee, tea, and pepper, became the objects of interest, helping to stimulate Vasco da Gama's voyage around Africa in 1498, which opened up the southern seas to European expansion.

Given the hazards of the diver's craft and the appalling conditions under which most divers worked, it is astonishing that anyone would willingly take up diving as a way of life. As Nels Johnson shows, access to livelihood throughout the Gulf was structured by kinship and debt, and pearling was one of the few occupations open to non-kin. Pride in one's abilities, intense bonding with coworkers, and a gambler's love of high stakes attracted people like Ahmad to the diver's life and retained them, even when other opportunities were available.

Prewar Kuwaiti society boasted one of the world's highest standards of living. Its impressive systems of health care, education, and welfare have transformed the lives of ordinary people. When he was interviewed in 1973, Ahmad was still going to fish each morning as in the old days. Alienated from his children and consumed with nostalgia for the old days, Ahmad is left cold by the new Kuwait. Its ways are to him forever strange. So extensive have been the changes he has lived through, it is as if he suffers from a kind of sociological version of "the bends"—a disease that strikes divers who, failing to decompress, surface too rapidly. It is an understandable reaction, one shared, moreover, by many of his generation. (See the biographies of Mohand N'Hamoucha, Migdim, Abu Jamal, and Haddou in this volume.)
—Eds.

I used to fish from a derelict jetty in Kuwait in the early 1970s. I never caught anything, but it was there that I met Ahmad, the former pearl diver whose working life will be recounted here.

Ahmad used to fish, using seaweed as bait, from a nearby beach. He made his livelihood from the fish he caught, selling them to the local residents, for whom he had become a fixture of the neighborhood. It was hard to estimate his age: to begin with, he did not know himself. But from things that he said and major events he remembered, he must have been in his mid- to late seventies when I knew him.

We often got into conversations about his past, conversations made difficult by his Kuwaiti brogue, which often forced me to resort to a Kuwaiti acquaintance for help in sorting out his story. The main topic of our talks was *al-ghaws*, "the diving," by which he meant the pearling industry that is now dead in the Gulf region.

Ahmad's story is one with several facets. It is his version of a life and so is not necessarily "accurate" in all aspects. But its importance lies in the fact that it is his perception of the world in which he lived, an expression of his culture that is important to record and preserve. This is also the story of a system of work, with all its social, economic, and political facets. Ahmad provides us with insight into an industry that was exploitative to a high degree, and no matter what our sympathies are for the individual, it is the system that is in need of close scrutiny. For that reason, it will be described in some detail.

Pearl diving was an economic mainstay of the societies of the Gulf before the discovery of oil. It was an ancient industry that had provided the world with valuable jewels for many centuries. The rewards of pearling were great for the entrepreneurs, middlemen, and boat captains who formed the elite of the industry. But for the divers who risked their lives and whose health was often seriously damaged in bringing up the pearl oysters, profits were few, and ironically the work often resulted in personal debt. To understand this, we have to look briefly at the societies in which pearling flourished and the social character of the work itself. Ahmad was one of those who dove for years but had nothing to show for his efforts, and this situation was a direct result of the social system in which he lived.

The settled societies of the Gulf coast were, and to a great extent still are, characterized by the politics of kinship. That is, tribal ties defined the individual's status, obligations, and loyalties. The prestigious families within a tribe controlled and manipulated the politics and economics of the wider group. This was a form of rule that was less dictatorial than it was autocratic, in that the preeminence of certain families was a result of respect based on a history of long-term leadership, wealth, and patronage rather than on pure physical coercion or threat. Nonetheless, the elite's rule was rigid and brooked little opposition. Kinship was the language of power: one obeyed the wishes of the elite because they formed the wealthiest and most influential stratum of one's blood kin.

Pearling up and down the Gulf coast was controlled by these old and wealthy families. They mobilized the men of their clans and tribes, among others, to serve in the pearling fleets. The ties of kinship allowed them to pressure men to participate and then held them, through ties of debt, in their service season after season. This system of debt ties permeated the whole hierarchy of pearling and will be discussed more fully later.

Ahmad began diving in his mid-teens. He entered the work through the usual channels: poverty, the illusion of opportunity, and debt pressures. He belonged to a poor clan of one of the major tribes whose territories lay at least partially within the modern borders of the state of Kuwait. Most of his relatives were nomads in the vicinity of Kuwait Town, though they ranged farther north into what is now Iraq. His extended family eked out an existence herding sheep, and some combined this with working as independent fishermen, alternating herding with fishing. Neither form of life was entirely satisfactory in Ahmad's eyes.

Kuwait Town itself, until the advent of oil, did not provide much in the way of opportunity. The town, up until the 1950s really a large village, served as a small port for trade, a craft center supplying nomads and townspeople with everyday needs, a hub of the Gulf boat-building industry, a political seat for important tribal figures, and, most importantly, a locus for the trade in pearls. Of these, only the last provided Ahmad and his kinsmen with any chance of improving their lives. Crafts such as gunsmithing, metalwork, boat building, and the like tended to be controlled by families who guarded access to their crafts, usually shutting out non-kinsmen to protect their livelihood. Boat building, a highly skilled craft and one of great importance to Kuwait, and indeed to the whole of the Gulf, was particularly difficult to enter. Ahmad at one point had attempted to find an apprenticeship to a boat builder but found the trade closed to him because he lacked the necessary family ties to the important craftsmen.

Pearling, then, was the only alternative open to Ahmad and others like him. But it was a gamble as an occupation. The profits of the season's diving were divided on a strict basis. Nobody was paid a salary, and so everyone from captain down to diver could count only on the chance of finding valuable pearls and sharing in the rewards at the end of the season. Shares had little to do with energy expended: the biggest shares went to the entrepreneur who funded the boat and to the captain who directed its operation. Shares were calculated only after the costs of the season's diving were deducted—leaving little to be doled out to the workers themselves. The divers and other workers had their food, water, and supplies deducted from their shares, and if the profits were so meager as not to cover those expenses, the diver found himself in debt to the boat captain.

The system of debt bound together all levels of the pearling system. The principle that ruled indebtedness was that a debtor had an obligation in traditional law to continue to work for the creditor until his debt was paid. Further, debts were heritable: a man's debt was not discharged on his death or disability but was transferred to his son or other close male relative, who was, in his turn, bound to work for the same creditor.

The weight of indebtedness fell on the divers and other workers on the pearling boats. Their shares in the profits, as mentioned before, rarely covered more than their supplies for the season. In addition, the workers had to borrow money from the captain or the backing entrepreneur in order to feed their families for the time they were at sea. Being illiterate, they could not ascertain whether the records kept of debts were accurate. The result was an ongoing debt to a captain or backer that could be paid off only in the unlikely circumstance that the diver found a remarkable gem, in which case his share of the season's profits was much greater than normal.

A diver was expected to appear ready for work at the beginning of the season. If he did not appear, his creditor would go in search of him. This was not a common occurrence simply because there were few hideouts for a runaway diver. I once asked Ahmad why he and others did not simply abscond and take up a new life elsewhere. He made it clear that the question was naive, if not downright foolish. Where, he asked, would he go? Running from a debt meant either going into the desert or taking ship, and both deserts and seaports were inhabited by people who took notice of strangers or, worse, already knew you and would be curious about your movements.

The system of debt was central to the maintenance of pearling. Traditional practice ensured this system by protecting the rights of creditors to the labor of their indebted divers and workers. Among these traditional practices was the imposition of stiff fines on those who gave refuge to an absconding diver, or a demand that the diver's debt be paid by his new protector. In fact, this system was so clearly tied to the pearling economy, and therefore to the economic viability of the Gulf towns, that in 1897 the British (whose sphere of political influence encompassed the Gulf at the time) engineered a treaty between Gulf principalities that formalized the control and return of recalcitrant divers and stipulated the fines to be paid by any who harbored them.

Besides poverty and the faint possibility of wealth, the factor of debt played a strong role in Ahmad's entry into diving. One of his uncles had died owing debts for family maintenance to a prominent boat captain. He died with no heirs, and pressure was put on Ahmad to go pearling in order to make good the debts. This pressure was not of a threatening kind: no heavies made unwelcome visits to Ahmad or his family demanding repayment. Rather, the pressure was moral, a question of honor. The captain was a fellow clansman, and all the pressures of shared kinship were brought to bear on Ahmad, as the oldest and nearest young male relative of the deceased man, to discharge the debt. It was put to him as a family matter: one could dodge the demands of outsiders, but a family debt had to be respected; otherwise, as he put it, his "face would be blackened," that is, his honor would be in doubt. This combination of poverty, illusory riches, and debt pressures led Ahmad to join others on the pearling banks some time in the years just after World War I.

An estimate of the size of the Kuwait pearling fleet in the early part of the century puts the number of boats at around eight hundred. The boats themselves were large, elegant, clinker-built sailing vessels known collectively in English as dhows, a word not known in Arabic, which refers to them by their specific styles (for example, *bum, baghlah*).

The boats left Kuwait in the hottest part of the year, when temperatures in excess of 110 degrees Fahrenheit in the shade were normal. The pearling banks lay relatively close inshore, and the boats anchored over them, moving when the captain felt that an area had been cleared of pearl-bearing oysters. The boats only came into shore occasionally, staying out on the sea for several months on end and coming in only briefly to reprovision.

Conditions on board the boats were difficult in the extreme. The first thing that Ahmad told me about the boats, which was confirmed to me time and again by other former divers, was the stench. The smell of rotting oyster remains—the detritus from opening dozens of shells a day—crept into everything. One old boat builder told me that he did not go into the port to work on the days when the pearling ended and the boats came straggling in; the smell was too much for him. Crowding was another major feature of life on board a pearling dhow. The boats held up to fifty men, and the decks were stacked with the gear needed for the diving itself, the personal possessions of the workers, the food and fresh-water provisions for the crew, and the cooking equipment and tackle used to fish for supplementary fresh food. The only shelter on board was a canvas canopy that shaded a large portion of the deck.

The occupants of the boat were divided according to their jobs. The captain (*nakhuda*) either rented the boat from a backer or owned it himself. He made the major decisions and so took most responsibility for the outcome of the season's work. It is worth noting here that the same system of debt ties applied to the captain as to the divers; if he fell into debt to his backers, he was bound to continue to work for them until it was paid. This, however, does not seem to have been a frequent state of affairs.

Ahmad began work as both a diver and a deck worker. The latter spent most of their time monitoring the progress of the divers and hauling them rapidly up from the sea bottom when signaled. Ahmad alternated these deck jobs with diving for the first few seasons and then gradually limited his activities to diving.

Diving was an arduous, exhausting business. The demands made on divers were extraordinary. The oyster beds lay at depths of from fifty to one hundred feet, and the deeper they were, the less efficient the divers became. The dives were performed in precipitous fashion. The divers stood on a heavy weight attached to the boat, which was then released and rapidly dragged the diver to the bottom. This sudden descent caused frequent pressure injuries to the ears and eyes of the divers. Ahmad, in fact, had lost the hearing in one ear over a period of years of doing particularly deep dives. After groping in the murky water for oysters, the diver put his catch in a basket and then signaled to the tenders to haul him quickly to the surface. The whole process—descent, collecting oysters, and being hauled to the surface—took just a matter of minutes, depending of course on the length of time a man could hold his breath. A healthy diver in good weather would make several dozen dives a day. A diver's equipment consisted simply of a nose clip, a basket slung around his neck for oysters, a tool for prizing the oysters loose, and leather finger stalls to prevent cuts.

Divers were generally debilitated, exhausted, and often ill or injured by the end of the season. This was in the nature of the work; diving with modern equipment is exhausting enough, but doing so in this traditional manner was physically destructive. The divers' diet may well have contributed to this. They were put on limited rations during the day, in the belief that they worked better on little food. The main meal of the day was at night and consisted mostly of rice and dates with any fish that had been caught during the day.

The hazards of diving were legion. There were the occupational hazards, such as pressure injuries, skin afflictions stemming from prolonged immersion in salt water, wounds that would not heal cleanly for the same reason, parasites, malnutrition, and so forth. Natural dangers were also present. Sharks were a persistent danger, although Ahmad himself claimed that they rarely attacked divers, especially if they were submerged. In his years as a diver, he witnessed only one attack, and that was on a man who was clinging to the side of the boat and was not actually diving. Jellyfish were also a definite danger. The stings of the bigger jellyfish, especially over large areas of the body, could be paralytically painful and even fatal. This was a possibility because jellyfish often travel in shoals that can cover sizeable areas of the surface. Protection against their stings was provided by a crude cotton suit that covered the diver from head to foot, leaving the face exposed. (The equipment needed by the divers was generally supplied by the boat captain. Ahmad, however, provided his own. He said that the captain had no real interest in maintaining the equipment, and so it was better to supply one's own, especially the protective clothing.)

Ahmad continued to dive for over twenty years. In that time, he married, had three sons, and fished for a living in the off-season. He managed to pay off his debts slowly, largely because of his skill at fishing. He would have continued to dive even after his debts were discharged, but the loss of one eye made it impossible for him to do so. This was something I could not understand; why would a man continue to risk his life working in an occupation that could put him back in debt? Ahmad's reply to my questions about this was that it was a gamble, but there was an element of excitement in it that could not be matched by doing the same job day after day, year in and year out.

The pearling industry died out in the Gulf rather rapidly after World War II. The reasons for this were many. Probably the major factor was the development of relatively inexpensive cultured pearls whose growth could be monitored and did not entail the risk of capital that was part of traditional pearling. The gradual pollution of the Gulf waters probably also contributed to the demise of pearling.

The whole of Gulf society changed in the 1950s with the advent of the age of oil. Citizens of the Gulf states shared in this wealth to varying degrees, depending on their social position and the nature of the government that ruled a particular state. But in any case, the vast majority of people began to live in great comfort and affluence, coddled by a welfare state that subsidized food, housing, education, and private businesses. Manual labor was carried out by immigrant workers—Palestinians, Egyptians, Kurds, Baluch, Afghans, etc. Such labor, never highly respected in the region, became despised, as it was increasingly associated with low-status outsiders.

There were exceptions to this pattern, however, and Ahmad was one of them. From our talks, it was clear that he was still married, his sons were very well off, but that he had as little to do with them as possible. Ahmad in fact had no respect for the new society and its affluence. He believed that people should work for their living, that there was nothing wrong with honorable labor, by which he meant skilled work such as his fishing. Unfortunately, this attitude, which is why he continued to fish for a living, was an embarrassment to his family. His history as a pearl diver was equally embarrassing, and that phase of his life, which was so important to him, was considered shameful by his sons—so much so that the only audience for his life story was made up of other old divers and sailors and a chance-met anthropologist.

Ahmad found the wealth and consumerism of Kuwait corrupting. He repeated time and again that his family had so many useless possessions and so much time on their hands that they were impossible for him to understand. His sons had several automobiles apiece (one of them, he said, laughing, even had a Palestinian chauffeur). His wife had a large, modern kitchen but continued to cook on a single gas jet, as she had done all of her life.

Through all this, he returned over and over again to the past times when diving, fishing, boat building, and herding were the everyday lives of "true" or "real" people. He clearly felt that his society was diminished by the passing of these things. He did feel that some things were better and often mentioned the state clinic that sat on the edge of his fishing beach as an improvement over the old Kuwait.

I could not understand this nostalgia for what seemed to me an oppressive system, especially in its use of debt to bind people to entrepreneurs and boat captains. I wondered why it was that the divers did not rebel. This was a question that I put to Ahmad and to elderly members of an old and wealthy Kuwaiti-Persian family who had been very active as entrepreneurs in the heyday of pearling. The question was one that puzzled them all. The answer was the same: people did not find pearling an oppressive occupation. All shared the dangers and the gambles, though they were different for the captain and backer from those faced by divers. And debts were debts; they had to be paid, and if a man inherited a debt from his father, well, it was only right that the son should honor it.

Ahmad was very much like many people, such as miners, who have spent their lives in an industry that objectively is exploitative and dangerous. They, however, still saw value in what they did, and their struggles gave them a sense of shared spirit with their fellow workers that is now lost. In the end, I suppose, it was the passing of this spirit that he really mourned.

A NOTE ON SOURCES

The interviews on which this article is based were conducted informally over several months in 1973. I was helped on occasion with the difficulties of Ahmad's Kuwaiti dialect by Hamad al-Mutairi, a student who was a local resident. My thanks to him.

SUGGESTIONS FOR FURTHER READING

There are few sources in English on pearling, though a considerable amount has come out recently in Arabic. The best firsthand account is that by Alan Villiers, who spent a year sailing in Kuwaiti trading dhows in the mid-1930s. He spent several months observing the pearling season, and his account can be found in his book, *Sons of Sinbad* (London: Hodder and Stoughton, 1940). For a pictorial account of Kuwaiti development between 1900 and 1950 with a focus on pearling, fishing, boat-building, see William Facey, *Kuwait by the First Photographers* (London: I. B. Tauris, 1998).

The best sociohistorical account of pearling can be found in a British government official publication, J. G. Lorimer's *Gazetteer of the Persian Gulf, Oman, and Central Arabia* (London: India Office, 1915). See also Salih Gharib and Shawqi Uthman, "Adawat al-ghaws fi al-khalij," *Al-Mathurat al-Shabiya* 2 (1987): 107–10 (photo essay on pearl-diving equipment of the Gulf); and Captain Rashid bin al-Fadil Bin Ali, *Routes of Guidance/Majari al-*

Hidaya: A Pearl-diver's Guide to the Oyster Beds of the Gulf, ed. and trans. Fayiz Suyyagh (Doha, Qatar: Arab Gulf States Folklore Centre, 1988).

The wider historical context of this article can be found in two books by Dr. Ahmad Abu Hakima, *A History of Eastern Arabia, 1750–1800* (Beirut: Khayats, 1965), and *The Modern History of Kuwait, 1750–1965* (London: Luzac, 1983). See also Jacqueline Ismael, *Kuwait: Dependency and Class in a Rentier State* (Gainesville: University of Florida Press, 1993).

A melodramatic, but basically accurate, view of pearling is provided by a film whose inaccurate English title is *The Cruel Sea* (*Bass, ya Bahr*).

Chapter 6

Mohand N'Hamoucha: Middle Atlas Berber

Edmund Burke, III

Pastoral transhumants, like the Thamazight-speaking Berbers of the Middle Atlas Mountains in Morocco, were especially sensitive to the changes that affected the Middle East and North Africa in the nineteenth century. With one foot in the world of nomadism and the other in sedentary agriculture, they were racked by conflicting tensions. The Aith Ndhir of central Morocco were more exposed than many neighboring groups to these contradictory pulls since their territory was near Fez, the capital city, and thus within range of the punitive power of the government (known to locals as the *makhzan*). The portrait of Mohand N'Hamoucha presented here may thus usefully be compared with those of other pastoralists in this volume. (See the chapters by Julie Oehler, Lois Beck, and Lila Abu-Lughod.)

There is a second context in which the story of Mohand N'Hamoucha must be situated—it is that of Morocco at the parting of the ways in the early twentieth century. Like Iran, Yemen, and Afghanistan, an independent Morocco survived into the twentieth century because of the rivalries of the European imperialist powers, as well as because of its lack of valuable resources and its forbidding topography. Between 1900 and 1912, the struggle for colonial possessions intensified, and the "Moroccan question" several times brought France and Germany to the brink of war. While a weak and indecisive Moroccan government dithered over how to respond to the French and Spanish colonial offensives, patriotic Moroccans sought to expel the enemy via direct action. Following the landing of French troops at Casablanca in August 1907, a powerful insurgency succeeded in ousting the incumbent sultan, Abd al-Aziz, and installing a coalition of urban notables and rural power brokers under the leadership of Abd al-Hafiz, the sultan's brother.

Mohand N'Hamoucha was involved in this rebellion and subsequently went on to play an important role in the efforts of his group, the Aith Ndhir, to oppose the modernizing policies of the government and the encroachment of the French on their historic pasturelands. His biography confronts contemporary Moroccans with the paradox of someone who was both a hero of Moroccan resistance and, subsequently, a French collaborator. We come to understand the reasons for his actions as we recognize the complex pressures he and his group were subjected to and the sharply narrowing range of options available to them. Mohand's perception of the challenges posed by colonialism changed over time, and with it, his survival strategy. (The responses to imperialism of other first-generation anticolonial resisters, like Bibi Maryam, may be purposefully contrasted with the nationalists whose biographies are to be found in part 2.) —Eds.

The deep, sunken eyes are gray-blue, steely, but touched with sadness, a sadness that comes from having outlived one's time. At ninety-four, still spry and able to scramble up a hillside or sit cross-legged drinking syrupy Moroccan mint tea and talk by the hour, Mohand N'Hamoucha had survived almost a century of changes that had transformed Morocco from a quasi-medieval Muslim monarchy to a modern state. When I interviewed him in 1967, he still had the clarity of mind and physical presence of a man thirty years younger. His weathered and deeply lined face was dominated by those eyes, impressively bushy eyebrows, a prominent nose, and a decisive mouth. Beneath the hood of his gray-and-white-striped *jallaba,* he was still an imposing man—tall, angular, and wiry, though no longer vigorous. As a young man, together with his brother Haddou and other members of his tribe, the Aith Ndhir, he had waged a twelve-year guerrilla struggle against the French invaders in the rugged Middle Atlas Mountains.

An authentic Moroccan patriot then, Mohand fought the French army from 1908 until 1919, at first with optimism and some hope of victory, then in a series of gallant rear-guard actions that took him and his small band of resisters from their accustomed pasturelands on the fringes of the wealthy agricultural plain between Fez and Meknes to increasingly more remote and forbidding mountain hideaways under merciless pressure from French air attacks and ground patrols. Eventually, their numbers badly depleted, their few animals starving, they surrendered to French authorities in 1919.

By this time, only isolated pockets of resistance remained—notably, Abd al-Krim al-Khattabi in the Rif Mountains to the north, and the redoubtable Ait Atta in the desert fastnesses of Jabal Saghru. By this time as well, the conquest of the Aith Ndhir and of "le Maroc utile" (the agriculturally rich central plains of Morocco) was long since an accomplished fact. The tribal territory, especially the farmlands of the Sais Plain, had by a series of legal subterfuges passed out of the hands of the tribesmen. French settlers, attracted by the fertility of the soil, the mild winters and warm summers, and the numerous streams, began to establish themselves there in numbers. The Sais Plain was indeed one of the best regions in Morocco for viticulture—to this day it produces some of the best Moroccan wines.

When Mohand and his companions surrendered in 1919, they did so only after having endured enormous privations in their desperate effort to stem the tide of history. Recognizing finally that Morocco had passed into a new historical phase and that further resistance was fruitless, they negotiated terms for their surrender. As a result of these negotiations, Mohand acquired land near Bouderbala not far from El Hadjeb, the chief town of the Aith Ndhir territory. He agreed to serve the French protectorate authorities as a *khalifa* to his brother Haddou, who was made a governor (*qaid*) of the tribe. Mohand's surrender evoked a few murmurs of discontent but no protests from other Ndhiris, who by this time had lost control of most of their best lands—and of their destinies as well.

Under the French, Mohand prospered. Eventually he owned a lot of property in the area. His sons grew to manhood under the French protectorate, went to French schools, and eventually found careers as doctors, lawyers, and architects in independent Morocco. In 1967 he recalled the past of the Aith Ndhir and of Morocco with a certain bemusement. Most of his contemporaries had disappeared. His sons, who are modern professionals, he regarded as *roumis* (Europeans). Their "French" ways are forever strange to him. By 1967, Mohand had become a living anachronism, misunderstood by his family, a remnant of the folkloric "traditional Morocco."

The career of Mohand N'Hamoucha poses a dilemma for Moroccans and for modern scholars. How are we to regard him: as a resistance hero or a collaborator? To understand him is to confront the complex decisions many rural Moroccans made as they contended with the shifting political and economic tides. A consideration of his career takes us into the changing world of a pastoral transhumant Berber tribe of the Middle Atlas Mountains in Morocco from the turn of the century till the mid-1960s.

Preprotectorate Morocco was a complex society marked by common allegiance to the Alawi dynasty and its corrupt and unreliable bureaucracy, the *makhzan*. Despite a superficial resemblance to the Ottoman Empire (both were Muslim-dominated agrarian bureaucracies governing ethnically mixed populations), nineteenth-century Morocco was not on the road to becoming a modern, centralized state with a powerful army and an efficient modern bureaucracy like Turkey. Instead, it resembled states like Ethiopia, Iran, Afghanistan, and Yemen, whose survival into the twentieth century owed as much to European diplomatic rivalries as to any real obstacles they might have been able to place in the path of a determined European takeover bid. As with these states, only the absence of significant resources, a rugged topography, and the combative reputation of its population helped Morocco deter eventual European conquest.

Compared with the much more ethnically diverse societies of the Middle East, Morocco was relatively homogeneous: the majority of its population were Arabic-speaking Sunni Muslims of the Maliki legal rite. About 40 percent of its estimated four million people spoke one of three major Berber dialects (though most adult males also spoke Arabic). There was also an important Jewish minority who made up about 5 percent of the total population. The topography of Morocco is dominated by mountains. To the north there is the Rif chain, which extends along the Mediterranean coast. Inland to the south and east, the Middle Atlas and High Atlas mountain ranges separate the relatively well-watered central plain from the pre-Saharan steppes.

Historically, from the tenth century on, Morocco had been the center of powerful empires, such as the Almohads and Almoravids, whose territories embraced Algeria, Tunisia, southern Spain, and even Senegal across the Sahara. By the nineteenth century, as a result of a long-term process of urban decline, shifting trade routes, and nomadic incursions, the *makhzan* had become weak and corrupt. The Moroccan interior from Rabat (the present-day capital) on the Atlantic coast to Fez inland was occupied by pastoral tribes, the great majority of whom spoke the Thamazight dialect of Berber. The Aith Ndhir were one of these groups.

The Aith Ndhir were pastoral transhumants who migrated seasonally with their flocks and herds. In the late spring, they left their homes on the edge of the Sais Plain south of Meknes to move to cooler summer pasturage in mountains above Azrou. In the autumn, following the first snowfall, they returned to their permanent dwellings in the plain. Although the distances involved were not large (thirty to forty kilometers), these migrations were moments of great tension. They involved traversing the territory of neighboring tribes and could upon occasion lead to pitched battles between groups eager to preserve claims to water and pasturage.

The seasonal moves of the Aith Ndhir intersected those of other tribes who also trekked with their animals. Indeed, these movements were complexly patterned into a kind of pastoralist game of falling dominoes. Middle Atlas Berber tribes took over pastures in summer that belonged in winter to their neighbors farther up the slope. In winter, the movement was reversed. Thus, for example, a section of the Igerwan tribe, western neighbors of the Aith Ndhir, summered in fields vacated by sections of the Aith Ndhir. These in turn occupied land that in winter that belonged to the northern groups of the Aith Njild, who displaced other Aith Njild clans farther up the mountain, who migrated over the passes to pasturage below Timhadit.

Until 1914, when they were reorganized by the French protectorate administration, the Aith Ndhir were politically decentralized. No chief was able to exercise authority within the group, other than during the semiannual migrations to and from winter pasturage. (Although there were six *makhzan*-appointed *qaids*, or governors, in 1900, their power did not extend beyond the circle of their immediate kinsmen and allies.) Internally, the group was divided into ten quasi-autonomous clans, each of which had its own territory which it jealously protected from all comers, including other

Ndhiris. Feuding between clans (and even within clans) in competition for resources was common. A healthy suspicion of everyone not directly related by blood was an important feature of Ndhiri society.

Acephalous societies like the Aith Ndhir, in which authority was widely diffused, look unworkable when viewed from the outside. In fact, their democratic ethos did not prevent the emergence of wealthy individuals and families. Also, the difficulties of forging alliances outside the kin bond were mitigated by a host of crosscutting institutions. These included religiously sanctioned alliances known as *tada,* membership in Sufi brotherhoods (in Arabic, *tariqa*), marriage alliances, and personal business partnerships. As we shall see, Mohand utilized all of these relationships in building his reputation and in sustaining himself during the period when he was involved in resistance activities.

While the term *tribe* suggests that Aith Ndhir was a "natural" grouping that possessed a degree of moral and political independence, the Aith Ndhir clans (known as *arbaa*) had in fact been assembled by the *makhzan* from the social rubble left after it had crushed the Aith Idrassen confederation in 1817. While the exact circumstances of the creation of the Aith Ndhir remain obscure, it was connected to the effort of the *makhzan* to establish loyal auxiliary forces along the strategic Middle Atlas corridor. In return for providing military service to the *makhzan,* the clans were given lands upon which to pasture their animals and build their dwellings.

By the end of the nineteenth century this system had fallen into disuse, however. In the collective memory of the Aith Ndhir, the group had always been free. (*Imazighren,* their name for themselves in the Thamazight dialect of Berber, means "free men.") In reality, they were an important block in the edifice of *makhzan* rule over the Middle Atlas through much of the nineteenth century. Only latterly, in the wake of the collapse of Hasan I's rule, did they become the fractious and unruly group described in the colonial sources. The historically contingent character of the Aith Ndhir may usefully serve to warn us of the misplaced concreteness of the term *tribe.*

Mohand's clan, the Aith Harzalla, had a reputation for cooperation with the *makhzan.* No doubt this was in part occasioned by the vulnerability of its lands in the fertile Sais Plain to *makhzan* pressure tactics. Because the Aith Harzalla and their neighbors, the Aith Bubidman, were situated nearer to Fez, they developed closer relations with the city and its government. This relationship was supplemented by economic and religious ties. Fez was an important market and center of Sufi activity, which radiated into the surrounding area. The influence of the city and the *makhzan* appears to have been a source of tension and occasional hostility within the tribe. Feuds would break out occasionally between the two main factions, usually over access to water, pasturage, or women. Both factions had close ties with the *makhzan* as well as with neighboring tribes.

These contradictions alone would not have been sufficient to propel Mohand N'Hamoucha into the leadership of the anti-French resistance of his tribe. To understand how this came about, we must see how his personal situation intersected with the changing fortunes of the Aith Ndhir over the period 1860–1912. Two main sorts of changes worked to undermine the old structures of Morocco: government efforts at centralization inspired by the Ottoman *tanzimat*, and the incorporation of Morocco into the world economy.

The impact of government rule on the rural populations of Morocco had traditionally been limited and dependent upon the balance of forces between the *makhzan* and the tribes. Tribes were jealous of their autonomy and refused to pay taxes or accept government-appointed *qaids* unless obliged to do so. Under Hasan I (1876–94), a politically astute and militarily powerful leader, this slowly began to change. Hasan embarked upon an ambitious program of reform that sought to develop a modern army and a modern state apparatus. Not surprisingly, this was viewed by the tribes as deeply threatening. By 1894, despite efforts to modernize his army and bureaucracy along Western lines (as the Ottomans had done in their *tanzimat* reforms), Hasan I's endeavor was crowned with failure.

Following the death of Hasan in 1894, the reform plan crumbled. With the strong sultan no longer in control, the tribes gradually adopted a more independent attitude toward the government and refused to pay taxes unless compelled. Hasan I's "modern" army, no longer receiving regular pay, melted away. By 1900, the reforms of Mawlay al-Hasan were but a memory. The stage was set for the tribes to seek to regain their autonomy. Under the regentship of Ba Ahmad, the court of the young sultan Abd al-Aziz resided at Marrakesh from 1894 until 1901. In that year, a European-inspired modernization program was announced.

When the court returned to Fez in the fall, construction was begun on a railroad and telegraph line intended to connect Fez with the coast. Since the line passed through the territory of the Aith Ndhir, they became alarmed and attacked it, destroying the new installations.

During the reign of Hasan I, the international context was also changing. Following the Congress of Berlin in 1878, European imperialism was once again on the march. Tunisia and Egypt lost their independence in 1881 and 1882, and the scramble for Africa began. As a result of French annexation of the Algerian Sahara, existing patterns of trade that linked Morocco with Egypt and the Arab East on the one hand, and Timbuctoo and the Muslim African states south of the Sahara on the other, were drastically altered. It was just a question of time before Morocco itself became the focus of European acquisitiveness. By 1900, French Algerian settlers were agitating for a more aggressive policy toward Morocco, extolling the economic and strategic opportunities for France that would result from the establishment of a protectorate.

While the internal political situation worsened, a second sequence of changes was simultaneously transforming the society in other ways. Taking advantage of the vague provisions of the 1880 Madrid Convention, Europeans began to acquire land in Morocco, especially around coastal cities like Tangier, Casablanca, and Essaouira. Commercial agriculture spread from the Atlantic ports far into the interior. Even isolated villages found themselves entering the cash economy as they sold their grain, wool, and dates in order to be able to purchase Manchester cottons, Chinese tea, Belgian sugar, and French firearms. Far-reaching social and economic changes were set in motion that had already begun to transform the old agrarian structures and the ways of life they fostered.

By the 1890s the export of Moroccan wool to the international market was growing. As a consequence the flocks and herds of the Aith Ndhir, who had been accustomed to a substantially autonomous existence, began to pass into the hands of Muslim and Jewish merchants based in Fez and Meknes, whose wealth increased accordingly. Each autumn vast herds of sheep were driven from the Middle Atlas to markets on the French side of the Algerian frontier. A tribal elite also began to emerge and to acquire tangible signs of status, including Winchester repeating rifles and houses in Fez and Meknes.

Mohand also benefited from these trends. In the 1890s he entered into a sheep-raising partnership with Qaid Umar al-Yusi, a business arrangement that was sealed by his marriage to Umar's daughter, Miriam. (Also the pasha of Sefrou, Umar was the most powerful figure in the Middle Atlas at the time. He governed the Aith Yusi and several other tribes to the south and east of Fez. His influence also extended over the eastern clans of Aith Ndhir.) This connection was an indication of Mohand's increasing status, although he was too junior to have a major voice in deciding the affairs of the group at this time. The intersecting crises that burst upon Morocco after 1900 weakened the authority of the tribal elders and provided an opportunity for individuals like Mohand to play a greater role.

The gradually increasing involvement of Europeans in Morocco meant more opportunities for Moroccans to develop potentially useful ties to Europeans. From them might flow business deals, increased political clout, and perhaps, eventually, coveted status as a protégé (Moroccans who benefited from official treaty status, including tax and other exemptions). But Europeans were also perceived as enemies, their religion inimical to Islam and their ways alien and potentially harmful. The two sides of the European connection must have posed a dilemma for individuals like Mohand. Still more, given the direct threat to the tribes posed by *makhzan* reform plans, it must have been unclear until fairly late in the game which threat was primary, *makhzan* reforms or European imperialism.

The economic and political changes outlined above reverberated throughout Moroccan society, setting in motion complex and occasionally conflicting responses among rural groups like the Aith Ndhir, who sought to cope in an atmosphere of uncertainty and heightened political tension. In such a context, personal relationships often influence the choices people make. Such seems to have been the case with Mohand. By his connections to the family of Qaid Umar, as we have seen, he was drawn into the circle of rural leaders in the Fez region. Through his connections with Muhammad ibn Abd al-Kabir al-Kattani, he was gradually led to become involved in opposition to the protectorate.

A fiery preacher and prominent member of the Fasi *ulama*, al-Kattani was the head of a Sufi brotherhood that had a significant popular following both at Fez and among the nearby tribes. In late 1904, on the eve of the first Moroccan crisis, al-Kattani threw himself into opposition to a proposed French plan of reforms, which he claimed (not unreasonably) amounted to a disguised protectorate. While we do not know just when Mohand became a member of the Kattaniya *tariqa*, it is likely that it was around 1905 that he first became a *fakir*. Other, mostly younger Ndhiris from his own and adjoining clans located closer to Fez became affiliated with the brotherhood about then as well. (Other Ndhiris were affiliated with the rival Wazzaniya Sufi order.)

Despite German diplomatic opposition to French reforms, in 1905 an international conference at Algeciras confirmed French claims to the country. The young sultan Abd al-Aziz was compelled to accept the Algeciras Convention, which granted French primacy in the modernization of Morocco. Following anti-European riots at Casablanca in 1907, he also had to acquiesce in the landing of French troops "to restore order." By the end of 1907, Abd al-Aziz's policies had provoked a major rebellion. It was led by his elder brother, Abd al-Hafiz, who opposed his acceptance of the Algeciras Convention and his passivity in the face of French aggression. The revolt spread to northern Morocco in January 1908, and Abd al-Aziz was deposed by the *ulama* and people of Fez. After promising to uphold Muslim law (the Sharia) and to oppose the French military forces in the Shawiya (the agricultural hinterland of Casablanca), Abd al-Hafiz was proclaimed the new sultan.

Muhammad al-Kattani had played a central role in the deposition of Abd al-Aziz and the enthronement of his brother at Fez. Early in 1908 he called for volunteers to go to the Shawiya to help oppose the French expeditionary force. Fired with enthusiasm, Mohand joined the others. His enthusiasm for *jihad* was soon deflated by the pusillanimous attitude of the Shawiya tribes, however. The struggle was not going well, and his group was not warmly welcomed. He and his companions returned home dejected.

This was to be the beginning of a series of disappointments. No sooner was he in power than Abd al-Hafiz began to back away from his uncompromising positions and to seek a *modus vivendi* with the French. In early 1909, he initiated a crackdown on his critics at Fez, firing several officials and attacking the Sufi brotherhoods. On 19 March, matters escalated further when he sought to arrest his biggest detractor, Shaykh Muhammad ibn Abd al-Kabir al-Kattani. Warned in advance, the Shaykh sought refuge among his supporters in the Middle Atlas. Late in the evening of 20 March, al-Kattani reached the territory of the Aith Ndhir. He came to Mohand's tent and, grasping a tent peg in a traditional appeal to Mohand's honor (*ar*), claimed the right of protection. Since Mohand was a staunch member of the Kattaniya Sufi *tariqa*, this was willingly granted. Soon, however, al-Kattani was again on the run due to the arrival of a search party of *makhzan* troops. Captured the next day at the edge of Aith Ndhir territory, he was brought back to Fez, tortured, and executed at the orders of the sultan. The killing of al-Kattani demonstrated the lengths to which Abd al-Hafiz was willing to go to repress inconvenient opposition. It also showed the extent to which he had put behind him the patriotic oaths of 1908.

When Mohand and I discussed this episode in 1967, half a lifetime later, his eyes still clouded with emotion at the memory of the betrayal of his spiritual guide and leader. Yet he had been in no position to defend his honor, let alone to exact revenge. On the contrary, by agreeing to help him, he and the other Ndhiri followers of the Kattaniya had endangered the livelihood of the group as a whole. Abd al-Hafiz had threatened to burn every village in the tribe if al-Kattani were not promptly turned over.

From the sultan's point of view, the fact that al-Kattani had been helped by the Aith Ndhir was a sign of their unreliability. To prevent the contamination from spreading, an unprecedentedly large *mahalla* of *makhzan* troops was dispatched to Aith Ndhir territory. The Aith Ndhir were ordered to pay a huge fine in kind and in cash immediately or suffer the consequences.

When the government forces were defeated in an initial skirmish in which Mohand was involved, it looked as though the Aith Ndhir might be able to avoid complying. But a reorganized *makhzan* army, supplemented by a French artillery officer, soon turned the tide. In response to this show of force, most of the tribe sought safety in the hills for their families and their animals. The few who tried to stand and fight were crushed. Fearing a similar fate, the bulk of the group remained in the mountains. To counter this ploy, the *makhzan* force camped on Aith Ndhir land and began "eating" its way through the tribal grain reserves. By spring this economic pressure had accomplished its aims. The half-starved tribesmen were compelled to surrender on terms more draconian than those originally proposed, including not only payment of a punitive find but also acceptance of a *makhzan* -imposed *qaid* and provision of a three-hundred-man contingent to the *makhzan* army.

The consequences were severe for Mohand, who was one of the three hundred hostages whose induction into the army at Fez was intended to guarantee Aith Ndhir acquiescence. In the army, he became a *qaid al-raha* and acquired the rudiments of military discipline that he was later to put to use against the French. The arrival at Fez soon thereafter of reinforcements under the command of the grand vizier Madani al-Glawi, lord of the Atlas, consolidated Abd al-Hafiz's victory. In order to win al-Glawi's full support, the sultan granted him full control of the tribes around Fez and Meknes. During the following year, al-Glawi turned loose his private army of black African slaves to pillage the region. More than fifty years later, the memory of al-Glawi's oppression was still enough to make Mohand angry all over again.

Early in 1911, things came to a boil. Goaded by the abuses of al-Glawi's henchmen and a misguided *makhzan* attempt to reorganize its army along the lines of the French Algerian *goum*, leaders of the Aith Ndhir began to meet secretly with those of other tribes of the region. They decided to take advantage of the Id al-Mulud festival to launch a rebellion. Traditionally, at this celebration of the Prophet's birthday delegations of tribesmen presented offerings to the sultan as a sign of their fealty. The conspirators decided instead to assassinate al-Glawi, capture the sultan, and expel the hated French military advisors.

Unfortunately, the revolt fizzled when the Cherarda tribe rebelled prematurely in February. Changing their tactics, the insurgents instead laid siege to Fez in an attempt to compel Abd al-Hafiz to dismiss his hated grand vizier and the French military advisors. At first it looked as if they might succeed. But this was to reckon without the Machiavellian skills of the French colonial lobby, who capitalized upon the alleged threat posed by the siege to Europeans at Fez to obtain the dispatch of a French relief column. After a forced march, French troops under General Moinier reached Fez at the end of May and occupied the interior. Mohand took part in these events, in which his tribe was a major participant, though he does not appear to have been a leader.

In the aftermath of the rebellion, Moinier's troops occupied El Hadjeb and turned it into a permanent military installation. They hunted down suspected rebels and imposed heavy fines and back taxes on the tribe. With the leaders of the 1911 rebellion imprisoned and others of the old tribal elite badly compromised by their dealings with the French, where were people to turn for guidance? If his people were to have a chance of throwing off the French yoke, it would depend upon younger men. In this Mohand needed no encouragement. As a *qaid al-raha* and a participant in the 1911 rebellion, his military prowess was already established. In the winter of 1911–12,

Mohand began to seek out like-minded individuals and to plan a major rebellion against the French.

Without the knowledge of the French, Abd al-Hafiz soon gave active encouragement to the rebels. In April 1912, he secretly convoked his *qaid al-rahas* (among them Mohand) and ordered them to prepare an attack. But before the rebels could act, *makhzan* troops at Fez mutinied, sparking a popular uprising within the city. Initially taken by surprise, the French were soon able to regain control, although the cost to their prestige was enormous. Suddenly, Moroccans saw that France was not invincible. In the Fez region the tribes hastened their preparations for a major offensive. Rumors that the Fez mutiny had almost succeeded, and that "Abd al-Hafiz had sold Morocco to France," soon brought new recruits flocking to join them. Under the leadership of the *sharif* Muhammad al-Hajjami, they planned a series of coordinated assaults on French posts in Fez, Meknes, El Hadjeb, and Sefrou.

On 24 May, French positions throughout the region came under Moroccan attack. At El Hadjeb and Sefrou, the *mujahidin* were led by Aqqa al-Bubidmani (though for the first time Mohand also was prominently featured). The coordinated uprising had caught the French off guard. At Fez, it was only after three days of intense fighting that superior French firepower eventually scattered the ranks of the attackers. At Meknes and Sefrou, the story was similar. Although the tribes were able momentarily to breach the French defenses, they were ultimately unsuccessful. Since Mohand's wife was a daughter of Umar al-Yusi, he was particularly motivated to take part in the latter offensive. Along with other bands of resistance fighters, he and his men continued to harass French patrols in the nearby hills until late summer.

After the relief of the siege of Fez, the focus of attention shifted in mid-August to southern Morocco, where another major insurrection threatened the French. Under the leadership of Mawlay Haybat Allah (known as El Hiba) Moroccan insurgents occupied Marrakesh, taking captive nine Frenchmen (including the personal emissary of General Lyautey and the vice-consul). Significantly, El Hiba presented himself as an opponent not only of the French but also of the corrupt rule of the lords of the Atlas. Mohand and his band of patriotic fighters were greatly encouraged by El Hiba's successes. But their hopes were dashed when the French succeeded in retaking Marrakesh in early September, expelling El Hiba and reestablishing the grinding quasi-feudal control of the great *qaids*.

Although the French were victorious, it was some time before French hegemony was secured. In the months that followed, French errors continued to provide an opening to Moroccan resisters. This was especially so in the Middle Atlas, where French policies took no account of the special character of Berber pastoralist society. The mixture of bribery and intimidation that had worked elsewhere to assure French control failed utterly when applied to groups like the Aith Ndhir, whose lack of identifiable chiefs and pastoralist life-style rendered them less vulnerable to such tactics.

With their greatly superior firepower and resources, the French were able to impose their control over the Aith Ndhir from their post at El Hadjeb. They established a local administration with the aid of opportunists like Driss Ou Rahu, whose corrupt and bullying ways soon made him detested by all. Mohand watched Ou Rahu's ascent with anger and disgust. Under the French, grievances continued to pile up. Allowing their local agents free rein was bad enough, but requiring the proud Aith Ndhir to recognize their submission to the *makhzan* was an intolerable humiliation. Prior to the defeat of El Hiba, Mohand had been a participant in some of the most dramatic moments of Moroccan history. In 1913 he emerged as a leader in his own right, a key organizer in his tribe of the struggle against the French.

One of the catalysts that propelled Mohand and his friends into action was the dramatic intervention of a hitherto obscure local *sharif*, Sidi Rahu. With a reputation for piety and probity already well established by 1912, Sidi Rahu was ideally placed to rally those who wished to continue the patriotic struggle. In late 1912, Sidi Rahu withdrew into the snowy forest above Ifrane and began a public fast aimed at galvanizing the conscience of the Berber groups nearby. Impressed by the *sharif*'s resolve, Mohand began to seek allies.

As if this was not enough to encourage Mohand to take up arms, a second factor now intervened. Having earlier refused to help al-Hajjami's patriots or to join El Hiba in opposing the French, the powerful Zaian tribal confederation decided that the time had come for action. With their large numbers, cohesion, and weaponry, the Zaian were able to intimidate smaller tribes like the Aith Ndhir, the Igerwan, and the Aith Njild. They threatened to prevent their access to summer pastures unless they immediately launched a major offensive against the French. Thus inspired and compelled, it did not take much for Mohand and his comrades to take up arms.

In March 1913 French complacency was shattered when a large force under Mohand's leadership launched a surprise attack on the French post at El Hadjeb. Other French positions in the region also came under attack at this time. Soon, a full-scale offensive was under way, in which the French suffered significant losses. For a time it looked as though French control over the entire region might be overthrown, as other groups to the north of Fez also became active. It was several months before they regained the upper hand. Only the application of relentless military pressure, coupled with a drastic reappraisal of their policies, permitted them to reestablish their hegemony.

Even though his tribal homeland soon fell to the French, Mohand fought on for the next five years. With varying degrees of success, he and his group of 30 to 150 men continued the struggle in the mountains. Gradually, his small guerrilla band had less and less scope for its activities. He and his men were driven ever deeper into the remote fastnesses of the Middle Atlas. Finally, in 1918, discouraged and exhausted by the years of life on the run, Mohand surrendered.

Over the next thirty years the French protectorate consolidated its hold on Morocco. In the new circumstances, Mohand prospered. After Mohand surrendered, he accepted a commission in the native auxiliary forces of the protectorate (the famous *goum marocain*) and became a minor official. In his new guise as a supporter of the French protectorate, Mohand was able to acquire considerable land in the region and to become a privileged member of the Moroccan rural elite. But unlike such French collaborators as Driss Du Rahu, Mohand continued to enjoy the respect of his people because of his years fighting the French. By the same token, his past as a resistance hero guaranteed that he was never really trusted by French authorities.

By 1967, when I interviewed him as a still vigorous ninety-four-year-old, Mohand had managed to survive the French protectorate. By then a respected tribal elder in newly independent Morocco, he wore his many years with pride. How he had managed to navigate the tricky shoals of the nationalist period, when French collaborators like himself were widely despised and distrusted by the eager young nationalists, I do not know. When I was introduced to him by the Moroccan governor of the Aith Ndhir, it was clear that Mohand was regarded with a mixture of respect and suspicion. As the *qaid* and I talked, it became apparent that, ironically, despite his advanced years, Mohand's past as an opponent of French rule, then as a cog in the protectorate machine, had tainted him as an oppositionist.

His survival a living testament to the complexities of the transition from precolonial times to the present, Mohand had become a living anachronism.

A NOTE ON SOURCES

This account was written on the basis of several lengthy interviews with Mohand N'Hamoucha in August 1967 at his home near Bouderbala. In addition, I have drawn upon research in French military archives in Ch{ac}teau Vincennes, Section d'Afrique, Maroc, Série C, D, and E; British foreign office political correspondence (notably the letters of the British vice-consul in Fez, James Macleod, preserved in FO 174); and published and unpublished French ethnographic writings on the Aith Ndhir and the Middle Atlas region, of which the most important are Abès, "Monographie d'un tribu berbère: Les Ait Ndhir (Beni mtir)," *Archives Berbères* 2 (1917) and 3 (1918); and Edouard Arnaud, "La région de Meknès," *Bulletin de la Société de géographie du Maroc* (1916).

SUGGESTIONS FOR FURTHER READING

The best ethnography of the Aith Ndhir is Amal Rassam Vinogradov, *The Aith Ndhir of Morocco: A Study of the Social Transformation of a Berber Tribe*, Museum of Anthropology, University of Michigan, no. 55 (Ann Arbor: University of Michigan, 1974). My *Prelude to Protectorate in Morocco: Precolonial Protest and Resistance, 1860–1912* (Chicago: University of Chicago Press, 1976) provides a general political history. For a discussion of many of the events mentioned here, see my "Tribalism and Moroccan Resistance, 1890–1914: The Role of the Aith Ndhir," in *Tribe and State in Northwest Africa*, ed. George Joffe and Richard Pennell (London: M.E.N.A.S., 1990). In French there are two excellent semifictionalized accounts of Middle Atlas Berber life: Said Guennoun, *La montagne berbère* (Paris, 1929); and Maurice LeGlay, *Chroniques marocaines* (Paris, 1933).

Chapter 7

Bibi Maryam:
A Bakhtiyari Tribal Woman

Julie Oehler

Middle Eastern tribes have received the attention of scholars only when their actions have impinged on the national government. Otherwise, their histories have generally been ignored. How much more is this the case for the role of tribal women in politics, which insofar as it is discussed tends to treat women as the appendages of male relatives, the better to deny the significance of their actions!

The Bakhtiyari are perhaps the best-known Iranian tribe. Luri-speaking pastoralists, until recently the Bakhtiyari migrated with their flocks and herds twice a year from summer pasturage in the cool valleys west of Isfahan to their winter grazing grounds near Ahwaz in Khuzistan on the other side of the rugged Zagros Mountains. Their seasonal migration covered over two hundred miles each way. Prominent contemporary Iranians of Bakhtiyari origin include Queen Soraya, the recent Shah's first wife, and Shapour Bakhtiar, his last prime minister.

Julie Oehler's biography of Bibi Maryam provides a window on the changing world of Bakhtiyari elite women in the early twentieth century. The daughter of the *ilkhan*, or paramount chief, Bibi Maryam played an important role in anti-British politics in Iran during World War I in defiance both of the Qajar government and the leading Bakhtiyari *khans*. She conducted Wilhelm Wassmuss, "the German Lawrence," into the Bakhtiyari lands, where he sought to rally opposition to the British, who were defending their newly discovered oil fields in Khuzistan.

While little is known of Bibi Maryam beyond this, that little is tantalizing. By reading the known facts against the grain, Oehler argues that in response to the transformation of Bakhtiyari society in the preceding decades, the role of the *bibis* drastically altered. As she explains, in the nineteenth century the *khans* acquired vast estates and were drawn into the national political game, leaving their wives, the *bibis*, to manage their affairs. This they did with gusto, organizing carpet production and entering trade on their own. Previously little noticed, the *bibis* began to take up positions often at variance with their menfolk. Bibi Maryam's role in the Wassmuss mission is one example of this trend.

Bibi Maryam's story also challenges prevailing notions of the bimodal gender division of labor in the Middle East, in which the public role of men stands in contrast to the family sphere of women's activity. In fact, such generalizations, while having some basis, do not begin to account for the great variety of possibilities for action available to women, depending upon their class, status, occupation, and residence. Thus, for example, rural women throughout the area have seldom worn the veil, except when going to town, and some women have been able to play an active role in the economy, buying and selling goods and property.

Other selections in this volume treat the lives of Middle Eastern pastoralists. One might compare Bibi Maryam's situation with that of Migdim, for instance, a contemporary Egyptian bedouin matriarch profiled by Lila Abu-Lughod. Lois Beck's portrait of Rostam, a present-day Qashqa'i tribesman, allows us to see how much has changed in the life of Iranian pastoralists since the early twentieth century. Finally, Edmund Burke's essay on Mohand N'Hamoucha, a Moroccan Berber pastoralist contemporary of Bibi Maryam's, suggests interesting comparisons across the region. —Eds.

In 1916, at the height of World War I, a force of Turkish soldiers, renegade Swedish gendarmes, and Persian nationalists undertook the hazardous journey from Ahwaz to Isfahan. Led by Wilhelm Wassmuss, a German officer later known as "the German Lawrence," its mission was to capture the recently developed British oil fields in the territory of the Bakhtiyari tribal confederation east of Isfahan. Wassmuss and his men were able to come undetected into the region because they were guided by Bibi Maryam, the daughter of the paramount chief of the Bakhtiyari, Husayn Quli Khan. Maryam assisted the force in defiance of the pro-British policy of the leading *khans*, as well as of a Qajar edict that anyone opposing the British or Russian war efforts would have their property and personal possessions seized and sold. Maryam's exploit required great personal strength indeed.

Why was a Bakhtiyari *bibi* (daughter of a *khan*, or tribal chief) traveling on this dangerous secret mission? In their discussion of this episode, Western writers always describe Bibi Maryam as "the strong-willed and independent" daughter of Husayn Quli Khan. This formula is convenient, for it simultaneously deprives Bibi Maryam of agency, by ascribing her actions to her father, while dismissing her leadership role as an aberration. Yet it helps to explain why a consideration of this brief episode of her life is potentially so interesting, for Bibi Maryam's behavior does indeed appear to defy the traditional role of women in Persian society. But how typical of tribal women was her behavior? How typical of tribal women of elite background? What were the possibilities for public action by elite tribal women in early twentieth-century Iran? Although the sources that mention Bibi Maryam are fragmentary at best, by reading the sources against the grain it is possible to see her actions as part of a larger response by elite tribal women to the rapidly changing social and political conditions in the early twentieth century.

Basically, what needs to be explained is not so much how or why one woman sought to outwit the system in which she found herself, but rather, what circumstances led her to resort to such a dangerous deed. Accordingly, we must examine the historic relationship between the Qajar government, the British, and the Bakhtiyari and its impact on the lives of the elite women of the tribe. As we shall see, the importance of the wives, mothers, daughters, and sisters of the leading *khans* changed as a result of the growing dependence of the Bakhtiyaris on alliances with the powers outside the tribe, first with the Qajars and later with the British. These powers, especially the British, sought to circumvent the traditional role of marriage alliances as the essential mediating factor in intertribal struggles for power.

Bibi Maryam was a woman of prominence among the ruling family of the Bakhtiyari tribes. Not only was her father, Husayn Quli Khan, the paramount chief of the Bakhtiyari tribal confederacy, but also she and her family played an important part in the country's nationalist struggles. Bakhtiyari involvement in Persian national politics began with the constitutional revolution of 1906–11. The revolution represented an effort by the intelligentsia, bazaar merchants, and *ulama* to limit the autocratic powers of the Qajar ruler and encourage a program of modernizing reforms. A protracted struggle ensued, one of the results of which was the intensification of the political contest between reformers and reactionaries in the country. By 1909, when Bakhtiyari tribal forces intervened at Tehran, the revolution had lost its way. For the next decade, Bakhtiyari *khans* played a prominent role in Persian national politics. Among them were many of Bibi Maryam's brothers, uncles, and cousins. From 1911 to 1913, one of her brothers was prime minister and others were key members of the new cabinet. Although after 1916 Bakhtiyari *khans* no longer served in the central government, several still held governorships of large districts throughout the country.

As is the case for most Middle Eastern women, we know very little about Bibi Maryam except those facts that relate to her role as wife and mother. These facts, however, reveal a great deal about the life of the women of her class and the changes that were occurring in the tribal structure. Bibi Maryam's social identity was derived from her birth and marriage, which provided her with the capacity for undertaking initiatives in her own right. In order to understand the complicated political world in which she maneuvered, we must first turn to a discussion of the politics of kinship and marriage among the Bakhtiyari elite, the strategy of alliances pursued by her husband's family, and the way that strategy was altered by the centralizing efforts of the Qajar government.

Bibi Maryam was one of twelve daughters and eight sons born to the Bakhtiyari chief Husayn Quli Khan. Her mother, Bibi Fatima, was the daughter of Ali Reza, the head of a rival branch of the Bakhtiyari known as the Chahar Lang. (Husayn Quli Khan himself belonged to the Haft Lang branch; more on these divisions below.) Bibi Fatima's marriage to Husayn Quli Khan sealed an alliance with Ali Reza and the Chahar Lang against the intrigues of other tribes or the Qajar state. Bibi Maryam and her sisters and brothers continued the practice of taking marriage partners from outside their clan as well as from among the children of their father's brothers. Maryam married twice, first to Ali Quli Khan of her mother's clan, then, after he died, to her cousin Fatula Quli Khan. Murdan Khan, her eldest son by her first husband, became an important figure in Bakhtiyari politics in later years.

The position of noblewomen among the Bakhtiyari declined significantly within the lifetime of Bibi Maryam. Bibi Maryam's struggles and those of other women of her class took place against the backdrop of this declining power. Formerly, Bakhtiyari marriage alliances insured harmony among the members of a tribe. As mothers, daughters, sisters, and wives, tribal women served as mediators in disputes between the men. A man did not want to be faced with the prospect of fighting against the husband of his sister or daughter. In this way, most divisions within a tribe were resolved before real trouble began. The preferred marriage for a woman was to her father's brother's son. But marriages to members of outside tribal factions began to occur more often as the Bakhtiyari sought to unite against the encroachment of the central state. During Maryam's lifetime, the tribal network of relationships based on blood and marriage greatly extended the power of her family. A consideration of the nineteenth-century experience will make this clear.

The Bakhtiyari were made up of loosely organized nomadic clans that considered themselves to be of either the Chahar Lang or the Haft Lang branch of a people who spoke Luri, the Bakhtiyari language, and shared biannual migration routes. For centuries, Bakhtiyari pastoralists migrated with their sheep, goats, and mules across the Zagros Mountains in southwest Iran. In the early spring the tribesmen and their families braved the high trails and swollen rivers to move their flocks from the winter feeding grounds on the plains of Khuzistan to the cool valleys west of Isfahan. Again, in the autumn, before the first snows covered the passes, the tribes gathered at the tribal meeting place in one of the northern valleys to prepare for the return to the warmer lands of the south. Transit between the summer and winter feeding grounds was difficult and dangerous. The western town of Ahwaz, at the mouth of the Karun, and the city of Isfahan, on the eastern edge of the Bakhtiyari lands, were separated by several mountain chains where the trail reached altitudes of more than eight thousand feet. As the river wound its way down from the high peaks to water the fertile pastures on both the eastern and western slopes, it cut deep channels into the limestone rocks. Narrow suspension bridges spanned the high banks in a few places, but more often the herdsmen were forced to descend into the steep gorges and swim with their animals across the cold, swift waters that blocked the trail.

In the nineteenth century, things began to change. The rivalries between the Chahar Lang and Haft Lang branches of the Bakhtiyari gradually gave way to a new political organization. The centralizing Qajar government played a crucial role in this transformation. In the 1820s and 1830s, Muhammad Taqi Khan, head of the dominant Chahar Lang faction, imagined that he and the Bakhtiyari could remain independent from the state. For several years, he refused to pay taxes or to furnish troops to the government.

Fath Ali Shah (1797–1834), the Qajar ruler, was faced with an empty treasury and the threat of revolt among his troops. He feared Iran would be completely overtaken by the Europeans after humiliating defeats resulted in the loss of the rich northern provinces to the Russians in the treaties of Gulistan (1813) and Turkmanchay (1828). When Muhammad Taqi Khan sought to withhold his taxes, and subsequently began negotiating a commercial agreement with the British, Fath Ali Shah became convinced a plot was afoot and ordered his arrest. He was put into prison in 1841, where he died ten years later. Relations between the Bakhtiyari and the Qajars continued to slide downhill in the years that followed. Nasir ud-Din Shah, who began his long reign as a liberal reformer in 1848, became increasingly reactionary after the British invasion of Bushire in 1857. British overtures to the Bakhtiyari, even in the form of commercial treaties, were viewed by the Qajars as an attempt to subvert the power of the Crown.

Husayn Quli Khan, Maryam's father, was in a position to profit from the mistakes of Muhammad Taqi Khan. In keeping with a traditional Qajar practice of using rival factions to check the power of tribal leaders, the government used *khans* from the Haft Lang branch of the Bakhtiyari to help capture Muhammad Taqi Khan. Husayn Quli Khan was one of those *khans*. As a reward for his loyalty to the government, he was recognized as the paramount leader of the Bakhtiyari. Thereafter, he used his ties with the Qajars to increase his status among the tribal factions. As a Qajar official, he was responsible for maintaining order in his tribal area, collecting the excess surplus from the peasants, and furnishing tribesmen to defend the state.

For the next few years, Husayn Quli Khan was left alone by the government and consolidated his wealth and power within the tribal area. He married wisely, formed alliances with neighboring groups, and successfully eliminated all rivals to his rule of the Bakhtiyaris. In 1867 Husayn Quli Khan was given the title of *ilkhan*, or paramount chief, by Nasir ud-Din Shah. He was also awarded what amounted to private ownership of large tracts of land that had once been held in common by the tribes, the proceeds of which he used to enrich himself and his family. On this occasion, his younger brother, Hajji Imam Quli Khan, was designated as the *ilbeg* (second in command) of the tribes. Thus was consolidated a new administrative division of the Bakhtiyari into Ilkhani and Hajji Ilkhani branches. The central government retained the right to give or take both titles at will.

The temporary security of this outside alliance with the Qajar government ushered in several significant changes in the lives of the newly created Bakhtiyari nobility. The permanent positions of *ilkhan* and *ilbeg*, and the subsequent land grants that went along with these titles, required Husayn Quli Khan and his sons and brothers, along with their families, to give up the role of pastoral nomadic chiefs. There was little time for the annual migrations for the leading *khans*, who as landlords now owned agricultural land complete with peasants and villages.

By the 1870s, the *khans* had settled down and built castles in the lush valleys of the summer pasture to the east of Isfahan. They began to invest their land rents not only in greater herds but also in the agriculture and small craft industries of the villages throughout the area. However, in spite of growing responsibilities at home, the *khans* were now required to spend more and more time in the Qajar capital in Tehran to give service to the Shah and lobby for continued royal support. The Qajars often kept *khans* under virtual house arrest in the capital in order to insure that their tribal retainers would remain faithful to the royal house. The move from nomad chief to elite landlord and agent of the government substantially altered the life-styles of the Bakhtiyari. This change was nowhere more pronounced than in the case of the elite women.

The wives and mothers of the leaders found themselves administering the household and its surrounding estates during the long absence of the men. Estates often included entire villages, where the *bibi*, in the name of the landowning *khan*, was in charge of the decisions about planting, water allocation, harvesting, and distribution of the crops. The *khans* claimed a percentage of everything produced by the villagers, from the grain that passed through the mill to the handicrafts made by the peasant women. This required that elaborate books be kept by the *bibis*, most of whom were literate by this time. During this period, a *khan* became increasingly dependent upon the opinions of his mother or wife of noble birth, not only because of her blood connections but also because of her role as administrator of the estate. During these years of the *khans'* absence, the *bibis* also gained an economic independence not known to previous generations of tribal women. Life on the estates, surrounded by peasants and village craftsmen, gave this new class of elite women the chance to run small businesses that were separate from those of the *khans*. A grain mill or carpet factory was often owned and run by a leading *bibi*.

Carpet making became a particularly lucrative business for the noblewomen. Most of the weavers were wives and children of servants on the estate. The *bibi* supervised every stage of the preparation. She selected the best wool and watched to make sure it was properly washed and dyed; she weighed out and mixed the dye with her own hands to make sure of the quality. The short, colored threads of wool were then woven into the warp, which was wound on simple horizontal wooden looms. The number of women on a loom depended upon the size of the carpet. The weaving of one carpet was a long process, and the women were paid little besides their food. Money from the sale of the carpets went into the *bibis'* private funds, and several of the *bibis* began to accumulate wealth in their own right and did not have to depend completely on their husbands. In later years, some of the *bibis* found it very profitable to switch from the traditional Bakhtiyari pattern carpet designs to the large flowers that were popular in England.

The increased independence of the women was one side effect of the changing Bakhtiyari society; there were others, however, that eventually came to threaten the position of the *bibis* as partners and power brokers for the *khans*. The necessary alliance with the Qajars was not without its cost. While leading *khans* found it increasingly necessary to seek the favor of members of the court, they soon learned that the Qajar family could not be trusted in this relationship. While the official ties with the Shah allowed Husayn Quli Khan to strengthen his alliances within the tribal confedera-tion, it did not eventually give him protection against the intrigues of other members of the Qajar court. His success attracted the jealousy of the crown prince, who was governor of the district of Isfahan and who feared the grow-ing power of the *ilkhan* in the neighboring tribal lands. The prince con-vinced his father that the Khan was preparing to side with the British in a growing dispute between the Qajars and the Europeans over trade in the southern part of the country, and in 1882 he persuaded his father to have Husayn Quli Khan killed.

The murder of Husayn Quli Khan began a new era for the ruling family of the Bakhtiyari. It demonstrated to his sons and brothers that although outside alliances were necessary, the Qajars could not be trusted. As *ilkhan*, Husayn Quli Khan was the Qajar representative in the tribal lands. He had worked for more than thirty years in the service of the Shah, collecting the taxes and furnishing tribal troops, yet he was cruelly murdered when it was feared he was becoming too strong. After his death, his brothers and his oldest son were put into prison so they could not immediately assume tribal leadership. They were released one by one over a three-year period so the Qajars could actively manipulate the competition between the different fac-tions of the family. The *khans* were forced to compete among themselves for the titles and the power and wealth that went with them. Any unity between the factions depended largely upon the security of the kinship alliances.

This conflict between brothers, cousins, uncles, and nephews was not a new factor in the tribal system in Iran. The absence of inheritance by pri-mogeniture or of clearly defined rules for the passing of leadership roles had for many years made the ascent to power a matter of contention throughout the tribe. However, once the Qajar government became part of the alliance system through which the *khans* struggled for position, marriage ties became even more important in keeping peace among the leading families. The *khan* most able to form the strongest alliances, especially through marriage, would end up with the most important tribal roles. For although the Qajar Shah had the right to grant the title to the *khan* of his choice, he almost always chose the leader with the strongest ties among his people. It would have made little sense to name an *ilkhan* that the tribesmen would not follow. The value and influence of the women of Bibi Maryam's class grew as the rivalry made their mediation essential to the peace and unity of the tribes.

By the time of the constitutional revolution of 1906–11, the ability of the women to mediate disputes had become even more important. The Bakhtiyari *khans* were drawn into the war between the royalists, who supported the absolute power of the Shah, and the nationalists, who wanted the constitution restored. In 1906, a revolution had forced the Qajar monarch to agree to a parliamentary system of government. The Shah died a short time later, and his son, Muhammad Ali Shah (1907–9), set out to revoke the agreement. The Bakhtiyari *khans* joined forces with the nationalists in 1909 to reinstate the constitution and force the Shah to step down in favor of his young son, Ahmad. The efforts of the Bakhtiyari *khans* were successful, and they became known as the heroes who saved the constitution, in large part due to the efforts of the women.

As part of the plan to unseat Muhammad Ali Shah, the supporters of the constitution asked the paramount chief of the Bakhtiyari, Najaf Quli Khan, to march on Isfahan and take over the governorship from the Qajar prince who held the office. From Isfahan the Bakhtiyari tribesmen marched to Tehran and with the help of a tribal army from the north defeated the troops of the Shah. The plan was almost spoiled by Khusrow Khan, a half brother of the *ilkhan*. Khusrow Khan had for years sought to persuade the Shah to make him *ilkhan* in place of his half brother Najaf Quli Khan. When he learned of the plot to take Isfahan, Khusrow Khan reported it to the Qajar governor and asked the court to make him *ilkhan* if he, rather than his brother, succeeded in capturing Isfahan.

When it became known that Khusrow Khan had decided to mount a challenge to the authority of Najaf Quli Khan, the women stepped in to resolve the conflict. From her home in the tribal district of Chahar Mahal, Bibi Sahab Jan, the wife of Najaf Quli Khan, wrote letters to her powerful brother, Ibrahim, the oldest son of Reza Quli Khan, and also to the wives of several of the other *khans*, urging them to help her husband. By the time Najaf Quli Khan reached Isfahan, the city had already been secured for him by Ibrahim. Khusrow Khan was unable to gather tribal support for his cause, and he joined the *ilkhan* in the march to Tehran to depose the Shah.

It is interesting to note that as long as the disputes were settled through kinship and marriage, there was very little physical violence or loss of life among the families of the Bakhtiyari leaders. Khusrow Khan offers a case in point; even though he was a known troublemaker, his half brother did not long consider him an enemy. In the same way, another Bakhtiyari *khan*, Luft Ali Khan, of the Hajji Ilkhani branch of the family, fought for the royalist cause in the revolution against the forces of his brothers and cousins who supported the constitution. When the fighting ended, he was immediately accepted back into the family and was later named *ilbeg* and governor of the district of Kerman.

Throughout the constitutional revolution and civil war the ties of kinship, held together primarily by the women, were very effective in helping to settle disputes among the tribal factions. With the *khans* away from home, women's roles as partners of their husbands and power brokers for their sons had grown stronger. Many of the leading *bibis* followed the news of the nationalist movement in Iran with keen interest because their husbands and sons were involved in the political struggles.

It is commonly acknowledged that the influence of the Bakhtiyari *khans* in Iranian politics reached its high point during the civil war. Not so well known is that the influence of their women also reached its apex during these times of nationalist struggles. The *khans* depended on kinship alliances to keep harmony in the tribal homeland. However, it soon became evident that blood and marriage ties would no longer be enough to check the growing disunity among the tribal factions. During the years just preceding the civil war, a new element entered the alliance of the Bakhtiyaris. The British, who had been active in Iran on a limited basis for more than a century, increased their commercial and political efforts. They sought alliances with the tribal leaders, much the same as the Qajar shahs had done fifty years before. They hoped to be able to use the tribal *khans* to help make the southern part of the country safe for British commercial pursuits. The Bakhtiyari had sought to find a European ally for some years. Husayn Quli Khan had realized that a powerful outside ally, as well as extensive kinship and marriage ties, was essential to holding power within the tribe.

After the death of Husayn Quli Khan at the hands of his Qajar supporters, many of the Bakhtiyari *khans* began to look more closely at the possibilities of seeking support from a European power. They were well aware that the British had proven unwilling to help the Bakhtiyari leader Muhammad Taqi Khan in his dispute with the Qajars in 1840; however, British interest in the tribal lands stepped up after 1901, when the British began to drill for oil in the southern part of the country. In 1907 oil was discovered in the Bakhtiyari lands, and in 1913 the British navy converted all its ships from coal to oil. These developments increased Britain's stakes in Iran, and soon the British legation supplanted the Shah's government as the most significant power in the tribal area.

In the early years of British commercial penetration, the European agents had worked through the Qajar government to try to insure the security of the trade routes in the south. This led to conflict between the Qajar shahs and the tribal leaders, and did not bring safety to the trade routes. After the oil drilling began, the British began to usurp the authority of the central government and signed separate agreements with the leading chiefs of the Bakhtiyari to guard and maintain the roads through the tribal lands; in return, the *khans* were promised shares of the oil revenues and money to pay for the road guards.

The younger *khans* were also anxious to become part of the European commercial and political power. Contracts to guard the drilling sites and the oil pipeline, as well as the roads leading to the fields, created new wealth and status. At a time when many of the leading *khans* were away fighting for the nationalist causes in the capital, lesser *khans* were busy vying for the money offered by the British oil company. Rivalry and jealousy had increased within the Bakhtiyari noble family as the leading *khans* were given positions of authority as members of parliament and as governors of the provincial cities. The lesser *khans* left at home in the tribal areas felt that they were not getting a fair share of the wealth that these positions offered. The young *khans* saw the alliances with the British as a chance to move up in the power structure.

The Bakhtiyari leaders who were paid to guard the roads were unable to control the situation. The *khans* not only failed to stop the raids by rival tribes, they also lost control of the situation within the Bakhtiyari tribes. While some Bakhtiyari tribesmen acted as guards, others robbed caravans and cut off supplies to the British oil fields to the west of Isfahan, making it difficult for their leaders to collect the fees promised by the British.

The problem of tribal rivalry became more intense after 1913 when the leading *khans* suddenly ended their political role in Tehran. When the fighting was over, the Iranian nationalist leaders, who were anxious to use the tribal forces to overthrow the Shah, found it difficult to deal with the Bakhtiyari *khans* once they became part of the government. After the parliamentary government was firmly established, the nationalist cause split along conservative and liberal lines. The Bakhtiyari approach to politics had always been pragmatic, and the *khans* were unsuited for the ideological struggles that went on in the Iranian capital in the years following the civil war. They withdrew from their positions in the parliament and returned to their tribal homes.

The return of the leaders to the tribal lands did not put an end to the disunity among the *khans* of the ruling family. The British at first found it to their advantage to continue the Qajar policy of causing dissension in the leadership by playing one *khan* against another. In this way, they could force the tribesmen to work for less money. Later, however, they found that they could not control the chaos caused by the competition among the factions. Robbery and raiding by the group out of favor with the British made it impossible for the *khans* who were hired to keep peace in the area. From the period following the civil war to the end of World War I, the roads in the southern part of the country were shut down. Trade goods could not be carried with any regularity throughout the area. This served only to worsen the miserable conditions caused by a downturn in the world economy.

The Qajar government refused to help the British control the Bakhtiyari *khans*. The central government was suspicious of British efforts to recruit the tribal leaders as partners in their commercial endeavors. The Qajars were not strong enough to keep the Europeans out of the area, and they feared that separate treaties between the British and the tribal groups of Iran would exclude the monarchy from the economic picture. World War I exacerbated the problems of the Bakhtiyari tribal factions. Anti-British feeling ran high, as the European power was blamed for the poor conditions and anarchy in the south. German agents actively recruited among the southern tribes, and the leading *khans* were attracted by the prospect of help from another European power to block British dominance of trade and oil rights in the south. By the outbreak of the war, it was not certain which side the tribal leaders would support. Though the Qajar government declared the country neutral, several of the Bakhtiyari leaders openly gave aid to the German-led Turkish forces. Other *khans* remained on the side of the British. The split in tribal loyalties increased the already wide divisions within the tribal leadership structure. Ironically, many of the Swedish officers who in 1911 had been brought to Iran at the urging of the British oil company chose to join the tribal factions who supported the German agents against the British.

The women were forced to watch the anarchy grow as the men of the Bakhtiyari were used by yet another group who sought to gain power in Iran. First the shahs, then the nationalist reformers, and finally the British made agreements with the *khans*, yet none were able to enforce the agreements. The divisions that came to the tribe after the discovery of oil were much more serious than any before. The women's roles as administrators and mediators became less important after oil was discovered on the Bakhtiyari land. The land rents and revenues collected on the estates were no longer the predominant sources of wealth. The large amounts of foreign capital involved in the oil fields altered forever the social and political conditions in the tribal lands.

The nature of the tribal conflict was altogether different after the British government, as outside enforcing power, claimed the right to name the *ilkhan* and *ilbeg* of the tribes. As has already been pointed out, before there was little violence involved in settling disputes, and even challenges like the one put forth in 1909 by Khusrow Khan were solved without bloodshed. In 1916, however, the *ilkhan* and *ilbeg* named by the British asked the Europeans for military protection for their trip back home, out of fear that the other *khans* would kill them. The conflicts by that time were far beyond the ability of the Bakhtiyari to settle through traditional kinship and marriage ties.

It is not improbable that many of the *bibis* hoped for a German victory in the war. A victory by the Central Powers offered hope of breaking the grip of British oil wealth that controlled Bakhtiyari society. In this context, Bibi Maryam's actions can be understood historically.

Wilhelm Wassmuss did reach Isfahan in the fall of 1916, but he did not succeed in capturing the city or the British oil fields to the east. He continued to avoid capture until the spring of 1918, and many of the Bakhtiyari and other tribal people in the southern part of Iran joined the pro-German cause. Bibi Maryam, along with some of the *khans*, had her property seized, as had been threatened. It is not known where she settled in the years following the war. Her oldest son, Ali Murdan Khan, joined the Russians in the north and managed to come out of the war years with a respected position among the leadership of the Bakhtiyari, probably through his connections with the Russians.

The years immediately following the war saw the complete disintegration of order in the tribal territories throughout Iran. The roads were impassable because of lawlessness, particularly in the south. Disease and famine were especially serious, and many tribespeople died. The Qajars continued their downward spiral in the face of the growing foreign intervention. The Russians were forced to retreat from active involvement in Iranian economic and political affairs as a result of the Bolshevik revolution in 1917. The British, however, persisted in trying to work with the Qajars and the Bakhtiyari to protect the oil fields. The Anglo-Persian agreement of 1919 was rejected by the government, and nationalist anti-British feelings ran high throughout the rural and urban areas.

When Reza Khan seized power in 1921, he was welcomed by many Iranians, including some of the tribal peoples. The Bakhtiyari soon learned that he was no different than the Qajars. The settling of the tribes became a top priority of the new Pahlavi shah. Although Reza Shah used anti-British sentiment to secure power, once he was installed he allowed the new Anglo-Persian oil company to lease the Bakhtiyari lands. The tribesmen were ordered to turn in their rifles, and the migration routes were closed to nomadic herdsmen. These measures resulted in a revolt of both the Bakhtiyari and the Qashqa'i in 1929. This rebellion, known as the battle of Safid Desht, was quickly and brutally put down. A major hero of the battle of Safid

Desht, imprisoned and later executed in 1934, was Ali Murdan Khan, the oldest son of Bibi Maryam.

A NOTE ON SOURCES

Bibi Maryam's life, like that of many Middle Eastern women, is little known. She appears briefly in Elizabeth N. Ross, *A Lady Doctor in Bakhtiari Land* (London: Leonard Parsons, 1921), and in Christopher Sykes, *Wassmus, "The German Lawrence"* (London: Longmans, Green and Co., 1936). In Persian, the main sources are Hajji Khusraw Khan, *Sardar Zafar Bakhtiyari* (Tehran: Intisharat-i Farhangsara, 1362/1983); and Iskandar Khan Ukkashah, *Zaygham al-Dawlah Bakhtiyari* (Tehran: Intisharat-i Farhangsara, 1365/1986).

SUGGESTIONS FOR FURTHER READING

The history of the relationship between the Bakhtiyari, the Qajars, and the British has been fatally contaminated by the language of the nineteenth-century "Great Game of Asia," as I discovered when I wrote my master's thesis in history, "The Bakhtiyari, the Qajars, and the British in the Great Game of Asia" (University of California at Santa Cruz, 1990). There is much, accordingly, to redo.

For the British perspective, see Edward G. Browne, *The Persian Revolution of 1905–1909* (London: Frank Cass & Co., 1910); Browne, *A Year amongst the Persians* (Cambridge: Cambridge University press, 1926); George N. Curzon, *Persia and the Persian Question,* 2 vols. (New York: Barnes and Noble, 1892); David Fraser, *Persia and Turkey in Revolt* (London: William Blackwood and Sons, 1910); Hermann Norden, *Under Persian Skies* (Philadelphia: MacRae, Smith Co., 1928); Morgan W. Shuster, *The Strangling of Persia* (New York: Century Co., 1912); Percy Sykes, *A History of Persia* (London: Macmillan, 1915); and Arnold Wilson, *S.W. Persia: Letters and Diary of a Young Political Officer, 1907–1914* (London: Oxford University Press, 1942).

On the history of tribes in southern Iran, see Gene R. Garthwaite, *Khans and Shahs: A Documentary Analysis of the Bakhtiyari in Iran* (London: Cambridge University Press, 1983); Garthwaite, "Khans and Kings: The Dialectics of Power in Bakhtiyari History," in *Modern Iran: The Dialectics of Continuity and Change,* ed. Michael Bonine and Nikki Keddie (Albany: State University of New York Press, 1981), 159–72; and Leonard Helfgott, "Tribalism as a Socioeconomic Formation in Iranian History," *Iranian Studies* 10 (1977): 36–58. Travel and eyewitness accounts about life among the Bakhtiyari (in addition to Ross) in the early twentieth century include Paul E. Case, "I Become a Bakhtiari," *National Geographic,* January–July 1946, 325–58, and the classic by Merian C. Cooper, *Grass* (New York: G. P. Putman's Sons, 1925).

For some anthropological studies of pastoralism in Iran, see, among others, Fredrik Barth, *Nomads of South Persia* (Oslo: Universitetsforlaget, 1964); Lois Beck, *The Qashqa'i of Iran* (New Haven, Conn.: Yale University Press, 1986); Beck, "Women among the Qashqa'i Nomadic Pastoralists in Iran," in *Women in the Muslim World*, ed. Lois Beck and Nikki Keddie (Cambridge, Mass.: Harvard University Press, 1978); Richard Tapper, ed., *The Conflict of Tribe and State in Iran and Afghanistan* (New York: St. Martin's Press, 1983); and Tapper, *Pasture and Politics* (New York: Academic Press, Inc., 1979).

On the political history of early twentieth-century Iran, see Firuz Kazemzadeh, *Russia and Britain in Persia, 1864–1914: A Study in Imperialism* (New Haven, Conn.: Yale University Press, 1968); Janet Afary, *The Iranian Constitutional Revolution, 1906–1911* (New York: Columbia University Press, 1996); and Nikki Keddie, *Qajar Iran and the Rise of Reza Khan, 1796–1925*, (Costa Mesa, Mazda Publishers, 1999). For a general survey of modern Iranian history, see Nikki R. Keddie, *Modern Iran: Roots and Results of Revolution* (New Haven, Conn.: Yale University Press, 2003).

PART TWO

Colonial Lives

Chapter 8

The Shaykh and His Daughter: Coping in Colonial Algeria

Julia Clancy-Smith

The vitality of popular religion in the Algerian countryside was one of the features of North African culture that was most noted by nineteenth-century European observers. The marabouts (in Arabic, *murabit*), as those of the popularly venerated saintly lineages were called, were the focus of devotion of large numbers of rural people, who saw in them repositories of charisma, or *baraka,* as it is called in Arabic. The blessing of a saint was believed to cure illness, revive sinking family fortunes, or cause barren women to conceive a male child. Marabouts were of many different kinds. They sometimes combined their saintly status with claimed descent from the Prophet or with the headship of a Sufi religious brotherhood, or *tariqa*. Some had strictly local clienteles, while others attracted the devout from all over Algeria.

The marabouts played a leading role in resistance to the French during the period of the conquest (1830–71). They helped organize, inspire, and lead the various piecemeal efforts of rural Algerians to oppose French colonial rule. The most famous marabout was Amir Abd al-Qadir, who, although of urban origin, traded on his religious prestige and his headship of the Qadiriya Sufi *tariqa* to rally the support of the tribes in western Algeria. In the Tellian Atlas of the pre-Saharan steppe, where resources were scarce and charisma was plentiful, rural holy men played an especially important role in resistance activities.*

The end of resistance in the steppe zone in the 1860s and 1870s signaled a change of strategy by the marabouts, who were gradually won over to supporting the colonial order by the liberal distribution of honors and rewards. Their options for further resistance were few, given the superiority of French military technology and French administrative prowess. Among the early learners of the new game was

---

*For a survey, see Peter von Sivers, "Rural Uprisings as Political Movements in Colonial Algeria, 1851–1914," in *Islam, Politics, and Social Movements,* ed. E. Burke III and I. M. Lapidus (Berkeley: University of California Press, 1988), 39–59.

Muhammad ibn Abi al-Qasim, the *shaykh* of the *zawiya* of al-Hamil and a leader of the Rahmaniya Sufi *tariqa*.

As Julia Clancy-Smith explains in her contribution, the *shaykh* took care to keep the French at arm's length so as to avoid compromising himself too much. He also untypically placed a high value on the upgrading of agriculture on his lands, sought to fend off French land-grabbers, and adopted an uncharacteristic attitude toward religion, preaching against the cult of the saints and extolling the pursuit of science. In another context, Shaykh Qassam, a Muslim religious leader in Palestine with strong Sufi connections (on whom see the biography below by Abdullah Schleifer), evolved in a rather different direction. Palestinians are still debating how he is to be seen. —Eds.

The oasis of al-Hamil is located some twelve kilometers southwest of Bou Saada and situated on the right bank of the wadi that funnels water to date-palm groves below. The village, constructed of dun-colored mud brick, sits amid the barren foothills of the Saharan Atlas upon a great rose-brown mountain. By the late nineteenth century, a Rahmaniya *zawiya* (Sufi establishment) dominated the village and valley below; like other desert Sufi centers of the period, it resembled a fortress more than anything else.

Al-Hamil's importance as a pilgrimage site was due to the presence of the Rahmaniya center, which by then boasted a well-known *madrasa* (theological college) and a fine library containing a number of rare manuscripts that represented a significant portion of Algeria's cultural patrimony. The *zawiya* had been founded in 1863 by Shaykh Muhammad Ibn Abi al-Qasim (1823–97), a venerated Muslim scholar, or *alim* (pl. *ulama*), as well as a Sufi (mystic) and *wali* (saint). Because of the Shaykh's piety, erudition, and unstinting generosity, the al-Hamil *zawiya* commanded an impressive popular following in the region and elsewhere. Muslim pilgrims, scholars, students, and the needy from all over North Africa flocked to the *zawiya*, which provided crucial religious, cultural, and socioeconomic services.

Muhammad Ibn Abi al-Qasim died on 2 June 1897, and a bitter struggle soon erupted in al-Hamil over who was to be his spiritual successor. Despite the village's modest appearance and seeming isolation, the stakes were quite high. Not only did the al-Hamil *zawiya* claim the single largest group of Rahmaniya clients in the department of Algiers, but it also held in various forms property whose net worth was estimated at well over two million francs, not a small fortune for the time. In some respects, the quarrel was similar to other disputes over social and spiritual turf that periodically divided North African Sufi orders and elites, particularly after the death of a charismatic *shaykh*. Indeed, two decades earlier, another powerful North African Sufi brotherhood, the Tijaniya *tariqa*, had split into two warring factions in Algeria during the 1870s over the matter of headship of the order. Open discord among the Tijaniya Sufi elite had caused momentary distress to the French colonial authorities of Algeria since such struggles frequently compromised the country's tenuous political calm. The troubles in al-Hamil were viewed at first in the same light by officials.

However, the uproar provoked by Shaykh Muhammad Ibn Abi al-Qasim's death in 1897 differed in one significant way from other such contests for Sufi hegemony. Leading one powerful Rahmaniya faction centered at al-Hamil was a female saint and Sufi, Zaynab (1850?–1904), who was also the daughter of the deceased *shaykh*. Opposing Zaynab bint Shaykh Muhammad was her cousin, Muhammad b. al-Hajj Muhammad, who enjoyed the support of the minor Rahmaniya notables and Sufi brothers not allied with Zaynab, as well as the backing of local French authorities in Bou Saada. The contest between the two factions eventually reached those at the pinnacle of the colonial hierarchy in l'Algérie Française, including the *procureur général*, the chief official at the Ministry of Justice, and even the governor-general himself.

Sidi Muhammad was from the Awlad Laghwini of the Jabal Tastara in the Bou Saada region. His was a minor clan of *shurafa* (sing. *sharif:* those claiming kinship with the Prophet's family). Sharifian descent could be a potent source of socioreligious authority if parlayed in the right manner. In addition, members of Muhammad's clan were credited with founding al-Hamil, which represented another source of local prestige. According to popular lore, the town's existence was associated with a miraculous event that occurred several centuries earlier. Sidi Muhammad's ancestors had caused a stick thrust into arid soil to be transformed into a verdant mulberry tree. This was taken as a sign of the family's supernatural powers. However, the translocal authority the *shaykh* wielded later in his life was the product of his religious knowledge, good works, and the miracles attributed to him by his numerous followers.

Shaykh Muhammad's early education was quite typical of saintly Sufi figures in North Africa at the time. He studied first in a local *zawiya*, and was beginning to learn the Quran by heart when the French army landed at Sidi Ferruch in July 1830. Further studies were undertaken in the Kabylia in northern Algeria at the *zawiya* of the Awlad Sidi Ibn Daud near Akbou, where he mastered Muslim law and theology. Sometime before 1848–49, the *shaykh* returned to the al-Hamil region, which had long been popularly regarded as a holy place. This part of Algeria was still outside of effective or direct French control, then mainly concentrated in the north, which made the small oasis all the more attractive.

In al-Hamil, Sidi Muhammad founded a *madrasa*, began family life, and was endowed with *karamat*, or the ability to work miracles. For North African society at the time, evidence of supernatural gifts operated both to create and to confirm holiness; thus the saintly personage was at once the cause and consequence of the miracle that he or she performed. Moral probity, *ilm* (knowledge, especially sacred knowledge), and personal piety, ratified by the Prophet's appearance, were virtues demanded of the holy person, who thereby became the object of collective veneration and popular support. By the middle of the nineteenth century, Sidi Muhammad was building up a clientele drawn mainly, although not exclusively, from the region of al-Hamil.

The years 1849–50 witnessed major political changes in the upper reaches of the Algerian Sahara and in the fortunes of various branches of the Rahmaniya *tariqa*, which by then counted followers and allied Sufi centers in much of eastern and central Algeria, both north and south. Between 1849 and 1871, many Rahmaniya leaders were drawn into armed confrontations with the French army; all ended in disaster. Humiliation, exile, or imprisonment in Christian lands, forced emigration to neighboring Muslim states, and destruction of Sufi centers and property were the rewards of those who opted for collective struggle. During the 1849 uprising near Biskra, Bou Saada was besieged, occupied, and given a permanent garrison to protect the newly created French administrative *cercle* of Bou Saada. In this period, Shaykh Muhammad Ibn Abi al-Qasim remained largely unscathed by the larger, more ominous forces around him, although he obviously drew some important lessons from the experiences of his Sufi peers in the Rahmaniya network elsewhere.

In 1857 he left al-Hamil for the Rahmaniya *zawiya* of Awlad Jalal in the Ziban, located southwest of Biskra, which had just suffered "pacification" at the hands of the French military. There, he studied under the direction of a regionally prominent Rahmaniya *shaykh*, Muhammad al-Mukhtar, who initiated Muhammad Ibn Abi al-Qasim into the order. By the time of Shaykh al-Mukhtar's death in 1862, Muhammad Ibn Abi al-Qasim had become his closest spiritual associate and the inheritor of his *baraka* (spiritual blessing) after his master's death. For a year he even ran the *zawiya*, until the opposition of Shaykh al-Mukhtar's family forced him to return to al-Hamil. There, he established an independent Rahmaniya center, using the older *madrasa* as a nucleus. Soon it rivaled the *zawiya* in the Ziban.

Before long a collection of buildings—a family residence, library, mosque, guest house, elementary school, meeting room for Sufi ceremonials, and student lodgings—graced the town of al-Hamil. These attested to the ability of the founder-saint to attract a diverse following, as well as the funds (largely in the form of pious offerings) needed to finance a multitude of social and religious services. In fact, Shaykh Muhammad engaged in financial operations for the good of the local Muslim community. Individuals were able to deposit money with him at the *zawiya* for safekeeping, receipts were issued, and account books kept, which suggests the existence of a sort of primitive savings bank. However, in contrast to some other Sufi elites elsewhere in Algeria, there is no evidence that the Shaykh ever solicited or received financial subsidies from the colonial regime. Until his death, he maintained his ascetic lifestyle and simple manners, a mode of behavior followed scrupulously by his daughter Zaynab.

For Shaykh Muhammad, one method of cultural survival was redemption through land use, although distance from the main nodes of colonial agriculture was the key element in the *zawiya*'s survival. In the region of Bou Saada alone, some nine hundred hectares of land were farmed for the benefit of the al-Hamil *zawiya;* outside the region, hundreds of hectares were placed under the *zawiya*'s control in the form of pious endowments. Shaykh Muhammad's involvement in the rural economy went far beyond the cultivation of existing arable land. Revenues and offerings were employed to open up new areas for agrarian exploitation by peasant-clients in an era when Algerian cultivators elsewhere were suffering cruelly from the progressive loss of land to settler colonialism.

By the early 1890s, several hundred students and scholars were involved in education at the al-Hamil *zawiya* at any given moment; it was visited by between seven thousand and eight thousand pilgrims annually. The curriculum of study offered was surprisingly eclectic, a blending of the "traditional" Maghribi religious education with what might be termed the "classical." In addition to *fiqh* (Islamic jurisprudence), *hadith*, the Quran, and Sufi doctrines, students learned chemistry, mathematics, astrology, astronomy, and rhetoric, subjects that had fallen somewhat out of favor in some rural North African colleges during the past centuries. Muhammad's intellectual prowess in the important discipline of *ilm al-nahw* (grammar) won him the sobriquet "imam of the grammarians." Yet his greatest contribution was to remind the community that the pursuit of science was a duty incumbent upon all Muslims, an attitude that harked back to the medieval Islamic era while anticipating the modern reformist movements of the early twentieth century.

Among the Shaykh's numerous writings was a treatise that constitutes a remarkable critique of the cult of saints as then practiced in Algeria. In it Muhammad questioned one of the sources upon which his own authority and prestige in the community were based. This suggests that his vision extended beyond the mere maintenance of the cultural status quo to the more daunting task of social regeneration through the acquisition of knowledge.

The steady influx of visitors from all over Algeria and the Maghrib required a permanent staff of some forty-six people to oversee the day-to-day affairs of the Rahmaniya establishment. Once again, the general situation in Algeria in the period contrasts with that in al-Hamil while also helping to explain the popularity of the Sufi center. From the 1860s on, the rural Muslim population was afflicted by drought, famine, and epidemics that made more precarious an economic existence already seriously compromised by massive land expropriations. At the same time, after 1871 the colonial bureaucracy passed fully into the hands of civilian administrators, who were notoriously parsimonious about extending financial assistance to the beleaguered Muslim population. Thus, the relatively thriving state of al-Hamil and its clients offer a striking contrast to conditions elsewhere. Much of the credit for this was due to the postures and strategies adopted by Shaykh Muhammad toward the unpleasant reality of foreign occupation.

North Africans were not the only visitors to Muhammad's *zawiya* in this period, although aside from the presence of the military administration Bou Saada did not attract permanent European settlements. This was naturally a critical factor in Shaykh Muhammad's relative freedom to construct a social space where the impact of asymmetrical power relations was attenuated. The commandant of Bou Saada, however, periodically called upon Shaykh Muhammad. On one occasion in the 1880s, he was accompanied by a group of French ladies, motivated by a mild curiosity in things Muslim and Saharan. During this visit, Sidi Muhammad Ibn Abi al-Qasim showed himself to be a cordial host, displaying an equanimity in the face of European eccentricities that can only be described as remarkable. Not only did the Shaykh open the doors of the very private women's quarters to the female visitors, but he also agreed to a formal sit-down luncheon *à la française* at the *zawiya*. One can only wonder at his thoughts as he was seated for two hours, with French women on either side of him for companions, before a table set with the curious culinary implements of European civilization furnished by the delegation. For the first time in his life the Shaykh had to maneuver with silverware, sit with women while eating, and engage in polite dinner conversation through an interpreter.

His hospitality earned him the sympathy of the French visitors, thus reinforcing the benevolent attitude of the military commandant, who was a powerful figure in the region's affairs and in those of the *zawiya*. Of this, Shaykh Muhammad was painfully aware. In an age when the *régime du sabre* had given way to the more corrosive system of civilian bureaucratic control and cultural conquest, a consummate diplomat like Sidi Muhammad could claim victory in wars waged far from conventional battlefields. Thus, his survival was due in no small part to his temperament, which enabled him to deal patiently and skillfully with Europeans.

Nevertheless, in contrast to other Algerian religious notables in the period, Shaykh Muhammad refused to learn French; Zaynab was unversed in French as well. A lack of proficiency in the infidel's language created a subtle sort of cultural distance between the Shaykh and those forced to work with him or through him to govern the local populace. Maintaining a balance between rapprochement with and distance from the conqueror was critical for highly visible social intermediaries like Shaykh Muhammad. An overly cozy relationship with the French might erode popular indigenous support, while remoteness could compromise the Shaykh's proficiency in wringing concessions for the community from colonial authorities.

In addition, Sidi Muhammad Ibn Abi al-Qasim prudently refused to accept any formal office, honoraria, or even decorations from the regime. This public rejection meant that his reputation remained untarnished, thus assuring the continued support of his constituency. In this he differed from some other religious notables of the period. Seduced by the temptation of minor positions in the administrative system, they frequently saw their followers transfer loyalties to other religious leaders. After enjoying an official post in northern Algeria for three years, which earned him the opprobrium of his clients, a local Rahmaniya figure made the *hajj* to Mecca to atone for his sins and recapture some of his lost socioreligious prestige and popular support.

French authorities rarely indulged in gratuitous praise of Algerian Muslim leaders. Yet Shaykh Muhammad b. Abi al-Qasim was often described as of "great intelligence, vast knowledge, and pure of morals." "His authority," it was said, "stretches from Bou Saada, Djelfa, Boghar, and Biskra to the region of Aumale, Médéa, Tiaret, and Sétif." Such a far-flung spiritual following demanded that the Shaykh travel periodically to visit the faithful, confer his blessings, and receive donations in kind or currency. In the places where he had stopped to rest, his clients constructed small shrines (*maqams*) commemorating his holy presence.

One of his last journeys brought him to Maison Carrée, outside of Algiers, in April of 1896. On this occasion, Shaykh Muhammad was greeted by some five thousand Muslim Algerians in the course of a single day. During this particular trip, Shaykh Muhammad performed one of his most widely publicized miracles—a demonstration of *baraka* that was at the same time a discreet affirmation of powers superior to those claimed by the French masters of Algeria. His followers swore that the Shaykh had employed his supernatural gifts to stall the departure of the train in which he had been riding so that he might perform his prayers undisturbed; the mechanics had been powerless to move the train forward until the saint had completed his devotions.

Shaykh Muhammad could not have undertaken travels to visit his numerous affiliated *zawiyas* and followers without the blessing of the colonial regime. By this period, many officials were frantic about the supposed threats to the French empire posed by pan-Islam and by politically active Sufi brotherhoods. These apprehensions led authorities to monitor closely the movements of Algerian religious notables. Written permits had to be obtained from the authorities in advance of travel, a privilege that was selectively conferred and frequently refused. Denial of travel permits to uncooperative indigenous leaders loosened the highly personal bonds between

Sufi masters and clients, thus undermining Sufi networks that had always been deemed inherently subversive by the French.

The positive attitude of colonial officials toward the al-Hamil establishment and its director—indeed the very prosperity of the family Sufi center—was directly tied to Sidi Muhammad's conscious decision not to oppose France head-on. Outwardly, at least, he maintained an amiable, if reserved, stance toward the regime, eschewed direct involvement in either profane politics or maraboutic squabbles, and even attempted to defuse movements of violent protest, during the revolts of 1864 and 1871, for example. This may perhaps be explained by the fact that as a young man he had witnessed several disastrous rebellions supported or led by Rahmaniya leaders, most notable the Abu Ziyan uprising of 1849 and the subjugation of the Kabylia.

By the eve of his death, Muhammad Ibn Abi al-Qasim was clearly one of the most influential Rahmaniya figures in North Africa. His *zawiya* was rivaled only by an older establishment directed by Sidi Ali Ibn Uthman (d. 1898) in the small oasis of Tulqa in the Ziban (in the region of Biskra). Significantly, the Sufi clan controlling the Rahmaniya center in Tulqa had also opted for accommodation of the colonial order from 1849 onward, a stance that won it the benign neglect of French officials.

While steering clear of contests pitting Muslim against European, the *shaykh* of al-Hamil risked the disapproval of the colonial order on more than one occasion. The most serious case of mild but determined insubordination was the fact that his house was made accessible to all. Shaykh Muhammad openly provided asylum to refugees from French justice, among them former rebels and leaders of insurrections—for example, the Awlad Muqran and Ibrahim Ibn Abd Allah, implicated in the 1864 revolt. Asylum was traditionally expected of saintly Sufi leaders, whose centers were havens of protection and hospitality in North Africa. To refuse the right of sanctuary to fellow Muslims would have diminished Sidi Muhammad's prestige in the eyes of the community and attenuated his ability to exercise moral persuasion in shaping collective behavior.

For Muhammad Ibn Abi al-Qasim, survival was more important than armed struggle. Or more precisely, survival for Muslim Algerian culture represented in and of itself such an immense struggle that violent confrontations with the colonial order gave way to subtler, perhaps more enduring, forms of resistance. Because he perceived the limitations imposed upon him and others like him, Shaykh Muhammad was able to work all the more efficiently within a colonial system of domination that was marginalizing large numbers of people while reinforcing the abusive powers of selected indigenous elites.

As Shaykh Muhammad advanced in years, unease regarding the question of his successor steadily increased in colonial circles. These fears were only partly tied to the internal affairs of the al-Hamil *zawiya* itself. Muhammad Ibn Abi al-Qasim appeared to be grooming his nephew, Muhammad b. al-Hajj Muhammad, for a future leadership role. This he did by presenting his nephew on several occasions to local French officials as well as to those in Algiers. Yet the aging Shaykh declined to appoint publicly an associate to succeed him, despite French insistence. On the other hand, the individual most intimately involved in the *zawiya*'s day-to-day management was his daughter Zaynab, although few anticipated her audacious behavior prior to 1897. In the eyes of military administrators, the relatively calm political climate prevailing in the area and among Muhammad's followers resulted from his spiritual authority and his public stance toward France. Would the new *shaykh* be equally well disposed toward the colonial order?

French worries about future trouble within the al-Hamil *zawiya* in the early 1890s can be understood only in relation to a whole constellation of imperial concerns stretching far beyond the Sahara, Algeria, or even the Maghrib. Visions of pan-Islamic plots haunted colonial administrators, both French and British, in Africa and elsewhere at the end of the century, as did older French obsessions with the inherently "dangerous" Darqawa and Sanusiya *tariqas* in Algeria. Since the leaders of the Darqawa and Sanusiya orders in the region sent their children to al-Hamil for education and visited there regularly, the French feared that a weak successor might fall under their influence.

By 1897, the issue of al-Hamil's spiritual direction was a matter of no small consequence, not only for the *zawiya* and its clients, but also for those whose administrative careers depended upon the maintenance of social tranquility and order in the Sahara. This then was the complex political legacy inherited by Zaynab bint Shaykh Muhammad. Zaynab, too, would fight to carry on her father's work. While her father had managed to avoid serious clashes, Zaynab chose to confront the colonial system directly to sustain the religious and social functions so vital for the community's well-being, if not its very existence. She therefore contested that system more vigorously than her father had deemed wise or even necessary.

Information about Zaynab's early years is scanty, and many things can only be posited or deduced from her father's biography. Most of our material comes either from European visitors to al-Hamil, who were often very sympathetic toward her, or from hostile colonial officials during the period of the contested headship of the *zawiya*. In some ways, Zaynab embodies the dilemma of women in other colonial societies structured not only according to gender and class but along "racial" lines as well. She was part of a social order that was doubly patriarchal—colonial and indigenous. Nevertheless, saintliness and the miraculous powers attributed to her after her father's death meant that Zaynab was an extraordinary person, at least in the eyes of the Muslim faithful. Sainthood and special piety placed her outside of the normal boundaries circumscribing female behavior and status in Muslim society. While the French obviously did not subscribe to the same cultural norms, they were reluctant to take any actions against Zaynab that might offend her partisans and lead to political unrest.

Although the exact date of her birth is unknown, it appears that she was born around 1850, soon after Sidi Muhammad had arrived in al-Hamil to found the religious establishment that later grew into a Rahmaniya *zawiya.* Zaynab spent most of her life in the oasis, although she may have been with her father during his years in the Ziban. Raised in the harem (private women's quarters) of the Shaykh's residence, Zaynab was educated by Sidi Muhammad, who took his daughter's instruction very seriously. She attained an advanced level of erudition, being well versed in the manuscripts and books housed in the *zawiya*'s library, and she later helped keep the accounts of the center's properties. Her erudition was admired by her father's followers and increased the already great prestige she enjoyed in the community as the Shaykh's daughter.

Following the custom of endogamy among North African saintly Sufi clans, Sidi Muhammad had taken a number of wives from other maraboutic families; even divorced wives continued to reside in the *zawiya.* The harem housed at least forty women—the Shaykh's mother, sister, wives, and a large number of females without male protectors who were entrusted to Sidi Muhammad's care. These women led secluded lives devoted to spiritual exercises, not unlike cloistered nuns. While she had many suitors, Zaynab took a vow of celibacy, a somewhat unusual action since Islam prizes matrimony and family life above all else. Yet for Zaynab, virginity was a compelling source of spiritual authority and social power. It permitted her to devote herself entirely to caring for the destitute, unencumbered by the burdens of domestic chores or child rearing. Zaynab's celibate state also conferred upon her greater freedom of movement in the community, for she was not afraid to show herself to others. Her frail appearance resulted from a lifetime of prayer, fasting, and other forms of asceticism that enhanced her virtuous reputation. One European visitor to the *zawiya* described Zaynab as "a saintly being whose face is marked by smallpox and small tattoos."

It is unknown whether Zaynab actually witnessed the somewhat humiliating departure of her father from the Ziban in 1863, although presumably she knew about the dispute in Awlad Jalal since she would have been thirteen years old at the time. To avoid a similar sort of dispute over succession, her father directed the *qadi* of Bou Saada to establish a family endowment in 1877 after Shaykh Muhammad suffered a heart attack. The document, which was akin to a legally binding will, alienated all of his personal property—houses, fields, gardens, flocks, a mill, the library's manuscripts, etc.— to Zaynab's benefit. Moreover, Zaynab was explicitly mentioned as receiving a part equal to any future male heirs of Shaykh Muhammad, although no sons were ever born (or survived to adulthood). All other female descendants would be accorded only the customary one-half of a male share of property. This departure from the usual inheritance practices dictated by Maliki law indicates the great love and respect accorded to Zaynab by her father. However, the fact that she had renounced the pleasures of marriage meant that she would have no heirs to complicate the matter of inheritance.

Some European sources claim that the Shaykh had raised his daughter—in the absence of male offspring—to assume command of the *zawiya* upon his death. However, apparently under intense pressure by local officials, Sidi Muhammad had written a letter to the military command in Bou Saada only two months before his death stating that he had chosen Muhammad b. al-Hajj Muhammad, his nephew, as his spiritual successor. It is uncertain whether Zaynab knew about this letter at the time. She later used the letter as the main basis for her grievances against French authorities in Bou Saada.

No sooner had Shaykh Muhammad been laid to rest than his nephew aggressively asserted his claim to the headship of al-Hamil. Accompanied by several followers, Muhammad b. al-Hajj Muhammad was immediately confronted by a resolute and hostile Zaynab, who publicly refused to acknowledge his authority over the *zawiya*. She forbade the students and *zawiya* personnel from obeying her cousin's orders and denied him access to the center's library, books, and buildings, instituting a sort of lockout by taking possession of the keys. Loss of control over the *zawiya*'s material assets signified that Muhammad b. al-Hajj Muhammad also forfeited the spiritual and social perquisites that accompanied that control. Of this, both Zaynab and her cousin were well aware. The confrontation degenerated into a series of brawls in which some of Zaynab's partisans were beaten. Moreover, Muhammad b. al-Hajj Muhammad went so far as to attempt to shut Zaynab up in the harem against her will. A desperate act by a desperate man, this unsuccessful stratagem only brought disgrace upon the pretender and caused Zaynab to go on the offensive.

The conflict soon widened. Zaynab sent letters to Rahmaniya members all over the Bou Saada region denouncing her cousin. She accused Muhammad b. al-Hajj Muhammad of putting forward spurious claims to succeed her father. She claimed that local French officials had forced her father to nominate her cousin as his successor at a time when his health was failing. She also informed the French authorities of her cousin's untoward behavior, demanding that they curb his injustice and thievery and reminding them of her father's "devotion to France and public order."

Zaynab's bold actions had repercussions not only among the numerous Sufi clients directly attached to her father's center but also among other independent Rahmaniya *zawiyas* in the Sahara. Several of the region's powerful tribes split into two groups—one was pro-Zaynab and the other joined her opponents. While information is lacking about the bases of tribal sup-

port for either of the contestants, it should be noted that tribal groups customarily split into two factions whenever they were confronted by politi-
coreligious struggles of this nature. In addition, the Rahmaniya *shaykhs* of
the Tulqa Sufi center sought to gain some advantage from the quarrel by
wooing religious clients away from the al-Hamil establishment, apparently
with some success.

Finally, while some of Shaykh Muhammad's followers regarded Zaynab's
cousin as an acceptable successor, their great respect for Zaynab prevented
them from breaking with her. The Shaykh's daughter bore a striking physical resemblance to Sidi Muhammad; her carriage and mannerisms recalled
those of the deceased saint. More important, many believed that she had
inherited her father's *baraka;* awe came to be mixed with reverence for her
person. An uneasy stalemate ensued.

French officials were stunned and infuriated, since they had anticipated
that Muhammad b. al-Hajj Muhammad would assume control of the *zawiya*
unopposed. On the eve of his death, the Shaykh had taken his nephew on
trips to Bou Saada to meet with colonial officers. This was interpreted as a
sign of his favor. When Zaynab's opposition to her cousin became known,
officials strove to limit the damage done by the upstart daughter by offering
their full support to her cousin.

Described by military officers as of "average intelligence yet ambitious,
haughty, and prone to excess," Zaynab's cousin seemed the most amenable
to manipulation by the colonial regime. Moreover, the lack of popular support for Muhammad b. al-Hajj Muhammad among the *zawiya*'s numerous
inhabitants and clients—he was regarded as avaricious—also meant that he
needed the French to exert his authority. In turn, Muhammad b. al-Hajj
Muhammad expected the authorities to force Zaynab to yield, something
that officials were unwilling, or perhaps unable, to do. This diffidence on
the part of those ostensibly in power alienated Zaynab's cousin from his
would-be colonial mentors, further complicating the matter of succession.

Zaynab's unexpected behavior provoked a great deal of bitter frustration
among local military officers. Dealing with a defiant Muslim woman was a
novelty, although by then the colonial regime had rather effective methods
for dealing with insubordinate Muslim men. Moreover, Zaynab was a saint
and venerated mystic with her own popular following, which rendered the
matter all the more delicate. Another element that placed colonial authorities in an awkward position was Zaynab's health. It was common knowledge
among the local French authorities that she suffered from a grave nervous
condition as well as from chronic bronchitis (perhaps tuberculosis). At first
it was calmly assumed that these afflictions would render her more recep-
tive to some sort of compromise. But Zaynab held firm.

The helpless rage expressed in official correspondence by some military
personnel led them to evaluate the actions of "the rebellious woman" in a

certain way. For example, Commandant Crochard, Zaynab's nemesis, portrayed her as the compliant victim of sinister intrigues within the *zawiya*. According to Crochard's reports, she was exploited by anti-French malcontents who perceived her cousin as hostile to their own political self-interest. "Among [Zaynab's] associates, there are no good men. . . . She is surrounded by people who are untrustworthy . . . capable of the worst excesses. . . . They know well that she can be manipulated," wrote Crochard. Thus her strength was interpreted as the product of female weakness. Such explanations, however, reveal the absence of colonial mechanisms for containing small-scale, nonviolent rebellions, particularly by Muslim women, and French military views of female nature in general.

Zaynab was serenely conscious of the advantages that seeming powerlessness confers, and in turn exploited this tiny breach in the prevailing system of domination. "She [Zaynab] knows that a woman is always treated with circumspection," an official report observed, "and she exploits this in order to embarrass and cause problems for the local [French] authorities whom she sees as favoring her cousin." By this time, her main adversary was Commandant Crochard, whose reports to his superiors became increasingly censorious of Zaynab's personality and behavior as his awareness of his own impotence grew.

With the French in Bou Saada against her, Zaynab cleverly petitioned those at the top of the colonial hierarchy for assistance. In August 1897 she hired a French lawyer, Maurice Ladmiral, to represent her interests in Algiers, and he brought the dispute to the attention of the head of the French judiciary, the *procureur général*. The latter, alarmed by Zaynab's accusations and the dimensions the conflict was assuming, contacted the French governor-general and the commander of the province in October 1897. While Ladmiral does not appear to have been a key player in the clash—he and his associate met with Zaynab only on a few occasions—the mere threat of the semi-independent judiciary getting mixed up in the affair caused unease in Algiers.

In laying forth her grievances to those at the top of the political heap, Zaynab revealed a surprising familiarity with the administrative structure of colonial Algeria and its weaknesses. This appears extraordinary since prior to 1897 she had remained largely within the oasis of al-Hamil. However, Zaynab had access to three important sources of information: her father, who traveled often and widely and treated her as a confidant; the political refugees long residing in the *zawiya;* and the thousands of pilgrims and students from all parts of Algeria who had visited over the years, invariably bringing news of conditions outside of al-Hamil. This knowledge of how the colonial order functioned allowed Zaynab to pit French official against French official, thereby enabling her to pursue her father's work of cultural survival.

After the death of Shaykh Muhammad, Zaynab emerged more fully into the public sphere normally reserved for men, in part because of the very opposition of Commandant Crochard, the head of the Bou Saada office. However, it was not necessarily the dictates of gender boundaries that had kept her on the sidelines until 1897, but rather deference for the old Shaykh's prestige and authority. Such deferential attitudes were also assumed by subordinate or junior male associates in Sufi orders toward highly respected, older *shaykhs*. Then too, Zaynab had always moved more freely about in the community due to her saintly status and celibate condition. In order to combat her cousin's claims to succession, Zaynab began to travel widely, visiting not only Rahmaniya notables and local Muslim dignitaries but also French officials, among them her lawyer. She also agreed to meet personally with her bête noire, Crochard, which resulted in several heated confrontations. Finally, Zaynab accepted pious offerings from the hands of the faithful in person, without recourse to a male intermediary, a sure sign that she intended to succeed her father in office.

Zaynab employed every means at her disposal to thwart Commandant Crochard's support for her cousin. The material stakes by this time were considerable since they included control over the *zawiya*'s substantial properties. Increasingly frank, the commandant portrayed Zaynab to his superiors in the following terms: "passionate to the point of hatred, bold to the point of insolence and impudence, very haughty and eager for deferential treatment, she displays in the worst way the qualities of her father; her charity is nothing but extravagance; she does not hesitate to lie or make false accusations to pursue the plan of action that she had in mind."

In concluding his vilification of Zaynab, Crochard gloomily predicted the ultimate ruin of the *zawiya* of al-Hamil and the end to its numerous social services due to the actions of a rebellious woman. Significant to note is that those qualities that were regarded as positive in Zaynab's father—philanthropy and largess, for example—were negative in a recalcitrant female. Crochard reveals his true apprehensions about the contested headship by lamenting that "this behavior of Lalla Zaynab has completely destroyed all that I had labored so hard to construct"—in other words, to arrange for a smooth, untroubled succession after Shaykh Muhammad's death. In late-nineteenth-century Algeria, small defiant acts could be as threatening—and effective—as larger, more militant gestures of noncompliance.

Zaynab eventually defeated the combined forces of French officialdom and her cousin. When it became clear that Zaynab would never yield on the matter without the use of force, the authorities in Algiers ordered Crochard to desist; the hapless Muhammad b. al-Hajj Muhammad was relegated to the sidelines for the next seven years. In addition, Zaynab successfully fended off another assault upon her management of the *zawiya* in 1899 that assumed the guise of fraudulent financial claims against the center's assets.

Feeling secure in her position as *shaykha*, Zaynab had the mosque in al-Hamil rebuilt in 1898, calling in Italian masons to construct a completely new structure, perhaps as a symbol of her hard-won spiritual authority. In part, Zaynab's victory was the consequence of her own determination and tactical skills as well as French powerlessness when confronted by a refractory Muslim woman. The feckless and greedy nature of her cousin also contributed to Zaynab's triumph since enthusiasm for him was at best lukewarm, even among his small cohort of followers. Finally, the backing of colonial authorities may have eroded what little prestige Muhammad b. al-Hajj Muhammad enjoyed in the local community. Nevertheless, Zaynab's father played a role in resolving the dispute by performing a posthumous miracle.

When the struggle over succession was in its most bitter stage, Lalla Zaynab took refuge one day at her father's tomb. There, she wept and prayed for hours until nightfall. Alarmed by her absence and emotional state, Zaynab's family and clients gathered at the cemetery and implored her to return to the residence. As Zaynab refused to heed their pleas, the old *imam* (prayer leader) of the *zawiya*'s mosque raised his voice to heaven and cried out: "O Lord, come and help us; who thus has inherited your *baraka*?" Immediately, all present heard Sidi Muhammad's voice issue from the grave, saying: "It is my daughter, Zaynab, who has inherited my *baraka*." From that day on, Zaynab's popular following was assured, its ranks swelled by those who had previously been undecided or unconvinced.

There is, however, one more significant, if less articulate, force, in the matter of Zaynab's victory—public opinion and collective consensus—for it was as much Zaynab's clientele, whether from the local community or from the wider Sufi network, that really decided the issue of succession. As stated earlier, Zaynab had inherited from her father a fund of sociospiritual capital that she then enlarged upon through her own piety, chastity, and generosity. Moreover, because *baraka*—that ineffable substance that combined blessings, supernatural powers, and charisma—was highly "contagious" under certain conditions, the struggle between Zaynab and her cousin was in reality over the dead Shaykh's *baraka*. It was public recognition of Zaynab bint Shaykh Muhammad's worthiness to inherit her deceased father's *baraka* that settled the dispute, together with the overriding colonial interest in maintaining "public order."

Contrary to French predictions that "the daughter of the marabout by herself will not be able to administer the *zawiya*'s vast fortune and holdings dispersed over three Algerian departments," Zaynab's seven-year stewardship of al-Hamil was successful. Threats by the colonial regime to sequester those holdings and incorporate them into the public domain if she refused to relinquish the headship to her cousin remained just that. One knowledgeable European source from the period observed that "Zaynab directed the *zawiya* with a quite remarkable mystical vigor" despite her deteriorating health and the taxing burden of caring for several hundred indigent *zawiya* clients per day. By 1899, local military officials reluctantly admitted that under Zaynab's direction the fortune left by her father remained intact and "the gardens around al-Hamil are flourishing, the farmland cultivated, and the numerous flocks owned by the *zawiya* are in a prosperous state."

Zaynab was not only the undisputed administrative head of the *zawiya* but also its spiritual leader. As her father had done previously, Zaynab initiated members into the Rahmaniya *tariqa* with her own hands. The number of annual pilgrims to al-Hamil remained as high as in the pre-1897 period, and the *madrasa* continued to offer advanced instruction to hundreds of students at a time. When Muhammad b. al-Hajj Muhammad's attempts to rally support to himself failed miserably, he earned the derision of the Muslims and the snubs of the colonial bureaucracy. Finally, it was once more the vox populi—the public veneration of ordinary people—that confirmed Zaynab's steadily growing spiritual authority, which extended far beyond the *cercle* of Bou Saada. Wherever she paused to pray during her travels in the region, the faithful immediately erected simple shrines to commemorate her visit and mark off the sacred space, as they had done for her father.

On 18 November 1904 Zaynab succumbed to the disease that had progressively undermined her health. She was buried the next day with an immense crowd in attendance. Her body was laid alongside her father's in the family cemetery—still a popular pilgrimage site to this day. Her cousin could at last assume the long-coveted headship of the *zawiya* of al-Hamil— or so he thought. However, Zaynab died intestate, almost certainly intentionally, leaving neither an officially nominated successor nor a valid, undisputed will. The result was to postpone the succession for a year while complex judicial inquiry proceeded through the courts. Eventually, the case ended up before the civil tribunal in Algiers, pitting the would-be Rahmaniya *shaykh* against fellow Muslim jurists.

When Muhammad b. al-Hajj Muhammad finally took over the Sufi establishment, the worst had happened. During the lengthy court proceedings, the *zawiya* had lost control over a good portion of its land and flocks, thereby forfeiting some of its material assets, and with these, part of its sociospiritual prestige. By 1910, the economic situation of the *zawiya* was so precarious that the new *shaykh* petitioned the French government to borrow money from the Société de Prévoyance, falling into the very trap that Zaynab and her father had scrupulously avoided—financial dependence upon, and by extension, moral subjugation to, the European masters of Algeria. By the eve of the Great War, however, colonial officials were no longer terribly preoccupied with rural Sufi leaders on the edge of the Sahara since the locus of popular protest had moved into the cities. Muhammad b. al-Hajj Muhammad's requests for credit advances were regarded more as a minor irritation than as an opportunity to influence the course of Muslim politics.

Viewed in the long term, Zaynab's victory was a Pyrrhic one. Fearing that her cousin would squander the *zawiya*'s resources, she fought successfully to retain full management of al-Hamil's spiritual and mundane affairs. By dying intestate, she exposed the Sufi establishment to a debilitating legal quarrel that ultimately led to direct French intervention in the internal affairs of the *zawiya*. Yet it could be argued that al-Hamil's social importance would have declined anyway due to the emergence of new urban-based political and religious forces after World War I, among them the reformist *ulama* of Shaykh Ben Badis. Nevertheless, the Algerian nationalist movement, and particularly the modernist *ulama* led by Shaykh Abdulhamid Ben Badis in the 1930s, were, perhaps more than they cared to admit, the cultural heirs of people like the Shaykh and his daughter.

A NOTE ON SOURCES

Archives d'Outre-Mer, Aix-en-Provence, Archives du Gouvernement Général de l'Algérie, carton 16 H 8, "Notice sur l'ordre des Rahmanya," 28 June 1895, and the report of 1897; carton 16 H 61; and cartons 2 U 20, 21, and 22 of the Sous-série 2 U, Fonds de la Préfecture, Département d'Alger, "Culte Musulman."

The work of North African scholars has also been most helpful: Muhammad Ali Dabbuz, *Nahda al-jaza'ir al-haditha wa thawratuha Al-Mubaraka* (Algiers: Imprimerie Coopérative, 1965), 52–75; Ahmed Nadir, "La fortune d'un ordre religieux algérien vers la fin du XIX siècle," *Le Mouvement Social* 89 (1974): 59–84; Youssef Nacib, *Cultures oasiennes, Bou Saada: Essai d'histoire sociale* (Paris: Publisud, 1986); and Muhammad al-Hafnawi, *Ta'rif al-Khalaf bi rijal al-Salaf* (Tunis: Al-maktaba al-'atiqa, 1982).

SUGGESTIONS FOR FURTHER READING

In addition to the author's *Rebel and Saint: Muslim Motables, Populist Protest, Colonial Encounters (Algeria and Tunisia, 1800–1904)* (Berkeley: University of California, 1994); and "Female Authority and Saintly Succession in Colonial Algeria," in *Women in Middle Eastern History,* eds. Nikki Keddie and Beth Baron (New Haven, Conn.: Yale University Press, 1992), the reader is referred to the following works.

On Sufism and popular Islam in colonial Algeria, Octave Depont and Xavier Coppolani's *Les confréries religieuses musulmanes* (Algiers: Jourdan, 1897) is the classic work. Also, Jamil Abun-Nasr, *The Tijaniyya, A Sufi Order in the Modern World* (Oxford: Oxford University Press, 1965), 77–81. For a critical evaluation of French works on Sufism, see my "In the Eye of the

Beholder: The North African Sufi Orders and the Colonial Production of Knowledge, 1830–1900," *Africana Journal* 15 (1990).

On Islam and resistance, see the contrasting studies by Fanny Colonna, Julia Clancy-Smith, and Peter von Sivers in *Islam, Politics, and Social Movements,* ed. Edmund Burke III and Ira M. Lapidus (Berkeley: University of California Press, 1988).

Isabelle Eberhardt is an important source on al-Hamil. See her diary, *The Passionate Nomad: The Diary of Isabelle Eberhardt,* translated by Nina de Voogt and edited with an introduction by Rana Kabbani (London: Virago Press, 1987); and the biography by Cecily Mackworth, *The Destiny of Isabelle Eberhardt* (London: Quartet Books, 1977). On Eberhardt, see my "The 'Passionate Nomad' Reconsidered," in *Western Women and Imperialism,* eds. Nupur Chaudhuri and Margaret Strobel (Bloomington: Indiana University Press, 1992).

French policy is described in Charles-André Julien, *Histoire de l'Algérie contemporaine,* vol. 1 (Paris: P.U.F., 1970); Charles-Robert Agéron, *Histoire de l'Algérie contemporaine,* vol. 2 (Paris: P.U.F., 1979); Kenneth Perkins, *Qaids, Captains, and Colons: French Military Administration in the Colonial Maghrib, 1884–1934* (New York: Africana Publication Co., 1981); David Prochaska, *Making Algeria French* (Cambridge: Cambridge University Press, 1990); and Yvonne Turin, *Affrontements culturels dans l'Algérie coloniale, écoles, médecines, religion, 1830–1880* (Paris: Maspero, 1971).

Chapter 9

Izz al-Din al-Qassam: Preacher and Mujahid

Abdullah Schleifer

Until recently Shaykh Izz al-Din al-Qassam was but little known outside of Palestinian circles, although he was one of the first Palestinian nationalists and an early practitioner of armed struggle. This is because the historiography of the 1936–39 revolt has emphasized the central role of urban elite politicians in the politics of the period, notably the part played by al-Hajj Amin al-Husayni, the *mufti* of Jerusalem, in the revolt.

Al-Husayni was the head of the Supreme Muslim Council and of the Arab Higher Committee, two of the leading Palestinian organizations involved in the events of the period. In stressing the role of al-Husayni and other elite politicians, historians have implicitly argued that Palestinian nationalism was essentially similar to the secular nationalisms that emerged elsewhere in the Arab world in the interwar years. Thus, the significance of al-Qassam was not well understood.

The focus has now begun to shift to the role of the peasantry in the 1936–39 revolt, and a much more complicated picture has begun to emerge. In the new picture, Zionist settlers, British officials, and Palestinian elite politicians share the stage with displaced and disgruntled peasants and villagers. The struggle between British imperialism, Jewish nationalism, and an emerging Palestinian nationalism can be seen as only one aspect of a complex pattern of conflict. Secular nationalist slogans, it now appears, had a limited audience among the displaced peasants and rural migrants who crowded the cities of mandatory Palestine. Peasant anger was fueled not only by Zionist land policies but also by the oppression of Palestinian landlords. Appeals couched in the language of Islam found a wider following among the quasi-literate Muslim peasants who formed the majority of the rural population.*

The life of al-Qassam helps to explain how many Palestinians came to be involved in politics during the interwar years. It brings together strands of Islamic radicalism

---

*On the evolving literature, see Ted Swedenburg, "The Role of the Palestinian Peasantry during the Great Revolt," in *Islam, Politics, and Social Movements,* eds. E. Burke III and I. M. Lapidus (Berkeley: University of California Press, 1988), 169–203.

grounded in the Salafiya Islamic reform movement, as well as political notions forged in the pan-Islamic politics of the late Ottoman Empire.

With al-Qassam we encounter an individual deeply imbued with what we might wish to call the Islamic social gospel and who was struck by the plight of Palestinian peasants and migrants. Al-Qassam's pastoral concern was linked to his moral outrage as a Muslim at the ways in which the old implicit social compact was being violated in the circumstances of British mandatory Palestine. This anger fueled a political radicalism that drove him eventually to take up arms and marks him off from the Palestinian notable politicians.

Abdullah Schleifer's biography makes clear that while al-Qassam has been claimed as a Palestinian secular nationalist hero, the Islamic dimension of his political life ultimately best explains his actions—but it does so in ways that make him more co-optable by today's Islamic militants. Because he was one of the first to elicit a deep response from ordinary Palestinians, al-Qassam's life can serve to illuminate the complex roots of Palestinian opposition to the British and the Zionists in the interwar period. —Eds.

On 21 November 1935 a three-column front-page headline in the *Jerusalem Post* announced that a British constable had been killed and another injured in a battle near Jenin with Arab gunmen described as "bandits" and "brigands." According to the official statement issued by the British authorities and quoted in full by the *Post*, "among the bandits known to have been killed were: Shaykh Izz-ed-Din al-Qassam . . . who disappeared from his house in Haifa early this month and was the organizer of the band."

Both British and Zionist intelligence circles were, in fact, better informed. They knew Shaykh Izz al-Din was the president of the Young Men's Muslim Association (YMMA), a popular preacher at the Istiqlal mosque near the Haifa railroad yards, and a roving marriage registrar for the Haifa Islamic (Sharia) Court. Al-Qassam had been under surveillance, had been brought in for questioning, and had been cautioned against his habit of publicly preaching *jihad* against both the British occupation and the Zionist colonization over the preceding decade. He was also suspected of having organized a series of clandestine armed attacks against Jewish settlers and British officials in and around Haifa beginning in the early 1930s, but for lack of evidence the authorities did not prosecute him.

Convinced that his arrest was imminent and that his capture could jeopardize the secret organization he had carefully built over the previous decade, al-Qassam moved up into the mountains near Yabud between Nablus and Jenin early in November. He took only twelve men from Haifa, those most openly identified with him. After one of his patrols had killed a Jewish policeman serving in the British force in an accidental encounter, he divided his group to better evade the inevitable pursuit. Nevertheless, al-

Qassam's group was discovered and surrounded by a large force of British police and soldiers. Called upon to surrender, al-Qassam told his men to die as martyrs, and he opened fire. Al-Qassam's defiance and the manner of his death (which seemed to stun the traditional leadership) electrified the Palestinian people. Thousands forced their way past police lines at the funeral in Haifa, and the secular Arab nationalist parties invoked his memory as the symbol of resistance. It was the largest political gathering ever to assemble in mandatory Palestine.

Five months later, a band of Islamic patriots (*mujahidin*), led by one of al-Qassam's companions in the flight from Haifa, ambushed a group of Jewish travelers in northern Palestine. In the weeks that followed, peasant guerrilla bands and urban commandos led by other Qassamiyun (as his followers were called) sprang up across Palestine. The 1936 Palestinian rebellion had begun.

The biography of al-Qassam serves to frame a story that enables us to better understand the political mobilization of the Palestinian peasantry and urban migrants who had been displaced by British policies, Zionist land-acquisition schemes, and the Depression.

Izz al-Din ibn Abd al-Qadar ibn Mustapha ibn Yusuf ibn Muhammad al-Qassam was born in Jebla in the Latakia district of Syria in 1882 (A.H. 1300). His grandfather and granduncle were prominent *shaykhs* of the Qadari Sufi order, or *tariqa* (pl. *turuq*), who came to Jebla from Iraq. His father, Abd al-Qadar, held a post with the Sharia court during Turkish rule but was better known as the local leader of the Qadari *tariqa* in Jebla. However, Shaykh Abd al-Malik al-Qassam, nephew of al-Qassam and the *imam* of a mosque in Jebla, says that Abd al-Qadar also followed the Naqshbandiya Sufi order, which played a noticeably militant role in resisting colonial conquest in nineteenth-century Syria, as well as in India, Turkestan, and the Caucasus, while reaffirming the religious orthodoxy of the *turuq*.

Al-Qassam, who followed the Hanifi school of jurisprudence, studied as a boy with a well-known *alim* (Islamic teacher) from Beirut, Shaykh Salim Tayarah, who had settled in Jebla and taught there at the Istambuli mosque. Shortly after the turn of the century, al-Qassam left Jebla for Cairo to study at al-Azhar. There, he studied with the well-known Salafi teacher Muhammad Abduh. This was probably between 1902 and 1905 (though the exact chronology is obscure). During his stay in Cairo, he also met another well-known Salafi, Muhammad Rashi Rida, like himself a Syrian. All reports agree that he returned as an *alim* from al-Azhar in 1909.

While a student in Cairo, al-Qassam became friends with a fellow classmate, Izz al-Din Alam al-Din al-Tanukhi, the son of a Damascus notable. Their friendship was to last until Qassam's death in 1935. Even at this time, his piety and self-sufficiency were noted by fellow student. One example was related by al-Tanukhi in his reminiscences to al-Qassam's son some years later:

> We were studying in al-Azhar together, and we were short of money. I asked the shaykh, "What do we do now for funds?" The shaykh asked al-Tanukhi what he could do, and al-Tanukhi said he could cook *nammurah,* an Arab sweet. Al-Qassam told al-Tanukhi to cook the sweets, and he would sell them. Al-Tanukhi's father was visiting Cairo at the time, and, passing by al-Azhar, he saw them together selling the sweets and asked his son what he was doing. Al-Tanukhi answered with some embarrassment, "This is what al-Qassam told me to do," and his father replied, "He taught you to be self-sufficient."

The story is instructive, for it is among the earliest of many anecdotes in which al-Qassam practices and encourages self-sufficiency as one of the moral elements, along with humility, courage, and asceticism, for training in *thabit* (steadfastness). This was understood by his disciples to mean the willingness to sacrifice and the practice of moral-ethical behavior. Al-Qassam was sensitive to what he perceived as the backwardness and moral debasement of the Muslims of his day. He believed that the only way Muslims could liberate themselves from foreign occupation (which was to become all but universal after World War I) and to progress would be by the revival of Islam.

In 1909 al-Qassam left Cairo and returned home to Jebla. He brought with him a heightened sense of the threats that faced Islam and of the moral struggle necessary to preserve it. He began teaching at a school maintained by the Qadari *tariqa,* where he not only taught the mystical disciplines of the Qadaris but also gave instruction in the Quran, its commentary and jurisprudence. He also served as *imam* at the Ibrahim Ibn Adham mosque in Jebla.

Al-Qassam undertook an Islamic revival in Jebla based upon the conscientious practice of religious obligations and orthodox voluntary practices. The simplicity of his manner and his good humor marked him off from the beginning. One story that still circulates in Jebla is how an important official came to the town to meet al-Qassam only to find him, to his great shock, eating a simple lunch with the man in charge of stoking the fire at the communal *hammam* (public bath). Similar stories circulate about his later life in Haifa, where he lived simply and with the poor in a society rapidly dividing along the strict class lines of a modern industrial city, although he was a salaried official of the *waqf.*

At Jebla, al-Qassam devoted himself to moral reform. He encouraged the community to keep regular prayer, to maintain the Ramadan fast, and to stop gambling and drinking. His campaign was so successful that those among the townspeople who were not noticeably pious either reformed or began to conform to Sharia standards in public. Because al-Qassam had acquired moral authority with the Turkish authorities responsible for the district, he was able to call upon the police in the case of rare but flagrant violations to enforce Sharia standards within the town. On a few occasions when he heard that mule trains were moving alcohol through the district he sent out his disciples to intercept the caravans and destroy the contraband. The religious revival in Jebla allegedly reached such a point that the women would go to the market unveiled on Friday at noon, certain they would encounter no man on the streets, since every male in Jebla was at prayer.

The family of his classmate al-Tanukhi had been exiled to Turkey by the Ottoman authorities for suspected Arab nationalist activities, but there are no indications that al-Qassam himself was ever involved in the anti-Ottoman Arab national movement. His behavior and the Turkish assessment would indicate that he was a loyal subject. In September 1911 the Italians invaded Tripolitania (Libya). This act of blatant imperialism stirred up strong passions among Muslims in the Ottoman Empire. They struck a special chord with al-Qassam, who was moved to preach against the Italian invasion and to take up a collection in Jebla to support the combined Turkish-Libyan resistance. He also composed the following chant for the townspeople:

> Ya Rahim, Ya Rahman
> Unsur Maulana as-Sultan
> Wa ksur aadana al-Italiyan
>
> O Most Merciful, O Most Compassionate
> Make our Lord the Sultan victorious
> And defeat our enemy the Italian.

The governor of Jebla attempted to take control of the fund-raising away from al-Qassam; when the townspeople continued to contribute to al-Qassam, the governor accused the Shaykh of plotting against the Ottomans, but an official investigation vindicated al-Qassam and resulted in the discharge of the local governor. Exonerated by the authorities, al-Qassam soon became convinced that fund-raising for the *jihad* against Italy was not sufficient. In June 1912, while preaching the Friday sermon at the al-Adham mosque in Jebla, al-Qassam called for volunteers to go fight against the Italians. Many townsmen came forward, but he only accepted those who already had received Ottoman military training. He also undertook to raise funds to finance the expedition and to provide a modest pension to the families of the *mujahidin* during their absence.

Accompanied by from 60 to 250 *mujahidin* (accounts vary), al-Qassam went to Alexandretta (Iskandarun), expecting the Ottoman authorities to provide them with sea transport to Libya via Alexandria. The same route had been used by Anwar Pasha, Aziz Ali al-Masri, and Abd al-Rahman

Azzam, who had already made their way to Libya to participate in the fighting against the Italians in Tripolitania. This, however, was not to be. A new government in Istanbul, mobilizing to meet the closer threat of a war in the Balkans, abandoned the struggle in Libya and came to hasty terms with Italy in mid-October 1912. After waiting at Alexandretta for more than a month, al-Qassam and the Jebla volunteers were ordered to return home by the Ottoman authorities. Some of the money raised for the aborted expedition was used to build a school. The rest was put aside for a time when it would be needed.

When World War I broke out, al-Qassam volunteered for service in the Ottoman army. Although *ulama* enrolled in the Ottoman army were usually offered assignment in their local town or village to register recruits, al-Qassam refused this offer and requested a military assignment. He was sent to a camp south of Damascus, where he received his training and remained as a chaplain assigned to the garrison.

In the chaos of the Ottoman collapse in the Arab East, with British forces in Syria and a French buildup in Lebanon, al-Qassam returned to Jebla and initiated military training for every able-bodied man in the town. With the funds put aside from the Tripolitania *jihad*, the proceeds from the sale of his property, and donations from local landowners, al-Qassam purchased arms for the Jebla militia. At that time Jebla was part of the "Blue Zone" or "Occupied Enemy Territory North" set aside by the Allies for French occupation. From late 1918 through 1919 French forces moved into the zone and consolidated their positions, while the Arab national movement struggled on in Damascus to establish an independent Syrian kingdom for Amir Faisal.

The period 1918–20 was marked by much turbulence and confusion in the Jebla area. Encouraged by the French, bands of Alawites (a heterodox Shiite group who inhabited the nearby Jabal al-Nusayri) occupied the orchards and farmland outside Jebla as part of a destabilizing move against the Sunni communities in the Latakia district. They were opposed by the Jebla militia organized by al-Qassam. When the Alawites were driven out of the Jebla area, the French quickly moved in. Al-Qassam withdrew, along with his closest disciples, into the mountains and established a guerrilla base near the village of Zanqufeh on Sahyoun Mountain. From there he was able to harass French forces and to train his men in military tactics and in the doctrine of *jihad*.

A Sunni notable in the district, Umar al-Bitar, had also taken to the mountains with armed followers to resist the French. He was killed in action, and his followers joined forces with al-Qassam's group. As the French consolidated their hold on the district, several large Jebla landowners who had been supporting al-Qassam were pressured by the French to pay their taxes or lose their property. They began to question the wisdom of continuing to fight and eventually gave up. (This experience undoubtedly made al-Qassam much more cautious when, years later, he began recruiting followers in Haifa.) Finding himself increasingly isolated, al-Qassam abandoned his base and moved toward Aleppo, where he joined forces under the command of Ibrahim Bey Hananu, who had been raiding French forces in northern Syria since May 1920.

In mid-July 1920 French forces pushed past Hananu's fighting forces and occupied al-Shughur Bridge on the road to Aleppo. They demanded (among other conditions in an ultimatum to King Faisal) that the government in Damascus punish the "criminals" resisting the French advance, or they would march on Damascus. Al-Qassam decided to flee. He and his men made their way through French lines with false passports provided by al-Tanukhi and thence by boat to Tartous, Beirut, and Palestine in 1921.

Like many other exiles from French-occupied Syria and Lebanon, al-Qassam settled in Haifa and joined the teaching staff of Haifa's Islamic school, the Madrasa Islamiya, which had branches throughout the city. Along with other Islamic institutions in the district, the Madrasa Islamiya was supervised and supported by the Jamiat Islamiya, a *waqf* (pious foundation). Supported and directed by Haifa's Muslim notables, the Jamiat was a vehicle for communal self-support and expression for the Muslims of Haifa and the surrounding rural districts. During the British Mandate period it became a meeting ground for Islamic and Arab nationalist opposition to the mandate.

Under its well-known principal, Kamal al-Qassab, an exiled Damascus notable, the Madrasa Islamiya became a radiating center of the Salafiya Islamic modernist movement and of Arab nationalism. Al-Qassab was a friend of Rashid Rida and Shakib Arslan, and he had played a major role in Faisal's short-lived Syrian Arab Kingdom. It was al-Qassab who rallied the Syrian National Congress to confront French claims in Syria directly in March 1920 and who inspired the people of Damascus to seize arms and confront French forces at the battle of Maysalun.

In the early 1920s al-Qassab and al-Qassam became allies in a controversy with some of the Palestinian *ulama* over the permitted ritual for Islamic funerals. They published a pamphlet denouncing the laxity of officially sanctioned practice and for their pains were denounced by the establishment *ulama* as Wahhabi heretics—a standard (but ill-founded) accusation in any polemic between the orthodox *ulama* and the Salafiya. Al-Qassam, who was the pamphlet's chief author, concluded his argument by reproducing Islamic legal opinions (*fatwas*) taken from leading *ulama* at al-Azhar and in Damascus condemning the practice. Al-Qassam was also opposed to other popular innovations in the practice of Islam, such as the pilgrimage by women to the shrine of Khidr in the foothills of Mount Carmel to sacrifice sheep in gratitude for the recovery of a child from illness or a son's graduation from school. After making sacrifice, the women would perform tribal dances around the shrine. Al-Qassam preached in the mosques of Haifa against this superstitious practice, which was opposed to the Sharia.

In the early 1920s al-Qassam met the Algerian Muhammad bin Abd al-Malik al-Alami. Shaykh al-Alami was a special roving leader (*muqaddam*) of the Tijaniya Sufi brotherhood. In the early decades of the twentieth century he established branches of the Tijaniya throughout the Arab East. Al-Alami had a great impact upon al-Qassam and his closest disciples in Haifa. According to Hanifi, only al-Qassam, Hanifi himself, and three others were initiated into the Tijani *tariqa* by al-Alami. It was around this small inner core of Tijani disciples that al-Qassam would build the new movement of Islamic patriots (*mujahidin*).

Over time, some important differences appeared between al-Qassam and al-Qassab. Both *shaykhs* believed in the inevitability of *jihad* against the colonial occupation of the Muslim world. Where al-Qassab concentrated upon developing a following among middle classes who he believed would lead the masses, al-Qassam found himself more and more drawn to the uneducated working classes. They, in turn, responded to his warm and modest personality. Al-Qassam's preaching was enthusiastically received, both at the Gerini mosque and subsequently at the Istiqlal mosque. (The latter was built by the Jamiat al-Islamiya to serve the spiritual needs of the growing number of Muslims employed in the new industrial district growing up in and around Haifa's railroad yards.)

Because of his easy accessibility, in contrast to that of many of the other *ulama*, al-Qassam would frequently be stopped on the street on his way to teach at the Madrasa Islamiya for advice and religious guidance, so he was frequently late for his classes. As director of the Madrasa, al-Qassab insisted that al-Qassam should keep regular hours, but since that was becoming increasingly impossible, al-Qassam resigned his teaching post.

In the late 1920s and early 1930s, al-Qassam intensified his contacts with the people of Haifa. He became an "outstanding personality" at the Mawlid al-Nabi festivals held, according to Syrian custom, whenever a family has some good fortune to celebrate—the birth of a child, his or her memorization of a portion of the Quran, a graduation, or a promotion. Al-Qassam would recite the *mawlid* ritual at such occasions since in a spiritual sense such events were "the birthday of the Prophet."

Slowly, patiently, he built a large group of followers, all personally selected. He studied the men who seemed most concentrated in their prayer and invocations and most responsive to his preaching at his Friday sermons. Later he visited them in their homes for more discussion and more observation. When he was certain of them, he formed them into perhaps a dozen circles, each circle unknown to the other. He taught them to read, using the Quran as text. All the time he preached the duty and inevitability of struggle against the British and the Zionists. Invariably, his followers were men without formal education, illiterate workers, or former tenant farmers recently driven off their land by Zionist land purchases, the Arab labor exclusion policies of the Jewish National Fund, or their own inability to meet steadily rising rents.

In Haifa, the effects of sudden development and the peculiar characteristics of the settler-colonization of Palestine were compounded. Because it was the major port, railroad center, and (by the early 1930s) oil refinery for the Arab East, Haifa had a greater attraction for the drifting Palestinian labor force than any other city in Palestine. The increase in Jewish immigration in the early 1930s stimulated a boom in building and allied trades in Haifa. This further intensified its influence, drawing in still more unskilled labor from the countryside.

Palestinian workers were crowded into shantytowns and were largely ignored by the traditional urban Palestinian elites, who were locked into an all-consuming political struggle between the big families for the leadership of Palestinian Arabs. Victimized by inflation that often required more than half the wages of an unskilled worker to pay the rent of a decent room, and thrust into a rapidly secularizing environment, the Palestinian worker found that his

> feelings were intensified by the spectacle of the handsome new boulevards erected in the more desirable parts of the towns by and for the [Jewish] immigrant population, and by the acres of Jewish working men's quarters erected by Jewish building societies. Sometimes too, he had the experience of being driven from work by Jewish pickets and he resented the fact that the [British Mandate] Government paid the Jewish workman double the rate it paid him for the same work. (Neville Barbour, *Nisi Dominus: A Survey of the Palestine Controversy*, p. 134)

The same process that led to the emergence of a new, displaced Palestinian Muslim working class was producing a Zionist-settler society and state. The traditional Palestinian elites were incapable of responding to either phenomenon. At worst, the avarice and petty political rivalries of the big family notables and the decadence of the religious leadership contributed directly to the settler-colonization of Palestine; at best, by opposing Zionist settlement while refusing to confront directly the British colonial authority protecting that colonization, the Palestinian elites limited the effectiveness of their opposition. Al-Qassam differed from the nationalists both in his diagnosis of the problem and in the remedy he proposed.

Unlike the elite politicians, who focused on the impact of imperialism on Palestinian society and saw a strong secular nationalist movement as a solution, al-Qassam saw the situation in religious terms. The remedy he proposed was *jihad*, the moral and political struggle for justice in the path of God. Instead of organizing demonstrations or a political party as the Palestinian nationalists were doing, al-Qassam sought to prepare the ground for a struggle at once spiritual, political, and military. In so doing, al-Qassam placed himself within the tradition of Islamic thought that saw a spiritual dimension to holy war. For him, as for others in this tradition, *jihad* had to begin with the individual moral struggle against evil. Only when the individual had turned away from evil could he move to the next stage, struggling physically to bring about the reign of justice.

Al-Qassam explained to his followers that the true *mujahid* (holy warrior) has been chosen by God and that the perfect *jihad* required the sincere perfection of all aspects of ritual duties, creed, faith, and submission to God's commands. For al-Qassam, the holy warrior was one who helped the poor, fed the hungry, comforted the sick, and visited his relatives. All of these good deeds must be crowned by constant prayer. The *mujahid* achieved this sincere perfection by practicing the "greater *jihad*." This al-Qassam described as the *jihad al-nafs* (the struggle of the individual soul against evil thoughts and desires—as contrasted with the lesser *jihad*, or armed struggle).

Good character, al-Qassam taught, was more important than bravery for the *jihad*. When God praised the Prophet, it was not for his bravery but for his good character or ethical standards. A man of good character will never accept humiliation but will fight, he preached. Therefore, the virtues precede bravery or militancy as a prerequisite to fighting; thus, the greater *jihad* is greater than the lesser *jihad*. In some ways, the Qassamiyun resembles the medieval Islamic *futuwwa* organizations, a combination of artisan guilds and religiously inspired chivalric fellowships. In building his circles among the Muslim working-class population of Haifa's shantytowns, al-Qassam was thus, intentionally or not, renewing an age-old social form.

A central focus of the *jihad* was the need to combat the moral degradation of the inhabitants of Haifa's shantytowns. Al-Qassam had a deep concern for these rural migrants, who lived separated from their families under appalling conditions and who were exposed to all manner of vice. He believed it was important to facilitate marriage as a barrier to corruption, which meant some sort of subsidy to young men who could not afford the *mahr* (bride gift), as well as keeping the age of consent low. He was also aware of the plight of those left behind in the villages. There are reports that he encouraged the *fellahin* in the movement to set up cooperatives for growing and distributing their crops. When an individual joined the Qassamites, he underwent a complete conversion experience, reintegrating himself into a world of moral purpose, ethical standards, and religious culture. This transformation took years.

In the earliest years, when a follower was inducted into the *mujahidin* al-Qassam would ask him to grow a beard, as a symbol of his dedication to *jihad*. This was a form of testing by which he could determine the depth of the disciple's religious devotion. When a follower decided to grow a beard, al-Qassam would appear at his house with other bearded Qassamiyun to "celebrate his decision." After the recitation of *fatiha* and other passages from the Quran bearing upon *jihad*, the new disciple was congratulated by the company and sweets were served. In later years this ceremony was replaced or supplemented by an oath, sworn over either a dagger or a pistol placed alongside the Quran. Because the first members of the Haifa circles were bearded, the group was known as *al- mashayikh*, "the shaykhs." It was by this name that the movement first came to the attention of British and Zionist intelligence. (After al-Qassam's death the *mujahidin* were to become increasingly known as the Qassamiyun.)

The *mujahidin* were instructed to carry a copy of the Quran with them at all times so they could read and recite the Quran whenever they found themselves unoccupied. Al-Qassam also encouraged them to practice the Sufi spiritual exercises of the Qadiriya, and he gave them simple invocations and chants to recite when about to perform a mission in the *jihad.*

As soon as a group of disciples had been formed into a secret circle, al-Qassam would give them basic military training and order them to continue to train among themselves. At least one retired Ottoman officer was recruited by al-Qassam to train the disciples, contrary to the claim by some of his biographers that al-Qassam in principle never recruited outside of the working classes.

Al-Qassam was very strict in his training. One informant described his method and the degree of obedience he commanded as follows:

> He would take us for training and shooting lessons and asked us to walk barefoot, and he made us sleep outdoors in the cold weather when we trained in the mountains. And he was tough on the disciples, making us go without food or water to be able to endure hunger and thirst. He would ask us to sleep once or twice a week at home on the floor on a straw mat and with a light cover, and he always insisted that we be secretive about our activities, so we were all in trouble at home with our wives and family because we couldn't explain why we were sleeping in this manner, and we would endure this because we were devoted to carrying out his orders.

At the same time, the disciples were encouraged to return to their villages outside of Haifa, either on regular visits or to resume residence, to cultivate the support of their local village head and to prepare likely recruits for a visit by al-Qassam. Then al-Qassam would visit the village, accompanied by the disciples and frequently by other members of his particular circle in Haifa, and the slow process of preaching, observation, guidance, military training, eventual initiation of disciples, and the formation of new circles would begin again. At times, the *shaykhs*, as the members of the oldest circles were known, were authorized to initiate directly tribesmen and villagers in the countryside into their movement.

By 1923 al-Qassam had secured land in the Beisan Valley, and he sent Muhammad Hanifi there to farm in order to have an eventual source of income to purchase weapons for the *jihad* as well as a center of communication with all parts of Palestine. In the summer al-Qassam came to Beisan and helped Hanifi plant his crops; in the winter Hanifi would come to al-Qassam, and together they visited the villages on horseback. Hanifi served as al-Qassam's deputy and as treasurer of the group. He was entrusted by al-Qassam with the contacts to all of the circles. The head of each circle was called either *arif* or *naqib*, both titles drawn from the technical vocabulary of the Sufi organizations.

Because the *mujahidin* knew only members of their own circle, or at most members of their parent circle, the total number of adherents was never known. From interviews with Hanifi, who visited all of the circles and arranged the dispatch of communications from al-Qassam to the *arif* of each village circle by courier, it would appear that the number of trained and initiated *mujahidin* was more than a thousand. These were concentrated chiefly in the northern districts but included disciples and secret circles throughout most of the countryside, even as far south as Gaza.

Al-Qassam's position as president of the Young Men's Muslim Association provided him with an acceptable explanation for his frequent visits to the villages around Haifa, where he was organizing branches of the association that became, outside of Haifa, the equivalent of a "front" or "cover" group for the local *mujahidin*. It also provided him access to the notables and to the younger and more radical Arab nationalists from the modern educated classes who were to coalesce around the Istiqlal Party, a loosely organized, nonsectarian party focused upon secular Arab, rather than Islamic, identity, founded in the 1920s. Although the Istiqlal was radical in comparison to the traditional parties of the big families, it was nevertheless profoundly respectable. Al-Qassam's relationship with the Istiqlal thus helped protect him from his political enemies.

Since the Istiqlal Party drew its inspiration from the Salafiya reform movement, and Arabism and Islam were associated in the popular mind, it colored its Arab nationalism with an Islamic rhetoric that employed such phrases as *jihad* and *sabil Allah*. There was thus the basis for an alliance of mutual respect. This vague approximation of rhetorical style was reinforced by the one basic political position shared by the Istiqlal and al-Qassam, that opposition to the Zionist colonization of Palestine could not be separated from opposition to the British occupation, since Zionist settlement was possible only by virtue of British protection. This position contrasted with the prevailing strategy among all the big-family parties, be they "moderate" or nationalist, to work politically, mixing cooperation and principles, to protest for a realignment of British policy in favor of the Arabs that would halt further Zionist encroachment on Palestine.

Al-Qassam's identity of view with the Istiqlal was limited to this one point, but from the perspective of Palestinian politics and their subsequent interpretation as secular history that identity of view was not only profound but inescapably reinforced by al-Qassam's continuous denunciation of the British in his sermons and less formal public talks. But al-Qassam shared this perspective with whoever else held it, and as late as 2 November 1935 the *Palestine Post* reported al-Qassam sharing the platform at a Haifa rally condemning Balfour Day with Jamal al-Husseini, leader of the Arab Party, rather than being in Nablus for the big Istiqlal rally organized by Akram Zuayter.

Al-Qassam's closest associate in the Istiqlal was the Haifa banker Rashid Hajj Ibrahim, a leading figure in the charitable society Jamiat al-Islamiya and the founder and first president of the Young Men's Muslim Association in Haifa. Hajj Ibrahim appealed to him several times to moderate his sermons, since it was becoming difficult for him to persuade the British not to arrest the Shaykh, who several times picked him up for interrogation. Because of his association with the notables and young professionals (men like Hajj Ibrahim) of the YMMA and the Istiqlal, however, he was not taken with sufficient seriousness by either British intelligence or his Arab nationalist acquaintances. In fact, despite some shared values, few adherents of the Istiqlal or the predominantly middle-class Young Men's Muslim Association of Haifa ever joined his cause. For his part, al-Qassam appears not to have joined any of the existing nationalist political parties, although he was claimed by both the Istiqlal and the supporters of Hajj Amin al-Husayni, who as *mufti* of Jerusalem and head of the Arab Higher Committee was the leading spokesman for the Palestinians in the mandate period.

More secularly minded nationalists tended to misunderstand the profoundly religious context for the activities of al-Qassam and his followers. They could not see why the Qassamiyun refused to take food from the peasants if it was not offered to them. Nor could they understand why they told the truth to their enemies about their objectives instead of lying to protect themselves. But from the perspective of the chivalric code of the medieval Islamic *futuwwa* organizations on which they were modeled, their behavior was impeccable. Both their Quranic sense of *shahid*, or witnesses against mankind, and their imitation of the Prophet, who "makes the truth victorious by the truth," then become understandable.

If al-Qassam and the products of his effort seem to defy even the best-intentioned modern Arab thinkers, it is because his life and thought—dedicated to *jihad* in all of its dimensions—transcended the identity systems and contradictions of modern Islamic political thought. He was capable of waging *jihad* in the contemporary milieu because he was able to absorb whatever of these conflicting schools filtered through his own traditional orthodox conscience, applying what he understood was compatible with orthodox Islam and rejecting what he understood was not.

Moving among jealous effendis, decadent *ulama*, and worldly religious reformers, a secret presence in the shacks of railroad porters and stonemasons, al-Qassam—illuminated by those spiritual virtues that he and his disciples perfected so earnestly—opened their tawdry and doomed natural world to the presence of the supernatural. This, by his own doctrine, was his greatest and only enduring triumph, and it is precisely this sacralizing triumph that has been denied him by his modern biographers.

A NOTE ON SOURCES

In writing this life of Izz al-Din al-Qassam, I have drawn upon interviews with many of his family, disciples, and acquaintances, especially Imam Abd al-Malik al-Qassam, Umm Muhammad al-Qassam, Muhammad al-Qassam, Shaykh Muhammad Hanifi, Shaykh Nimr al-Khatib, Zuhayr Shawish, Muhammad Izzat Darwaza, Farid Troublsi, Atif Nurallah, Rashid Ibu, Hajj Hassan al-Hafian, Abu Ibrahim al-Kabir, Abu Adnan Sursawi, and Shawki Khayrallah.

Also consulted were the following collections of personal papers, held at the Institute for Palestine Studies: Tegart Papers, Zu'ayter Papers, Zuhayr Shawish Papers. Memoirs and other works in Arabic include Muhammad Izzat Darwaza, *Hawl al-haraka al-arabiya al-haditha* (Sidon, n.d.); Ahmad Shukayri, *Arabaun sannatin fi al-hayat al-arabiya waal-dawliya* (Beirut, 1969); Abil Hassan Ghanaym, "Thawarat al-Shaykh Izz al-Din al-Qassam," *Shuun Filastiniya* 6 (January 1972); Subhi Yasin, *Al Thawra al-arabiya al-kubra fi filastin, 1936–1939* (Beirut, 1959); and Ghassan Kanafani, *The 1936–1939 Revolt in Palestine* (Committee for a Democratic Palestine, n.d.).

SUGGESTIONS FOR FURTHER READING

On al-Qassam, see especially the author's "The Life and Thought of Izz-ididin al-Qassam," *Islamic Culture* 5, no. 23, pp. 61–81 (from which the present chapter is adapted), and the following: A. W. Kayyali, *Palestine: A Modern History* (London: Croom Helm, 1978); and Nels Johnson, *Islam and the Politics of Meaning in Palestinian Nationalism* (London: Routledge, 1982).

The standard political history of Palestinian nationalism in the mandate period is the two-volume work of Yehoshuah Porath, *The Emergence of the Palestinian Arab National Movement, 1918–1929* (London: Frank Cass, 1974) and *The Palestinian Arab National Movement: From Riots to Rebellion, 1929–1939* (London: Frank Cass, 1977). On the origins of Palestinian nationalism, see Rashid Khalidi, *Palestinian Identity: The Construction of Modern National Consciousness* (New York: Columbia University Press, 1997); and Muhammad Muslih, *The Origins of Palestinian Nationalism* (New York: Columbia University Press, 1988).

For the perspective of a British Mandate official, see Neville Barbour, *Nisi Dominus: A Survey of the Palestine Controversy* (London: George Harrap, 1946); for an Arab perspective, George Antonious, *The Arab Awakening* (Beirut, 1969); for contemporary Zionist perspectives, Amos Elon, *The Israelis: Founders and Sons* (New York : Penguin, 1983).

In addition to the above, the following more specialized works may serve as an introduction to the substantial bibliography on the Palestinian mandate: Ann Mosely Lesch, *Arab Politics in Palestine, 1917–1939: The Frustration of a Nationalist Movement* (Ithaca, N.Y.: Cornell University Press, 1979); Philip Mattar, *The Mufti of Jerusalem: Al-Hajj Amin al-Husayni and the Palestinian National Movement* (New York: Columbia University Press, 1988); Edward Said and Christopher Hitchens, eds., *Blaming the Victims* (London: Verso, 1987); Rosemary Sayigh, *Palestinians: From Peasants to Revolutionaries* (London: Zed Press, 1979); and Kenneth Stein, *The Land Question in Palestine, 1917–1939* (Chapel Hill: University of North Carolina Press, 1984).

Chapter 10

Abu Ali al-Kilawi:
A Damascus Qabaday

Philip S. Khoury

While the Ottoman *tanzimat* reforms and the opening of the empire to the world economy stimulated a host of important changes, the social and cultural life of cities evolved at a slower rhythm. In Syria, it was not until the interwar period that many of the old ways were replaced by new ones, and then under the auspices of the French colonial mandate government. In other parts of the region, much the same process can be observed, although the pace of change differed.

As Philip S. Khoury explains in his contribution, the old ways were especially persistent in the urban neighborhoods, or quarters. At the popular level, the quarters of Damascus possessed their own identities, distinguished by traditions and customs. A prominent feature of life in the quarters was the neighborhood youth gang and its leader, the *qabaday,* an individual reputed for his strength, prowess, and honor. Endowed with a quasi-chivalric ethic, youth gangs redressed grievances and defended the honor of their quarter in ritual combat against the gangs of other quarters. These fights featured displays of prowess in horsemanship, wrestling, and swordsmanship and have their roots in earlier Islamic history.* Through their alliances with local notables, *qabadays* and their gangs controlled the streets of the quarter and maintained the dominance of the notables into the twentieth century.

Abu Ali al-Kilawi, the subject of Khoury's essay, was one of the last of the Damascus *qabadays.* His career is situated between the older, notable-based clientele style of politics and the politics of the new nationalist movements. As a result of the failure of the 1925 insurrection against the French, the inadequacies of the *qabadays,* most of whom were illiterate, became increasingly evident, and Abu Ali, despite his heroism, became virtually obsolete. From this time on, the turn toward new political organizations and ideas became irreversible.

Not quite part of the underworld, but not entirely respectable, *qabadays* have largely disappeared from most places today. With the coming of modernity, their place has been taken by more explicitly criminal elements and by other voluntary

---

*On the organization of the quarters in earlier times, see Ira Lapidus, *Muslim Cities in the Later Middle Ages* (Cambridge, Mass.: Harvard University Press, 1965).

associations, including labor unions, youth groups, women's groups, and religious groups.[†] —Eds.

The period of the French Mandate (1920–45) was a pivotal time in Syrian politics. The country was in a transitional phase, uncomfortably suspended between four centuries of Ottoman rule and national independence. France had occupied Syria and Lebanon in 1919–20 and imposed a new form of colonial rule known as the mandate system, which received legal sanction from the League of Nations in Geneva. The French constructed an administrative system that separated Lebanon from Syria and then divided Syria into separate units along religious and regional lines. These and other measures caused serious discontent throughout much of the country. The result was a national revolt that lasted two years (1925–27) but that was ultimately crushed. The failure of the revolt convinced nationalist leaders to drop armed confrontation as a strategy. In its place, they substituted a more gradualist approach to the nationalist goals of Syrian unity and independence that relied on a combination of boycotts, strikes, demonstrations, and diplomacy. The architect of this new strategy was the National Bloc, an alliance of traditional elites in Damascus and other Syrian towns that in the 1930s became the most important nationalist political organization of the French Mandate era. It would steer the course of the nationalist movement until independence was finally achieved at the end of the Second World War.

Although the Ottoman Empire had collapsed and new forms of social and political organization were available, there remained a distinctive Ottoman cast to Syrian politics and especially to Syria's urban elites. The foundation of Syrian political life during the French Mandate, as in Ottoman times, were the major towns, of which Damascus was the most important. The towns were characterized by deep cleavages between different religious sects and ethnic groups, between the rich and the poor, between the various trades, and between long-settled urbanites and recent migrants from the countryside. In some senses, the most acute cleavages were those between the different quarters, which were separated from one another by walls and gates, a reflection of their narrowly defined interests and desire for protection from outsiders.

Even though the quarters retained their distinctiveness and purpose throughout most of the French Mandate years, their cohesiveness had already begun to be eroded by new social forces. This was the direct consequence of the structural changes that had been sweeping the Middle East since the early nineteenth century—changes in administration and law; in

---

[†] See, however, the Lebanese case: Michael Johnson, *Class and Client in Beirut: The Sunni Muslim Community and the Lebanese State, 1940–1985* (London: Ithaca Press, 1986).

commerce, industry, and agriculture; in the movement of goods, peoples, and ideas. The towns of Syria, and particularly their quarters, were affected by all these changes. New patterns of trade and production hastened the impoverishment of some quarters and the enrichment of others. New concentrations of wealth, coupled with the spread of modern education, accelerated the process of class differentiation. New landholding patterns uprooted peasants and encouraged their migration to the towns, where they often settled in quarters vacated by the recently rich and educated, or in impoverished suburban quarters.

Although the winds of change in Syria intensified after World War I, their impact on urban politics should not be exaggerated. For instance, the exercise of local political power was characterized by a remarkable degree of continuity, which was not disrupted by the substitution of French for Ottoman rule. For the most part, the men who were important in local affairs under the Ottomans were the same men, or their sons, who wielded political influence under the French. Political leaders, now grouped into an array of nationalist organizations like the National Bloc, continued to organize their patronage networks as they had in late Ottoman times. Urban leadership remained the basic building block of political influence in Syria. And at the heart of urban politics were the quarters, the traditional domain in which political leadership operated and from which it derived much of its support.

One figure in the quarters who could give the nationalist leader a decisive edge in competition for clientele during the French Mandate (1920–45) was the local gang leader, the *qabaday* (pl. *qabadayat*), or, in the patois of Damascus, the *zgrirti*. Probably no individual with independent influence in the quarters was closer to the common man than was the *qabaday*. He was something akin to an institution. Each quarter had its own set of historical figures who were glorified from one generation to the next. In time, an ideal type was formed, one that characterized the *qabaday* as strong, honorable, the protector of the feeble and the poor as well as of the religious minorities, the upholder of Arab traditions and customs, and the guardian of popular culture. He was hospitable to strangers, always pious, and lived clean. This image placed far less emphasis on the *qabaday*'s darker side, his shady dealings, his preference for physical coercion, and even his "mortal" crimes for personal gain. The common people clearly differentiated between the *qabadayat* and the *zuran*, or hoodlums, who ran protection rackets (*khuwa*) in the quarters and bazaars, although in reality such distinctions were hazy.

A *qabaday* might eventually become fairly well-to-do, but what distinguished him from the dignitaries of the quarter were his significantly lower social origins, his general want of formal education, his outspoken preference for traditional attire and customs, and the much narrower range of his interests and contacts, all of which accorded him a less exalted status than that enjoyed by merchants or religious leaders. He survived best in the traditional milieu of the self-contained quarter with its inwardness and nar-rowly defined interests. There he was needed to provide physical protection from hostile external forces, and extralegal mechanisms for settling per-sonal disputes. But by the time of the mandate, the *qabaday* had begun to feel threatened by the pressures created by rapid urbanization, the growth of a market-oriented economy, and the rise of new classes and institutions outside the popular quarters. This period was a transitional phase in the life of the Syrian city and in the organization and functions of its quarters; the *qabaday* survived it, although not without difficulty.

A *qabaday* might rise to leadership in the quarter by several different paths, and it is difficult to separate myth from reality when tracing the emer-gence of any particular strongman. It is, however, possible to trace the career of at least one prominent *qabaday* of the mandate period in Damas-cus, his links to the principal national independence organization, the National Bloc, and his contribution to the independence movement.

Abu Ali al-Kilawi [al-Gilawi] claims to have been born in 1897, in Bab al-Jabiya, an old popular quarter situated near the entrance to the central commercial artery, Suq Midhat Pasha, and including the charming Mosque of Sinan Pasha. The origins of the Kilawi family are obscure. They seem to have first settled in al-Maydan, the southernmost quarter of Damascus, some time in the early nineteenth century, where they were engaged in the transport of wheat from their native Hawran to flour mills in al-Maydan. They may have belonged to one of the tributaries of the Rwala bedouin who roamed with the Rwala chieftains of Al Shalan before the mandate. The Kilawis also claimed descent from Abu Bakr, the Prophet's companion and the first caliph, and billed themselves as members of the *ashraf* (descen-dants of the Prophet), although the great religious families of Damascus did not recognize their claim. According to Abu Ali, the family's surname had been al-Bakri until the end of the nineteenth century. When his father died unexpectedly, the family dropped al-Bakri for some inexplicable reason and adopted instead the surname of Abu Ali's maternal grandfather. During the mandate, the Kilawis were not regarded as members of the aristocratic al-Bakri family of Damascus; however, they were very partial to the Bakris and especially close to Nasib Bey al-Bakri of the National Bloc.

Abu Ali had two older brothers. He happened to be much closer to the oldest, Abu Hasan, who assumed the leadership of the family upon his father's death and under whose wing Abu Ali grew up learning the ways of the quarter. Abu Ali attributed his rise to the status of a *qabaday* to several factors, all of which suggest that he did not inherit the title. One factor was his own physical strength, which he displayed early in life despite his slight build. The youth of Bab al-Jabiya and other quarters engaged in different forms of informal competition that helped lay the groundwork for the rise of a *qabaday*. Abu Ali, for example, excelled in wrestling (*musaraa*). To the beat of two drums, the youth of the quarter would congregate in an open field or garden where wrestling matches were staged between boys dressed in leather shorts worn above britches. By the age of sixteen, Abu Ali was reputed to be the best wrestler in the quarter.

By this age, the youth of the quarter had already begun to practice the martial arts and, in particular, swordsmanship. Wielding a long, silver-handled sword in one hand and a small metal shield (*turs*) in the other, two young men would face each other, twirling their swords through different orbits over and around their heads while interspersing blows against their own shields and those of their opponents in a complicated cadence. The boy who could handle his sword most adeptly and innovatively advanced in the competition, and the best five or six contestants were asked to form a troupe. This troupe would then have the honor of performing on all festive occasions in the quarter, such as weddings and the Prophet's birthday. In his day, Abu Ali was the leader of such a troupe of swordsmen, and from it he began to build his own personal following.

Horsemanship was Abu Ali's other forte. After their father's death, his brother, Abu Hasan, used his family's relations with the bedouin tribes south of Damascus to convert the Kilawi transport business into a horse-breeding and trading concern. The center for their new activities was a small stud farm that the family owned just south of al-Maydan. In time, the Kilawis became renowned horse dealers throughout the Arab East, purveying purebred show animals and racehorses to the royal families of Transjordan and Saudi Arabia and to other Arab dignitaries. By the time he was twenty, Abu Ali was considered to be the best horseman in his quarter, a reputation that soon spread throughout Damascus and the rest of Syria. By the mid-1930s, the Kilawi stable of show horses had become an attraction at all national parades, and Abu Ali always rode at the head.

Successful business enterprises helped to vault the Kilawi family into the social limelight of Bab al-Jabiya. Neighbors began to ask for favors or assistance, and in no time they built up a solid core of followers and clients from among the poorer elements of the quarter, some of whom were personally loyal to Abu Ali. The result was that Abu Ali was able to put together his own gang, composed mainly of unemployed youth and casual laborers.

In the early 1920s, as the Kilawis began to accumulate capital, they were able to purchase a fairly large apartment in the heart of their quarter, one with a special salon for entertaining. This salon also was used as an informal courtroom where the Kilawis, now much trusted in Bab al-Jabiya, served as administrators of extralegal justice, arbitrating or mediating disputes between individuals and families who for one reason or another were not comfortable going before the religious or civil courts. The Kilawis also lent their salon to poorer families for wedding parties and other social functions, and it eventually became one of the main political meeting places in the quarter.

Abu Ali claimed that he and his brothers never asked for money or other material rewards for their hospitality and services. But they did expect personal loyalty to the family, which they acquired as the Kilawi network grew and the family name came to be mentioned with both reverence and fear.

One of the most prominent features of urban life in Damascus were the *arada*, or traditional parades, held in the quarter to celebrate some religious event such as a circumcision, the return of the pilgrimage, or the Prophet's birthday. These occasions allowed the youth of one quarter to compete with the youth of neighboring quarters in wrestling matches, sword games, horse racing, and the like. The honor of the quarter was always at stake in these events, as were specific controversies over turf and freedom on movement. Certain quarters were known to be long-standing rivals, most notably Suq Saruja and al-Salhiya, and Shaghur and Bab al-Jabiya. Yet another way in which Abu Ali al-Kilawi reinforced his status in the quarter was to lead his stalwarts in street fights against rival gangs of Shaghur.

By the early twentieth century, however, the parades had begun to assume secular dimensions as they came to mark political events such as the election of a deputy, the return of an exile, the Young Turk revolt of 1908, or the Italian invasion of Libya in 1911. This politicization accelerated during the mandate, and acts of defiance against the French and their collaborators highlighted the continued independence of life in the quarters. But, equally important, as political consciousness rose in the quarters, the fierce rivalries between them were transformed into an alliance of the quarters against the French. The narrowness and insularity of quarter life began to break down as the scope of political activity widened.

The Great Revolt of 1925 hastened the erosion of many of the traditional social and political barriers and rivalries between quarters and helped to bind them together in a common front against the French. There is little doubt that the many stories of individual heroism that quickly became part of the local history and mythology of the Great Revolt helped many a young man to enhance his reputation in the popular quarters of the city, enabling him to achieve the status of *qabaday*. In fact, there was a noticeable turnover of *qabadayat* at this time, owing to the emergence of new heroes during the revolt who replaced those who had been killed. Probably the most respected and esteemed *qabaday* of his day was Hasan al-Kharat, the night watchman of Shaghur, who led a rebel attack on French positions in the Syrian capital and was later killed by French troops. His elimination permitted another rising star of the revolt, Mahmud Khaddam al-Srija, to assert himself as the undisputed strongman of Shaghur.

Abu Ali al-Kilawi frankly admitted fifty years after his own participation in the Great Revolt that it also enabled his family to consolidate their position as the *qabadayat* par excellence of Bab al-Jabiya. When the revolt erupted, the Kilawis and their armed gang prepared their quarter for insurrection against the French. Abu Ali joined the rebel band of Nasib al-Bakri, whose family had patronized the Kilawis for some time. After the French regained control of most of Damascus in October, Abu Ali followed Bakri's forces into the gardens around the Syrian capital known as al-Ghuta. One particular episode contributed to his immortalization in the minds of future generations. Seriously wounded in a single-handed attempt to liberate his rebel comrades imprisoned in the Citadel of Damascus, he managed to flee on horseback, taking refuge among his traditional enemies in Shaghur. Two days later, a weak but determined Abu Ali al-Kilawi recruited some young men of Shaghur and rode back with them to Bab al-Jabiya, where he rounded up more followers and returned to the Ghuta to rejoin the Bakri band.

Like the great merchants and the *imams* of the local mosques, the *qabadayat* rarely joined the National Bloc or any other political organization. Rather, their affiliation and loyalty was to one or another of the Bloc chiefs. Abu Ali al-Kilawi's allegiance was to Nasib al-Bakri, not to the Bloc's executive council. The *qabadayat* were typically more important to a nationalist leader's political machine in the quarters than were the merchants or religious figures. The Bloc chief's resources were limited, especially when in and out of jail or in temporary exile; therefore, the recruitment and maintenance of his clientele required considerable finesse. He generally preferred to devote his personal attention to winning and sustaining following among the wealthier families of the quarters. With these he made certain that he was able to maintain regular personal contacts at all times. When the National Bloc chief began to distance himself from his ancestral quarter, he had to depend more heavily on intermediaries to dispense favors and services to the larger mass of poorer residents with whom he probably never came into direct contact. Merchants, whose status was based on wealth, philanthropy, and religious piety, were among those intermediaries who assumed this function for the politicians. But as class differentiation evolved during the mandate, merchants began to take less and less interest in the poor and their individual problems. They neither found time for, nor were they well disposed toward, the poor. Philanthropy itself did not require regular contact with the lower classes. Some members of the Muslim religious establishment also placed a greater distance between themselves and the common people. Others, however, including preachers in the popular quarters, actually strengthened their influence among the destitute and the illiterate. Although leading religious dignitaries and lower-ranking *imams* generally supported the nationalist chiefs, they also formed benevolent societies (*jamiyat*) that assumed a militant anti-Western and antisecular political character by the mid-1930s and eventually posed an unwelcome challenge to the authority of the nationalist leadership in the quarters.

The *qabaday*, in contrast, posed no such threat. He hailed from the common people, was under the protection of one or another nationalist leader (*bey*), was often indebted to him for loans and services, and, in any case, lacked the education, status, and statesmanlike qualities to reach the chief's level of political leadership. Thus, while the National Bloc leader, assisted by his personal secretary and family, policed the core of his patronage network, the *qabaday* looked after its periphery, servicing it directly whenever possible and guaranteeing its support when the *bey* required it.

Although some *qabadayat* were able to attract their own personal followings by performing such services as the mediation of disputes, the protection of the neighborhood, and small philanthropic activities, they had neither direct control nor access to large material resource bases that might have allowed them to build their own independent patronage networks. In the final analysis, they were beholden to the nationalist politicians in many of the same ways that other clients were. The only significant difference was that the *qabaday*'s apparatus for recruiting and policing his chief's clientele gave him direct access to the *bey*'s immediate entourage, in particular to his personal secretary. In this way, the *qabaday* could count on preferential treatment and a few more privileges than could the average client on the periphery of the chief's network. Although the scope for social mobility was not wide, a number of *qabadayat* managed to enrich themselves through connections with their patrons.

At any given time the residents of a quarter might refer to several individuals as *qabadayat*. A quarter could support more than one strongman, although it was not uncommon to associate the *qabadayat* with a single family. Residents of Bab al-Jabiya referred to *awlad* al-Kilawi (the sons of al-Kilawi) as frequently as they did to any one member of the family. It was the family, through its connections, that provided protection and assistance to the quarter. Abu Ali did make a name for himself, in particular as the family rabble-rouser, the gifted equestrian, and the local enforcer. But he frankly admitted that his oldest brother, who had some education, made the family's major decisions, ran its business, and dealt with the National Bloc politicians and their deputies, was in charge. Abu Ali was in effect Abu Hasan's lieutenant, prepared to execute his commands. When Abu Hasan died, the leadership of the Kilawi family passed to Abu Ali (his other brother was regarded as a high liver and a playboy, which disqualified him), who had already begun to educate his eldest son to fill the role of family lieutenant.

Part of the mythology surrounding the *qabaday* was that he never took money from politicians or their secretaries, or from merchants in the quarter, for carrying out various instructions, such as mobilizing the youth of the quarter to demonstrate or enforcing a strike or boycott. Abu Ali admitted that the National Bloc offered him money at various times and cited several attempts by merchants close to the Bloc to pay him to keep the general strike of 1936 going. Defending the ideal image of *qabaday*, he also claimed that to accept such offerings ran against his honor. He did not deny, however, that some *qabadayat* broke this code of personal honor and morality by accepting cash and other benefits for merely fulfilling their duties. For example, after the National Bloc took office in 1936 in the wake of the general strike and the Franco-Syrian treaty negotiations in Paris, Shukri al-Quwatli, the minister of finance and the national defense, saw to it that Mahmud Khaddam al-Srija, probably the most renowned *qabaday* of the 1930s in Damascus, received a regular stipend from a *waqf* (religious endowment) originally designated for the poor in his native Shaghur for services to al-Quwatli, the leading politician of that quarter.

Given the combination of resources that fed any National Bloc chief's political machine, the support that these leaders received from the quarters was uneven. A politician like Nasib al-Bakri was extremely well connected to numerous *qabadayat* like the Kilawis, the Dib al-Shaykh family of the Amara quarter, and to other veterans of the Great Revolt of 1925, in which he had featured so prominently. Bakri, who cut a much more socially and religiously conservative figure than did his more cosmopolitan Bloc comrades, and who had the religious prestige of his family behind him, moved easily among the tradition-bound masses of the popular quarters. By contrast, Shukri al-Quwatli, Jamil Mardam, and Fakhri al-Barudi (the other major Bloc figures in Damascus) were all extremely influential in their respective quarters, and particularly with merchants, but could not claim large personal followings in other quarters, despite the respect they commanded. Unlike Bakri, however, they serviced much more diversified political machines: each had a significant following in the modern sectors and institutions of Damascus, especially among the educated youth and the emerging professional middle class.

Although the popular quarters remained important units of political and social organization during the mandate period, their importance to the independence movement gradually declined. The advancement of urban political life produced new focal points outside the quarters. These were the modern institutions that were closely identified with the growth of a professional middle class whose fundamental interests lay beyond the quarters. The dominant sentiments of this class of lawyers, doctors, engineers, educators, journalists, and other members of the intelligentsia transcended the narrowness of quarter life. Their primary loyalties were to city, state, and nation rather than to family, clan, confessional group, or quarter.

The National Bloc recognized that the newly educated cadres were in need of youth leaders who were more sophisticated than the tradition-bound and often unlettered *qabadayat*, leaders with whom they could identify socially, culturally, and intellectually; simply, the *qabadayat* were increasingly unappealing and ineffective as role models for the growing numbers of educated youth in the cities who found their anchoring outside the popular quarters.

Thus, while the *qabadayat* and others with influence in the quarters continued to be important political actors during the mandate, they were merely experiencing a temporary reprieve from political obsolescence. This could perhaps best be seen in the changing composition and character of demonstrations against the French in the 1930s. By then, educated young men organized by Boy Scout troop or by political party were at the head of these demonstrations. Everything about them seemed different, from their secular slogans denouncing French imperialism and invoking pan-Arab unity, national liberation, and (by the end of the mandate) even socialism, to their European dress and modern uniforms. Many belonged to the rising middle classes and hailed from the wealthier or newer quarters of Damascus. But even those who did not preferred to march under the banner of their youth organization or school rather than alongside the traditional quarter bosses, the *qabadayat*. Moreover, their role models were a set of young leaders who were more ideologically motivated than the *qabadayat* and whose political bases lay outside the popular quarters in new, more sophisticated institutions and structures, such as the government schools, the university, and various youth organizations.

These new youth leaders regarded Abu Ali al-Kilawi and his fellow *qabadayat* as relics and obstacles to progress. *Qabadayat* like Abu Ali regarded them as party hacks, men whose highest commitment was to an elitist organization, not to the common people. Like Abu Ali, these new political personalities served as intermediaries, but more for the National Bloc organization as a whole than for any single individual in it. They operated in a milieu that ultimately proved to be more important to the future of the Syrian national independence movement and to urban politics in general. They clearly belonged to the future, while the *qabadayat* increasingly belonged to the past.

But these new urban youth leaders who supplanted the *qabadayat* in postindependence Syria were themselves destined for obsolescence. Profound structural changes in economy and society that had begun during World War II unleashed new forces with new methods and aims that were beyond the towns and outside the traditional framework of urban politics. Elements from the countryside now struggled against more established urban elements for control of the towns and of government. In the 1950s and 1960s dispossessed rural peoples belonging to Syria's compact religious minorities used the army and the major radical nationalist party (the Baath Party) as their vehicle for social and political mobility and ultimately to seize control of government. In the process, they effectively brought an end to independent urban politics in Syria.

A NOTE ON SOURCES

My account of the life and political career of Abu Ali al-Kilawi is based on several days of conversations with him and with several other *qabadayat* in the spring of 1976. It also draws upon his unpublished memoir, "Thawra amma 1925: Al-Faransiyyin fi suriyya." Also of help was Ahmad Hilmi al-Allaf, *Dimashq fi matla al-qarn al-ahsrin*, ed. Ali Jamil Nuaysa (Damascus: Wizarat al-Thaqafa, 1976). See also the published memoirs of several prominent Syrian nationalist politicians of the French Mandate era, including Fakhri al-Barudi, Abd al-Rahman Shahbandar, Lutfi al-Haffar, and Khalid al-Azm. Some of their private papers and those of other nationalist leaders are housed in the Center for Historical Documents in Damascus.

Other unpublished sources include René Danger, Paul Danger, and M. Ecochard, "Damas: Rapport d'enquête monographique sur la ville, 1936," found at Bibliothèque de l'Institut Français d'Études Arabes in Damascus; the French Mandate collection (Al-Intidab al-faransi) in the Center for Historical Documents (Markaz al-Wathaiq al-Tarikhiyya) in Damascus; the French Mandate archives at the Ministère des Affaires Étrangères in Nantes; Série E. Levant: Syrie-Liban 1918–1940; the *mémoires de stage* pertaining to Syria in the Centre des Hautes Études Administratives sur l'Afrique et l'Asie Modernes (CHEAM) in Paris; and the British Foreign Office files (FO 371, FO 226, FO 684) for the French Mandate located in the Public Record Office in London (Kew).

SUGGESTIONS FOR FURTHER READING

On Syrian politics during the French Mandate, see Philip S. Khoury, *Syria and the French Mandate: The Politics of Arab Nationalism, 1920–1945* (Princeton, N.J.: Princeton University Press, 1987). For comparisons with the Ottoman period of Syrian history, see Philip S. Khoury, *Urban Notables and Arab Nationalism: The Politics of Damascus, 1860–1920* (Cambridge: Cambridge University Press, 1993); and Linda Schatkowski Schilcher, *Families in Politics: Damascene Factions and Estates of the 18th and 19th Centuries* (Stuttgart: Franz Steiner, 1985). The best study of the post-independence era is Patrick Seale, *The Struggle for Syria: A Study of Post-War Arab Politics, 1945–1958* (London: Oxford University Press, 1965).

On the phenomenon of *qabadayat* and the challenges posed to them by new social and political forces in the twentieth century, see Philip S. Khoury, "Syrian Urban Politics in Transition: The Quarters of Damascus during the French Mandate," *International Journal of Middle East Studies* 16 (November 1984): 507–40, from which this essay is adapted. Michael Johnson has studied the *qabadayat* of Beirut; see his "Political Bosses and Their Gangs: Zuama and Qabadayat in the Sunni Muslim Quarters of Beirut," in *Patrons and*

Clients in Mediterranean Societies, ed. Ernest Gellner and John Waterbury (London: Duckworth, 1977), and his *Class and Client in Beirut* (Atlantic Highlands, N.J.: Ithaca Press, 1986).

For a general interpretation of how urban politics changed in Syria in the nineteenth and twentieth centuries, see Albert Hourani, "Revolution in the Arab Middle East," in *Revolution in the Middle East and Other Case Studies,* ed. P. J. Vatikiotis (London: Rowman and Littlefield, 1972). Also James Gelvin, *Divided Loyalties: Nationalism and Mass Politics in Syria at the Close of Empire* (Berkeley: University of California Press, 1998); Philip S. Khoury, "Syrian Political Culture: A Historical Perspective," in *Syria: Its Society, Culture, and Polity,* ed. Richard Antoun and Donald Quataert (Albany: State University of New York Press, 1991); and Elizabeth Thompson, *Colonial Citizens: Republican Rights, Paternal Privilege, and Gender in French Syria and Lebanon* (New York: Columbia University Press, 2000).

Chapter 11

M'hamed Ali:
Tunisian Labor Organizer

Eqbal Ahmad and Stuart Schaar

An examination of the life of M'hamed Ali, whom Tunisians consider the founder of their trade union movement, reveals a complex personality who has undergone a wide variety of experiences and influences. M'hamed Ali reflected, as he shaped, the trends and forces that came together in Tunisia during the early twentieth century. His first known political activity, his support of Libyan resistance against the Italians in Tripolitania, exposed him directly to the pan-Islamic movement, whose nonterritorial, universalist ideology was later to mark Arab nationalism. (For other examples of the role of pan-Islam as a predecessor of nationalism, see the chapters by Lisa Anderson, Julie Oehler, and Abdullah Schleifer.)

During World War I, M'hamed Ali was one of a small number of Tunisians who served in the Ottoman forces (in support of Germany and the Axis powers) as a way of opposing French colonialism in the Maghrib. The end of the war found him in Berlin, where he was exposed to the revolutionary currents of the German workers' movement. This experience made him a militant supporter of workers' rights.

After the war, a confused period in Tunisian politics ensued. The French protectorate government was opposed by a number of rival nationalist formations, notably the old Destour Party and the Néo-Destour Party. The Néo-Destour represented the rising younger generation, and the original Destour represented their parents. Class and regional elements also played a role in the split. (Such struggles can be found in many national liberation movements in this period.)

This conflict was paralleled and intersected by the three-cornered struggle over workers' rights. Here the French protectorate's labor policies were opposed by the Confédération Générale des Travailleurs (CGT), which was affiliated with the French Communist Party and most of whose leaders were European, and by the nationalist Confédération Générale des Travailleurs Tunisiens (CGTT), one of whose founders was M'hamed Ali. In the interwar years, the CGTT emerged as a leading defender of the Muslim working class and a strong ally (and sometime rival) of the Néo-Destour. M'hamed Ali participated in the major conflicts of the period, playing a decisive role. Sent into political exile by the French, he died in Cairo in 1927.

M'hamed Ali's biography allows us to reflect upon the always problematic relationship between nationalism and the labor movement in the Middle East. In Tunisia, as elsewhere, a burning question was which should have priority—the national struggle or the class struggle. M'hamed Ali's analysis of the power of the colonial state led him to throw his energies into the national struggle. It was not an uncontested decision, and much of the debate in the 1920s (in which he played a central role) focused on devising the parameters of worker support for the nationalist movement.

In thinking about the Tunisian case, comparisons with Egypt and Morocco, both of which were marked by strong labor movements, are especially useful. Close readers may also want to note M'hamed Ali's peasant origins in seeking to gauge the roots of his militancy. (For other biographies of peasants in this volume, see the contributions of Joost Hiltermann and David McMurray). —Eds.

In the history of the modern Maghrib, M'hamed Ali, whom the Tunisians consider the founding father of their still influential trade union movement, is a unique personality. He lived during the formative years of Tunisian nationalism and reflected the trends and forces that converged in Tunisia during the early twentieth century. His first known political activity, on behalf of the anticolonial resistance in Tripolitania, brought him in direct contact with the pan-Islamic movement, which spearheaded early anti-imperialist resistance in the Muslim world. It also placed him in contact with the nonterritorial, universalist trends that have marked Arab nationalist movements.

In the 1920s, when Tunisian nationalism was being transformed into a mass movement, M'hamed Ali played a key role in creating a national federation of workers independent of the French Confédération Générale des Travailleurs, or CGT. In the process, he became a central figure in the rivalries and polemics between nationalists and socialists in colonial Tunisia, a political struggle that played a large part in shaping the ideological premises of Tunisian nationalism. Finally, as a member of the young, progressive wing of the Destour Party, M'hamed Ali belonged to that generation of youthful, often rural, radical nationalists who later founded the Néo-Destour Party and led Tunisia to independence.

Perhaps as a result of the many gaps in the historical record, the life of Muhammad Ben Ali Ben Mokhtar Al-Ghaffani, alias Dr. M'hamed Ali Al-Hammi, alias Titon, popularly remembered as M'hamed Ali, has given rise to much controversy. Even his date of birth is in question.

M'hamed Ali was born in a rural community where, until recently, births and deaths were for remembrances rather than recording, and it was common for families to say that a boy was younger than he really was in order to assure him a longer term of employment. Similarly, little is known about his

life and activities in Germany at the end of World War I—an early testimony
to the anonymity of migrant workers in Europe. His death in exile conforms
to this pattern. Although patriots and scholars have researched the time
and place of his death, his birth date, and schooling, few details are known.
It is clear that the obscurities concerning his life and the controversies surrounding his politics are a direct result of his social and political origins.

We now believe that M'hamed Ali was born in 1896 in El Hamma, an
impoverished village in southern Tunisia near Gabès. El Hamma has but
few economic resources, chiefly date palms and a few carpet weavers. As a
result, its hardworking people have been forced to migrate to the coastal
cities, where they enjoy a considerable reputation as dockers and construction workers. The image of these rural migrants as sober, straightforward,
and loyal workers has accounted for their popularity with the Tunisian and
colonial bourgeoisie, whom they have served as porters, guards, chauffeurs,
and butlers.

While he was still a young child, M'hamed Ali's mother died. His father,
a poor peasant, took the boy to the home of a sister in Tunis. There he studied Arabic at a *kuttab* (Quranic school). His first job was as an errand boy at
the central market. Later he was hired as a domestic in the household of the
Austrian consul, where he added a smattering of German to his Arabic and
French. Most importantly, he also learned to drive an automobile, becoming the consul's chauffeur. As there were few Tunisian Muslims who could
drive at the time, the possession of this critical skill was to provide him with
many opportunities for personal advancement.

His political education came in the years prior to World War I, when after
years of quiet the Tunisian political situation suddenly became inflamed.
The emergence of the Young Tunisians, a small group of would-be nationalists who were the contemporaries of the Young Turks in the Ottoman
Empire, was an important moment in modern Tunisian politics. M'hamed
Ali was drawn to them because they aimed to reawaken Tunisian Muslims
from their political torpor. The Young Tunisians called upon Tunisians to
rid themselves of indolence and fatalism and "from all prejudices that
shackle their evolution, destroy their faculties, and hold them outside the
movement that carries humanity toward progress," as Muhammad Lasram,
one of their number, put it.

The Young Tunisian weekly, *Le Tunisien*, was founded in Paris in 1907
and developed ideas on the future Tunisian state. About the same time, the
Young Tunisians also established a political party, the Parti Évolutionniste.
Its aim was to bring about greater Franco-Tunisian cooperation and thereby
to facilitate the emergence of a modern Tunisian state in which all citizens
would have equal rights. Their concern with rights was a major source of the
popular appeal of the Young Tunisians. It was their willingness to address
the racism that defined relations between them and the Europeans that

attracted the attention of M'hamed Ali. The normal tensions that existed in Tunisian society between classes, and the class struggle that might have emerged in a noncolonial setting, were submerged in conflicts between the foreign and indigenous communities over racial issues.

In 1911 the Italians invaded Tripolitania. Then an Ottoman province administered by a governor appointed by the Ottoman sultan, Libya was the only North African province not yet conquered by European imperialism. Already France had occupied Algeria in 1830 and Tunisia in 1881, and 1882 had witnessed the takeover of Egypt by the British. The invasion of Tripolitania by Italy provoked deep emotions among Tunisians and crystallized their discontent into bitterness and fear. This was all the more the case because of the large numbers of Italian immigrants in Tunisia, some of whom were known for their racism.

The Italian invasion challenged the premises of pan-Islamic propaganda, which was then ascendant in the Ottoman Empire. Pan-Islam raised the hope that the Muslim people could be restored to their place in history. The chief instrument of that restoration was to be the Ottoman caliphate. Revitalized as an ideological force by the Ottoman ruler Abd al-Hamid (1876–1908) and used by the Young Turks as a tool of policy, the caliphate was a symbol of Muslim unity. Italy's attack on Turkish power so close to home threatened the dreams of ordinary Tunisians, shattering their lingering hopes and producing a nervous disquiet.

The invasion of Tripolitania prompted M'hamed Ali's first known political involvement. At the time he was in his early twenties and was employed as a chauffeur in the household of a wealthy Tunisian. In response to the Italian invasion, the Young Tunisians, led by Ali Bach Hamba, had formed a committee of solidarity with Tripolitania. They also began publication of a pan-Islamic journal, *Al-ittihad al-islami* (*Islamic Unity*). More practically, they took up a collection to send a medical supply unit to assist the Ottoman forces in opposing the Italians. In order to transport the medical supplies to Tripolitania they needed an experienced driver. Someone who knew of M'hamed Ali's background as a chauffeur suggested that he might be the right person for the job. Thus, in the autumn of 1911, M'hamed Ali embarked on a journey that took him to Tripolitania, Turkey, the Arab Middle East, and Germany. In the process, he was introduced to the pan-Islamic, reformist, and nationalist currents prevalent in the Ottoman Empire, as well as to socialist milieux in turbulent postwar Germany.

In Tunisia the climate produced by the Turko-Italian war sharpened the conflict between Tunisians and the French colonial authorities. In November 1911, rumors of an alleged French plan to confiscate the venerated Muslim cemetery of Djellaz on the outskirts of Tunis spread among the Muslim population, sparking a major protest that soon spilled over into violence. The French authorities launched a full-scale attack to dislodge the

Tunisians from the cemetery and established martial law. The resultant loss of life and heavy repression heightened political tensions. Three months later, the accidental killing of a Tunisian child by an Italian trolley-car conductor provoked a recrudescence of political turmoil. It soon led to a boycott of the Tunis streetcar lines. Trolley-car workers also demanded equal pay for Muslim employees and better treatment for Muslim passengers. The episode marked the entry of Tunisian workers into national politics. General national grievances began to be expressed along with specific worker demands. This was to become a pattern for the future. While the Young Tunisian leaders did not originate the boycott, they supported it. On 12 March 1912, the police arrested seven of them and deported four, including their leader, Ali Bach Hamba.

While Tunisian politics were heating up, M'hamed Ali was involved in the Young Turk efforts to bolster the Libyan resistance to the Italians. As a result of his expertise, he was hired as the personal chauffeur of Enver Pasha, the Young Turk leader. Following the Italian victory in the Libyan war, he accompanied his important friend to Istanbul, where he studied Turkish and perfected his literary Arabic. During World War I, he claimed to have headed the servicing section in the Ottoman army's automobile fleet. In 1918, following the conclusion of the war, M'hamed Ali fled with Enver Pasha from Turkey to Germany. When his mentor moved on to the Soviet Union in 1919, he remained in Berlin. There he resided, except for brief trips to Tunisia in 1922 and 1923, before finally returning home in March 1924.

In Germany, M'hamed Ali moved in socialist and labor union circles. Between November 1921 and January 1924, he worked in an aircraft-manufacturing plant and intermittently studied political economy at one of several free universities in Berlin. Tahar al-Haddad, who cofounded the Confédération Générale des Travailleurs Tunisiens (CGTT) with him, recalls his friend's enthusiastic references to the German labor movement. According to Haddad, it was the revolutionary zeal of German workers that inspired M'hamed Ali to devote himself to the betterment of Muslim countries. Whether or not M'hamed Ali obtained a degree at Berlin is uncertain. Although his enemies often asserted he had not, he himself would neither confirm nor deny it, though he allowed those who wished to believe it to do so. In refusing to confirm it, he implicitly denied the importance of status symbols. In laying claim to it (when arrested, for example) he used it as an instrument of struggle.

In 1924 M'hamed Ali returned to Tunisia, where he soon became a leader of the young, progressive nationalists, who included Haddad, Mahmound Bourguiba, Othman Kaak, and the Algerian Ahmed Tewfik al-Medani. These young radicals sought a socially progressive and economically dynamic Tunisia. They explicitly opposed the so-called Old Turbans in the Destour, who spoke of Islam and Muslim culture with the tenacity of wounded devotees. M'hamed Ali and Haddad questioned their cultural heritage with the agonizing uncertainty of honest appraisers.

Unlike Destour Party leaders such as Abd al-Aziz Talbi, author of *La Tunisie Martyre*, M'hamed Ali and his associates did not consider Tunisia simply a "martyr" of French aggression. On the contrary, they credited the French with jolting the Tunisian consciousness and with introducing Tunisians to modern techniques of economy and administration. To them, the subjugation of Tunisia to France was the result of internal weaknesses. They believed that meaningful emancipation could come only from a total reform of the society and the individual.

Instead of directing their energies toward dramatizing Tunisia's legal claims to independence and pinning their hopes for political reform on Woodrow Wilson, the League of Nations, and the French socialists, men like M'hamed Ali and Haddad insisted on looking inward. They placed a strong emphasis on self-improvement and self-reliance and on the search for the organizing principles of society. They also believed that it was necessary to root out the causes of backwardness, however sanctified by tradition they might be.

In the 1920s, direct contact with Marxists was commonplace among Tunisian nationalist and labor union leaders. A few liberals within the Destour Party had joined the Socialist Party during the war, when all other political groupings had been outlawed. Contact with the European Left in Tunisia pushed the nationalists toward the adoption of progressive positions. The French workers' organization, the Confédération Générale des Travailleurs (CGT), was affiliated with the union in France and had a great influence on men like M'hamed Ali and Tahar al-Haddad. It recruited Tunisians into a modern workers' organization based on progressive ideology. In this way, Tunisian workers came to have admiration for the ideals of 1789 while deploring the colonialist excesses of the French government. Haddad acknowledged this debt when he praised the Socialists, who recognized the "injustices and inequalities within the working class" and in whose CGT branches "Tunisian workers . . . participated in the strikes, in the organization and expansion of unions, and attended meetings." There, he went on, "they heard leaders . . . proclaim the liberty and equality of man; declare that the religion of the worker was his labor and his enemy was capitalism, that neither race nor religion distinguished the workers from each other, for these are the tools that capitalism employs in order to divide them and to defeat their objectives."

Because of attitudes like these, Tunisian labor leaders had a dual view of France. Although they resented being the dominated and scorned majority in an ethnically divided country, they were attracted by the Left's vision of liberty, equality, and fraternity in a society in which race and religion were transcended. At a time when the colonized were seeking to understand the causes of their subjugation, the European Left offered an interpretation of imperialism that was both satisfying and easy to understand.

Still, the colonial situation was full of contradictions. The Tunisian working class competed for jobs with a substantial number of privileged European workers—some 44,000 out of 107,500 salaried workers in 1926. In effect, they had become second-ranking workers in their own country. Competition with Europeans was unequal, discrimination in pay scales and wages galled many, and racist attitudes of European coworkers could hardly promote human dignity. Haddad's contemporary description of the crisis of the interwar period brings out these contradictions:

> Artisanal production has decreased; numerous professional people have gone bankrupt, and they have joined the ranks of the unemployed, who in turn are joined by the inhabitants of the southern infertile lands and by members of the tribes who are evicted from their lands by French colonialism. These are convenient circumstances for the grand French capitalists, who exploit the mining resources of Tunisia, who construct railroads . . . and factories such as limestone and cement works. These capitalists have been able to find by the hundreds, even thousands, an army of unemployed whose numbers increase with the passage of time. Capital recruits only as a function of its needs; it has been able to use the masses for hard labor at low pay, while others, and they are numerous, have to wander on the roads and in the towns, either begging or robbing.

M'hamed Ali, too, was deeply moved by the backward and miserable condition of Tunisians. He described "the wretched condition of so many of our people who live like animals." At night it was his practice to walk in the *medina* (the old Arab quarter), indignant at the sight of the poor, half-starved and seminaked, sleeping on sidewalks, receiving from "heaven its gift of heavy rain" and yet satisfied with their *maktub* (fate), while, he noted, "our leaders" sleep "in their fancy beds with their wives, their children and their golden dreams."

Despite M'hamed Ali's frustration with the Tunisian elite, the new order tended to bring Tunisian classes into closer, if superficial, contact. Before the protectorate, Haddad noted,

> important families abhorred labor, and they became high functionaries in the administration or they lived off an annual income from the exploitation of their lands by agricultural laborers. It is with the same disdain that they considered commerce, which for them was comparable to manual labor. Commercial activity meant that they would cater to a clientele to whom they would have to be nice. . . . They found that an unsupportable burden and a bit humiliating.

But the immigration of about 110,000 Europeans into the protectorate by 1900 led the Tunisian notables—at times impoverished by their loss of function and land—to join the ranks of the old merchant families and new self-made people to form a local bourgeoisie.

Simultaneously, the leaders of the European colony—mostly French—assumed the role of a new aristocracy. The lives of the Tunisian upper crust increasingly became filled with empty forms and ceremonies. Their dominance was significantly reduced; their way of life was threatened. European settlement accentuated this threat and compelled the Tunisian bourgeoisie to seek mass support in the emergent Tunisian working class.

Given these contradictory tendencies, M'hamed Ali concluded, as did Haddad, that conditions in Tunisia were not yet ripe for class struggle or a full-fledged social revolution. While accepting the general theory of class struggle, they denied its validity for colonial Tunisia, where the process of industrialization and class formation had been delayed and distorted. In their analysis, race took precedence over class in defining the major social cleavages in colonial Tunisia. The chief concern was not so much with the local class struggle as with getting rid of the European occupiers. While M'hamed Ali and his friends did not rule out the possibility of an internal revolutionary conflict in the future—at least Haddad articulated this position—in the organizational sphere M'hamed Ali stressed the need for Tunisians to bury their differences and unite in revolt against foreign domination.

World War I and the debilitating political and economic environment of the 1920s accelerated this potential for revolt. New disappointments accentuated old anger among increasingly larger sections of the population. Some 65,000 Tunisians had fought for France during the war, and of these, 10,900 had died or disappeared. An additional 30,000 had worked on construction brigades in the metropolitan area. Therefore, nearly a quarter of the active Tunisian male population had had direct contacts with the metropolis. Their sacrifice, loyalty, and service led them to expect rewards from France. Instead, they returned home to face unemployment, high prices caused by inflation, and a fiscal system that violated basic social justice. The tax system hurt the already exploited Tunisians and gave settlers and French capitalists major privileges.

This crisis was exacerbated by major crop failures in postwar Tunisia. The 1919 crop was mediocre, and the 1920 harvest was one of the worst since the great famine of 1867. In 1921 it was a bit better, but from 1922 until 1924 less grain was harvested than was needed to feed the population. The French protectorate government was forced to import wheat at high prices. As a result, the cost of living rose by 29 percent between 1923 and 1924 and workers began to clamor for higher wages. The postwar economic crisis thus wiped out whatever profits Tunisians had gained during the war. In addition, Tunisian war veterans, like the workers who labored alongside the Europeans or the many who unsuccessfully sought work, were no longer ready to accept the status quo that treated them as inferiors. Inevitably, the national question came to seem the key to everything else.

In 1924 the political situation came to a head. With M'hamed Ali as the chairman of its management committee, the young nationalists launched a consumer cooperative movement in June and July, seeking thereby to expand the outreach of the nationalists and to impart new skills and a new sense of self-reliance among Tunisians. The management committee under M'hamed Ali had just started its work when Tunisian workers openly defied the orders of the leadership of the CGT. In August, the dockers of Tunis and Bizerte, some of whom had grown close to M'hamed Ali through the cooperative movement, went on strike, demanding wages equal to those of French port workers. When the CGT leaders in Tunis advised moderation and calm, the workers formed an independent strike committee and solicited the help of the intellectual and youthful elements within the Destour Party.

The striking dockers appealed for help to the leadership of the cooperative. M'hamed Ali responded to their call at the risk of exposing himself to charges of confounding objectives. Conflict, however, was inherent in the dual goals he set for Tunisians to achieve, namely, winning national autonomy and achieving social and economic progress for the masses. He had hoped to launch the cooperative movement to enhance the political strength of the nationalists, but he gave greater long-range importance to economic and social progress. Yet, when faced with the critical alternative of abandoning the striking workers and thereby losing his potentially most important constituency, which favored the securing of his reformist program, he opted for political and syndical activism.

The dockers found ready support in the young Destourians, particularly M'hamed Ali, Tahar al-Haddad, and Tewfik al-Medani. After two weeks of peaceful picketing and an unsuccessful appeal to the *bey* and his prime minister, the strikers, under M'hamed Ali's leadership, appealed for help to the public. Popular street demonstrations, clashes with the police, and widespread support for the striking workers forced the Destour to endorse the workers' demands publicly. Under severe economic pressure, the maritime company in Tunis accepted arbitration. A compromise settlement was worked out, by the terms of which some of the workers' demands were granted. On 6 September, the twenty-four-day Tunis dockers' strike ended, and that of the Bizerte dockers ended soon thereafter.

The strikes crystallized widespread discontent and set in motion a chain of events that was to lead by November to a permanent split in the CGT. The strikes had demonstrated the effectiveness of organized mass political action. They also revealed widespread and deep discontent among people who were willing to sacrifice heroically in order to win minor economic, but major psychological, battles against foreign exploiters. A propaganda committee under M'hamed Ali concentrated on winning popular support and the nationalist party's backing for the striking workers. Financial and moral support permitted a prolonged strike and ultimate victory. It also confirmed the young trade unionists' belief that a trade union could become viable and strong only with mass and party backing based on a nationalist appeal.

The initially hostile attitude of the French-dominated Socialist party and CGT further alienated the Tunisians from the metropolitan federation and intensified the move toward the creation of a national—and ultimately nationalist—labor movement. Arguments and debates started between the French socialists and M'hamed Ali's group. The split between Tunisians and European workers in the CGT eventually culminated in the establishment of a nationalist union, the CGTT, in November 1924. This development was the outgrowth of a protracted period of conflict and debate on the left. During the summer, striking workers, lacking the support of the CGT labor federation, established several autonomous local unions. In Tunis, the dockers, textile workers, streetcar employees, cement-factory workers, and some traditional handicraftsmen formed their own unions. Workers in Bizerte and other coastal towns also left the CGT at this time.

The European Left vehemently opposed the formation of a nationalist organization on the grounds that such a labor union would be inimical to the principles of labor solidarity. They charged the union seceders with racism, communalism, and negativism. The multiplication of autonomous Tunisian unions alarmed CGT officials in France. Léon Jouhaux, secretary general of the CGT, arrived in Tunis on 24 October 1924 and urged M'hamed Ali to help maintain workers' unity and solidarity. At a public meeting on 31 October, Jouhaux conceded that although the CGT rejected in principle any differences of race or color, in practice the European workers in Tunisia had given the Muslims a genuine cause for complaint. But he warned that separatism would only perpetuate evil practices and attitudes while intensifying divisions within the working class.

The Socialist Party (SFIO) in Tunisia presented a serious moral and political challenge to the nationalist labor movement because it could not be easily dismissed as imperialist and its objections had to be answered and accommodated. The Socialists were as consistent in opposing the pretensions and the continued privileges of the settlers as they were in objecting to what they regarded as the "narrow, communal, counterrevolutionary" character of nationalism. The real issues, they argued, were neither national, racial, nor religious; the working class should not permit fragmentation by dividing along such lines. European and Tunisian workers faced common enemies: the dominance of capitalism and the clergy in an alliance of special privilege perpetuated by the dead hand of tradition. The answer, they stressed, was to build a movement, liberate humanity from superstition, instill a revolutionary spirit in people, and build mass institutions to defeat imperialism. The

Left could point to their efforts in this direction. The Socialist Party and, after the December 1920 split, the Communist Party were the only interracial political institutions in Tunisia, and their unions were the only ones in which both Europeans and Muslims were full members.

Not all Tunisian workers favored splitting the CGT. In response to M'hamed Ali's proposal to establish a national Tunisian union federation, some workers, led by Ahmed Ben Milad and Mokhtar al-Ayari (who nevertheless became a founder of the CGTT), at first opposed him. They argued that the plan smacked of religious prejudice and violated the principle of universalism. M'hamed Ali pleaded with them:

> The creation of a Tunisian federation does not mean that we shall not be united with the workers of the world as a whole. France, Germany, and England have national federations. Why are we denied similar rights? The only reason for their [the European Left's] attitude is that they would like to consider us a part of France. Is not imperialism a denial of equality? Why such accusations from Socialists and Communists? Are they also deceiving us?

On the ideological level, nationalist labor leaders were placed on the defensive. They often took their cues from the CGT program and ideology and defined their goals in the moral, universal, and progressive terms that they had learned in the parent organization. In order to counter the harsh criticism from the European Left, M'hamed Ali and his comrades had to define their goals clearly and make distinctions between political exigencies and long-term objectives. In so doing, they might win over Europeans who, like the Communists after their initial hesitation, could aid them to gain their freedom.

"If we achieve social progress, remove our internal weaknesses inherited from the past, and begin to view the world clearly and with a broad outlook," Haddad wrote,

> then we will be able to convince many Europeans that we deserve a free life. The Europeans do not trust our feelings; when we ask for freedom they think that we hate their presence among us, that freedom to us only means the license to wander aimlessly around the streets of our nation even if this delays industrialization and leaves natural treasures buried in the ground. They mistrust us. What they say seems true when matched by our immobility and our satisfaction in exposing only their injustices and our hatred.

When the CGTT was formally established in November 1924, M'hamed Ali was named its secretary general. He headed a provisional executive committee of twelve members, six of whom were veteran trade unionists. Initially, the new federation made rapid gains. Its leaders demonstrated unusual organizing ability, and the masses proved ready for mobilization.

After consolidating their position in Tunis, they moved into the provinces. M'hamed Ali in the south and Mokhtar al-Ayari in the north registered unexpected successes. At its first congress in January of 1925 the CGTT publicly flaunted its achievement. A majority of employed Tunisians had gathered under its banner. For the first time, activists had tried and succeeded in mobilizing and organizing an important segment of the mass. For the first time, a Tunisian militant, M'hamed Ali, had reached the grassroots by articulating concrete and specific demands. Yet its very success exposed the union to repression.

The protectorate authorities were alarmed when union organizers reached the farms of French settlers, and Tunisian workers began calling for land reform and speaking out against colonial exploitation. The French chief of police, who arbitrated labor disputes, called on M'hamed Ali to dissolve the federation and merge with the CGT. Instead, he responded by intensifying his efforts. He won over more affiliates, which only increased the ire of the Socialists, who then controlled the French government. Significant weaknesses soon appeared among the nationalists. The Destourian leaders who had hitherto supported the CGTT discreetly began to prepare to abandon them in return for reforms that they were negotiating with the French Socialist government. Only Communist leaders backed the CGTT, but this enthusiastic support further exposed the Tunisian workers to the red-baiting practiced by the settler lobby.

The contradictions within the nationalist camp, added to those within the Left, exposed the CGTT to repression. Events did not cooperate either. Just as the CGTT was holding its first congress in Tunis, a wildcat strike broke out in a cement factory in Hammam-Lif on the outskirts of the city. Three days later, it spread to farm workers and limestone quarry workers at the *domaine* de Potinville, which was owned by the powerful French businessman Félix Potin. The CGTT leaders knew the risk they were running, but there was no alternative other than to support the strikers. The expected French crackdown was not long in coming. On 5 February 1925 M'hamed Ali, Mokhtar al-Ayari, and J. P. Finidori were arrested. Following protest demonstrations, three other militants—Muhammad al-Ghanouchi, Mahmoud al-Kabadi, and Ali Daraoui—were apprehended and charged with conspiring against the security of the state.

The French authorities easily isolated the young leaders. A Destourian delegation to Paris, led by its secretary general, Ahmed Essafi, had already negotiated the appointment of a Tunisian reform commission, and Essafi's group hoped for more political concessions. Charging that the nationalists were Communist dupes, French settler interests sought to sabotage the provisional agreement. French police raided M'hamed Ali's living quarters and found forty books in German, leading them to claim that he was a German agent sent to Tunisia to sabotage the French colonial enterprise. Destour leaders answered the anti-Communist propaganda with an equally anti-Communist declaration. A few days later, they repudiated the CGTT, abandoned its imprisoned leaders, and adopted the Socialist Party position.

M'hamed Ali and the other leaders were placed on a ship destined for Naples and sent into exile. Soon after his arrival there, Italian authorities arrested M'hamed Ali and expelled him to Turkey, where he was also declared unwelcome by the authorities. Ten days later, he arrived in Port Said in Egypt. From there, he set out for Morocco to join the Rifian revolt of Abd al-Krim. Before reaching his destination, M'hamed Ali was again arrested in Tangier and deported to Egypt. There, he was cared for by friends from Berlin until he moved on to Arabia, where, according to correspondence found in Shaykh Abd al-Aziz Talbi's papers, he died in 1927. After independence, the Tunisian government had his body transferred from Arabia to Tunis, where it was accorded a hero's burial.

A NOTE ON SOURCES

An earlier version of this article appeared under the title "M'hamed Ali and the Tunisian Labour Movement" in *Race & Class* 19 (1978): 253–76. Material used in this essay was initially collected during fieldwork in Tunisia in the early and mid-1960s. It also draws upon archival research in 1976 in the General Archives of the Tunisian government, series on the history of the national movement, especially carton 11. The authors would like to thank Mr. Moncef Dellagi, former director of these archives, for his invaluable assistance. Also consulted in the late 1980s were archives in the Ministry of Foreign Affairs, especially the series Tunisia Ler Versement (Nantes) and the series Tunisia 1917–40 (Paris). French and Tunisian newspapers were also consulted.

SUGGESTIONS FOR FURTHER READING

Three books are especially valuable in dealing with our subject. Tahar al-Haddad, *Al-ummal al-tunisiyun wa zuhur al-haraka al-inqabiya* (Tunis, 1927); Ahmed Ben Milad, *M'hammed Ali: La naissance du mouvement ouvrier tunisien* (Tunis, 1984); and Mustafa Kraim, *Nationalisme et syndicalisme en Tunisie, 1918–1929* (Tunis, 1976).

For works in English on this period of Tunisian history, see Eqbal Ahmad, "Trade Unionism in the Maghreb," in *State and Society in Independent North Africa*, ed. Leon Carl Brown (Washington, D.C.: Middle East Institute, 1962); Jacques Berque, *French North Africa: The Maghrib between Two World Wars* (New York: Praeger, 1962); Charles Micaud et al., *Tunisia: The Politics of Modernization* (New York: Praeger, 1964); Edouard Méric, "The Destourian Socialist Party and the Nationalist Organizations," in *Man, State, and Society in the Contemporary Maghrib*, ed. I. W. Zartman (New York: Praeger, 1973). See also Kenneth Perkins, *A History of Modern Tunisia* (Cambridge: Cambridge University Press, 2004).

Chapter 12

Hagob Hagobian:
An Armenian Truck Driver in Iran

David N. Yaghoubian

Hagob Hagobian was one of the survivors of the Armenian massacres during World War I. His life thus began with the crushing of hopes for an independent Armenia homeland in eastern Anatolia. Hagobian grew up in an orphanage in western Iran and through his ability to take advantage of the chances that came his way was able to establish a financially secure position in middle-class society in Iran before emigrating to California in the 1970s.

As told by his grandson, David Yaghoubian, the story of Hagob Hagobian is that of a self-made man. His survival strategy revolved around his ability to exploit kin and ethnic networks, as well as his intense desire to better himself and his family. His biography sheds light on Iranian society between the 1920s and the 1950s. Of particular interest is his membership in the truck drivers' guild, an indication that the old Islamic guild system flourished into the twentieth century and even showed a capacity to adapt to changing times. The role of Armenians in trade and commerce in Iran is well attested.* Hagobian's involvement in this line of work would therefore not have been exceptional.

What emerges from the biography of Hagobian is the role of Armenians in artisanal trades, notably in the development of the trans-Iran trucking industry. We also witness how World War II brought rapidly changing circumstances: first destroying, then providing, remarkable opportunity. Since Iran was a crucial strategic crossroads in the support of the Russian front, long-distance trucking boomed for some and increased their personal fortunes. Hagobian's experience was entirely different: his truck was confiscated and he was deprived of his means of livelihood, although he later regained his modest wealth and his former position through perseverance. Ultimately, Hagob Hagobian was able to utilize his hard work, determination, and social networks to make a success of his life in Iran, before emigrating to the United States.

---

*For a brief summary, see Philip Curtin, *Cross-Cultural Patterns in World Trade* (Cambridge: Cambridge University Press, 1988), ch. 9.

A number of other lives recounted in this book also feature migrants (see the contributions of Akram Khater and Antoine Khater, David McMurray, and Sami Zubaida). A comparison of them can yield some important insights. In each case, the varying strength of family and ethnic networks, different strategies, and a different personality helped to shape a different response. —Eds.

The frightened Armenian boy stood in the doorway of his family's home as his mother rushed past him in a vain attempt to protect her husband as he was being attacked by a band of Kurdish men. Following the violent struggle, the Kurds quickly rode away, leaving his parents' bodies in front of the farmhouse. Although Hagob Hagobian was the oldest of three brothers, at the age of seven he was far too young to understand the enormity of what had happened. Seeking help, he sadly led his smaller brothers away from their farming village of Khan-Baba-Khan into the countryside of northwestern Iran. It would be many years before Hagob could begin to understand the political and ethnic ramifications of the violence that orphaned the young boys in 1916.

Intercommunal violence resulting in scenes such as this was widespread in eastern Anatolia and Azerbaijan during and after the First World War. The violence was in many ways the result of the Young Turk policies concerning Armenians living in the Ottoman Empire, who had been persecuted as a group since the reign of Sultan Abdul Hamid began in 1876.

Hagob and his brothers found refuge at the Near East Relief Orphanage in Tabriz, the provincial capital of Azerbaijan. An American-sponsored Presbyterian mission, it was home to them for the duration of their childhood. Orphaned children from other areas affected by the Armenian genocide and intercommunal violence arrived at the center almost daily. One such child, Arshalous Harutoonian, a baby girl believed to have been born in Baku, was brought to the orphanage early in 1917 and years later would become Hagob's wife.

The orphanage not only provided a safe haven and the necessities of living but coordinated its efforts with the local Armenian priest to educate the children. With the help of older orphans and adult volunteers from the Armenian community in Tabriz, the priest and orphanage staff instructed the children in the Armenian language and taught them about their rich cultural heritage, rooted in Christianity since the fourth century C.E. The boys and girls also attended classes in Farsi, English, mathematics, music, and handicrafts such as sewing and carpet weaving, which were taught by local craftsmen. While Hagob did not have much interest in his academic subjects, he worked for hours on end weaving carpets with other children. This activity produced revenue for the orphanage to reinvest after the items were sold in the bazaar and provided the children with job skills and a way to help pay for their care.

Reza Khan toured Tabriz in 1924 following his rise to power, and the children of the orphanage were gathered to sing for his welcoming parade. In 1925 Reza Khan had the last Qajar shah deposed and proclaimed himself shah and founder of the new Pahlavi dynasty. Soon after this event, Hagob moved into a sparsely furnished room with several boys from the orphanage who at fourteen were considered old enough to support themselves. Each boy occupied a *takht*, or wooden bed frame, and owned his own bedding and some clothing. A woven cotton carpet, or *zelo*, covered the bare floor in the room, which was heated on the coldest nights by a wood-burning stove. Bread, cheese, and sweet tea made up the customary meal, and when work was steady the boys bought heartier meals of rice, lamb, and vegetables.

At the age of fifteen, Hagob supported himself by working at small jobs, one of which was unloading goods from carts and the few trucks that made deliveries around Tabriz. Chosen for his capacity to work hard and his great interest in trucks, Hagob became an apprentice truck driver at sixteen. This was a prized position for a young man, as it provided some income, travel, and the opportunity to work around the rare and powerful vehicles that the master drivers piloted across the mountains to Tehran and then south to the Persian Gulf. Hagob Hagobian spent more than a year learning the specifics of the trade from his sponsoring driver in Tabriz. As an apprentice truck driver, he learned to perform daily maintenance chores, load and balance the cargo on the vehicle, and repair the vehicle under varying circumstances. Successfully completing his apprenticeship in 1927, he became a *shagaird-e-shoofer*, or driver's assistant, and began the actual driving portion of his training.

In order to become a master driver, or *arbob*, an individual had to pass a complicated and difficult licensing procedure in which he was judged on his truck-driving skills by an experienced government representative. One of the tests required that the driver maneuver the truck in reverse gear along a figure-eight-shaped path outlined by boulders. Once licensed, the driver proudly wore an insignia that represented his trade.

Hagob began his actual driving practice by alternating driving and resting shifts with his *arbob*, a fellow Armenian, on runs between Tabriz and Kermanshah. While on a layover in Kermanshah, he met a cousin from his home village of Khan-Baba-Khan who joyfully informed him that Hagob's maternal uncle and two of the uncle's five children, as well as a paternal aunt and her three children, had also survived the events of 1916. Fleeing south toward Baghdad through Azerbaijan and Kurdistan in western Iran, they had found calm and safety in Kermanshah, where, familiar with the language and customs, they began their lives anew. Hagob had fortunately found what remained of his family.

In 1933, after passing his driver's test and attaining the status of *arbob*, Hagob made arrangements for his marriage to Arshalous, who was now a young woman of eighteen living with a family in Tabriz, where she sewed to support herself. In a borrowed truck they drove together from Tabriz to Kermanshah, where she was introduced to Hagob's family. At the American Presbyterian mission in Kermanshah, they were married, with their best man, a fellow Armenian truck driver, and relatives in attendance.

Soon after the ceremony, Hagob and his new wife moved to the growing city of Tehran to be near the hub of the trucking and transportation industry of the country. Having no relatives with whom to share a home, as was customary in most Armenian families, Hagob and his wife made temporary arrangements to share rooms with friends from the orphanage in Tabriz who lived in Tehran. Before the birth of a son in 1934, the young couple moved into private rooms located on a narrow *koutcheh,* or alleyway, in an area of the city where some of their neighbors were other Armenian refugees from East Anatolia and Azerbaijan as well as Russian-educated Armenian professionals who had immigrated to Iran following the Bolshevik revolution. This small but growing Armenian community was affiliated with the local Armenian church. Churches became the locus of social interaction and cultural education for many in the Armenian diaspora.

Hagob began driving long-distance hauls between Tehran and the Persian Gulf and soon acquired his own truck through the assistance of his former employer. For an agreed-upon monthly payment made possible by their mutual trust, Hagob took possession of the truck immediately and repaid the debt through the truck's income.

Tehran and the Persian Gulf ports were the focal points of the country's economic activity. Agricultural goods and handicrafts were brought to Tehran from surrounding areas by animals, a small but increasing number of trucks, and Iran's single railroad line. From Tehran these goods were redistributed to other Iranian cities or moved south to the Persian Gulf, to be exported or exchanged with goods and materials being shipped into the country.

In the nineteenth and early twentieth centuries, Iran's slowly growing economy was tied to the European and world markets through the export of cash crops such as cotton, tobacco, sugar, opium, pistachios, raisins, and grain, which were cultivated domestically. Commodities necessary for the development of Iran, such as steel, cement, and machinery, had to be imported from Europe and other areas. The Persian Gulf became the trading ground for these items, as the raw agricultural goods were shipped out and traded for building materials and processed products. Iran's oil, which was granted in concessions to the British government early in the twentieth century, was not yet a major factor in the Iranian economy. It would be decades before it began to play a major role. In the 1920s and 1930s the volume of import/export goods that required transport increased at a steady rate as Iran's economy and infrastructure were developed under Reza Shah. His goals were to move the country swiftly to industrialization and Western-influenced social change.

The economic, military, and political changes that had been occurring elsewhere in the Middle East in the nineteenth century, such as the *tanzimat* reforms in the Ottoman Empire and similar changes in Egypt, did not appear uniformly in Iran until nearly half a century later. There were several reasons for this. One was Iran's geographical distance from Mediterranean and European economic activities. In addition, major powers such as Russia in northern Iran and Britain in southern Iran pursued their own interests in Iran. The later shahs of the Qajar dynasty allowed spheres of influence to exist for the foreigners and independent tribal confederations within Iran. Iran's cohesive Shiite *ulama* were another challenge to the governing powers throughout the nineteenth and twentieth centuries.

The reign of Reza Shah (1925–41) can be seen as a turning point for the modernization of Iran, as the changes brought about during his rule, many of them a reversal of nineteenth-century trends, were indeed far-reaching. The interrelated ideals surrounding the changes that took place included a strong secularist bent, total dedication to the doctrines of nationalism-statism, and a desire to assert Iranian nationalism by a rapid adoption of the material advances of the West and nationalization of foreign concessions. It was during this period that Reza Shah changed the name of Persia to Iran by decree.

In order to adopt the material advances of the West, it was necessary for the country's interdependent economy and infrastructure to grow simultaneously; this became Reza Shah's main agenda during his reign. Because of Iran's large territory (628,000 square miles) and rough terrain, the country badly needed a modern system of transportation and communication. Reza Shah's regime turned to this vital task at an early date. In 1924 the government undertook a complete study of the country's transportation problems, and a list of priorities was drawn up and adopted.

Until this time, neither Iran's single railroad line nor its extremely limited water transport system were sufficiently developed to handle the increasing transportation needs of the 1920s. Thus, the moving of goods from place to place until the end of the 1930s was achieved through the widespread use of trucks, which replaced the ancient mode of land transportation, primarily animal-drawn wagons and beasts of burden such as camels and donkeys. To facilitate motor transportation, the government's main effort went into improving and maintaining the existing roads. By European standards the roads were considered well planned, but their surface conditions and grades were very poor. In 1925 alone, the Majles appropriated over 9,170,000 rials for road construction and repair. In 1926, registration and licensing of vehicles were introduced, with revenue from these measures being designated for road construction. An independent Ministry of Roads, with wide powers and elaborate plans for expanding the country's highways, was created in 1930. Apart from attention to roads, several steps were taken to encourage the use of motor vehicles. These included tariff exemptions for trucks and buses as well as reduced registration and licensing fees for transport vehicles.

The increase in miles of roads and numbers of available trucks greatly reduced the transit time, risk, and associated costs of motor transport. For instance, in 1920, it cost two hundred dollars a ton and required two months to move goods from the Gulf ports of Tehran. By 1929, motor transport of goods was more prevalent, and the same trip took one to two weeks at a cost of fifty dollars a ton. The number of registered motor vehicles in Iran rose from about six hundred in 1928 to over twenty-five thousand in 1942. Miles of roads increased from two thousand miles in 1925 to fourteen thousand miles by 1942.

Hagob Hagobian and his fellow truck drivers independently contracted to deliver cargo. In addition to the paid cargo, truck drivers routinely carried any item that might conceivably be required on a trip. Thus, a truck driver packed authentic and makeshift replacement parts, extra sets of tires, gasoline, food, water, and personal gear.

Trucks and their components were imported from abroad, and there was an acute shortage of all parts. U.S.-manufactured single-cab six-wheel trucks such as Hagob's 1934 International were the industry standard in Iran. The early trucks were especially vulnerable to the frigid air and ice of the mountains, as well as to the desert environment, where heat and sand were brutal on the machinery. When trucks broke down, the men had to improvise ways to repair them, although they had had no formal training. Up to two full sets of spare tires might be needed during one round-trip, due to the ravages of the unpaved roads.

The hijacking of vehicles by bandits and associated violence were commonplace in the Iranian countryside in the 1920s. This continued to be of concern to Hagob and his fellow truck drivers even after Reza Shah largely suppressed such activities in the mid-1930s. Because of the many unpredictable dangers, truck drivers in Iran caravanned in groups, finding strength and security in their numbers. Driving in shifts, the truck crews of two, ordinarily the *arbob* and his *shagaird-e-shoofer,* alternated sleeping and driving eight to ten hours, with the driver at the wheel keeping the other trucks in sight.

The challenging nature of the truck-driving profession in Iran during this formative period necessitated a truck driver's involvement in a guild.

The guild served a variety of crucial needs through a network of shared information and credit based on mutual trust. In the 1930s Hagob became part of a guild consisting of Armenian and Assyrian members, who maintained their ties for decades. He and the others proudly wore their guild's insignia, a jeweler's handcrafted replica of the front portion of a transport vehicle.

In addition to the physical protection that guild members found in the truck caravan, commercial bonds based on a member's spoken word were maintained, through which members could borrow money, parts, tools, and equipment. Vital information regarding the nature and availability of cargo at port, and road conditions, as well as basic communication between drivers and their families, was exchanged in an efficient network of verbal transmissions on the road. Further, guild membership served to limit and keep exclusive the truck-driving ranks and to guarantee the honesty of its members and the safety of the cargo to the cargo owners, thus establishing confidence with them. The guild was also able to help maintain a stable price structure.

Nevertheless, group involvement did not solve all of the problems associated with trucking in its initial stages. Perhaps the greatest danger of the job during an entire trip was the risk of an accident on the precarious mountain switchbacks that had to be crossed to get to and from the Gulf. Many Iranian truck drivers, including some from Hagob's guild, died after having made a crucial error on an ungraded turn, as their overloaded or poorly serviced vehicles plunged down the mountainside.

A haven to which Hagob Hagobian and his driving colleagues could go for rest and some restocking of supplies was the rural teahouse, or *tchai-khaneh*. The teahouses, in effect truck stops, were the former caravansaries, which for centuries had been way stations for travelers and traders in camel caravans. Hagob and his fellow truck drivers paused at the shelters to eat a hot meal, buy supplies, and spend a night before beginning another grueling twenty-four-hour shift. If time permitted, the drivers would enjoy the common pastime of playing cards and *nardi* (backgammon) while drinking tea. Due to the unpredictable hygienic conditions of the *tchai-khanehs* and a general fear of disease and parasites, truckers rarely accepted the rooms and beds that were offered. Instead, they slept in or on top of the trucks, using their personal sleeping gear. This practice also served the function of providing security for the valuable trucks and cargo, which were vulnerable to thieves if the drivers slept elsewhere.

Iranian truck drivers, predominantly Christian Armenians and Assyrians, enjoyed a unique status in the nation as the operators of novel and complex machines. The *tchai-khaneh* owners were Muslims, who, in Islamic tradition, provided a hospitable environment to every guest. Thus, although they came from different religious backgrounds, the *tchai-khaneh* owners and truck drivers formed a trusting and enduring relationship that became an integral part of the transportation industry of Iran.

At a time when these multiple systems of support were becoming efficient and trucking had become profitable, World War II created new troubles for Hagob Hagobian and some members of the Iranian truck-driving industry. As the transportation needs of the occupying forces took precedence over private ownership and private transportation, many large vehicles were impounded for war use. At the onset of the Allied occupation of Iran in 1941, Hagob's truck was being loaded by his assistant in Tabriz while Hagob was visiting his family in Tehran. Aware that trucks were being commandeered by Russian troops, some drivers and their assistants removed the tires and other crucial operating parts in time to avoid their loss. In Hagob's absence, his truck and its cargo were confiscated. His repeated appeals to the Soviet Embassy in Tehran were futile, and he thus lost his only means of livelihood; he never received compensation.

Further complicating his existing problems, Hagob became ill in 1942 with malaria. By mortgaging the family's Persian carpets to the state bank, a common practice in Iran, and with support from his relatives in Kermanshah, his family, which grew in 1943 to include a daughter, survived unexpectedly trying times. Hagob returned to his trucking activities in 1945 with the help of a loan from relatives that enabled him to purchase a dump truck. For the next several years, Hagob transported construction materials to job sites in and around the growing city of Tehran in partnership with fellow guild members. By the early 1950s he had purchased a ten-wheel truck and again began more profitable long-distance hauling to the Gulf. This was becoming a quicker and safer journey with the continued construction of modern roadways.

Again earning a stable income, Hagob repaid his debts and over the next few years began planning and saving for his son's higher education. He took advantage of a program offered by the Iranian government that paid half of the educational expenses for students who passed a qualifying examination and received an acceptance from an accredited university abroad. In 1956, Hagob sent his son to the United States to earn a university degree. In 1964, while still engaged in long-distance hauling from the Persian Gulf to Tehran, Hagob sent his daughter, accompanied by her mother, to the United States to begin her university education. A serious trucking accident near Kermanshah in 1966 necessitated his wife's return from abroad to care for him and forced his retirement. During the next decade, Hagob Hagobian and his wife were visited frequently by their adult children, who had established careers in the United States, but the continual separations were insufferable for a couple who had spent their youth as orphans. Therefore, in 1975 Hagob and Arshalous Hagobian moved to the United States to be with their children's families and resettled in a California community in which Armenians in the diaspora had again established their churches, schools, and cultural centers.

A NOTE ON SOURCES

This essay is primarily based upon interviews with Hagob Hagobian conducted between March and June 1989.

SUGGESTIONS FOR FURTHER READING

For a general history of the Armenian *millet* in the Ottoman Empire, see Leon Arpee, *A History of Armenian Christianity* (New York: Armenian Missionary Association of America, 1946). On the role of the Armenian trading diaspora, Philip D. Curtin, *Cross-Cultural Trade in World History* (Cambridge: Cambridge University Press, 1984). The emergence of nationalism is treated in Louise Nalbandian, *The Armenian Revolutionary Movement* (Berkeley: University of California Press, 1963). On the Armenian massacres and related intercommunal violence, Richard Hovanissian, ed., *The Armenian Genocide in Perspective* (Oxford: Oxford University Press, 1986). For an overview of the history of religious minorities in modern Iran, see Eliz Sansarian, *Religious Minorities in Iran* (Cambridge: Cambridge University Press, 2000).

For some general histories of modern Iran, see Ervand Abrahamian, *Iran between Two Revolutions* (Princeton, N.J.: Princeton University Press, 1982); Amin Banani, *The Modernization of Iran, 1921–1941* (Stanford, Calif.: Stanford University Press, 1961); and Nikki Keddie, *Modern Iran: Roots and Results of Revolution* (New Haven, Conn.: Yale University Press, 2003).

On Iranian economic history generally, see Charles Issawi, ed., *The Economic History of Iran, 1800–1914* (Chicago: University of Chicago Press, 1971); Issawi, *An Economic History of the Middle East and North Africa* (New York: Methuen, 1982); and Homa Katouzian, *The Political Economy of Modern Iran: Despotism and Pseudo-Modernism, 1926–1979* (New York: New York University Press, 1981). Also Malcolm Yapp, *The Making of the Modern Near East, 1792–1923* (London: Longman, 1987).

On the development of Iranian roads and the advent of trucking, see Charles Issawi, "The Iranian Economy, 1925–1975," in *Iran under the Pahlavis,* ed. George Lenczowski (Stanford, Calif.: Stanford University Press, 1978); and Wilfrid Knapp, "The Period of Reza Shah, 1921–1941," in *Twentieth-Century Iran,* ed. Husain Amirsadeghi (New York: Holmes and Meier, 1977).

Chapter 13

Naji: An Iraqi Country Doctor

Sami Zubaida

Like the traditional Jewish communities of North Africa, the Jews of Iraq were predominantly urban and heavily involved in trade and commerce. (In 1947, they numbered 117,100 and constituted 15 percent of the population of Baghdad.) A small minority of wealthy Jewish merchants profited from its international connections and protégé status, while the vast majority of Iraqi Jews lived in poverty—as did most Iraqi Muslims. Through the Alliance Israélite Universelle, the Jews of Iraq were exposed early to modern ideas and thus were able to benefit from the new opportunities that developed in the colonial state after 1919. Arabic-speaking and highly acculturated, the Jews of Iraq were better integrated into their society. Most Iraqi Jews, as most Iraqis, were apolitical. Some of the intelligentsia and craftsmen, however, were attracted to democratic and leftist politics; many others had communalist feelings that translated into Zionist sympathies. Indeed, some were among the leading lights of the Iraqi Communist Party.*

Dr. Naji, the subject of Sami Zubaida's contribution to this volume, was a member of the Baghdadi middle class who was able to take advantage of the British colonial presence to move into the modern professions. Through Zubaida's biography of Naji we come to understand the extent of his integration into Iraqi society, his commitment to the people among whom he lived and worked, and the personal ties and political affiliations that governed his professional choices. Naji's medical career unfolded in a series of provincial postings away from the capital. His upbringing, friendships, and talents helped ensure him a successful career as a provincial doctor.

In Iraq, where large, tribally organized ethnic groups (including both Kurds and Shiite Arabs) coexisted with an urban intelligentsia and a small but radical working class, the ability of the British to play upon traditional interests gave a certain desperate quality to the anticolonial struggle. The fact that the bearers of nationalism, especially pan-Arabism, were Sunni Arabs, whereas the tribal populations were

* Hanna Batatu, *The Old Social Classes and the Revolutionary Movements of Iraq* (Princeton, N.J.: Princeton University Press, 1978).

mostly Shiite Arabs (51 percent of the population in 1947) and Kurds (18 percent), no doubt further increased the stakes and gave a certain lurching quality to Iraqi politics.

By the end of the British Mandate, the marked tolerance of traditional Iraqi society had begun to erode. Not until 1968, when the political atmosphere shifted sharply following a Baathist coup, did things change decisively. A wave of political persecutions and ethnic attacks led to the violent suppression of the Iraqi Communist Party and to the emigration of many Iraqis, including Dr. Naji. —Eds.

Dr. Naji was a Jewish doctor who worked, often under adverse and difficult conditions, in the provinces of Iraq from his graduation in 1936 until the end of the 1950s. Naji was born in 1915, at the start of World War I. Many Jews, especially those educated and qualified, were conscripted. Naji's father, a pharmacist, played his part as an officer in the Turkish army. He was involved in the fighting that raged in southern Iraq between the Turkish and British forces, including the protracted Turkish siege of the British in Kut-ul-Imara. Demobilized after the Turkish defeat, Naji's father ran a canteen/snack bar for the British forces in Amara in the same region. The family was from Baghdad, where the Jewish community, long native to Iraq, inhabited particular old quarters of the city and established themselves as craftspeople, shopkeepers, peddlers, and service workers; there was also a tiny minority of prosperous businessmen, landowners, and bankers and professionals such as doctors, lawyers, and teachers. After the end of hostilities, Naji's family moved back to Baghdad, where they found the population suffering from grinding poverty after the deprivations and shortages of the war years.

World War I was a major watershed in the history of the Middle East. Following the defeat of the Ottoman Empire in 1918, the political map was redrawn by the victorious Allies. The British emerged with control of Palestine, Transjordan, and Iraq; the French with Lebanon and Syria. Under the terms of the Versailles peace settlement, subsequently ratified by the League of Nations, British and French authority were given legal recognition. Under the terms of the British Mandate, the ex-Ottoman provinces *(wilayat)* of Baghdad, Basra, and Mosul were grouped together in the new state of Iraq. Between 1921 and 1932, the new entity was ruled by a "national" government headed by a monarchy, but under British supervision and control. In 1932, Iraq became formally independent, though still under British control and treaty obligations. Not until 1958 was the monarchy overthrown in a bloody revolution.

Under the monarchy, Iraq was ruled by King Faisal, who, having been displaced by the French as king of the Syrian Arab Kingdom in 1921, was installed by the British. In an effort to limit his ambitions and to provide a basis for his rule, the British promoted the power and interests of the heads of the large Arab tribal confederations. These local leaders, the *shaykhs*, had already come to possess as private property formerly tribal and state lands as a result of Ottoman policy, thereby accruing enormous fortunes. These landowners and their nominees became the main force in parliament. As a mandate, Iraq was formally a democracy with an elected parliament. However, elections were generally rigged, and parliaments were often dissolved when they became awkward, allowing the country to be governed by decree. In the 1930s, government revenues came increasingly to depend upon the control of the exploitation of oil resources under the control of the British-owned Iraq Petroleum Company. Tax evasion, especially by the wealthy landlord class, was endemic, and tax revenues were negligible. The regime was corrupt.

Iraqi society under the monarchy was thoroughly politicized, particularly urban society. The opposition especially targeted the corrupt regime and its British masters. There were two broad political streams: pan-Arab nationalism and "Iraqist" democratic forces. The chief force within the latter was the Iraqi Communist Party, generally reputed to be the strongest Communist party in the Arab world. Arab nationalism found its chief support among army officers, who staged a series of coups d'état starting in 1936 that displaced particular cabinets or ministers but did not challenge the monarchy or British domination. The sole exception was the pro-Nazi Rashid Ali coup of 1941, which directly challenged the British by seeking German support. As we will see, this event and the British military intervention that it sparked gave rise to violent attacks on Jews in Baghdad and other urban centers.

Religious and ethnic divisions played (and continue to play) an important role in modern Iraqi politics. An estimated 18 percent of the total population of 4.8 million in 1947 were Kurds, whose struggle for national and cultural rights has constituted a dominant factor in the history of the country to the present day. The 80 percent of the population who were Arabic-speaking were divided along religious lines into Sunni and Shiite Muslims and included small Christian and Jewish minorities. Sunni Arabs, although a decided minority (possibly as small as 20 percent), have always been politically dominant. With the exception of the Kurds, who are Sunni, ethnicity in Iraq has tended to be ethnically coded by religious community. Most Arab nationalists have been of Sunni origin, while most Kurds and Shiite have tended to support Iraqi nationalist solutions and groups. In the 1950s, these opposition forces came together in a common front that cooperated with the Free Officers, who initiated the 1958 revolution. The ensuing regime of Abd al-Karim Qasim was characterized by struggles between Arab nationalists and Iraqists (the latter led by the Communist Party). In 1963, Qasim was in turn overthrown by another coup led by a nationalist officer. From it the Baathist regime of Saddam al-Husain eventually emerged.

This then was the Iraq into which Naji was born. There was never an exclusive "ghetto" in Baghdad itself, although a version of the Ottoman *millet* system had been maintained by the new state of Iraq for the autonomous corporate organization of Christian and Jewish communities. Naji's family settled in a predominantly Sunni neighborhood in an old quarter of Baghdad. Their immediate neighbor was a *mullaya*, a female reader/teacher of the Quran, and the young Naji memorized large portions of the holy book under her tutelage. He attributed his special strength in the Arabic language to this early training, although Arabic (with a peculiar Baghdadi accent) was the native tongue of Iraqi Jews. Later, the family moved to a house in Dahhana, a Shiite quarter. The family was well regarded in the neighborhood, with many friends on dropping-in terms.

Young Naji was sent to a Torah school to learn Hebrew and religion. He learned French at home from his mother, who had been one of the first batch of girls to go to one of the schools of the Alliance Israélite Universelle, which had opened schools in Baghdad and Basra in the late nineteenth century. These schools taught in both French and Arabic, as a result of which sectors of the Jewish community were incorporated into colonially related elites. (A parallel process also operated within the Christian community.) Nonetheless, in Iraq this did not lead to a separation into colonial cultures and languages with different political orientations, as happened elsewhere in the British Empire.

Eventually, Naji was educated at a Jewish primary school close to his neighborhood. His school, like all others, followed a national curriculum. All pupils who remained at school until the appropriate age took the government *baccalauréat* examinations at different levels. Some of those who finished school then proceeded to jobs and careers in government or in private employment, where they worked alongside people from other communities. Some went on to higher education in the newly opened colleges, most notably in medicine, pharmacy, and engineering, but also in law.

Naji enjoyed his childhood as a happy, harmonious period, with wide social contacts in school and in his neighborhood. This harmony continued into his secondary-school experience at Al-Idadiya al-Markaziya, the central and most renowned government school in Baghdad, where many of the later leaders and notables of the country were educated. There, it would seem, the difference of the Jews was implicitly noted and accepted by most pupils, who then made a special effort to emphasize the equality of all in the new nation-state. Jewish pupils were defended, for instance, against any hostility that might arise in the street or in the schoolyard. Yet such hostilities, although sporadic, were still to be expected. A few students avoided or shunned their Jewish classmates, primarily out of religious prejudice.

Naji and his older brother graduated from secondary school in 1930 with very good marks in the official *baccalauréat* examinations, which made them both candidates for entry into the Medical College, considered the highest achievement for graduates. The Medical College was founded in 1927 by the British Mandate government under predominantly British direction and expertise but with increasing Iraqi participation. The intake of students in the early years of the college included many Jews, a fact that led to unease in high quarters. Tacitly, a quota of Jews was introduced. The fact that two brothers applied at the same time was perceived as an undue share of the quota for one family, but their father had connections with British medical authorities and both brothers were admitted.

Naji's college days in the 1930s were marked by an atmosphere of serious dedication to the fledgling Iraqi state among the educated youth and by a sense of common purpose regardless of communal barriers. But as the decade progressed, nationalist sentiments and agitation grew, with an increasing awareness of the Palestine question and the Arab struggles in that country. The development of militant nationalisms in Europe, especially Nazism, was an inspiration to some Arab nationalists in Iraq and elsewhere, especially insofar as it was directed against the British. This accumulation of factors brought the position of the Jews into question. These ideological trends were by no means universal, but they affected an important sector of intellectuals and army officers; this led to various attempted or temporarily successful coups d'état, which were usually thwarted by British interests. Naji experienced changes in the political and social atmosphere in his later years at college, with some professors and students raising questions about the loyalty of the Jewish students, sometimes in whispers and sometimes openly. But the Jews also had their defenders, who maintained comradely relations and held on to the ideology of common citizenship.

Naji graduated in 1936. There followed a period of training in different medical branches. This was marked by rivalry among graduates for entry into the more desirable branches of the profession. Naji got on very well with the British specialist in ophthalmic surgery, with whom he spent eight months. During this time, the surgeon came to rely on him a great deal, both in the conduct of operations and in the organization of work schedules. This close relationship was resented by more senior doctors in the field, who agitated against such a young man being entrusted with serious responsibilities. When his patron went on leave for a few months, Naji's detractors took the opportunity to oust him from that department and push him into radiology, regarded as an inferior and undesirable specialty.

Naji did not settle there. The medical establishment seemed rather disorganized and lax, and Naji was able to frequent the department of general surgery, where he made himself useful and where the senior staff assumed that he was allocated to them. He would make an appearance in the radiology section for one or two hours a day, then slip into surgery. While doing this, Naji continued his efforts to be allocated officially to a desirable branch but failed. He approached another British eye specialist, who immediately asked his religion and discouraged him when he learned that Naji was a Jew. A Scottish bacteriologist was very welcoming but could not fulfill his promise of an attached post. When the training period was over, Naji was posted to his first appointment.

Admission to medical education in Iraq entailed a contract with the government for five years' medical service. The graduate doctor could be posted anywhere in the country. Baghdad and the other major cities held the most desirable posts, generally allocated to those with family connections and influence in the right quarters. The socially weakest and poorest, including most Jewish graduates, ended up in the remote country areas with the least amenities and entertainments and the most poverty and disease.

The Jewish country doctor became a regular feature of the Iraqi scene in the 1930s and 1940s. A number of these country doctors, including Naji, remained in this form of service long after their compulsory contracts expired. Many pressures kept Naji in government service. His ultimate objective was to travel to Britain for further training and specialization. Financial limitations and family commitments led to constant postponement of this action. Lack of finances was also an obstacle to setting up private practice in Baghdad. In the late 1940s, things became difficult, and the government sought to prevent doctors from leaving the service by issuing a decree forcing those who resigned to practice where they last lived. It was also thought at the time that an official position would provide exemption from arbitrary arrest and political persecution.

Naji's first appointment was to Hashimiya, a small town on the Euphrates near Hilla, about a hundred kilometers south of Baghdad. He was put in charge of the small public health center (*mustawsif*) there, manned by three medical orderlies/nurses (*mudhamiddin*). He felt utterly overwhelmed by the sheer magnitude of poverty, deprivation, and disease that he found among the tribal and peasant population. There was a great array of diseases. Naji reflected philosophically that working in a place like Hashimiya taught a young doctor more than many years of experience would have taught him in a wealthier environment. The most prevalent disease was chronic malaria. Another was bilharzia, which when left untreated led to terrible degenerations like cancer of the bladder. Naji examined so many patients with cancer of the bladder that he could diagnose it just by the feel of the particular spot when he pressed it.

Being the only doctor in the area, Naji also had to do police forensic work such as performing autopsies. Given the tribal custom of the blood feud, which prevailed and was tolerated by the authorities, there were frequent occasions for such work. Naji was also required, in this and in subsequent postings, to supervise the other health centers in the district, which were operated under *mudhamiddin*. To that end, he undertook regular tours, sometimes traveling in difficult terrain to places that could be reached only by horse or mule. Work had to be accomplished under primitive conditions, with poor equipment and inadequate supplies of even the most essential medicines, including anesthetics. Up to six hundred patients a day presented themselves for treatment. Yet there were no facilities for surgery, and even simple cases of hernia had to be referred to Hilla, the provincial capital, which had a hospital. Cancer cases were hopeless.

Poverty was the ally of disease. Naji wished he could feed his patients rather than just treating them. Most of the population were sharecroppers working the land of their tribal *shaykh*. The terms of their contracts left them with little to eat, and they were always deeply in debt. Public health measures were so rudimentary that Naji's duties included the supervision of spreading crude oil over stagnant water lagoons as a measure against malarial mosquitoes.

The terms of employment of a provincial government doctor allowed him to engage in private practice in his spare time. Under these conditions, Naji had no spare time. He was still expected by local notables, landlords, and officials to attend to their medical needs, for which he may or may not have been paid. At this stage, he could not open a private clinic, although he managed this later in his career.

Naji spent three or four years in the province of Hilla. He was temporarily transferred from Hashimiya to Hindiya to replace another Jewish doctor who had been drafted into the army. He returned to Hashimiya, and then finally went to a permanent posting in Hindiya until January 1941, when he was transferred to the town of Hit in another region on the Middle Euphrates. As a government doctor, Naji took his place in the society of officials and notables of the town and the region. At the top of the hierarchy was the subprefect (*qaim maqam*) of the town. (The prefect, or *mutasarrif*, lived in the provincial capital.) While the doctor was responsible to the local health directorate, which in turn answered to the ministry in Baghdad, the prefectures had considerable say in matters of health policy, premises, and facilities, so Naji also had to deal with the local bureaucracy.

Officials, as well as professionals and technicians such as engineers, shared a particular status and social life in the province, centered upon the Officials' Club (Nadi-al-Muwadhafin). This is where those so inclined would meet afternoons and evenings, chat, play games, and drink. Naji was part of this circuit, although, he recalls, he had little time to engage in these diversions and he did not gamble or drink. Local notables would hold banquets for the high-ranking officials, which would have included the doctor: in terms of protocol, wherever the subprefect was invited, the doctor too would be included, on occasions ranging from public ceremonies on national days to weddings in notables' households. More routinely, a servant would cook

Naji's meals or bring him cooked food from a local restaurant. For some of his time in the Hilla region, his brother, also a doctor, was posted in the nearby town of Diwaniyya, and he would occasionally spend the night there. On public holidays and leave periods, he would go to his home in Baghdad.

Many parts of provincial Iraq included small Jewish communities among their populations. There were Jews in the Hilla province, mostly in Hilla itself. A few were merchants and landowners (although these latter tended to move to Baghdad and appoint managers to run their estates). Most were poor peddlers and craftsmen, while a few were teachers and local officials. Naji did not socialize with the local Jews. He had not made a conscious decision against it, but they were simply not his kind of people. He said of the Jews of Ana (a later posting) that they were like the local "Arabs." ("Arab" in that context meant bedouin or "native" and was used in that sense by all urbanites.) They dressed and talked and lived like other locals, and as such they were very different from Baghdadi Jews, especially the intelligentsia. As an educated man and an official, Naji had much more in common with Muslims and Christians like himself. The only provincial Jews with whom he had regular contacts were those employed by the health service, like Murad the Jew, who was the driver of the official car. Others included medical orderlies, nurses, and midwives.

Naji recalls a young Jewish girl who worked as a midwife in Hindiya. She was from a poor family, with a blind father, and it was her pay that kept them. Her mother would always accompany her on emergency calls outside the town. One night she and her mother accompanied Naji to attend to a difficult childbirth. They cleared all the people and the animals from the room but missed a lamb who was hidden in the shadows. Naji used forceps to pull out the baby, and as his head emerged the lamb bleated, at which the young midwife jumped in horror and shouted to her mother outside that the woman had given birth to a lamb!

Naji was an energetic and attractive young man, devoted to his work and patients, and he was warmly regarded by colleagues, subordinates, and patients, as well as by the local notables. He was a relatively high-ranking government official, and one on whom many people depended for their lives. Although he was Jewish, his professional persona and his personal qualities predominated. Shiite Muslims (the dominant religion in that region) observe certain taboos on contacts with non-Muslims, who are considered ritually unclean. Yet, in the many years of his life in Shiite regions, Naji regularly treated patients, frequently shared people's food, and even slept in their houses, only encountering the observation of that taboo on rare occasions with unusual individuals. He was sought out, and occasionally entertained, by religious dignitaries as well as other notables. Once, during an epidemic, for example, Naji encountered difficulties trying to secure premises for quarantine. The landlord of the designated house tried to renege on the deal at the last minute. To obtain the key, Naji had to be very firm and exert his full authority, to the extent of slapping the man. This was not unusual conduct in the circumstances, but Naji was surprised at his own behavior: "I was a government official," he reflected. "I forgot that I was a Jew!"

Violence, like poverty and disease, was a regular feature of life in the provinces. The "code of honor" and the blood feud were prominent principles. This was recognized by the new Iraqi state in its enactment of a "tribal law," which embodied customary codes and as such was lenient regarding "crimes of honor." Naji recalled receiving hospitality from a *shaykh*, whom he found to be a most kind and genial person. When relating his impressions to some local people, they informed him that the same *shaykh* had the year before slaughtered all four of his daughters because he had heard that one of them had chatted and laughed with a young man.

On occasion, Naji was put under considerable pressure from powerful quarters to act against the regulations in ways that would leave him liable and vulnerable. This arose particularly over the issue of death certificates. In Hindiya, a powerful local *shaykh* asked him to issue a certificate for one of his tribe who, he claimed, died of cancer. The *shaykh* would not present the body, on the grounds that it was already on a train on the first lap of the journey to Najaf, where it was to be buried. (Shiite Muslims who are able to do so bury their dead in the holy city of Najaf.) Naji insisted on examining the body before issuing the certificate and persisted even after the intervention of the *qaim maqam* (subprefect). In the end, the body had to be produced: the man had been shot at close range in the stomach. The story then was that the man had shot himself to escape the severe pain of his cancer. Naji, in his persistence, was mindful of the example of a Christian colleague in another area, who had been similarly approached while gambling at the club. He had readily agreed to issue a death certificate without examining the body, only to be confronted later by relatives of the deceased, who contested the specified cause of death and had the body exhumed to show that the man had been murdered.

While discrimination against Jews did not affect Naji in his daily work and life, at least not in the Hilla province, it was present in his official dealings with the Ministry and the Directorate of Health both at the provincial and central levels. As the 1930s progressed, there was increasing discrimination against Jews. The Ministry of Health was more thoroughly penetrated by pan-Arab nationalists and, at that time, Nazi sympathizers, than most other government departments. For Naji and other Jewish doctors, this meant confinement to the less desirable provincial postings, slow promotion in terms of salary increments, and almost a complete barrier against promotion to consultant or specialist ranks. This also meant barriers to any further training. Naji's great ambition was to travel to Britain for further training and specialization. The constraints of his contract, finances, and then the Second World War prevented the realization of this ambition.

While in Hindiya, Naji wrote numerous reports urging the establishment of a hospital in the town, and his campaign was ultimately successful. He worked hard at establishing the hospital and equipping it, but soon after he was posted to Hit, in western Iraq. This region was very important in the events of 1941. It is the part of Iraq nearest to Syria, which was the center of pan-Arab nationalism. Until the latter part of 1941, Syria was governed by Vichy France, with a governor noted for his pro-Nazi sympathies. As such, it was a center for Nazi propaganda and covert military aid to rebel movements with those sympathies. The predominantly Sunni Arabs of the western region were more open to pan-Arabism than their Shiite compatriots, since the rest of the Arab world is mainly Sunni. For all these reasons, the region was to be an important stage for the Rashid Ali revolt of 1941, which had distinct pro-Axis elements and culminated in a massacre of Jews in Baghdad. It was a dangerous place for a Jewish doctor.

Hit was another small town with a health center (*mustawsif*). Soon after arriving there, Naji had to cope with an outbreak of smallpox in an outlying tribal area. He alerted the authorities and established a quarantine around the affected areas, forbidding movement out of the boundaries, but the order was difficult to enforce. All infected persons were confined to a quarantine house, where they were treated. Inadequate facilities and medicines led to a death rate of about 30 percent of those affected. Naji embarked on a vaccination campaign around the area and ultimately succeeded in containing the outbreak. He did all this in addition to his normal duties. When the doctor in the larger nearby town of Ana was drafted into the army, Naji was ordered to take over there. He left the Hit center in the charge of a medical orderly and spent the months of the troubles in Ana.

The months of April to June of 1941 witnessed the height of the crisis in Iraq. The Rashid Ali government refused to extend the facilities for military movements that the British authorities claimed were required by treaty obligations. The British air base of Habbaniya was surrounded by units of the Iraqi army. The pro-British regent (for the child king) and his entourage left Baghdad. The British Middle East Command drew up plans for a military campaign against the "rebel" government. Hostilities broke out in May, leading to a brief and unequal war in which British air strikes played the decisive part. British forces reached the outskirts of Baghdad in the first days of June. These were the days of the breakdown of order in Baghdad and the unleashing of the anti-Jewish pogrom known as *farhud*, in which several hundred lives were lost and many atrocities committed. It ended with the reestablishment of order under a British-controlled government and the return of the regent. These were the most dangerous months for Naji.

At that time, Ana was a town obsessed with the war and with the national struggle that became so firmly linked to it. Nazi sympathies were common among the intelligentsia and the notables of the town but had also spread to the common people. There were a few exceptions among people known as Communists or as British sympathizers. Anti-Jewish sentiments were common but, for the most part, restrained. The local Jewish community was well integrated into the bonds of neighborhood and custom of the town and was usually protected. All the same, one Jewish teacher in the town decided to go to Baghdad on leave.

Naji himself was received politely but not always warmly. He received the warmest hospitality from traditional religious households, to the extent of being a regular guest at the Thursday night *dhikr* parties of one such house, where he enjoyed the Sufi religious ceremonial with music and chanting. His staff, nurses, and porter (*farrash*) were loyal. The *farrash*, especially, brought him intelligence as to what was happening and was generally protective.

The most vociferous protagonist of Nazism was a schoolteacher of Syrian origin. Naji would give the occasional lesson in health care at the local school, and on one occasion he received a visit from the teacher and his class at the health center. The attention of the teacher was attracted by a nail in the wall with a piece of string attached, which he proceeded to examine closely, telling the pupils that this must be a wireless device for transmitting intelligence to the British forces. Such suspicions and accusations were common during this period, and it was only the firm intervention of the *farrash* that prevented a hostile reaction. On another occasion, Naji was called in the middle of the night to attend the body of a murdered woman. He found a young Jewish woman stabbed in the chest, her young child crying. The rest of the household had fled. Eventually, the killer was arrested, a teenage boy from the school whose modern nationalist ideology had moved him to transgress the traditional neighborhood bonds.

One time, six wounded guerrillas were brought to the health center for Naji's attention and had to be kept there until they had sufficiently recovered. Naji discovered that they were part of the volunteer force of Fawzi al-Qawuqji, a Syrian commander who would eventually be killed in Palestine in the first Arab-Israeli war. He had brought his forces of Syrian, Palestinian, and Iraqi volunteers to the aid of Rashid Ali in his struggle against the British. With the imminent defeat of their ally, they were retreating toward Syria when they were hit by British air strikes. Naji cared for them like he would have any other patients, maintaining a professional detachment. Eventually, Fawzi himself came to Ana, and when visiting his men he hesitated visibly before shaking the hand of the Jewish doctor to thank him. Toward the end of this period, Naji felt himself to be under real threat. Sitting in a café one evening he heard a local police officer taunting his companions for tolerating a Jewish doctor in their midst and expressing mock surprise that he was still alive. Naji conspired with his *farrash* to steal the ignition key of the subprefect's motorcar as an emergency measure to facilitate escape in case of attack. Fortunately, the attack did not come.

In the meantime, Naji was very worried about his family in Baghdad. Communications were difficult even at the best of times. The local post office manager, a keen supporter of Rashid Ali, was nevertheless sympathetic to the plight of the Jewish doctor and aided him in establishing telephone contact with neighbors of his family in Baghdad, who were unharmed. Naji's sentiments similarly blurred ideologies when it came to personal friends. After the defeat of the rebellion, the restored government carried out retribution against rebel cadres. One such figure was a medical colleague and friend of Naji's, who when pursued by the authorities received shelter in the Jewish doctor's quarters until the storm passed over and he was able to return to Baghdad.

Another of the dilemmas Naji had to face in Ana during this period was over the *mutasarrif*'s (prefect's) attempt to requisition the premises of the health center for his own use. Fearing the threat of British air attacks, the prefect abandoned his quarters in Ramadi. Unable to reach Baghdad because of flooded roads, he took refuge in Ana, and he considered the health center premises to be the most appropriate place for his temporary residence. Naji successfully resisted this attempted invasion of the busy center and the dislocation of patients and activities it would cause. But he was later to regret this victory. After these events, back at his post in Ramadi, the prefect punished Naji by sending him to a desert outpost on the Syrian frontier, Rutbah, where he was to stay until the end of the war.

Rutbah was a British army outpost guarding a crucial frontier crossing and the oil pipeline to Haifa. The garrison also supervised the construction of a military road to connect Baghdad to Haifa and included a depot for the servicing and repair of motor vehicles and tanks. It included two small hospitals, one military, one civilian (for the workers on the projects). Naji supervised the civilian hospital. The military hospital had British military doctors, but they were frequently shifted around in accordance with war needs and Naji also worked there when required. Naji was responsible to the British military command as well as to the health directorate in Ramadi. He was given a small house near the civilian hospital but did not feel secure there, so he moved into a room in the hospital. He shared mess privileges with the British officers.

Naji felt isolated in this desert outpost, which had the added disadvantage of not providing any scope for private practice, a factor that was to become more and more important for his livelihood. At the same time, however, Naji found the British forces diverting and the company of British colleagues stimulating. He observed the interactions and conflicts between Sikh and Gurka troops with the local Arab population and what seemed like the eccentric religions and customs of strangers.

In Rutbah, Naji had to cope with a typhus epidemic, to which he himself fell victim. The commanding officer decided to send him home to Baghdad and provided a military car to take him there. After a difficult journey through the desert, sedated with morphine, he arrived home in a very weak state. He took to bed for several weeks in the care of his parents. When he recovered, he felt weak and depressed and decided to resign his post. The director-general of health in Baghdad called Naji to his office and cajoled him into withdrawing the resignation, giving him an immediate promotion in terms of salary grade, the first he had been offered in all his years of service, and promising a future posting to a more desirable center. Naji went back to Rutbah, but the posting to Ramadi, the provincial center, was not to come until near the end of the war in 1944.

In Ramadi, Naji was in charge of surgery at the hospital in addition to general medical duties. At first, there was only one other doctor in the public service. Naji was under enormous work pressure but managed to run a private practice, which was a matter of increasing financial importance. At this point, Naji was contributing most of his income to the family budget, partly for saving but most importantly to support a sister studying medicine in Egypt and his elder brother, who was now studying in Britain for eye specialization. The idea was that both would return to work in Iraq and then be able to support Naji's further study in Britain. This was not to happen.

After World War II, political crises and popular upheavals followed one another in close succession in Iraq. The clique of politicians around Nuri al-Said, through whom the British had grown accustomed to rule, continued to dominate the official political life of the country. But it experienced growing difficulty in controlling an increasingly politicized society. Mounting economic difficulties, inflation, and unemployment at home were compounded by momentous events in the region that heightened national sentiment. In 1947–48, there occurred the United Nations' partition of Palestine, the declaration of the state of Israel, and the first Arab-Israeli war. In 1956, following the failed tripartite intervention aimed at deposing Nasser and reestablishing British control over the Suez Canal, the prestige and appeal of Nasser reached new heights throughout the region. Through all of these events, the Iraqi government remained publicly loyal to Britain. Anti-British demonstrations on a grand scale erupted in January 1948 against a proposed military agreement with Britain known as the Portsmouth Agreement. Hundreds of demonstrators were killed by machine-gun fire. Faced with a near-popular insurrection, the government fell, and the Regent abandoned the treaty. Repression was intensified, including notably the public hanging of three prominent Communist leaders. Martial law was established later that year on the pretext of Iraqi participation in the fighting in Palestine. A further crackdown against the opposition was instituted.

The events leading up to the partition of Palestine and the foundation of the state of Israel in 1948 had negative consequences for the Jews of Iraq. There were threats of another *farhud*. Zionist societies and circles were eventually uncovered, which provided the pretext for unleashing a campaign of arrests and persecution of innocent Jews on charges or suspicions of Zionism and Communism. The two were conveniently equated to facilitate the campaign against Communists and leftists at the same time. Jewish public servants faced added harassment, if not sacking. In 1946, at the beginning of this period, Naji received an order posting him to Rawanduz, a remote center in the Kurdish mountains of the northeast. On this occasion, he was able to mobilize the intervention of a recent prefect of Ramadi who liked him, as well as that of the new British consul in Baghdad, an acquaintance from the Rutbah days whom he met by chance in the railway station in Mosul. The order was eventually withdrawn and Naji returned to Ramadi.

The following years, from 1947 until the termination of his government appointment in 1955, were to be particularly difficult for Naji. In Ramadi, he had to work under an antagonistic Egyptian director of health. Jealous of Naji's success in private practice and exploiting his vulnerability as a Jew, the director wrote adverse reports on his work as well as inciting local thugs to harm him. All of this was reported to Naji by a patient, an Armenian carpenter working in the house of the director who overheard his machinations. On the night of the declaration of the state of Israel, Naji had to take refuge with friends in Habbaniya. The hostile director's efforts succeeded later in 1948, and Naji was posted to Abu Skhair, a small town in the south. The irony of the situation was that the same director of health was himself transferred to take charge of the province of Diwaniyya, where Abu Skhair is located, and Naji was again in danger. His petitions to the Directorate of Health in Baghdad eventually succeeded in getting him posted to another small town, now in the province of Amara, in the southeast.

The disadvantages of these small-town postings were not only isolation but also loss of income from private practice. At this point, Naji needed the money badly. Most Jews were preparing to leave Iraq under a policy by which Jews could renounce their Iraqi nationality and eventually travel to Israel. Jews who registered under this policy were to have their assets sequestrated under a new decree issued after they registered. The result of these events was the collapse of property prices in Baghdad as Jews scrambled to sell whatever they could. Naji's father had invested the family savings, including Naji's, in building a house, which was no sooner completed than it had to be sold at an enormous loss as part of the family's plan to leave Iraq. Naji was left penniless.

A combination of factors prevented Naji from resigning. There was a regulation, introduced shortly before, that stipulated that a doctor who resigns a public post can work only in the town to which he had been posted, in this case a small town with little prospect of work. At the same time, a government post, however precarious, was judged to provide some immunity against official persecution. Naji feared that were he to resign, he would be framed on some charge of Zionism and Communism and imprisoned. At this point, he was also barred from travel outside Iraq and his passport was withdrawn.

The Amara director of health, on a visit to Naji's outpost, realized his potential and offered him the temporary post of surgeon in Amara itself, a populous provincial center. Naturally, Naji was delighted. He threw himself into work at the hospital and built up a thriving private practice. These happy days were to be short-lived, however, terminated by the appointment of another director who had been Naji's junior at medical college and who proved to be a dangerous enemy. The aim of this new director was to curtail or end Naji's successful private practice, which rivaled his own, and to try to get him transferred yet again to some small town. But in the meantime the director exploited Naji's vulnerability as a Jew for his own private profit.

The director forbade Naji to conduct any operations except at his order. He would then only authorize operations for which he had obtained an unofficial and illegal fee. He also contrived to put Naji on night emergency duty at the hospital continuously for six months, at the same time expecting him to perform all his other medical and surgical tasks. He attempted to drive Naji to resignation by withdrawing all the night-duty facilities: first food, then the bed, then other furniture. He then resorted to charging Naji with holding Zionist/Communist meetings at his house. Only the intervention of an honest prefect saved Naji from arrest and investigation. Finally, he succeeded in having Naji transferred back to his previous small-town outpost of Ali al-Gharbi, where he remained for one year. During that time, Naji enhanced his reputation further among the local population by performing difficult operations without hospital facilities, sometimes on the patient's own bed at home, with a high success rate.

Naji's final episode of public service was the campaign against a particularly virulent disease, bejel, a kind of syphilis that is not sexually transmitted. Bejel had to be treated with penicillin injections. Naji was put in charge of the operation in the marshes region of southeast Iraq, centered in Amara, but spent most of the time traveling the desolate region by car, motorboat, canoe, horse, and donkey. This post was to occupy the years of the early 1950s until the termination of Naji's appointment in 1955, on a charge of being politically undesirable.

After that, Naji decided to spend a few weeks resting in Amara before traveling to Baghdad. During that time, he was inundated with crowds of private patients demanding treatment. He had acquired a reputation in the area of being a miracle worker. This induced him to stay in Amara until further troubles at the end of the 1950s forced him to go to Baghdad, where he conducted a thriving private practice until the next Arab-Israeli war in 1967. The aftermath of this war and the Baathist regime inaugurated by a coup d'état in 1968 combined to make life for the Jews very difficult. A wave of government terrorism spread in the country, and the Jews were specifically targeted. Mass arrests, torture, and public hangings (on spying charges) culminated in the exodus, legally or illegally, of the few remaining Jews via Iran in 1970 and 1971. Naji was among those arrested, but his reputation and contacts saved him from the violent fate of the others. Naji left Iraq in 1970.

A NOTE ON SOURCES

This account is based primarily upon extensive interviews with Dr. Naji (not his real name), who is now living in London. They were corroborated and supplemented by interviews with other Iraqis who knew him personally or by reputation.

SUGGESTIONS FOR FURTHER READING

The most important book on modern Iraqi history is Hanna Batatu's monumental *The Old Social Classes and the Revolutionary Movements of Iraq: A Study of Iraq's Old Landed and Commercial Classes and of Its Communists, Ba'thists and Free Officers* (Princeton, N.J.: Princeton University Press, 1978). See also Peter Sluglett, *Britain in Iraq, 1914–1932* (London: Ithaca Press, 1976). On contemporary Iraq, see Marion Farouk-Sluglett and Peter Sluglett, *Iraq since 1958: From Revolution to Dictatorship* (London: I. B. Tauris, 2001).

For an anthropological study of the Iraqi countryside in the period, see Robert Fernea, *Shaykh and Effendi: Changing Patterns of Authority among the El Shbana of Southern Iraq* (Cambridge, Mass.: Harvard University Press, 1970). On the women of El Shbana, Elizabeth Fernea, *Guests of the Sheik* (New York: Doubleday Press, 1965).

For a history of the Jewish community of Iraq by one of its members, see Nissim Rejwan, *The Jews of Iraq: 3,000 Years of History and Culture* (Boulder, Colo.: Westview Press, 1985).

1. Assaf Khater. Courtesy of the Khater family.

2. Mohand N'Hamoucha. Photograph by Lawrence Rosen. Used with permission.

3. Shaykh Muhammad
Ibn Abi al-Qasim of al-
Hamil, Algeria. From
Octave Depont and
Xavier Coppolani, *Les
confréries réligieuses
musulmanes* (Algiers:
Jourdan, 1897).

4. Shaykh Izz al-Din al-
Qassam. From *Before
Their Diaspora: A
Photographic History of the
Palestinians, 1876–1948*,
with introduction and
commentary by Walid
Khalidi (Washington,
DC: Institute for
Palestinian Studies,
1984, 1991).

5. M'hamed Ali, a Tunisian worker. From Zin Abd al-Din al-Sinusi, *Ketab al-janat* (Tunis, 1925), p. 48, consulted at the French Archives, Nantes, 1er versement Tunisie no. 2171. Photograph and retouching by Roger Haile. Used with permission.

6. Hagob and Arshalous Hagobian and their son. Courtesy of the Yaghoubian family.

7. Migdim, a bedouin
woman. Lila Abu-
Lughod/Anthro-photo.

8. Medhi Abedi and
Michael Fischer.
Photograph by Susann
Wilkinson.

9. Haddou, a Moroccan migrant worker. Photograph by David McMurray.

10. Abu Jamal and his grandson, Muhammad at Netanya Beach, 1986. Photograph by Joost Hilterman.

11. Khanom Gohary at the woman's collective, Tehran, 2004.

12. Talal Rizk and his wife, Lily Delgado, Jeddah, 2004.

PART THREE

Postcolonial Lives

Chapter 14

Migdim:
Egyptian Bedouin Matriarch

Lila Abu-Lughod

Around 1800, bedouin pastoralist tribes constituted 5 to 10 percent of the population of the 3.5 million or so Egyptians. They inhabited a wide area, ranging from the Western Desert to the Nile Valley, even including portions of the Delta. The bedouin played an important economic role in the trade that linked Egypt with Bilad al-Sudan (Land of the Blacks) in the interior of Africa, as well as with the Muslim states of the Maghrib. Powerful bedouin tribes like the Hawwara and the Hanadi were greatly feared by peasants and villagers for their depredations of agriculture.

During the nineteenth century, as a result of the deliberate policy of Muhammad Ali (who ruled Egypt from 1807 to 1841 on behalf of the Ottomans) and his successors, the Egyptian bedouin were gradually sedentarized. Proud bedouin *shaykhs* were gradually transformed into a rural gentry owning vast estates, while their tribesmen became (not without some resistance) agriculturalists. A centerpiece of the changes introduced in the nineteenth century was the government-mandated switch from production of subsistence crops to long-staple cotton for the world market. The bedouin played an important part in the peasant revolts against these changes in the 1820s and 1830s. But by the end of the century, their violence curbed, the bedouin had become a somewhat discontented, but relatively docile, part of the rural population.

By the late 1970s, the life of the Awlad Ali, a bedouin people to the west of Alexandria, bore but a scant resemblance to that of the tent-dwelling pastoral nomads depicted in such films as *Lawrence of Arabia*. By then living in scattered villages along the coastal road that leads to the Libyan frontier, the Awlad Ali had long since abandoned their camels for Toyota pickups, although some remained herders until the 1950s, even to the 1970s. Yet, as Lila Abu-Lughod shows in her portrait of Migdim, one of the Awlad Ali, the bedouin have not lost their sense of cultural identity. Because their sense of self is linked not to way of life but to genealogy and a code of morality emphasizing honor and modesty, their sense of themselves remains intact.

Most accounts of life among the bedouin are based upon the work of male anthropologists, who because of the social conventions of bedouin society have lacked access to the private world of the family. The view they have provided us of bedouin society is inevitably limited to the public arena of trade, politics, and religion. Yet androcentric views alone are clearly inadequate if we wish a fuller understanding. One of the great merits of Abu-Lughod's contribution to this volume is that it breaks with this tradition. Through Migdim, a bedouin matriarch with whom Abu-Lughod lived between 1978 and 1980 and again in 1986, we acquire an understanding of bedouin life from a female perspective. It is a life full of surprises, one that breaks more than a few stereotypes about Arab societies and Arab women.

It is particularly interesting to compare Migdim's story with Julie Oehler's account of Bibi Maryam, another tribeswoman. (See also the other portraits of women in this book.) If we keep the focus on tribal peoples, Migdim's life can be compared to Rostam, a Qashqa'i rebel portrayed by Lois Beck, and Mohand N'Hamoucha, a Middle Atlas Moroccan Berber profiled by Edmund Burke. —Eds.

On a quiet day toward the end of 1979, I asked Migdim whether she would tell me her life story. She said, "When you get old you think only of God, of prayer, and of the oneness of God. What happened has passed, you don't think about it. You don't think about anything but God." And she refused to say any more. Then, as now, the only decoration on the walls of her one-room house was a faded black-and-white photograph behind fingerprinted glass. It showed her as a younger, upright woman, standing proudly next to her eldest son, both wearing the distinctive white clothing of Meccan pilgrims.

She was busy in those days. Although she was bent nearly double and walked only with the help of a stick, she had the many social duties of a world where the mutual visits of relatives are the stuff of social relations. As the matriarch of one large family and the oldest sister of another, she was expected at many weddings, sickbeds, and funerals, as well as at feasts to welcome home those who had been released from prison or had returned from the pilgrimage to Mecca. Even when she was at home she was always busy with something—spinning, winding wool into thread, sewing burlap sacks together to patch the old summer tent, seeing to the goats, giving advice, or bouncing a grandchild on her lap.

By the time I returned in 1986, exactly seven years later, she could hardly stand up any more and could not walk except to go out to the bathroom or to do her ablutions for prayer. She had more time for me then, since her sons were gone most of the day and the women and girls in the camp had their chores and were not always free to sit with her.

When I asked her to tell me her life story or any girlhood memories, she said, "I've forgotten all of that. I've got no mind to remember with any more." But then she went on, "We used to milk the sheep. We used to pack up and leave here and set up camp out west. And there we would milk the goats and milk the sheep and churn butter and we'd melt it and we'd put the clarified butter in the goatskin bag and we'd cook wheat until it was done and we'd make dried barley cheese."

She laughed, knowing how formulaic this "story of her life" was, but that was all I got from my direct questions. Yet, as we sat together over the next few months, many tales of her life and the lives of those around her came out. For her, like the other women I knew in this bedouin community, the convention of "a life" with a trajectory made little sense. Instead, there were memorable events, fixed into dramatic stories with remarkable details. I have put together some of these stories to try to convey some sense of both what her life has been like and how she constructs it for others, especially the daughters-in-law, nieces, and granddaughters who surround her.

If there is any convention of telling women's life histories among the Awlad Ali bedouin I knew in Egypt's Western Desert, it is the capsule summary offered when someone asks about a woman she has just met or heard about for the first time. Women say, "She's from such and such a family, and a man from such and such tribe married her and she had two sons and three daughters." These three facts of a woman's life define some crucial circumstances: where she lives and what kind of support and standing she has in the community and, more important, who matters to her.

I have honored this convention in the stories that follow, stories about Migdim's marriage and her efforts to shape her large family's destiny. Her complicated relations with the sons so desired by women in patrilineal societies suggest the tensions between the ideals of a system and a woman's experiences over a lifetime. What she struggles over with them, as well as what she keeps alive through story memories, suggests to us too what the twentieth century has meant for a desert community that lived by herding sheep. Her life and that of her family have been shaped by how they coped, first with the aftermath of the battles of European armies during the Second World War, and then with the Egyptian government's land reclamation projects. A life, even a woman's life defined by marriage and children, is always located in time and place.

One of the most vivid of Migdim's stories was the tale of how she resisted marriages her father tried to arrange for her. I even heard more than once, almost word for word, the same account of how, over fifty years ago, she had ended up marrying Jawwad. I first heard it one evening that winter, in the presence of her sons' wives and some of her granddaughters. The first person to whom she was to have been married, she explained, was a first cousin. His relatives came to her household and conducted the negotiations and even went as far as to slaughter some sheep, the practice that seals the marriage agreement. But things did not work out.

"He was my father's brother's son," she said, "and I didn't want him. He was old, and he lived with us. We ate out of one bowl. His relatives came and slaughtered a sheep and I started screaming, I started crying. And my father had bought a new gun, a cartridge gun. He said, 'If you don't shut up, I'll send you flying with this gun.'

"Well, there was a ravine, and I went over and sat there all day. I sat next to it saying, 'Possess me, spirits, possess me.' I wanted the spirits to possess me, I wanted to go crazy. Half the night would pass, and I'd be sitting there. I'd be sitting there, until my cousin Brayka came. And she'd cry with me and then drag me home by force, and I'd go sleep in her tent. After twelve days of this, my cousin's female relatives were dyeing the black strip for the top of the tent—they were about to finish sewing the tent I'd live in. And they had brought my trousseau. 'I'll go get the dye for you,' I said. I went and found they had ground the black powder and it was soaking in the pot, the last of the dye, and I flipped it over—pow! on my face, on my hair, on my hands, until I was completely black.

"My father came back and said, 'What's happened here? What's the matter with this girl? Hey you, what's the matter?' The women explained. He went and got a pot of water and a piece of soap and said, 'If you don't wash your hands and your face, I'll . . .' So I wash my hands but only the palms, and I wipe my face, but I only get a little off from here and there. And I'm crying the whole time. All I did was cry. Then they went and put some supper in front of me. He said, 'Come here and eat dinner.' I'd eat, and my tears were salting each mouthful. For twelve days nothing had entered my mouth.

"The next afternoon my brother came by and said to me, 'I'm hungry, can you make me a snack?' I went to make it for him, some fresh flat bread, and I was hungry. I had taken a loaf, and I put a bit of honey and a bit of winter oil in a bowl. I wanted to eat, I who hadn't eaten a thing in twelve days. But then he said, 'What do you think of this? On Friday they're doing the wedding, and today is Thursday and there aren't even two days between now and then.' I found that the loaf I was going to eat I'd dropped. 'Well,' he asked, 'do you want to go to so-and-so's [to seek refuge] or do you want to go to your mother's brother's?' I said, 'I'll . . . ,' but then it seemed as if there was an eclipse, the sun went out, and nothing was visible. I said, 'I'll go to my maternal uncle's.' I put on my old shoes and my shawl on my head and started running. I ran on foot until I got to my uncle's. I was in bad shape, a mess."

She complimented her uncle's wife, who had taken her in,—"May God have mercy on her, she was a good woman"—and explained to the man what the problem was. But her uncle sent her back the next morning, with instructions to his son to accompany her and to deliver greetings to her father and to ask him to oblige him, as he had comforted his niece. If he were to postpone the wedding, perhaps she would come around. Migdim continued: "So I went home. After that I didn't hear another word. The trousseau just sat there in the chest, and the tent—they sewed it and got it all ready and then put it away in their tent. And autumn came, and we migrated west, and we came back again. When we came back, they said, 'We want to have the wedding.' I began screaming. They stopped. No one spoke about it again."

Grandma Migdim continued her story with two more episodes of attempts to arrange marriages for her until she accepted one. When she remembered how her husband's family had come to ask for her hand, one of her granddaughters interrupted, "And Grandma Migdim, did you eat and drink at that engagement?" She answered, "Yes, I ate and drank." But then, as if to guarantee her virtue by assuring us that she had not had any special desire for this man, she continued, "Although I swear by my soul, that it wasn't in my thoughts nor was it in his. Not at all. It was his father who'd seen me when I was young. I was energetic and really smart. He'd say, 'That girl, if only my son could have her.'"

One of her daughters-in-law commented, "Bread and salt were running between you." She was referring to the notion that God wills certain people to share meals, that is, to live together. Migdim agreed, "Yes, it was bread and salt."

Migdim had seven children who lived, four boys and three girls. Her four sons and their families now made up the "camp" (once tents but now houses) that was her community. One daughter had married a neighbor and so also lived close by. The other two had married into other families and lived elsewhere, coming for visits on special occasions like weddings and illnesses and at the major religious feasts. Once as she watched a group of her little granddaughters playing from her doorway, Migdim sighed, "Little girls are nice. This one goes to get water, that one helps you. But in a week they can leave you, and their place will be empty. . . . Daughters aren't yours. When they marry that's it—they stay with their families and that's that. They leave you with nothing. But boys, they stay." Her daily life, as a result, revolves around her sons, their wives, and their children and even grandchildren.

Giving birth to children can be memorable, and Migdim had her own stories of childbirth to tell. There were no doctors around in her day, and she even maintains that, unlike most women, she did not like having other women around to help her when she gave birth. Of her fourth child, a son, she says, "I gave birth to him alone. I had no one with me but God. We were out west, inland from Alamein. That day I did the wash. I washed up everything. . . . In the morning I had washed my hair and braided it with henna and cloves. I cooked too—a pot of rice with yogurt sprinkled with some butter from the goatskin bag. . . . My sister-in-law and my husband's aunt were visiting and they asked for lentils. So the other women started making some bread and cooking the lentils. It got to be sunset—the days were short that time of year.

"Jawwad had gone to sleep in the tent, taking the two older children. . . . I went to sit with the old women for a while as the girl cooked the lentils. My little boy fell asleep in my lap, so I said 'I'll go put my son to bed.' They said, 'Stay until we eat supper, then we'll all go to bed.' I said, 'I'll come back soon. But if I don't come, it means I don't feel like eating.' We'd had something to eat in the afternoon, and in those days people didn't used to eat much.

"I went off to put the boy to bed. I got three cramps while I was putting him down. Well, I didn't come back for supper. I circled around the tent, tightening the guy ropes. They called to me, 'Come have dinner, come have dinner.' The sun had gone down, and they called out, 'Come have dinner.' But I didn't want any. I scooped out a hole in the sand and went to sit by it. I brought out a straw mat and a donkey's burlap packsaddle, and I put them down and sat on them, outside by the corner of the tent. When the labor pains hit me, I'd hold onto the guy rope's tension bar. One hand between my legs and one holding on to the rope above. The sheep came home after sunset, close to the time of the evening prayers, just as the child was coming out. . . . When the child broke through I lifted myself up by the pole, lifted my clothes up until the child dropped.

"When my sister-in-law came out to pee she heard. She ran into the tent and told the women, 'Migdim has given birth!' They came running. 'Where? Where?' they asked, and I told them, 'The child has a forelock [a boy]. The child with its forelock dropped.' So they lit a fire and wrapped the boy, and they moved me inside. They cooked a pot of *asida* [a special food for new mothers] that night and made tea. And Jawwad was sleeping near us, in the corner, and didn't wake up. The women had set up a compartment for me in the middle of the tent. He was sleeping with the children in the corner and didn't wake up.

"In the morning my mother-in-law slaughtered a chicken and was cooking it for me over by the hole I'd made. A woman neighbor of ours come over. 'Poor dear! When did she deliver? Why just yesterday she was doing the wash, and there was nothing wrong. Poor thing!' I tell you from the minute the old woman said, 'Poor thing'—God protect me, God protect me—I was seized by cramps. Something (may it be far away from you), something rang in my ears. And something covered my eyes so I couldn't see. I prayed, 'There is no god but God, there is no god but God,' until my mouth went dry. That was all the woman had said when they had to come running. Something blinded me, blinded me and knocked me out. My mother-in-law came and started moving my head, she made me sniff a burning rag. Well, I tell you, I didn't taste that chicken she was cooking. I never even saw it. I have bad cramps after I give birth. My cramps are bed then.

"I delivered my other children alone," she added. "I had no one with me but God." When I asked her why, she answered, "The women laugh and they talk and they bother you. You'll be as sick as can be, and they'll be making a lot of noise around you. I don't like them." When I asked if she would also cut the umbilical cord herself she said, "No, after the baby has dropped they come. They come and they cut the cord." Then I asked why they say that the woman who has just delivered is close to God. She laughed at my piece of knowledge. "Yes, they say it. By God it's difficult. Ask the woman who has given birth, ask her about death. She has seen it."

Death is not something people like to talk about. In fact, whenever women tell stories about bad things that have happened to people they interject phrases like "May it be far from you" or "May it only happen to enemies." Migdim was still sad about her brother's recent death. But she had lost other dear ones. Her husband, Jawwad, had died young. She connected his death to the death of his younger brother, killed by an exploding mine about seven years after what they knew as "the war between the Germans and the English." This kind of death was not uncommon after the battles of the Second World War had ended and the armies departed. In their desperate postwar poverty the bedouins had survived by scavenging scrap metal. They used the Arabized English term "to rubbish" for this activity.

Migdim did not like telling this story. When I asked one day how this younger brother-in-law of hers had been killed, her answer was brief. "We had migrated out west that spring. He went rubbishing riding on a donkey with a friend. I didn't believe he was dead because when he left the camp he had been heading east. And he had money—he had no need to go rubbishing. But he ran into friends who persuaded him to go. They came across a mound and found a bomb. The other man started taking it apart. My brother-in-law said, 'I won't work on it.' But instead of moving far away, he sat near him. The man kept trying to take it apart, but it exploded.

"The bomb exploded and killed the man. He flew, who knows where he landed. Who knows where it threw him. But my brother-in-law, all that came his way was a small bit, it landed (may it be far from you), landed in his chest. That year part of the family was camped near the train station at Alamein. They hadn't come with us. People brought him to them at night, in a car, and he died that night. They brought him in a car from the desert, from the camp of the man who had been rubbishing.

"We had all migrated from here and had set up camp way up in the desert south of Alamein. Someone soon came—the one who brought us the news came in the morning. He ran into the camp shouting his name, told us that he had died and was at the camp in Alamein. When he told us we jumped up and began running northward. My sons were young then, and they started running on foot, so I put on my belt and started running with them, wailing. We found everything in chaos. People came from everywhere. I found him all wrapped in a blanket and wailed his name.

"When Jawwad went in to see him, he shuddered. He told me, 'I trembled, and something pounded me from head to foot.' . . . He got sick, Jawwad, and he remained ill after the death. Ill for a year. And then a year after his brother had died, Jawwad died. And the old man, their father, died between them in the month of Ashura.

"My younger son wasn't very old then—he was still small. But he sang about his kinsmen who had died: 'He took away those around you, o eyes, despair hasn't been easy on you.'"

As her older son now describes it, this dangerous business of scavenging occupied many people after they returned to their territory from the camps in the Nile Valley to which the English had evacuated them during the war. He explains, "After they drove the Germans out, the English left. Then the Arabs could return to their territory. They went back as soon as they could. But they found that the armies had left the area of the battles covered with mines and bombs and big guns that had not gone off. We found hand grenades, some that had been tossed but had not exploded, some that were untouched. They had left everything: mines, broken tanks, cars, even whole garages with their dead in them. For six or seven years they were collecting their dead."

Migdim's niece tells the same story of those early days after the war. Their wells had been destroyed, they had lost much of what they had. And they had not been able to plant barley for their bread. They had nothing. "When the Germans came to Alamein the English stopped them. They pushed them back. So we came back to our land. We found the world in chaos. There were broken airplanes, ruined cars, and broken big guns. And big tins of biscuits. We used to find spoons and forks, rope, nice shoes, and burlap sacks from the sandbags. And nice bottles, nice little glass bottles. We used to collect them. White and green and red. Just lying around.

"The boys would collect them and sell them. And there were tires, you wouldn't believe the new tires! They used to carry them off on camels and go to sell them. Later there was the work in iron. The flints of big guns. They started gathering that, iron. And the copper, it was everywhere. They began collecting that. . . . But the bombs, they got aluminum from those. At the time it was worth a lot. So they started digging in the ground to get out the mines. They would collect four or five detonators, five or six detonators, and they'd take them far into the desert. Then they would light a fire and set them off. They would explode. When they'd cooled, they'd come and collect the stuff and sell it. Many of them got hurt. There are poems about that."

Migdim's son elaborated. "Dealers from Alexandria and Cairo came to buy the copper, one kind yellow and another red, and the gunpowder. . . . People would go into the desert in cars and on foot, any way they could.

One time someone would pick up a mine, and it would explode in his hands. Another time someone would touch a bomb, and it would explode. Another time someone would try to undo a detonator to get out its cartridges or gunpowder, and it would blow up. Then five or six people would die together. It became like a war—explosions all the time. . . . A car would stray from the track, and a mine would go off and blow it up with whomever was in it. It was like a war." He estimates that at least twelve thousand bedouins have been killed through these accidents. To this day, people and camels are being killed by unexploded mines they accidentally set off, even though no one works in scrap metal anymore. Reflecting on this period, he concludes, "Some people got rich. People got rich, but it destroyed families."

After the deaths of her husband, brother-in-law, and father-in-law, Migdim's sons found themselves forced to take responsibility for the family. They had to get themselves back on their feet after the devastations of the war. And as an important family, they had a reputation to uphold. There were many decisions to be made, and Migdim was usually consulted or informed about family affairs. Her sons, when not traveling, spent their evenings with her, chatting together in her room by the light of a kerosene lantern. They also often stopped in during the day when they found themselves free. Her youngest son was the most affectionate in the days I was with them. Even as a forty-year-old man, he often came to sit close to her on the mat, stretching his legs out to tuck them under her blanket. Her sons were relaxed in her company, and as they had all gotten older, they were usually solicitous of her needs. They trusted her to run things in the household, among the women. She organized much of the work that needed doing, and she distributed the goods they brought home, from food to dress fabric.

Migdim, however, often complained about her sons. They sometimes made her angry—when they would not take her advice, when they put themselves in danger by getting involved in arguments with other families, when they made bad decisions about women. For example, she recounts that she had refused to sing or ululate at the marriage of one of her daughters. "I was opposed to it. It was against my will," she asserted. Her brothers had agreed to give her in marriage to her first cousin, although Migdim felt she was too young. And when the girl kept running away and hiding under a straw mat in the goat pen, her mother didn't tell the groom's family where to find her. The marriage ended in divorce after a few years and no children.

She also often got angry with her sons for their behavior toward their wives. Her daughters-in-law often came to her with their grievances. If she thought her sons were indeed treating them unfairly or poorly, she would speak to the men. On the other hand, her daughters-in-law praised her for being discreet about conflicts that arose between women of the community; she was careful not to involve the men in these. Most of her daughters-in-law recognized how often she took their side and looked out for them in situations in which they had little say.

As her sons got older and wealthier, they began to take second and even third wives. In her day it had been rare for men to have more than one wife. It was still unusual, except for those who were rich and important. She yelled at her sons each time they decided to marry again, even as she recognized that men wanted to marry women so they could have more sons, men to make the family strong. One evening when one of her sons half-jokingly remarked that if death did not beat him to it, he would build a new house and get another wife, she had a fit. "You idiot! Bringing together many women is no good. Look at your household. Everything is left spilled, everything's a mess. That's because you have too many women. Each one says, 'It's not my responsibility. I won't pick it up. Let someone else do it.'" She had objected to his decision to marry a third wife and had even done her best to discourage the woman from marrying her son. She did not succeed that time, although she had managed earlier to dissuade the parents of another girl her son had wished to marry. She had told them he was a difficult man and that he already had two wives and too many children.

Her youngest son married a second wife after his first wife suffered several serious illnesses and miscarriages and was forbidden by the doctor from having any more children. When he started spending time at the household he set up for his new wife, away from his mother, she complained to everyone about how miserable she was. She moaned that it was terrible to be alone, not to have a man in the house any more; no one to say good morning to, no one to say good night to, no light in the men's guest room. But the women teased her about this. How often, they demanded, had her own husband, Jawwad, slept at his mother's house?

It was not just because her sons paid less attention to her when they married new wives that she objected. She was protective of the mothers of their children, the women who had been there for years, and of the children themselves. This complex mixture of jealousy and protectiveness toward her daughters-in-law and grandchildren figured clearly in a conflict Migdim had with her sons in the summer of 1987—a conflict over land.

A small family that had lived in their community for over thirty years wished to build a new house. The head of the household, now an old man, had come originally to help herd their sheep and goats but had since saved up for a sizeable herd of his own. He and his wife, who was the strong one in the family, had a modest house built on the property of their host family, quite close, in fact, to Migdim's small house. It seems they wanted a little more land to build on, and they wanted title to the land so they could feel secure that their sons could remain there.

Trouble simmered for weeks as the younger generation of boys and young men, Migdim's grandsons, worried about giving away family land that would become scarce. There were at least thirty boys in the family—where would they all build when they married? She supported them in this. When her sons came to consult her, she told them not to give over the land. Yet they went ahead and tried to beat up their own sons for threatening one of the old shepherd's sons. Migdim was furious. The day after it happened she ranted about her older son. "He's not my son, and I'm not his mother! . . . My son should respect my wishes. . . . He's my son. He came out of me. What could be closer to me? Yet he goes and signs it over to that family when I said not to. By the Prophet, isn't that wrong? Seeing how I said not to?"

This was obviously not just an argument about a piece of land. Nothing in this community can ever be an isolated incident, not when everyone has lived together so closely for so many years. For Migdim, this matter concerned the women's community, and particularly her relationship to her neighbor, the shepherd's wife. About eight years earlier, the woman's youngest daughter had become Migdim's eldest son's third wife. Just a few weeks before the incident over the land, this young woman had decided to go against the usual arrangements for the sharing of domestic work among the wives, grown daughters, and daughters-in-law of the household. Her husband had agreed that she could separate from the others and begin to cook and bake just enough for herself and her five small children. She claimed the work load was too heavy for her and that it was unfairly split. Her withdrawal had been discussed a lot in the women's community, defensively by the other two wives, who feared being blamed for having been unfair, and angrily by Migdim and the mother and sisters of the man's senior wife (who was also his first cousin), not to mention the other women in the community, who took sides with the older wives.

Migdim had been opposed to the marriage in the first place. When she was informed that he had arranged the marriage while she was away visiting her sick brother she blew up, insulting her son and calling him names. His first wife was his first cousin. She had not wanted to marry him yet had stayed and produced a line of sons. She was like a sister to him, and they had long since ceased sleeping together. His second wife was someone he had fallen in love with, the daughter of a shepherd's family that had lived near them for a while. He had longed for her. As his mother reminded him one day when he was complaining about the lousy bread she baked, he had raved, in the days before he married her, about how delicious her bread was—and that was before they had white flour, when they used only coarse brown barley. Migdim sympathized with both these wives, but especially with this good, simple woman. Her son was mistreating her by not buying her a proper gift of gold to match what he had gotten for his new bride. That is a senior wife's due.

A couple of months after he had married this eighteen-year-old girl, he stopped by his mother's house, trailed by several of his little children. They played with him, but he soon tired of them and sent them off. Migdim complained about the number of children in the community. She criticized her son because his children had just accidentally killed a small goat they were playing with and she had only barely rescued a lamb from them. Four of them had climbed on its back to get a ride. She counseled her son, "A holy man said the man with many wives will go to hell. If he doesn't treat them exactly alike, if he brings something to one and not the other. Even if he looks at one and not the other. It's a sin, sin, sin."

Her son just laughed and said, "No, it's the one with only one wife who's going to go to hell." But his mother was just getting started. She went on to complain about the amount of gold he had bought for his new wife. "The old woman just buys, and you pay." The least he could do was buy his senior wife a little ring or something. "Shame on you," she said. Again he laughed and said, "Gold isn't everything." Then Migdim started in on the problem of having so many children. Who is going to feed them? Where will they all live? Her son responded with a religious line: "He who created them will provide for them. Every being on this earth is born with his God-given livelihood. God will provide for them." She muttered and grumbled, but her son just laughed.

If the conflict was over loyalty to kin versus generosity to longtime friends, over new wives against old, and exacerbated by the jealousy of an aging matriarch steadily growing weaker, the crisis was also one about land itself. Land was becoming scarcer and more valuable now that the Egyptian government had begun to reclaim desert land through irrigation projects. What had been good only for growing rain-fed barley or for grazing sheep could now be planted with other crops, especially fruit orchards, which were beginning to bring in much more money than herding. The government had also decreed that all the land held by Awlad Ali bedouins had to be purchased formally in order to secure title. It was now all becoming private property and the disputes over it had riven the whole bedouin community. The trouble with land, unlike a herd, is that it does not increase. That is why Migdim's grandsons were so worried.

By the late 1980s, Migdim's sons, like most wealthy bedouin, had shifted almost completely away from herding sheep and into other economic activities, including agriculture. These changes have had many consequences for the community, especially for women's day-to-day lives. When Migdim reminisces about what the area was like for most of her life, she is nostalgic. All of it, she describes, was sown with barley and wheat, so that in the spring, if there was rain, it turned green and there was no place to set up the tents. They would leave to migrate west to Alamein with the herds. There they milked the sheep and stored up enough butter to last the whole year. Speaking of the past generation, she commented, "The old ones had been blessed, really fortunate. They were happy. They had camels and sheep. They lacked nothing. . . . My sons, though, they say the old ones did the wrong thing [by sticking with herding]. But all that we have is due to them. The government came and took their land, and so these young men had to buy it from the government. This business of agriculture they're now in, may God release them from its troubles."

They had planted their land slowly. Migdim had brought a few cuttings from her father's olive trees (he was one of the few in the area to have planted olive trees, following the advice of and taking cuttings from the local British administrator). They had watered them and they grew. But the olive orchards that now take up much of their land were planted around 1960, when an Egyptian man who worked for the government came and told them he wanted the land to build a house on. They didn't want to give up what they considered their land, of course, and they heard that if the land was planted, no one could seize it from them. So day and night they worked, digging holes in the daytime and planting trees from Migdim's father's orchard by night. In fifteen days they had planted the whole orchard, with the help of many neighbors, relatives, and friends, and had surrounded it with high posts and barbed wire. When the government people came to inspect the land they found it all planted and so said the man could not have it. Migdim remembers that day well. The man left in his car, and Migdim's sons, on horseback, followed him all the way back to town, firing their guns into the air in celebration of victory. It was the first time a bedouin had won a land claim against the Egyptian government.

Migdim's one-room house sits, like most of the rest of the "camp," on a ridge that affords a wide view of these olive orchards, their new fig and guava orchards, and the scattered clumps of houses that extend to the horizon. There are so many people and houses now. She remembers when it was empty; nothing between here and her relatives' houses. This crowding means that the girls no longer go off to gather firewood—because there isn't any—and their trips to get water are short because their kinsmen worry about the girls passing by so many houses of people from outside their tribe and encountering at the tap so many others who are strangers. Migdim and the other older women bemoan this loss of freedom for women.

When she gets together with other women, she often rails against the younger men of the community for being so strict about the movements and behavior of their young sisters, cousins, and wives. "The boys are terrible now," she began one such conversation. Her daughter agreed, "The boys are terrible. I swear by my father we have one son who's black in word and deed. And he's so young." A visitor added, "Why, when we were young, remember, we used to go off to herd the goats on our own. Not any more!"

Migdim's daughter continued, "Yes, that's how things were, may God have mercy on past generations. They weren't like this new generation. . . . The men now are awful."

Migdim's attitudes are contradictory. She defends her granddaughters and grandnieces and even her daughters-in-law when the young men, and sometimes the older ones, criticize them or accuse them of talking to men or going places away from home. But then she complains that the young women of today have no modesty. When she was young, she claims, they used to veil with heavy black shawls, not today's flimsy pieces of cloth that do not even hide women's faces. When a great-granddaughter of hers comes in crying because she has lost her hair clip, Migdim scolds her: "It's shameful for girls to wear hair clips. Why do you want a hair clip? Are you wanting to get married?"

Yet the world she remembers is one in which behavior that would now be considered scandalous was perfectly accepted. For example, Migdim thinks wedding celebrations have lost their appeal. She tells her newest daughter-in-law that they used to celebrate weddings for a week with evenings of singing and dancing. "Weddings now are like a shrunken old man," she comments. At weddings in the past, young women, including her husband's sisters and nieces, had danced veiled, in front of semicircles of young men who serenaded them. Young men and women had always exchanged love songs at these weddings. "Stuff that couldn't happen now!" they agree, thinking of the sex-segregated affairs that weddings have become since they settled into houses.

Traces of that older world are kept alive in the women's world, with the older women remembering together and the younger ones listening to these tales of what would now be scandalous. Most of Migdim's time is spent with women. If she is feeling alright, able to sit and to eat, she always has the company of the members of her household—the two daughters-in-law whose husbands no longer sleep with them, and their children, including one young man who has recently married his cousin and had a son. Her great-grandson is a joy to her. Whenever he comes into her room she greets him warmly, as she does all her little grandchildren and great-grandchildren, "Welcome, welcome, welcome!" A chubby blond boy, he has become steady on his feet and wanders around her room getting into things.

One of her favorite games is to call out to him, "Come here, my little Kafy. Come gimme some snuff. I want to sniff some snuff. Where's the wild parsnip?" He toddles over to her, lifting up his robe so she can pretend to sniff his little penis. She pretends to sneeze, the way one does when one has taken snuff. This is outrageous behavior, but old women can do what they want. A visiting granddaughter is shocked. "What a black scandal!" she says. She teases the toddler, "Go put on your underpants!" But Migdim laughs and does it again. She sings to the boy, too, holding his hands in her own, wrinkled and tattooed, teaching him to clap. She often sings old lullabies to him, songs about little boys who grow up to ride horses, carry guns, and become tribal leaders. These are songs the younger women do not know.

Migdim is getting old and her health is not good. She is diabetic but does not know what to do about it except to avoid rice and fried foods. When she has a fever, cries because her head hurts or her eyes burn, loses her appetite, or is unable to sit up, everyone in the community comes to see her. Sometimes her daughter moves in with her, to bathe her, feed her, and wash her clothes for her. As she feels better, the mood lightens. All day her room will be packed with women and children who disappear or go quiet when one of her sons comes in. Otherwise, even if her grandsons or great-nephews stop by to chat, things are lively.

The conversations, especially among older women, can get quite bawdy. Once when I was there with my tape recorder, the women entertained Migdim with old folktales about the sexual desires of old women. They laughed at the shamelessness of such women, and perhaps at themselves, these women with grown sons, mostly widowed or divorced. There is something disturbing in the hostility between mothers and sons these tales convey, something that hints at the ambivalence of that important relationship.

I missed the beginning of the first story Migdim's daughter-in-law was telling. "A man asked his elderly mother, 'Mother, do you want me to get you a husband?' She said, 'No, no, my son. That would be shameful. No, that's shameful.' But he said, 'No, no. He'll keep you company.' So she said, 'May God grant you success if you do. If you do it, may God bless you.'"

The storyteller laughed and went on. "He went off and killed a hyena. He killed the poor thing and wrapped him in a white shroud. and he brought him to her—she was blind—and he put him down next to her and said, 'Mother, be careful. His name is Hasan. He's sleeping now. Don't wake him up, he was up late last night. Let him wake him up on his own first. And don't move him. Let him sleep until he's slept enough.' And he put him down next to her and left.

"She started shaking him, trying to wake him up—her son was nearby, even though it was evening, and she assumed he had gone—she tried to wake him up. She said to him, 'Hey handsome! Hey handsome! Sit up, handsome. Look, here's a jar and here's another jar. There are some more as well that are hidden.' She was talking about jars she had filled with gold and buried. She had buried them all over, and she was showing him, the hyena, as her son watched!"

This reminded Migdim of another story; she called up a few lines from it, and Migdim's daughter-in-law picked it up. "She would always say, 'May God grant you success, if only.' Anytime he talked to her she said, 'May God grant you success, if only.' He went and asked someone, 'Why does my mother only say, "May God grant you success if only." What is this "if only"?' He was told she wanted a man. 'If only' means only if you bring me a man."

Migdim laughed hard as she listened to the story. It continued, "So he went to her and said, 'Mother, I've gotten you a man, and he says you should come. I'll take you to him.' She said, 'Fine, let's go.' He went and put her in a hyena's lair. It was rainy and cold. He put her in the lair and left her there. When she heard the wind in the night whistling and going *oooh* and *rrrr*, she thought it meant that this was this was the night of her wedding and that she was going to get married. Soon her groom would come to her.

"Well, he came to her. The hyena wanted to eat her." Migdim interrupted, "Yes, he started eating her." Her daughter-in-law continued in a high voice, imitating the old woman but laughing as she tried to finish, "'Ooh! By God, by God, the groom is licking and stroking, licking and caressing me.' He was actually tearing her apart."

As they all laughed, one of the young women listening, Migdim's granddaughter, burst out, "Damn these bedouin stories!" Again imitating the old woman, her mother-in-law repeated the old woman's words,

"'The groom, he's licking and caressing!' He tore at her and bit her until he ate her up! (May it be far from you!) She assumed he was really her bridegroom, curse her! He came in the morning, her son, and found her dead."

Her daughter-in-law went on, "Shame on him." Migdim filled in the beginning of the story. "Her son had gone everywhere with her and done everything for her, but still she would never say to him, 'May God grant you success.' All she'd say was 'If only.' So he put her in with the hyena. 'I'll bring you an old man,' he said. 'And here is his house.' 'His house?' she'd said, 'God grant you success my son, God grant you success.'" At this point Migdim remembered my little tape recorder, resting discreetly near her, and laughed, "Lila's machine is working now, taping our words." Then she chanted a rhyme to it:

> A pity, you who this cap belongs to
> A pity, you who this cap belongs to
> A pity, you who this cap belongs to
> They said you were a man among men
> He died without me laying eyes on him
> A pity, you who this cap belongs to.

The caps of red felt were the standard dress of the older generation of bedouin men. Migdim explained the story that went with this rhyme to the excited questions of the women gathered there. They had never heard it. "Here's what it means. The old woman is lamenting the old man. Her son is a joker! He was teasing her. He said to his mother, 'I found'—what he found was a cap, a cap in a room on the floor—and he brought it to her and said, 'I found you a husband, but as we left the market he dropped dead. This is his cap!'" The other women exclaimed, "What a bastard! A joker!" Migdim laughed too as she finished, "So she started lamenting: 'Woe is me, such a pity . . .'"

My tape went on for a while, recording the laughter and repetitions of the rhyme, the comments on the son that he was a bastard, a real joker, and one woman's comment, "Hey, if he'd said the old man was alive, she would have gone off to look for him!" One by one, the women sighed, chuckled, and got up to leave. They had things to do—cooking, baking, weaving, washing, taking care of children.

Migdim is almost blind now, despite the eye operation she had many years ago, and she always has to ask whether it is time for prayers. When I am there I tell her by looking at my watch. "Yes, it's after three o'clock, time for afternoon prayers," I say now. She positions herself to face southeast, unrolls her prayer rug in front of her, and without standing, because she cannot, she begins her prayers. When she finishes, she feels around under her blanket until she finds her prayer beads. She starts counting off on them the names of God. As she folds up her prayer mat she ends, as she often does, with "Praise be to God. Praise be to God. May God keep evil away from us. May God keep weddings going forever among Muslims. May God always bless Muslims with celebrations."

She is happiest at the weddings of her many grandsons. Whatever disappointment or anger she sometimes feels toward her sons seems to disappear as she sings songs praising them as fathers of these boys. At the last wedding in the community she sang a song that placed her where she wanted to be: at the center of her family—

> May they always be blessed with happiness
> the sons of my sons with me in their midst.

A NOTE ON SOURCES

This life story has been adapted from my book, *Writing Women's Worlds: Bedouin Stories* (Berkeley: University of California Press, 1993). Migdim (a pseudonym) was one of several women I came to know well over the years I lived, visited, and did anthropological fieldwork in a small Awlad Ali bedouin community in the Egyptian Western Desert. My initial fieldwork in 1978–80 was funded by the National Institute of Mental Health; subsequent long stays in 1986 and 1987 were supported by a Fulbright Islamic Civilization Award and a National Endowment for the Humanities Fellowship for College Teachers. I am grateful for this support as well as for the generosity of the bedouin families who took me in.

SUGGESTIONS FOR FURTHER READING

Those who would like to know more about the Awlad Ali bedouin community of which Migdim is a part may read my book *Veiled Sentiments: Honor and Poetry in a Bedouin Society* (Berkeley: University of California Press, 1986), and a more recent article exploring the transformations it is undergoing, "The Romance of Resistance: Tracing Transformations of Power through Bedouin Women," *American Ethnologist* 17, no. 1 (1990).

There are several good studies of the bedouin in other parts of the Arab world, but very little specifically on bedouin women. Yet, the excellent and fast-growing literature on Middle Eastern women touches on many of the issues raised by Migdim's life, and especially her complex relationship with her sons. A good place to begin is Hilma Grandqvist's *Marriage Conditions in a Palestinian Village* (1931–35; reprint, New York: AMS Press, 1975). Fatima Mernissi's *Beyond the Veil* (Bloomington: Indiana University Press, 1988) offers a harsh view of the effects of these mother-son dynamics in urban Morocco.

For more on women in Egypt, see Evelyn Early, *Baladi Women of Cairo: Playing with an Egg and a Stone* (Boulder, Colo.: Lynne Rienner, 1993); and Beth Baron, *The Women's Awakening in Egypt: Culture, Society, and the Press* (New Haven, Conn.: Yale University Press, 1994).

For other narratives of women's lives in the Middle East, see Nayra Atiya, *Khul Khaal: Five Egyptian Women Tell Their Stories* (Syracuse, N.Y.: Syracuse University Press, 1982); Fatima Mernissi, *Doing Daily Battle* (New Brunswick, N.J.: Rutgers University Press, 1988); Erika Friedl, *Women of Deh Koh: Lives in an Iranian Village* (Washington, D.C.: Smithsonian Institution Press, 1989); Elizabeth Fernea and Basima Bezirgan, eds., *Middle Eastern Women Speak* (Austin: University of Texas Press, 1977); and Boutheina Shaaban, *Both Right and Left Handed: Arab Women Talk About Their Lives* (Bloomington: University of Indiana Press, 1991).

On women and gender issues in the Middle East there is abundant literature. On the role of women in Islamic history, see Leila Ahmed, *Women and Gender in Islam* (New Haven, Conn.: Yale University Press, 1992); and John Esposito and Yvonne Haddad, eds., *The Daughters of Abraham: Feminist Thought in Judaism, Christianity, and Islam* (Gainesville: University of Florida Press, 2001).

More easily accessible are collections like Lois Beck and Nikki Keddie, eds., *Women in the Muslim World* (Cambridge, Mass.: Harvard University Press, 1978); and Nikki Keddie, *Women in Middle East History: Shifting Boundaries on Sex and Gender* (New Haven, Conn.: Yale University Press, 1992).

For women in the contemporary Middle East, Laurie A. Brand, *Women, the State, and Political Liberalization: Middle Eastern and North African Experiences* (New York: Columbia University Press, 1998) is helpful.

Chapter 15

Rostam: Qashqa'i Rebel

Lois Beck

What is the place of national minorities in the contemporary Middle East? The question is important, because many Middle Eastern states include large ethnic, tribal, linguistic, and religious minorities. In Ottoman times, religious minorities were afforded a measure of protection as *dhimmis* by Muslim doctrine, while ethnic, tribal, and other minorities could exist as fellow Muslims without threat to their way of life as long as they accepted the authority of the sultan.

In an age of nation-states this social complexity was later found to be vexatious. Here, the nationalist fiction of ethnically uniform societies clashed with the protean complexities of the real world. Homogenizing national education programs, which sought to turn all citizens into Moroccans or Iranians or into Turks or Arabs, were perceived as a threat by minorities who were attached to their own traditions. But the plethora of potentially competing nations within each of the Middle Eastern states constituted a possible challenge to the national unity and was therefore perceived by governments as subversive.

Anthropologist Lois Beck's portrait of Rostam, a Qashqa'i tribesman of southwestern Iran, poses the question sharply. Beck's intimate knowledge of the Qashqa'i spans more than two decades, including two periods of research among them since the 1978–79 revolution. Her encounter with Rostam provides us with an understanding of the fluid and sometimes conflictual relations between the Iranian state and the tribal minorities and with a glimpse of the shifting alliances of underground and exile politics in the 1970s.

The youngest son of a Qashqa'i nomad, Rostam found himself propelled into opposition to Muhammad Reza Shah's government when Rostam's father was killed by an army officer. Rostam was initially motivated by a desire to take revenge for his family, but his feelings later evolved into a more broadly based ideological commitment. His growing commitment brought him into contact with Kurds and other minorities fighting for their political and cultural rights, and ultimately with political exiles and leftists abroad. His death at the hands of the Islamic Republic's revolutionary guards has ensured that his memory will be preserved among the Qashqa'i and his heroism is undoubted. In the end, however, his death is not without its quixotic aspects. Why is this so?

There is an aura of tragedy about the encounter between the Qashqa'i and the central government, for each side pursued what it perceived as worthy goals. Qashqa'i efforts to salvage their way of life collided with the Shah's efforts to centralize and control the rural inhabitants of Iran and bring about what he perceived as the benefits of modernization. (These policies were continued, although in different ways and for some different purposes, by the Islamic Republic.) For Qashqa'i opponents like Rostam, such plans amounted to ethnocide. For the Shah and his officials, Qashqa'i opposition was perverse, if not treasonous. The brutality of the Shah's agents (and the greed of those who coveted the Qashqa'i lands) insured the opposition of individuals like Rostam. In the wider context, it seems unlikely that the Qashqa'i could continue to follow their way of life in an increasingly populous and modernizing Iranian society. In that sense, one may legitimately wonder about the ultimate futility of their resistance, even as one honors it.

Because a significant proportion of the 50 percent of Iranians who do not speak Persian as a first language and who do not identify with Persian culture are tribal minorities (Baluch, Turkmen, Bakhtiyari, Qashqa'i, Shahsevan, Lurs, and many Kurds and Arabs), there have been many such clashes since the 1920s, when Reza Shah began to create what he viewed as a modern nation-state. Thus, the situation of the Qashqa'i has parallels elsewhere in Iran. More generally, one also thinks of other minorities: the Kurds of Turkey, Iraq, and Iran; the Berbers of Algeria and Morocco; the Druze of Syria, Lebanon, and Israel; and the bedouin in many states. (See the contributions by Lila Abu-Lughod, Edmund Burke, and Julie Oehler elsewhere in this volume for more on tribal people.) —Eds.

Golgaz handed her son Rostam a miniature Quran to kiss and then placed it on a tray and held it high. Tears filling his eyes, Rostam stooped to pass under the tray and then, without a backward glance, walked away from his mother's tent. She feared she would never see him again, as she always feared whenever he left home after another furtive visit. Each time he departed abruptly, without warning; each time he could never manage to stay more than a few hours with her. She did not understand why he seemed so driven to leave his family and tribal territory. She did not know what kind of life he lived while he was gone, and she worried about his safety and his encounters with strangers. She had always expected that he would remain with her, marry her brother's daughter, and present her with grandchildren. Now he was gone again, and she wept.

Rostam was born in 1949 during the arduous spring migration, and his family and tribal group of Qashqa'i nomadic pastoralists traveled from winter pastures in the foothills of the Zagros Mountains of southern Iran to summer pastures three hundred miles away to the north, high in the alpine valleys of the Zagros. When Golgaz's labor pains began, her husband, Morad, notified men in his camp that he would not travel the next morning as planned. The men replied that the location provided good grazing for their flocks and said they did not mind postponing the move for a day. In the meantime, they sent their camels and other pack animals, used for transporting all their possessions, into the mountains for browsing. Several women from nearby tents came to assist with the birth and help with domestic tasks. A baby boy was born after several hours of labor. He was Golgaz's eighth surviving child, and delivery had become increasingly easy with each new birth. The women cooked a strengthening mixture of wheat flour, sugar, and ginger in clarified butter for her. Golgaz's sister Guhar told the family's eldest son about his new brother, and he passed the word to Morad. People in camp rejoiced at the arrival of a new "warrior," and men fired rifles into the air in happiness and celebration and in order to frighten evil spirits away from the infant.

When her son was forty days old, Morad gave him the ancient Iranian, pre-Islamic name Rostam. Many Qashqa'i families used ancient Iranian and Arabic/Islamic names for their sons and Turkish names for their daughters. Morad held close to the traditions of his ancestors and chose names of people legendary in tribal history for all his children. He believed that his lineage descended from central Asian Turkish warriors who were part of Chingiz Khan's armed guard.

When Rostam was six years old, his father decided to send him to the tent school newly established in the winter and summer pastures of his tribal group. The school was part of a tribal program created by a Qashqa'i entrepreneur with financial assistance from the United States and Iran's Ministry of Education. With eight children, as many boys as girls, Morad did not need Rostam's labor full time, and he appreciated the benefits of literacy and knowledge. He especially hoped to equip Rostam with the skills necessary for him to interact with the surrounding Persian-dominated society. None of Morad's other children had attended school, but he had taught his sons the rudiments of reading and writing. He had received several months of instruction in reading and writing as a youth. His father had supported the *ilkhani*, the leader of the 400,000-strong Qashqa'i tribal confederacy, and the *ilkhani* had allowed the young Morad to attend school in his camp for a brief period.

Rostam attended school regularly and appeared to flourish there. His teacher was a Qashqa'i man who was comfortable in his surroundings. The government had earlier tried to send young urban Persian men to teach the Turkish-speaking Qashqa'i, but the experiment had failed. In 1960, having completed the five years available, Rostam did not object when his father suggested that he continue his education in a town school. His three brothers performed with skill their tasks in animal husbandry and agriculture, and his absence from home did not much affect the family economically. During autumn, winter, and spring for several years, Rostam lived in Farrashband, the town closest to his tribal group's winter pastures, and attended school. He and several other Qashqa'i adolescents rented a room from a Persian merchant there. After examinations in late spring every year, he rode by horse to summer pastures far to the north in the mountains northeast of the rolling plain of Khusrow Shirin, lived with his family there, and helped with pastoral and agricultural tasks. He assisted his family at the beginning of the autumn migration and then rode by horse alone to Farrashband when classes resumed.

In 1962 Muhammad Reza Shah proclaimed a White Revolution, which included a comprehensive land-reform program. To exert state force over the still powerful Qashqa'i tribal elite, government officials announced plans to implement land reform first in Fars province, where the Qashqa'i *ilkhani* and his family had governed vast stretches of land. Morad and his father and grandfather had used pastoral and agricultural land near Farrashband that the Qashqa'i *ilkhani* had controlled, one area now targeted by government officials for confiscation. Morad and other members of his tribal group depended on this land. In charge of some tribal affairs since the Shah exiled the Qashqa'i *ilkhani* from Iran, an army officer ordered the headmen of seven Qashqa'i tribal groups to appear at his headquarters in the town of Firuzabad. There, he notified of the government's intention to confiscate their land and assign it to Persian-speaking nontribal peasants in the region.

Morad was outraged by the announcement. He had done nothing to warrant being excluded from his ancestral pastures, and the peasants now said to be taking his place had never cultivated crops there. Confronting the army officer, Morad and several kinsmen angrily stated their grievances. The officer beckoned to his armed escort and ordered Morad and his kinsmen to leave; when the unarmed men refused, the officer yelled at his guards to seize them. Years later, people were still uncertain about what happened next. But after the skirmish, Morad lay dead, and his nephew Bizhan lay badly wounded. The officer ordered his guards to seize Morad's cousin Jehangir and then telegraphed army headquarters in the city of Shiraz to seek reinforcements because, he claimed, the Qashqa'i had attacked his headquarters. Several Qashqa'i headmen who had witnessed the violent confrontation left town in order to notify Morad's family and group of the catastrophe.

Rumors of some sort of trouble in Firuzabad reached the Qashqa'i boys in school in Farrashband; Rostam hastened home to find out what had happened. As he hurried up the mountain slopes to his group's winter pastures, he could hear wailing in the distance and he feared for the fate of his family. As he rounded a bend near his father's winter campsite, he heard his mother's laments and knew instantly that someone close to her had died. He saw her crouched in the dust by the tent, beating her hands against the sides of her head and ripping at the front of her tunic. Her hair, always carefully tended in many neat braids down her back, was disheveled, and she made no effort to cover her head or neck. Repeating a verse of a Qashqa'i dirge, her sister Rokhsar lamented, "Go tell my sister, 'Rip the front of your tunic, loosen your braids, and scatter your hair on the tombstone.'" Rostam's father's brother Hushang came forward to tell him that his father had been killed, and then the uncle sadly assembled a few men to go to Firuzabad to retrieve the body.

Two days later, near sunset, the men returned to camp with Morad's body draped over the back of a horse. They had hoped to return sooner, but army officers had refused to release the body. Hushang had sought assistance from Hajj Abdul Rasul, a Persian merchant and moneylender in Firuzabad with whom Morad had been acquainted, and the man had pleaded with the authorities to allow the family to bury the body in compliance with Islamic tradition.

Men and women of Morad's lineage and subtribe gathered at his tent while Morad was washed and prepared for burial, and then they accompanied Khalifeh, the one man in their group able to recite the required Quranic passages, to a nearby graveyard. On the seventh day after the death, people convened again at Morad's tent for ritual observances. A sheep had been slaughtered for the commemorative meal, and women not closely related to Morad prepared meat and rice. Rostam and his brothers served as hosts of the gathering and accepted people's condolences. At the beginning and ending of the meal, men mournfully recited a few Quranic verses and everyone wept.

Soldiers in Farrashband notified Hushang that Bizhan, wounded in the skirmish, had died in jail. Hushang brought his body back to camp, and the group sadly held another funeral. The two murdered men, considered victims of the Shah's regime, had left wives and children behind. Also retained by the army after the skirmish, Jehangir was reportedly moved to prison in Shiraz.

Remaining at home with his mother and siblings, Rostam decided to postpone returning to school in Farrashband. His family needed him. Military authorities periodically summoned Hushang to Farrashband and Firuzabad to interrogate him about the activities of men in his group. One day they announced that they were moving ahead to seize his group's winter pastures, to punish it for the violence, and they ordered the group to leave immediately for summer pastures. They hoped to forestall any organized protest against the events that had occurred and took advantage of the nomad's mobility and changing seasonal residences. On the forced migration north, the small group entered higher, colder altitudes where no grazing was yet available for their animals. During the trek, Rostam heard that the government had also confiscated pastureland from other Qashqa'i groups whose members had protested against new land policies. Several men told him about skirmishes between Qashqa'i men and the rural police (gendarmes), who had attempted to restrict the nomads' travel between tribal territory and towns. Qashqa'i men were routinely harassed by the army and gendarmes when they traveled outside tribal territory, but these harassments were escalating. Rostam learned of the government's imminent plans to confiscate all guns and rifles held by the Qashqa'i. Coupled with the murder of his father and cousin and the loss of pastureland, the announced confiscation was a turning point for Rostam. Guns were the Qashqa'i people's primary means of defense and offense and were the major symbol of Qashqa'i power and autonomy.

As the nomads neared Shiraz, Rostam heard rumors that two young Qashqa'i men, distant kinsmen of his, had escaped after a confrontation with gendarmes and had sought refuge in the mountains nearby. When a shepherd returned to camp with the news that he had met the two men, who appeared to be without food, Rostam told his sister to bundle the sheets of flat bread she had just baked and to pack dates, onions, tea leaves, sugar, and a small metal teapot. Carrying the supplies and armed with a rifle, Rostam abruptly left camp without a word to anyone. He followed the directions given by the shepherd. After six hours of hard climbing up the mountain slopes and across a small valley to another slope, he reached a rock face shaped like a gazelle's head and he called out using wild bird songs. Soon an answering call came, and he showed himself. A man some distance away waved his felt hat (identical in its unique shape to Rostam's own and the marker of Qashqa'i identity), and he approached. Two young men near the mouth of a cave exchanged customary greetings with Rostam. The rest of the day he sat in a secluded spot in the sun with Shapur and Kaikavus and talked about the events that had occurred during the past month. The two men had of course known about the murder of Morad and Bizhan. They told Rostam of their own plans to obstruct the movement of army convoys to and from Firuzabad. He said he would join them. First, he noted, he wanted to return home briefly to see his mother and collect ammunition and supplies. The three young men agreed to meet four days later at a secluded location in the mountains northwest of Firuzabad.

When Rostam met up with Shapur and Kaikavus again, they plotted their revenge against the army officer responsible for the two men's deaths. Word that Shapur and Kaikavus had become *yaghi* (rebels, outlaws) had spread among the dispersed Qashqa'i nomads in the vicinity, and several of their cousins joined them. Two young Qashqa'i men who had recently been released from prison also sought them out, and within several months a small band of fluctuating size, but at times as large as fourteen people, had formed. They plotted small-scale, lightning attacks against isolated gendarme posts in order to seize arms, ammunition, and supplies. They held pity for the frightened conscripts who were their own age or younger and who came from impoverished families, and they avoided engaging them in violence. The rebels impeded the movement of military vehicles in and near Qashqa'i territory by setting up road barriers and firing on the stalled vehicles from rocky hideouts in mountain passes. Members of the band took pride in demonstrating the military's weakness and vulnerability and asserting their own and QashqaQashqa'ii power. They were quite successful in these aims, and their reputation spread. Young men admired their courage, and older men reminisced about the rebels and outlaws they had known in the past. Adolescent girls sang romantic ballads about the rebels. Families of the rebels provided provisions, and other Qashqa'i nomads were generous in their help. Especially given the proximity of the Persian Gulf and the active smuggling trade there, arms and ammunition were not difficult to acquire. The rebels always wore their two-flap felt hats, a cartridge belt, and often a diaphanous beige cloth cloak called a *choqqa* that they tied with a tasseled cord. Qashqa'i warriors had worn these cloaks during battles in the past.

Rostam stayed with the small group on and off for several years. Members came and went. Periodically, with caution, he visited winter and summer pastures to see his mother and other family members. He arrived at night, slipped off during the day to hide in the nearby mountains, and left in the night, newly provisioned and glad for the familial contact. The government had carried out its threats to confiscate the group's winter pastures, but most of the nomads were fortunate to have found new pastures in nearby mountains, and they cooperated with neighboring Qashqa'i groups in the cultivation of the crops necessary for their own and their animals' sustenance. Occasionally, Rostam traveled to the city of Shiraz by taking a circuitous route and blending with other rural people who were on their way to and from market. In Shiraz, he met other young men who opposed Muhammad Reza Shah and his regime. Some were university students who told him about political activists elsewhere in Iran and who provided him with some understanding of revolutionary ideologies and struggles in other parts of the world.

By 1965, bolstered by escalating military aid and new technology from the United States, Iran's army and gendarmerie were increasingly effective in their surveillance of and control over Qashqa'i territory. Small Qashqa'i rebel bands similar to that of Shapur and Kaikavus had found it difficult to secure safe mountain retreats, travel freely, and escape from attacks. The government attempted once again to disarm the Qashqa'i, and the young men could no longer carry arms openly during their travels. After the army and gendarmes attacked and killed or captured other Qashqa'i rebels and outlaws, Shapur and Kaikavus decided to disband their own group and find other means of protest. Both men were killed several months later in a skirmish with gendarmes.

Rostam returned home, and this time he decided not to hide. As far as he knew, he had never been identified by state authorities as a member of an outlaw band. When officials had inquired about his whereabouts, for the purpose of conscripting him into the army, his uncle reported that he was a high school student in Shiraz. A year had passed since the last inquiry. Rostam was not comfortable staying at home for long periods, however. His elder brother who had married and fathered children now headed the household, and Golgaz was glad for the company and help of a daughter-in-law and grandchildren. Her second son's bride also proved to be a competent, cooperative worker. The family was still able to hire a shepherd, a young impoverished man, for their sheep and goats, and the brothers cultivated wheat and barley in winter and summer pastures. They sold and traded sheep, goats, wool, goat hair, and dairy products in Firuzabad and Shiraz for cash and needed commodities such as salt, rice, and tea. They were indebted to urban merchants and moneylenders, as were practically all Qashqa'i, and high and rising interest rates troubled them. The family survived economically without Rostam's presence, however, and he did not see a role for himself at home. His mother wanted him to marry and establish a family, but he said he was not ready. Besides, he noted, no girl in his extended family appealed to him. He was entitled to a share of the household's animals but only after his three brothers had set up their own independent households. As youngest son, the "son of the hearth," Rostam was by custom the one eventually responsible for filling his father's place at home and caring for his mother, but he saw with some regret that his elder brothers had already assumed that role.

After several months at home, a restless and bored Rostam returned to Shiraz and sought out the friends he had made there. Although he wanted to continue to act against increasing government restrictions on the Qashqa'i and the loss of their political autonomy, enhanced military surveillance and control made that difficult. The government's treacherous capture and execution in 1966 of the rebel Bahman Qashqa'i, nephew of the Qashqa'i *ilkhani*, was another turning point for Rostam. He considered attending high school in Shiraz but then rejected the idea. He was not qualified or adequately prepared to attend university.

Rostam accompanied his friend Selahaddin, a young Kurdish man from a small village near Sanandaj in northwestern Iran, back home for the New Year's holiday in March. He intended to return to his own family after a week but was drawn to Selahaddin's friends and was excited by their discussions of the problems of Kurds in Iran and neighboring Iraq and Turkey. He decided to remain in Kurdistan for a while. Sympathetic to this sensitive young man who no longer had a father, Selahaddin's father invited him to stay with his family. As Rostam helped out there, he saw that although the family lived in a village, its livelihood was similar to that of his own family in its dependence on both pastoralism and agriculture. During the evenings and on Fridays, he met young Kurds and became aware of the plight of this nation of people oppressed by the states under whose authority and control they fell.

In 1967, disturbed about news of renewed military attacks against Qashqa'i rebels and outlaws near Firuzabad, Rostam decided to travel to Europe to meet with Khusrow Khan, one of the exiled leaders of the Qashqa'i confederacy. Several Kurdish friends wanted to talk with Kurds in exile from Iraq and Turkey, and Europe was the safest, most accessible location for their gathering. Travel by bus from Tabriz to Munich was inexpensive, and the young men hoped to find ways to meet their expenses while visiting Europe. Rostam located Khusrow Khan Qashqa'i, who was widely known to frequent a certain café and a nearby antiquities shop in Munich. Rostam's Kurdish friends traveled on to Paris. Khusrow Khan was distressed as he heard Rostam's firsthand reports about the severe measures the Iranian government was taking against the Qashqa'i. Forced into exile thirteen years previously, Khusrow Khan had received money from the Iranian government that its agents said compensated him for land it had confiscated from his family. He used some of it to support the living expenses of young Qashqa'i men abroad, including Rostam. He hoped to build support for the future, when he would return to Iran and resume tribal leadership.

Rostam remained in Europe for ten years and supported himself by a variety of temporary unskilled jobs and some aid from Khusrow Khan. Periodically, he visited other European cities and met members of other national-minority groups in Iran, particularly Kurds and Baluch. He encountered many expatriate Middle Easterners and heard them tell familiar stories. He was struck by the common fate of almost all their groups: military surveillance and control, economic oppression and neglect, and cultural discrimination.

Rostam was initially drawn to leftist groups in Europe that were composed of people from Iran and other Middle Eastern countries, but none of them spoke directly to the concerns he held. He grew to be particularly distrustful of many Iranian leftists of Persian background. Although Persian Iranians seemed sympathetic to the political problems he had faced in Iran, they appeared to him to be more interested in exploiting the Qashqa'i as a strategic and military weapon in their larger struggle. They said they cared about minority rights, but their ideas and programs for a new form of society in Iran did not adequately address minority issues, and they seemed overly concerned about changing the conditions of what they termed the "backward" minorities. They viewed the nomadic pastoralism practiced by Rostam's family and other QashqaQashqa'i as archaic and pointless, they described Qashqa'i economic and political systems as feudal, and they perceived Qashqa'i social systems as patriarchal and oppressive. They said they intended to eradicate these practices and systems and transform these people into a proletariat in a unified Iran. Rostam was offended by their attitudes and knew that these goals were ridiculous and, besides, impossible to achieve.

In 1971 and 1975, Rostam returned briefly for visits with his family. Although he had originally left Iran legally, he had not fulfilled the military service required of Iranian men and he worried about being apprehended by the authorities. The Shah's repressive secret police, SAVAK, was active and powerful, and Rostam feared staying more than a few days with his mother. SAVAK had infiltrated Qashqa'i society; no one knew exactly who all the agents and informers were, although rumors of their identities proliferated. On each visit, Rostam entered and exited Iran illegally through Kurdistan with the help of Kurdish friends. He considered staying in Kurdistan and assisting the struggle for minority rights there, as an affiliate of one of the leftist groups that were active. Most of these groups held non-Kurdish members; as a Qashqa'i, he believed he would fit in. He also considered joining the Marxist-oriented rebellion in Dhofar in the southern Arabian peninsula. Muhammad Reza Shah was providing military aid to the sultan of Oman in his efforts to end the rebellion in Dhofar, and a few Iranians opposed to the imperialist aims of the Shah and supportive of the rebellion had gone there to foil the effort.

When Rostam returned to Munich in 1975, uncertain as to his future, he met again with Palestinian men and women who were engaged in their own nationalist struggles against the state of Israel and other enemies. Many of them had received military and other training in camps of the Palestine Liberation Organization in southern Lebanon, and he asked them about the possibility of going there. They provided him with false documents, and in 1977 he passed through Turkey and Syria to Lebanon. Rostam spent a year in a PLO camp there and then returned to Munich.

The rise of protest in Iran against Muhammad Reza Shah in 1978 excited Iranian youth in Europe. Rostam joined their discussions and grew increasingly agitated to return to Iran. He expected Khusrow Khan Qashqa'i to formulate a plan for the Qashqa'i people in the escalating struggle in Iran and was disappointed to find that he had not yet voiced any specific policy or program. In late 1978, when Khusrow Khan traveled to the United States in order to discuss the situation in Iran with Qashqa'i and other people, Rostam returned to Iran, again through Kurdistan, and went immediately to see his family in winter pastures.

During the previous decade, Rostam's brothers, uncles, and other patrilateral kin had purchased small plots of land and built two-room, mud-brick houses near their former winter pastures, for they expected that the economic and political conditions for nomadic pastoralism would continue to worsen. Their expectations had not proven false, and they were glad that they had settled before the government had forced it upon them. They had named their new village Moradabad, after Rostam's father as well as the reputed founder of their lineage. One of Rostam's brothers and a hired shepherd continued to migrate seasonally between winter and summer pastures with the family's sheep and goats.

Rostam spent many evenings talking with his kinsmen about the years of his absence and his ideas concerning how to improve the status and position of the Qashqa'i in Iran. He spoke of his association with Khusrow Khan, a man they all admired, especially for his military stand against the Shah in the 1940s and 1950s, and they eagerly anticipated his expected imminent arrival. Several young men talked about volunteering their services to Khusrow Khan as his armed guards, a role performed by their fathers and grandfathers for previous paramount Qashqa'i leaders. Rostam sought out the Qashqa'i teacher assigned to his group and was surprised to find that although they shared a hatred of the Shah, the teacher laughed about the prospects of the paramount Qashqa'i *khans* ever assuming a position of leadership in Iran again. The time for "tribal" leadership was over, he proclaimed. Iran had entered the "modern" era, he declared.

In early January 1979 Naser Khan Qashqa'i, Qashqa'i *ilkhani*, returned to Iran after twenty-five years of exile in the United States, and hundreds of Qashqa'i people came to Tehran to greet him. By then, the tide had turned against Muhammad Reza Shah, and on 16 January he fled Iran, never to return. Two days later, Naser Khan and a large escort traveled by car to Shiraz in the south. Several thousand Qashqa'i people gathered in secure Qashqa'i territory south of Firuzabad to welcome him. As he joined the gathering, Rostam expected Naser Khan to announce a course of action for the Qashqa'i in these turbulent times, when state institutions were weak or nonexistent, but he did not, partly because of advanced age and his caution in acting after having been in exile for so long. His personal style of leadership, one traditional for Qashqa'i leaders, was to hold council with the tribespeople he respected, allow a consensus to emerge from these often large public gatherings, and then possibly act if it was warranted. When Khusrow Khan arrived in Iran some days later, the situation became tense and complicated, for the two *khans* (who were brothers) held different notions about the roles they should play and the actions they should take in support of or against the new revolutionary Islamic regime. Unlike many of Iran's national minorities, the Qashqa'i were Shii Muslims, but they did not share the fundamentalist interpretations of Islam propagated by the Ayatullah Khomeini and his supporters. The *khans* debated their plans but reached no decisions. Out of loyalty to Khusrow Khan, whom he still regarded as his patron, Rostam remained close and served as a lieutenant. He delivered messages, carried out instructions, and tried to involve other Qashqa'i youth.

Some Qashqa'i men who had associated with Khusrow Khan in Europe had also returned to Iran, and they too were puzzled by the lack of specific programs and policies. Several joined nationwide Persian-dominated leftist groups then active in Iran, but Rostam did not trust many of their members and feared they would exploit him because of his Qashqa'i tribal connections. Although many non-Qashqa'i leftists continued to view him as politically naive, they did expect that he and his "tribe" would be useful in any forthcoming military struggle in Iran. They appreciated the vast numbers of armed and militarily prepared Qashqa'i men and their strategic location near oil fields, a major urban area (Shiraz), and the Persian Gulf.

After national elections in 1980, Khusrow Khan Qashqa'i was elected to the first parliament of the newly proclaimed Islamic Republic of Iran. Muslim clerics and their supporters formally questioned his credentials and then sent revolutionary guards, the new regime's main military arm, to arrest him. Days later, after beatings from revolutionary guards, he was released from prison and sent to his sister's home in Tehran. Instead, he headed to Qashqa'i territory in the south. Revolutionary guards attempted to intercept him and then began to plot attacks against his small group of family and other supporters. Several hundred Qashqa'i men, including Rostam, joined in the defense, and a small insurgency rapidly formed in Qashqa'i territory. Members of three pan-Iranian leftist groups, all non-Qashqa'i men and a few women, attached themselves to the insurgency. Naser Khan, his son Abdullah, Khusrow Khan, and their respective supporters disputed about the presence of the non-Qashqa'i leftists. Unable to agree, the three men set up separate but affiliated camps for a while. Rostam remained in Khusrow Khan's camp and continued to serve as a trusted assistant.

Because of the close proximity of the insurgent camps to Rostam's family near Farrashband, he was often able to visit home. Revolutionary guards, gendarmes, and the army exercised little control over the rugged mountainous area, and Qashqa'i people and others were often able to travel with impunity. Rostam's mother feared for him each time he left home after a brief visit, but his stories about the sometimes pleasant life in the insurgent camp (especially the camaraderie established among the Qashqa'i members) and the infrequency of attacks against it reassured her.

By the spring of 1982 the small group of Qashqa'i rebels was isolated, beleaguered, and demoralized. Revolutionary guards had increased the intensity of their attacks. Concrete expressions of support from within the Qashqa'i confederacy, which had been low-level from the start, were diminishing. Abdullah, son of Naser Khan, died suddenly of suspicious causes, possibly intentional cyanide poisoning, several hours after a battle with revolutionary guards. Dispirited about his son's death and in poor health himself, Naser Khan was encouraged to leave Iran. Even loyal supporters of Khusrow Khan worried about the advisability of continuing to maintain the insurgency. Revolutionary guards intensified their surveillance of roads in the camp's vicinity and travel was impeded. In July, a mediator in Shiraz, supportive of the small Qashqa'i group, arranged for Khusrow Khan and the remaining fighters to receive amnesty if they surrendered to the Shiraz authorities. After much deliberation, Khusrow Khan and some others from the camp secretly entered Shiraz to await the conclusion of the negotiations. A spy from within the insurgency, some Qashqa'i later stated, reported on Khusrow Khan's location, and revolutionary guards seized him. Khusrow Khan was later tried, sentenced to death by an Islamic court, and tortured. Then, according to many reports, he was publicly shot in Firuzabad (some say Shiraz), possibly after having already been killed. Controversy concerning the circumstances of his death continued for years, and soon many legends arose about him. Some members of the insurgency had remained in their mountain stronghold and attempted to find their own way to sanctuary. Most of the key members of the insurgency were later executed or arrested or driven into foreign exile.

Rostam had waited in the mountains until he thought that Khusrow Khan had safely reached Shiraz, and then he had traveled alone by foot toward Farrashband. En route, he was ambushed by revolutionary guards sent out from Firuzabad to watch for stragglers from the insurgent camp. They shot Rostam as he struggled to escape and then roughly loaded his body into the back of a Land Rover.

No one in Rostam's family ever discovered where the revolutionary guards took him or where he was buried. Golgaz often visited her husband's grave and pretended that her son was buried next to his father. As she bent her head toward the ground, she murmured that only the earth could hear her and that only the soil of that undug grave could bear and share her endless pain and grief. "O heavenly earth, let my beloveds be held in your caring arms, and let my Rostam sleep in your lap. When they are awakened [on the Day of Judgment], tell them that I was not here to complain but to inform them that new *alamdars* [flag holders in wars] have been born to fight for their tribe."

A NOTE ON SOURCES

The names of many people in this account, including the name Rostam, are pseudonyms, and I have changed some place-names. This account is augmented by my anthropological, historical, and archival research on the Qashqa'i people of southern Iran. I was in southern Iran in 1963–64 when Qashqa'i rebels were active, and I was acquainted with several of their families. I conducted anthropological field research among the Qashqa'i in 1970–71, 1977, and after the revolution in 1979 and 1991. I also conducted interviews with and collected oral histories from many Qashqa'i individuals (in Iran and in exile abroad), particularly current and former tribal leaders, members of the Qashqa'i insurgency of 1980–82, and men and women who had been fugitives from the Iranian government. A former classmate of mine at Shiraz University in Iran, who became a medical doctor, treated wounded Qashqa'i rebels in the 1960s and later told me about their lives. Two Qashqa'i men, Manucher Dareshuri and Mohammad Shahbazi, offered helpful suggestions for this essay, as did Gene Garthwaite.

SUGGESTIONS FOR FURTHER READING

My two books on the Qashqa'i will provide readers with the historical and anthropological context of this account: *The Qashqa'i of Iran* (New Haven, Conn.: Yale University Press, 1986), especially chapters 11 and 12, dealing with Iran under Muhammad Reza Shah Pahlavi and the Ayatullah Khomeini's Islamic Republic; and *Nomad: A Year in the Life of a Qashqa'i Tribesman in Iran* (Berkeley: University of California Press, 1991). See also "Local Histories: A Longitudinal Study of a Qashqa'i Subtribe in Iran," in *Iran and Beyond: Essays in Middle Eastern History in Honor of Nikki R. Keddie*, eds. Rudi Matthee and Beth Baron, (Costa Mesa, Calif.: Mazda Publishers, 2000), 262–88. In "Tribes and the State in Nineteenth- and Twentieth-Century Iran," appearing in *Tribes and State Formation in the Middle East*, ed. Philip Khoury and Joseph Kostiner (Berkeley: University of California Press, 1990), I discuss the historical importance of tribes and tribal confederacies in Iranian history. Pierre Oberling provides a brief account of Qashqa'i rebel activity in the 1960s in *The Qashqa'i Nomads of Fars* (The Hague: Mouton, 1974), 210–15. In *The Last Migration* (London: Rupert Hart-Davis, 1957), Vincent Cronin offers a fictionalized account of a military confrontation between the Iranian state and the Qashqa'i in the early 1950s. For a novel about a young Kurdish peasant in Turkey who became an outlaw and bandit, I suggest Yashar Kemal's *Memed My Hawk* (New York: Pantheon, 1961). Eric Hobsbawm's *Bandits* (New York: Pantheon, 1981) offers a historical study of the phenomenon of social banditry, while David Hart discusses the applicability of Hobsbawm's notions to the Middle East in *Banditry in Islam* (Cambridgeshire: Middle East and North African Studies Press, 1978). Farhad Kazemi and Ervand Abrahamian in "The Nonrevolutionary Peasantry of Modern Iran," *Iranian Studies* 11 (1978): 259–304, discuss forms of political protest in rural Iran. On social movements in the modern Middle East, see Edmund Burke III and Ira Lapidus, eds., *Islam, Politics, and Social Movements* (Berkeley: University of California Press, 1988).

Chapter 16

An Iranian Village Boyhood

Mehdi Abedi and Michael M. J. Fischer

What a personal odyssey is Mehdi Abedi's! From boyhood in the small village of Dareh, south of the city of Yazd in south-central Iran, to schooling first in Yazd and later in the city of Qum (the seminary city of Iran) on the eve of the Iranian revolution, and finally to Rice University in Texas where he is now an anthropologist, his life has been one of remarkable changes. In this selection, Abedi (with Michael M. J. Fischer) tells of growing up in Dareh in the 1950s and 1960s.

His story is a warmly nostalgic look backward at a world that has now vanished forever as a result of the many changes modern Iran has experienced. Although Dareh is but a small village, one is struck immediately by the enormous vitality of its social and cultural life and by the density of human interactions. We meet a colorful group of characters who appear to have stepped out of the pages of a nineteenth-century novel—the headman, the Hajji, the washer of the dead, the midwife, the barber, and the various individuals who served (with more or less competence) as teacher in the village school.

At the center of everyone's interest was the annual enactment of the passion play at Ashura, the Shiite festival that commemorates the killing of Imam Husayn by the evil Umayyad general Shemr. For the small boy Abedi was then, it must have been a wonderfully exciting time. Selection for the roles in the play became the occasion for intense competition among the villagers. All over Iran, similar passion plays were held on this occasion and were no doubt acted with the same gusto. In the Ashura passion play, the Islamic revolutionaries were to find a rich symbolic vocabulary to denounce the Shah (portrayed as the new Yazid) and his allies.

Fischer and Abedi's account also touches upon the latter's life and education in the nearby city of Yazd (where his family resided in the winter months) and the central place that Islamic education played in his life. Through Abedi's experiences, we come to understand the cultural roots of the Iranian revolution and how firmly grounded the Shiite tradition is among the Iranian people. At the heart of this tradition is the Quran, which was memorized by some urban and rural Iranian boys as well as by some girls. For many Iranians, it is clear, religion offered much that was spiritually nourishing—although it could also be utilized by politically ambitious clerics. Ironically, the Shah's educational reforms worked to increase further the influence of the *mullahs* and of the Shiite clergy through the founding of new seminaries and schools and the expansion of the media.

Finally, one must note that Abedi's story is unique in having been written in close collaboration with his coauthor and friend Michael M. J. Fischer. Is this account biography or autobiography? Or is it a new genre? How do we situate this story alongside the more recognizably biographical contributions to this volume? —Eds.

Dareh (Valley) is the name of the little village in which I was born. In the legal documents it is called Dareh-i Miyankuh (the Valley of the Middle Mountains). It is a poor hill village in a narrow valley of the middle ranges of the Shirkuh Mountains, above the basin plain on which sit the larger villages Mehriz and Manshad to the south of the city of Yazd in central Iran. Not even many Yazdis have heard of it: from Yazd you take the road to Kirman as far as the Abdul Malik Coffee House, then turn right onto a gravel road, past Mehriz, toward the mountains, and when you come to a branch in the road, you can see the bottom of the village. Villagers distinguish three neighborhoods, or *mahalleh:* upper, lower, and middle. We lived in the middle.

The people of the village tell stories about the good past, the days when water was plentiful, much wheat and barley was produced, melons were grown, and everyone was happy. By the time I was old enough to know the village, it was extremely poor, and more than a third of its population had left to work in Yazd or Tehran. Its primary produce was dried mulberries. My memories are of famine conditions of the postwar and post-Mossadeq period, when children were told to fill their bellies by foraging for berries (*angur-i kuhi* and *panirok*). American wheat was sent, but it was often spoiled and uncleaned.

Among the spiritual or religious features of the village were, beginning at the bottom of the village, the *husayniyeh* (arena for the passion plays on Ashura), the graveyard and a hyena's grave for curing sick animals, a mosque and public bathhouse, and, on the hillside behind the bathhouse, a rock formation that was said to be an imprint of the sword of Imam Ali. In our yard, in the middle neighborhood, there was a holy tree. In the upper village, there was a second mosque and an older holy tree. Above the village was a cave where the Imams were said to have left their footprints, and a mountain ridge in the shape of a camel led by a man and pushed by another. All these sites were visual reminders of moral lessons. The camel shape of the mountain went with the legend that during a time of drought and famine two villagers decided to declare war on God, and so they set out with their camels to reach the highest point so they could talk to God. God turned them to stone, and so they remain as a constant warning to people against blasphemy; Big Brother brooks no revolt. Similarly, the sword of Ali was a warning against those who express animosity toward the First Imam: the story was that an enemy had tried to ambush Ali, and in his lightning speed to draw his sword, Ali hit the hillside, leaving an imprint. The hyena grave (*qabr kaftar*) at the desert's edge was used for animals as saints' tombs (*imamzadehs*) were for humans: when animals fell sick they were circumambulated seven times around this grave, and sacrifices, offerings, and vows were made.

The bathhouse was used both for cleanliness and ritual purity: menfolk used it before dawn, womenfolk afterward. Menfolk were less concerned with bathing and more that they be ritually pure before going off to the fields. Womenfolk enjoyed spending time in the bathhouse socializing and picnicking. But the bathhouse was also associated with *jinn*, perhaps through an association with moisture, and so one was never supposed to go there alone. *Jinn* were said to attack neither those who were totally fearless nor those who were extremely timorous, but only the majority in between. They did not attack the timorous lest they have heart attacks and die; all *jinn* in this village were Muslims and did not want to have the blood of anyone charged to them. They feared the totally fearless lest they be seized and have their necks wrung. There was a woman, Zan-i Hajji Daqqaq (Wife of Hajji the Cloth Finisher), who lived between the *husayniyeh* and the mosque, who was possessed by *jinn*, and who served as an example to all of what might happen if you failed to exercise caution. She was constantly talking to the *jinn*, screaming at them, cursing them, calling on Hazrat-i Abbas to get them to leave her alone. Her sons had to lock her in when they left for the fields. She must have done something to a *jinn*. She was a living reminder that whenever you pushed a stone down a hillside, as kids loved to do, or whenever you threw out hot water, or even whenever you stepped somewhere, you should first call out to warn any invisible *jinn* in the way: *bismillah-i rahman-i rahim* or *parhiz o bismillah-i rahman-i rahim* or just *parhiz* (beware). If you did get tormented by a *jinn*, a *jinn-gir* (*jinn* catcher) would come to divine its name.

The holy tree in our yard had a story that I helped produce. People believed that trees have senses and understanding, especially such that one could talk to them. So if a fruit tree stopped bearing, if one had tried fertilizers and transplanting and nothing else seemed to work, one might try a ritual called *bebur nabur* (cut, don't cut). One placed a saw at the tree's base and one person pretended to begin cutting it down. A second person would then plead for the tree: "What are you doing, don't you realize this is an apple tree?" First person: "You mean it looks like an apple?" Second person: "No, it gives apples" (thus suggesting to the tree its duties). First person:

"Why then does it not give apples? It looks like a simple plane tree to me."
Second person: "Please, I beg you, give it one more year, and I guarantee it
will bring forth fruit."

We had a tall apple tree in our yard that gave pleasant shade but no fruit.
My brother was working in Tehran and had promised to bring us some special black cherry seedlings. My father decided to cut down the apple tree to
make room for the new seedlings, but for some reason I jumped at him and
began a kind of *bebur nabur* dialogue with him, and Amu Ali, the village
muezzin (caller to prayer) joined me. My father relented. Sometime later, I
happened to kill a snake in the mountains and I buried it at the base of the
tree because snakes were thought to be excellent fertilizer, and I would
whisper to it: "Please, I want to be proud of you, do your duty and bear
fruit." Miraculously, the next year the tree produced an overabundance of
apples, but in the following winter, as if exhausted by its efforts, it died, and
did not sprout again in the spring.

Near the mosque in the upper neighborhood there was an ancient plane
tree that was even more venerable. Someone on an Ashura day had said he
had seen it bleeding in sympathy with the martyrdom of Husayn. And so
people believed that if they attempted to cut its branches, especially on the
festival of Ashura, something terrible would befall them.

Such folklore provides the weft in the rich anecdotal tapestry of the village's sense of its place and its social composition through the lives of its
highly individualistic characters. It is a human tapestry viewed with much
humor, as well as suspended judgment: only God knows what is possible;
and in a materially hard world, folkloric elaboration provides humane comfort and endless material for storytelling sociability. A few characters may
serve to illustrate.

At the top of the upper village lived a wealthy Hajji and usurer (*nozulkhor*)
who had connections with both the police and the clergy. (Ayatullah Saduqi
of Yazd used to stay at his house.) One day, a truck delivered a bag of melons for him. The driver called out to Hajji that he was dropping off the purchase, and left. I and some other boys stole the largest melon on top. When
Hajji discovered his loss, he cursed us and our fathers at the top of his lungs.
We waited until very late to return home, hoping our parents would be too
tired to beat us. They were not. We were beaten soundly enough so that our
cries wafted through the village to Hajji. The next day, we planned revenge
on Hajji. We decided to stone his windows. Hajji's house was the only one to
have glass windows. We did not realize that when the lights were on he could
not see out, so we waited until he turned out the lights before throwing
stones. When the lights came on, we stopped. Hajji's house was the highest
up the mountain slope, so we simply climbed above it to throw stones. Hajji
could not figure out what was going on: somehow he did not think it was us.
Instead, he yelled at his two wives that one of them had thrown hot water

carelessly on the heads of the *jinn* and he read out the prayer against the *jinn*. Then he called a diviner. We were afraid the diviner would discover us, and I was very close to confessing to my mother, but fortunately I held back, figuring there would be time if he actually knew. The diviner, however, concluded it must indeed by the *jinn* and that the house was haunted. As a result, Hajji sold his house and moved to town. It was not until years later that I told my father what had happened, and was surprised to learn that none of the boys had told their parents.

Among the other characters of the village there was first Hasan Kadkhoda, the headman, with his pipe and handmade tobacco pouch. He used to be the servant to the previous *kadkhoda*, Hajj Mirza Agha. As was always pointed out, he was a "nobody." Hajj Mirza Agha had fourteen wives and many sons. Being a large landowner, he needed cheap labor. Instead of hiring labor, he married many women, mostly widows, who were happy to be assured daily bread. In contrast, Hasan Kadkhoda had only one wife, and she had only one eye. She was a bitch, and we children were terrified of her loud mouth.

Then there was Rubabeh, the midwife. She was about seventy and lived with an unmarried daughter who had been blinded by smallpox in childhood. Rubabeh was the female healer of the village, curing with herbs. She also baked the most delicious bread. She had a saintly reputation for her piety, her healing, her religious knowledge, and for helping bring so many babies into the world. She herself was also the mother of several men of solid reputation.

There was also Maryam, the female washer of the dead. She was even older than Rubabeh. Most children feared her due to her occupation, but I was used to her since she visited our house frequently. My mother liked her, and my father would tease her by asking her to be his concubine. She was always murmuring prayers, and there were stories about the times God had answered her prayers immediately. Before falling asleep at night, I was told, she repeated the principles of her religion (*usul-i din*) and the names of the Imams so that if she should die in her sleep, they would be able to answer the questions of the angels of death. Whenever there was a drought, people would ask her to pray for rain. I once asked how she did it, and my father suggested that we kids go with her up the mountain to the cave where the Imams had left their footprints. So, one day, two of my sisters and I went with her. This pilgrimage was my first "long trip." Since it was the middle of summer, I knew that Maryam could not ask for rain: there are proper times for asking things of God. But at the cave Maryam began to shout and cry. As her voice echoed in the mountains, I experienced a mixture of fear, excitement, joy, and awe. We then entered the cave: there was a puddle of water and some birds flying about. Maryam said the birds were messengers of God. We sat down for a meal and departed before sunset. My father admired Maryam and would say she was worth more than several men. He would frequently tell the story of the year the month of Muharram fell in the winter and he tried to cancel the annual passion play, which he supervised, because of the snow. Maryam objected, saying snow was a blessing and if we abandoned the religious activities of Muharram, next year there would be no snow, and hence also no water in the spring for irrigation. She took a shovel in hand and shamed the menfolk into helping her clear the village square for one of the best Muharram *taziyehs* (mourning rites) ever held.

Ali "Dallak," the barber, shaved the men, pulled bad teeth with his pliers, and ran the village bathhouse. During his military service he had learned to read and write, and so was something of a religious authority. He circumcised all my age-mates. I was circumcised when I was two. I remember that he called me: "Amu [reciprocal for paternal uncle-nephew], come here, let me see your little dodo and how it has grown." Then snip with a razor. I was so scared I pissed on him. I was then handed over to a woman. My mother was not there, but my father was. There was no ceremony, and certainly no talk of being a man. Children were not supposed to know about sex. The foreskin is supposed to go to an unmarried woman, who chops it up in a mortar and pestle and eats it, to help her catch a husband.

And, of course, there was my father, who always bragged about his calligraphy, his ability to understand religious issues, and his ability to cure illnesses with talismans. If a girl could not find a husband, if a woman's husband no longer liked her and wanted another wife, for any ill, my father had the book of talismans and prayers. He was the male healer for the village, combining herbs, powders, liquids, and tablets, as well as talismans and prayers. For curing, in most cases he did not charge. He had a shop in which he also sharpened knives, sickles, and saws, repaired broken china and stone cooking pots. For this he was paid by the villagers in kind: eggs, yogurt, dried nuts, and other agricultural products. Even peddlers from outside the village often took payment for their wares in kind.

My father was also the supervisor of the passion plays for some forty years, and people would gather at our house from both the upper and lower village on the festival of Ashura. From there a grand procession of floats and *dasteh sineh-zani* (flagellants, mainly boys and young men) would go to the *husayniyeh* down at the bottom of the lower neighborhood.

For two months before Ashura ("the tenth" of the month of Muharram, anniversary of the martyrdom of Imam Husayn on the plains of Karbala), my father would prepare, collecting clothing for costumes, carpets and props for the floats, and reserving particular horses to be ridden. Many items were stored at our house, endowed by the villagers for the passion plays. But no one would refuse a request to lend a fine carpet or *chador* (veil) or animal. The villagers firmly believed that ill would befall anyone who did not participate in the Ashura events. the best horse in the village was reserved for Shemr, the evil general of the Sunni Syrian army, because he had to be able to catch Husayn. The second best horse was reserved for Ali Akbar, the elder son of Husayn, because it took time for Shemr to catch him and traditionally Ali Akbar would fall from his horse so that he could be caught by the aging Shemr. The laziest horse in the village was used to carry the Fourth Imam, the only male who survived the massacre at Karbala because he was sick and did not fight. For a month or so, my father would supervise rehearsals of the chief actors. Shemr was usually played by the husband of my eldest sister. Shemr had to be tall and have a loud voice with which to frighten people. He was dressed from head to toe in red. Occasionally, when he was available (he lived in the city), my brother-in-law's brother would play Shemr, because he had blue eyes (as Shemr is said to have had). Husayn had to be a man in his forties with a full beard. Imam Sajad, the Fourth Imam, was played by a sick old man, in many villages an opium addict, but in our village there were no opium addicts—almost no one was rich enough to support an opium habit—so the part was played by one addicted to a *qaliun* (water pipe).

There were only so many lead roles. Most men participated as porters for the heavy floats. In other villages the floats might be carried by trucks, but our village was too steep and narrow. The floats illustrated all the major events in the life of Imam Husayn for the ten days preceding his martyrdom and the days immediately following, when the women and children were taken off as prisoners to Damascus. The procession was accompanied by lines of black-shirted men beating their breasts with their hands or chains and chanting rhythmic dirges mourning the fate of Husayn. They all wore Arab *kafiyahs* or headbands (*aqqal*). Only the sick and disabled stood on the sidelines with the women and girls.

Beginning when I was five, I was cast for several years as the barely nubile bride of Qassam (the son of Husayn, the Second Imam). I was given this role partly, no doubt, because I was the son of the producer of the show, and partly as a reward for (or out of my father's pride in) my already being able to recite the Quran. In addition, I was part city boy, cleaner, better dressed, and better behaved than the other village boys—the sort who might be trusted not to blow their nose in the fine silk *chador* reserved for the wife of Qassam. The role was intended to make the young girls cry, identifying with the tragic fate of this young widow. I had little white sugar balls (*noql*) to hand out, received as blessed sweets. In second grade, I finally refused to play a woman any longer. What triggered the refusal I no longer exactly remember, but I remember bursting into angry tears at either being pinched, winked at, or obscenely teased as if I were a girl.

Such teasing and humor had a regular place: the man who played Zeinab (sister of Husayn, who led the women and children after the massacre until the sickly Fourth Imam could assume his leadership role) always had a big mustache, and when someone would make a rude comment to him, he would show his mustache from under his *chador*. Typically he had an obscene tongue as well and would respond to such propositioning with retorts like "Yes, I'll sleep with you. Bring your mother, too." There was less such humor during our passion plays than the ones I saw in the city, but afterward there would be a lot of ribald mockery of the *taziyeh*. Shemr and Zeinab would replay their repartee from the passion play in obscene variations such as the following:

> *Shemr.* Agar to Zeinab-i, pas doldolat chist?
>
> If you are Zeinab, then what's that penis?
>
> *Zeinab.* Khoda danad ke in gusht-i ziadist.
>
> God knows it is an extra piece of meat.

And indeed some of the acting could stick to the actor. Thus, someone named Mahmad who played the role of Shemr might come to be called Mahmad Shemr, even if it caused him to bristle and see red.

Once the procession of floats reached the lower village, it would enter the *husayniyeh* and circumambulate counterclockwise. The men were the actors on the *husayniyeh* floor, while women sat up on the walls (*ghurfeh*, "reviewing stand"). Shemr would gallop into the center, calling for Husayn to show himself and announcing to the audience: "I'm neither Shemr, nor is this the land of Karbala; I'm just playing the role." This formula was partly used to fend off the danger that the onlookers would become so enraged at his killing of their beloved Imam that they would kill him. ("In some villages," goes the archetypical Iranian comment, "people actually killed the person playing Shemr.") Partly the formula was to allow Shemr to shed tears, to empty himself as it were, so that he could then take on the hard-hearted role. Then Husayn would enter, crying to the people: "Is there no one to help me?" Ali Akbar would then gallop in, dressed in a white shroud stained with blood and sewn with the arrows that had penetrated his body. He always was played by someone of draft age and was the heartthrob of the girls.

The time frame of the passion play was in fact a mythic, rather than a chronological, one, for, of course, all the events were presented on the floats simultaneously prior to and during the action in the center of the *husayniyeh*. Thus, the head of Husayn was already on a pole, and the good Christian who attempted to intercede on Husayn's behalf was seated on a chair, dressed in safari khaki and shorts, pith helmet, with binoculars, watching the events. The climax of the play came first with Shemr killing Ali Akbar: the lad would fall off his horse and roll in the dust as Shemr cut off his head while Husayn stood by and cried, or feigned crying. (Both actual and pretend tears were regarded as having merit.) Finally, Shemr would kill Husayn, and everyone would rush into the middle, beating their heads in grief.

Afterward, people rushed to eat the special wheat stews (*ash-e gandom*) that were cooked in massive cauldrons. These communal meals were supplied either from perpetual endowments, vows made during the year, or by richer villagers. They usually contained the meat of a freshly slaughtered lamb. I remember with amusement scenes of people eating stew communally off big trays, jockeying to make sure they were sitting next to someone relatively clean with whom to share their dipping.

Such communal meals were also important during the holy month of Ramadan (during which Muslims are enjoined to fast from dawn to dusk). In Ramadan one received double merit for good deeds. The rich paid their debts to God by cooking cauldrons of stew to distribute, sharing the meat of a slaughtered lamb, and sending gifts of dry provisions (e.g., rice) to their neighbors. My grandfather served in his day as the village timekeeper: he was one of the first in the village to have a pocket watch, and just before dawn he would sing hymns of praise (*monajot*) to the First Imam to waken people. Traditionally, villagers would start their fast with the rooster's crow. The first pocket watches did not change things much since people only could tell time when the two hands came together at noon and midnight. Thus, watches were called *zohr-kuk* and *qurur-kuk* (crow of noon, crow of midnight). Just before dawn, my grandfather would sing out the formula *abast o teriak* (only time for a "sip of water and a pull of opium"). It is said that my father's father (he died before I was born) would often substitute the phrase *kaseye tut-i khoshk o kuzeh ab* (only time for a "bowl of dried mulberries"—the main produce of our village—"and a jug of water"). Then he would conclude with *tanbal kahnha ya allah* ("Get up you lazy bums!"). After he died, this role was taken over first by Amu Ali (Uncle Ali), of whom it is said, the first time he saw a radio he recited the *shahadah*, the credo of Islam, and in mock surprise he exclaimed, "So here is the proof of what the preachers say, that at the end of time people can hear each other no matter what the distance." (Radios were enormously popular, and after the first one came to the village, everyone else immediately had to have one.) Then Akbar-i Ramazan took over the role of calling people to the fast: he eventually became the father-in-law of my father, when my father took a second wife after the death of my mother.

My mother was a city girl, the daughter of Gholam Husayn Vasel, a shopkeeper, Sufi, *zurkhaneh* (traditional gymnasium) master, popular storyteller, wit, and interpreter of Rumi's *Masnavi*. He had married the daughter of a rich merchant, Hajj Muhammad Karim Esfahani, who had come to Yazd from Isfahan. Hajj Muhammad Karim's wife was named Maryam, and her father was Yusuf Aghaii, a Jewish rabbi who had converted to Islam in a striking episode. My mother would often say: "The children of Yusuf Aghaii are scattered throughout the world. But we do not know very many of them." What she meant was that children of converts assimilate among Muslims without leaving much trace, but they carry a certain kind of character legacy.

Several morality plots interlace in her invocations of my great-great-grandfather. First, there was the story of Yusuf Aghaii's conversion. As you know, Jews were not allowed into the produce bazaar during the day but only at the end of the day. Being *najes* (carriers of pollution), they could not touch the produce, lest it be declared polluted. To ensure that Muslims got first pick as well as religiously pure food, Jews had to wait until the end of the day to shop. Late one day, Yusuf Aghaii went to buy some yogurt. He dipped his finger in it to see if it was still good and rejected it as sour. The shopkeeper raised a ruckus, crying that Yusuf had defiled the entire container of yogurt. A crowd gathered and things started to turn ugly. Yusuf, in an effort to escape, said: "I may be as good a Muslim as you." The shopkeeper retorted: "Let us go to the *mujtahid* and see." So the crowd took Yusuf to the *mujtahid,* who publicly forced him to eat some yogurt and meat together, thereby violating Jewish dietary rules. It is said that thereafter the Jews rejected him, but that his father, also a rabbi, asked to be allowed to name Yusuf's first child: it was a girl, and the name chosen was Maryam. Now Yusuf had studied both Hebrew and Arabic in Jerusalem, and so, it is said, when he became Muslim he did not need to study any Islamic jurisprudence: he knew it all and was as learned as any *mujtahid.*

One day when I came home as a child, very upset that I was not a *sayyid* (descendent of the Prophet, entitled to wear a green or black turban), my mother consoled me by saying that we were another kind of *sayyid,* that through Yusuf Aghaii we were descended from Haroun (Aaron), the brother of Moses, and that this could be seen in our entire family's gift of gab and rhetorical flair. Haroun, of course, was known for his silver tongue, and the story is well known that when the baby Moses was brought to the pharaoh, the pharaoh tested him by placing before the child some dates and some red-hot coals. The diviners had suggested that if it were just an ordinary child, it would be attracted to the bright red objects, but if this were the future prophet, it would know better and take a date. The child in fact began to reach for the coal, but the angel Gabriel took its hand and caused Moses to pick up the coal and put it on his tongue. Hence Moses stuttered, and when he went to plead his people's case before the pharaoh, God advised him to take Haroun along. And so the majority of Jews are relatively quiet types, but the descendants of Aaron are loquacious and persuasive. And hence: "The children of Yusuf Aghaii [Jewish converts] are scattered throughout the world, but we do not recognize them as such."

Jews, of course, were ambivalent figures in my mother's discourse. She would use Yusuf Aghaii both as reproof when she scolded me and as explanation when I did something intelligent. In the negative vein, she used to cite the popular *hadith,* "al bala lil awlia" (the people of catastrophe/sadness are friends of God), identifying Jews as not friends of God: when Jews raised their faces to God, the angels would immediately demand God grant their wishes so that the stench of Jews would disappear. But when the faithful prayed, the angels would tell God to delay granting their wishes so that they might look longer on their faces. Thus, it was often repeated that Fatima, the daughter of the Prophet, had to wait eighteen years for her wish to be granted.

My mother's father, Gholam Husayn Vasel, must have been a prosperous young man to have married the only daughter of Hajj Muhammad Karim, but he was a Sufi in the true sense, spending all he had and not valuing the material world. Originally, he was a *mazari* (processor of henna). He owned a factory and helped others to establish similar factories in Yazd and Ardakan. (Yazd is still known as a center of henna processing. The raw material comes from farther east in Kirman province.) He had traveled a great deal and composed an epic poem about his adventures, which ended:

> Abul Qassem sits like a mouse.
> Creditors raise hell.
> One claps his forehead,
> Another beats his breast.
> Most upset of all is the broker.

Indeed, Gholam Husayn had to sell the business to pay off his debts. He later bought a small grocery. It caught fire and burned. For the last fourteen years of his life he was blind, and he died destitute. He seemed not to mind: the world was but a passage to the real life. But I think it was after the death of his young wife that he lost interest in the world. He raised his son and three daughters with difficulty, managing to educate them and marry them off, albeit none lived up to his mark. His son, Abul Qassem, a tailor, married the daughter of a *mullah* but had no offspring. His youngest daughter, Khojasteh, married a coppersmith and had three sons and a daughter, all of whom are educated and relatively prosperous. The eldest daughter, Marziyeh, married a sugar-shop employee, who suddenly disappeared for seven years, then reappeared with a good education from India and became a customs clerk in Ahwaz. They had a daughter (Rakhshandeh) and three sons: Muhammad-Ali Sirjani became a physician and major in the army and died a suspicious death in the recent revolution; Mahmud became a high school teacher, and Mehdi died at age eighteen shortly before I was born, contributing to the conundrums of my own naming.

My mother's father's death is among my earliest memories. When I related this memory to my mother many years later, she was quite surprised.

His bed was in the middle of the summer room and everyone sat around him. The barber came and trimmed his gray beard, but when he touched the mustache, grandfather stopped him, waving his hand to say, not this part. Then, a few minutes later (my mother corrected me that it was a few days later), when I was crawling near the courtyard pond with a little bell around my neck, my mother suddenly came into the courtyard, wailing.

My mother, Farkhondeh, was the middle daughter. Beautiful, with thick black hair down to her knees, always braided and hanging on her back, she was witty, a living encyclopedia of poetry, a *hafez* of the Quran (a *hafez* is one who memorizes the entire Quran), a weaver, and a professional dress weaver. The neighborhood women loved her and called our house *bagh-i delgosha* (garden of the open heart), because she had a way of making even the saddest person laugh and because despite our poverty she was the most generous of souls. She had her most beautiful moments with God, when she melodiously sang the Quran and prayers. Despite my love for my father, I must say, she was a world wasted in his house. Once, I asked her why she had married him. She said it was her fate.

My father, the spoiled only son of a relatively well-to-do farmer, had been encouraged by his parents to marry a city girl. My father's father owned a house in Yazd in the same neighborhood as my mother's family. Periodically, he would come from Dareh to collect the rent and to sell dried mulberries. My mother's family had fallen on hard times and so was happy to give their daughter to a villager who could at least guarantee steady food. Otherwise a villager could never have dreamed of marrying a granddaughter of Hajj Muhammad Karim. In the village, my father owned some land and was well connected. His father's sister had married the eldest son of the then *kadkhoda* (headman), Hajj Ismail, who must have owned half the village. His village occupations and religious roles I have already described in the preceding section.

If the date on my birth certificate is to be believed, I was born on the tenth of Shahrivar 1331 Shamsi (31 August 1952). I was the sixth surviving child. My oldest sister, Safa, had already married two years earlier and had a son. She married the eldest son of my father's only sister. My brother Ahmad was the second child, and there were three other sisters: Ezzat, Fatemeh, and Robab. My mother was to have, all told, fourteen pregnancies, of which seven survived. (I have a younger brother.) According to my mother, she was baking bread in the basement kitchen when she felt the labor pains. Everyone had gone to the fields to pick fruit. The old midwife, Rubabeh, was a neighbor and could be called in an emergency, but my mother thought she had time to finish the bread. When she realized there was no time, it was too late, and she could hardly move. She called out a few times, but no one heard. She began reciting prayers, hoping someone would stop by. So I was born. She cut the cord, wrapped me in some clothes, put me under a basket with a stone on top, so no animal could get at me, and went to call Rubabeh. When everyone returned, there was joy that I was a boy, that is, on everyone's part except my elder brother, who felt his special status threatened.

My father named me Mehdi, but since my eighteen-year-old cousin (mother's sister's son), also Mehdi, had just died, my family decided to address me as Gholam Husayn, or Gholi for short, the name of both my grandfathers. The name Mehdi was used only on the birth certificate, and I was seven before I learned my real name. That happened because when I was registered for school in Yazd my legal name was given, and when the teacher called out "Mehdi Abedi" at first I did not respond, though I had a vague feeling it might be me. I had never liked the name Gholi, which I associated both with the word for ghouls (*ghul*) and the word for a small bell (*ghuri*) that had been tied around my neck as a toddler. So I went home and said I wanted to be called Mehdi. The custom of changing an infant's name, if there was a death or illness in the family, or even of "selling" the child to another set of parents, was a kind of evil-eye avoidance, to confuse the forces of harm so they could not find or identify the child. It is of historical interest that the name Mehdi was not particularly popular earlier in the century but became very popular for children of my age cohort. This was no arbitrary flux of fashion but a kind of campaign launched by Muslim believers to thumb their noses at the Bahais (who claimed that the Mahdi had already come in the person of Bahaullah).

Similarly, at the same time it became popular to call the Mahdi or Imam Zaman, Ala Hazrat (His Majesty), to deny the use of that title by the Shah. Pro-Khomeini activists, however, soon called for a ban on this practice, as well as on all monarchical titles for the Imams: thus they asked that one no longer refer to the Eighth Imam, Imam Reza, as Sultan or Shah-i Khorasan; nor should one call Ali, Shah-i Vilayat. Instead, the Imams ought to be called Abd-i Saleh Khodah (Righteous Servant of God). The struggle between religious sources of legitimacy and royal ones was symbolized in cities like Yazd by the *azan*, the call to prayer, which served as a public timekeeping device, and by the drum and trumpet sounds (*naqqareh khaneh* and *surna*) at dawn and dusk issuing from atop the governor's palace. My mother used to say she could always especially tell from the vigor of the latter how stable the government was: when loud and martial, the governor was in full control; when the sound was more playful, it was a harbinger that the musicians could feel the governor on the defensive and liable to be deposed. When Reza Shah was deposed, she reported, people said the trumpets' sound bursts seemed to be saying *tu kos-i zan-i shah* (up the Shah's wife's) . . . .

I did not get to Hafiz with the *mullah* Monavvar. I got through the Quran, at which point I celebrated my first *noql kardan,* a ceremony in which sweets and coins and nuts mixed together would be sprinkled over the young scholar's head, which other children could scramble for; and there would be a gift for the scholar. I remember with some embarrassment that my mother wanted to do the ceremony, but we were so poor that she could only afford the *noql* and not a gift. I knew the situation, and so I also scrambled for the *noql* and coins, probably to the dismay of my mother.

When I was five, we spent the winter in the city (Yazd) and I was sent to a pious woman *mullah* to learn the Quran. In the Yazd area, *mullah* is the proper term for one who teaches the rudiments of literacy. (Hence, Jews were often addressed with the title *mullah* because they were almost universally literate.) Her name was Monavvar and she had about ten students, each at a different level. While teaching, she also made bags for a henna company, and we sometimes helped. She taught me the alphabet and the reading of the first sura of the Quran. I already knew much of the Quran by heart, because my mother was a *hafez* and she often recited parts of it. It was a tradition to have a celebration (*noql kardan*) when students finished the first sura; the first, second, and eighth *joz* (thirtieths) of the Quran; and of course when they finished the whole Quran, at which time they were assumed to have acquired literacy in Arabic. In addition to the round sugar balls mixed with nuts and coins that were sprinkled over the scholar's head and the gift for the scholar, the teacher also would be given gifts relative to the family status of the child.

Following memorization of the Quran, students went on to the Persian poet Hafiz as an introduction to Persian literacy. Various things might follow Hafiz: the *Masnavi* of Jalal al-Din Rumi was particularly popular. All of this was just reading, not writing. My older sisters learned the Quran and Hafiz this way. They can no longer really read, but they can open Hafiz and "read" the familiar verses they have half memorized. Such literacy was referred to as *siahi ba sefidi farq gozashtan* (knowing black from white, that is, the print from the page). This is the connection between the Persian term for literacy, *savad*, and the Arabic word for black, *sud*.

Following the celebration, we went back to the village, where I was sent to another *mullah*, an old shroud weaver. Despite the high infant mortality rate, there was barely enough work for her to make a living making shrouds, so she also taught the Quran. Each student had a little carpet or goatskin on which to sit, which we kept at her house. Going to this *mullah* could be terrifying, for she would threaten to send us to the *surakh-i mar-mush khaneh* (the snake-mouse hole, namely, the dark basement, which was particularly scary in a village mud house perpetually falling into ruins), or she might use her knitting needle to draw blood from the back of our hands or she might bastinado the bottoms of our feet if we did not do our lessons properly. I did not like her and soon quit.

I was placed with another *mullah*, a young widow, a weaver with long, dark hair. Her husband had died during a hunting trip from a fall in the mountains. She had a lovely voice and would sing with the rhythm of her loom. She taught us the rules of ritual cleanliness and the daily prayers. We were mischievous kids, and there were opportunities for mischievousness when we were sent to the river to do the ablutions for prayer. There were trees that provided cover from being watched too closely. Our leader was a girl of about eight or nine. She liked to take her pants off, and we liked to watch. In the villages, children who are around animals learn about sex earlier perhaps than children in the city, even if they do not connect sex with pregnancy. We would play at sex, comparing penis sizes, having erections and fellatio. One day of course someone saw us and raised a fuss. The big girl never came back to learn the Quran.

I had learned just over half the Quran when I quit. My mother decided it was enough for the time being. It was a bad year of drought. Many villagers had left to work as construction workers in the city. There was nothing to eat except bread made of American wheat. For some reason it was uncleaned, and one day a piece of bread baked with this wheat got stuck in my mouth. When my mother pulled it out, it was found to contain a large thorn. She angrily threw away the rest of the bread and declared that she would no longer live this miserable life in the village and subsist on charity. She would go to the city and work as a maid for her mother's brother and she would take me: I was old enough to earn a little money. My father got very angry. But a few days later we packed for the city and left.

A NOTE ON SOURCES

This essay is simplified and excerpted from a longer piece recently published as the first chapter of our *Debating Muslims: Cultural Dialogues in Tradition and Post-modernity* (Madison: University of Wisconsin Press, 1990), where we explain the collaborative process of writing:

> We have worked together on a variety of projects since 1970 when Fischer as a young graduate student in Yazd hired Abedi, still in his teens, to translate Islamic texts. We helped each other to learn the other's language and culture. What began as Abedi's effort to convert Fischer and Fischer's use of Abedi's argumentation as an anthropological access into the world of Shi'ism, gradually turned into a deep friendship and genuine set of collaborations. Abedi's autobiography consists of stories Abedi has shared over the years; some he wrote down at Fischer's urging, some were elicited orally in rich memory-laden "bull sessions." We had fun retelling them and shaping a chapter around them, Abedi reminding Fischer about Yazdi places, people, events and practices. Yazd was home to Fischer for some two and a half years (1969–1972), and he helped

celebrate the birth of Abedi's first son, Reza, there. In 1975 Fischer spent the academic year in Qum, and Abedi came with his wife and child to live with him for three months, and to work as a research assistant on the project that eventuated in the book *Iran: From Religious Dispute to Revolution*. In 1981 Abedi came with Fischer to Rice University to pursue a Ph.D. degree in anthropology, and as we completed this manuscript, we also celebrated the birth of Abedi's second son, Maysam Morad. [xxxii]

SUGGESTIONS FOR FURTHER READING

For accounts and memoirs of Iranian life, see Erika Friedl, *Women of Deh Koh: Lives in an Iranian Village* (Washington, D.C.: Smithsonian Institution Press, 1989); Shusha Guppy, *The Blindfold Horse: Memories of a Persian Childhood* (Boston: Beacon Press, 1988); Michael M. J. Fischer, "Portrait of a Mullah: The Autobiography of Aqa Najafi Quchani," *Persica* 10 (1982): 223–57. See also Farideh Goldin, *Wedding Song: Memoirs of an Iranian Jewish Woman* (Hanover, N.H.: Brandeis University Press, 2003). Memoirs of Iranian elites include Sattareh Farman Farmaian, *Daughter of Persia* (New York: Anchor Books, 1993); and Manucher Farmanfarmaian and Roxanne Farmanfarmaian, *Blood and Oil: Memoirs of a Persian Prince* (New York: Modern Library, 1999).

See also the novels by Fereydun Esfandiary, *Day of Sacrifice* (New York: McDowell, Oblonsky, 1959), and Taghi Modarressi, *The Pilgrim's Rules of Etiquette* (New York: Doubleday, 1989).

On Iranian Shiism, see Roy Mottahedeh, *The Mantle of the Prophet: Religion and Politics in Iran* (New York: Pantheon, 1985). See also Michael M. J. Fischer, *Iran: From Religious Dispute to Revolution* (Cambridge, Mass.: Harvard University Press, 1980); Said Arjomand, *The Turban for the Crown: The Islamic Revolution in Iran* (New York: Oxford University Press, 1988); and Hamid Algar, *Religion and State in Iran, 1785–1906* (Berkeley: University of California Press, 1969).

Chapter 17

Gulab: An Afghan Schoolteacher

Ashraf Ghani

As in Morocco, Yemen, and Iran, other Islamic states where pastoralist tribal forces maintained their power into the twentieth century against weak governments, the politics of Afghanistan have been characterized by sharp conflict between the forces of tradition rooted in the countryside and the forces of change based in the cities. In fact, the Afghan experience can be seen as an exaggerated variant of that of the region as a whole. Yet Afghanistan is also different from these other states. It ranks at the bottom of most international development statistics in meeting basic human needs. This disturbing fact can be starkly represented as follows: the total annual consumption of energy in all forms by an Afghan tribesman, it is said, is equivalent to the amount of energy it takes to produce one soft-drink can. Because of the huge gaps between rich and poor, modern and traditional, rural and urban, in Afghanistan, the struggle between groups favoring change and those seeking to maintain the old ways has taken on a particular intensity. It is therefore understandable that a murderous civil war should have erupted.

The life of Gulab, the Pashtu-speaking schoolteacher from the city of Khost in eastern Afghanistan, whose biography is here presented by Ashraf Ghani, can be situated in the midst of and characterized in terms of this struggle. Gulab is the classic man in the middle. In 1978, on the eve of the civil war, he found himself besieged by the demands of conflicting political groups, each of which claimed to have *the solution* to Afghanistan's problems, and each of which sought his support. The choices were mutually contradictory. To select one was to deny a part of himself. Hence Gulab's paralysis. Ghani's portrait of Gulab makes clear what the stakes were for ordinary Afghans and why the situation was so explosive.

Through Gulab we come to understand the importance of the internal social and political divisions of Afghanistan. Some divisions are linguistic, like that between the Persian (Dari)-speakers, based in the west of the country and in the cities, and the mostly rural and tribal Pashtu-speakers, in the central and eastern districts. Others pit the rural forces, dominated by the tribal aristocracy, against the government and merchants in the urban centers. Islam itself is divided between local and Sufi groups, which tended to support the status quo, and a host of competing and mostly urban groups inspired by radical Islamic doctrines imported from Pakistan, Egypt, and Iran. We learn that the radical Islamists and their equally radical Marxist opponents were both predominantly urban; both required a sharp break with established customs. Until the start of the civil war in 1978, neither had much appeal for the predominantly Pashtun tribal groups.

The biography of Gulab provides a guide to the turbulent world of Afghan politics in the 1970s. To situate his life more precisely, we might here briefly summarize the central dynamics of modern Afghan political history. Until the early 1970s, Afghanistan was a monarchy dominated by urban-based supporters of modernization, grouped around the Pashtun leader Muhammad Daud in alliance with elements of the mostly Pashtun tribal aristocracy. Because of Afghanistan's strategic location between Iran and Pakistan and its common frontier with the Soviet Union and China, the Cold War years were ones of active competition in Afghanistan between Soviet and American influences, mitigated by a tacit agreement between the two superpowers not to compel Afghanistan to choose sides.

The status quo was challenged in 1973, when Daud suppressed the monarchy in a coup d'état in order to introduce a program of drastic reforms. Because of a political miscalculation, his regime failed to develop a solid political base and was compelled to resort to repressive policies and an alliance with the United States to stay in power. The competition between Islamist and Marxist groups for supporters intensified. Eventually, the political contradictions of the government provoked a coup by the army and the intelligentsia, in which Marxist factions played a leading role. When the new regime adopted an ill-considered series of radical measures (including a far-reaching land-reform program, an end to usury, and an end to Islamic marriage practices), this challenged the power of the tribal aristocracy and generated widespread popular opposition. It is at this point, just before the outbreak of the civil war, that we leave Gulab. The history of Afghanistan since this period has been tumultuous, to say the least. The biography of Gulab helps understand how the unraveling began.

The portrait of Gulab may be profitably compared with the biographies of other provincial youth in this book, including Mehdi Abedi, Rostam, Nasir, and Ahmed Chaabani (husband of Nadia). —Eds.

Just as the thick dark of the night was giving way to the pale light of early dawn the ringing of the alarm clock shook Gulab out of his sleep. He hastily got out of his cot and, after making his ablutions, rushed to the local mosque. With a sigh of relief he noted that other people were still arriving. He was keenly aware that some people were keeping a close record of his attendance, as well as of his other activities. As he mechanically performed the rituals, his mind wandered over the conflicting demands that were ripping his life apart.

Like everybody else in the mosque of Khost in southeastern Afghanistan, Gulab had been born in the vicinity of the town. He was thirty or thirty-one years old. As dates of birth were not recorded, he did not know his exact age, but he knew the tribal lore well. He remembered the times spent with his father memorizing the names of his seven paternal ancestors, as required by custom. His father had made sure that Gulab and his three brothers knew the names of the various lineages and clans that jointly made up the Pashtun ethnic group. They were also told about the groups that were allied together and those that carried on feuds.

When Gulab was a boy, his father owned four acres of irrigated land and about forty watered by rainfall in a village fifteen miles east of Khost. He was also involved in the illegal trade between Khost and towns across the border in Pakistan. The biggest item of trade at the time was wood. Some of the now barren mountains were forested then, and others had a much thicker layer of green. But people had to make a living and nobody was concerned about the changing nature of the scenery or the erosion that deforestation would precipitate.

In those years, Khost was not a particularly healthy place. It was infested with malaria and the people preferred their cooler villages on the upper hills to the damp and flat valley in which the town was located. Few people wanted to settle in Khost for long. Yet a government garrison had been stationed in the town since the mid-nineteenth century, and the governor of Paktia province spent the winters in the town.

But it had not been Gulab's lot to avoid Khost. He remembered his first trip there well. One day when he was about six years old, he and his brother Sur Gul, who was a year younger, were told to put on their fine clothes and were taken to the town. In those days, there were no trucks or buses linking the villages to the town and the boys were put on a donkey while the older men walked. One of Gulab's two sisters was married to a man whose village was about two miles from Khost, and the brothers were told at first that they would be staying there for some time. In fact, they were to attend the school in Khost for the next six years.

Gulab's father was illiterate. He had not allowed his eldest son to go to school and, as it later turned out, was not going to permit the youngest one to enroll either, but his dealings with the governmental machinery had convinced him that it might be useful to send his two middle sons to school. So, in 1956, Gulab and Sur Gul found themselves in school.

The two boys were terrified by the discipline. Whenever they felt the need, teachers and headmasters used the stripped branch of an almond tree on the students. Most of the students were much older than the two brothers; some had spent two or three years in the same grade without learning to read or write. As the central government held the headmaster accountable for the number of enrollments per year—public schooling was in theory compulsory—those students unwilling to attend the classes were dragged there by the school's orderlies. A generous bribe to the headmaster was the only way their parents had to release them from their misery. After their pleas to return to the carefree life of the village were rejected, Gulab and Sur Gul accepted the inevitable and passed their exams regularly. Despite their acclimation, they cherished their three-month summer vacations, which they spent in their home village sharing the schemes of their age-mates.

Graduation from the elementary school brought about a longer period of exile for the two brothers. Through some connections in Kabul a member of their lineage learned that the government had established two special high schools for students of the border areas. Unlike other schools in the capital, in the special schools the language of instruction was Pashtu. In addition to room and board, students were granted a monthly stipend. The relative persuaded Gulab's father to enroll Gulab in one of the high schools and to send Sur Gul to a military school, also located in Kabul.

This time, the trip was longer and more strenuous. After tearful partings from their mothers, who entrusted each with a bundle containing clothes, some home-baked cookies, and a cone of refined cane sugar, a band of thirty boys from villages surrounding Khost headed toward Gardez, the provincial capital. Steered by five elders from different clans, the group took three days to walk the one hundred or so miles separating the two towns. They spent the nights in mosques or guest houses of the various clans along the way. It rained on the last day of their trip, and when they reached Gardez not only were they soaked but the sugar in their sacks had melted, permeating all their clothes with a special smell. The owners of the tea-houses that also served as guest houses refused to receive them at first, until one of the elders accompanying them found a local friend who intervened on their behalf.

Gardez was much larger than Khost; its size and the number of soldiers pacing its streets awed the boys. They listened with fear as some shopkeepers described the methods of torture that the governor administered to those who dared defy his orders. However, the sight of the trucks on which they were to be taken to Kabul overjoyed them. The trucks were loaded with wood on which they had to sit, but this was the first time most of them were to ride in a vehicle and they were thrilled at the prospect and pleased to not be walking. They sang Pashtu martial and love poetry and were amazed at the speed of their journey. The trucks were making about ten to fifteen miles an hour!

Covered with dust from the dirt road, they reached Kabul after about ten hours' travel. Henceforth, Gulab's and Sur Gul's lives were to be inter-twined with the rapid tempo of political change in the capital. Nobody had any inkling of what the future held in store, of course, and when he was taken to his room in the school and shown his bed, all that a tired Gulab desired was blissful sleep. The night was quiet, but with dawn the new adjustments began.

Life in school resembled that in a military barracks, and there were elaborate rules for what could and what could not be done. The rest of the city remained a great mystery to Gulab and his fellow students. On holidays and Fridays they walked around the town and even at times managed to see a movie, but they never made any real contact with the local people. Gulab slowly mastered the Persian language, but the opportunity to use it was basically confined to the classroom and his weekly rounds in the markets of Kabul. Gulab spent six years in the school, yet not once did he have a meal in a house. The only home he visited was that of the principal, but not for social purposes. The principal was building two new houses for himself, and to avoid hiring labor, he assigned teams of students to work on the site.

In these years, Gulab's perception of Afghanistan underwent radical changes. Textbooks told him of an indestructible country that had managed to resist all attempts at annexation and conquest for some three thousand years. While he readily imbibed this part of the nationalist credo, he was more ambivalent about the portrayal of rural revolts. The textbooks painted an image of a progressive central government whose designs were destroyed by the bigotry of the rural people. Not far from his school was a monument called the Minaret of Knowledge and Ignorance, which celebrated the victory of the reforming government over the rebels of Khost in 1924. But Gulab had heard a different story about Khost. The elders of the village had told him that they had been resisting a despotic government's interference in their customs and its demands for revenue. At home, Gulab himself had repeatedly sung some of the antigovernment poetry of the period. To say the least, he was confused by the discordance of the two versions.

During their three-month summer vacations, Gulab and his brother went back to their village near Khost. Transportation now reached the town, and the boys rode on the back of trucks. They were becoming adolescents, and there was talk of looking for suitable matches for them. As the last year of high school approached, the boys' family arranged their engagements to two girls from nearby villages. Since they had never seen the girls before, they spent long hours wondering what they looked like. Custom allowed the future mothers-in-law to arrange for the couples to meet without the knowledge of their husbands, who played the role of stern patriarchs. Gulab and Sur Gul were finally permitted to see their future wives in the presence of their mothers, but nobody quite knew what to say and they just stole glances at each other. By that time, vacation was over, and the boys had to return to school.

Life in school was suddenly transformed. A spate of high school student unrest and widespread political agitation at Kabul University had erupted following General Muhammad Daud's ouster as prime minister, a post he had held for about a decade. The movement had taken five years to reach Gulab's school, which was finally in the throes of overdue change.

Food in the school had always been bad. It was common knowledge among the students that part of the funds assigned to their upkeep was diverted to pay for the principal's new houses. Nobody had dared to complain, taking for granted that all government bureaucrats were corrupt. On hearing that the Ministry of Education had considered similar complaints from the students of Kabul University, some of Gulab's classmates decided to follow their example. They even convinced a number of students, including Gulab, to accompany them to the university to talk to the college students.

This was Gulab's first visit to the university. He was amazed to see so many extremely well-dressed girls and boys and, at first, took them to be part of the staff, only to learn they were all students. A number had their own cars, and others used chauffeur-driven government cars. When he expressed his surprise at this wealth, a friend commented that these students came from a class other than that to which people like Gulab and himself belonged. Seeing the expression of bewilderment on Gulab's face, the friend explained that the word "class" expressed the difference in wealth and social standing of different segments of society.

Gulab knew that in his village there were people called *mala*, which meant "filled with food," and those called *wigi*, which meant "hungry." He knew that the size of landholdings in Khost was unequal. But a considerable part of the land of one person, if not all of it, would not be enough to pay for one of the cars the students were driving. A thought suddenly flashed through his mind: if the sons displayed so much wealth, how wealthy must the fathers be!

The sight of the university made such an impression on Gulab that he could not absorb the advice he and the other students were given on how to voice their discontent. The idea of bringing their complaints to the Ministry of Education, however, was circulated among his fellow students, and although most were frightened, they all agreed that the situation was intolerable. A few days later, some students challenged the authority of the principal by refusing to eat their supper. Infuriated, the principal reacted by trying to beat one of them. Others came to his rescue and a melee broke out between students and orderlies. Some teachers intervened and soon a representative of the Ministry of Education arrived at the scene of the fight. After inquiries that took almost a month, the school got a new principal, the food improved, and there was no more talk of working on housing sites in the evening.

Soon it was time to prepare for the entrance exam to the university. Only by accident did the students, who were familiar only with writing essay examinations by rote, learn that it was to be of the multiple-choice type. A friend from the university volunteered to explain what this meant and even gave them a trial exam. When the examiners came from the university, they took only a couple of minutes to explain the procedure before administering the exam.

After some six months of anxious waiting, Gulab learned that he had been admitted to the School of Natural Sciences. He was granted a place in the dormitory, where he was to share a room with five other people, none of whom was from the vicinity of Khost. Two were Pashtu-speakers, but the other three spoke hardly a word of it. Also, all professors lectured in Persian. Gulab made a strong effort to understand what was said in class, but he was acutely aware that the students from Kabul made fun of his accent. Not wishing to risk ridicule, he grew reticent in class and would not take part in discussions.

Life in the dormitory was different. Gulab thought it funny that he was becoming closer to his Persian-speaking roommates than to the Pashtu-speaking ones. These last two came from major landowning families and everybody was soon aware that they had used forged documents on their family income in order to qualify for the subsidies provided by the university. They carried sufficient cash to go regularly to restaurants and movies. When in a good mood, they even spoke of their exploits with women and told Gulab that they made regular visits to prostitutes. Gulab, who had never been told that one could have access to a woman outside the bonds of marriage, now realized there were many things he did not know and braced himself for future surprises.

Gulab's three Persian-speaking roommates came from a background similar to his own. One, from the valley of Darwaz in the province of Badakhshan, told Gulab that his village was right on the banks of the Oxus River, which bordered the Soviet Union. Gulab was amazed to learn that there was a large town on the Soviet side of the border and that it had an airport where some fifteen to twenty planes landed every day. Gulab had been to the airport of Kabul only once, but the description of the Soviet airport convinced him that it was much larger than the Kabul airport. And he marveled that the airport of the Soviet capital must be even larger than that of a provincial town.

He also learned that people in Badakhshan spoke several languages and that Persian was not, in fact, his friend's mother tongue. It was the same with another of his roommates, who came from a small village in the province of Balkh, in northern Afghanistan, and whose mother tongue was Uzbek. Only the third roommate, who came from Hazarajat in central Afghanistan, was a native Persian-speaker, but even his accent was not like that of Kabul. Although the boys at first hesitated to trust each other, they gradually found that they had a lot in common. Other differences, however, gradually came to the fore.

All were aware that there were students who were members of various political parties, and Gulab had even heard some of them deliver speeches on oppression and class struggle in a corner of the campus where a forum was regularly held. Toward the end of the first semester, one of these boys, who lived in the next room, approached Gulab and asked whether he would be interested in reading some of their literature. Gulab said he would not mind, and the student gave him three novels written in Pashtu by Noor Muhammad Taraki, who was to become president of Afghanistan some ten years later, after the coup of April 1978.

These books centered on a description of life in rural Afghanistan and of migrant Afghan labor in British colonial India. Religious dignitaries were condemned as parasites, and the consumption orientation of the rural and urban upper classes was deplored. But the books also had a positive message. In each one, the chief character was made to declare that if the working people united they could put an end to this condition of inequality and abolish the stratification of society.

Gulab was favorably impressed and asked his contact for more material. Meanwhile, he discussed the books with his three roommates. To Gulab's surprise, one of the boys told him that although the author claimed to be a socialist, he was in fact a Pashtun chauvinist and that most of his followers were Pashtuns. The second said that he could not possibly agree with an atheistic author, and that Islam, although abused like any other religion, was capable of being generated from within. True equality, he said, had only existed during the reign of the first four caliphs. The third one disagreed with all of them, declaring that the Soviet Union, which had inspired the author in advocating a method of peaceful struggle, was no longer revolutionary. He maintained that the only revolutionary country in the world was the People's Republic of China, that the only true harbinger of the future was the Maoist group in Afghanistan. Taken aback, Gulab did not know how to respond. When his three friends realized that he had not, in fact, joined the party of Taraki, they each urged upon him their own literature and implored him to meet with their comrades who would explain their course of conduct to him in detail. Although Gulab agreed to take a look at their material, he had to prepare for his examinations and did not get around to reading it until the next year. But the discussion in the room continued, and while Gulab listened, each of the three boys stuck to his position and attacked that of the others.

One day just before the beginning of the summer vacation, Gulab's brother Sur Gul, who was attending the military academy and whom Gulab now saw only occasionally, came to his room in great excitement. He had been granted a scholarship to pursue his studies in the Soviet Union and would be leaving in six months. Training was provided by the USSR, the only country offering military aid to Afghanistan. The brothers rushed to the bus station—by now, buses were running to Khost—and told a relative who was a bus driver to inform the family of Sur Gul's good fortune. A week later, Gulab and Sur Gul left for home.

The family had changed during their absence. Gulab's father and elder brother were now involved in smuggling Pakistani cloth to different provinces in Afghanistan and in taking wood from Paktia province into Pakistan. The father was also negotiating to become the agent of a company that imported spare truck parts to be smuggled into Pakistan. The family, with a group of friends, had bought some camels for transporting the goods across the border. They had also invested in a mini-truck, and Gulab's youngest brother, who had not been sent to school, was transporting people and goods between Khost and the surrounding villages. The family members were wearing better clothes and eating more meat and rice than during Gulab's childhood.

Upon the boys' arrival, the topic of conversation became Sur Gul's impending departure and the responsibilities of the family. Although everybody had heard that the Soviet Union was an atheistic country, the father and elder brother were not particularly worried by this and were happy that Sur Gul had been granted the scholarship. An officer who was related to a business associate had told Gulab's father that recipients of these scholarships advanced very rapidly in their careers and were bound to be entrusted with important government posts. Obviously, all the family would gain from his influence.

The discussion turned to the marriage of the two boys. As Gulab was older, he was expected to marry first. The plans had been that Gulab's marriage would take place in a year and Sur Gul's in three years. But Sur Gul's imminent departure changed the whole picture. The family could not meet the expense of two marriages on such short notice and yet did not know how to avoid hurting Gulab's feelings and violating the custom. Sensing the dilemma, Gulab came forward and said there was no need for him to marry at the moment, that he would go and explain the problem to his future in-laws. The father and the elder brother agreed and advised Gulab that when he paid his visit he should take a sheep and some special presents. Without the consent of Sur Gul, it was decided that his wedding would take place in a month.

On the eve of the occasion, Gulab's father, his four sons, and some of the elders of the village drove to the bride's village and gave her father the last installment of the bride-price. Half of the money had already been given at the time of the engagement. The total sum amounted to fifty thousand *afghanis*—the price of one acre of irrigated land—and the family spent another ten thousand on the marriage ceremony itself. The teenage bride was brought to Sur Gul's village and during his five years in the Soviet Union she stayed with his family.

Meanwhile, Gulab gained the confidence of his future mother-in-law and several times she allowed him to visit his fiancée alone. Gulab found her quite pleasant and was fairly happy with what fate had brought him. He was so busy during all these months that he completely forgot about the literature that his roommates had given him. He saw the books again as he was preparing his bag just before leaving for Kabul.

The political climate of Kabul was as intense as ever, and Gulab soon found himself in the midst of conflicting demands. There were frequent demonstrations, speeches every day in the special corner of the campus, and intense discussions in the dormitory on the merits and shortcomings of various parties. Professors took sides more or less openly and actively tried to build a loyal following among the students. There were allegations that grades reflected the political beliefs of the students more than their competence. There were also rumors that some of the professors took bribes and that most of the rich students were passing without studying. There was even talk that some members of the faculty took advantage of female students. Everyone was full of accusations and Gulab did not know who to believe.

As he slowly read over the material that he was given, one question bothered him more and more. What did all this have to do with Afghanistan? He read the Chinese attacks on the Soviet Union and those of the latter on the former. He read fragments of a piece on how out of ten hours of work the workers were given wages for only five, but there were very few industrial workers in the country. Even the literature of the Muslim group dealt with Syria and Egypt. Gulab spent most of the year considering the merits of the pieces he was reading and preparing for his exam.

From time to time, his father and two brothers from the village would visit him on their way to other provinces in Afghanistan. Gulab's father even spoke of buying some land in northern Afghanistan. Gulab's involvement in the family economy was minimal; he was never asked his opinion and kept his thoughts to himself. But even in his own mind he did not know how to react to the relative expansion of his family's resources.

When Gulab returned for his vacation, plans for his wedding were under way and he was soon married. By the time he left, his wife was expecting a baby. Gulab, of course, had no income of his own, and all the expenses of his wedding and the maintenance of his wife were paid by the family. He took advantage of every major holiday to visit home, but as the trip took two days each way he could not make it as often as he wished.

By Gulab's third year of studies, things at the university were in turmoil. Demands for the establishment of a student council led to a full-scale student strike and the government stopped supplying food to the dorms and asked the students to leave. Although the university was officially closed for some time, committees of students and faculty met regularly and became even firmer in their demands. Students raised funds from inside the country, and even Afghan students from abroad sent money to provide food for the university. It was during this strike that Gulab became known as a sympathizer of Taraki, although he had not officially joined his party. One day he was taken to Taraki's house, which was located only a couple of miles from the campus. Taraki was a plump man with a clean-shaven head. In his humble manner, he told the group that their demands were legitimate and that history would prove them right.

Gulab was becoming fairly active in the strike when he received a message that his father was seriously ill. He reached home just in time to witness his father's last words, a request that his sons remain united. With the death of his father, the authority in the house passed over to the elder brother. Since harvest time was approaching and the family had been deprived of an active member, the elder brother asked Gulab to oversee the management of the house. Gulab stayed the summer until the university reopened. During this time, his wife gave birth to a son.

Back for his final year at the university, he continued his political activity, which now included trying to recruit others to his beliefs. He was told by members of Taraki's party to make use of his knowledge of local conditions to attract the sympathies of students from the region of Khost. Although some joined, others were quitting. The membership of the various groups was not stable and there was much crossing over. Gulab himself did not feel particularly bound and still did not join Taraki's party officially. There were more strikes, more protests. All of the city was gripped by the debates in parliament on the question of languages. A proposal for turning Pashtu into an official language was being considered, but for months the quorum was not met. There was also pending a treaty with Iran on the division of the waters of the Helmand River, which had become an issue throughout the country; this was portrayed as an act of national treason by all the opposition parties. Just as Gulab was preparing for his final examinations in the university came the coup of 1973.

General Muhammad Daud, cousin and brother-in-law of the king and prime minister from 1953 to 1962, overthrew the monarchy and declared the republic. A large number of the posts in the cabinet were given to junior officers, who according to rumors were sympathetic to the parties on the left. Yet open political life in the country came to an end, continuing only underground.

Gulab received his B.A. in chemistry and was assigned to teach high school in the valley of Aryoub in Paktia province. Aryoub was not very far from Khost, but as it was not on the road between Kabul and Khost, Gulab had never been there. As he rode on the back of a truck toward Aryoub, he was amazed by the beauty of the forest that unfolded in front of his eyes. Unlike the semibarren valleys that surrounded Khost, the mountains were all densely covered with trees. To his dismay, he learned that even from here the wood was increasingly taken to Pakistan. The only government-owned forest was located near the border, and only there did some reforestation take place.

Gulab did not expect the school where he was to teach to be built like the one in Kabul, but he was not prepared for what he saw. The high school, which served about six hundred students, was an old mud house, and most of the classes were held in the open air. Whenever it rained, classes had to be canceled. Next to the school was an unfinished two-story concrete structure; Gulab was told that this was to be the new school but that contractors and government officials had stolen from the allotted budget and it remained uncompleted. The minister of public works of the new regime had come to the valley, but despite the petition he was presented with by the teachers, the only outcome of his visit was a report in the national newspapers stating that he had been satisfied with the 95 percent completion of the work.

Although all of Gulab's teaching of chemistry was confined to illustrations on the blackboard, he found the students attentive. Only he and the principal, who had a B.A. in literature, were graduates of the university. The other ten teachers had anywhere from six years of schooling to specialized training in teachers' institutes. Despite the seeming geographical isolation of the place, currents of ideas from the rest of the country were very much present. Students quickly started asking Gulab about the political movements in Kabul, and he found out that the teachers had very definite commitments.

Whereas students and teachers were divided along lines similar to those found in Kabul, there were also movements among the peasantry aimed at the revitalization of Islam. A number of theology students, trained in schools in Pakistan, were coming back and trying to teach the peasants what "true" Islam was all about. Gulab also heard of the emergence in a neighboring valley of a soldier as a holy figure; in six months, the man had a major following. When the more orthodox *mullahs* challenged him to a debate, his lack of knowledge of Islamic sources was exposed and he was forced to leave.

While in Aryoub, Gulab sent the major part of his salary home. His wife and child were not with him, and he found his assignment cumbersome. Two years went by. Finally, through some friends and relatives he secured a contact in the Ministry of Education and managed to be transferred to Khost. The town had changed considerably. There was a German-operated hospital, as well as a center for reforestation. Shops built of concrete were replacing the old mud structures, and buses and taxis left almost every hour for Kabul. Half of the road to Kabul had been paved; this section could be traversed in about two hours, while the unpaved portion required from four to five hours. Students and teachers were politically active, and the deputy governor, who had had no formal education himself, kept a wary eye on their activities.

Gulab's elder brother had visited Mecca and was now known as Haji. He had expanded his operations and had even bought a house in Khost, where all the male members of the family stayed when they had to remain in town. The youngest brother had also married. Sur Gul was back in Afghanistan and had a post in the armored division in Kabul, but he did not have a house of his own in the city and his wife had to stay with the rest of the family in the village. Every other week he went to see her and his daughter. (Gulab too had a daughter now.) Although Sur Gul did not share his thoughts with the other members of the family, he confided to Gulab that he had secretly joined Taraki's party and that conditions in the country were coming to a head-on collision. Dissatisfaction with Daud was growing because officers in the regime were being fired and the regime was drawing closer to Iran.

When, one day in April 1978, Gulab heard on the radio that as a result of their demonstrations in Kabul Taraki and some other members of the party were arrested, his thoughts went to the safety of his brother. Two days later, however, Daud was killed while resisting a coup and Taraki became president, prime minister, and chairman of the revolutionary council. Two of Gulab's professors were appointed to the cabinet, as well as some friends of Sur Gul from the armored division. Gulab soon learned that Sur Gul, having played an important role in the coup, had been appointed garrison commander, fulfilling the duties of a general. Because Sur Gul was now too busy to leave Kabul, he asked that his wife and daughter be sent to join him. He had been given an apartment and could provide for them. When Gulab took Sur Gul's family to Kabul, he was asked to join Taraki's party and was told that if he wished, his transfer to another ministry in Kabul could be easily arranged. He answered that he would join the party but preferred to stay in Khost for a while.

Most of the people in the country were stunned by the takeover by Taraki's party and could not really believe it. Many were happy that the old regime had come to an end, and people in Khost were pleased that Taraki was giving his official speeches in Pashtu. Neither the king nor Daud had ever done so, although ethnically they were Pashtuns. But after some months disturbing news started to emanate from Kabul. There were rumors of mass arrests and torture of people whom Gulab had gotten to know in his years at the university. There were also rumors that Russians were in charge and that in response to local armed resistance the government had dropped bombs on villages in the province of Jalalabad. Parties of people arrived from Kabul and crossed the border to Pakistan. Soon, a number of them were crossing back into the Khost region, openly declaring that they were going to fight the government. Religious dignitaries asserted that religion was in danger, and landlords and moneylenders said that the state was going to confiscate all the belongings of the wealthy. Everybody was taking sides and people seemed hesitant to speak in front of Gulab.

Government officials said that they were not afraid of any party and that whoever opposed them was reactionary and would be punished. They soon showed that they were not talking lightly. One day, people who came from the Aryoub Valley brought the news that planes had bombed the neighboring valley. One after the other, reports of bombing came from every corner of the country, including almost every valley of Paktia province. Business came to a standstill, and few dared go to Kabul.

In the midst of all this uncertainty, Sur Gul sent his family back to the village. He wrote that he could not live with an ignorant rural wife and was going to marry a member of the party from Kabul. This news made Haji and Gulab's youngest brother so furious that they disowned Sur Gul. Haji also announced that he was going to join the opposition and cross the border; the youngest brother said he was going with him.

Gulab by this time was under considerable pressure and did not know what to make of the situation. On the one hand, he was witnessing considerable suffering; on the other, every day the radio was proclaiming the glories of the revolution and its achievements for the toiling people. But then came another piece of news. Taraki had been removed from office and replaced by his deputy, Hafizullah Amin. Some weeks later, Taraki's death was announced. Then came news of a huge attack by some four hundred tanks on the town of Gardez, a display of muscle by the central government intended to intimidate the rebels. Khost, by that time, was more or less isolated, and few dared move out of it. Gulab was still teaching in the high school, but the number of students was decreasing. Whereas previously nobody had ever asked him whether he prayed, now he had to attend the local mosque and pray with the congregation. The people who showed concern were not strangers; they were his in-laws and kinsmen, who told him openly that unless he sided with them they could not guarantee his safety.

Thus, all his life unrolled in front of his eyes in the early chill of a December morning in the mosque of Khost. Gulab realized that he had to make a decision soon. He could join his brother in the capital by becoming a member of the bureaucracy and embracing the ideology of the emerging regime, but he would have to sacrifice his ties to the community where he was born. He could ally himself with his other two brothers in rebelling against the central government; in so doing, he would affirm traditional family ties at the risk of becoming an émigré, severed from his homeland. Neither route could promise safety and security, for the future was too uncertain.

Just as the prayer ended, a soldier came running in, shouting that the Russians had taken over the capital and that President Amin had been shot. There was sudden silence, then a great flurry of noise and activity. Gulab knew that there was no more opportunity for postponement. All his life he had been hesitant about making clear-cut decisions; now he could no longer delay. Either choice was going to be painful.

The sounds in the mosque slowly emerged, and there was a cry of *Allah u-Akbar*—"God is great." Yet as he looked out of the window, Gulab could see the red flag of the regime unfurling in the wind on top of the government building.

Gulab is one of some thirty thousand teachers in Afghanistan. In a country where the majority of the people are illiterate, teachers had a very important role to play in implementing the social policies of the new regime. Most of the membership of the leftist parties also came from the ranks of the teachers. All were confronted with more or less the same choice.

A NOTE ON SOURCES

This essay is based upon fieldwork conducted in Kabul and the provinces of Afghanistan, including the town of Khost, during the period 1973–77.

SUGGESTIONS FOR FURTHER READING

Unfortunately, most of the works on the Afghan civil war in English are generally poorly informed and highly ideological. Readers interested in learning more about contemporary Afghanistan should begin with Martin Ewans, *Afghanistan: A Short History of its People and Politics* (New York: Harper-Collins Publishers, 2002). Louis Dupree, *Afghanistan* (Princeton, N.J.: Princeton University Press, 1980) is also worthwhile.

On the civil war, Olivier Roy, *Islam and Resistance in Afghanistan* (Cambridge: Cambridge University Press, 1986) is recommended. See also M. Nazif Shrani and R. Canfield, eds., *Revolutions and Rebellions in Afghanistan* (Berkeley: Institute for International Studies, 1984); and Hafeez Malik, ed., *Soviet-American Relations with Pakistan, India, and Afghanistan* (New York: St. Martin's Press, 1987), especially the present author's "The Afghan State and Its Adaptation to the Environment of Central and Southwest Asia," 310–33. Also, my "Persian Literature of Afghanistan, 1911–1978," in *Persian Literature*, ed. Ehsan Yarshater (Albany: State University of New York Press, 1988); the evolution of urban elite Farsi culture is discussed on pp. 428–53.

For the subsequent role of the CIA and the evolution of the Taliban, see Ahmed Rashid, *Taliban: Militant Islam, Oil, and Fundamentalism in Central Asia* (New Haven, Conn.: Yale University Press, 2000); and Steve Coll, *Ghost Wars: The Secret History of the CIA, Afghanistan, and Bin Laden, From the Soviet Invasion to September 11, 2001* (New York: Penguin Press, 2004).

Chapter 18

Abu Jamal:
A Palestinian Urban Villager

Joost Hiltermann

Abu Jamal has seen a lot: the end of the British mandate over Palestine and the incorporation of the West Bank into Jordan in 1948, the defeat of Jordan and the Israeli occupation of the West Bank and Gaza after the June 1967 war, the "iron fist" policies of the Israeli military government in the early 1980s, the outbreak of the *intifada* (the Palestinian uprising that began in December 1987 and continued until the initiation of the Oslo Accords in 1993). Abu Jamal has managed to survive by taking whatever jobs fate chanced to blow across his path. Thus far, he has been (among his other occupations) a shepherd, a Red Cross relief worker, a soldier in the Jordanian army, a laborer, a waiter, the manager of a small café, a construction worker, and a welfare recipient. With this background, Abu Jamal escapes sociological classification. He is illiterate and a widower (his wife died in 1986). Due to an accident on a construction site in West Jerusalem, he has been unable to work since 1973. Most of his large extended family are landless peasants; many work in the fruit and vegetable trade in Ramallah. Abu Jamal lives in a house rented from an absentee owner in the West Bank town of Ramallah, supported by his sons and a meager Israeli welfare allowance.

The Israeli occupation has affected Abu Jamal and his family in countless ways, drastically constraining his movements, his possibilities for work, his access to services. Life has become increasingly hard. None of his four working-age sons have been able to acquire a regular trade, though they have learned to read and write. All have spent periods in Israeli jails for resistance activity, and the fines imposed by the authorities have been a heavy drain on the family treasury. The two oldest daughters are married and live at Se'ir near Hebron. Two young sons and three daughters live at home.

The outbreak of the first *intifada* in December 1987 was followed by sharply worse living conditions for Palestinians. The strikes and increased militancy of the Palestinians were a response to the brutal "iron fist" policies of the military authorities in the preceding years (under the terms of which beatings, jailings, and shootings of Palestinians escalated). They also represented the emergence of a Palestin-

ian leadership within the Occupied Territories capable of undertaking an unprecedented mobilization—in coordination with PLO officials based in Tunis. Because of
repeated strikes and Israeli-imposed curfews, living conditions worsened. One
means of coping was the development of the informal sector of the economy (in
which Abu Jamal was a participant): itinerant peddlers, backyard gardens, chicken
farms, etc.

Joost Hiltermann first wrote this sketch in 1987 and revised it in 1989. By this latter date, the first *intifada* had been going for two years. His essay reflects the Palestinian sense of optimism about its effects on Israeli society then current and the
hope that some solution to their desperate situation might yet emerge. By mid-1993,
for many Palestinians these hopes seemed realized with the initiation of the Oslo
peace process. By 2004, as the second *intifada* raged on, peace and process
remained elusive.

The portrait of Abu Jamal can be usefully compared with the contemporary lives
of Ghada, a Palestinian woman, and June Leavitt, a settler. —Eds.

The sun was setting over Ramallah as I bent my head and, after a short
knock, stepped into the dimly lit house in the Haret al-Jiryis in the Old City.
Abu Jamal sat glowering in a corner of the small, damp room, his hands
raised over the coals that lay smoldering in the *kanoun*, drawing intently on
his cigarette of homegrown tobacco—what is known in the villages as *hisha*.

Abu Jamal had no reason to be cheerful: his son Nasr had decided to
divorce his wife of six months, Nuha, who returned to her father's house in
Se'ir. She was what is commonly referred to as *hardana*, disgruntled and
unwilling to go back to her husband until he came to fetch her. Now Abu
Jamal was faced with the prospect of rocking the family boat—Nuha's father
being his cousin, after all—in addition to having to pay the deferred
amount of the bride-price (*al-mahr al-muakhar*) for the divorce, if in fact it
was to take place. Given his precarious standard of living, it was probably the
second punishment he feared most.

Abu Jamal does not fit in any neat sociological category. Historical
processes have thrown him and his family among the in-betweens of human
society, who constitute, however, a major component of Palestinian society.
Raised in a family of peasant origins, he is definitely not a peasant: he lives
in the city, feeding off the crumbs it provides him and his offspring. He is
definitely not a worker in the proletarian sense, as he has moved around in
the lower reaches of all possible economic sectors: agriculture, industry,
services. If ever he had a career, it is fair to say that his was a career in hon-
ing his survival skills, at scraping through by the skin of his teeth. He and his
wife raised eleven children, who will support him until his death.

Abu Jamal was born the oldest son of Abd-al-Fatah Ghanam al-Furukh, in
Se'ir, a village northeast of Hebron, in the year 1936. Abd-al-Fatah moved
with his small family up to Ramallah the same month that Abu Jamal was

born. A landless shepherd, he was unable to sustain himself, his wife, and child in the native village, and the city beckoned with the prospect of work in the booming stonecutting industry and with the support of those relatives who had preceded him in his journey northward.

Unable to find housing near the Manara, the square that is the hub of the twin towns of Ramallah and al-Bira, Abd-al-Fatah moved around from place to place, finally settling in the old city of Ramallah in a house owned by the Shunara family. Aziz Shunara, like many Ramallah Christians, had made the big move to America, leaving his property for rent at a rate that, due to rent-control regulations, is low today compared with new housing: one hundred Jordanian dinars per year (or about twenty-five dollars per month). By the early 1980s, the al-Furukh clan (*hamula*) had become firmly ensconced in the original town of Ramallah, its twenty families (*dawr*) making up perhaps one-fourth of its population. They share this small area of one square kilometer surrounding the fifteenth-century mosque with other Se'ir families (the Shalaldas, the Umturs, the Jaradats) and a number of families from Dhahriya, south of Hebron. Now, relatively few of the original Christian families remain in these old parts.

Immigration from the economically depressed Mount Hebron (Jabal al-Khalil) region northward, which started in the late nineteenth and continued throughout the twentieth century, permanently altered the character of Ramallah's old city. The Hebronites are referred to as Qaysis, as opposed to the Yamanis; both are putative lineages whose members make up the population of the modern Middle East. The differences between the two groups, if they exist at all, are political, not ideological, and families are known to have switched allegiances in the past. Both lineages are represented in Ramallah and the villages in the subdistrict; clashes between them over territorial claims and rights of passage characterize local history. When the first Hebronites came to Ramallah in search of work, being Qaysis, they became retainers for the local landed Qaysi families, working as sharecroppers in the olive and fig cultures and taking the side of the Qaysi families in the latter's conflicts with the Yamanis. They later moved into the building trade and the service sector; in the 1940s, for example, most porters in Ramallah were Qaysis from Hebron.

Being an underclass, the Qaysis from Mount Hebron, who are Muslims, have suffered their share of discrimination at the hands of the established Ramallah families, Qaysi or Yamani. In fact, most Christian Ramallah families refer to themselves as Qais, which, though the same word, is pronounced quite differently from the "Qaysi" with which they designate the Hebronites; in Ramallah, the word Qaysi has now become synonymous with riffraff. The Hebronites, however, continue to refer to themselves as Qaysis with a fair measure of pride. When I asked him about it over a dish of rice and *liya* (the fatty deposits stored by goats near their buttocks, a village delicacy), Abu Jamal declared in his strong southern peasant accent, "Ana min al-Geisiya!"—"I am a Qaysi!"

As a boy in the 1940s, Abu Jamal contributed to the income of the growing family by shepherding, running errands, and carrying goods for people. He attended the school run by the Roman Catholic church in Ramallah but quit after three years. As a result, he never learned to read or write. He has two vivid recollections of World War II. He remembers the blackouts in 1945, when residents were ordered by the British occupying forces to cover their windows with blankets or paint them blue; and he recalls the British soldiers celebrating in the streets of Ramallah after the final victory of the Allied forces. Memories of the war of 1948, and what Palestinians refer to as the Disaster (*al-Nakba*) that followed it, lie closer to the surface. "We were not scared," Abu Jamal recalls now, "because the war stayed far from Ramallah. We trusted that the Arab nations would expel the Jews, sooner or later. Our people used to carry out acts of sabotage and raid Israeli farms and camps. In Ramallah we did not notice much of this." With the defeat of the Arab armies, an uneasy peace came to the area, and with it thousands of refugees expelled from their native lands. Abu Jamal worked the next two years for the Red Cross, distributing relief packages to the newly dispossessed.

At age fifteen, Abu Jamal journeyed to Aqaba to haul goods in the Hashimite Kingdom's southern port: wheat, phosphates, whatever arrived in or departed from this busy port city, Jordan's gateway to the Fertile Crescent. He would return home every forty days or so and stay with his family for a week until new ships arrived and the demand for labor peaked. In 1952 he voluntarily joined the Jordanian army. He remembers training, guard duty, patrols, and occasional skirmishes with the Israelis entrenched across the Green Line, only meters away.

Four years into his army service, at age twenty, Abu Jamal wedded the daughter of his aunt and uncle in Se'ir, as is the custom in Palestinian villages. Um Jamal was barely thirteen when she was sent to Ramallah into marriage. Close kinship ties dictated a minimal bride-price—itself one more reason, aside from the traditionally strong identification with the clan, for a young man of humble means to marry within the immediate family. The oldest son, Jamal, was born two years later. Twelve children followed, two of whom died at an early age. Um Jamal was strong of character, and her stewardship over the family through times both rough and very rough was natural and unchallenged. She was the one who encouraged the children to study, and she would even help them with their homework, though she herself could neither read nor write. Her influence extended beyond the immediate family; others in the neighborhood, as well as more removed members of the clan, treated her with a great deal of respect. When she succumbed to illness and died in 1986, she was deeply mourned and missed by all who knew her. Her youngest child, Ahmad, was only five years old at the time.

At the birth of his first son in 1958, Abu Jamal left the army and set off on a career as roving laborer in Ramallah, performing irregular tasks such as loading and unloading trucks and moving from coffee shop to coffee shop as a waiter. By 1965, he had saved up enough cash to open his own café near the Manara, where he developed his considerable skills as a comic orator and working-class socialite, the antihero who plays the clown at village gatherings and is the butt of many an affectionate joke. Still today, he is fondly referred to as Abu Shaham—the Fat One—by his friends and relatives.

The Israeli occupation came brusquely on the unsuspecting Palestinian population of the West Bank and Gaza in 1967, as Abu Jamal recalls:

> Airplanes came flying over. But it was more of a game than a real war. The Arab leaders were lying to us. People were scared. They had Deir Yassin [a Palestinian village near Jerusalem whose 261 inhabitants were massacred by elements of the Irgun, Stern gang, and Palmach on 8 April 1948] in mind. Some were so scared, they fled across the bridge [into Jordan]. I was scared, but I could not leave; I did not want to leave. When the situation got dangerous, we used to go down into the cellar underneath the house. When the Israelis came, we moved to Ein Kinia [a village west of Ramallah] to hide. There was water there for the kids, and shade. Jordanian soldiers were taking off their uniforms and putting on civilian clothes. After one day, we returned to Ramallah. The Israelis said that everybody should go to their houses and raise a white flag on the roof. So we put up a white flag and kept it for about a week, like everyone else. We were under curfew, and soldiers searched all the houses.

Normal life remained paralyzed that June, and food was scarce. "There was no flour in the shops," Abu Jamal relates. "So we went down to the UNRWA offices, which were closed, and broke them open to take the flour that was inside. Soldiers were looking on and asked what we were doing. 'We are hungry,' we said. 'We want to eat.' They said they wouldn't stop us."

Abu Jamal's career as a coffee-shop operator did not survive the war. Although he reopened the café later in 1967, he grew increasingly apprehensive about his position in such a public area as a coffee shop, given the proliferation of collaborators, the scourge of the Israeli occupation, and the influence they had on the atmosphere among his customers. He shut down the shop shortly thereafter and sold the business finally in 1971. For two years he worked in the building trade for Israeli contractors ("with the Jews") in West Jerusalem, until he dropped a stone on his foot. After a three-month stint in the hospital, he retired from the labor force. Since then, he and his family have scraped by on the meager welfare check he managed to draw from the Social Affairs Department of the Israeli Civil Administration in the West Bank and on the occasional income from his chicken trade, usually illicit. Toward the late 1970s, the burden of providing the family's subsistence was gradually transferred onto the backs of his sons as they reached their teens.

Today, Abu Jamal lives in the house of the absentee Aziz Shunara, which consists of two small buildings, each containing two rooms, located on the square that abuts the Ramallah mosque. Abu Jamal's cousin (who is Um Jamal's brother) and his cousin's wife (who is Abu Jamal's sister) live twenty meters across the way; other relatives are just around the corner. Relations with the remaining Christians are cordial, and confessional differences, which do exist and sometimes are even articulated, play a minor role in the life of the neighborhood.

The bonds with the village remain strong, both because of its significance as the family's birthplace—as Abu Jamal explains—and because of continuing close family ties. Relatives travel back and forth almost daily, if not for family visits, then at least for the frequent major family occasions like births, weddings, and funerals, or religious feasts like the Id al-Fitr and the Id al-Adha. Intermarriage ensures that these bonds will not soon diminish. Those members of the clan in Ramallah who still own land in Se'ir return seasonally to the village, where many have retained an abode or where their children have chosen to settle. Most of the landless Ramallah contingent work in the fruit and vegetable trade around the *suq* in the old city or are employed irregularly either in Ramallah or inside Israel, usually in construction.

Some of the al-Furukhs have come into money through the years and have moved into new housing elsewhere in Ramallah or in al-Bira. Some of the young men even ventured across the ocean in search of greater opportunity, often finding life in the United States harsh but profitable. Many of these married a second wife in the States to obtain the much-coveted green card, and some of them never returned to their first wife and the children they sired in Ramallah. Abu Jamal's younger brother Musa managed to make it to the United States in 1978, married, stayed, earned some money, and then was shot to death under yet unsolved circumstances in Boston in 1983. His wife in Ramallah, a mother of six, was forced to look for work in order to survive, since Musa's American wife received most of the small estate. She now cleans houses and offices at five dinars (approximately fifteen dollars) per day and must otherwise rely on the irregular labor of her oldest son, a boy of sixteen.

In spite of, or perhaps because of, tight kinship bonds, fights among close relatives are frequent and reverberate throughout the extended family. Marriages are a major source of friction, and because of the custom of marrying both a son and daughter off to a daughter and son of a brother or first cousin, the whole clan may get embroiled in minor disputes. At one point, in the summer of 1988, relations soured between Abu Jamal and his cousin (his sister's husband) Abu Anwar across the square following a disagreement about the (negligible) inheritance of the husband of Abu Anwar's sister in Se'ir, who passed away in July 1988. Abu Saket's death triggered a fight between Um Saket and her oldest son Saket—as well as Abu Anwar's family in Ramallah, on the one hand—and Saket's wife, Jamila, who is Abu Jamal's daughter—and therefore with Abu Jamal's family in Ramallah, on the other. False rumors fed the squabble. Abu Jamal, for example, claimed that Abu Anwar had poached some of Abu Jamal's chickens from the boxes in front of his house, a charge vehemently denied by Abu Anwar, who subsequently launched a smear campaign against his cousin in the neighborhood. Rejected by her husband Saket, Jamila became *hardana* and returned to Ramallah; Nasr's wife, Nuha, who is a daughter of Abu and Um Saket, was sent packing to Se'ir in exchange. After a couple of weeks, the combatants grudgingly assented to make peace.

Life under military occupation has taken its toll on the family of Abu Jamal. His sons are involved in various trades but usually for short stretches and at low wages. Although they can read and write, they have not learned any particular trade or skill. Jamal, the oldest son, was managing a coffee shop in an office building at the Manara until he was arrested for membership in a group that was planning armed attacks against the occupation in the summer of 1985. He was sentenced to two and a half years in prison. Nasr, the second son, has intermittently worked at the local Tako tissue-paper factory at 60 dinars (180 dollars) a month, including overtime. He spent ten months in jail in 1985–86 on the accusation of being a member of a group that threw a Molotov cocktail at a car driven by agents of the Shin Bet, the Israeli internal intelligence service. Two other sons, both in their late teens, work odd jobs. Khalid took over Jamal's place in the coffee shop when the latter was in prison, and Umar has also worked at the tissue-paper factory, at a mere 45 dinars a month, since he is not married. Umar spent three months in prison in 1986 on a charge of throwing stones; as part of Umar's sentence, Abu Jamal had to pay a fine of 140 dinars (about 420 dollars).

That same year, Abu Jamal himself was caught transporting chickens from a hatchery in Bet Shemesh inside the Green Line to Ramallah in the West Bank without a license (i.e., without paying taxes) and was ordered to pay a fine of 140 dinars to the authorities. In addition, his chickens and the boxes containing them—at a total value of 450 dinars—were confiscated. It is sometimes difficult to believe how families like Abu Jamal's are able to save up money for the only major expense of their lifetime, the weddings of their sons. According to his own calculations, Abu Jamal shelled out between 4,000 and 5,000 dinars, part of which he borrowed from friends and relatives, for the wedding in July 1986 of his son Nasr—the one who later made several attempts at divorcing his wife, which itself would have cost the family 1,000 dinars, along with the predictable upset in familial ties.

The biggest jolt to the family was the death of Um Jamal in August 1986. Mourning the absence of her two imprisoned sons and virtually pining away because of the uncertainty surrounding the fate of a brother who apparently "disappeared" in Syria, she was not able to muster the necessary physical resources to withstand a bout of hepatitis, nor could her family muster the necessary financial resources to put her up in a hospital to protect her from the constant demands at home. At age forty-two, Um Jamal had come to wield considerable power in the family, virtually running it single-handedly, as Abu Jamal was either away looking for chickens to transport or socializing in the coffeehouse near the *suq*. The gap had to be filled by the second generation: Abu Jamal's younger daughters (the older ones having married and moved back to Se'ir), like Ferial, who upon her mother's death had to quit school, and Jamal's wife, Anam, who at age twenty-four had five children of her own to take care of.

Abu Jamal's immediate family circle was thus further reduced. His own father, Abd-al-Fatah, died in 1970. But his mother, Luliya—the Hajja (an honorific title given to a woman who has made the pilgrimage to the Muslim holy places at Mecca and Medina), is still around, a spunky old woman in her seventies and a real tease, who will alight anywhere on the ground in the small neighborhood but who will never ever sit down on a chair. One of Abu Jamal's brothers and two of his sisters died at a very young age; another sister did not survive an illness at age eighteen (an "act of God"—*min Allah*). Now two sisters remain: Um Anwar, who lives across the square with her family, and Um Abbas, who lives with her children in Se'ir while her husband travels back and forth between the village and Ramallah, where he sometimes works selling watermelons and other goods in the market. A picture of Abu Jamal's father, Abd-al-Fatah, a beautiful black-and-white reproduction of the man in his later years, still adorns the wall of Abu Jamal's house.

Traditional village mores remain the organizing force of the Ramallah community, an idée fixe indelibly impressed in the consciousness of these semi-urbanized villagers. It is as if the social structure of Se'ir has simply been lifted out of the original village to be reproduced intact in the city, minus the social relations generated by immediate access to land and the fruits it engenders. The weight of Ramallah's economic life gravitated long ago toward the dividing line with al-Bira, leaving the old city a peninsula bordering on the main part of town, a virtually self-subsistent (but barely so) economic and social entity with links, not primarily to the Ramallah and al-Bira commercial hub, but to the native village, and through the village, to the money that is repatriated by its offspring in the Gulf states and in the United States. The longevity of the community is in doubt, however, as more and more of its members seek their fortunes elsewhere. The older generation is fading, and the Ramallah municipality, faithful to the plans first developed by the late mayor Karim Khalaf, has begun to earmark some of the aging houses for demolition.

In the mid-1980s, women activists linked to the recently founded women's committees tried to interest the women in the neighborhood in their social and cultural activities. So far, they have had little success. One reason is the traditional prohibition on village women from moving outside their houses and outside the immediate family circle. Another reason lies in the political affiliation of the committees, which tend to identify with the more progressive blocks in the Palestinian national movement. Abu Jamal's family, like most of the families in Ramallah's old city, displays an unwavering identification with the mainstream grouping in the national movement, and their allegiance to Abu Ammar (Yasir Arafat) as a leader remained absolute and unquestioned. In fact, the political action of the residents of the old quarter extends as far as the edge of their communal territory and is usually a direct response to overt repression.

Before the uprising (*intifada*) that began in December 1987, these people were at the heart of the demonstrations against the Israeli occupation— for example, in December 1986, following the killing of two students in Birzeit, and in February 1987, during Amal's siege of the Palestinian camps in Lebanon. Their activity consisted of throwing stones at soldiers and burning tires in the general area of the *suq* and the mosque. Although the demonstrations involved mostly children and teenagers under eighteen (especially girls), the older generation gave their full moral support. One turbulent day in late 1986, I ran into Abu Jamal near the *suq* carrying bags of vegetables and groceries; he had taken it upon himself, in the absence of Um Jamal, to do the shopping for the family. Yet—with a whiff of tear gas still in the air from that morning's encounter with the army—this was positively the only day since the death of Um Jamal in August that I saw Abu Jamal with a spark in his eyes and a big grin on his face, as he, like everyone else, was momentarily bathing in a rediscovered sense of self.

The *intifada* tapped long-dormant energies in the neighborhood, while providing new outlets for pent-up frustration and resentment against the occupation. Altercations between children and soldiers, previously the exception, became part of daily life in 1988, and the Haret al-Jiryis was affected as much as any area in Ramallah or elsewhere. In contrast to earlier times, few displayed fear of facing the army, and families have been immeasurably proud of those among their children and siblings who were touched directly by the army's "iron fist." On 8 February 1988, for example, soldiers came to the Haret al-Jiryis to suppress demonstrations that were taking place throughout the town. They ordered residents to remove the barricades of stones, old metal, and other scrap materials that local youths had erected in the narrow alleyways. People refused, which led to an argument. In the melee, someone threw a rock at the soldiers, who responded by spraying rubber bullets at the group of people that had amassed on the square near the mosque, and beat men, women, and children at random, following them even into their homes. Abu Jamal's youngest son, Ahmad, was hit in the buttocks by a rubber bullet. Abu Jamal's daughter-in-law Anam was beaten and could still not move her badly swollen arm after a week. Anam's four-year-old daughter, Amal, was hurt, too. Both had been inside their home at the time of the incident, attacked by soldiers who forced their way into all the houses in the neighborhood.

Many youngsters have been arrested during the uprising, but usually on flimsy charges or on no charges at all, and they would often be released after a few days of punitive detention in prison camps, where they were forced to run the gauntlet of soldiers' rifle butts and verbal and physical abuse. In mid-December 1987, two weeks into the uprising, soldiers came to the house of Abu Jamal and arrested Nasr and Umar, as well as their cousin Khadir from across the square, and took them to the prison camp in Dhahriya, which was opened specifically to accommodate those arrested during the uprising. There they spent twelve days, along with hundreds of other boys averaging age sixteen, packed together in tiny rooms, deprived of washing facilities, and forced to use an overflowing trash can as a toilet, with few blankets and little food. They were released without being interrogated or charged. The family heaved a sigh of relief; they had been saved the extended anguish and steep lawyers' costs that usually accompany the arrest of one of their children. Two weeks later, the soldiers came and arrested another of Abu Jamal's sons, Khalid, who did a similar ten-day stint in Dhahriya and was then released, also without charges. He shrugged as he recalled his experience later; shared collectively by so many of his peers, it had become part of an unremarkable routine.

Not so for deaths. Abu Jamal's family so far has been spared the loss of one of its relatives, but the neighborhood has felt the army's fire. On 20 February 1988, a soldier of the Druze Border Guards fired three bullets at point-blank range at Abdallah Ataya, a young man from the village of Kufr Naima, who was fleeing through the *hara*, killing him instantly. In tune with the spirit of the uprising, the whole neighborhood pitched in and erected a marble monument on the spot where he fell, committing the event to the collective memory. Months later, Um Anwar would recount what happened, describing in detail how the young man's brain had lain splattered across the alley that runs next to her house.

As the violence continued, flaring up and receding throughout the year, people tried to make do despite the turmoil, adjusting their life-styles to the new realities of the uprising. For some, the hardships suffered by others brought unexpected benefits, though no one gained economically from the uprising in absolute terms compared with the previous period. The commercial strike, for example, that was set by the Unified National Leadership of the Uprising to start every day at noon proved a boon to those whose contribution to economic life had always been marginal. In an effort to reduce their losses, shopkeepers in the major towns converted their merchandise to wholesale after twelve o'clock, charging street vendors and peddlers with the task of selling their wares from street carts or neighborhood stalls. This informal economy proliferated, defying official strike hours and thriving throughout the afternoon and into the early evening.

Seizing the opportunity, Abu Jamal opened a candy and lemonade store in the doorway of his two-room house, competing with his sister's family across the square for the patronage of the children in the neighborhood, whose regular supply from the corner grocery had been cut off. Even though half his merchandise was consumed by his own children, his income was supplemented by the wages brought home by his sons Khalid and Umar. (The latter found work in an Israeli bakery in Holon across the Green Line.) Nasr, meanwhile, still married to the recalcitrant Nuha, traipsed mopishly around the neighborhood, unemployed, incurring the scorn of family members, who were unanimous in designating him as incorrigibly lazy. At the same time, Abu Jamal continued his chicken trade, but the increased police checkpoints on West Bank roads raised the risk of his illicit Bet Shemesh runs, and the income from his feathered contraband was thus reduced to a trickle. By the summer of 1988, he was quietly expressing the intent of doing the rounds of local charities, because although he was loath to admit it, he could no longer make ends meet.

Once the euphoria and pain of the first violent months had worn off, the uprising gradually evolved from a much-discussed exception to the regular way of life, and families like Abu Jamal's made the transition almost unnoticed. One day, eight months into the uprising, in the late afternoon, Abu Jamal was sitting on a stone in front of the house of his sister, Um Anwar, clutching a cup of tea. As usual, the discussion among the various members of the family centered on the latest events in the neighborhood: demonstrations, clashes, army patrols late into the night, soldiers perched in a newly established watch post on the roof of a nearby building, throwing stones at those in the *hara* who dared to leave the sanctity of their homes after nightfall.

Suddenly, kids, the oldest perhaps seven, came running out of the little alley past the monument to Abdallah Ataya crying "Jaysh! Jaysh!" (The army! The army!). The whole *hara* leaped to their feet, seeking to verify the news. "Where are they?" "In the *suq*!" "How many?" "Just one!" "Only one? It can't be!" "Only one," an older boy who turned the corner confirmed. "It is a trap [*kamin*]!" Scores of children, boys and girls, rushed, stones in hand, past the mosque to the road that issues into the *suq*, then halted, waiting for the *jaysh* to appear, ready to defend the neighborhood—ready, too, given the army's inclination to open fire without warning, to give their lives.

After a few minutes, things returned to normal, as the *jaysh* failed to make an appearance except for the fading whine of a jeep engine in the distance toward the Manara. Abu Jamal sat down again in the falling twilight, sighing, lamenting, "Oh, oh, oh, the world is a mess. They are making a mess of everything." "But," his nephew, sitting next to him, retorted, "the uprising is doing a lot of damage to Israel!"

Presently, Abu Jamal looked up from the small cup in his hand, a broad grin smoothing out the furrows that mark his face. He beamed as he repeated after the boy, forgetting for a moment his own economic predicament and his intention to turn mendicant. "Yes, it is doing them harm. It is doing them a lot of harm!" And he adjusted his blue hand-knit cap with a slow motion of his hand, rolled himself a cigarette of *hisha,* and calmly drank his tea.

A NOTE ON SOURCES

This essay is based upon conversations with Abu Jamal and his family over a period of more than four years (1985–89), when I got to know them and they me on an intimate basis. I lived a mere five-minute walk from their neighborhood for three years before moving to Jerusalem, and after that I visited them intermittently until my departure in December 1989. The present essay is a revised and expanded version of my article, "Seasoned Migrants to the North," which appeared in *MERIP Reports*, May–June 1987.

SUGGESTIONS FOR FURTHER READING

Palestinian society under Israeli occupation has been the subject of a number of important recent studies. See, in particular, Said Abu Rish, *Children of Bethany: The Story of a Palestinian Family* (Bloomington: Indiana University Press, 1989); Naseer Aruri, *Occupation: Israel over Palestine*, 2nd ed. (Belmont, Mass.: Association of Arab-American University Graduates, 1989); Ibrahim Wade Ata, *The West Bank Palestinian Family* (London: Routledge and Kegan Paul, 1986); Paul Cossali and Clive Robson, *Stateless in Gaza* (London: Zed Books, 1986); and Rita Giacaman, *Life and Health in Three Palestinian Villages* (London: Ithaca Press, 1988). My own book, *Behind the Intifada: Labor and Women's Movements in the Occupied Territories* (Princeton, N.J.: Princeton University Press, 1991), examines the role of Palestinian labor unions and women's organizations in the politics of the West Bank and Gaza.

The human rights of Palestinians under occupation are examined in al-Haq, *Punishing a Nation: Human Rights Violations during the Palestinian Uprising, December 1987–1988* (Ramallah, West Bank: Al-Haq, 1988). The journal of Raja Shehadeh, a Palestinian human rights activist lawyer and cofounder of al-Haq/Law in the Service of Man, although set in the period before the uprising, conveys the realities of life under the occupation. His *Samed: A Journal of Life in the West Bank* (New York: Adama Books, 1984), also published as *The Third Way: A Journal of Life in the West Bank* (London: Quartet Books, 1982), is of particular interest.

A number of American and Israeli authors have discussed the impact of the occupation on the Palestinians and on Israeli society. See, especially, David Grossman, *The Yellow Wind* (New York: Farrar, Straus & Giroux, 1988). Also Amos Oz, *In the Land of Israel* (New York: Harper & Row, 1987); David Shipler, *Arab and Jew: Wounded Spirits in the Promised Land* (New York: New York Times Books, 1987); Thomas Friedman, *From Beirut to Jerusalem* (New York: Farrar, Straus & Giroux, 1989); and David MacDowall, *Palestine and Israel: The Uprising and Beyond* (London: I. B. Tauris, 1989).

The PLO, U.S. policy, and the international context of the occupation are discussed in Noam Chomsky, *The Fateful Triangle: The United States, Israel, and the Palestinians* (Boston: South End Press, 1983). On the dynamics of war and peace, see David Hirst, *The Gun and the Olive Branch* (London: Faber and Faber, 1977).

There are a number of books on the first *intifada*. See, especially, Glen E. Robinson, *Building a Palestinian State: The Incomplete Revolution* (Bloomington: University of Indiana Press, 1997); F. Robert Hunter, *The Palestinian Uprising: A War By Other Means* (Berkeley: University of California Press, 1993); Roger Heacock and Jamal Nassar, eds., *Intifada: Palestine at the Crossroads* (New York: Praeger, 1990); and Zachary Lockman and Joel Beinin, eds., *Intifada: The Palestinian Uprising against Israeli Occupation* (Boston: South End Press, 1989). For an Israeli view, Ze'ev Schiff and Ehud Ya'ari, *Intifada: The Palestinian Uprising—Israel's Third Front* (New York: Simon and Schuster, 1990).

More recent works that cover this period include Rashid Khalidi, *Palestinian Identity: The Construction of Modern National Consciousness* (New York: Columbia University Press, 1997); and Baruch Kimmerling and Joel S. Migdal, *The Palestinian People: A History* (Cambridge, Mass.: Harvard University Press, 2003).

Chapter 19

Haddou:
A Moroccan Migrant Worker

David McMurray

David McMurray's portrait of Haddou, a Moroccan migrant, presents us with yet another facet of the new Middle East: Arab labor migration to Western Europe. The presence of ever greater numbers of Arab workers in the European economy is a sign of the internationalization of labor (as is the presence of Mexicans and Hispanics in the United States) and the globalization of the world economy. The sources of this migration are complex; its consequences for the future of relations between Europe and the Middle East are considerable.

As in the United States, where World War II hastened the dissolution of the black peasantry in the South and led to the massive civil rights movement of the 1960s, the end of the war brought momentous changes for North Africa. One result, to be schematic, was the independence movement of the 1950s and 1960s. A second was a large-scale peasant migration to the cities, not just of North Africa, but increasingly of Western Europe as well.

As part of the latter trend, Haddou, a Moroccan Berber from the region around Nador, left his home in northern Morocco in the 1960s and voluntarily expatriated himself to seek work. By this time, migrants from North Africa had already established a beachhead for themselves in Western Europe, where they did jobs that no Europeans would do anymore. Initially, migration was a seasonable phenomenon. But by the late 1970s and 1980s it had led to the emergence of large permanent communities of migrants—with an increasingly problematic insertion into European society. The rhythms of Haddou's life largely follow this script, though not without complications.

On one level, Haddou's biography can be read as a story of economic success. In this, it merits comparison with that of Talal Rizk. We can trace his ascent from his early, low-paying jobs as a young man in northern Morocco to positions of growing income and security in France and Germany. By careful planning and much hard work, he had achieved his original goal: to construct an imposing home in which he could live in his old age surrounded by his married sons and their families. In his dreams, then, he resembles Assaf Khater, whom we encountered in part 1 (as well as many successful Sicilian and Polish immigrants to the New World who elected to return to their villages of origin to vaunt their newly gained wealth).

Yet this reading contrasts with Haddou's own sense of his life. Despite a measure of worldly success, he has not, for all of that, achieved happiness. His years of hard work and voluntary deprivation have gone for naught, and he finds himself in his fifties alienated from his family, his authority not respected. As far as his children (whom he sees only one month out of a year) are concerned, his primary role is to bankroll their desires for the latest consumer items. Even his eldest son, Driss, who now also works in Europe, is a disappointment to him. Instead of sending monthly remittances to the family, as the Moroccan family-centered ethos requires, Driss spends his income on himself and his Dutch girlfriend. (Haddou's feeling of betrayal and his sense of the breakdown of family values give him a lot in common with the Palestinian Abu Jamal, whose life is also presented in this volume.)

By the mid-1980s, when this essay was written, Haddou was no longer content with an annual migration to his village of origin. The years of deprivation and lone-liness had taken their toll, and his estrangement from his children had chilled his welcome. He had begun to establish himself and his wife, Thraithmas, in Düssel-dorf. While it is unclear what he eventually decided. One possibility was that he would gradually sever his ties with Morocco and make his home in Germany. If so, he would join the increasing numbers of Turks, West Africans, Yugoslavs, and other recent migrants who have put down roots in the new multiethnic Europe. —Eds.

Haddou sat on the bed, thumbing through his passport. It was full of entry and exit stamps from his many trips between his family in Morocco and his job in Düsseldorf, Germany. As the pages flipped, he stopped again to look at the visa he had received from the German government just that after-noon. He had to smile, for this newest visa guaranteed him a court hearing before any deportation measures could be taken against him. It made him feel relaxed. He did not need to fear every time the boss yelled at him or every time the border guards interrogated him. He had had very few close calls over the years, but you could never be too careful. He thought of that time when while riding his bicycle to work the cops stopped him, claiming he had run a red light. They said to him, "Hey, where do you think you are, Turkey? Here in Germany we obey the law. Do that again and you'll be rid-ing that bike back in Istanbul!" Haddou was upset that they assumed he was a Turk. It further irritated him that they assumed he disobeyed the law when in fact he bent over backwards to keep his nose clean. With the new visa he would not have to jump every time a police car passed him.

He looked up at the railway calendar on the opposite wall next to his tele-vision set. He could not make out the date exactly, for now, at fifty, his eyes were going bad. He put it up mainly for decoration anyway. The calendars were free, given out at the train yard where he worked. He often thought of getting glasses but did not, because he suspected that the railway company might consider him unfit to continue working. His job consisted essentially of copying down the numbers of each boxcar on each train as it came into Düsseldorf. So if he was having trouble seeing and they found out about it, well . . .

Haddou's thoughts always drifted back to Morocco whenever he found himself alone in his railroad company apartment. Thinking about the visa this time set him to remembering what his life had been like before he started migrating to Europe.

As far back as Haddou could remember, he had worked. Everyone did. Everyone except his oldest brother, that is. Haddou's father determined that his four younger sons would work and pool their wages so that the eldest would be able to attend school in Fez. Even Haddou's father pitched in. He supplemented the produce from their small farm with wages earned in Algeria. Every year in early May Haddou's father would leave for Oran province in Algeria to work the harvest on the farms of the French *colons* (settlers). He would then hurry back to harvest his own barley crop the month after.

Haddou's first job was as a ticket taker on the local bus route between Kariat Arkman, a small town near his *char,* or lineage settlement, and Villa Nador, the Spanish provincial capital of the whole region. He got the job during the great drought of 1944–45, when he was only seven years old. Prior to that he had worked on the family farm, watching the goats or helping with the planting and harvesting. The drought proved to be so bad, however, that his father was forced to sell the goats—and that was after the goats had eaten what little of the barley actually sprouted that year.

The whole of northern Morocco was under Spanish protectorate control from 1912 until 1956, the year of Moroccan independence. Villa Nador sprang up in the late 1920s as the easternmost Spanish administrative center. Nador paled, however, in comparison with Melilla, a purely Spanish city less than fifteen miles from Nador on a peninsula jutting out into the Mediterranean. Melilla had been a Spanish garrison and trading center on the coast since the end of the fifteenth century. It exerted a stronger influence than Nador over the surrounding countryside by providing menial jobs for the local Moroccans and by consuming much of the surplus produced on farms in the area. Eventually, Haddou found a job running produce into the Spanish city. Every morning throughout the early 1950s he loaded up a donkey cart with eggs or vegetables or fruit—depending on the season—and delivered them to the Melilla market.

When in his late teens, Haddou finally landed a good-paying job working in Kariat Arkman in an automobile upholstery shop. Since the business was owned by a Spaniard and all of the customers were Spaniards, when the Spanish population in the region began to decline after independence, so, unfortunately, did the business. Before it closed, however, Haddou managed to save enough money to get married. That same year he and a friend from the shop decided to emigrate to Europe to look for work.

Haddou got up from his bed to make himself a cup of tea. He had a one-burner hot plate and three little teacups. While he was measuring out the tea leaves into the pot, he thought back to his first job in Europe and the very beginnings of his "dream house" idea, as he called it.

Haddou had started as an unskilled construction worker on a job in the outskirts of Paris. He lived in a shack on the site to save money. Many other North Africans lived there also. They guarded the site during the night in exchange for their room. That is how Haddou met the big bosses. Every Saturday evening after work had finished, the architect, contractor, and their cronies returned to the job site. Haddou would open the gate to let them in, after which they would enter his guard hut and pull out the cards and liquor and proceed to play poker until early in the morning. Haddou's job was to wash their cars and then wait outside and stand guard in case of trouble. Since he was a Muslim, they reasoned, he did not want to go out on the town or to play or drink with them. He could thus be trusted to stay nearby, sober and alert. He could also be trusted to guard their liquor stash during the week. They did not have to worry about his taking a nip behind their backs. They did not see the need to pay him extra for his special duties either.

One Saturday night as Haddou sat in the dark, the cars all clean and shiny, the architect came out to stretch. Haddou seized this opportunity to request once more that the architect sketch out a floor plan for Haddou's dream house. He did not know what he wanted exactly from the architect, he just knew that the man was very well educated and very talented and that whatever he designed Haddou would be proud to build. This time the architect obliged Haddou. He quickly sketched on a scrap of paper the rough design and dimensions of a floor plan.

Haddou carried that scrap with him for years, unfolding it every time he thought of his future dream house. He slowly managed to save enough from his wages to put a down payment on a small plot of land on the edge of the city of Nador. That was in the late 1960s. By 1975 he had saved enough to start construction of the house. His land no longer stood on the edge of the city. Nador had grown so much in the interim through migrants relocating their families in the city that Haddou was now starting out to build his house on one of the nicest streets in Nador.

Haddou took his architect's design to a local draftsman to be filled in. He then hired a construction foreman to round up a crew and get started. They came from the region of Ouarzazate in southern Morocco, just like most of the other construction workers in Nador. Haddou liked them because they worked hard for little money and without complaint. They had migrated in search of work just like himself.

The house rose slowly over the next decade. Each year Haddou saved enough to pay for a few months of work. The first year they laid the foundation. The second year they raised the support pillars and laid the first floor. The third year, as soon as the ground-level garage was enclosed, Haddou moved his young family in. He wanted them to start attending the city schools as soon as possible—even if that meant setting up house in the garage. He did this because his vision of the family's future included good schools and then good jobs for all of his boys. He had grown up in the countryside without benefit of education and did not want that to happen to his children.

The dream house actually contained four apartments of five rooms each, two apartments to a floor, each the mirror image of the other. When they grew up, Haddou figured, each of his boys and their respective families would get an apartment. As the house was being built, he occasionally reflected on how similar it looked to all of the other buildings in the neighborhood. This was odd because the French architect had never been to Nador and thus did not know what the houses looked like there. What Haddou found out later was that the majority of draftsmen in Nador were unlicensed and more or less trained by each other. Therefore, the same three or four blueprints were reproduced with slight variation by most of them. Haddou's architect's design had been quietly but efficiently reworked by the local draftsman to conform to Nador standards.

All of this reminiscing was making Haddou homesick again. He finished his tea, put the passport back in his pocket, and reached for his coat. By the time he stepped outside his apartment in the company's housing complex, it was almost dark. He walked to the phone booth on the corner, entered, closed the door, and dialed the number he had dialed countless times before. Hassan, his second son, heard the ring and picked up the phone at the other end, in Nador, Morocco. "Is your mother there?"

Haddou always asked first about his wife, Thraithmas. He was crazy about her, as devoted to her now as he had been at the time of their marriage. In 1958 she had begged him not to go to work in Europe. He assured her that he would return regularly. Unfortunately, he had had to wait a long time before his first vacation. His eldest son, Driss, was already over two years old by the time Haddou initially saw him. Even now, after thirty years of marriage, Haddou and Thraithmas has spent less than three years total in each other's company.

In the beginning of his sojourn in Europe Haddou kept in touch with his family in Morocco by means of professional runners, whose job it was to transfer money and messages back to Morocco. As the migrant communities grew in Europe, runners were replaced by migrants, and Haddou came to depend on fellow workers from his tribal region to help keep up contact with his family. The migrants took turns relaying greetings and gifts back and forth for each other's respective families. Those who could write sometimes used the mail, but many complained that their letters never arrived or had been opened before arrival. Moreover, the petty bureaucrats in the post office in Nador often forced the migrants' families to buy "lottery tickets" or pay some other form of bribe before receiving their letters from overseas. The postal workers, who made very little money working for the state, were jealous of the uneducated migrants and their relatively large European salaries. They thus seized the opportunity provided by their positions to profit from the migrants.

The migrants' other option was to arrange to make a long-distance telephone call from one public telephone to another. This often proved difficult, however, for international connections took a long time in the early days, reception was bad, and the whole province had to use the same little office in Nador, which created long lines.

The first big change in means of communication came with the spread of the tape recorder, particularly the cassette recorder. The actual voices of the migrants could now be relayed to the families instead of just their secondhand salutations. A minute or minute-and-a-half conversation cost as little as the stamps on the package.

By the mid-1980s, the private telephone had become the communication medium of choice. The wait for phone installation sometimes lasted three or four years, but the freedom it provided from theft, censorship, waiting in line, and general worry was worth it. Most importantly—from Haddou's point of view—the telephone reinstated the migrant as master of the house, whether he was there or not. Migrants in Haddou's position, that is, those who moved their families into the city from the country while they continued working in Europe, customarily demanded that their wives remain in the house during the migrants' absence. Worrying about the well-being and fidelity of the women back home occupied a good share of the migrants' time. Haddou was no different. Once they installed the phone in his house in Nador, however, Haddou could call any time of the day or night to find out if his wife was there. During any given week, he called at least three times, always at a different hour and on a different day so as not to establish a pattern. That way no one in the house could plan their activities around his phone calls. He also kept the phone dialer in Nador locked so no one could call out but could only receive calls. He could thus monitor and manage the activities of his whole family from thousands of miles away. In effect, Haddou transformed the telephone into a technology trap.

Haddou also controlled the household by controlling its purse strings. He sent a monthly stipend through the Moroccan Banque Populaire. The bank had established branches throughout Europe and gave the migrants a fair exchange rate to make it easier for them to send money home. The bank had to do something because most migrants did not trust the banking system. Migrants traditionally brought the biggest share of their earnings home with them at vacation time. Money changers in the Nador market or in the nearby Spanish port town of Melilla then bought the migrants' European currency and sold them Moroccan dirhams. Haddou and the others who worked abroad did this because they feared that the government might some day confiscate their earnings if they deposited them all in Morocco. Besides, the migrants did not want Moroccan officials to know how much they earned so that they could avoid paying Moroccan taxes. They still brought the lion's share of their earnings home this way. Now, however, Haddou also transferred about fifteen hundred dirhams (approximately two hundred dollars) a month to his account in Nador. His son, Hassan, would write a check on the account for the family. Haddou would then telephone instructions as to how the money was to be spent.

Yet try as he might to enforce his will upon them, Haddou's family found ways to subvert his authority during his absence. Even his loving wife, Thraithmas, dipped into the family's monthly stipend. For example, every week or two Thraithmas's mother came to visit. She would stay for a few days and then return home with a little money and some tea, sugar, or meat given to her by her daughter. The mother gladly accepted the food paid for by her daughter because she was dependent on a pitifully small pension from the Spanish government, given in recognition of her husband's death during the Spanish civil war. Over seventy years old and beginning to stiffen up, she was also glad of the chance to forgo the hour's walk needed to reach the weekly market nearest her country home.

Hassan, who was in charge of the accounts, skimmed the most. He exaggerated the extent of his school and clothing expenses regularly. Occasionally he pocketed money earmarked for bills and then spent the money in cafés and on other forms of entertainment enjoyed by the richer boys on the block. Even little Murad, Haddou's youngest son, pocketed the change from the daily shopping trips it was his duty to perform. The whole family habitually ran up credit at various stores, which Haddou then had to pay off during his vacation.

These problems with the children began early and at the top for Haddou. Driss, the eldest, disappointed him first by not passing his *baccalauréat* (high school graduation exam) and then by becoming a migrant. Haddou had always intended that he alone would migrate, so that none of the others would have to leave home. Unfortunately, when Driss was visiting his maternal uncle, a migrant in Lille, the Socialist government of France declared an amnesty for all foreigners working without papers. Driss's uncle quickly talked his boss into hiring Driss so that he could apply for papers and a visa. The plan worked, and Driss got a job in a warehouse in northern France. But that was only half of the problem, according to Haddou. What was worse, Driss begged off contributing to the household budget from his own salary by claiming that the European cost of living ate up all of his savings. Yet Haddou knew only too well that Driss's major expense happened to be his weekly trips and gifts to a certain Dutch girlfriend Driss had met while she was on vacation in France.

The family's insubordination troubled Haddou constantly. He felt he had worked all of his life just to provide for them and yet they were not appreciative. All they ever asked for was more money; all they ever complained about was their "small" family stipend. He had poured his savings into a piece of property and then built a four-apartment building on it, all for them. He had never asked for anything more than to be allowed to retire back in Nador on a comfortable German pension, to live surrounded by his children and their families, all under one roof in a building of his own creation. Was that too much to ask? Now, however, his eldest son wanted to quit his job in France and move in with his girlfriend in Holland. Since his second son had failed the *baccalauréat,* he would not be able to go to university or find a decent job in Morocco. Maybe the two youngest sons would mature and prosper, though they seemed no more likely to fulfill their father's dream than the older brothers.

The frustrations of being an absent head of household preoccupied Haddou as he walked back from the phone booth to his apartment. Haddou partly blamed himself for the family's failure. He had not been there to raise the children properly and knew he could not make up in one month for eleven months of absence. He also suspected that his children did not entirely respect him, for he, like many other migrants, had never lived in the city and thus had few of the social graces typical of the nonmigrant fathers of his children's friends. What was worse, Haddou had none of the contacts needed to ease his children's access into good schools and jobs. Years of giving and receiving favors and of sitting in cafés with men of influence were needed to develop a network of acquaintances. Haddou had spent his adult life out of the country, which meant that his circle of acquaintances was strictly limited to men he had known before he migrated. He was thus in the unenviable position of having an income and house commensurate with a high status but none of the personal prestige needed to get others to do his bidding. The children, he sensed, resented him for this.

On the other hand, Haddou knew how to work for something he wanted, and the children did not. They expected it all to be laid out before them. They disdained manual labor and assumed, instead, that only white-collar jobs were respectable. Take last winter when the sewer pipe backed up. Haddou jumped right in and dug up the pipe, while the boys disappeared. They were embarrassed to have the neighbors see their father digging in the dirt. Yet what did they think their father did all year to earn money that kept them from having to work? He deserved their respect, if only for that.

At least Haddou's daughters were loyal. Fatima, the older one, had last year married without complaint a successful migrant working in Holland. The man had approached Haddou requesting that Fatima live abroad as his second wife while his first stayed in Nador with their children. People in the neighborhood were aghast that Haddou consented to give his daughter away as a second wife. They said that showed what a country bumpkin he was. A good city family would never stoop so low. But Haddou defended his actions by claiming that the man was from his tribal region, earned an excellent income, owned a nice house in Nador, and was a migrant—in short, he was just like Haddou himself and therefore a good match for his daughter.

Haddou's other daughter, Malika, never gave him cause for concern. Her high school grades were impressive; she did particularly well in French. Yet she also helped her mother with the cooking and cleaning in the house and even found time to take sewing classes from a seamstress a few blocks away. In Haddou's eyes, Malika was the model daughter. He daydreamed on occasion of keeping her unmarried and at home so that she could tend to his needs in his old age. He justified this by saying it would be a pity to separate Malika from her mother, because they were so close. Unlike the others, Malika never asked him to raise the monthly stipend.

Haddou could not help smiling as he closed the door to his apartment and took off his coat. It was Malika, after all, who had said he looked like Charles Bronson and that he should stop working and start making movies. Bronson's mustache was smaller and his eyes not as round as Haddou's, but otherwise he had to agree with her: the resemblance was striking. Maybe he would buy a VCR this time to take back with him on his upcoming vacation to Nador. That way, the whole family could watch Bronson movies together.

Haddou chose to take his vacation and return to Nador during the month of December. The winters were cold in Germany and he no longer wanted to compete for space with the hundreds of thousands of Moroccan migrants who returned in July and August. He disliked the crowded Spanish highways and the crush at the boat docks and the Moroccan border caused by the summertime returnees. It had grown so bad in recent years that some migrants now wasted a week of their vacation time just getting home. Once back in Nador, the streets became jammed with the migrants' Mercedes. Every summer weekend, one procession after another of honking cars, followed by fireworks displays, created a ruckus, all due to the dozens of weddings taking place simultaneously. This was caused by the migrants' families back home, who found brides for the unmarried male migrants and arranged for their weddings to coincide with their vacations. The locals, too, preferred to marry in the summer, hence the noise and confusion of that season.

The changed nature of the wedding celebration also added to the mayhem. Prior to the influx of peasants and migrants into Nador (in 1960

Nador's population was seventeen thousand; in 1985 it was eighty-five thousand), weddings would take place within the confines of the village and kin group. However, the tremendous growth of the city, the creation of neighborhoods full of strangers, and the dramatic rise in family income following labor migration to Europe led to the development of open, lavish matrimonial displays. The families of newlyweds used fireworks, Mercedes-Benz corteges, and professional electronic orchestras to compete with each other and to make a big splash in front of the neighbors and relatives.

Haddou personally disliked the lavish displays because the only marriage he had been responsible for, that of his elder daughter, Fatima, had been a secret affair carried out quietly behind closed doors and windows, due to the shame attached to his daughter's becoming a second wife. He justified his displeasure at large public weddings in more sweeping and general terms though, by citing the wastefulness of such extravagance. Why should he, a hardworking father with dependents, squander his savings on celebrations meant to impress strangers? On the other hand, he did not mind competing with his neighbors when it came to building a big house or decorating its facade. That kind of social competition required no face-to-face interaction or mastery of urban etiquette.

Making sure his children were reasonably well dressed and had imported electronic toys to play with on the street was another form of social display of which Haddou approved, for as a migrant he was in a position to purchase such foreign articles cheaply. Haddou, like all the other Moroccan migrants, always brought home presents for the whole family. In his family, the boys normally received shirts and pants, while Thraithmas and Malika got scarves and dresses. The boys proudly wore their German clothes— when they fit—but the women tended to leave theirs in the closet since the clothes Haddou picked out were often too ugly or too risqué (sleeveless, for example) to be worn in Nador.

Haddou also brought back items from Germany for the house. Like many Moroccans, Haddou considered foreign-made goods to be superior to domestic products. In fact, so strong was the allure of commodities from industrial Europe that Haddou carried back items as small as faucets and door handles made in Germany, not to mention tea glasses, pots and pans, and tablecloths. Driss, the son with the self-professed high living costs, tended to buy cheap presents for the family from Spain, Taiwan, or Hong Kong when he returned, and then to claim that they were really made in Germany or France.

One year Haddou brought back a Mercedes-Benz for a colonel in the Moroccan air force. He had met Haddou on the train to Rabat. They started talking, and the man ended up contracting with Haddou to purchase a car in Germany and then drive it back to Rabat for him. The colonel, in turn, saw to it that Haddou met no resistance from Moroccan officials. Thus protected, Haddou seized the opportunity to load the car down with items for his own household, including a television, a sewing machine, folding chairs, and bundles of towels. No one asked him for bribes on that trip.

Haddou set about brewing another pot of tea. He realized as he thought about his own vacation that he had to make a decision soon on whether to bring Thraithmas to Düsseldorf that year. Since the mid-1980s, when Murad had turned ten and could be left in the care of his brothers and sisters, Haddou had begun to bring Thraithmas to Germany to stay with him for a month each year. When it was time for his mother to go, Hassan would wake up while it was still dark, go down to the taxicab stand, and bring a car right up to the front door. Thraithmas would heavily veil herself and then quickly step out of the house and into the car. She and Hassan would then take the taxi to the Oujda International Airport long before anyone in the neighborhood awoke. Once in Düsseldorf, Thraithmas would change out of her Moroccan dress and into Western clothing. Haddou insisted on that. He remembered too well when she first arrived in Germany, wearing her *jallaba*. All eyes were upon her, staring at her as if she were a freak. When she wore her Western clothes, no one paid attention. Luckily for Haddou, unlike her mother, Thraithmas had never tattooed her face with the markings of her natal region, so nothing about her attracted the Germans' curiosity.

Haddou deeply appreciated her visits. She brought with her delicacies from Morocco: almonds, prepared barley dishes, pickled lemons, olive oil, fresh mint. She also made his favorite food, *limsimen*, a fried bread of many layers made by folding the dough again and again. More than anything else, Thraithmas's visits broke the monotony of Haddou's existence in Düsseldorf. Without her, his routine consisted of waking early, making tea on the small hot plate, riding his bicycle down to the rail yard, and then working as long as they needed him. He would ride home after finishing, change his clothes, and go out to buy a little food for supper. He then watched television for awhile or flipped through a magazine before going to bed. The weekends were mainly reserved for washing clothes and straightening up his room.

The only excitement of the week occurred on Saturday afternoons, at which time Haddou liked to walk down to a certain tearoom in a nicer neighborhood where German women gathered. There he would sit for a few hours, listening to their conversations. Sometimes when the place was full, women even sat at his table. They would start to ask him about his homeland or about his religion. Haddou enjoyed these little exchanges very much because they were practically his only informal contacts with the locals. During the rest of the week he talked to Germans only as a worker talks to a boss or as a customer talks to a storekeeper. The women at the tearoom were the only Germans who showed Haddou any consideration.

With Thraithmas around, Haddou had no need for the Germans. What is more, when he woke up in the morning she had his tea ready. When he got home at night, she was cooking his supper. During the day while Haddou was working, Thraithmas would often go across the hall and sit in the apartment of the railway widow who lived there. They watched television together and communicated through gestures. That was enough. They just enjoyed each other's presence. When Haddou returned at night or on weekends, he and Thraithmas sometimes went shopping in one of the big discount department stores. She doubly enjoyed these outings because she, like other relatively wealthy migrants' wives, was not allowed to go out shopping in Nador. By going out with Haddou in Düsseldorf she could also buy more tasteful clothes for the family back home—at least clothes that fit. She also enjoyed buying inexpensive perfumes, soaps, and candies to place around the house in Nador on special occasions and to give to guests when they visited.

Perhaps more than anything, Haddou appreciated Thraithmas's visits because they provided him with a sense of stability and worth. Her calm and respectful manner toward him, her familiar way of speaking, her correct behavior, all reminded him that he belonged, as a proud believer and father of a family, to an Islamic community with a set of values and way of living totally distinct from his present European surroundings. He had not always felt this way. During those early years in Paris, no one had been overly concerned with strictly maintaining the religious practices and precepts of their Islamic homeland. They were too busy working. Besides, there was only one mosque in all of Paris.

Sometime during the 1970s a mosque opened in Haddou's quarter of Düsseldorf. It began as a room where Muslims could gather and pray. An Egyptian led the prayers. Haddou visited the mosque once or twice, but he did not know the other men. They seemed too serious anyway and were too interested in trying to run his life. One day while Haddou was in the train yard recording the boxcar numbers of the most recent train to arrive, a Turkish worker from the mosque approached him and asked him to join an Islamic group then forming. They wanted to petition the boss for the right to stop work during prayer times. Some companies in France had even set aside rooms to be used as mosques—right inside the factories. Maybe the Germans could be persuaded to do the same thing.

Haddou refused to have anything to do with the man or his group and their objectives. He said he was in Europe to earn money, not to pray. God had given him two hands and a strong back to use to provide for himself and his family. Who was going to put food on the table back in Nador if he decided to spend all day at the mosque? In any case, he did not need a bunch of bearded migrants telling him what was and was not Islamic.

And look at the way the religiously militant migrants were greeted back home! The cops at the Moroccan customs bureau treated them like criminals. They knew who the troublemakers were because the government spied on the migrants in Europe. The consulates and the Moroccan migrants' associations were full of spies who kept track of everyone. When the migrants got to the Moroccan border, the customs agents went through all their possessions, looking for religious tracts. They even began confiscating the migrants' audio and video cassettes. Supposedly, the militants smuggled the sermons of subversive preachers into the country on these tapes.

Locals in Nador also complained of the way the bearded migrants came home and preached to them about the "true" Islam. The locals viewed them as hicks from the countryside who had spent most of their adult lives in Christian Europe. Now they were coming back every vacation to Islamic Morocco and had the gall to preach to the people who had never abandoned their country and its religion.

Haddou had to admit, however, that it was the risk of being fired from his job and then deported from Germany that weighed most heavily on him and kept him from getting involved with the group. The Germans used any excuse to get rid of foreigners. Even with his new visa, he did not entirely trust them, so he was going to continue to make sure he never arrived late for work or left early. If they wanted him to work night shifts outside in the train yard in the middle of winter, he would still be there. He would even continue to have his paycheck deposited directly into his account so that the bank could automatically pay his rent and utilities bills. That way, he would never miss a payment and give the Germans a reason for firing him.

Haddou had to admit that he respected the Germans as well as feared them. They worked hard, built good products, and kept their streets and parks clean—more than he could say for the Moroccans. The Germans were also honest with you. If you asked them a question, they would tell you the answer. If a Moroccan knew, he would never tell; if he did not know, he would make something up. On the other hand, unlike the Moroccans, the Germans were morally bankrupt. The family meant nothing to them. Old people were all sent off to live alone in homes for the aged. Daughters and wives went about scantily clad, even drinking and talking to strangers if they so desired. The men were too weak to keep their families in line. What was worse, they were all racists, young and old. It was best to steer clear of them, for nothing good ever came from mixing. The Germans knew nothing of the proper Islamic way of life. Haddou knew this through one of his friends who had married a German woman. At first the man had been enthralled with his new wife and her Christian way of life. He danced and drank and even began to eat pork. Soon, however, their marriage deteriorated and he rediscovered his Islamic heritage. Nonetheless, she refused to maintain an

Islamic household. The couple ended up with two kitchens in the house: one for her pork and alcohol dishes and the other for him, free of impurities. The man now spent most of his free time at the mosque in the company of other strict believers.

"Why don't you just go home?" Haddou thought to himself on many occasions. This is what the racists wanted, too. Haddou's answer was always the same: "To do what?" Most Moroccan men's answer to this would be to set up a shop and sell something. But Haddou felt himself to be unsuited to the life of a small merchant. They were not involved in productive activity anyway, just buying and selling what others had made. In any case, he needed contacts to make a good profit. Otherwise no one would buy from him, and the Moroccan bureaucracy would slowly bleed him to death without a patron to protect him. Even if he wanted to make some kind of productive investment, the banks were not safe, laws were not enforced, and besides, in what kind of manufacturing could he invest in Morocco that could possibly compete with foreign manufactures? The government favored imported goods by keeping import tariffs low. What was worse, the Moroccan consumer was convinced that quality came only from abroad. The only domestic products worth buying consisted mainly of foods and traditional clothing. If he chose to produce them, who would buy his modern shoes, for example, when they could purchase imported Italian shoes? Or who would buy his Moroccan-made shampoo when they could buy it from France or Spain? Even dinner plates imported from Taiwan were preferable to those produced locally. The Moroccan government made matters worse by throwing its support behind commercial activities producing for export. In the region of Nador, that meant growing citrus fruit for Europe. But citrus grew locally only on irrigated land, and most of the good, irrigated land had been bought up long ago by wealthy men with contacts. They had been told of the planned irrigation system before everyone else and had bought the land at a cheaper price in order to take advantage of the development. Today that land was too expensive to buy. Equally vexing was the fact that many of the prices for crops grown on unirrigated land were controlled by middlemen and the government in such a restrictive manner that they barely repaid the farmers' investments—and then only during good years. No subsidies existed to carry the farmers during the bad years, which in recent times had far outnumbered the good.

Given these conditions back home, Haddou never could understand why so many Europeans expected the migrants just to pick up and leave. They acted as if the migrants had come uninvited. On the contrary, he and the millions of other migrants from around the world were in Europe because the European governments, factories, and shop owners originally asked them to come work. The first time Haddou went back on vacation, during the early 1960s, his boss had given him hundreds of work contracts to hand

out to people in the Moroccan countryside who might want to join him in
Europe, so eager was the boss to expand his migrant labor force. No,
migrants did not originally knock down the door; it was opened for them.
Unlike the better organized and more demanding European workers,
migrants could be made to work harder and longer or to do dirtier and
more dangerous jobs, thus providing greater profits for their European
employers. As Haddou saw it, the real dilemma was that Moroccans were
dependent on Europe no matter what they did. They could stay home
and—if they were lucky enough to find a job at all—produce goods for
export to Europe, work on assembling and distributing products legally
imported from Europe, illegally smuggle products in from Europe, or, like
himself, they could just pick up and go to work right in Europe. Directly, or
indirectly, in Morocco or abroad, they were all working for the Europeans.

Being a migrant in the modern world is serious business. Moroccans like
Haddou know this well, for he and close to a million of his compatriots have
left their families and homeland in Morocco in order to earn a wage a thousand miles away in the countries of Europe. They have had to learn how to
navigate through the Moroccan bureaucracy, which selectively issues or
withholds necessary papers and passports, as well as how to master the complex European system of visa and residency requirements, which deter-
mines how long—or even whether—they can stay. Along the way they have
been victimized by an array of corrupt Moroccan and European officials.

The migrants' vulnerability increased during the 1970s and 1980s. On
the Moroccan side, their allegiance to the state has come under suspicion,
particularly with the growing influence of Islamic revivalists in the migrant
community. On the European side, the growing power of rightwing groups
places a further burden on the migrants, who now find themselves threatened physically by racist thugs and legally hemmed in by restrictive
legislation.

Yet it would be a mistake to see Haddou and migrants like him as merely
pawns, pushed about by political and economic forces out of their control,
for in spite of official harassment, forbiddingly long distances, and minimal
time spent with their families, migrants continue to invest their own sacrifices with meaning by committing themselves to the betterment of the lives
of their dependents. As the career of Haddou reveals, however, the male
migrant's vision of what constitutes a good life, a good family, or even a
good father is often at odds with the perceptions of others close to him. It
may be difficult to agree with the way Haddou managed his familial affairs
and relations, but it is not difficult to respect his ability to sustain, in the face
of what amounted to almost lifelong hardship and privation, his commitment to what he valued most: the construction and maintenance of an economically stable and emotionally nurturing household.

A NOTE ON SOURCES

My wife, Joan Gross, and I spent most of 1986 and 1987 living in Nador studying the impact of migration on the region, which is how we came to know Haddou and his family, whose stories, of course, provided the sources for this article. For obvious reasons, we have not given his real name. Fulbright, Social Science Research Council, and American Institute of Maghrib Studies dissertation grants made our stay possible.

SUGGESTIONS FOR FURTHER READING

On Moroccan migrants, see my book, *In & Out of Morocco: Smuggling and Migration in a Frontier Boomtown* (Minneapolis: University of Minnesota Press, 2001). On the Moroccan context, most important is David Seddon, *Moroccan Peasants: A Century of Change in the Eastern Rif, 1870–1970* (Folkestone, England: Dawson, 1981), one of the best sources of information in English on the history and development of the region of Nador, as well as on the early years of migration from that region. Henk Driessen's ethnography of Nador's sister city, Melilla, *On the Spanish-Moroccan Frontier: A Study in Ritual, Power, and Ethnicity* (New York: Berg, 1992), is particularly valuable. A very readable memoir about life among Riffi women to the west of Nador is Ursula K. Hart, *Behind the Courtyard Door: The Daily Life of Tribeswomen in Northern Morocco* (Ipswich, Mass.: Ipswich Press, 1994).

Most Moroccan researchers write on the subject of migration either in Arabic or French, the two national languages of Morocco. One important work in French is Tahar Ben Jelloun's account of the sexual frustrations of migrants, *La plus haute des solitudes* (Paris: Seuil, 1979). Zoubir Chattou, a Moroccan researcher, has written a very interesting and important work on the travels and travails of migrants from the region to the southeast of Nador, in and around the city of Berkane: *Migration marocaines en Europe: Le paradoxe des itineraries* (Paris: l'Harmattan, 1998).

Several Moroccan novels concerning various migration experiences have been translated into English. Some of the most interesting come from the collaboration of Paul Bowles and Modammed Mrabet, notably their *Love with a Few Hairs* (1967; reprint, London: Arena/Anchor Books, 1986), which chronicles the life of a migrant to Tangier from the eastern Rif. Bowles has also translated Mohamed Choukri's *For Bread Alone* (London: Grafton Books, 1987), the autobiography of another Rifi from Nador province who was forced to migrate to Tangier. See also Driss Chraibi, *The Simple Past* (Washington D.C.: Three Continents Press, 1989). Finally, Ali Ghanem's *A Wife For My Son*, trans. G. Koziolas (London: Zed Press, 1984) describes in depth the familial stresses and strains accompanying an emigrant's attempt to work in Europe while maintaining a family in Algeria. It has recently been made into a film.

There are two other studies that could also be used to compare and contrast migration experiences from elsewhere in the Arab world with those of Morocco. The first is Petra Weyland's *Inside the Third World Village* (London: Routledge, 1993), which is a study of Egyptian emigration. The second is Anh Nga Longva's study of the impact of immigration on Kuwaiti society, *Walls Built on Sand: Migration, Exclusion, and Society in Kuwait* (Boulder, Colo.: Westview Press, 1997).

PART FOUR

Contemporary Lives

Chapter 20

Nasir: Sa'idi Youth Between Islamism and Agriculture

Fanny Colonna

Translated by E. Burke, III

Political Islam spread rapidly throughout the Middle East after the 1979 Islamic revolution in Iran. In part, this was a response to the inability of regional states to revive their sagging economies or to maintain social services in the face of economic globalization and a 2 percent net annual population increase. It also was driven by the repression of the Left—a change that disproportionately benefited Muslim religious associations and parties of the Right. Already in the 1980s, opposition groups had begun to organize their activities through established Muslim organizations. After the 1991 Gulf War, these trends continued. Economic inefficiency, rising unemployment, and the growing income gap between rich and poor exacerbated social tensions and weakened the legitimacy of states.

No place was this truer than for Egypt, where Islamist groups of various types had by the 1990s become deeply institutionalized within the mainstream society and constituted the principle opposition to the corrupt regime of President Husni Mubarak. The bleak economic outlook and the political failings of the regime were compounded by increased government repression. Already by 1991 there were 25,000 Islamist prisoners in Egyptian jails, as a result of which the activist Islamist *jama'a* went permanently underground. By some estimates, fewer than half of the 500,000 Egyptians who entered the labor market each year could expect to find a decent job. Most could never expect to have more than a series of low-paying "McJobs." Elections were marked by fraud and intimidation on a wide scale, and were routinely manipulated. In this context, the hopelessness of the younger generation was increasingly alloyed with popular resentment. The result was paradoxical.

On the one hand, it led to the emergence of an insurrectionary group of radical Islamists whose attacks on the security forces had by 1992 led to a generalized insurgency against the regime. The insurrection was inspired by the activist Jama'a t al-Islamiyyah but largely carried out by autonomous local radical organizations. It was particularly virulent in Middle and Upper Egypt and in certain working-class districts in Cairo. After an intense campaign of assassination of local police and public officials, the radicals directly attacked the tourist economy. In Fall 1997 they massacred more than sixty tourists near the tourist city of Luxor. The subsequent repression was ferocious and by the end of the 1990s seemed largely successful, though at a huge cost in terms of the violation in human rights.

On the other hand, a far more important development was taking place: the emergence of moderate, conservative, and often apolitical forms of Islamic activism. While drawing upon the organizational capacity of the politically moderate Islamic Brotherhood, the new activism had no single coordinating body. Instead, by the 1980s a host of mostly middle-class groups had established a network of faith-based charitable organizations that sponsored neighborhood medical clinics, schools, legal aid societies, and day care centers. They aimed to demonstrate the relevance of Islamic principles to modern conditions, and asserted their respect for human rights, democracy, and social justice. These moderate Islamist groups embraced all age cohorts and classes, and were inclusive of women. This so-called quiet revolution was deeply institutionalized in all corners of Egyptian life. Its call for democracy and social welfare programs constituted an implicit challenge to the increasingly repressive Mubarak regime.

Nasir, the subject of this portrait, was twenty-eight years old in 1997 when he met Algerian researchers Fanny Colonna and Kamel Chachoua in Aswan, a city in Upper (Southern) Egypt. He had recently returned to the city of his birth after attending university in Assiout, a nearby city known for its strong tradition of student radicalism, which since the 1950s had evolved from Marxist to Islamist.

Nasir's stay in Assiout (1987–91) had been immediately preceded by a series of unprecedented attacks upon the Coptic community of Upper Egypt (1986) and the insurrection (and intense repression) of radical groups affiliated with the Jama'at al-Islamiyya.

While deeply attached to Islam and its moral agenda, Nasir is not tempted by the radical option. Instead, he looks forward to buying a plot of land and practicing his skills as an agronomist. His choice is both deeply personal and at the same time representative of other rural youth in his age cohort who also have been reluctant to break with the dominant Egyptian culture of civility and social consensus. His desire for an agrarian lifestyle also reflects the decisions of other Egyptian young men who have been similarly attracted by the Islamic vision of a re-moralized society. Foreign observers have been slow to note both of these developments.

Nasir's biography raises important questions about Egyptian society and the legacy of Nasser's revolution. Nasser's social policies sought to cope with the rising birth rate through both the democratization of education and the decentralization of the university system. Nasir's experience makes us ask: Can one have both remarkable intellectual advances and a university open to everyone at the same time? His portrait also merits comparison with the biographies of other young men profiled in this book, especially his contemporaries, Talal Rizk and the husbands of Nadia and Ghada. —Eds.

Aswan has very lively street scene that starts around 7 P.M. each evening. But it abruptly shuts down around 11 P.M. Wandering aimlessly along the Corniche the evening of our arrival, we came upon a fairly imposing building still open despite the hour (it must have been after 9 P.M.). It turned out to be a public library dedicated to the memory of the great Egyptian writer and journalist, Mahmud al-ʿAqqad (1894–1964), who was a local figure. One can still visit the great man's bedroom with its old-style bed and touch his slippers, his cane, his tarbush (fez). On the bookshelves one sees his personal library, most of it written in languages other than Arabic. Some portraits of his family and various groups hang on the walls. His diary lies open on the table, ready to use. But the place has become a kind of cultural center for the young men and women of Aswan. The employees, both men and women, were also young, and this led us to strike up a conversation. Some were librarians in training, students or recent graduates waiting for a job to open up for them. They were exactly the kind of people we were looking for. We—that is, other than myself, two young Algerian sociologists and a French photographer straight from Paris—decided to return later on.

We were there to study the lives of college graduates, young or old, trained in Egyptian universities or elsewhere and returning to their place of origin. Certainly, our original plans did not call for striking up idle conversations with strangers without an appropriate introduction. But despite our careful efforts in Cairo to find local contacts, things did not go as planned once on the spot. Nobody answered our phone calls, and most of our local contacts seemed either to be away or not responding. Most researchers encounter this type of situation at one time or another, but that doesn't make it any easier to manage. Our first unscripted meeting with local people was thus completely welcome.

To pass the time, Kamel Chachoua, a member of our group of Algerian researchers, made the rounds of the local bookstores, where he found three of al-ʿAqqad's books, one of which was his autobiography, whose title (in Arabic) was *Ana (I)*. Al-ʿAqqad was from a family of some distinction but not much wealth, though he was sufficiently good as an architect to receive an award from the city fathers. Aside from the library along the Corniche, we'd noticed an imposing but not quite finished mausoleum as we came in from the airport. A large bust of al-ʿAqqad in black granite of almost pharaonic dimensions stood before it.

The picture of Aswan that emerges in al-ʿAqqad's autobiography depicts a town known to the Greeks from late antiquity, a crossroads of East and West, North and South even before the coming of Islam. By al-ʿAqqad's time, it had become a major attraction for British tourists bent on finding a warm place to pass the winter. (Al-ʿAqqad was to become a superb translator of books in English.) This helps explain the elegant atmosphere of this border city, five hundred miles from Cairo, the last town along the Nile before the Sudanese border, known for its antiquities, verdant botanical gardens, luxury hotels (quite out of the price range of our research team!), the mausoleum of the Agha Khan that stands on the edge of a dune on the other side of the river, and, finally, the Cultural Palace, nationally known for its theatrical offerings. All of this without counting the regional television station, Channel 8, the most inventive in all of Egypt while we were there.

Knowing all these accumulated cultural layers, Kamel decided to invite Nasir, a librarian intern whom he'd met on our first evening in Aswan, to talk to him about his daily life. Their conversations—conducted in Arabic and recorded in their entirety—took place in the afternoons in the office of the al-ʿAqqad library. Breaking with our practice, I decided not to take part. Nasir's interviews were especially well adapted to this approach, both because of their reflexivity and introspective quality, as well as because of the universal aspect of his life experiences and his way of speaking about them. The spontaneity and improvised character of the interchange between Nasir and Kamel was no doubt strongly shaped by the similarity in their ages and backgrounds. In an effort to provide context for the reader, I've included my author's comments for this portrait. The speaker is Nasir, unless otherwise identified.

Nasir began, "As a student, I can travel in a foreign country and study in a place different from the one in which I was born. How about you? You want to know how I experienced this? What was the impact of this trip on me? At the beginning of this phase of my life, I was eighteen years old. It's the time when it's normal, when one feels that one belongs to a family. You can't fit in or go out without an older person. Here in Egypt, when one of us leaves for a foreign country we say, 'I'm going into exile.' This means that I am going somewhere that I won't be able to fit in. The departure is a major source of worry for the entire family. How will you live? Find a room to stay? You'll need money to help you fit in. Furthermore, since I am used to living at home, I don't know how I'll manage with the new living environment. Or if I'll be able to study or get myself organized. Inside the home, it's the father who rules the family; he's the one who spends the money, who oversees everyone's life. I seek his advice about everything. I tell him: I want to go up to Cairo for a few days for a visit, and he tells me whether to travel by myself or with someone else; that is, he's thinking about my personal security. A father's affection for his son makes him afraid on his behalf, afraid that he won't return, or that something will happen to him. As an eighteen-year-old Egyptian boy, I was very much under the influence of my family. Family ties are very strong."

Kamel asked, "Are they stronger in Aswan than in Cairo?"

"Maybe yes, maybe no," Nasir replied. "In Cairo there's much more freedom. A young man can go on short trips, go to Alexandria or Ismailiya in just two hours. In three hours he can go to Port Said. He goes in and out whenever he wants. But for me in Assiout, where I went to university, the distances involved are much greater; the trip is very tiring, and you have to go in a group with people you know, friends or neighbors. I have to call my parents and tell them I got there okay, I have to reassure them, tell them that I'll be back tomorrow. That's how we go on trips. If you are going to study, you stay for a longer time: a year or two, even three or four. When I pass the entrance examination for the university, we have a big party. I've become a man of accomplishments, educated, at a higher level, a man with diplomas, who will have responsibilities. My father and mother look at me as if I were still a kid. As for me, I have some potential. I had my skills and talents, an energy that allows me to get along, to live away from home with my friends. I can study and go to lectures. Inside my room, I can count on myself, since private life is totally autonomous. I have to do my own cooking, since the place where I live provides nothing. In Aswan, when I get home from school, everything is ready. But in Cairo, when I come home from the university, everything is different. I have to do everything myself. If I am exhausted, how can I find the time to cook dinner? At night, I can cook—or what I call cooking—rice and some vegetables or meat. I cook my next day's meal so that when I get back I won't get tired out. This requires a lot of organization. Who can teach me how to organize my life? . . . Life itself," he said with some bitterness. "Our lives. I confront it and afterwards I wonder. Let me tell you a story.

"I was living in a rooming house with many other students. I didn't know how to cook; I couldn't even cook pasta. At home my mother was the one who cooked pasta, and I had no idea how to do it. I learned that this is how you cook pasta: you takes the pot [in Egyptian, *halla*, a conical pan]—you know, of course, what a *halla* is, I can speak frankly? You take the *halla* and put some butter (*samna*) or oil in it, you take some normal pasta and you mix them until they are browned and then you pour in the water. So what did I do? I took the *halla*, I poured in the water and the pasta and I left it to cook for three hours or so while I took a nap. I figured that I would check on it when I woke up. But in fact you must boil it and then pour off the water and add the tomato sauce before eating it. I just left it in the water to cook until it got so swollen up that it all congealed in a sticky mess. I went to sleep. It was the first time I'd ever tried to cook for myself. It was because I had to count upon myself alone. I could not imagine calling upon my neighbor to ask him for help. Boy, did I have a shock when I found it all stuck together! Of course, I had no idea. Later on, I asked how to do it. My roommate explained the whole thing to me. My first stage was thus to learn how to cook pasta." Nasir concluded with a bit of humor. "I learned how to count only upon myself. I worked and learned how to make pasta by myself. At first, it was a lot of trouble. Learning how to live alone shocked me a bit at first.

"I began to organize my time. I went to class from eight in the morning till four in the afternoon. The food had to be prepared beforehand and my clothes washed and ironed. I had to organize my things so they didn't bother me. First, I began to understand how important having a sense of time is. Second, I began to grasp my responsibility. Being a man is a responsibility, since God has called upon man to be honest. And what is honesty? It's our capacity to endure the problems that we confront in our lives and to learn how to bear them. Later, I saw that there were other things that I need to learn, such as organizing my personal expenses. You tell yourself that you've got the two hundred Egyptian pounds that your father has sent you. With it you need to provide housing and pay your personal and scholarly expenses, books and things like that. So I took a pencil and I began to calculate my budget, which I'd never done before. Beforehand, if I wanted a shirt, I told myself, 'I'll buy myself one,' or pants, . . . go buy some. Now, however, I have to figure out how much I can spend and then I check the local shops for the one that looks nicest to me at the best price and that's the one for me!"

Nasir's adventure took place at Assiout between 1987 and 1991, after he'd completed his secondary education at Kima School in Aswan, near the factory of the same name. A large city on the Nile, halfway between Cairo and Aswan, Assiout has a population of a million and, together with the nearby city of Minya, is one of the birthplaces of Egyptian Islamism, and more specifically, of the activist milieu of Jama'at al- Islamiyya, about which Nasir spoke later on in the interview. The university was founded in the 1950s. Ever since the establishment of regional universities, students have been recruited geographically. "Lots of high school graduates from Aswan are oriented toward Assiout: the University of Assiout is considered as the mother for us, from all points of view." In 1979, however, even before it became the epicenter of violent Islamist student unrest and equally violent state repression in the 1980s, the university witnessed a major riot by the *jama'at* and the seizure of two nearby cities during an official visit of President Sadat. It is also interesting to note that Assiout had previously been known as a strong center for Marxist student activism, whose propaganda and "didactic" interventions strongly marked the lives of those who were students there at the time. It is even possible to see a strong resemblance between the ways the former Marxists talk about their leftist phase at Assiout and the way Nasir describes the Islamist milieu and its methods of religious and political activism a decade later.

While rapidly evoking his attendance at the mosque, and at information and discussion groups, as well as listening to the radio and the circulation of news via rumor networks, and discovering the existence of people poorer than himself, Nasir comments: "Transplanting oneself from one life to another has lots of advantages. Many beneficial things go into forming a personality, as they did mine. I became more deeply involved in life than previously, and daily met a huge number of persons, especially students. You learn to differentiate good people from bad, to figure out who likes you and who is your enemy, who will stick by you. Adoration and prayer are the two things that were the most beneficial for me personally. When you enter a mosque and you see that the majority are young men . . .

"Most were *young* men?" asked Kamel.

"Yes, previously, when you entered a mosque, the quarters of the congregation were old men. This is a change that comes from Allah. There are also university students who take part in politics in a positive manner. If the price of something goes up, . . . you can talk to people without any problem, *confidentially*. Before, I lived in my house and I didn't know anything. If the price went up, it went up! What can I do if it went up! But there are people who are affected whom one finds everywhere—poor, tired, overwhelmed people. There are rich people and poor people; there are different classes. I began to understand that there were really poor people, and to become aware of my own social class, where I am situated on the social scale, at what level. Lots of benefits.

"Also, my personal situation evolved for the better. I began to become socially integrated and to understand the news. Previously, when the news appeared, I did not know about it. When Iraq was bombed [1991)], for example, I was in the final year of my university studies. We were really affected by this event and felt solidarity with the Iraqis. We would have wanted the Arab countries to be more involved so that nothing happened to Iraq. Among students, we began to think alike about this subject. We discussed and spoke with one another about what Iraq should do and about the position of the U.S. I regularly listened to the radio, which I had never previously done. Previously, I just watched the news bulletin on TV and the *salaamu alaykum*. Now, I grabbed my radio and spun the dial for up-to-date news."

"You spoke and argued amongst yourselves?" asked Kamel.

"Yes, we argued," said Nasir. "Some of my brothers said that it was a good thing that Saddam attacked Kuwait. As for me, I listened, I had an opinion. I had an opinion thereafter, he murmured softly. Because I had never had an opinion before about anything. Henceforth, I had an opinion. Sometimes, if my opinion was right, others would be convinced by it. I began to understand for myself that I was thinking correctly."

"All this took place at Assiout, at the university?" asked Kamel.

"Yes," said Nasir. "I changed my attitude; it was like an internal exodus. I think that this was one of the principal and most positive benefits that I received."

Confidence, based upon a kind of lived *fraternity,* would appear to be the link between this mixture of spiritual and temporal (especially political) concerns that provided a kind of unity to Nasir's education. When he speaks of his "brothers," it's not just words.

Nasir's personal inclinations pushed him toward the science department, but his father insisted that he major in agronomy. The region of

Aswan was at one time very well suited for agriculture, and at first Nasir thought that he wanted to "take a government plot and plant it so that it bore its fruits." He allowed himself to be convinced and joined the School of Agronomy "on this basis," as he said, that is, on the basis of his father's wishes and the renunciation of his own. "In our country," he added lucidly, "as Egyptians, one of the biggest mistakes made by families is that they favor certain subjects which, even though they might offer a good theoretical training, do not in the end lead to work opportunities and while, on the other hand, other subjects can lead to jobs. For example, [in] the School of Education, you graduate as a teacher. Before graduating, you sign a contract and you're right away in a job." But his father wanted him to study agronomy because his family had always been peasants: "Their roots are peasant, the whole family loves farming." He had promised his son that he would buy him some land "as a first step." Then, once he had begun his studies, Nasir "found himself," discovering that he was really attracted to agriculture, that he loved farming, "because of his love of his studies and the prospect of an exciting future." From that point on, he tried to find a way to farm.

Even if Nasir's dream of owning land seemed unrealizable, and despite living in a place and attending a school where agricultural values were not dominant, he remained faithful to his father's wishes. The surrounding region has little in the way of arable land, and as we've already seen, agriculture is far from the chief activity in Aswan. Aside from tourism, the city is mostly a commercial center for trade between Egypt and the Sudan. In fact, his father's love of farming is unclear, since he is probably of Nubian descent and migrated to Aswan from Lower Egypt or the western oases. Nasir's ultimate fate would remain undecided, since his father would not be able to follow up on his earlier promise to buy Nasir land (we don't know the reason why).

"Why did you return to Aswan?" asked Kamel.

"After I graduated?' Nasir asked, and then responded to his own question. "It was because of my attachment to my family, as I told you already. We Egyptians, when one of us goes away—it's probably the same in Algeria—he misses Algeria, right? I missed my village, my birthplace, even [though] I was in Egypt. I am from Aswan. If I go to the north, I will miss my region, there's nothing I can do about it. I can't work normally. Even if I find a job outside Egypt, we find something in ourselves that keeps us tied to our village. Among ourselves, when friends get together, we ask one another: Where are you from? Are you from Kafr al-Shaykh? And you, where are you from, Mansura?

"We all think of our village. *Our land keeps hold of us.* If I am sent to work in Alexandria, I depart, but I'll be impatient to return to see my family. I can ask to be transferred, there are lots of branches in my specialty. But until now, nothing has come up to lead me away from Aswan."

"No opportunity, really?" asked Kamel.

Nasir replied, "I am responsible for my mother and my little brother and this keeps me always here. And, *al-hamdu lillah*, I have a job, I earn a good living, I don't see what might lead me to leave Aswan. Now I am financially responsible for the family. I'm the one who pays the bills. That's just the way we are. *Sa'idis* (people from southern Egypt) are more strict than *Baharis* (people from northern Egypt). Here in the Sa'id (also known as Upper Egypt), men are responsible for themselves, from Beni Souief, Assiut, Suhag, Qena, Luxor to Aswan. Family ties are stronger than among the *Baharis*. We are the sons of Egypt and maybe it's the same in Algeria, but between North and South, that's the way things are. Sure, everyone has his own way of thinking and his own habits and rituals, and here in the Sa'id our customs say that your cousin is like your brother. There are obligatory family occasions. Family solidarity is very strong. Whenever there's a wedding, everyone comes. In moments of sadness (may God preserve us from them) or for funerals, we're all there for one another. It is important that each family has a man of the family," Nasir says, three times. "He who speaks for the family. If he's weak, no one will consider him as worthwhile. He must be strict [*shadid*, strong and unbending] when he states his opinion. Even if he's wrong," Nasir laughingly insisted.

"That's the way things are. But *al-hamdu lillah*, there are no wrong opinions. For an opinion is also a suggestion that can apply to this or that subject. I can tell him my opinion, the fruit of my experience as a thought, and I tell him, do it like this. If he follows my advice, that's good."

"Are there ever disagreements with fathers over marriage within families, for example, yours?" asked Kamel.

"I'm not married yet!" Nasir emphasized.

"But there are possibilities?" suggested Kamel.

"Yes," Nasir replied. "Just now, there's a woman in whom I am interested. I've requested her hand, but then there were problems and we've separated. But now I want her all over again. I want her; I want us to get back together and to get married. There are problems about this at home. My parents don't want any more of this. They say the girl is no good!"

"Are there things you're not telling me?" asked Kamel.

"No," said Nasir, "but you never know what can happen. Maybe it's my fate! I go to request her hand or speak with the girl in the garden and what happens? [Another] girl tries to create difficulties with my fiancée, who is her friend. She invents bad stuff about me. And they believe her, they believe that I have this or that defect: 'He doesn't earn a thing, he's a spendthrift,' or some other vice. Creating all sorts of problems, you see. There was a disagreement with her family. They were neighbors who lived on the same floor in the same building. And as is often the case, when families live next door, there were problems. Fate intervened, and we have parted. It was a normal engagement, however. . . . Now I am trying to raise the question again, but now my parents oppose it. Everyone is against it. I took their advice, but they said, 'We'll find you another girl who will be better for you.' But it's not theirs to decide. The choice is in my hands.

"Still," Nasir went on, "I need to bring about a resolution. That is to say, the family needs to come together on the same plan, or nothing will happen. There are difficulties that come from education, for example. I received a different education from my father. But to the extent that my behavior matches what he expects, an agreement is possible. For example, if I want to marry a girl or if I want to work in this or that region, I attempt to simplify the way I present it to him. I see that it is difficult for him, so I try to simplify it, so that my parents can understand and that they are capable of taking it in, so that we don't have a fight. In the case of marriage, for example, I'm the one who will choose. But the most important thing is their agreement. I don't want to lose my family because of my choice of spouse. Because what really matters is your brother. Spouses can be replaced. That's why I tried with them by using this or that strategy to convince them that there's nothing wrong in so doing. If it doesn't work, then I'll shut up right away.

"What do you think of that?" he asked Kamel with a laugh.

"These problems exist in Algeria, too," Kamel replied prudently. "We also live through such situations."

"You also," said Nasir. "Well, *al-hamdu lillah* [thank God]. The same, it's true."

Nasir was quiet for a few seconds, then said thoughtfully: "We Arabs in general have the same blood. Despite the differences in our cultures and our histories . . ."

"We have the same way of doing things," replied Kamel.

"But at bottom," said Nasir, "in the beginning, we feel it within ourselves, this common blood, we feel it, and I hope it's been good for us!"

At the time of the interview, in 1997, Nasir was twenty-eight years old. It's a normal age to begin thinking—that is, other than in one's dreams—of getting married, at least according to the prevailing Egyptian norms. Along with having a job, marriage is the sign of the real entry into adulthood. It is a social necessity that now comes, for Nasir's generation, some ten years later than would have been the case for his parents' generation. This is why there is such a long, unspecified period, which in his case had lasted for six years, between his graduation and his assumption of a real social role. The reader may have noted above that one of the worst things the family of a girl can say about a boy is that he doesn't have a job, or that he is a spendthrift. This is why we've emphasized Nasir's responsibilities within his family of origin, both financial (which he claims to have shouldered from his student days) as well as moral and ethical (for which the Islamist groups and his new religious observance prepared him). In a word, we're talking about a different passage to adulthood from the process of socialization that shaped his parents.

But, in any event, marriage is always the result of a negotiating process, as it is here for Nasir, since it must satisfy both families—not to mention the two people directly concerned! The way in which Nasir formulates his dilemma, as the need to reach an agreement without imposing his point of view but also without either giving up what he wants or curbing his determination, shows in both his personal and public demeanor. Another example is the way he agreed, while a student, to major in a subject that was not his choice but that he claims he came "to really love." Nasir is always looking for compromise.

On the subject of the availability of job opportunities, Nasir thinks that "in Egypt, there's a lot of opportunity, thank God, in all sorts of areas." But in regions like Aswan, where there's little investment yet, or where there are few projects that can create jobs, each year the universities have more graduates than there are jobs available. In Aswan, between two hundred and five hundred graduates per year enter the labor market. From one year to the next, it's always the same problem, and it only gets worse. The private sector in Aswan tries to attract executives with advanced degrees. But, as Nasir notes, "for a long time we have naturally always sought jobs as bureaucrats, working for the government. Government jobs provide a fixed income and security of employment. There's lots of free time." In fact, the 1996 census shows that 40 percent of the working population of around 220,000 people work for the government. This is almost as many as the 53 percent of the working population who work in the commerce and tourism sector.

After he graduated from university in 1991 and finished his military service (about which he didn't say a word), Nasir returned to Aswanto look for work, "because you have to." He found a part-time afternoon job working at a fish farm—a relatively recent development project, connected to the completion of the High Dam—which was more or less connected to his studies in agriculture. He is proud of the fish farm facility, describing it as "a beautiful place where everyone, both Egyptians and tourists, can come. It's very productive and it's a great job."

"And here?" asked Kamel, speaking of the library where the interview was being conducted, "How is this job?"

"You mean the cultural level?" asked Nasir. "It's like every library. During the school year, we work really hard. We keep track of the books we've got, the lost books. We withdraw the damaged books from circulation. We've set up the regulations, how to return the books."

"And what have you got to read?" asked Kamel with delight, since he himself is a voracious reader.

"Well," replied Nasir, "if you see a bureaucrat in his office, you notice that he's often got a book in his hands. When things get boring, when no one's there, he can pick up a book and sit and read. As for me, I've read books on medicine, pharmacy, all sorts of subjects."

Nasir's is a "professional life" broken into two parts (his job at the fish farm in the afternoon and at the library in the evening), with no connection between them, but both jobs have in common both their special character and the seriousness with which he performs them. In any event, Nasir speaks of them with respect and not as dead-end jobs. Still, both of Nasir's part-time jobs look a lot like what the Egyptian newspapers call "little jobs," those to which most recent graduates are condemned and which can scarcely be reassuring to the family of the girl in whom he is interested. Here, as elsewhere, what is striking is the way Nasir keeps himself going and is able to speak positively about his present condition. Maybe it is a result of working at it, but one can easily imagine an opposite, much more pessimistic reaction, under the circumstances. Indeed, the Egyptian press is full of stories on "the youth question" that are much more negative and angry.

Nasir claims that "Sa'idi youth are just fine, very studious" (96 percent of boys over ten years old are in school, along with 92 percent of the girls, which is quite unusual), and that "most of the Cairo doctors are from the Sa'id." We've heard this same theme of a provincial brain-drain to the capital in Luxor. "At Aswan," says Nasir, "there may be lots of nice people, but we've never met them. They must be doing their doctorates in Paris. My cousin, for example, was a teacher. And he was gifted with a brilliant mind. But once he'd finished studying in Cairo, he went to France, got a doctorate, and decided to stay and work in France. He's been traveling a lot, and his family hasn't heard from him for a long time."

"How would you explain the character of Sa'idi intelligence?" asked Kamel.

According to Nasir, Sai'idis don't have any particular character, but Sa'idi youth "are simply waiting for the moment." In the Sa'id, the social and economic standard of living is rough. Baharis have lots of plans. They have them all the time. But in the South, there's the drought, difficult conditions of life; whereas in the North, there is the center of the state, ministers and very important industrial and commercial activities. The Sa'id has lots of resources, though; if we look at them today, we can figure out that "the future will be great. Whoever has the chance to study in Cairo and can travel to a European or Arab country will [be able to] do whatever he wants."

Nasir doesn't seem to be displaying the slightest bit of "cultural regionalism" here. But the idea that Aswan could become a cultural center of southern Egypt, while perhaps a utopian idea, has been realized by a certain number of "cultural entrepreneurs" who work in television and the theater. Such people are common in Luxor, farther north, as well.

"What about social life, how important is religion in other areas of life at Aswan?" asked Kamel.

Nasir explained that the people of Aswan are best characterized as good, and described this goodness in nearly universal terms. People are good; family ties are strong everywhere. They are good people, healthy, who like laughing, dancing, weddings. They like joking, going for walks, running. As for the young people, they are happy." According to Nasir, "Young people need to preserve their values better. They sometimes lack a certain seriousness," or, as he said, they "are too licentious."

Nasir continued, "You see, young people need to be more serious. Where will they find this seriousness? Not in nature, for even if people are good, they aren't necessarily serious. However, one sees lots of serious young people, even strict, austere. They get it from their fathers and their grandfathers; they learn this rigor from them. They get married young. It's not uncommon that young people of our age are already married and have children. We [you and I] aren't married yet [actually, he's wrong, since Kamel, who is Algerian and has lived in France for several years, has been married for the past ten years and has two children]. But there are young people who marry their maternal or paternal cousins. We find that they have a sense of responsibility from their earliest years."

"But," Kamel mused, "students who study in Assiout and other universities outside Aswan, who have had the same experiences as you and have the same social and political consciousness, what are the effects upon them of returning to Aswan? Do some of them get involved in politics and try to change things at the local level?"

"As I was saying," Nasir replied, "there is a greater openness in the University of Asiout. The culture and political conscience of the student population of ten thousand is generally high. We know the news from the sermons that we listen to in the mosques. For example, there's a problem somewhere in the world—Muslims have been killed in Palestine, or there's a new video on Bosnia. If one wants to inform oneself on the world outside, one begins by gathering information on Muslim society [here, Nasir makes a slip of the tongue and says *mutajamma'at* (armed groups) instead of *mujtama* (society), before correcting himself]. Everyone is aware of the news, as I said. It's only the young people who want to do something, to struggle, run, fight, make something."

"But when they return back to Aswan, for example?" asked Kamel.

"When you return home," said Nasir, "you have acquired a certain cultural level, you know what's happened. You know that Muslims need to unite to become one. They need help. As for you, you can begin with your family and teach them about this country. For example, they think that the United States is good for Egypt, that they give us money. No, they only give money for this or that reason. You can tell them about the relationship between Arafat and Rabin and the secret agreements they've reached. Or that the Palestinians sold their land to the Israelis. These are things that no one around here knows. Because when you return from such a university you've learned a lot."

"So when you got back to Aswan," asked Kamel, "did you undertake serious political discussions, dialogue with your family?"

"Yes, we began a discussion. When there's a problem of some sort, we state our advice."

"Previously," Kamel insisted, "you didn't do that?"

"No," replied Nasir, "we didn't do anything like that. Society didn't allow us to do it."

Kamel observed that the influence within the family, the neighborhood, between friends, all comes from a form of action from the bottom up. He compared it to what was attempted from the top, that is, by the local government at Aswan. Did other returning students like Nasir undertake the same political education, but at a higher level?

"In fact," Nasir continued, "lots of problems derive from the highest level. But the government offers no possibility [for engagement]. It's happy just to maintain order. When demonstrations (*baltaja*) break out, they provoke movement, create tensions, because demonstrations are forbidden, and we have to put up with the fact that some people go to prison. Putting a student in prison can ruin his future! Thus, if someone has a certain level of culture, he gives his opinion about liberty to the extent possible, without turning the world upside down with demonstrations. For participation in demonstrations can be used against him. There were problems at Aswan."

Actually, we'd been told in Cairo that there were many communist voters residing in Aswan, the largest number in the country. There seems no doubt that this is linked to the presence for more than ten years of Soviet workers and leaders who were involved in the construction of the High Dam (completed in 1971), one of the great successes of Nasser. The communist activities in Aswan didn't only involve students, but a broader base.

"But the students weren't involved," said Nasir. "With respect to those of us who were returning, there were no problems. But at a high level, the newspapers of the opposition party [he doesn't say which one] keep people informed of what's going on all over the country. Every country has its defects, each policy has its defects, but people want to know for themselves. When we meet one another, we exchange opinions." (It is not clear who Nasir is speaking about here. Probably former Assiout students with the same political orientation as his.) "However," he went on, "if you think I can change something or do something, or that someone besides myself can do something, that's not likely. We can't do anything."

"Do you write for the newspapers?" asked Kamel.

"No, I don't write," replied Nasir. "But there are opposition newspaper that are known for good writing, since we have some freedom of the press today. Jama'a Islamiyya, you've heard of them and of what's happened, what we call the 'incidents'? The attacks, the tourist trains hit, the foreigners who were their targets and other things like that? These actions were attributed to [*mansuba*] Jama'a."

"*Mansuba?*" asked Kamel. "Only *attributed*? It's not certain?"

"The government blames them on Jama'a," said Nasir. "But if Jama'a did that, they'd be wrong. One must preserve one's religion. I am in the path of righteousness, I pray and I keep to my religion. I can raise people's consciousnesses, I can [hope] to bring about a change, but I don't ruin the country. There are poor people."

Kamel asked, "Are the armed *jama'at* like those we've got in Algeria?"

"Yes," said Nasir, "we're very, very upset at what's going on there."

"Who belongs to Jama'at Islamiyya in Egypt?" asked Kamel. "What is their level of consciousness, their education, what social class do they come from?" Kamel hesitates a lot, not knowing how to formulate his questions without appearing to be either pushy or negative. "Are they young? How far did they get in their studies?"

"They are different ages," replies Nasir. "But most were students who graduated and are married and have a family. Some of them are dues-paying members, others are there as *mu'ahid* [volunteers]. Today, this organization has a negative influence. What has happened recently is almost like what's gone on in Algeria: murders, killings and massacres, terrible things that no one wishes. If you are someone who defends your religion, you don't just kill non-believers. No one asks this of you. You're asked to deal with those who want to hurt you. And to preserve the stability of the country, stability being the most important thing. Whatever your politics, the worst thing in Egypt is that tourism is attacked. Lots of people live entirely from tourism—for example, at Luxor. During the recent period of difficulties, they were left without work. Who benefits from that? In Europe, you know well, they have freedom; you can express your opinion and that's that, you walk in the street, you don't damage people's cars, you don't put bombs under vehicles, or next to people's doors, you don't blow anyone up. As for me, I know the law. You don't do such things in the street. There's a certain behavior to maintain. No one hurts another, that's the real Islam. I don't shame anyone and I don't kill anyone. That's my view. The Jama'a Islamiyya were fine before. I don't know what's happened, why they began destroying and killing. All that is unreasonable. The countries of the unbelieving foreigners see Muslims killing one another. They say: 'What I must do is to fight Islam.' They are right to say it!"

One assesses the profound anxiety that underlies the words of Nasir in the face of a spiral of violence that appears to be unending and without any positive political effects. The period in which this interview took place was preceded by three years in which some of the most bloody and spectacular actions of the *jama'at* took place, including two attempted assassinations, one of the Minister of Information, the other of Naguib Mahfouz, the

Nobel Prize-winning author, as well as another attempt on the life of President Mubarak while he was visiting Ethiopia. In the Fall of 1997, just after our encounter, a massacre took place at Luxor in which sixty foreign tourists were killed under terrible circumstances. This, too, was attributed to the *jama'at* and was followed by a heavy repression, which in turn led to the announcement of a unilateral truce by the terrorist organization. What is reflected in Nasir's words is the complete absence of any rhyme or reason for the destructive violence, as well as the teaching received by the group's members during their years of political education in Assiout. Nasir says little or nothing about his own political education, or where it led him and the others in their involvement in the movement.

What Nasir says about the need to preserve stability so as not to ruin the country as a whole, or about the living standards of people in the south who make their living from tourism, or even about the international image of Egypt, illustrates perfectly what some far-sighted Egyptian political scientists call "the regime of civility." As a result, Nasir's views are representative not only of those of the educated provincial youth but of other social strata as well. The regime of civility is an implicit social contract that consists of absolutely avoiding any kind of confrontation. It doesn't presume that all citizens agree upon the same values or even, in the end, upon common objectives. It is neither directed at opposing progress nor at preserving the status quo. It has shown itself to be perfectly compatible with the requirements of what is called "re-Islamization" (and thus with the ideals of Nasser, in particular), of which it is in fact the product. It also implies the choice of means: education, persuasion, preaching, adapted to shaping society—insofar as such a thing exists—from both the top down and the bottom up, by the governors and the governed (even though, in Nasir's version, only the bottom-up version is considered). In this sense, the words of this orderly young man provide a remarkable key to understanding behaviors and forms of consensus—a word that appears constantly in Egyptian political vocabulary—that are apparently unexplainable to the foreign observer.

Kamel asked about how everyday life, outside of work, was for Nasir and his peers. "What kind of leisure activities are available?" he asked, and observed, "There's only one working cinema, which is near the Al-Sadaqa train station." Nasir is not concerned; he thinks that movies are not a good distraction, that they exert a bad influence. He prefers libraries that have lots of good books. However, he has to admit that young people are not eager to read, especially as few have any free time since they have to spend all their time looking for "employment opportunities" to make a living. Some young men work twelve to thirteen hours a day. If Nasir has a free moment, he "runs to the nearest library to take up any book on religion, there's no time for anything else." Otherwise, young people like naturally to dance. They also like singing—the two go together in local culture—and the region is rich in singers with wonderful voices. "Some," he says, "like Mohamed Mounir, have a national or even international reputation."

Kamel asks about the types of leisure activities Nasir favors, and his hopes for the future.

Nasir says that he has no plans: "To have a plan, one must have the means." He goes on: "If I had the means, the first thing I'd do would be to buy some land. I'd take up agriculture and completely give up working for the government. I'd like some good land. I'd never consider working in a shop. I don't like it. I want to be a farmer. I'd like to buy some land, put [it] into shape to farm, and live there."

The stubborn persistence of Nasir's farming dream echoes strangely, upon hearing it once again, as one notes the number of Islamist militants who have chosen to become farmers . This is true from one end of the country to the other. Even local intellectuals who were on the same cultural wavelength but never became militants have chosen farming, even though such a choice undermines, in some cases, the mercantile occupations of this cultural group. There seems to be a kind of affinity between working the land and the Islamist vision of the world

Nasir is quiet for along time.

"Thanks," says Kamel, who is left by Nasir's quiet determination almost without a voice.

"*Nawwartuna* [You're the one who has illumined us]," replies Nasir with civility.

A NOTE ON SOURCES

The portrait of Nasir is adapted from a chapter in Fanny Colonna, *Récits de la province egyptienne: Une ethnographie Sud/Sud* (Arles: Sindbad/Actes Sud, 2004. The entire interview with Nasir was audio-taped in the subject's language of interaction (in this case, Modern Standard Arabic). The larger book project includes two dozen interviews of Egyptians from North to South from a dozen small towns and villages (but not including Cairo). Research on the book was conducted from 1996 to 1998. It was financed for several years by CEDEJ and the Ford Foundation for the Middle East, both located in Cairo. Colonna wishes to thank them all here, along with everyone who generously agreed to speak about her or his daily life.

SUGGESTIONS FOR FURTHER READING

For an introduction to provincial Egypt, Amitav Ghosh's *In An Antique Land* (London: Granta Books, 1992) is without equal. Christophe Ayad, *Géopolitique de l'Egypte* (Brussels: Editions Complex, 2000), and two books by Eberhard Kienle, *A Great Delusion: Democracy and Economics Reform in Egypt* (London: I. B. Tauris, 2000), and *Politics from Above, Politics from Below: The Middle East in the Age of Economic Reform* (London: Saqi Press, 2004), give a broad recent panorama, albeit one somewhat distanced from Egyptian society. This is also the focus of Paul Amar and Diane Singerman, eds., *Cosmopolitan Cairo: World Capital of Myths and Movements* (Cairo: American University of Cairo Press, 2004).

For an excellent discussion of marriage among lower-class urban Egyptians, see chapter 2 of Diane Singerman, *Avenues of Participation: Family, Politics, and Networks in the Urban Quarters of Cairo* (Princeton, N.J.: Princeton University Press, 1985). On political culture and civil society, see Jean-Noel Ferrié, *Le régime de civilité en Egypte: Public et réislamisation* (Paris: CNRS, 2004). See Mohamed Berrada, *Comme un été qui ne reviendra pas, Le Caire, 1955–1996* (Arles: Actes du Sud, 2001) for a description of the literary salon of Mahmud Aqqad.

On Egyptian Islamism, see, among other works, Gilles Kepel, *Jihad: The Trail of Political Islam* (Cambridge, Mass.: Harvard University Press, 2002); and Genevieve Abdo, *No God But God: Egypt and the Triumph of Islam* (Oxford: Oxford University Press, 2000).

Chapter 21

Ghada: Village Rebel Or Political Protestor?

Celia Rothenberg

Israeli checkpoints are a major aspect of Israeli control and administration of Palestinians in the West Bank and Gaza. The Israeli government regards the checkpoints as necessary for the security of Israel and the occupied territories. Palestinians, however, see them as a source of daily restriction, abuse, and humiliation. Checkpoints have become symbolic arenas for Israel to demonstrate its vigilance and strength, and for Palestinians to demonstrate their resistance.

Since the Israeli occupation of the West Bank and Gaza Strip following the June 1967 War, military checkpoints have become a constant point of friction between Palestinians and the Israeli authorities. They have also increasingly become a focus of criticism. The 2003 U.S. State Department Report on Human Rights Practices for "Israel and the Occupied Territories," and the 2004 U.N. Commission on Human Rights report, "Question of the Violation of Human Rights in the Occupied Arab Territories, including Palestine," both speak of routine physical abuse, as well as cases of torture and even random killings. The latter refers to "the methodical intimidation and humiliation of [Palestinian] civilians at checkpoints."* Since the outbreak of the second *intifada* in 2000, these reports even note instances in which sick or injured Palestinian individuals or ambulances have not been allowed to pass a checkpoint on their way to a hospital.

Attacks on checkpoints have taken many forms. During the first *intifada* (1987–92), they ranged from verbal abuse to stonings and physical aggression. It was in this context that, early in 1992, Ghada, a young Palestinian woman, approached the checkpoint near the West Bank village of Artas armed with a kitchen knife and set in motion the events described here. It is important to keep the political chronology in mind. Only after the start of the second *intifada,* in Fall 2000,

---

*The two reports are available on the Web at http://www.state.gov/g/drl/rls/hrrpt/2003/27929.htm and http:// http://domino.un.org/unispal.nsf/0/631c8deb907650e985256e6000520f3b? OpenDocument, respectively.

have checkpoint guards become the targets of Palestinian snipers and suicide bombers.

As Celia Rothenberg's portrait of Ghada demonstrates, the symbolism and accessibility of the checkpoint was but one of Ghada's motivations. Using the story of Ghada as a lens, Rothenberg examines the West Bank Palestinian village from the viewpoint of women: the realities of cousin marriage, the impact of divorce, the lack of economic opportunity, as well as the burdens of Israeli occupation. In this way, we learn of the complex motivations behind Ghada's desperate act.

Ghada's experience helps us see the impact of global politics on the lives of individuals. After the creation of Israel in 1947, Artas ended up under Jordanian rule. With the collapse of the local economy, Ghada's parents sought a better future and moved from the West Bank to Kuwait, where Ghada was born in 1970 and grew up. But following Saddam Hussein's invasion of Kuwait, many Palestinians (including Ghada's middle-class parents) were forced to relocate to Amman, Jordan.

The 1990–91 Gulf War turned Ghada's world upside down. Not only did it have a disastrous impact on her family's fortunes, but it also propelled the decision that led to her unhappy 1990 arranged marriage with a cousin in Artas. The impact of war upon ordinary families in the Middle East, a central theme of the contemporary period, is thereby underscored.

Ghada's biography also illustrates how Palestinian women's lives are shaped both by the Israeli occupation and its checkpoints, as well as by the patriarchal culture of the village and family. Rothenberg's portrait helps us to understand the multiple pressures that weighed upon Ghada. It also reveals that divergent sources of domination may, at times, work together to constrain women's lives. Here, the discourse of Palestinian nationalism and resistance mingled with Ghada's own personal feelings of being trapped and led to her desperate decision.

Ghada's life can be usefully related to the lives of Nadia and Farkhondeh Gohary, two other contemporary women profiled in this volume. But it also bears comparison with the lives of the other women chronicled in this book. The situation of Ghada's first husband may also usefully be compared with that of the other urban men who appear in this book, including Abu Jamal, Talal Rizk, Nasir, and Khanom Gohary's husband. —Eds.

One night in early 1992, after her grandparents had once again sent her back to her husband's home following a particularly bad argument with both her husband and mother-in-law, Ghada felt she could take no more. Village social mores and the Israeli occupation had colluded too often against Ghada, trapping her in both the West Bank and in her miserable marriage. At twenty-two, Ghada found herself with few practical ways to end her unhappy marriage and very few options afterward, even if she were able to do so. Married to her first cousin, Ghada felt tremendous pressure from her extended family members to make the marriage work. Her father was determined the marriage should continue, as he did not want her to return to his already crowded home in Amman as a divorced woman who could very likely become a perpetual burden. Besides, as a woman living in the West Bank, her movements were subject to Israeli control: it was no simple matter to cross from the West Bank to Jordan, even if she were to decide to go to her parents' home without their welcome.

And so Ghada took a kitchen knife and strode to the army checkpoint between Jerusalem and Bethlehem. Her plan was simple: she would stab a soldier in the hope that the Israelis would throw her out of the country. She assumed she could then return with honor to her family in Amman, as she would have been expelled by the Israelis rather than considered a failure at her marriage. Finally, she thought, she could escape her husband and mother-in-law and teach the Israelis a lesson at the same time!

I came to know Ghada, a young Palestinian village woman, during my fourteen months of fieldwork in the West Bank (1995–96). Ghada was particularly well known in the village of Artas for her attempt to stab an Israeli soldier. Villagers told me that she was living evidence of how severe Palestinian oppression at the hands of their Israeli occupiers truly is: "A young woman, armed with only a knife, attempted to stab a fully armed Israeli soldier, villagers would say. "Surely, this is proof of just how desperate times are here." Israelis, on the other hand, told Ghada's story somewhat differently: "You see," they said, "this is how unpredictable Palestinians can be. The solider was not bothering her or harassing her in any way—and she walked up to him, pulled a knife, and attempted to kill him!" While there is truth in both versions of the story, they are also both significantly incomplete, and each version serves to justify a single agenda at the cost of failing to recognize the complexity of Ghada's experiences.

The site of Ghada's attempted stabbing was the military checkpoint between the Israeli-occupied West Bank and Israel's "Green Line" border. This is the closest checkpoint to the village of Artas, Ghada's family home. Artas is home to about three thousand Palestinian Muslims and is located just a few kilometers south of Bethlehem and a short fifteen-minute drive from Jerusalem, excluding potential waits of up to several hours to cross Israeli checkpoints leading into the city. The village is built down a hillside and into a fertile, green valley where generations of villagers have cultivated the land and where a lovely convent was built in 1901 by a Uruguayan archbishop.

Artas is part of the Bethlehem district, an area encompassing Bethlehem and its surrounding villages, which at the time of my fieldwork, in 1995 and 1996, came under semi-autonomous Palestinian control. The Bethlehem district is considered to be in the highlands, bordered on the west by the coastal plains of Israel and on the east by the Jordan Valley. Artas rises upward on the southern slopes of Jabal Zahir (Mount Zahir) and spreads down into the valley; the village faces Jabal Abu Zaid in the south. On the opposite side of Jabal Zahir sprawls one of the West Bank's largest refugee camps, Deheisha, home to around ten thousand Palestinians who fled from inside Israel's Green Line border in 1948. It is possible to enter Artas from the north by the paved road that links it directly with Bethlehem. From the west, Artas can be reached by following the main road that runs from Jerusalem, past Bethlehem, and ultimately to Hebron; between Bethlehem and Hebron, this road passes a small turnoff which leads to Solomon's Pools and into Artas.

When I met Ghada in the mid-1990s, Artas was home to a mosque and a kindergarten; there was also a spring that was still used for washing clothes. The village had sex-segregated schools for girls and boys (providing education until the ninth and eleventh grades, respectively). Pupils who wished to complete high school and the high school certificate exams (*tawjihi*) had to commute to Bethlehem, a factor that contributed to the girls' high dropout rate in particular. A doctor would see patients twice a month in a one-room structure located along the road from Bethlehem, although many Artas residents would go to the hospital in Bethlehem or to medical centers in Jerusalem when they needed to see specialists or when they experienced a medical emergency. There were a few small shops scattered throughout the village, selling primarily sweets, household cleaning items, and a small assortment of convenience goods.

Neighborhoods often seem to extend as much vertically as horizontally in Artas, because the village sits on a relatively steep slope. Newer homes of relatively wealthy residents have cement-poured walls lined with white stone. Older homes were built from stones pulled from the surrounding rocky mountainsides. Many of these older homes provide foundations for additions. During my fieldwork, many families built additional stories onto their older homes, and since my departure I have been told the practice has accelerated. Additions have reached the point of blocking many villagers' views of the valley and hillside.

Villagers from Artas, or Artasis, describe the history of their village as the story of a place caught in the middle of four mountains, a metaphor for their feelings of entrapment by the series of occupiers—the Ottomans (1516–1917), British (1917–48), Jordanians (1948–67), and Israelis (1967 to the present, in varying degrees)—who have come to Palestine. In the same way that mountains are immovable, so, too, have the occupations seemed to linger. In the mid-1990s, the Palestinian Authority assumed control of civil matters in parts of the West Bank, including the area containing Artas. Yet the history of occupations has made many villagers skeptical and pessimistic about what will come next, either from their own government or from a new (or old) foreign power.

The Ottoman Empire conquered the area in the sixteenth century and governed it until the League of Nations (a precursor to the United Nations) granted the British a mandate to govern the area in 1922. This mandate made Palestine into a virtual British colony. Palestinians in the West Bank quickly faced not only the presence of a colonizing power but also from increasing Jewish immigration from Europe, from the loss of lands sold to the new immigrants, and from a host of other economic and political issues stemming from the British occupation itself. Tensions among the Jews, Palestinians, and the British colonial rulers continued to grow and reached a breaking point in 1936, when urban and rural Palestinians took up arms against the British and the Zionists. The Palestinian Great Revolt was suppressed by 1939. Although not immediately successful in ending the mandate or the Zionist enterprise, the revolt did pressure the British into limiting Jewish immigration and more strictly regulating the sale of Palestinian land.

It was not until after the end of World War II, in 1947, that the British announced their intention to withdraw from Palestine and turn the mandate over to the United Nations. A special committee of the United Nations proposed a partition plan for Palestine that divided the area into a Jewish state, a Palestinian state, and an internationally administered area around Jerusalem. The war that immediately broke out between the Zionists, Palestinians, and surrounding Arab states following the approval of the U.N. partition plan is referred to by Israelis as the War of Independence. Israel declared its independence on 14 May 1948, and by 1949, Israeli forces had occupied considerably more area than the United Nations partition plan had allotted to the Jewish state. The events of 1948–49 are referred to by Palestinians as *al-Nakba*, the Disaster. In addition to the establishment of Israel in the majority of historic Palestine, Egypt occupied the coastal region known as the Gaza Strip, and Jordan occupied the West Bank. No internationally administered area was established nor was a Palestinian state. The borders of the new Israeli state, established following the 1949 armistice agreements, are often referred to as "The Green Line" or "Green Line Israel." Nearly one half million Palestinians who either fled or were expelled from this territory ended up in refugee camps in the West Bank, while some two hundred thousand others were taken in as refugees by surrounding Arab nations.

The Jordanian occupation of the West Bank lasted from 1948 to 1967. It was during that occupation, in the 1950s, that Ghada's father began searching for work outside of Artas. At the time, many village families barely supported themselves by working as agricultural laborers and in other low-wage jobs typically available in nearby cities. Kuwait had begun to exploit its oil fields at approximately the same time that the state of Israel was founded. While many Palestinians fled or were forced from their homes by Israel's declaration of statehood, Kuwait, because of its newly found oil, was in desperate need of labor in all sectors of its society. Palestinians, who were in need of work and new homes, were eager to be employed. Ghada's father went to Kuwait, found a job, and then returned to Artas to bring his wife and young children to live in Kuwait with him. Many other Artasis followed suit, so that Ghada's family had many friends and relatives from Artas with whom they could visit and live in Kuwait. This was true to such an extent that many villagers who had lived in Kuwait described their neighborhood as a "little Artas." Indeed, if you ask Ghada where she is from, she will answer Artas, in spite of the fact that she was not born in Artas and did not grow up there. Ghada was born in Kuwait in 1970, and lived there until her marriage in 1990.

After the Israeli occupation of the West Bank and Gaza Strip in 1967, Ghada's parents found that they were forced to stay in Kuwait, and they ended up raising their family of seven children there for nearly thirty years. Immediately following the Israeli occupation, Israel conducted a census of all the residents living in the occupied territories and issued to them permanent resident status and identity cards. Thousands of Palestinians like Ghada's family, who were not in the territories at the time of the census, were not allowed to claim permanent resident status or to return to live in the West Bank. As a result, Ghada's family remained in Kuwait. Under the Israeli occupation, Palestinians from the West Bank who are looking for economic opportunities have become an even more significant part of the Kuwaiti labor force. But these Palestinians have typically held Israeli-issued identity cards, and have been able to return to the West Bank to live when their Kuwaiti work contracts finish.

Unable to return to the West Bank, families like Ghada's were also in a difficult situation in terms of their residency status in Kuwait. The Kuwaiti government initially welcomed families like Ghada's from the West Bank to fill the country's need for labor, but by the early 1970s Kuwait began to fear that the presence of nearly 150,000 Palestinians in Kuwait could threaten the country's stability. The Kuwaiti government thus chose not to grant citizenship status to foreign workers—even long-term, resident non-Kuwaitis like Ghada's family. Foreigners were allowed to reside in Kuwait only for as long as they were working, and non-citizens were not allowed to retire there. The Kuwaiti government also restricted the access of Palestinians and other non-Kuwaitis to free public education, limited the number of spots available to non-Kuwaitis in higher education institutions, and created numerous other "Kuwaitization" policies that advantaged Kuwaitis over non-Kuwaitis, no matter how long the latter had lived in the country. These policies were not nearly as problematic for other groups of foreign nationals as they were for Palestinian families like Ghada's family, who had no country to which they could return.

Ghada attended elementary school and high school in Kuwait, dropping out in her later high school years. She claims she was both uninterested in and not particularly talented for school; the latter assertion is difficult to believe when speaking with her. She projects an obvious brightness, quickness, and vivaciousness; perhaps she was simply unmotivated. Ghada's experiences in school were somewhat atypical when compared to many of the young Palestinian women whom I met who had grown up in Kuwait. Most of these young women spoke a second language—most commonly, English—and had well-developed academic skills. Whatever Ghada's reasons, she quit school early and spent most of her time helping her mother at home and visiting with her family and neighbors. Her father earned a good wage in Kuwait as a truck driver and Ghada's family was generally happy.

Although Ghada's family's planned trip to Kuwait turned into an extended, semi-permanent stay, her family always kept in close touch with the relatives they had left behind in Artas. Pictures, letters, phone calls, money, and other tokens of affection and symbols of connection flowed back and forth between the families, usually via visitors who would personally deliver the items. Sometimes relations would become strained due to the separation of family members from one another, but relations were always carefully maintained and fostered nonetheless.

Another central source of strain for these extended family relations came from the differing economic and political circumstances under which family members lived. While Ghada's family lived in Kuwait, other members of her extended family lived under Israeli occupation in Artas. The occupation of the West Bank soon meant that Israel controlled almost all aspects of Palestinian life—the economy, the civil society, and the daily movement of Palestinians into Israel's pre-1967 territory (including East Jerusalem), as well as throughout the West Bank itself. Since 1967, Palestinians seeking to build houses have had to obtain an Israeli permit (which is almost always denied). Aggravating the housing shortage is the Israeli practice of the demolition of houses suspected of harboring resistance fighters, terrorists, or their families. The Palestinian water supply has also been controlled by Israel, as has access to the electrical and telephone grid. Israel also established scores of Jewish settlements in the West Bank and Gaza on confiscated Palestinian lands. These settlements, and the matrix of roads linking them together, were intended to further strengthen Israel's hold on the occupied territories and complicate any hope for the establishment of a Palestinian state in the area.

A daily reminder of Israel's occupation of the West Bank and Gaza Strip, and its control over the Palestinian population, is the existence of Israeli "checkpoints"—installations along the roads marked by gates and armed soldiers. Movement throughout the West Bank is strictly controlled by the strategic placement of these checkpoints, through which cars and pedestrians must pass in order to enter, travel within, or leave the territory. Crossing these checkpoints is difficult for Palestinian villagers, who must obtain proper documentation from the Israelis. If a person does not have such documentation, a crossing might still be attempted by walking around the checkpoint or by simply hoping that the Israeli border guard will choose not to look closely at everyone's papers that day. It is not uncommon for men and women to be pulled out of taxis and busses that are going through the checkpoints to be questioned, physically and verbally harassed, and even imprisoned. Crossing checkpoints is very tricky, time consuming, and at times dangerous—something that Ghada's relatives and other Artasis had to negotiate daily.

Crossing those checkpoints at the border between the occupied territories and Israel can be particularly tense and adds an international dimension to daily life in Artasis and to the local economy. Palestinians feel they need to be able to travel in and out of the land they consider their own, to traverse the short distance between Bethlehem and Jerusalem to get to work, to visit hospitals, and for shopping needs, just as Israelis feel they must attempt to control traffic across Israel's pre-1967 borders in order to maintain national security. This situation is complicated by the fact that many men in Artas and from other villages in the West Bank have at times found work inside Israel. Wages are often higher there, and it is often difficult to find work in the economically depressed West Bank. But this source of work has proved to be unreliable. Border crossings are often closed, cutting many Palestinians off from their sources of livelihood, medical help, and other necessary goods and services. Thus, the economic life of the village is closely linked to the politics of these international checkpoint crossings that are a clear and central symbol of the Israeli occupation of the West Bank and the control that the occupation imposes on Palestinian lives.

The first large-scale uprising against Israeli occupation began in 1987 and lasted through 1992. This uprising was called an *intifada,* an Arabic word that means "shaking off," and in this case refers to the attempt to shake off Israeli control. The *intifada* began in the Gaza Strip and quickly spread throughout the West Bank. Vocal demonstrators and stone-throwing Palestinian youths facing off against armed Israeli soldiers became the hallmark images of this first *intifada* that quickly gained the attention of the world's media. Palestinian women sometimes participated in these affrays as well, throwing stones at Israelis who were armed with guns.

Images of Palestinian women attempting to shield children, gathering stones, or simply fighting against Israeli incursions became common in the Western media. These pictures were among the most well-known images of the *intifada,* primarily because so many Westerners were surprised to see Arab women taking an active part in street politics. Western imagery of Arab women in the Middle East has often focused, to the point of distortion, on the subject of women's honor, veiling, and the norms of male-female interaction. Such imagery distorts the complexity of Arab women's lives, to the point that Palestinian women who take part in street politics are perceived by many Westerners as exceptional in the Arab world, their actions having little to do with the "real" world of politics and public spaces presumed to be dominated by men. Clearly, this has not been the case for Palestinians; nor has it been true of women in Egypt, Iran, or Algeria, and many other Middle Eastern countries in times of revolution. Indeed, from the point of view of the Palestinian women themselves, their political and public involvement in the Israeli-Palestinian conflict is both necessary and required of them by the situation. At the same time, as Ghada would find out, some traditional village mores regarding women's honor and reputation have persisted even in times of crisis and resistance.

Palestinian women's involvement in political organizations, many of which evolved during the first *intifada* and have continued to function until the present, is also notable. Palestinian women's organizations are most typically based in urban areas and are generally led by educated, middle-class women who work for an end to the Israeli occupation and the internal strengthening of Palestinian society in a variety of ways. Some provide organized support for the families of Palestinian men killed in the *intifada* or imprisoned in Israeli jails, while others organize demonstrations and rallies, or provide classes for women in health education, food preparation and storage, and literacy.

In addition to street battles and the self-strengthening and protest activities of local political organizations, Palestinian resistance to Israeli occupation during the first *intifada* included numerous other nonviolent strategies as well. Shopkeepers often participated in lengthy strikes by refusing to open their shops and sell their goods. Although this strategy hurt their own profits, it also damaged the Israeli economy by discouraging tourism and the sale of Israeli goods. During the *intifada,* many Palestinians also tried to boycott Israeli goods to inflict further damage on the Israeli economy. For many women, this meant being creative in making their own homemade substitutes for Israeli products they refused to purchase. While not as easily seen, and perhaps not recognized as an inherently political act, such critical consumerism is quite political.

In contrast to the Palestinian cities, where women's resistance has flourished, in the village context, numerous obstacles to participation exist. Village women often lack the time to participate in organized committee actions due to the demands of housework and childrearing activities. Also, their male relatives may forbid them to take part in activities outside of the home that may bring them into close contact with men. As a result, village women are sometimes thought to be apolitical and in need of greater political awareness by some members of urban women's committees. Yet the range of ways in which Palestinian village women have taken part in protesting and challenging Israeli control is extensive, if often unobserved by others.

While Ghada's family was living in Kuwait, her extended family members were living through a time of occupation and uprising. Although Ghada's family was subject to laws that privileged Kuwaitis over non-Kuwaitis, their experience of hardship and political and economic uncertainty was far removed from that of their extended family in the West Bank. In one particularly infamous incident, this reality was brought into sharp relief when another Palestinian family in Kuwait sent their relatives in Artas a videotape of a lavish wedding they had held at a fancy Kuwaiti hotel. Artasis, in the midst of *intifada,* were deeply hurt that their relatives were holding large, expensive celebrations while they in the West Bank were suffering and curtailing celebrations. Still, throughout the uprising, these long-distance families kept close ties, greatly valuing their connection to their homeland and relatives.

In the summer of 1990, during this time of occupation and *intifada,* Ghada's family came to Artas for a visit from Kuwait. While the family was visiting its West Bank relatives, the Gulf War began. Iraqi President Saddam Hussein invaded Kuwait in August 1990 and then quickly annexed the country. Historically, Iraq has long claimed Kuwait, but Saddam Hussein argued that he invaded Kuwait primarily because of its overproduction of oil, which had hurt Iraq economically, especially in the wake of the Iran-Iraq War (1980–88). When Saddam Hussein refused to comply with a U.N. deadline to withdraw his troops from Kuwait, the United States launched Operation Desert Storm. By late February, when the war ended, Iraqi troops had been expelled from Kuwait but Saddam Hussein remained in power in Iraq.

Israeli travel restrictions during the Gulf War significantly extended Ghada's family's planned brief visit to Artas. During this time, Ghada's *ibn 'amm,* her father's brother's son, or first paternal cousin, who lived in the village, asked for her hand in marriage. First-cousin marriage is a relatively common practice throughout the Middle East. Many people in the village believe that cousin marriages are preferable to marriages with more distant relatives or between unrelated persons. After all, they reason, cousins know one another well and are likely to be familiar with each other's ways of living and shortcomings. Thus, they believe, families can be trusted to look after the welfare of the young wives of such marriages.

Despite the fact that it was Ghada's cousin asking for her hand, Ghada's father was against the marriage. Ghada's fatherly intuition led him to dislike the young man—cousin or not—and doubt that he would be a good husband and father. Further, although he was Ghada's cousin, he and Ghada did not know one another well since they had grown up in different countries. But Ghada was insistent. Now twenty years old, Ghada was known to be a headstrong young woman; she insisted she was in love with the young man and that they wanted to marry. So the young couple soon married in a simple ceremony with little celebration, with her father's reluctant blessing. Foregoing large and expensive wedding celebrations, as Ghada did, was a common way for Palestinians to express their sense of community solidarity in the struggle. The *intifada* was not a time of celebration, since so many Palestinians were suffering, imprisoned, or grieving. Many families stopped entirely or practiced only symbolically giving the *mahr*, the dowry, for marriages as well. The *mahr* is money and goods given by the groom to his bride's family. This wealth is used to compensate the family for the loss of the bride's labor to the household, as well as to act as her insurance policy should she get divorced. Recognizing how difficult times were for families, many women also felt that expensive wedding presents were unseemly and refused them, although to do so may have been very much against their own best interests.

After the wedding, in 1991, Ghada's natal family returned to Kuwait. But the Kuwait that they knew and had considered home had changed in their short absence, as a result of the Gulf War. Many Kuwaitis believed that the Palestinians supported Saddam Hussein's invasion and occupation of their country. Saddam Hussein's missile attacks on Tel Aviv had been publicly cheered by some Palestinians living in the West Bank, while his attempt to link Iraq's withdrawal from Kuwait to Israel's from the occupied territories gave them hope. The fact that PLO Chairman Yasir Arafat sided with Iraq during the crisis sealed the image of Palestinians as collaborators for most Kuwaitis.

For the nearly 200,000 Palestinians who lived in Kuwait, being accused of supporting the Iraqi invaders was devastating, especially since the majority of them had either remained neutral during the crisis or had aided the Kuwaiti resistance. Their individual political views and situation during the war were overlooked, and they found themselves no longer welcomed by their Kuwaiti neighbors, who had suffered at the hands of Saddam's forces. As a result, Kuwaiti Palestinians came under greater suspicion and many were forced to leave the country. Because they held Jordanian-issued passports, not Israeli identity cards, Ghada's family, who had been residents of Kuwait for more than thirty years, moved to Amman (Jordan) after the war. Although they were not forced out of Kuwait, they felt that they would be in danger if they stayed and that the future for Palestinians in Kuwait was bleak.

Villagers in Artas were also seriously affected by the global politics of the Gulf War. Artasis not only cross the tense Green Line border with Israel to go to work, visit the hospital, and shop, but also to receive international remittances from relatives who lived abroad. Villagers need the money that their relatives send them, from places like Kuwait and the United States that offer more and better work opportunities. Such remittances support many families in the West Bank. After the Gulf War and the expulsion of many

Palestinians from Kuwait, remittances slowed or stopped altogether for many families. Amman, in Jordan, which had a high unemployment rate before the Gulf War, became flooded with Palestinian migrants looking for work. While Ghada's parents struggled with the pressures of finding work and a home in Amman, their extended family in the West Bank also suffered with a significantly reduced cash flow in a village occupied by the Israeli military.

From the beginning of her marriage, Ghada experienced substantial conflict with her husband's family, with whom she lived. Ghada and her mother-in-law (who was also her aunt) did not know one another very well. They had difficulty adjusting to one another's presence in the house and could not get along. Her mother-in law felt that Ghada did not accord her due respect and deference. For her part, Ghada felt that her mother-in-law expected her to be her servant. Since Ghada and her husband lived in a single room in her in-laws' house, the problems were continuous.

Ghada's living arrangements were not unusual. The practice of living with one's in-laws is one reason that marriage to a relative whom a woman has known for most of her life is often viewed as an attractive marriage option. While not all Palestinian marriages are cousin marriages, brides and grooms almost always at least meet and often know one another before their marriage. If they are not related to each other (as in the case of an arranged marriage with someone from outside one's family and/or village), they will usually have encountered one another only briefly and in public. They have typically not had a chance to get to know one another, or the other's family, very well. For this reason, most young brides prefer living with relatives they know over moving to the home of an unknown family. Although technically Ghada was marrying a close relative, Ghada's marriage was nevertheless similar to the marriage of two strangers.

Often, after young husbands have had an opportunity to earn enough money, married couples will build their own home in the family compound and live in a nuclear family arrangement. Often they build an apartment directly on top of their family's home. This practice is both pragmatic and practical: families tend to prefer living close to one another. Also, with little space in the village for building new homes, land is difficult to buy, and obtaining an Israeli permit to build a new house is practically impossible. However, Ghada's husband was unable to build his own home due to the economic devastation that the Gulf War had brought to the West Bank, as well as to the hardships of the *intifada*.

To escape her mother-in-law and their cramped living quarters, Ghada often fled to her maternal grandparents' house. However, they always encouraged her to return to her husband's home. In this way, older, more experienced family members seek to encourage newly married couples to live together and to reconcile after disagreements or fights. The pressure to remain married is particularly strong for cousin marriages, for exactly the same reasons that they are arranged: the marriage has great potential to work out well as it is the marriage of the children of two siblings. On the other hand, if a cousin marriage does not work out, the resulting turmoil can be disastrous for extended family relationships.

In principle, women are legally entitled to ask for a divorce under the Jordanian Family Status Law (which applies to the West Bank) as well as customary village practices. There are a few options for women who wish to divorce. Although under the Jordanian Family Status Law a woman may request a divorce due to the breach of a clause in her marriage contract, few women exercise this right. A woman may also ask for a divorce if her husband fails to enact his marital duties. Or a woman may ask for divorce if she can pay her husband a mutually agreed upon sum, but in this case her husband must consent to the divorce.

Bride-wealth, known in Arabic as *mahr*, typically consists of gold, money, and other valuables, particularly household goods, given by the groom and his family to the bride. (It contrasts to the European tradition of dowry, typically paid to the groom's family by the bride's family). Under Muslim law, bride-wealth becomes the sole property of the bride upon her marriage. To reduce the risk of frivolous divorce, the bride's family often insists that the marriage contract specify the dower be paid in two installments: half at the time of marriage, the other half payable only in the event that the husband divorces or pre-deceases the wife. However, the rules change when it is the wife who requests a divorce. According to law, she must forfeit the second part of her dowry. This meant that Ghada's desire for a divorce would have significant financial consequences for her and her family.

Another disincentive to a woman initiating a divorce is the harm it might bring to her reputation in the village. Divorce is generally frowned upon, particularly when the marriage is between cousins, and very much so when it is initiated by the woman. Initiating divorce also lessens a woman's chances for remarriage. Finally, since according to law any children of the marriage belong to the husband and his family once they reach puberty, many women also fear they will lose custody of their children if they initiate a divorce.

Although Ghada did not yet have children, she felt that she could not ask for a divorce while living with her in-laws. Her father, although initially against the marriage, told her that she was now a married woman who must learn to make the marriage work. He made it clear that if Ghada were to initiate a divorce, she would not be welcome to return to her natal home. Nor was Ghada's husband interested in divorcing her at that time, as he, too, was concerned with the effects of their divorce on extended family relations. He claimed to want the marriage to work out; he also did not want to pay Ghada the second part of her dower.

Later, looking back on her life, Ghada often wondered what she would have done had she managed to obtain a divorce early in her marriage? How might she have supported herself? Where would she have lived? Ghada had finished only a few years of high school and had never held a job. There are very few economic options for single women with little education in the West Bank; indeed, there are only a few options for educated women. Working outside of the home also makes a woman a less attractive prospective marriage partner to villagers with traditional values. Should a woman be seen outside the neighborhood interacting with strange men, her reputation would be threatened. Women with less than perfect reputations are less desirable marriage partners. Thus, when considering employment, unmarried village women must constantly balance their need for cash with their desire to be perceived as honorable women worthy of marriage.

Even educated village women who hold professional jobs are likely to live with their families, although urban women may have a few more options for living on their own. It is very difficult for a young single woman to find a place to live on her own in a village setting; few families would be willing to rent her a space even if she could afford the rent. Renting an apartment or a room in a city such as nearby Bethlehem was far too expensive for Ghada to even consider. In short, Ghada would have had a very difficult time trying to make it on her own. Her extended family in Artas might have housed her temporarily, but the additional economic strain of a young-adult woman would have been difficult. Her family also would have pressured her continuously to reconcile with her husband.

Ghada's personal circumstances—an unhappy domestic situation and a pronounced lack of viable alternatives—are inextricably entwined with her identity as a Palestinian villager living under Israeli occupation and the political dynamics of the Arab-Israeli conflict. One might imagine that if Ghada's parents had lived in Artas, they could have provided her with daily support and advice, and offered her a home to go to when she simply needed a break from the daily strains of her marriage. Then, perhaps, her marriage might have survived. But Israeli restrictions made it impossible for Ghada's family to return to the West Bank. Alternatively, one might imagine that if the Palestinians had been welcome to stay in Kuwait after the Gulf War, then perhaps Ghada's parents would have been able to lend the young couple enough money to build a home of their own and thereby create some distance between Ghada and her mother-in-law. But this, too, was impossible.

Ghada was also unable to visit her family in Amman as a way of easing the tension in her husband's household. While it is technically possible that she could have obtained the necessary Israeli permit to travel to Amman, her husband would have needed to co-sign the forms. This he was unwilling to do, since he (rightly) feared she would not return. For this reason, Ghada's parents pressured her to stay in the village to make the marriage work out. It was against this background that in the winter of 1992 Ghada devised an alternative plan: to attack an Israeli soldier at the nearby checkpoint and precipitate her immediate deportation to Amman. It was a brilliant solution: at one stroke, she could return to her parents, escape her marital home, and become a heroine in the process.

Ghada took a kitchen knife and walked the few kilometers to the well-lit checkpoint. As she approached, however, her suspicious behavior attracted the attention of the Israeli guards. Before she could do anything, she was apprehended by the Israeli military police and arrested. After an interrogation, Ghada was imprisoned for three months. During her imprisonment, at a facility for female Palestinian political prisoners, she miscarried in the first term of her pregnancy. Upon her release, she was expelled to Jordan and forbidden to re-enter the West Bank for ten years. So Ghada got her wish: she returned to her family in Amman. Meanwhile, her husband was also imprisoned for participation in *intifada* activities.

Ghada's attempted crime—the stabbing of an Israeli soldier—was a complex political act, and a unique, personal expression of dissent. Of course, this attempted stabbing was also a critical commentary on the nature of many young women's restricted social lives, their options and their agency. Ghada's action was thus both political, as an expression of nationalist sentiment, as well as a strong gender critique. By it, she drew attention to the fact that she was not only a Palestinian woman subject to the restrictions of Israeli occupation, but also a village woman subject to the restrictions of her family, her husband, and village social practices.

Ghada's husband was released from an Israeli prison in 1993, by which time the Israeli-Palestinian peace process had begun and many previous travel restrictions had been lifted. He was able to obtain permission to visit her in Amman, where her family pressured her to reconcile with him. A month later, the newly reconciled couple obtained the necessary permissions to return to Artas together, her banishment put aside.

But no sooner had she and her husband returned to the village than serious family discord flared again. Her husband's family had finally built the young couple a small separate apartment, but to no avail. The fighting between Ghada and her mother-in-law was almost continuous. Both of them were known as *qawiyya*, women who are perceived as particularly—perhaps excessively—"strong." Together, their differences were irreconcilable. In 1995 Ghada's husband, pressured by his mother and family to put an end to this problematic marriage no matter the consequences for familial relations, divorced her. According to the Hanafi branch of Islamic law applicable in the West Bank, a man may divorce his wife twice; the husband may revoke the divorce if he does so within three months of declaring it. Ghada's husband had divorced her twice before, following bitter fights. When a husband divorces his wife for a third time, the divorce is final and the couple is able to remarry only if the ex-wife has married a different man in the interim and become divorced from him. Ghada's husband returned to live with his family, leaving Ghada and her newborn baby girl alone in the little apartment in the family compound. It was during this period in her life that I met Ghada and first heard her story.

Following this final divorce, Ghada remained in the small apartment for some time, awaiting the payment of the second half of her bride-wealth. Her brother came to visit and see how she was doing. Her grandparents still said they welcomed her in their home, but she said she felt ashamed and awkward when she visited them. Finally, in 1996, Ghada's parents came to the village and took her and the baby back to their family home in Amman. Since Ghada's return to Amman, her life has not been easy; Ghada's family has experienced hard economic times.

Some of Ghada's siblings were able to relocate to the United States, Jordan, and Oman. Dispersed families are common among Palestinians, who have had to find ways to survive throughout difficult economic times and political turmoil. The eldest daughter of the family, Fida, married a relative who had emigrated to New Jersey. He had returned to Jordan to visit his family and look for a wife. Together, they returned to the New Jersey suburbs to build a life together. Fida felt this was her best hope for creating more opportunities for herself and her future children, no matter how much she would have preferred to remain close to her family and parents. Ghada also has a brother living and working in Oman.

Ghada's other siblings still live in Amman. One sister is in her early thirties. She is unemployed and unmarried. Often, Palestinian women have a difficult time finding a marriage partner if they are past their mid-twenties. It seems unlikely that Ghada's sister will ever marry. Unmarried adult women are not typically free to set up their own homes and live alone; families would not allow it. Rather, unmarried women far more typically live with their parents and, upon their parents' deaths, with a married sibling. These women may work for a wage, if they can find a job, but must still do the housework. Two unmarried brothers also live at home—one works as a taxi driver in Amman, and another works in construction. Ghada's youngest brother is finishing high school.

In 2004, in Amman, Ghada remarried. Her new husband is much older than she is—a widower and the father of five children. Young women who are divorced and have a small child often find that if they wish to remarry their choices are limited. For divorced women, becoming a second wife is common (according to Islamic law, a man may marry up to four women if he can support them all equally). Or, a divorced woman may become the wife of a much older man who already has children, as has happened for Ghada. Many of Ghada's family's friends and relatives feel that Ghada was lucky to obtain even this match. After all, her honor is stained, not only by her divorce but also, somewhat paradoxically, by her time in prison. While some in the village view Ghada's time in prison as evidence of her bravery and proof of her patriotism, others question what may have happened to her while in prison at the hands of unknown men.

Although practices and interpretations vary in the West Bank's cities, towns, villages, and refugee camps, most women and men agree that the honor of young women is of central importance. This honor is maintained in many different ways. The primary way is through young women's relative seclusion from unrelated men. A young woman should not be seen with a young man to whom she is not related, she should not be seen walking the streets alone (which Ghada did on her way to the checkpoint—and at night), and she certainly should not be alone with a men, as Ghada was in the prison. Remaining a virgin is a central prerequisite for marriage, and a woman who gets a bad reputation, for whatever reason, risks very serious familial-imposed punishments. These may range from being killed (known as an "honor killing"), to being married off to a "faraway old man," that is, to a man with whom the girl's family has little ongoing connection, making the marriage a kind of banishment for her. After marriage, women are expected to maintain a perfect reputation for fidelity and modesty. Ghada's actions and her incarceration left lingering questions in the minds of village residents, and lingering fodder for the local gossip-mill.

When Ghada's daughter grows older, it is possible that she will move to her father's home in Artas (as we've seen, children legally belong to their father's family). Ghada, however, will almost certainly remain in Amman in her new husband's home. Ghada's ex-husband has remarried a young woman from a village nearby to Artas. The difficulties divorced mothers of young children face in remarrying are not faced by men. Her ex-husband now has a new child, works as a car mechanic, and lives with his new family in the small apartment originally built for him and Ghada.

A comparison of Ghada's life to those of her two husbands illustrates how gender influences a divorced woman's options in traditional Palestinian society. Her first husband was able to easily remarry, to a young woman who had never before been married. His family had little fear for his future, unlike Ghada's family. Men's and women's honor is differently affected by divorce: women largely suffer more. The circumstances of Ghada's second marriage reflect this inequity. Ghada would have preferred a man closer to her in age and perhaps with fewer children for whom she would need to provide care. But because of her "questionable" past, locals, as well as most of her family members, felt that Ghada was lucky, and indeed her family was lucky as well, to have any prospect for remarriage at all. Ghada's second husband was also able to remarry easily. A woman in a similar position— widowed and the mother of five children—would have found it very difficult indeed to find a husband who wished to assume the burden of caring for the children. The children, upon reaching adolescence, would be considered members of their biological father's family in any case, making the effort and expense of raising and caring for them too burdensome for most men outside the family.

The first *intifada* ended when the Oslo peace accords were signed by Israel and Palestinian government leaders in September 1993. In these accords, Palestinians were promised that, following an interim period of five years, a self-governing authority would be established. Yet the process was constantly hindered, sidetracked, and obstructed by a variety of Israeli measures and decisions, as well as ongoing attacks by Palestinian militants. The second Palestinian *intifada* began in September 2000. At the time of this writing, the situation in the West Bank remains volatile and many of the gains made by the Palestinians in the 1990s have virtually been lost. As of 2004, the chances that Ghada's family will be allowed to return to the West Bank are slim.

Perception is critical in the Middle East. Different observers understood Ghada's actions in different ways. Israelis who had heard of Ghada through news reports recalled that she carried out a "near successful" attack on a soldier for no apparent reason. Villagers pointed to Ghada's story as evidence of Israeli oppression. Both Israelis and Palestinians interpreted Ghada's attack according to the demands of their respective nationalist political agendas, while ignoring the central, formative aspects of Ghada's experience. Israelis drew attention to the violent and unjustified nature of the attack—the soldier was not bothering Ghada. He was simply guarding the border: he was not shooting rubber or real bullets, nor was he harassing Palestinians in the street. By characterizing Ghada as irrational—indeed, as a "terrorist"—Israelis neatly sidestep the prickly issue of their control over the West Bank and its far-reaching implications for the lives of villagers there.

It is important to reject one-sided explanations of "why" Ghada attempted to stab an Israeli soldier and to look instead at the multifaceted nature of the oppression that she experienced—stemming from her marriage, her community, and her identity as a Palestinian under occupation. Ghada is both a village rebel and a political protestor, but not in the ways most Israelis and Palestinians may think. Her story rejects a simplistic explanation, but by doing so, a far richer picture emerges—one that acknowledges Ghada as a complex, modern actor in today's Middle East. Exploring the interconnections among those more powerful than Ghada—the Israeli military, her in-laws, the Kuwaiti regime, and her own family—is requisite for understanding Ghada's life, and the episode of the attempted stabbing, in particular. The danger inherent in emphasizing only one dimension of Ghada's experience is demonstrated by the tendency of Israelis and Palestinians alike to use her story in ways that serve and entrench their respective nationalist discourses while ignoring the important nuances of gender, opposition, and resistance underlying the conflict.

A NOTE ON SOURCES

I learned the details of Ghada's story during fieldwork for my doctorate in Artas in 1995–96. Ghada, her relatives, and her friends and neighbors told me their versions of her story. A short version of this story was originally published in *Middle East Report* (1999). My fieldwork was supported by the Research Institute for the Study of Man and the University of Toronto (including the Melissa J. Knauer Award). I am grateful to these institutions for their support and to the people of Artas for sharing so much with me.

SUGGESTIONS FOR FURTHER READING

The literature on Palestinian women and their involvement in the *intifada* is now vast. Of particular interest for their detailed analyses of the cultural aspects of Palestinian lives during the *intifada* are articles by Julie Peteet, including "Male Gender and Rituals of Resistance in the Palestinian Intifada: A Cultural Politics of Violence," *American Ethnologist* 1, no. 1 (1994): 31–49; and "Icons and Militants: Mothering in the Danger Zone," *Signs: Journal of Women in Culture and Society* 23, no. 1 (1997): 103–29. See also Iris Jean-Klein's "Mothercraft, Statecraft, and Subjectivity in the Palestinian Intifada," *American Ethnologist* 27, no. 1 (2000): 100–27; "Nationalism and Resistance: The Two Faces of Everyday Activism in Palestine during the Intifada," *Cultural Anthropology* 16, no. 1 (2001): 83–126; and "Into Committees, Out of the House?" *American Ethnologist* 30, no. 4 (2003): 556–77. Ellen Fleishmann's *The Nation and Its "New" Women: The Palestinian Women's Movement, 1920–1948* (Berkeley: University of California Press, 2003) provides key historical information about earlier organized Palestinian women's participation in explicitly political organizations.

Studies that do not focus exclusively on the *intifada* include my own ethnography about women, men, and their stories of spirit possession in Artas, *Spirits of Palestine: Gender and the Jinn in a Palestinian Village* (Lanham, Md.: Lexington Press, 2004). Hilma Granqvist's ethnographies of Artas (part of the Societas Scientiarum Fennica series Commentationes humanarum litterarum, 1931, 1935, 1947, 1950, and 1965) are remarkable for their scope and detail on the subjects of marriage and kinship, death and burial, and birth and childhood. Annelies Moors examines *Women, Property, and Islam: Palestinian Experience, 1920–1990* (Cambridge: Cambridge University Press, 1995). Rhoda Kanaaneh, in her book, *Birthing the Nation: Strategies of Palestinian Women in Israel* (Berkeley: University of California

Press, 2002), provides a fascinating analysis of Palestinian women's family planning choices in the Galilee. Suzanne Ruggi has looked briefly at honor killings in her article, "Commodifying Honor in Sexuality: Honor Killings in Palestine," *Middle East Report* (Spring 1998): 12–15.

Works on Palestinians outside of the West Bank, Gaza Strip, and Israel include Julie Peteet's examination of Palestinian women's involvement in the resistance movement in Lebanon, *Gender in Crisis: Women and the Palestinian Resistance Movement* (New York: Columbia University Press, 1991). Ann Lesch's article, "Palestinians in Kuwait," *Journal of Palestine Studies* 20, no. 4 (1991): 42–54, is valuable. Nicholas Van Hear's comparative study of migrant communities, including Palestinians in Kuwait, is also important: *New Diasporas: The Mass Exodus, Dispersal and Regrouping of Migrant Communities* (Seattle: University of Washington Press, 1998).

Chapter 22

Khanom Gohary: An Iranian Community Leader

Homa Hoodfar

The Islamic Revolution of 1979 brought sweeping political and social change to Iran. Although both men and women found they had to cope with a new system that limited political and personal freedoms, women's rights were uniquely curtailed. This was an especially bitter pill for Iranian women, many of whom had participated in the revolution with expectations of greater political and personal freedom.

While the Islamic constitution guaranteed the right to vote for women, the new government's codification of Islamic law took away divorce and child custody rights that women had acquired under the Pahlavi regime. It also legalized polygamy, temporary marriage (*muta*), and child marriage. The new government also imposed mandatory *hijab* (Islamic dress) for women, and required segregation of men and women in public spaces. The early years of the revolution saw a virtual purge of women from upper-level public-sector management and government positions, including the judiciary.

Nonetheless, Iranian women have remained economically innovative and politically active, making important gains in both arenas since 1990. Faced with discrimination in the public sector, female entrepreneurs and professionals flocked to the private sector, often building successful businesses on community needs imposed by new gender-segregation laws. (For example, the number of female doctors dramatically increased since the examination of female patients by male doctors was forbidden). Iranian women also took full advantage of opportunities for equal education. In 2002, female literacy reached 82 percent (from around 60 percent at the time of the revolution), a figure superior to any other Middle Eastern country (and on a par with many so-called developed countries).

Women have also made their mark on Iranian politics and the institutions of civil society, from the *majles* (parliament) to professional associations, charities, and community-based organizations. In 1997, Dr. Masoumeh Ebtekar became Iran's first female vice-president. The reformed judiciary includes many female judges in advisory (though not ruling) positions. During the late 1990s, a higher percentage of women served in the Iranian *majles* than in the U.S. Senate. In 1999, a senior *ayat-*

ullah declared that women should be considered the equals of men in social and political life, and should not be restricted from serving even as president or Supreme Leader.

In recent years, female Iranian political activists and reformists have made international headlines. Fatima Hagiqatjou, an outspoken *majles* deputy during the February 2004 political crisis, and human rights activist Shirin Ebadi, winner of the 2003 Nobel Peace Prize, are two well-known examples. Much less well known are the thousands of female community leaders who serve as a primary link between the government and local communities. "Khanom" Farkhondeh Gohary, the community leader and activist whose story is told here by Homa Hoodfar, is one such woman.

Gohary's reluctant entrance into community leadership and civil society came in 1995. At the age of thirty-four, as the owner of a small business in the southern Tehran suburb of Shahr-e Ray, Gohary became a neighborhood facilitator for the Healthy City initiative. As Hoodfar's portrait illustrates, Khanom Gohary's personal life experience, her awareness of the needs of other local women, and her activist spirit unleashed an indomitable one-woman force for community improvement. Armed with knowledge, tenacity, and a mastery of *ta'roff* (Iranian ritual courtesy), she became a volunteer health worker and local coordinator for the Iranian Ministry of Health's Family Planning Program. In 1998, she was elected head of the Neighborhood Women's Council. Gohary has simultaneously demanded government responsiveness to women's health and social welfare issues while striving to promote popular awareness, individual responsibility, and community participation.

Farkhondeh Gohary's biography reveals some of the ways Iranian women have coped with the challenges posed by revolution, war, and gender discrimination. But it also presents an interesting paradox. While generally distrustful of politics, Khanom Gohary's successive roles are all endeavors directly sponsored by the Iranian government. Does her life story serve as a testament to individual agency and persistence, or is it an example of the emergence of Iranian civil society since 1990? More generally, does Hoodfar's contribution suggest that social and political change in Iran is motivated from the bottom up or the top down?

The experiences of Gohary and her mother with marriage and divorce can be contrasted with those of Nadia and Ghada, two other contemporary women profiled in this volume. The situation of her husband merits comparison with the lives of other urban working-class men profiled in this volume, including Nasir, Abu Jamal, Talal Rizk, and Haddou. —Eds.

Farkhondeh Gohary was born in 1961. Her parents were from a small northern town on the Caspian Sea but moved to Javadeih, a modest, working-class area of Tehran, after her father, a corporal in the military, was transferred. Gohary grew up in Javadeih, home to many newly arrived migrants from other parts of the country. Gohary's mother was quite happy to have moved to the capital, where her husband's job provided a secure monthly salary, which was not the case for many low-income households. Still, it took the family many years to feel at home in Tehran.

Gohary's parent's marriage was not a happy one. Although there was no financial necessity, Gohary's mother worked from home as a seamstress, both to help with expenses and because she enjoyed the limited economic independence her work provided. Raised by her own widowed mother on a meager income, Gohary's mother had learned early the value of a woman's economic skills. Moreover, her sewing fulfilled other needs: she was gregarious and greatly enjoyed the company of other women, and sewing gave her a pretext for entertaining. From her own earnings, Gohary's mother would buy tea, sugar, sweets, and pumpkin seeds for her clients and visitors, and her husband could not object to the expenditure and thus have reason to curb his wife's social interaction.

Nonetheless, the couple often argued about her social life, an issue that would not have arisen in an earlier era, when men were either at work during the day or at the teahouse with friends. Traditionally, teahouses have been gathering places for men to socialize, catch up on local and national news, and, in small towns, hear about job opportunities. The family home has, at least during the day, traditionally been the domain of women. However, in Tehran, under the new state employment structure, workers had the afternoon off and generally went home, resulting in a loss of autonomy for many women in terms of how they organized their time. Some women considered this new situation a curse of modernity. Teahouses fell out of fashion (and in any case did not really appeal to Gohary's father, who had no childhood friends or familiar colleagues in Tehran with whom to spend time drinking tea). Many women were relieved, though loathe to admit it to their husbands, when in the 1970s inflation and the high cost of living, along with stagnant salaries, forced many public sector and government employees to seek second jobs, keeping them out of the house for longer periods during the day.

There were other sources of tension between Gohary's parents. Her mother, who took adult literacy classes and found other ways to further educate herself, was attracted by the things she perceived as urban and contemporary. She wanted a hygienic, modern home, and came to view marriage as a partnership, and her husband grew weary of her expectations. She objected to his insistence on raising chickens despite their crowded urban living situation. Though many other formerly rural households did continue to raise fowl, this custom grew to be increasingly problematic in the city, in terms of hygiene and odor. Perhaps more importantly for Gohary's mother, raising poultry was considered unsophisticated—a sign of peasant backwardness and thus something that Gohary's mother, like many of her contemporaries, desired to distance herself from. Combined with several other sources of disagreement, tensions between Gohary's parents rose to the point where the couple separated, and actually divorced twice, only to reconcile at the urging of relatives who were concerned for the couple's four children. Finally, Gohary's parents divorced for a third time in 1972, with no recourse to reconciliation. Under Islamic law, which is applied to family law in much of the Muslim Middle East except Turkey, while a wife's consent, as well as that of her male guardian/father is essential, divorce is a unilateral right of the husband. Without a husband's consent, a woman can only obtain a divorce under very limited circumstances. A wife has to wait three months and some days after her divorce before she can marry again. A divorce can be annulled within the first three months. Husband and wife can reconcile; however, if they divorce for a third time, it is final and cannot be overturned, which was the case with Gohary's parents.

Although a new family law was introduced around this time, few people actually used the family court to divorce; men simply went to any marriage registration office and registered the divorce. In accordance with conventional religious practices and custom where men receive custody of sons over the age of two and daughters over the age of five, Gohary and her siblings remained with her father. Though the new Family Protection Act made it possible for women to go to court over divorce and custody matters, few were aware of the new law or had the skills and money to access the court system. (The law was later repealed, as religious leaders considered it un-Islamic and an infringement on male rights.)

Gohary's father's own mother had died very young in childbirth, a common occurrence in the days when women married and bore children very young and without prenatal care. Gohary's father, himself raised by a stern father and a strict stepmother, did not want to subject to his children to a similar hardship and thus decided not to marry again. Gohary believes this was due, at least in part, to her father's continued love for her mother even after the divorce. Reflecting on the situation years later, Gohary expressed the belief that widespread social change in the 1950s and 60s, including the expansion of education for girls and wider employment options for women, along with the influence of the mass media (in particular radio), affected men and women differently. While women began to see marriage as a partnership, men expected respect and obedience; the result was often disappointment and acrimony. Nevertheless, divorce stigmatized not only the couple involved but their children as well. Having suffered the consequences of divorce, Gohary vowed she would never put her own children in that situation.

Her parent's final divorce in 1972, when Gohary was twelve, was a turning point in Gohary's life. Being the eldest and a girl, Gohary found herself responsible for the care of her eight-year-old sister and three brothers aged ten, six, and just under two, as tradition dictated. Her duties included cooking, cleaning, and nursing the children when they were sick. Though Gohary was in her first year of high school when her parents divorced, her education was not a priority for her father. He was not particularly concerned if she missed school, as long as she kept the house in order and cared for her siblings. Consequently, Gohary did not do well in school; after doing the housework and cooking, she was too tired to do her homework. However, she went to classes whenever she could because it took her out of the house and allowed her to pretend she was a regular teenager.

Like many divorced men, Gohary's father, knowing that his ex-wife had no recourse, prohibited the children from seeing their mother. While this seemed not to trouble the boys, it disturbed Gohary and her sister deeply. Behind her father's back, Gohary arranged meetings with her mother while her father was at work. This often resulted in confrontations and clashes at home, though she knew that ultimately her father, unlike many, would forgive her and understand her desire to see her mother. As an adult, Khanom Gohary often uses the stories of her troubles as a child of divorced parents to illustrate that unjust laws and family institutions must be corrected so that children do not have to suffer what she did.

Within a few years of her parent's divorce, potential suitors began visiting Gohary's home. Traditionally, when a girl turns sixteen, the families of potential suitors meet with her family, and when a mutually satisfactory match is found, if the couple agree, their engagement is announced. Gohary always knew when a suitor was coming because her father would bring home sweets and fruits and tell her to clean the house for guests. She was not really interested in marriage at the time, and her father's main concern seemed not for her happiness but that she marry a man of his choosing. Gohary was determined to hold off marriage as long as she could, but a new suitor from a neighboring street, whose family came originally from the Turkish-speaking province of Azerbaijan, changed her mind. Her father opposed the match: Turkish men had a reputation for being very strict with their women and, from Mr. Gohary's perspective, the suitor's family was too poor and unsophisticated for his daughter.

In those days, marriage was often considered primarily in terms of an alliance between families and kin groups and not in terms of a relationship between two individuals. However, Reza, the new suitor, was determined, and he and his family persisted. Reza made no secret of his feelings for Farkhondeh Gohary, and she grew very fond of him, letting neighbors and relatives know that she wished to marry him. Her disgruntled father announced that he would only consent to the marriage once Reza had completed his military service and started working. Because of the disrespect Farkhondeh's father had shown Reza and his family, Reza's older brother and his parents now also objected to the marriage. The situation became increasingly tense and uncertain for the young lovers, who could not even speak to each other under the watchful eyes of the neighbors.

Conventionally, young women in Iran (as in the rest of the region) have had little say in deciding the course their lives will take—including who they will marry—unless they have the support of an influential mother, which Farkhondeh Gohary did not. Farkhondeh managed to send messages encouraging Reza to complete his two years of military training and service, and promising to wait for him, knowing that without a military certificate he would not find a job and her father would continue to use this as a reason to oppose the marriage. But every few months, Reza, posted in some small town, would hear that Gohary's father was pressuring her to marry someone else and he would leave for Tehran without authorization, ending up in military detention and punished with extra time in the service.

Still young and beautiful, Gohary's mother, who had found a job as a seamstress at a large public hospital after her divorce, married a man ten years her junior. He was handsome and modern and seemed to appreciate her. While many around her were skeptical about her marriage to a childless, younger man, for Farkondeh Gohary, facing turmoil under her father's roof, the situation presented new options; she contemplated moving in with her mother. In 1977, after yet another argument with her father over her relationship with Reza, Gohary, by this time eighteen, moved in to her mother's home. With his eldest daughter gone and no one to run his household, her father married a thirty-five-year-old woman from his home town. This relieved Gohary from worry about the well-being of her siblings, for whom she continued to feel responsible.

This was the beginning of a new chapter in Farkondeh Gohary's life—an unusual transition to adulthood that, for women, typically occurs only with marriage. Her mother helped her get a job at the hospital. Although she could not move out on her own (which was socially unacceptable even for young men), having some degree of financial independence meant she could pay her own expenses, buy small items for her trousseau, and plan her marriage. Life seemed finally to be getting brighter. However, her new happiness was short-lived. Her mother's new brother-in-law decided he wanted to marry Gohary. Gohary resisted. Her stepfather accused her of being disrespectful and pressured her mother to insist Gohary marry his brother. Once again, she realized how hard it was for a woman to try and shape her own life.

News of the situation reached Reza and again without permission he left his military post and came to Tehran. Gohary's stepfather made a scene and the police were called. In the middle of the night, Gohary ran to her sympathetic maternal uncle's, who arranged for a Quran reading between her and Reza. This meant they were now engaged according to Islam and could see each other. Her mother and stepfather continued to cause problems, and her father publicly disowned her. One night in 1978, yet another angry scene forced Gohary to seek refuge with Reza's family and the couple decided to marry the next day. Reza's parents agreed to help them register their marriage and to postpone a proper wedding for later. Registering the marriage required health certificates and blood tests. Fortunately, preparations had been undertaken earlier and the paperwork had been processed; although the papers had expired, for a small bribe the registrar agreed to record the marriage.

Despite all of these preparations, the couple realized that according to Muslim and Iranian law a woman's first marriage would still require paternal consent: Gohary could not marry without her father's formal permission. Though he had repeatedly said that he would never agree and that he no longer considered her his daughter, Reza's family finally managed to bring Gohary's father to the registrar. The Quranic verse of marriage was read and the documents signed (however, not before further argument over the amount of the dower). The couple were finally married, but after the registration was complete they were left on their own in a melancholy mood. Though marriage is usually a celebration with friends, family, and well-wishers dancing until dawn, theirs had been a somber affair, far from the wedding Farkhondeh had dreamed of someday having.

Even now, in her forties, Gohary gets upset when she talks about how she suffered for daring to choose her own husband. While she believes that families should be consulted and should guide young people in such decisions, she feels that in many cases, including her own, the parents' disapproval of their daughter's choice has more to do with a desire to use women to control family alliances than it has to do with looking after the daughter's best interests. Gohary points out that many laws and customs ensure obedience from women, who continue to pay heavily for resisting them.

With the help of a few friends and relatives who gave them some basic items, a few months after their marriage Gohary and Reza rented a room and started their life together. Within the year, the Iranian revolution was underway, yet the anti-Shah slogans and demonstrations in the streets had little impact on Gohary's daily life. She had her own problems, and at the hospital where she worked people were preoccupied with the health of loved ones rather than with national politics. It was not until the autumn of 1978, when the Shah appointed an opposition prime minister and fled the country and the likelihood that he would not return sank in, that the upheaval became a general topic of discussion and concern in the neighborhood.

Like many in her neighborhood, Gohary had always believed politics was all about privileged men fighting over shares of the pie, whereas poor people and women had to look out for themselves and not pin their hopes on any government. Now, in the increasingly politically charged climate, she noticed that younger women in the neighborhood were wearing the *chador* (a large cloak which covers a woman from head to toe) in public. While in Gohary's neighborhood older women had always tended to wear the *chador*, younger women like her generally did so only for religious events or on occasions for which they lacked appropriate outfits. Suddenly, it seemed there was increasing pressure from the more religious and politicized residents of the neighborhood for all women to wear *hijab*, and specifically the *chador*. Parents and male kin encouraged their daughters and female relatives to don the *chador*, arguing that doing so afforded women increased security and protection. Stories began circulating of boys and young men throwing eggs and pebbles at women who were not wearing the *chador*.

Though faithful and observant of many Muslim rituals and traditions, Gohary began to feel uneasy about the new pressures being put on women and the fear of violence that was affecting women's mobility in the city. In her husband's quite conservative family, all the women observed *hijab*, and they began pressuring Reza to get Gohary to wear the *chador*. At first she resisted, but after Reza's family insisted it was for her own security as she moved about the city on her way to and from work, sometimes late in the day, Gohary finally agreed. This compromise only strengthened her dislike of politics.

Although happy to be married to the man she loved, and to be working and thus somewhat financially independent, Gohary grew increasingly concerned about Reza's failure to find a job. She knew part of the problem was that he hadn't finished his military service, and she convinced him to go back. By this point, his commanding officer was so fed up with Reza's repeated absences without leave that he agreed to reduce the remainder of Reza's service to two months. Shortly after Reza's return to Tehran, the Shah's regime collapsed entirely and the Islamic Republic was established. The new religious-political leaders began intensively promoting the idea of a return to traditional family structures, with women running the household and men supporting the family. This meant that an unconventional family like Gohary's, with an unemployed husband and a working wife, quickly became the talk of the neighborhood.

Gohary began to worry that perhaps her father had been right about Reza's capacity to provide for his family and become a responsible husband and father. The social and political climate, combined with all her concerns, led Gohary, pregnant for the first time with her son Majid, to leave her job and thus force Reza to find work. Within a few weeks of Gohary's stopping work, Reza found a job as an accountant and thankfully progressed well in his new profession.

A year and half later, in 1981, their first daughter Sonia was born. The next several years were difficult. The Iran-Iraq War (1980–88) had started, and Gohary worried lest her husband be sent off to fight just as she was about to give birth to their second child. She managed to have the hospital administration write a letter that prevented Reza from being drafted to the front. In 1985, her second daughter, Mona, was born, and finally her youngest child, a son named Said, was born. With this third child, Gohary decided to request a tubal ligation. At the time, the Islamic regime was promoting pronatal policies and it was difficult to access reliable contraception; thus, most couples relied on the rhythm or withdrawal methods, which were hardly infallible.

Gohary's father-in-law, a traditional man, had always felt badly that his younger son had never been given a proper wedding party like his brothers. Through his connections, he got a bargain on a domestically assembled Paykan, the most common car in Iran, and presented it to Reza. Within a few months, the price of this car had appreciated significantly, and Gohary, who was unhappy rooming in a house with several other families, encouraged Reza to sell the car and buy a house in the "informal housing" neighborhood near Shaher-e- Ray, where prices were relatively low. He agreed, and they found a house with two small rooms, a small kitchen and washroom, and a tiny courtyard. This is where the family still lives, though they have added a second story as the children got older. Gohary and Reza agree that buying the house was the wisest decision they could have made. They are secure in their own home, and real-estate prices have gone so high that they likely never would have had another such opportunity.

The years of the Iran-Iraq war were devastating for the south in particular. Tens of thousands of civilians and hundreds of thousands of troops were killed, many of them teenagers. Countless southerners were displaced by the fighting and fled to Tehran and other cities not directly affected by war. This movement of population put added pressure on the urban housing market and prices skyrocketed. As Iraqi losses multiplied after 1984, Iraq grew increasingly anxious to bring the war it had started to an end, but the Iranian regime had by then gained the upper hand, after initial defeats, and continued to fight while the so-called superpowers gladly sold guns to both sides. Eventually, the war made its way to Tehran, as Iraqi bombs targeted the city.

Iraq's bombing of Tehran, whose enormous urban constituency has the greatest impact on national politics, was intended to increase pressure on the regime to end the war. Greater Tehran, estimated at between 10 and 11 million residents at the time, compromised one-fifth of the country's population. Random bombings and the sudden scream of sirens made life in Tehran increasingly difficult, at times unbearable. Gohary spent many sleepless nights trying to calm her frightened children as the sirens wailed. With the influx of southerners and the stories of Tehrani citizens being bombed in their beds, the costs of war became increasingly more evident and the residents of Iraq's largest city grew ever more anxious and distressed. While the low-income neighborhoods of the southern edge of the city were less likely targets than the middle-class and affluent neighborhoods of north Tehran, which were home to many top officials and important decision makers, the human cost of the war weighed heavily on the poor, who provided the bulk of the young soldiers for the masses of troops the government sent in to flood the battlefields. Many sons were lost and many mothers heartbroken. It soon became evident that the cost in soldiers who had been severely wounded was equally devastating, with a lack of adequate services for handicapped veterans and the government's desperate polices to try and cope.

Gohary remembers how, in the early years of the war, religious leaders would urge young women to marry handicapped soldiers. The leaders spoke of how the women's love and care of war heroes who had sacrificed limbs and eyes in the defense of Islam and the Islamic revolution would guarantee them a place in heaven. This worked for a time, with the government actually subsidizing weddings and the setting up of newlywed households for disabled war veterans. Communities often contributed as well. But young brides received no training or support in caring for their handicapped husbands, many of whom suffered psychological as well as physical ailments and required more than cooking and housekeeping. These marriages were often miserable, and the women ended up seeking divorce, which was difficult to obtain.

There were other issues contributing to women's growing cynicism about the state as an agent of social justice, ostensibly acting on Islamic principles. The collective experiences of a generation of war brides and war widows were evidence that the regime's family policies had wreaked havoc on families. Many young soldiers who lost their lives had been married, since the convention of early marriage prevailed among the poorer and generally more traditional segments of the population. This left multitudes of young widows, often with small children, who were encouraged by the regime to become second wives. The *mullahs* entreated married women to allow their husbands to take second wives, presenting this option as a most worthy action in the eyes of God. Though many women remained skeptical, others responded to the state's urging, often to their later regret.

Agencies and individual brokers existed solely for the purpose of arranging such marriages, which often caused great distress in the domestic lives of first wives. And for many of the young war widows who grudgingly accepted marriage as second wives for lack of other options, the provision that upon their second marriage legal custody of any children from the first marriage would, according to conventions of conservative Islamic Sharia, go immediately to the paternal grandfather and his brothers, was devastating. If a widow remained unmarried, paternal kin still had legal custody of children once boys reached the age of two and daughters the age of five. This was women's reality, despite the fact that motherhood is publicly honored in Iran and is upheld in the Iranian constitution as the most important contribution to the nation. The custody issue, which has always been a concern of women, was totally unacceptable to these young mothers. None of this endeared the regime to women. The situation increasingly brought the regime's treatment of women and its idealized vision of Islamic family into sharp focus, which then made these issues topics of debate and discussion not only among the educated and elites but among women from all walks of life. By the mid-1980s Gohary, like many women in her milieu, was increasingly pondering the treatment of women by the Islamic regime. There were, however, few open platforms for complaint aside from the circulation of stories about women's harried lives and political jokes and commentary criticizing the government. Given the long history of censorship and government control over media by successive regimes in Iran, this had for a long time been one of the most prevalent and effective methods of airing public opinion. Women, in particular, grew increasingly skeptical of the regime's manipulation of them, and many who had become politically interested and involved at the onset of the revolution lost interest in political participation and mass demonstrations. Indeed, the pressure from women and from a loss of legitimacy eventually led Ayatollah Khomeini to announce in 1988 that the widows of Martyrs could retain custody of their children even if they remarried and to introduce some moderate revisions to the marriage laws. Though many women felt the reforms did not go far enough, they were evidence that change was indeed possible and that the laws of Sharia were not in fact written in stone. While these changes inspired more influential women to further mobilization and lobbying, many were by that point too disillusioned with the regime to bother with politics.

Gohary recalls how the unhappy stories of young brides and young widows were told and retold at every *sofreh* (commonly held, women-only religious gatherings, usually taking place in someone's home) she attended in those years. She and many other middle-aged and older women in her neighborhood watched these developments and the manipulation of young women with dismay. The situation caused her to look more critically at the law and at customs enforced in the name of Islam. The pervasiveness of the problem and women's seeming powerlessness to demand the justice promised but not delivered by the government left her and many of her friends ever more frustrated with politics. Many were by this point disillusioned with the regime and convinced that an Islamic state was no different than any other form of government. As a result, they became more tightly focused than ever on the lives of their own families.

However, "even in the family, life was not rosy," said Gohary. Her in-laws, devoted to their two sons, were victims of the younger generation's preference for nuclear-family living, which left little emotional or physical space for accommodating the elder generation. Constant problems between Gohary's in-laws and their elder son's wife made life in their older son's home unstable and stressful. The situation eventually motivated Gohary (despite her husband's protests) to move her in-laws into her own modest two-room home. Indeed, it proved difficult to share two small rooms between four children and four adults, and after a couple of years Gohary rented her in-laws an apartment nearby so she could continue to help them with daily chores. While extended-family living may remain preferable to some, in Gohary's view it is no longer a workable structure for the poorer classes, especially in the cities, where housing is at a premium and apartments are tiny. Gohary is determined to ensure that she and her husband remain financially and emotionally autonomous and do not become a burden to their own children. Still, she does hope that as her own children mature and marry they will live nearby.

By 1990, with her children older, her household tasks thus less time-consuming, and expenses continuously rising with four children to educate, she began to contemplate returning to work at the hospital, thus assuring herself an old-age pension. As the only adult working outside the home, Gohary's husband, like many men with families, had to work long hours and sometimes a second job, often returning home too tired to even speak with her. Yet he did not support the idea of her returning to work. Gohary grew resentful of being limited to her household duties and suspicious that perhaps her husband had taken a temporary or second wife. Such scenarios occurred with increasing frequency following the establishment of the Islamic regime, which legalized and legitimized *muta* (temporary marriage) and encouraged war widows to become second wives. With the regime presenting these practices as in accordance with God's will, women bitterly joked that it seemed men's pleasure in this world would also be rewarded in heaven. Gohary and her neighbors were well aware that the Quran states that a man must provide for and love all his wives equally; the same verse also notes that generally this is impossible and thus a man should have only one wife. The neighborhood women also wryly joked that jurists got so excited reading the beginning of the verse that they never actually got to the second part.

As Gohary's worries about her husband having a second family tormented her, their relationship deteriorated. Her husband dismissed her uneasiness as petty, unfounded jealousy. She emphatically explained to me that it was not jealousy but thwarted expectations of justice and resentment of the double standard for men and women that upset and depressed her. In her heart, she could not accept that God would sanction differential treatment for men and women, who were otherwise expected to observe the same religious duties, including fasting, praying, alms-giving, and making the pilgrimage to Mecca.

With the encouragement of friends, Gohary decided to train as beautician, using skills and talents she had honed over years of informally acting as a beauty consultant for her neighbors. This, she thought, would provide some economic security if life and marriage treated her badly. While her husband initially objected, eventually he grudgingly agreed that Gohary could set up a small business, and she converted the pantry at the front of her house into a storefront. Her shop soon became a meeting-place for neighborhood women to exchange news and discuss family problems, joke about politicians, find out about potential jobs for their husbands and sons, and make matches for their children, and Gohary's life grew increasingly busy and satisfying. Her presence and support for women had brought her much respect among her neighbors. Indeed, they always referred to her as Khanom Gohary. "Khanom" is a title of respect in referring to women, much like Madame but expressing less formality. Although neighbors usually refer to each other by first name, in the case of Khanom Gohary, everyone referred to her as Gohary or Khanom Gohary because Gohary also means "jewel." On several occasions, women with whom I spent time in the neighborhood told me that Khanom Gohary is definitely the jewel of the neighborhood.

During this period, the Iranian regime began instituting some "bottom-up" development programs. In addition to serving practical needs, such programs were politically advantageous, as the regime sought to bolster its image as the government of the oppressed and disadvantaged and to regain support from the poor who remained its largest constituency. Among these programs was the Healthy City Project, a model initially promoted in many developing countries through the World Health Organization. The project aimed to establish a coordinating body for the activities of various government ministries, in particular, for those ministries that delivered water and electricity, health services and education, and those dealing with roads and public transport. Another key aspect of Healthy City was its focus on public health—health being broadly defined to include mental and physical well-being but also sanitation and public awareness of hygiene and nutrition. Perhaps its most important goal was to increase public participation and empower citizens to take a more active role in community development. The project focused on issues relevant to the community and sought to bring tangible improvements to the neighborhoods, thereby encouraging further public participation. The first of these projects was set up in Shahr Ray—which included Gohary's neighborhood—in early 1993. A government representative canvassed the area, encouraging women to participate in weekly "Neighborhood Health" sessions that would take place in a different home each week.

Khanom Gohary and the neighborhood women were asked numerous times to participate, but their distrust of the state made many of them reluctant. Khanom Gohary's view of the state as serving the wealthy and powerful was typical of the cynicism many poor Iranians feel toward the government and political involvement. Eventually, a very pregnant facilitator approached Gohary, who was persuaded to attend a Neighborhood Health session by the young woman's enthusiasm and commitment. The meeting changed her life. The discussion of pressing health issues, including children's illnesses, dirty streets, and a lack of clean running water, and the solutions suggested, inspired her. She considers this meeting, in 1995, a turning point. Following the meeting, she mobilized her neighbors to participate, offering a 50 percent reduction to beauty shop clients who agreed to come to a session. This was a coup for the Healthy City Project in the neighborhood.

On days when meetings were held, generally in the morning when husbands were at work and children at school, the host household would hang a little flag on the front door or gate announcing the meeting to neighborhood women. This practice of hanging a flag was borrowed from women's religious meetings, which are often held in the early afternoon. The flag announced that all women are welcome and warns that men are not. By convention, males of the household stay away until the flag is removed. Khanom Gohary tells a funny anecdote about one Thursday meeting when she forgot to remove the flag from her door after the session. Since the family always ate lunch together on Thursdays and Fridays (the Iranian weekend), she had hurriedly prepared the meal and sat down at the table with her children to wait for her husband's return. The hour passed one o'clock, and then two o'clock, with no sign or word of her husband and she began to worry. Finally, a neighbor's child rang the bell and said that her husband was wondering how long the meeting would go on, as he was tired of walking the neighborhood. Gohary realized her poor husband had been walking up and down the street for two hours waiting for the flag to be removed.

The meetings and networking with neighbors who shared many of her concerns invigorated Khanom Gohary. She was convinced that by working together neighborhood women could solve some of their common problems. Many of the women's worries revolved around issues of family finances and children's health and education. There were worries about the implications of marriage laws, the problems of divorce, and child custody. The women worried not only for themselves but for their daughters and sons, for there seemed to be discord between customary practices, which varied from region to region, and the codified law that had assumed increasingly more influence over women's lives under the Islamic Republic. Few of the women were versed as to what the laws said vis-à-vis their legal rights and responsibilities. Gohary contacted a legal expert and arranged for her to speak to the group and answer some of the women's questions. The legal rights session was a great success and was followed by several others. On hearing of her initiative, the directors of the Healthy City Project encouraged and supported Gohary. On reflection, Khanom Gohary wonders if there has ever been a time in Iran when women have been as concerned with or involved in matters of community and law and justice as they have been since the early 1990s. She is not sure if this has occurred because of political circumstances or because women are less willing to accept the injustices imposed on them. However, she clearly distinguishes between this kind of activism and what is done under a political organization.

As Khanom Gohary got more involved in the concerns of neighborhood women, she began to understand her own family and domestic problems in a much broader context, and her relationship with her husband improved as they struggled together to address the structural problems underlying their hardships. This, says Khanom Gohary, brought them closer than they had been in years. Gradually, women from neighboring *koutcheh* (alleys) began coming to her for advice, or to request that she organize meetings for them as well. The more involved Gohary became, the more energetic she felt, and her husband was quite happy to support her efforts. Full of new-found energy, she decided to join the volunteer health workers program launched by the Ministry of Health to help with family planning and child health issues.

A few years earlier, in 1988, the government of Iran had reintroduced family planning. While in the early 1970s the Shah's regime had launched a relatively successful family planning program to limit family size, the clerical leadership of the revolution renounced it as an imperialist plot to limit the Muslim population. When the theocratic regime came to power following the overthrow of the Shah in 1978, the program was cancelled and pronatalist policies were introduced, which provided incentives for couples to have more children. According to the 1986 census, the Iranian population was estimated to be over 50 million—an increase of almost 17 million since the previous national survey in 1976—indicating the highest rate of population growth in the modern history of Iran. The revolutionary regime had initially committed to universal free education and health care, food subsidies, and pensions for the elderly, and these commitments were enshrined in the constitution. Such a dramatic increase in social welfare presented a major challenge, given the government's limited resources. As the clergy gained administrative experience, they recognized that providing education and health was key to building a strong nation and that a huge population was ultimately disadvantageous.

The regime reintroduced a family planning program, directed primarily at the low-income population and approved by Ayatollah Khomeini in 1988. From every mosque clerics began to urge people to limit their number of children. Using simple language and religious arguments they explained the regime's drastic reversal of its family planning policy. "We cannot depend on imperialists for our daily bread," argued the *mullahs*, and given the country's limited land-base it was thus imperative for self-sufficiency that population growth be reduced. Though all Muslims are expected to marry and procreate, the *mullahs* pointed out that Islam dictates that in difficult times efforts should be made to control fertility and that there are no religious restrictions on preventing conception. The contentious issue of abortion was not addressed in the regime's family planning program. To succeed in slowing population growth, especially in light of the regime's earlier promotion of motherhood as the ultimate duty and glory of womanhood, Iranian women had to be convinced that fewer children were better. The government hoped to reduce the average family to one or two children, and went so far as to limit child benefits for public-sector employees to a maximum of three children. The critical task was to convey the message to those women in the poorest suburbs of large cities, who had little or no education, and particularly to women in Tehran, which was experiencing very rapid growth. The government also recognized that in areas where the child mortality rate was high women would be unwilling to limit their fertility.

Trying to gain women's support, the Ministry of Health drew on the experiences of Thailand, China, and a few other countries to design a program whereby local women, in conjunction with community health centers, would be trained in basic maternal and infant health care, particularly prenatal care, immunization, and nutrition. The training program was designed to empower neighborhood women to share vital information and to teach them how to interact with clients. Each of the volunteer health workers would then have between sixty and eighty households under her jurisdiction, acting as a link between these households and the local health center. The first of these programs was launched in and around Khanom Gohary's neighborhood.

In 1992 Khanom Gohary had declined an invitation to join the volunteer health workers. Now, in 1995, with a new sense of purpose and recognition of the impact of grassroots activity, she took on yet another role, training to become a volunteer health worker. Not all the neighborhood women were open to the idea of health education and a local clinic. Their reluctance in many instances stemmed from suspicions on the part of mothers-in-law and other elderly women, and husbands as well, as to what exactly the women would learn at these healthcare workshops.

Sometimes men worried that their wives were going to receive "sex education." Although what this might actually involve was unclear in their minds, they were nevertheless uneasy that it might disturb the equilibrium of their marriages. Khanom Gohary well understood the obstacles she faced in getting the neighborhood women to participate in the reproductive health initiative, and she developed ways to address their fears. She visited mothers-in-law and husbands, explaining in simple, clear language the importance of having children vaccinated and of women spacing their pregnancies and receiving prenatal care. Her nonthreatening manner helped her almost always succeed in her outreach. Sometimes it was the young women themselves who were discomfited by the prospect of going to a clinic, either because of the idea of being examined or because they had rarely ventured farther than the immediate neighborhood. Some were wary of being treated with disrespect at the government-run clinics. Gohary often ended up accompanying women to the clinic, though this meant time away from her own business. She solved this problem by taking several women at one time, reasoning that as they got to know one another the women would provide mutual support for each other. Her efforts to bring women together created bonds of solidarity between neighbors who had come to Tehran from different parts of the country. While differences in dialect and traditions had previously impeded these women from getting to know each other, the meetings and appointments arranged by Khanom Gohary often proved to be catalysts for forming friendships.

Khanom Gohary knew that bureaucrats and government agencies had often treated women from the low-income neighborhoods with disrespect, seeing them as uneducated and incompetent. One result was that many of the women were uncertain they would be able to learn about health care and pass this knowledge on to others. Coming from a background similar to theirs, Gohary empathized and often shared stories of her own experiences with new volunteers and trainers. She was frequently asked to speak at Healthy City information and training sessions.

Khanom Gohary's self-confidence and reputation expanded in 1995. A local clinic had organized a session in an area that had many health-related problems and where there had been no success in getting neighborhood women to information sessions. The local volunteer health worker had arranged for the meeting to be held at the neighborhood mosque, which was likely to draw more women than a home-based session. It was advertised that a doctor would be speaking and would answer any health-related questions. Khanom Gohary arrived, along with the doctor, a very young, unassuming woman. Gohary asked the doctor to allow her to speak first, and she then proceeded to tell the women in attendance stories about other neighborhood health initiatives and the kinds of information that women were getting and sharing. Before long, Khanom Gohary, whom the women in the audience addressed as "Khanom Doctor," was being bombarded with questions. During a pause, she asked for a volunteer to help organize health sessions in the neighborhood. There was silence. The women began murmuring that they were not educated, not skilled, were familiar only with their own alleys, etc. Then Khanom Gohary told them that one year earlier she had said exactly the same thing, and now she was the spokesperson for the program and they had all mistaken her for a doctor! She then introduced the actual doctor, who spoke briefly about the importance of women taking their own and their families' health matters into their own hands. The doctor noted that good health was a gift bestowed by God and thus all good Muslims were duty-bound to look after their health. To do otherwise is to be an ungrateful Muslim—*mosalmon nashokr*—the doctor told the audience. She also told them that even more than praying or fasting, helping with the well-being of others earns much *savab* (blessings from God). The strategy was a great success, with many of the women who attended the meeting becoming volunteer health workers or otherwise involved with the Healthy City program. Khanom Gohary continued to help launch initiatives in different neighborhoods.

As neighborhood women became more aware of the role of hygiene in improving health, and realized that playing in dirty alleys and eating badly handled food were contributing to their children's illnesses, Khanom Gohary and her neighbors took action. Though some areas lacked even basic municipal services like regular garbage collection or clean running water, the women cleaned their sections of the alleys as best they could.

In 1996 Khanom Gohary and other women petitioned the municipality for better services, but they were barely given the time of day. The municipal administrators had no knowledge of, or interest in, either the Healthy City Project or the neighborhood health initiative, despite the national government's promotion of the program as a priority for the underserved urban majority. Khanom Gohary contacted the head doctor at the local health center and asked him to use his influence to help get the neighborhood cleaned up. Though he agreed, nothing came of it, as he had little authority outside the clinic. Khanom Gohary, still somewhat naive about the hierarchy of power and influence regulating government bureaucracies, was dismayed, as time passed and nothing came of her efforts.

After weeks of pondering how to tackle the system, she decided to set up a neighborhood women's council to pressure the authorities. The election of President Khatami in 1997, who ran on a pro-reform platform that emphasized women's rights and their role in civil society, engendered a lot of talk about neighborhood councils but few details concerning exactly how they would form and function. Khanom Gohary had heard descriptions of such councils while attending workshops but was uncertain as to how they actually operated. She forged ahead, deciding to work out the details as things evolved. Given the very high population density in the area, she divided the neighborhood into zones, then invited the women in each zone to the local mosque for an initial meeting. Khanom Gohary and the other neighborhood volunteers knew from experience that if the meetings were held more than a few blocks from their homes, many women would not attend, either because their husbands would object or because they would not be comfortable venturing too far. A substantial majority of the women in this low-income area of Tehran were first-generation, rural-urban migrants still struggling to adjust to urban life.

Khanom Gohary says she learned a great deal about her neighborhood, Iranian society, and the obstacles that impede women from organizing themselves and participating in public life as she worked to set up the neighborhood women's council in 1998. When she delivered letters inviting the women to the local mosque for a preliminary council meeting, she often encountered men who would simply tear up a letter in front of her, saying "My wife doesn't need this; her job is taking care of her home." Her attempts to explain that the council would help women take better care of their homes and families fell on deaf ears. Men who knew her would say, "Khanom Gohary, our wives are already too demanding. We don't want them to further question our authority." Others were skeptical, dismissing the idea of the council as another government trick to distract people while it continued to mismanage the country.

Meanwhile, older people who remembered Tehran in the 1950s told Khanom Gohary that the city had had local associations at one time, whose primary activity had been to lobby for better municipal services. However, as the Shah's regime became increasingly dictatorial in the 1970s, the government had begun interfering with the running of the neighborhood associations and they died out.

At these initial meetings to organize the neighborhood women's council, Gohary talked about the filthy streets, alleys, and gutters; the children's need for safe, clean playgrounds; the need for better bus service; for streetlights so women could safely walk outside after dark; and the importance of establishing local libraries. While the women attending agreed that these improvements were necessary, they were skeptical that a women's council could obtain them. Khanom Gohary said that the first step would be to collect signatures on a petition and the second would be to go in large numbers to the municipality with the signed petition and loudly voice their demands. "A busy mother won't nurse the baby until it cries," she told the women. "Nothing will be done unless we show that we refuse to accept this state of affairs." Twenty-six women came forward to sit on the council, seven of whom were elected to represent the zones that comprised the area, with Gohary elected head. Within days, in the Fall of 1998, the Neighborhood Women's Council had registered its official status and had its own stamp for council documents.

The campaign to enhance the neighborhood began with letters on council letterhead sent off to the electricity and water offices, the municipality, the ministry of health, the public transit authority, the sports federation, and the ministry of education. The council prepared petitions and collected signatures, first for streetlights, then for cleaning the streets, and so on. As head of the council, Gohary went directly to the various departments, petitions in hand. At first she was not taken seriously; then she threatened to bring her case to the media and to more senior national government officials. Soon, streetlights were being installed or fixed. For years, parents had asked the municipality to clean the empty lots that were used as unofficial garbage dumps so that neighborhood youths would have somewhere to play football and other sports. The collective pressure of the petitions and the threat of media exposure did the trick. Next came improved bus service. With each of the council's victories the list of issues to work on grew longer, as neighborhood residents gained faith in the council's ability to address local problems.

One early success was the removal from a side street of an abandoned car that had served as a locale for drug dealing by day and prostitution by night. This situation highlighted just how resourceful Khanom Gohary had become. She verified the situation, visiting the neighborhood and speaking with residents. She then phoned and wrote to the municipality and the police, and was informed by both that the removal of abandoned cars did not fall under their jurisdictions. Frustrated, she remembered a TV journalist who had been impressed by her activities and had promised to try and help. She phoned him and explained the situation. The reporter hesitated, considering the consequences for the mayor, the TV station, and various ministries. He told Khanom Gohary he'd check things out and get back to her within a few hours. Before he could call back, local residents called her to say that the municipality was removing the car. Camera crews arrived to film the scene for local TV. When Khanom Gohary arrived on the scene, the mayor intercepted her and asked why she was plotting against him. Khanom Gohary replied with a gentle smile that the Women's Council was only concerned with making the area safe and that if the mayor didn't respond the council was obligated to pursue alternative routes. Following this incident, Khanom Gohary's requests for meetings with the mayor and other officials were no longer turned down.

Reflecting on these experiences, Khanom always says that she is usually shy but working for her community gives her courage to deal with the media, officials, and bureaucrats, regardless of their power and social status.

One of the council's important strategies has been getting men as well as women to collect signatures and talk about issues with the community. Khanom Gohary frequently asked the husbands of council members to deliver letters or collect signatures from neighborhood men. This has been helpful, not only because many men have motorcycles but also because it makes it evident that the council is acting on behalf of everyone and is not simply a tool for pressuring husbands. One result was that more and more people began coming to the council, not only with complaints about municipal services but with family problems as well.

Gohary believes that increased public and media discussion of the affairs of the Tehran City Council and other municipal councils around the country have given the neighborhood councils greater legitimacy. And when municipal elections for Tehran City Council were held in 1999, Khanom Gohary and two other women from the neighborhood council ran, despite a total lack of campaign funds. Although none of them won, Gohary received more than a thousand votes, while the other two women each received close to seven hundred votes. In hindsight, Gohary feels that only one of them should have stood for election, with the other two supporting the campaign, but at the time none of the women had had any formal political experience and they believed the more women candidates the better because they thought it would give the women more visibility.

Zoning has been a major point of contention for Gohary and other local activists. While their area is considered part of Tehran for the purpose of municipal elections, when it comes to the distribution of resources, it seems, they are not considered to be part of the city. Local residents believe the neighborhood Women's Council is the body which best serves them, and they bring their problems there, not to the Tehran City Council offices. The Women's Council tries to work with representatives from the city to address local problems.

From its inception, the council's concerns went beyond dealing with government-run services. The Women's Council spoke with local food shops about improving hygienic practices to reduce health risks from contamination. Though some shops complied, others refused to listen to "a bunch of women who thought they were now the boss." The council members dealt with this by encouraging households not to patronize those shops, and if this produced little result, they threatened to ask the local clinic to call in the food and drug safety commission. Though the clinic protested to Khanom Gohary that such an intervention would be outside their mandate, she pointed out that training women about health and hygiene was pointless if the broader community did not participate. There were, however, only a few occasions when the council had to resort to such tactics; most shopkeepers responded to the boycotts. The woman also asked shopkeepers to more prominently display dried fruits, raisins, and juices instead of sweets and sodas, to support their attempt to improve children's eating habits. These efforts fostered a growing sense of community and empowerment as women took greater control over their families' well-being.

As momentum gathered and improvements became evident, more and more women were inspired to become public health volunteers or participate in other ways. However, husbands were not always supportive. In such cases, the women often asked Khanom Gohary to intervene. Gohary was by now middle-aged and increasingly respected in the neighborhood. A visit by her to the reluctant husband, during which she would describe how her own marriage had dramatically improved after she became a volunteer health worker, often helped to convince him. She would also speak about how increasing their knowledge of health and other issues helped families address social and economic pressures, and she would emphasize that the programs for women also helped them understand the pressures faced by their husbands and better support them. Because Khanom Gohary frequently voices her appreciation of her own husband's support, other men feel encouraged to support their wives' participation in community affairs. Khanom Gohary's gift has been to recognize that change must be implemented through appropriate and pragmatic strategies that don't cause domestic upheaval or dissent within families.

Gohary's work has continued. In 2000, the neighborhood women had nowhere to gather for activities and frequently sat on their stoops in the alleys to chat. There were few sports facilities for women; the open spaces used by boys for recreation were off-limits to girls. Khanom Gohary, then the mother of eighteen- and fifteen-year-old daughters, encouraged young women to visit the public library, but it was far away and parents were reluctant to allow their daughters to travel. As well, young men hung around the main public library and this made it an even less socially acceptable destination for girls. Khanom Gohary and the council decided to lobby for a small local women's library, but there was little political will and no budget for a project that the primarily male municipal administrators saw as unnecessary. She lobbied the local mosque, but they would only agree to support a religious library. Since she envisioned the library as providing general interest books on health and household organization, as well as novels, educational materials, and religious texts, she continued to lobby the municipality, and finally (just to get rid of her, as she put it) the authorities agreed that if she found a space they would provide two sets of bookshelves and a few other materials. Given the shortage of housing and space in the neighborhood, finding space was actually the primary challenge, but Khanom Gohary was determined. After considerable thought, she suggested to her husband that they turn her beauty shop into a women's library. Though this meant a loss of income for the family, by then, Khanom Gohary's involvement with the Women's Council left little time for running her shop. With her husband's agreement, the council worked to convert the tiny beauty shop into a library (*ketabkhane*). Khanom Gohary proudly spoke of the moment she appeared at the municipality to inform the official that her own shop would become the library. The shocked official muttered, "God help your husband." Six weeks later, the library opened with 150 books. The opening day of the *ketabkhane* became something of celebration for the women of the neighborhood, each of whom knew exactly how much work, hope, and energy had been invested. Gradually, the collection expanded, as Khanom Gohary contacted publishers and women's organizations with requests for book donations. By 2004, this tiny library held over 1,500 books and had a membership of 400 households. Under Khanom Gohary's guidance, the council has supported the establishment of other local libraries and Khanom has been interviewed by various newspapers and NGOs about the library project.

The neighborhood women are very proud of their little library, and they often gather outside the door to discuss books and issues they have come across in their reading. Though the men, especially younger men, including Khanom Gohary's own sons, are somewhat unhappy that they can't use the library, Khanom Gohary reminds them that they have much more freedom to move around the city than the girls do and can travel to the public library or ask their sisters to get books for them. She points out that they wouldn't want their own sisters or daughters encountering unrelated men in the library and that other families feel the same way.

Having four children herself, Khanom Gohary was well aware of the ongoing challenge of trying to keep teenagers productively busy, and so a few years ago she set up a youth organization. Together with neighborhood teens, the organization began publishing a newsletter that by 2002 had four issues in print. The fifth is still on hold due to lack of funds. Khanom Gohary has also organized several field trips for teens, as well as computer classes, film screenings, and other activities.

When I asked her if she regretted not becoming a social activist earlier, she paused, and then said no. She explained that it was only after the war and the advent of a degree of liberalization under President Rafsanjani that economic and social development became a government concern, with projects like Healthy City and the Volunteer Health Workers and the government's encouragement of public participation. "Before that, they wanted us to take to the streets in support of the government. I did not go because I do not trust politicians and was not interested in politics. After Khatami's election in 1997, social participation and civil society became more legitimate." She said she felt she had to campaign for Khatami when he ran for a second term, despite her dislike of politics. Opposition supporters had began visiting the neighborhood and speaking to people in the streets and in the mosque, arguing that Khatami's policies were responsible for corrupting and westernizing Iranian youth, especially girls, who were watching foreign movies, wearing tight *roupoosh* (long coverall coats, traditionally loose), and allowing their scarves to fall off their heads. The opposition supporters urged the people in the neighborhood to vote conservative and curb the situation, which they argued would otherwise lead to terrible youth immorality. Khanom Gohary vehemently disagreed with this perspective. While concurring that Khatami might not have delivered much, the fact that issues concerning youth had been raised under his presidency gave Iranian youth hope and a sense of worth. As a mother of four, with young teenagers at home, she encouraged women to go and vote for Khatami, if only to keep youth issues on the government agenda.

Khanom Gohary and the women she works with continue to seek solutions to neighborhood problems. Unemployment is high, and many men have no job security. Accidents, illnesses, and layoffs are always an issue.

There are endless births, deaths and weddings, and a chronic shortage of funds to deal with them. The Women's Council had heard of volunteer health workers in other neighborhoods who set up savings clubs that functioned as community banking and credit systems. Several well-acquainted women in Khanom's neighborhood decided to set up a "bank" that would be funded by an fixed initial contribution from each woman. Khanom Gohary was appointed as the new bank's trustee and was responsible for keeping the books and doing the bank transactions. Although this type of banking system is new in Iran, people refer to it as a "*gharzol-hasaneh,*" which refers to a traditional system of honor-based, interest-free loans provided to those in need. The women's system is more accurately a cooperative savings club that helps members with short-term financing. Members decide collectively who gets the available loan. It might be for a son or daughter's marriage, or to temporarily assist a family whose main breadwinner is out of work; or, a drawing might be held to pick the loan recipient. The loans, which are paid back over time, are often used for items like sewing machines to start small, income-generating projects. Savings clubs are now springing up throughout the low-income neighborhoods, and even among the middle classes. Khanom Gohary managed to finance the addition of two badly needed rooms to her house with the help of the savings club. She believes the system is an invaluable tool for poor families with little collateral, and especially for women trying to set up small, home-based businesses. Women rarely fail to repay their loans, as this would cause suffering to their own friends and neighbors.

A group of women had discussed starting a small business in the neighborhood, which would allow them to work a few hours each day and bring in a small income. After much searching, they identified an old government building that has been unused since the Shah's regime. After a very long process of negotiation with the municipality and various ministries, Khanom Gohary secured its use. Gohary and the core group researched and met weekly to determine what type of enterprise would be most profitable and require the least training, thereby allowing as many women as possible to participate. They decided to set up a business drying fruit and herbs and established a co-op, selling shares to members to raise the capital to buy machinery. In mid-June 2004, with a great sense of accomplishment and much celebration, the enterprise began production. When I spoke with Gohary on the first of June that year, she was busy preparing for the opening. She told me that aside from her family her greatest joy has been working to improve the life of her neighborhood and the people in it. It has been far more rewarding, she said, than winning a seat in government or being a member of parliament would have been, where, she said, people talk much and achieve little.

When I asked her what the highlight of these past years has been, she paused and then spoke of her family—about the day the results of the university entrance exams came out and her elder son and daughter both qualified. "That day," she said," "I could not sleep. I was beside myself and wanted to sing and shout and share my happiness with my friends." Gohary hopes her younger children will follow suit. She was also pleased about her elder son's marriage to a beloved classmate, and relieved that her children would not face the kind of struggle she and her husband did during their courtship. She has emphasized to all her children, including her daughters, that the choice of a mate is theirs, though Gohary and her husband are there to guide and support them and hope they will choose wisely. Her daughter, who is a student at one of the most prestigious engineering universities in Tehran, is very supportive and proud of her mother's activities and told me she feels extremely lucky to have such an understanding mother.

If there is one day, however, that stands out as the most memorable day of Khanom Gohary's public life, it is the celebration of International Women's Day on 8 March 2001. Gohary was invited by an activist to speak about how she had changed her own life and the lives of so many in her community. Until then, Khanom Gohary had never heard of International Women's Day; the official Iranian Women's Day is the birthday of Fatimeh, the prophet Mohamed's daughter. Gohary accepted the invitation, thinking it would be an event similar to a volunteer health worker meeting. She arrived with her eldest daughter and a friend to find an audience made up of hundreds of obviously well-educated, middle-class, primarily secular women. She said she suddenly felt as if all her body was on fire and there were hundreds of butterflies in her stomach. Her daughter, also surprised by the scale of the gathering, kept saying in jest to her friend, "We'd better pretend we're not with her because she is going to embarrass us. What is she going to tell all these woman?!" Khanom Gohary grew even more nervous when she saw that all the other speakers had prepared written speeches. But there she was, and she could not run away.

When her turn came to approach the podium, Gohary apologized to the audience for not having prepared a speech, telling them that if she had realized there would be so many people she would not have accepted the invitation to speak. She told the crowd that she had never heard of International Women's Day until she was asked to come to the gathering and share the story of what she and her friends had done in their neighborhood to change their lives. Gohary told them about the volunteer health workers, the Women's Council, the local women's library, and the other projects.

When she was done, the audience clapped for a very long time and Gohary felt elated—relieved that they had appreciated her story and that she had not embarrassed her host! Many of the women who came up to congratulate her afterward have kept in contact, sending books for the library and inviting Gohary and her neighborhood colleagues to meetings and workshops. For days after the meeting Khanom Gohary reflected on the day and her speech and spoke about it with her friends. A few years ago, she could not have imagined having such an experience.

Recently, in the summer of 2004, when I asked Khanom Gohary if the next step might be to run for parliament or city council now that she has so much experience, she shook her head emphatically and said she was not interested in playing politics and that government was not for her. Her concern was and remains finding ways to improve her life and the lives of other women facing similar circumstances.

A NOTE ON SOURCES

I heard about Khanom Gohary while working on the Islamic Republic's Family Planning Program in 1998. Later, in 2000, I met with Gohary on several occasions as part of a project examining the Intersection of Citizenship and Family Law, supported by the Canadian Social Science and Humanity Research Council. In 2001, I recorded an interview with Gohary in which she talked about her life. In December 2003, we spent another day together while I interviewed her further. She, in turn, interrogated me about marketable production projects that would not require much capital or training—that is, an enterprise flexible enough to allow women to work around their domestic responsibilities while earning a little income to help relieve some of the financial burdens of their households. When I last met with her, in June 2004, she and several other women were very busy testing machines, cleaning the office, and getting ready for the opening day of the co-op. As women came and went, and in the midst of countless interruptions to attend to one thing or another, Khanom Gohary spoke excitedly of the co-op's plans for future expansion, and of the day when they might be able to export their products abroad to bring in greater profits.

SUGGESTIONS FOR FURTHER READING

For an overview of the situation of women in Iran, see Nikki, Keddie, "Women in Iran since 1979," *Social Research* 67, no.2 (Summer 2000): 405–38; and Parvin Paidar, *Gender and Democracy: The Encounter between Feminism and Reformism in Contemporary Iran* (U.N. Research Institute Program Paper, no. 6, October 2001). For a discussion of different forms of grassroots activism, see Homa Hoodfar, "Volunteer Health Workers in Iran as Social Activists: Can 'Governmental Non-governmental Organizations' be Agents of Democratisation?" WLUML Occasional Papers, no. 10. (Women

Living Under Muslim Law, 2000), www.wluml.org/english/pubs/pdf/occ-paper/OCP-10.pdf); and Homa Hoodfar, "Muslim Women Mullahs as Volunteer Reproductive Health Workers," in *Cultural Perspectives on Reproductive Health,* ed. Carla Makhlouf Obermeyer (New York: Oxford University Press, 2001). For understanding the role of religion in Iranian society, see Roy Mottahedeh, *The Mantle of the Prophet: Religion and Politics in Iran* (New York: Pantheon, 1986). On issues of marriage and divorce, read Shahla Haery, *The Law, Desire, and Temporary Marriage in Iran* (London: I. B. Tauris, 1989); and Kim Longinotto and Ziba Mir-Hosseini, *Divorce Iranian Style* (London, 1998), film.

Chapter 23

Nadia: "Mother of the Believers"

Baya Gacemi

Translated by E. Burke, III

When Nadia met Ahmed Chaabani in 1990, she was fourteen years old and he was around eighteen. She was the eldest of nine children in a peasant family of Hai Bounab, a neighborhood of the village of Eucalyptus in the Mitidja Plain south of Algiers. She was not much interested in school. Mostly she was interested in Ahmed Chaabani. Ahmed was the third son of a widow and came from a desperately poor family. He had missed out on school, and the villagers of Eucalyptus pegged him as a youth with an attitude problem. But for Nadia, Ahmed was the love of her life. Against the wishes of her family, they were married in 1992. Baya Gacemi's portrait of Nadia provides a rare local perspective on the political turmoil that engulfed Algeria in 1992.

At the time of his marriage to Nadia, Ahmed was active in the Algerian black market—a risky but remunerative occupation in the economically stagnant Algerian countryside. But he soon underwent an unpredictable transformation, becoming a devout Muslim. Nadia had not been a devout Muslim and the makeover Ahmed imposed on her was drastic. As Ahmed's wife, she became "the Mother of the Believers," admired as such, but in fact the virtual house slave of her husband and his gang. When, after the Algerian elections in early 1992, Ahmed became the local Islamist gang leader, or *emir*, things got worse.

Algeria achieved its independence in 1962 after eight years of armed struggle and civil war, which were immortalized in the Gillo Pontecorvo film *The Battle of Algiers* and in Frantz Fanon's bitter critique, *The Wretched of the Earth*. As one of only three Middle Eastern countries to experience settler colonialism (the other two being Libya and Palestine/Israel), Algerian history had been marked by a prolonged and bitter struggle over land. (For the operation of the land question in Palestine, see the biographies of Abu Jamal and Ghada in this volume.) One hundred thirty-two years of French rule had seriously weakened the Islam of the urban *ulama*, even as it strengthened the power of the rural marabouts (Sufi holy men), many of whom agreed to collaborate with the French. (Julia Clancy-Smith's double biography, "The Shaykh and his Daughter," chapter 8 of this volume, introduces us to one such maraboutic family.)

Independent Algeria faced extraordinary challenges: a galloping birth rate, few trained professionals, and a fractured elite. Nonetheless, the first decades were dramatic and surprising. Algeria became a model socialist state, with a vigorous petroleum sector and a dynamic agricultural sector. Third Worldism, the belief that there was a middle road to development between the American and the Soviet models, served Algeria well at first. But, by the death of President Boumedienne in 1978, this model was foundering, not only in Algeria but in all states, like Egypt, Syria, and Iraq, that had pursued it. Jobs, housing, and education were lacking, and there was a large and growing underclass of semi-educated youth. The rise to power of President Chadli Bendjedid (1979–92) coincided with the end of the Cold War (the Soviet Union had been a key ally) and a sharp increase in corruption. Eventually, Algerian nationalism, which had been the bedrock of the state, imploded, and its main institutions (the army, the Party of the National Liberation Front, and the national trade union—the UGTA) splintered. Riots in Algiers in October 1988 marked the emergence of political Islam on the national stage.

Nonetheless, the eruption of Islamist violence in 1992 after the cancelled legislative elections came as a major shock. Just two years later, Muslim parties headed by the Islamic Salvation Front (FIS) won a majority of the seats in the first round of the elections. The army forced President Chadli to resign, cancelled the second round of the elections, legally dissolved the FIS, and arrested its leaders. The subsequent civil strife led to many massacres, in which not only the Armed Islamic Group but also the state itself have been implicated. In this context, disadvantaged young men like Ahmed Chaabani became militant Islamist leaders. More than thirty thousand Algerians have been killed to date (including hundreds of journalists and intellectuals). Algerian journalist Baya Gacemi's portrait of Nadia must therefore be understood as an act of courage. Algeria's collapse has had an enormous human cost and is still ongoing. The biography of Nadia provides a window into just how high this cost has been.

The portraits of both Nadia and Ahmed can be usefully contrasted with others in the volume. Nadia's life may be looked at in the perspective of Sumaya, Ghada, and Khanom Gohary, among others. Ahmed's situation, if not his response to it, resembles that of other rural young men chronicled in this volume, including Nasir, Gulab, Haddou, and the Iranians Rostam and Mehdi. —Eds.

Eucalyptus is a village twelve miles from Algiers in the rich Mitidja Plain. Its chief crop is citrus fruits (oranges, lemons, mandarin oranges).* Every year its fields were verdant and its orchards green. Hai Bounab is a hamlet in this commune. Starting with the French settlers, the Mitidja region has always been enormously productive. To see this little bit of paradise one might wonder how the people who live here could be provoked to violence.

---

*For reasons that will become evident, neither Eucalyptus, Hai Bounab, nor Douira can be found on a map. Nonetheless, Nadia's story is true.

After the independence of Algeria in 1962, the new socialist state began to redistribute the land to those who worked it. Under the agrarian reform program, the lives of peasants were completely transformed. Agricultural laborers became salaried workers on the ex-colonial lands and enjoyed the same status as factory workers. It is here that Nadia lived, and here that her father, an agricultural worker on one of these large agricultural estates, worked. Neither of Nadia's parents had known French colonialism at first hand. (Her father was a small child in 1962, when Algeria gained its independence, while her mother was born in 1961). Thus, their primary experience was with Algerian state socialism.

Nadia's parents were cousins. They had grown up in Douira, a farm village ten miles west of Algiers. Their parents had decided that they would marry each other when they were still young. Nadia's mother was barely fourteen when they got married in 1975, while her father was seventeen. Nadia was born a year later in 1976. They were a poor peasant family, but their home was filled with warmth and affection. This greatly helped them to deal with the frustrations and privations of daily life. In any event, they weren't in abject poverty. Since her father was a farm worker at the time, they always had lots of seasonal fruits and vegetables. They managed to get eggs, milk, and sometimes meat and honey from the farms nearby, and traded their surplus with one another. The farms of the region produced a variety of crops on their several hundred acres, as well as sheep and cattle. The socialist agricultural revolution, which had begun in 1974, was then at its height. It called for a redistribution of land, in accord with the slogan "The land to those who work it."

Hai Bounab consisted of three small groups of houses in a village of about one hundred dwellings. In each house lived two or three married sons and their families, together with grandparents, aunts, and sometimes cousins. They all belonged to the same tribe, which had come from the region of Médea, sixty miles south of Algiers, and they all got along together well. Their happiest day was in 1992 when for the first time a school was opened in their village. They all pitched in to share the cost of the celebration. The workers who had built the school were also invited, along with the employees of the city government and the local police. The villagers were especially happy for their daughters, who would no longer have to walk across the muddy fields to get to school and come home in the winter after dark.

The people of Hai Bounab were all Muslims. Before the Armed Islamic Group came on the scene in 1992, they practiced just what their tradition told them. Nothing more. Indeed, rather casually, it must be said. There wasn't even a mosque in the hamlet. The few people who wanted to attend Friday prayers had to go to the mosque in Eucalyptus. Mostly, it was the old people who did so, taking advantage of the trip to meet their friends along the way. It was the same with politics—few people were interested. They had too much work in the fields to waste time like that. A few of the neighbors had joined an Islamic political party, the Islamic Salvation Front (known as the FIS), before it was outlawed by the government in 1992, but even its members restricted their activities to the main town, Eucalyptus, and didn't come to Hai Bounab.

At first, the people of Hai Bounab had believed in the victory of the Armed Islamic Group, known in Algeria by the acronym GIA. Or at least they claimed to. Nadia must have believed in it, since she agreed to marry Ahmed Chaabani, the "*emir*" of the hamlet and its surrounding territory. Anyway, the people of the village all contributed to the victory of the GIA, both by their silence and through their active support. For more than three years (1992–95), despite their many abuses of power, the Armed Islamic Group was the law in the village. The villagers only rebelled against the GIA after they began to terrorize them. The changeover, when it came, was as rapid as it was violent. But, as we shall see, by this time Nadia was no longer aware of the consequences of her actions. She just loved her husband and pardoned everything he did. And, as we shall see, she paid a steep price for this.

By the time she was sixteen, in 1992, Nadia was quite a handful. The eldest of nine, she had quit going to school at the age of ten because she just wasn't interested in it. In all, she attended school for only three years. At the time, the school was far away and there was no bus. Furthermore, her parents, like many others with large families, preferred to keep their daughters home to help their mothers. Like other girls her age, Nadia loved playing and laughing with her girlfriends from the village, and she took advantage of every opportunity to escape the vigilance of her parents. Very early on, she became interested in boys. While her parents tried to keep an eye on her, Nadia was very clever and had a strong will. When her mother would send her to fetch water at the village fountain (since running water wasn't available in the village at that time), Nadia persuaded her girlfriends who also had to fetch water to band together in a group. This way, they felt better able to meet boys. Nadia became their acknowledged leader.

Far different was the background of her future husband, Ahmed Chaabani. Before coming to Hai Bounab, he had lived with his mother and his brothers in an isolated village in the Mitidja Plain. Ahmed's family was originally from Kef Lakhdar in the Tellian atlas near the city of Médea, and that's where he grew up. His father was a well-known philanderer, which gave him a poor reputation at Benramdane. Ahmed's uncles all disliked his father because he brought shame upon them. Ahmed's father had a series of affairs with women from nearby villages. This eventually provoked the wronged husband of one of these women to kill him. The man invited him to dinner and put poison in his food. Ahmed's father died several days later, suffering terribly. It was only when it was noticed that his hair was falling out

that it occurred to his family to take him to the hospital. The doctor diag-
nosed poison, but by then it was too late to save him. Although Ahmed's
uncles had a strong hunch who had done it, they didn't go to the police.
The family was so ashamed of the affair that they preferred to keep quiet.
At the time, Ahmed's mother was two months pregnant with her fourth son
(Ahmed was the third). As Nadia learned later from Ahmed, his uncles
threw his mother out of the house on the day of the funeral because they'd
always hated her. However, they kept custody of Ahmed and his brothers.

Ahmed and his two brothers were very upset by their mother's departure,
especially since it coincided with their father's death. What made it worse
was that their uncles and aunts treated them like slaves. Although the boys
were children, they were viewed as labor power. Ahmed's oldest brother was
about eight at the time, and Ahmed was scarcely three. Being the youngest,
he was the wildest, and was beaten regularly when he got out of line. Despite
his age, he was sent with his brothers into the pasture to look after the sheep
and cattle. He often stayed there the whole day, often without eating. When
he and his brothers came home in the evening, they were given the left-
overs, if there were any. Also, Ahmed and his brothers weren't allowed to go
to school, even though their cousins, who lived in the same house, were.
Their uncle explained that he couldn't afford to send all the boys to school.
Someone had to stay home and look after the animals. Somehow, Ahmed
managed to learn the Arabic alphabet at a local Quran school he attended
for a few months. Building on this shaky foundation, he was later able to
learn to read and write. More than anything, Ahmed loved the thought of
making money. Fairly soon he was able to convince other stock raisers in the
area to allow him to look after their flocks and herds along with his uncle's
animals. Along with his other brothers he had but one goal—to earn
enough to rejoin their mother. This they finally managed to do when
Ahmed was fifteen years old.

The Chaabani brothers were hard workers. Feeling stronger due to the
presence of her four sons—including the one born after her husband was
murdered—their mother also set to work earning money. She made candies
that her sons sold in the nearby markets. She also had some laying hens and
sold eggs to the villagers. Spending little and saving most of what they made,
the Chaabanis accumulated a bit of money. Nonetheless, it wasn't enough
to permit them to buy or rent a real house and escape the chicken coop
where they lived. One day, fortune smiled on Ahmed. He found a wallet in
the street containing 30,000 dinars (equivalent to about $600, a fortune at
the time). Gossiping neighbors claimed he had stolen it, which he swore to
God was not the case. This money, together with their small nest egg,
enabled the family to buy a tumbledown shack in Hai Bounab right next
door to Nadia's family.

At Hai Bounab, Mrs. Chaabani continued her moneymaking schemes. Thanks to their businesses, the family was able to buy a van that the brothers used to start a bus line between Hai Bounab and Baraki (three miles away). Later, they opened a shop in one of the rooms of their house, where the second son sold groceries. Then they bought two cows and began selling milk, yogurt, and butter. Their mother managed all of the family's money. Little by little, the Chabaanis became one of the wealthiest families in the hamlet. They finished the construction of their house and furnished it comfortably. By the early 1990s, they were living relatively well in comparison to other villagers.

Just about this time, when Ahmed was around eighteen, he took to disappearing for days at a time. He wanted to make a lot of money, and fast. Not having the commercial spirit of the rest of the family, he began to organize trips with his friends to as far away as Setif, a city located some two hundred miles east of Algiers, to buy black market goods which he'd resell in Algiers. These included dishes, clothing, food—all of foreign origin. Even though he had no passport, Ahmed figured out how to go to Libya on buying trips using just his national identity card and a driver's license by taking the back roads into the desert along the Libyan/Algerian border. He would returned with jewelry, cosmetics, even cars. The cars he resold, or dismantled for parts.

Nadia and Ahmed met for the first time when Nadia dropped in to see if she could help Mrs. Chabaani doing household chores. From that moment, Ahmed and Nadia fell hopelessly in love. When their relationship, which was against the local mores, became too obvious, Nadia's parents decided to send her to live with her uncles at Cheraga, a village close to Algiers. There, she remained under the watchful eye of her uncles, her slightest act under their surveillance. By being seen flirting in public, she had brought shame upon her family. For two years she didn't see Ahmed, though she received news of him from time to time. One day in 1992 her father came to tell her that Ahmed had asked to marry her. He'd already done so twice before but had been refused. In the meantime, Ahmed had become an Islamist and a member of the GIA. He was now the terror of the village and his word was law.

Although Nadia's father was still totally opposed to the marriage, he was frightened of the GIA like everyone else. "If I don't allow the two of them to marry, I know Ahmed will use it against me," he told his wife. Instead of provoking Ahmed to kidnap Nadia and putting up with the shame this would bring, he decided to bow to Ahmed's will. The years apart from Ahmed had not changed Nadia's feelings for him, and she was happy to see him again, never considering the possible consequences. Anyway, she refused to believe what people told her about him. Her brothers told her that Ahmed had become a terrorist, but she was convinced it was just a lie they told to make her break up with him.

While Nadia was living with her uncle near Algiers, a new person had arrived in Hai Bounab, a man named Rabah. He had been sent by the GIA to take over the hamlet and its inhabitants. The previous year, although the FIS and the other Islamist parties had won the December 1991 legislative elections, the government had annulled the results and declared a state of emergency. Outraged by this, some of the Islamists had begun a guerrilla campaign aimed at overthrowing the government and setting up an Islamic republic. As soon as Rabah arrived in Hai Bounab, he had sought to recruit some of the youth of the village, while his wife and three daughters tried to convert the women of the village. Rabah had no trouble finding a few men ready to join the GIA. His preaching appealed especially to unemployed youth who were fed up with the peasant lifestyle and were ready for anything, including taking on the government. Until their conversion, many had been ignorant of the rudiments of the Islamic faith. Overnight, thanks to the teachings of Rabah, they became pillars of the faith. He taught them to interpret the Quran according to the approach favored by the Islamist movements. They saw it as the source of a political program, not just of religious and ethical precepts. Among themselves, the members of "the group" addressed each other as Brother. By giving the appearance of justice and egalitarianism, they had managed to take over the town. They resolved disputes between neighbors or even within families. For whatever reason—fear, cowardice, or conviction—the villagers now proclaimed their support for the GIA. Those who had reservations kept quiet, or left town. Rabah, in the meantime, not only taught them the Islamist version of the faith, he also watched them closely so as to identify those who might be willing to take up arms when the time came.

One of those he selected was Ahmed Chaabani. This was just the sort of thing Ahmed needed. Previously, the people of Hai Bounab had regarded him with disdain because of his involvement in illegal activities. Suddenly, by joining the local GIA, he became a somebody. His whole attitude changed virtually overnight. He became polite and deferential to his neighbors. In return, the people of the hamlet obeyed his commands and no one dared to cross him. Two days before his wedding to Nadia, Ahmed built a rudimentary house with cement block walls and a tin roof for them to live in. (There being no zoning regulations at the time, no one bothered with land titles or building permits. All one needed to do was to construct some walls around a space and call it home).

It was on her wedding day that Nadia became acquainted with the new Ahmed. Overnight, his behavior toward her changed. In the first week of their marriage, after Ahmed had been away the whole day, he appeared suddenly in the middle of the night. Alone with his new wife, he admonished Nadia severely: "Have you said your prayers? If you come in looking like that, it is because you haven't done so and are impure." He then began yelling at her, expressing his shocked that she wore makeup, dyed her hair, and plucked her eyebrows. He began praying and calling upon God, before finally proclaiming: "From now on, I forbid you to go to the hairdresser. And this is the last time I want to see you with makeup. You can no longer go to the women's bath [the *hammam*]. To do so is a sin. A woman must not take off her clothes even in front of other women."

Nadia began to wonder if everything her brothers had told her about Ahmed wasn't in fact true. So to test him she asked: "Sing me a song of Cheb Hasni [a *rai* singer who had been killed by the GIA] the way you used to. Do you know that I cried the day he died?" Ahmed replied in a voice that chilled her to the bone: "I forbid you to cry for this *taghout* [tyrant]. He deserved what he got. His songs were leading the youth away from the right path [*al-tariq al-mustaqim*]." Then he ordered her to stand behind him and to pray with him. They prayed for two hours. After they had finished, he picked up a Quran from the night table and told her to read him some *suras* (chapters).

It became clear to Nadia at that moment that Ahmed had become a different man and that she had made a big mistake in marrying him. But she thought she could change him. What really counted for her at that time was to be his wife and to live with him. That same night he began to talk about his "brothers" and what was expected of her: "You have become their sister. You must make their meals and wash their clothes. In this way, you will contribute to the establishment of an Islamic state in Algeria." Someone had to do it, he reasoned, since "the brothers" were fighting the tyrant, as God had commanded. "You must help them in this cause. In this way, all who support them also participate indirectly in the struggle. When I become *emir*, you'll have the title of "mother of the believers" [*umm al-muminin*] and God will include you among the elect." He succeeded in convincing her. This kind of talk frightened Nadia, but she also found it seductive. Ahmed got up and left before dawn. As he departed, he said, "When I return, you must have breakfast ready for me and my brothers."

From that day on, Nadia became the maid for the group. She cooked their meals, washed their clothes, and put them up in her home. This she did out of love for Ahmed, but also out of pride. Some months later, she accepted her new status as "mother of the believers," the title that the members of the GIA bestowed on the wives of its leaders. But even before this, the men had begun requiring her to prepare more and more refined and time-consuming dishes. They had all come from poor families and were happy to enjoy their new situation, and to acquire things they had previously only dreamed about. It was Nadia's duty to provide them. She spent entire nights cooking their meals for the next day. She even had to bake bread for them (instead of getting it at the bakers). Each time they came, she had to make a holiday meal. There were always ten or twelve brothers around the table, and not always the same ones. They changed depending upon the GIA's activities in the area. She only knew a few of them by name. When they were around, she wasn't allowed to speak to them. Nadia was only allowed to see them through a curtain. According to their code of conduct, they weren't permitted to see the wife of one of the group, even if she was veiled. If one of them wanted to address her, he had to turn his back to her. After several weeks of this, Nadia felt harassed. She was spending all her time in the kitchen. Even when they weren't there, she couldn't sleep because her husband ordered her to remain awake in case he and his friends dropped in.

In contrast to Nadia's mixed feelings about her marriage, the families of Hai Bounab regarded the wedding of Ahmed and Nadia as a godsend, just as it was for the local GIA group. From that moment on, she alone would be responsible for the unrewarding job of providing meals for the group. Previously, the other families in the hamlet had all shared this task. Those with the means to do so paid for everything. The poorer families took turns preparing the food, while "the brothers" did the shopping. It was each family's duty to invite them to eat. It was regarded as an honor for the villagers to have "the brothers" to lunch or dinner. It was also a way of staying in the good graces of the GIA.

Everywhere the GIA spread, they established new rules. They banned schoolteachers from teaching in French. Those who refused were threatened with death. Most, the majority of whom were women, opted to accept this order. Once they had reached the age of nine, girls weren't allowed to go to school or to go out at all without putting on a veil. The children of Hai Bounab were organized to spy on their neighbors. At least until the GIA burned down most of the village schools in the area, boys were allowed to go to school. The latter were readily induced to work for the group, whom they idealized. They saw them as powerful role models who laid down the law and whom everyone feared. Also, "the brothers" always had lots of money and nice new cars, which they stole from the wealthy. They got their money through a kind of protection racket. Everyone in the neighboring village was required to pay a "revolutionary tax." Or else. Those who had no money gave what they could—blankets, mattresses, dishes, anything. At first, the GIA had helped the poor, but as time progressed they became a burden. They began to intimidate the villagers into cooperating with their plans.

From the moment they arrived in Hai Bounab, the local GIA leaders were interested in Ahmed. This was because of his reputation as a fighter, as well as his knowledge of the hamlet and the surrounding region. But especially because he was from Kef Lakhdar, an Islamist fief in the Mitidja region. This region was very important for the GIA. The groups from

Algiers and the rest of the Mitidja had lots of connections with the people of this town. Because Rabah knew that Ahmed had grown up there and that some of his family still lived there, he asked him to be the liaison between Hai Bounab and Kef Lakhdar. Ahmed had another thing going for him—he didn't yet have a police record and, as a result, he was able to travel freely. At first, Ahmed had shown little interest in religion or in becoming a militant. Indeed, quite the opposite. So, before he was accepted into the group, Rabah decided to test his discipline. He told Ahmed to attend mosque regularly. Only after he'd proved himself, did Rabah accept him as a member.

Ahmed quickly became a key member of the group. Initially, his role was to pass on information. Only after the group felt he was completely trustworthy did they allow him to come to their hideout. This is where Ahmed would bring the meals prepared by the neighbors the times when they didn't want to leave their hideout. He also did errands that required him to go to Algiers to get things from the department stores or particular specialty shops. Or he was sent to black-market dealers—especially to get the clothing and other things the GIA members required. To help him get around, the group gave him a motor scooter. According to the theorists of the GIA, men and women each had their own prescribed garb. Ahmed's job was to bring the group a special amber-scented Saudi perfume, as well as *siwak* (special twigs for brushing the teeth), henna, kohl, copies of the Quran, and religious tracts. He also brought jeans that they cut off at the knee so that they conformed to the Islamist dress code and didn't bother them when they ran. Usually, the members wore Afghan-style baggy *sirwal*, though some preferred jeans. Over the jeans, members would wear green or maroon *kamis* tunics. When they ran, they'd tuck the *kamis* into their belts. Some of them wore green or black turbans. Sometimes they'd get local tailors to make their outfits. The most clothes-conscious members wore traditional baggy *sirwal* pants, puffed out and embroidered around the knee with silk thread. For their part, women were instructed to wear dark-colored long dresses that covered their forearms and their necks and were cut so as not to reveal a woman's shape. Above all, women members were to avoid anything transparent or tight fitting.

Soon after they were married, Nadia became pregnant. Yet the news had no effect on her husband's comings and goings or on his insistence that she cook for the group and put them up whenever he wanted. Ahmed explained that the group needed to be together, in case of a nighttime police raid. They dug a hiding place in the courtyard, where they slept. They even wore their running shoes to bed so as to be able to escape in case of danger. At Nadia's insistence, Ahmed was persuaded to take off his shoes from time to time so that she could wash his feet, which gave off such an odor that they made Nadia gag. When he was around, he didn't let Nadia sleep under the blankets, so that she could remain awake and could listen for noises. "Fighters need their sleep to be ready for the *jihad*," he told her, "but you, you must watch over them. You can't allow yourself to slip into a deep sleep." During the day, he and his brothers went out to launch attacks.

The GIA, however, did not think Ahmed was sufficiently committed. So he was ordered to go underground three months after he married Nadia. One day, men Nadia did not know came looking for him. Ahmed disappeared for a week that time. When he returned, he seemed a changed man. He'd lost a lot of weight; he wore kohl around his eyes, dressed his hair with olive oil, and wore a strong amber-scented perfume. He wore a green *kamis* (tunic) and a black turban. He also had a sawed-off shotgun slung across his shoulder. During the week he'd been in the mountains, he'd neither eaten nor drunk. This was to test his ability to put up with the rough guerrilla lifestyle. His body was bruised all over. He explained that he had been beaten every day with all sorts of objects to gauge his ability to endure pain and test his resistance to torture. He'd learned how to shoot and use weapons. Ahmed became a guerrilla. His initiation took place a scant few weeks prior to the November 1995 presidential elections.

Ahmed for the most part refrained from telling Nadia what he was up to, since he knew she hated violence. But sometimes when he was in a good mood and she pressed him with questions, he'd let some details slip out. On days when he returned very pleased with himself, she understood that he and his brothers had just killed a lot of people. "Victory over the *taghout* is coming along well," he'd say in a triumphal tone. Once, he told her how one of his friends had killed his own brother, because the brother had allowed himself to be drafted into the army. One time, when the latter was home on leave, he ran into his brother, the GIA member, who straightaway cut his throat in front of their mother. She almost went mad as a result.

The first murder to take place at Hai Bounab was that of young Nacer, a teenager who was fifteen years old. He liked to hang out with the self-defense group that the authorities had organized in the hamlet. However, the GIA had ordered the town's inhabitants to have nothing to do with Nacer or his family, not even to speak to them, and they obeyed this order. One evening, the GIA group came to his house and asked his mother to cook them dinner. Of course, she did so. After the meal, they got up and asked Nacer to step outside with them. They put a bullet in his head right outside the house. He was buried the next day and no one ever said anything to the police.

Another time, the group came across a man in an orchard. "What do you do for a living?" they asked him. The identity card they found in his pocket established that he was a policeman. Since they had him dead to rights, he couldn't lie, but he tried to wriggle out of it by saying that he was a cook. But this was precisely the wrong thing to say. "Well," they said, "then you must be the one who fattens the hogs." No matter what he said, he couldn't have avoided what came next. As Ahmed told Nadia later, they "had fun with him." They began by poking out his eye with a rusty wire they found on the ground. "We'll let you keep your other eye so you can see what's going to happen to you," they said. Then they began to chop him up, starting with his toes and finger joints, ending up with his body, which they cut into pieces. Ahmed laughed out loud when he told Nadia this story.

In the group, there was a professional killer whose job it was to torture and kill under Rabah's orders. He was a fifteen-year-old boy, very short in stature. He had become an emotional automaton after witnessing his four brothers (all of whom were GIA members) gunned down in a battle with the army. Soon afterward, a helicopter bombed their house, killing their mother inside. He was the only one to survive. Ever since, he'd been obsessed with vengeance and killing.

To justify his actions, Ahmed had obtained a *fatwa* (an Islamic legal opinion). He told Nadia, "It's not me who kills. When my hand throws a bomb, it's not me who does it. It is God who has ordered me to do it and who guides my hand." When Nadia asked him whether it didn't bother him that so many innocent people died every day as a result of their operations, he responded coldly: "This is a war. There are always innocent victims. The people participate in this way, in paying with their lives. Anyway, the innocents are lucky to die this way, since they will go straight to paradise. They are martyrs to the cause."

Initially, the local police were unbelievably lax. Maybe they weren't prepared for the fact that they were facing an armed insurrection. Perhaps they were afraid. Whatever the case, they certainly knew about the armed groups. They also knew that a GIA group ate and slept in Hai Bounab, but they made no serious effort to verify this. When they heard that someone had been killed, they didn't ask how it happened or who did it. The violence and abuse continued, and the people, believing they had been abandoned by the authorities, began to think that the GIA was the stronger and started to support them. After Rabah was killed in a shootout in July 1995, Ahmed became the GIA *emir* in the village.

In November 1995, following presidential elections in which General Liamine Zeroual became head of the Algerian state, things began to change. The presidential election, which took place in a climate of violence, marked a major turning point. The unbelievably high rate of voter participation showed the GIA that the people were against them. Also, the longer it took the GIA to seize power, the more murderous they became and the more their actions seemed incomprehensible. The election results for the first time made Algerians (especially those living in the countryside) understand that they had succeeded in standing up to the GIA by going to the polls, and that they could also expel them from their bases. After that, they began to ask the police for weapons and to join self-defense groups to fight the GIA. Nadia's life changed utterly from that time onward. As the "wife of the *emir*" and the "mother of the believers," she'd become used to being treated as a princess by the villagers. Now she became an outcast. The people of Hai Bounab no longer wanted anything to do with her. Soon, Hai Bounab became a hostile place for Nadia and her family members, who were forced to flee the village.

Ahmed's promotion to "*emir*" thus came just as the tide began to turn and the people began to give up supporting the GIA. The previous two or three years, during which time the group was able to act with impunity, was now definitively over. For Ahmed and Nadia, the November 1995 presidential elections marked the reversal of their fortunes. Soon after the elections Ahmed took to the hills to escape the police, leaving Nadia, by this time very pregnant, at home. For the next three months, the group was hunted, on the run, always afraid. Nadia, who encountered the police every day, was humiliated on a daily basis.

Moving from one hiding place to another, their lives became a series of desperate escapes. Nonetheless, Ahmed continued his terrorist activities. In the village, no one bothered Ahmed until the day (mentioned above) that he and his gang killed a fifteen-year-old boy because his brother was in the self-defense force. After that atrocity, the police finally decided to put an end to the group in Hai Bounab. Nadia herself began a life on the run, with no one willing to take her in. Not knowing where to turn, she wandered the lanes of the hamlet by day and knocked at people's doors by night to find a place to sleep. About a week went by when Ahmed suddenly reappeared. He decided to take her to a village that was completely pro-GIA, and where the police didn't dare to show their faces. But soon he decided to leave that village because he was afraid of staying in one spot too long, leaving Nadia behind.

One day, while Nadia was wandering the streets of Hai Bounab looking for her mother-in-law, she saw her in the distance walking along the dirt road, her head bare (she who never removed her veil) and covered with blood. Periodically, she would stop and throw herself to the ground and roll in the dirt, waving her arms about madly. It was obvious she had no idea what she was doing. Nadia saw her approach two bloody corpses by the side of the road and kneel down beside them. She tried to hug them, all the while wailing loudly. Then she got up and walked about aimlessly, roaring like a wild beast. To get back at Ahmed, the self-defense forces had killed his two older brothers and dumped their bodies by the side of the road.

Not knowing where else to go, Nadia walked aimlessly along the road, crying. Almost everyone who saw her—those who previously had treated her like royalty—closed their windows and doors in her face. Another time, Ahmed, who would come to see her periodically when he was able, took her to stay at a farm in Ouled Allel, a nearby village. He put her up with the widow of another terrorist who lived there with her children and her mother-in-law.

The women spent their days cooking for the armed groups of the region, who were more numerous than in Hai Bounab. But their house was really too small to shelter so many people. Nadia slept with Ahmed in the kitchen with another couple, though it had neither doors nor windows. A thin curtain separated the two beds. Seeing that this could not last, Ahmed sent Nadia to stay with a family in Bertouta, yet another village in the region.

The new family was very wealthy. They were delighted to welcome Nadia to their home. The Ghali family was well known and highly respected locally. After dinner, the wife prepared a bath for Nadia in their large and luxurious bathroom where everything was made of marble. She gave Nadia clean clothes to wear that belonged to one of her daughters. Then she asked: "Would you be willing to meet my sons, or do you prefer not to be around them?" Nadia agreed to meet them, but wouldn't shake their hands. Mrs. Ghali had six sons, one of whom was underground and a second in the GIA. The whole family, men and women, each in its own way, helped the GIA. They were pious and deeply observant. Their daughters spent the evenings reading the Quran. The boys took care of the family business and supported the Algerian Islamist cause. Although Nadia was happy living at the Ghalis, after two weeks Ahmed came and took her away again. The family was too bourgeois for him, and cramped his style. But the two weeks spent there were for Nadia the calmest and most relaxed she'd been since she'd married Ahmed. It was the only period in her married life when she was able to sleep as much as she wanted in a comfortable bed in a heated house, and where she wasn't made to work like a beast of burden.

The next house that Ahmed found for Nadia belonged to an old woman who had lived all by herself in Hai Bounab since her sons had fled to Algiers to escape the GIA. The woman had refused to join her sons in the city, or to abandon her home. One day, while she was away, Ahmed and his "brothers" knocked down the door and installed Nadia and Fatma, the wife of another GIA member, and her three-year-old daughter. When the woman returned home, they threatened to kill her if she refused to take them in. "We don't dare leave two young women by themselves. It would be best if you kept them company, as if you were their mother." The brothers were afraid that the police and self-defense forces, knowing the women to be alone, might come and bother them. Later on, they returned with a truck full of goods. There was enough to fill an entire house: furniture, a stove, bedding, blankets, dishes. They also brought two large boxes full of food. They had stolen everything from the homes of two members of the self-defense forces whom they'd killed the day before. "It's war booty," they explained. In this way, "the group" spent two weeks living normally. On this occasion, they even organized the wedding of one of their number. They gave the bride a complete set of furniture and household goods. But, as before, this period of calm did not last. One day the old woman went to the police and told them her story.

She even embellished it a bit. Two days later, the entire household was awakened at dawn to the sound of gunfire. This happened in March 1996.

After the police had observed their comings and goings for the preceding two days, combined elements of the army, the police, and the self-defense groups had surrounded the house and launched their attack at around 6 A.M. But, as was their habit, a member of the group had been on guard outside, and his shots alerted the others of the danger. Ahmed and his men numbered nine altogether. Fatma was sleeping upstairs with her husband. From the sound of the first shots, they knew that someone had betrayed them. Ahmed and his buddies scattered. Since houses were built right next to each other in that neighborhood, it was easy to escape by jumping from one window to another. Of course, the terrorized neighbors cared more about their own safety and didn't make a peep. At any rate, they feared the GIA more than the police. Once Ahmed and his associates had reached the nearby orchards, they were able to get away since they knew the territory like the backs of their hands. The two women and their children were left to face the police alone and were led away. The police then invited the old woman and her daughter to return to their house.

Terrified at the thought of losing her husband or betraying him, Nadia wished she were dead. At the police station, she thought of Ahmed and his family, her parents, and her nine brothers and sisters, whose fate now lay in her hands. The police treated her respectfully and with consideration. When the commanding officer began to interrogate her, she confirmed that her husband was a member of the GIA and a terrorist. He began to question Fatma and Nadia in turn. The rest of the time they were left together in the same room, which allowed them to keep one another's spirits up. Later that evening, they were taken to the police headquarters at Baraki, the main city of the district. There, the two women were asked to take off their jewelry, belts, and cloaks. Fatma and her daughter were put in an office that had a bed. Nadia was put in a tiny cell with just enough room to spread out a mattress. It had no windows or light and was filthy. Although they were aware that she was pregnant, the police gave her a bloodstained foam mattress to lie upon. The blood was fresh. She felt a moment of panic but was too exhausted to protest. She took off her veil and used it as a sheet. Images of what she'd seen when she'd gone downstairs to the toilets swam before her eyes—naked men covered with blood lying on the floor of a sort of cellar. Stagnant puddles of water were on the floor. She wondered if she could put up with such things. She was lucky—she was not tortured. She spent three nights in the cell without eating. Meanwhile, Fatma slept in a clean bed with her daughter and didn't miss a meal. Her girl was given powdered milk for babies that the police brought for her. She also received soap to wash herself and her daughter and laundry soap to do their clothes. The police chief of Baraki was nice to her.

On the third day, the two women were taken to the regional court at Blida where they were remanded to the prosecutor. By a stroke of luck, the prosecutor turned out to be a distant relative of Nadia's father with whom she was on good terms. He knew Nadia very well. When he saw her arrive, he laughed out loud: "Couldn't you find a better husband than this hoodlum?" Then he reassured her, "Don't be afraid, I'll take care of you." The two women were questioned by the judge and sent back to the police station at Eucalyptus. They came out of it well. The captain of the police at Eucalyptus summoned Nadia's father and ordered him to take the two women with him, but not to let either of them return to Hai Bounab. "Send your daughter away," he insisted, "no matter where. And take Fatma back to her parents." The two women were both put on parole.

As soon as they were outside, Nadia's father told her that forty GIA thugs had come to their house the previous evening and were still there. The group had learned from their spies that the police had released Nadia and Fatma. They were waiting for the women to take them away, and in the meantime they were holding Nadia's brothers hostage. In spite of this, her father gave Nadia a choice between going elsewhere and putting her brothers at risk, or rejoining her husband and his friends and defying the orders of the police. It was a cruel choice. After a moment's thought, her father decided to take Nadia and Fatma to the home of a woman he knew, who put them up for the night. He returned the next morning, his face marked by despair and worry. He hadn't been able to reach a decision. Although he had never in his life shown any courage or determination, now he had to choose between the anger of the police and that of the terrorists. He didn't hesitate for long. He decided to face the police, since they seemed less inhumane than the GIA. "At the worst, the police will throw me in prison or beat me, whereas the terrorists will slit the throats of my wife and children right before my eyes," he said to himself.

Nadia and Fatma were received as queens by the GIA group, their families, and hangers-on. They departed with "the group" and were set up in the home of a woman GIA supporter in a nearby hamlet, Ouled Allel. This woman, who had five adult daughters and three teenaged sons, helped the group a great deal, even though it was against her husband's wishes. She housed and fed them and provided logistical support to Ahmed and his gang. Her militancy had even led her to construct a virtually invisible hiding place on the roof of her house for group members on the run. Yet, despite her genuine welcome, there were too many people in the little house. Their host family numbered ten persons. In addition, all the GIA members in the district regularly took their meals there.

Ahmed decided to send Nadia back to the Ghali family in Bertouta. She hoped she would be able to stay longer this time in their large and comfortable house, the only place where she had ever felt really relaxed. But no sooner had she arrived than she was literally chased away by Mrs. Ghali and her children, who treated her as if she had the plague. The house itself looked completely different, as the exterior walls were pockmarked with bullet holes. As Nadia later discovered, several days before, there had been a firefight between the security forces and a GIA group who had been staying with the Ghali family. One of the Ghali boys had been arrested. Disappointed, Nadia returned to the house in Ouled Allel where she'd been staying. That night, Ahmed told her he'd found them yet another house. Even though it was raining hard, they decided to leave right away since they suspected that the authorities were close behind them.

Pleased by the thought that she might have a roof over her head, Nadia went with him, not knowing where they were going. The two eventually entered a more isolated area with neither electricity nor paved roads. To keep from attracting attention, they had to cut across the fields and take scarcely used paths. After the first few minutes, Nadia found herself in mud up to her knees in the pelting rain. Her pregnancy was in a difficult phase and she began to hemorrhage and to suffer from severe pains. Ahmed gave her his hand to hold her up. It wasn't enough. Shivering with the cold and doubled over by cramps, she had a hard time wading through the mud in the dark. Ahmed tried to carry her on his shoulders, but he too was struggling with the mud and the darkness. After fifteen minutes, Ahmed set Nadia down, but in the dark and in his haste he placed her directly in a hole filled with muddy water. Instantly, she was soaked to the skin and her clothes became waterlogged. He carried her the rest of the way till they reached the house of one of his relatives, where he and his group were staying. There, Ahmed left her. But when he and his men departed, they ran right into a police patrol. In the resulting gun battle, Ahmed was wounded in the right arm. Several days later, Nadia found out that he was still alive and on the run. She knew she would not see him for a while, so she decided to try to return to her parents' house. Her mother agreed to take her in only on the condition that she register with the authorities. Nadia agreed. She would not see Ahmed again for seven months.

In August 1996, Nadia gave birth to a boy in the local hospital. Never had she felt so alone, so depressed. No one came to see her except her elderly grandmother, who was quite ill. Nadia gazed for a long time at her newborn son, who she had wanted so much. She was so upset, she refused to nurse him. Her mother only came to see her when it was time for her to come home from the hospital. The strain by this time had begun to affect her father. He was waiting for her at the door. "Take your baby and get out of here," he yelled. Fortunately, her mother was able to persuade him to let her stay while she regained her strength.

Seven months later, Ahmed returned, in the middle of the night, as was his habit. He arrived with three others. While two men stood guard outside, the other one came in with him. Ahmed had changed a lot. His beard now reached to his chest. He wore a black turban and an Afghan-style outfit that was so dirty one could no longer tell its color, as well as a dirty maroon jacket. When he took it off, Nadia noticed that he wore crossed leather cartridge belts and that his arm was bandaged. He could still move it a little, but it was useless otherwise. A heavy atmosphere fell upon the house. Then he broke the silence, saying, "I didn't forget you. I sent you a message via my uncle telling you that I was in poor health and that I'd return as soon as possible." The message hadn't arrived. He also conceded that the local population no longer supported him. In other words, that his protection racket no longer worked and that the generous supporters who had believed in the cause had become increasingly scarce. In the countryside, things had gone from bad to worse. As the GIA continued to lose control, its tactics became increasingly violent. Its well-publicized massacres shocked everyone and no one understood why they were so cruel. When Ahmed departed at daybreak, he told Nadia that henceforth she was free to go wherever she wanted. She was sure that she had seen him for the last time.

Nadia found herself in a familiar situation. But this time she felt strangely relieved because both the police and her husband had said she could go where she wished and do what she wished. But where? Her mother agreed once again to help locate a place for her and her baby. But it was all in vain. No one wanted them. Unable to bring himself to abandon Nadia and her baby, her father offered to make a final effort—he would rent a room for himself, Nadia, and his grandson in an Algiers slum (known locally as a Bidonville). Soon the three of them had moved in together. The hardest thing to bear for Nadia was to watch her father fall deeper and deeper into despair. Away from his wife, he was lost. One could see the distress on his face. Sometimes he'd explode and yell at Nadia. As time went on, he became more and more out of control. "You married him against my will because you wanted to," he repeated over and over. "Now I'm the one who has to put up with you and your problems."

At first Nadia's father just yelled. Then, one day, he really blew up. For the first time, he hit her, with a brutality she'd never anticipated. Then he seized her by the hair and kicked her. Finally, he grabbed a large stick and beat her severely with it. Her back was all bloody. She no longer reacted or even sought to protect herself. Indifferent to her physical pain, which was paltry compared to her mental anguish, Nadia lay still on the ground and just let it happen. Once he'd discharged his rage, her father collapsed on the ground like a sack of sand and began sobbing. "For you I left my home and children. Everyone rejects me and humiliates me," he said. He wept for a long time. Then he was quiet. The sadness of the whole world could be seen on his face. Two days later, Nadia was so sick she still couldn't get out of bed. Sick with fever, she vomited. She felt pain all over her body, especially her stomach. Eventually, her father took her to a nearby hospital. But by this time she was running a high fever, and her wounds, not having been treated, had become infected. The doctors kept her in the hospital for thirteen days.

Everyone in Hai Bounab had originally supported the GIA, or at least not dissented publicly if they had any misgivings. They had been delighted to see the police and local home guards get killed. They saw anyone connected to the state in any way as rich and powerful, able to exploit connections they did not possess. But once the GIA started to attack the civilian population, including people who had nothing to do with the state, and to kill entire families randomly, this sympathy turned to horror. In August 1997 a wave of massacres of defenseless civilians occurred at Rais, Beni Messous, and Bentalha in which hundreds of people were killed. That same month, in Hai Bounab, five girls were decapitated for no apparent reason. From that point on, the villagers understood that the violence could happen to anyone. The previous week, a list had been found in an abandoned house with the names of people to be killed. Half the inhabitants of the village were on the list because they were suspected by the local GIA of wavering in their support. Once the townspeople realized that no one was exempt from the violence, they switched sides. The anti-GIA mobilization was as dramatic as their previous support for the GIA had been. The police even offered the townspeople arms to defend themselves. In retrospect, the unprecedented cruelty of the GIA, more than anything else, caused those who had previously supported them to change sides.

As for Nadia's father, his greatest desire would have been to kill Ahmed with his own hands. He asked for a gun, but the police refused to give him one as long as his son-in-law was still alive, perhaps because they did not entirely trust him. He told them that he alone knew best how to track Ahmed down, since he knew all of his hiding places. Today, Nadia's father is glad to have a rifle, like the other inhabitants of Hai Bounab.

In August 1997, lacking the funds to renew their rental contract on the Algiers apartment, Nadia sought out her uncle once again to request his assistance; this time, he didn't dare turn them away. But the family's finances were extremely limited, so her uncle's aid was destined to be short-term. There were now eleven people in the house, and of the men, only one of Nadia's brothers, who was nineteen, had a job, working on a construction site. The brother had not spoken to her for six years, ever since she had begun to keep company with Ahmed. Her father needed desperately to find a safe place for Nadia to live so that he could take his family back to Hai Bounab. But few people were willing to accept even the widow of a GIA terrorist as a tenant. In complete despair, Nadia sought assistance and sanctuary from charitable agencies, but none were able to take her in since they were all full. However, one day while she was watching TV, Nadia saw the director of a women's shelter in Algiers describe the services they provided. Inspired, Nadia traveled by bus to Algiers to see her and ended up telling the woman her life story without leaving out any details. Moved by her plight and obvious sincerity, the women's shelter agreed to provide some money to help her and her whole family. Then the director found her a room with the family of one of her friends. Today, Nadia has been placed with a different family, and has renounced all ties to her family and to the citizens of Hai Bounab. Nadia has turned the page.

The last time Nadia saw her husband alive, she noticed that he was in a lot of pain because the wound on his arm had not healed. But she also thought that his sufferings were due in part to his recognition that the GIA had lost the struggle with the Algerian state. (This would have been in January 1997). She had sensed that he just wanted everything to end, having discovered that the path he had taken led nowhere. Finally, he got what he wanted. Some time after their last meeting (probably in November or December 1997), Ahmed was killed in a skirmish with security forces in the mountains. As was their custom, his comrades cut off his head and took it with them so the authorities wouldn't be able to identify him. Only his body was ever found, located at the bottom of a ravine. Ahmed was eventually identified by the wound on his arm.

A NOTE ON SOURCES

This essay is based entirely upon the testimony of Nadia (a pseudonym), who was interviewed at length at a battered women's shelter by Algerian journalist Baya Gacemi in February 1997. The interviews were conducted in the midst of the bitter and protracted conflict that wracked Algeria in the 1990s (a struggle that has not yet come to an end). They provide the principal source for Gacemi's book, *Moi, Nadia, Femme d'un Emir du GIA* (Paris: Le Seuil, 1998), soon to be published in English translation by the University of Nebraska Press. Because of the extreme danger involved both to the villagers of Hai Bounab and to Nadia's family, their names have been changed in the text. For the same reason, the author was unable to conduct follow-up interviews, either with Nadia or in Hai Bounab. Nadia has cut all ties to her family and friends and has gone on with her life.

SUGGESTIONS FOR FUTURE READING

Most studies on Algerian history since 1990 are written in French. For a modern history of Algeria to 1980, see John Ruedy, *Modern Algeria: The Origin and Development of a Nation* (Bloomington: Indiana University Press,

1982). For an Algerian nationalist perspective, see Mohamed Bennoune, *The Making of Contemporary Algeria, 1830–1987* (Cambridge: Cambridge University Press, 1988).

On the role of women in Algeria since the revolution, see Susan Slymovics, "Hassiba Ben Bouali, If You Could See Our Algeria," *Middle East Report* 25, no. 192 (1995): 8–13.

Works in English on the struggle of the 1990s include Hugh Roberts, *The Battlefield Algeria, 1988–2002: Studies in a Broken Polity* (London: Verso, 2003); John Entelis, *Islam, Democracy, and the State in North Africa* (Bloomington: University of Indiana Press, 1997). Robert Malley, *The Call from Algeria: Third Worldism, Revolution, and the Turn to Islam* (Berkeley: University of California Press, 1997) covers the transition to Islamism.

On Islamism in Algeria, see Graham Fuller, *Algeria: The Next Fundamentalist State?* (Santa Monica: Rand Corporation, 1996); and Francois Burgat and William Dowell, *The Islamic Movement in North Africa* (Austin: University of Texas Press, 1993). For a current view, see Francois Burgat, *Face to Face with Political Islam* (London: I. B. Tauris, 2003).

On the political economy of Algeria, the reader is referred to Dirk Vanderwalle, ed., *North Africa: Development and Reform in a Changing Global Economy* (London: Macmillan, 1996); and Ali Aissaoui, *Algeria: The Political Economy of Oil and Gas* (Oxford: Oxford University Press, 2001).

Chapter 24

June Leavitt: A West Bank Settler

Tamara Neuman

Tamara Neuman's portrait of June Leavitt, an Israeli settler who lives with her husband Frank in the West Bank settlement of Kiryat Arba, draws upon her subject's published memoirs as well as her own fieldwork to craft a portrait that considers how and why this exceedingly complex individual chose to live literally and figuratively at the center of the Israeli-Palestinian conflict.

Kiryat Arba, widely considered one of the most radical of the Ultra-Orthodox Jewish settlements, was established just east of the Palestinian city of Hebron soon after the Israeli occupation of the West Bank and Gaza in 1967. As Neuman suggests, Leavitt's unconventional blend of spirituality and nationalism, based upon her own somewhat secular formulation of Judaism, has enabled her to serve as an effective unofficial spokesperson for the settlement in times of crisis. One such occasion was the 1994 massacre of Palestinians by Baruch Goldstein, a resident of Kiryat Arba. This event provoked a wave of Israeli and international media scrutiny of Kiryat Arba that portrayed the settlers as Ultra-Orthodox extremists. Since Leavitt was not the average orthodox Kiryat Arba settler, she was able to offer the media an alternative image.

Although June Leavitt's background is far from typical of the settlers, it is important to recognize that settlers come from a wide variety of backgrounds. A 1999 poll concluded that there is no such thing as an average settler. Whereas 31 percent of settlers polled were of American or European origin, 32 percent came from Africa or Asia, while 29 percent were raised in Israel by Israeli-born parents, and another 6 percent had Russian origins. Fully 70 percent of settlers polled were born in Israel. Although Leavitt's personal blend of Judaism, spiritualism, and nationalism isn't easily categorized, it is almost certain she would not claim to be part of the 53 percent of settlers who consider themselves either Orthodox or Ultra-Orthodox (her own views lie somewhere between "traditional" and "secular"). However, she and her husband Frank joined the settler movement for religious/ideological reasons, rather than economic ones, as is the case for most settlers. Also, they arrived in Israel prior to 1988 (also like most settlers). The Leavitts (like almost three-quarters of the settlers polled) staunchly oppose evacuating settlements in the occupied territories in exchange for financial compensation. This final figure is critical because Israeli settlements remain one of the greatest obstacles to a final peace agreement.

Americans are linked to the settlements in ways that might surprise them. For example, in 2001, the Israeli government spent over $533 million dollars on settlements in the West Bank and Gaza Strip (more than half the annual amount of direct economic aid provided to Israel by the United States). Allocations to settlers, who comprise fewer than 3 percent of the total Israeli population, were substantially larger than to Israeli citizens living within the pre-1967 boundaries of Israel, and were driven by a political agenda favoring settlement rather than economic considerations. After three years of violent *intifada,* which has undermined Israeli's sense of security and left its economy in shambles, in 2003, 56 percent of Israelis polled said they would support a withdrawal from all settlements in the West Bank and Gaza Strip if a final peace agreement with the Palestinians could be reached. Hence, American subsidization and approval of Israeli settlement activities and ongoing occupation will be critical in any future resolution.

In this context, as an activist and advocate for settlers/settlement who has herself refused evacuation orders from the Israeli government in the past (1982), it is all the more important to consider June Leavitt's commitment to the settlement movement and the complex, syncretic belief system that motivates her activism at present.

June Leavitt's biography can be interestingly juxtaposed to the portrait of a contemporary Palestinian woman, Ghada, whose story is told by Celia Rothenberg. —Eds.

I first met June Leavitt during the Purim holiday of 1996, a charged time because it coincided with the second anniversary of the Goldstein massacre. By that point, I had already spent more than a year going back and forth between Jerusalem and Hebron in order to conduct field research for an ethnography of settlement life. I was urged to seek out the Leavitt family by an upstairs neighbor who characterized June and her husband, Frank, as "thoroughly secular" (*hilonim le-gamre*). Elhanan quickly added that he respected these two more than people who were religiously observant. Coming from a devout resident of Kiryat Arba, a West Bank settlement of approximately 6,400 residents located on the eastern side of the Palestinian city of Hebron, his deep respect for this couple struck me as unusual. In retrospect, it seems that he saw the Leavitts as being potential mentors within this relatively insular community of modern Jewish Orthodox settlers. It is true that there were certainly parallels between my academic pursuits and the Leavitt's creative and intellectual interests. June was a writer, and Frank a philosopher. Yet there were clearly important differences. A concern with how these differences operate often underlies ethnographic research, but in this case it provided an invitation to understand how a synthesis had been forged between New Age spirituality, liberal intellectual pursuits, and far-right politics.

At the time, though, my curiosity was piqued by Elhanan's regard for these "secularists." "Secular" and "religious" are relative categories often revealing more about a speaker's assessments than the internal character of these groups. In the context of Kiryat Arba, the term "secular" was often reserved for non-observant outsiders, and thus used with considerable derision. Yet it is only within the last decade that the gap between "secular" and "religious" has become a concern to settlers. Before this period, there had been a closer cooperation between Gush Emunim (Bloc of the Faithful), the extra-parliamentary religious movement that spurred the settling of the West Bank and Gaza from 1967 to the late-1980s, and a range of secular-minded supporters spanning the political spectrum. Though Gush Emunim only supplied about 20 percent of settlers at any given time, they provided the primary ideological inspiration and leadership for settlement in this period. One of the early stated aims of the Gush Emunim movement was to bridge the religious-secular divide for the shared purpose of maintaining control of the occupied territories. This earlier ideal dissolved into a pragmatic emphasis on religious-secular difference by the later bureaucratized phases of the movement. Gush Emunim no longer exists as a social movement devoted to Zionist revitalization. Rather, its primary legacy has been a series of middle-class and institutionalized national religious settlements, formally linked to a network of municipal councils overseen by the Israeli state. Institutionalization of the movement has also created separate religious tracks for education and military service, which serves to further entrench a considerable secular-religious divide.

This growing secular-religious incompatibility was evident in the ambivalence expressed about June Leavitt's journalistic forays by the time I initiated my study. For no sooner had I begun to contact the Leavitts, than I learned that Elhanan's high regard for the couple was not shared by other Kiryat Arba residents. Another neighbor, Meira, employed as a secretary in Jerusalem and a former U.S. compatriot, criticized June Leavitt on the grounds that she never wrote anything positive about Kiryat Arba in her diaries. Meira pointed out that June only depicted the depressing and sensational side of life in the settlement, that the Leavitts were actually Chabadniks (connoting Lubavitch Hassidic converts not terribly competent in Jewish tradition), and that they would probably leave the settlement if they had the financial means to do so. In her view, they had only stayed in Kiryat Arba because no income had materialized from June's writing and Frank was still struggling to secure a more permanent position at the university. To these criticisms Meira's husband Roni, originally a native of Baltimore, responded, "For *Time*, what she wrote is perfectly fine." His comment reflected a conscious concern with the image of the community and a dispute over whether it should be characterized in a purely positive light or whether genuine dilemmas could legitimately be made public. Like the small group of other American immigrants living in Kiryat Arba, he seemed particularly conscious of the impact that June's media images had in the battle to influence public opinion. June hadn't actually published in *Time,* but she was publishing editorials and portions of her diary in similar kinds of widely distributed news magazines.

When I first met June and Frank for lunch at their sparse apartment, I was at once struck by their distinctive style. She still had an artsy, sixties, and casual look about her, and Frank had an equally counterculture appeal that I hadn't expected to see in Kiryat Arba. The Leavitts immediately inquired about my research, though they seemed to be expressing their deeply felt concerns about privacy, anonymity, and consent, both from a personal standpoint and on behalf of the community. Upon agreeing that privacy and consent were crucial issues in fieldwork, June interjected that she had run into related problems as a writer within the community. She remarked that she tried to address the issue of consent by reading descriptions back to people before they were published, but that this turned out to be constraining because everyone improved upon their flaws, saying that they didn't have wrinkles or that their hair was actually blond rather than red. Thus, she said that she resolved to write what she wanted but, at the same time, to fictionalize a number of details in order to mask the true identity of people. In her case, the issue of consent exceeded the ethical obligation to inform people that she was writing about them. Consent merged with the larger quandary of finding a way to represent the community and its aims in the most positive light.

In the course of our conversation, I was struck by the fact that June also asked whether I intended to live in Hebron itself and whether I anticipated interviewing the "Arabs of Hebron." Her question was sparked by my mention of the Western Wall riots of 1929, which I often brought up as an entrée into popular historical understandings that animated religious claims to place. The 1929 riots are one of the key events that settlers use to justify their "return" to Hebron, on the grounds that they are simply reclaiming Jewish property unjustly taken over during an Arab massacre. While this property was indeed taken over, these claims overlook the many dislocations and material losses that have taken place on both sides of the conflict during Ottoman, British, Jordanian, and Israeli rule in the area. June stressed, countering my expectations, that I should seek out the "Arabs in Hebron" since some had actually saved Jews in the riots and one had even been named "a righteous gentile," a position that was clearly at odds with other settler accounts of the riots. She added that she didn't know how I would contact the Arabs, but that she thought that it was important nonetheless. It was significant that in spite of her encouragement to initiate some sort of dialogue, an unusual stance in its own right, June nevertheless used the term "Arab" rather than "Palestinian" to signal that she, like other settlers, didn't view Palestinians as having a distinct peoplehood. On another occasion, Frank reiterated June's view that I should talk to "Arab neighbors," including "those on good and not so good terms," and that I was mistaken if I imagined that there were "no social connections between Arabs and the residents of Kiryat Arba." His view also struck me as unconventional. In my fieldnotes, I register my confusion: "I wonder if they are testing me, my ideological limits, rather than genuinely believing that I should talk to Palestinians. I am shocked at their apparent 'liberalism.' Was it just for my benefit or do they themselves believe it? Both are possibilities."

I later learned from June's diaries that she and Frank had actually begun "speaking to Arabs" a year earlier. Critical of the way Israeli officials were handling the peace negotiations, and feeling themselves to be pawns of elite interests, the Leavitts actually embarked on a diplomatic venture of their own. June's diaries describe a short-lived 1995 foray to Gaza with her husband and another friend to speak to Major General "Natzer Yusuf," a member of the Palestinian Authority who they believed might eventually be given responsibility for overseeing all of Hebron. She represents the meeting as an attempt to see whether settlers would be able to remain under the control of the Palestinian Authority if it took over the area now inhabited by Jewish settlers.

Nearly two months later, on a Saturday, I bumped into the Leavitt family in a Jerusalem pool teaming with families escaping the somber strictures of the Sabbath. This time, I was caught by surprise since, on that day of the week in particular, I imagined myself at a considerable distance from the presence of settlers living in Kiryat Arba. The Leavitts were in a downcast mood because they had just dropped off their son for his required military service, and so they had decided to go to the pool for recreation. They had also brought along a friend, a woman with teased and bleached hair, who was active in "Bridges for Peace," a Christian Evangelical organization located in the Talpiot neighborhood of Jerusalem. The organization was established to help Jews achieve their mission of returning to Israel and to support the building of settlements in the occupied territories. I was told that one of its programs involved handing out Rabbi Kook editions of the bible to new immigrants, the edition having been put out by the yeshiva affiliated with the chief Ashkenazi rabbi during the Mandate, who had later been recuperated as the spiritual founder of the Gush Emunim movement. Rav Kook, and more particularly his son, Zvi Yehuda Kook, viewed settling the land of Israel as hastening the redemption of the Jewish people. Near the pool, Frank asserted that he thought I had been talking to the wrong kind of people in the settlement. He again emphasized that I ought to seek out those who had closer contact with Arabs, as well as religious converts, of which there were many. He also spoke of the lack of receptiveness of Kiryat Arba residents to "environmental concerns," as well as of his frustrated attempts to educate them. Finally, Frank proposed that I change the focus of my investigation altogether and consider working on "the ethics of a community under duress." Frank, as it turns out, had devoted much of his scholarly life to thinking about medical ethics and, in part, to the tensions between universal and "tribal" commitments when administering medical treatment in "war torn" communities such as Kiryat Arba.

In the course of our conversation, I became aware of the many contexts the Leavitts were able to negotiate and the ease with which they situated themselves in each of these settings. I realized that June and Frank took different positions from other residents of Kiryat Arba, and it was often unclear to what degree they even identified with the community they lived in. As I was thinking these thoughts, our conversation abruptly ended when everyone else headed to the pool, and Frank asked if I would be willing to watch over a swim bag that contained his handgun. Invoking my role as a participant-observer, I refused, and with considerable annoyance, Frank took his gun out of the bag and walked off to join his family. Though incidents like these would seem to indicate that the Leavitts did squarely operate within the parameters of the security regime that exemplifies settlement, the liberal values embodied by their style didn't mesh with a self-evident militant and religious worldview. At a broad level, these incongruities suggest that ethno-nationalist commitments often entail a merging of opposite sensibilities. Yet one is left with the practical problem of understanding how tokens of a liberal lifestyle get revalued so that Birkenstock shoes, meditation, yoga, weaponry, and radical-right politics no longer seem to be entirely antithetical. This sort of synthesis forged by the Leavitts becomes far more intelligible in view of their early formation as settlers.

June Leavitt's diaries state that she was raised in an upper-middle-class secular Jewish family on Long Island and attended college in Madison, Wisconsin, during the height of the Vietnam war. I recall her saying that she majored in sociology and wrote poetry, hoping to fulfill her ambition to become a journalist. During these formative years, she was awkwardly immersed in antiwar protests and 1960s counterculture—awkwardly because, in her view, it was a milieu that she did not actively choose but happened upon, coming from a sheltered suburban background. As she recounts the period, June writes that she felt out of place and was plunged into psychological chaos, the vortex that ensued from empty rebellion against dominant symbols of American culture. She accuses her immediate peers, and by implication the Left at the time, of a certain crassness in staking out the terrain of their rebellion—in effect requiring a uniform dress code (blue jeans), sexual promiscuity, uncut and unruly hair, and often pointless acts of destruction (such as setting fire to an A&P supermarket). She credits her college experience with the decision to eventually come to Israel since it turned her away from the "American emphasis on material success." Interestingly enough, June often gives voice to the kind of antimaterialism that many settlers believe govern their actions. Even outright acquisitions, such as property or building takeovers, are thought to be driven by the antimaterialist idealism of restoration. The irony here is that even these ideals have a significant material underpinning, given the difference in land values and the low cost of living for Israelis in areas under occupation compared with that within recognized Israeli boundaries.

June's liberal and experimental moment during college, which she later rejected, had a lasting influence on her personal style and politics of protest, not only in terms of her distinctly period look and antimaterial claims but in defining many of her hobbies and interests. In this, she resembles other residents of Kiryat Arba (and even within the Jewish enclave in Hebron) who merge many of the indices of a progressive or countercultural lifestyle—organic food, environmental consciousness, natural healing, meditation, New Age spirituality—with a discourse on origins that vitalizes ethno-nationalist claims. These two incompatible sensibilities meet in the mystification of soil, language, and blood ties that defines the collective. In the case of June Leavitt, they become the endpoints of a search for self and spirituality.

After graduating from the University of Wisconsin in 1972, June moved to the Lower East Side of Manhattan. By 1974 though, it appears that she grew tired of the urban grind and longed for a life that was closer to nature. In her diaries, she writes that she had a compelling desire to live the life of "an Indian in a tepee." Following her dream of finding a community with an organic connection to nature, and on the advice of a friend who had heard of a back-to-the-land movement out in Plainfield, Vermont, she hopped on a bus and went in search of her ideal. Shortly after her arrival, while wandering in the backwoods, she met her future husband Frank, a homesteader with a beard, blue eyes, and long hair. He was originally from Ohio, and had studied philosophy as an undergraduate at John Carroll University, a Jesuit college in Cleveland. After spending the remainder of the summer with Frank in this town known for its hippy culture, she decided to follow him back to Wendell, Massachusetts, a farm community where he owned five acres of land. She fondly recounts that they built their first home there in the style of a Mongolian yurt, chopping trees and hauling all the materials themselves. Their lifestyle was deliberately simple, using kerosene lamps for electricity and pumping their water from a well.

June writes that she was content with the life she had created for herself. On the other hand, her partner Frank, who had been teaching philosophy to students studying to become Greek Orthodox priests, suddenly felt himself lacking his own strong religious connections. As June tells it, Frank grappled with his lack of faith and toyed with the idea of either becoming baptized as a Christian or further exploring Judaism. To resolve this dilemma, he flipped a coin. When it came up tails, he decided to seek out a rabbi. Yet it was not until he was crumpling old newspapers for a fire that he saw the face of the Lubavitcher rabbi in Amherst peering out at him, and knew instinctively that this was the man he ought to contact. It seems that from the perspective of a back-to-nature farmer in rural Massachusetts, the face of this sullen, white-haired rabbi in black garb represented a further departure from the contradictions of modern urban life and a quest for an authentic form of spiritual experience. Amherst was located only about seventeen miles from their home in Wendell, and there the couple became affiliated with the Lubavitch community. Lubavitch Hassidism, like other Hassidic sects that have their roots in eighteenth-century Poland, is an inward-looking mystical sect of Jewish Orthodoxy. It is distinguished from other Ultra-Orthodox sects by having a network of emissaries in remote places precisely in order to bring secular Jews back into the fold. In more recent times, it has made extensive use of the Internet for its ends and thereby altered the thinking of other Hassidic groups who have rejected the use of technology for these purposes.

In 1976, not long after establishing a relationship with the Lubavitcher rabbi in Amherst, Frank decided to pursue his interest in Judaism more seriously. With June following suit, they moved to Crown Heights, Brooklyn, a working-class neighborhood which was at the center of the Lubavitch movement. There they studied in sex-segregated religious schools designed to teach those who were new to the religious tradition. The main rabbinical inspiration of the Lubavitch movement was Rabbi Menachem Schneerson, known for his hawkish pronouncements on the Israeli political situation and religious interpretations which concluded that not "one inch of land" in Israel could be rightfully returned in the context of a peace accord. This stance is unique for the Hassidic community, which often refuses to recognize the founding of the modern Israeli state as an event having any religious legitimacy whatsoever. In addition, Rabbi Schneerson's followers took him to be the messiah, an idea nothing short of heresy for other Hassidic sects. Crown Heights itself played a significant role in Frank and June's early religious formation. Messianism became enmeshed in the racial tensions that existed between the self-contained Hassidic Jewish community and the African American community that competed for sparse municipal resources. The neighborhood also became a center of activity for the militant and vigilante Jewish Defense League (JDL), led by the notorious Rabbi Meir Kahane, a spiritual mentor of Baruch Goldstein who would later become the Leavitt's neighbor and the perpetrator of the 1994 massacre in Hebron.

In order to be able to reside together in this sex-segregated Ultra-Orthodox community, the Leavitts decided to get married, and they organized a traditional Hassidic-style wedding back in Amherst. Yet after six months of living in Crown Heights, June inevitably began to long for a way of life that was closer to nature. The Lubavitch community owned property in the

Catskills, and with the promise of being able to teach Lubavitch children basic farming methods, the couple returned to their homesteading lifestyle, but this time as Ultra-Orthodox Jews. During this period, June Leavitt gave birth to her oldest son, the first of five children. Ultimately though, the Leavitts broke with the Lubavitch movement over what June vaguely referred to as "financial matters."

The combination of such American-based experiences and sensibilities seems to have eventually fueled a passion to reclaim what they considered to be lost Jewish territory in the Middle East: the 1960s and its culture of protest, antimaterialist values, a deep appreciation for nature and land, the valuation of a self-sufficient way of life, a spiritual quest bound to an inward-looking community, exposure to messianism, Jewish "fundamentalism" and its hawkishness vis-à-vis the land of Israel, and finally the racial strife which tainted the atmosphere of Crown Heights. This diasporic synthesis, however, was then interjected into the specific framework of post-1967 settlement in the West Bank and Gaza.

While settlement proved to be instrumental in Israeli state-formation from 1882 though 1947 in its pre-state phase, and then served to further secure Israel's borders after 1948, it was subsequently remade as a key religious strategy for holding onto Israel's vastly increased territorial acquisitions after the 1967 war. Yet the shift from a quasi-secular nation-building strategy to one justified exclusively on religious grounds occurred incrementally. Following 1967, settlement began as a government initiative roughly intended to implement the Allon plan, which envisioned creating an Israeli security belt along the Jordan River Valley while allowing densely populated Palestinian areas to be returned to Jordanian rule. Though the plan was never fully realized, it shaped the Labor government's settlement policy for the next decade. Its parameters were soon challenged by popular initiatives that attempted to locate settlements throughout the entirety of the West Bank. These early challenges drew on religious rationales in order to expand possibilities for the placement of settlements, focusing on locales deemed religiously significant rather than simply strategic. Kiryat Arba, founded in 1968, was important in this respect because it was the first settlement to emerge from religious activism. These initial confrontations between religious students and the government coalesced by 1974 into the formal establishment of the Gush Emunim, a national religious movement devoted to settling the occupied territories.

Gush Emunim's popularity was in part related to the widespread dissatisfaction with the Israeli Labor government after Israel's near-defeat in the 1973 war. This support increased with official government backing in 1977, when the Likud government came to power for the first time, and then again after 1978, when the government resolved to consolidate its hold on the West Bank after negotiating the Camp David accords. In brief, the

Israeli state attempted to harness not just religious sentiment but religious radicalism for its expansive purpose in this period. As a result, the Gush Emunim began losing its momentum as a bona fide popular movement by the mid-1980s, and its leaders eventually became thoroughly integrated into the governing municipal structures that continue to unite disparate West Bank settlements into a coherent constituency. Most settlers now view Gush Emunim as a thing of the past and instead identify with the national religious (*da'ati le'umi*) or Modern Orthodox camp in opposition to the antimodernist (*haredi*) Ultra-Orthodox community. Yet there are also some Hassidic groups, such as the Lubavitchers, that participate in national religious settlements because of their hard-line stance on Israeli territory.

In 1979 the Leavitts emigrated to Israel, moving initially to the Galilee within the Green Line, and then beyond it to the settlement of Atzmona within the Rafiah salient (also known as the Yamit Strip) located along the northern Sinai coast west of the Gaza Strip. Of her choice, June Leavitt simply writes that after a rich life in the forest she could not see herself going back to living in a city or an already established community. Driven by a strong pioneering spirit and a connection to the land, and probably pushed by their outsider status as new immigrants, the Leavitts gravitated toward the Gush Emunim movement, which at the time was financing opportunities for participation in popular settlement initiatives. With the assistance of the Gush Emunim, they came to Atzmona, founded after the 1978 Camp David accords, as a way of demonstrating resistance to the imminent withdrawal of the Sinai. In this respect, Atzmona differed from other Sinai settlements, of which Yamit was the largest, because it did not fall under the rubric of government-founded security settlements. Built in 1975, these security settlements were intended to serve as a "buffer" between Egypt and Gaza. By the time of the 1982 Israeli withdrawal of the Sinai, many long-term residents of these security settlements had been well compensated and began leaving the area when Gush activists stepped in. The Leavitts participated in this critical period of resistance. The purpose of the Gush Emunim was not only to resist withdrawal but to dramatize the anguish of leaving the land. The theatricality of the moment reached its height when settlers threatened to commit suicide if they were forcibly removed. Though their eventual defeat was seen as a major setback for the movement, it etched the Sinai withdrawal in national memory and created an important precedent.

In the Sinai settlement of Atzmona, the Leavitts lived in the provisional housing (mobile homes known as *caravanim*) associated with illegal outposts, which lacked basic amenities such as electricity or refrigeration. While there, they proceeded to work in agriculture and live a communal lifestyle. In addition, June took charge of domestic duties (food preparation and childcare), while Frank devoted himself to the study of Torah. This gendered division of labor served to reinforce a "return," not only to the homeland but to the "authentic" Jewish family as the foundation for religious community and nation. Gender-specific roles such as these serve to reinforce religious nationalist sentiment through a focus on population, linking women's fertility to nationalist aims on the one hand, while enlisting men to defend the "vulnerability" of women and children on the other. Given the controversy that emerged over the return of the Sinai within Israel, June and Frank also began to serve as spokespeople, particularly when English-speaking journalists arrived on the scene. Protesting the government's decision to the very end, they continued to live in Atzmona after its water supply had been cut off. In April 1982, they were forcibly removed by a large convoy of military jeeps, buses, and soldiers and relocated to the Gaza Strip. Atzmona was then rebuilt within the Gaza Strip, where it has continued to exist as part of Gush Katif, the southern bloc of settlements located along the Mediterranean coastline.

Israel's 1978 treaty with Egypt, in turn, strengthened Gush Emunim's resolve to expand the West Bank settlement of Kiryat Arba directly into the urban center of Palestinian Hebron, forming the basis for the settler stronghold known as the Jewish enclave. This stronghold is unique among West Bank settlements because of its location directly within a densely populated urban municipality. The Likud-dominated government of Menachem Begin had an overlapping interest in supporting settlement to strengthen its hold in the occupied territories following the Camp David accords, albeit at a distance from major Palestinian population centers. Overlooking this constraint in the context of a favorable political climate, women and children initiated a standoff with the military in 1979 that lasted for more than a year. They squatted in the Dabouya Building, later renamed Beit Hadassah, until it eventually became the basis for Hebron's Jewish stronghold. Three years later, a second building, the Ussama Ibn Al-Munther School, renamed Beit Romano, was also taken over, and it was here that the Leavitts again played a significant role.

While still in Gaza, Frank was invited by a rabbi to participate in the newly established Hebron yeshiva of Beit Romano. Moving the entire family into one room of the building that had been taken over, the Leavitt family thus traded their earlier residences in the Sinai and the Gaza Strip for Hebron, all key zones of confrontation around settlement expansion. Yet, June Leavitt's diary portrays squatting in the school as part of a relatively neutral and legal process. Describing a chain of historical events that undergirds her view of the takeover of Palestinian property as a process of returning Jewish property to its rightful owners, she writes:

> We moved into a decrepit building which had been built a hundred years ago as a yeshiva by a wealthy Turkish Jew named Romano. The Turks had taken it over and made it into a jail. After them the British had turned it into a police

station. When the war of independence broke out in 1948, and the Arabs gained control of the building, they turned it into a school. In 1982 after a lengthy court proceeding in which Jewish ownership was demonstrated, the Arabs were evicted.

As in other cases of property or land takeover by settlers, ownership of Palestinian property is often subject to legal "reinterpretation," given the incomplete documentation of property that has resulted from sudden changes of regime as well as from the conflicting sets of legal codes that have been inherited from these different periods. While squatting in Hebron, Frank befriended Rehavam Zeevi, a strong supporter of settlers seeking to establish a Jewish enclave in the municipality and a former Israeli general who in 1988 started the Moledet Party—a secular far-right political party advocating the "voluntary transfer" of the Palestinian population to surrounding Arab countries. These attempts to establish a Jewish enclave directly within a Palestinian urban area were one of several contexts that resulted in the coming together of religious and far-right secular interests. Moledet is considered to have comparable aims to the extremist religious Kach Party, which was banned from running for parliament (and then banned outright) because of its racist and provocative platform. It is unclear whether Frank continues to uphold the views of Moledet, but June claims that he was active in founding the party and remained in contact with Zeevi until his assassination in 2001.

After living in the center of Hebron in Beit Romano for approximately two years, the Leavitts decided to move their family to the confines of Kiryat Arba, the older and larger settlement located on the eastern side of Hebron. The decision to move out of this risky, high-conflict zone by 1985 was made, according to June, because they felt that their children deserved a more secure location to grow up in. It seems that they were also in a better position to leave because they had accomplished their aims; the Israeli government had by then fully sanctioned the building of a Jewish enclave in Hebron. This meant that permanent structures were built to house settlers in the Palestinian municipality and that municipal services (including electricity and water) were extended, along with the installation of a military brigade to insure the security of the settlers. Today, the Jewish enclave in Hebron consists of approximately five hundred people, many of whom are the young children of vanguard settler families living directly in the frontlines of the conflict.

In contrast to this stronghold directly in the city center, Kiryat Arba provided the semblance of a relatively peaceful gated community located a few miles away in the agricultural outskirts of Hebron. As an established settlement, Kiryat Arba contained many of the amenities of other small Israeli municipalities, including a municipal council, recreation center, supermarket, dry goods stores, a gas station, elementary schools, synagogues, and several playgrounds and parks. Its residents were somewhat more diverse, including different waves of immigrants and others living there primarily for economic reasons. The older section of the settlement still consists of clusters of four- to five-story apartment buildings resembling those in other working-class Jerusalem neighborhoods. While strategically located on a hilltop, it predates the militaristic architecture of newer West Bank settlements which often consist of rows of red-roofed single-family housing structures overlooking Palestinian agricultural fields and villages. Everyday life in Kiryat Arba, as in other religious settlements, centers around family activities and religious study. Large families are valued both as a locus of religious community and as a means of changing the demographic (and ethnic) composition of the occupied territories. As a result, the population of Kiryat Arba tends to be young, with at least half its residents being seventeen or under. This focus on family and community is augmented during election rallies, protests, and mass celebrations of religious and national holidays, events which draw hundreds of settlers to the area of Hebron in a public demonstration of solidarity with the settlers who reside there.

June writes that in 1987 she and her husband quietly underwent another spiritual transformation. After having first embraced Ultra-Orthodox (*haredi*) Judaism, and then Modern Orthodoxy (*da'ati le'umi*), both she and Frank decided to shed the external markers of belonging to the national-religious community, doing away with both headscarf and knitted skullcap. This shift toward being "inwardly religious," while unpopular with their friends and neighbors in Kiryat Arba, nevertheless allowed the Leavitts to move freely between different social contexts without announcing themselves as being part of any one sector of Israeli society. Together with an extensive grounding in settlement activism, this ability to navigate between factions later provided the Leavitts with the opportunity to serve as unofficial spokespersons for Kiryat Arba in the context of events that placed Kiryat Arba in the international spotlight. In 1994, Baruch Goldstein, a Brooklyn-born doctor and former Kiryat Arba municipal council member, committed a massacre that left twenty-nine Palestinians dead and hundreds of others wounded in Hebron's main, seventh-century mosque Al-Haram al-Ibrahimi/Me'arat ha-Makhpelah (most commonly referred to in English as the "Tomb of the Patriarchs," a designation inherited from the mandate period). In the aftermath of the event, even those who had been supporters of settlement became deeply critical of what was purported to be the growing "fanaticism" of the religious Right, further polarizing the divide between secular and religious Israelis. Israelis across the political spectrum and international observers alike cast Kiryat Arba as the locus of religious extremism, while res-

idents of the settlement and their religious supporters (from the far right
end of the national religious community) defended Goldstein's actions, and
upheld him as a heroic savior.

A year after the massacre, June emerged as a sophisticated apologist for
the settlement. Through the medium of her diary, and op-eds in newspapers such the *New York Times*, she led a crusade to humanize Kiryat Arba and
to defend its most extreme residents, including Goldstein, whom the Leavitts had long admired but with whom they disagreed. In *US News & World
Report*, a diary entry by June Leavitt dated 25 February 1994, the day of the
Hebron massacre, registers her shock regarding Goldstein, and her sadness
for his wife and children. She invokes the "extremism" of the settlement
community only to ultimately sacralize Goldstein's actions:

> How long he planned to rise up like an ancient Samson and slay the ancient
> enemy, no one knows. Family and friends sensed something was brewing. But
> he was very introverted. His family tried to soothe the uneasiness they felt by
> saying, "You're doing enough for the Jewish nation already, Baruch." He
> would just smile.
>
> If there were a God, and if he came to people and made them do earth-
> shattering things, then he would come to a man like Baruch. Cold and hard
> like ice, with a fiery devotion to things higher and deeper than this world.
>
> God would choose a man who could unblinkingly sit with his son and lis-
> ten to the Book of Esther in the night, and in the morning put on his Army
> uniform, take his rifle and much ammunition, creep out of the house, know-
> ing the chances were he'd never see his sleeping wife or children again.

It is in passages like these that June Leavitt weaves her apologia of Goldstein's actions, invoking the domestic sphere and portraying Goldstein as
both a devoted family man and amiable neighbor of many years. In dis-
cussing the massacre, her preoccupation clearly lies with members of Goldstein's immediate family and with the impact of his actions on the settlement, rather than on the many Palestinians killed or wounded. While these
inversions between victim and victimizer figure prominently in June Leavitt's writing, she is not alone in using them. Rather, June's diaries serve to
personalize the theme of victimization, a theme often used as a rhetorical
call to action in the political speech of national religious settlers. In her
view, Goldstein was acting in response to an impending threat, which he
likely averted. She sees him as a devoted physician who saw too many of his
friends injured by attacks resulting from the 1993 Oslo peace accords.

Given the intensification of the Israel-Palestine conflict, there is little
consensus on what the Oslo accords (the first framework for negotiations
between Israel and the PLO) were intended to achieve. However, most
agree that Oslo's fatal flaw was not only its ambiguity but its complete postponement of key issues pending permanent status negotiations. Thus, the
issues of the settlements, refugees, Jerusalem, security arrangements, and

border relations, among others, were left undetermined, allowing infrac-
tions on both sides to occur during the interim period. While there was no
explicit prohibition on expanding settlements in the Declaration of Principles, the interim agreement signed two years later included a clause stating
that no party could take any step to "change the status of the West Bank and
Gaza Strip pending the outcome of permanent status negotiations." In the
decade following the signing of the Oslo accords, however, the settler population in the occupied territories (excluding East Jerusalem) doubled,
amounting to twice the growth rate for Israel proper. While this population
increase was not the sole cause of renewed violence, settlement expansion
was one of several key factors that led to the deterioration of Palestinian support for the political process.

June Leavitt's more recent diary entries comment extensively on the
period of violence known as the al-Aksa *intifada*—the Palestinian uprising
that began in September 2000 when Ariel Sharon staged a visit, along with
thousands of security personnel, to the al-Aksa mosque, one of the holiest
Islamic sites in Jerusalem. In her rendition of subsequent events, she positions herself as a mother caught in a proverbial "storm of terror," doubtful
of the spiritual quest that has led her to live in Kiryat Arba. Understandably,
she is deeply fearful for the well-being of her friends and immediate family
who, during this period, are being targeted with considerable frequency on
the roads that lead from settlements into the Green Line (the 1949 armistice
line that served as Israel's border with Jordan until the 1967 war). Throughout this diary, it becomes evident that June is plagued by self-doubt. By
expressing this private sentiment publicly, she breaks with settler proscrip-
tions around expressing fear and the attitude that personal ambivalences
best be kept a private matter. As one reads further, one is struck by a number
of other uncharacteristic stances. Finding herself in the midst of convulsive
violence, we see June taking Bach flower remedies, practicing yoga, and con-
sulting a bioenergy pendulum to steady her frayed nerves. This spiritual
mélange is enhanced by her choices for a course she is teaching on spirituality in literature, where she revisits the teachings of Judaism, Christianity,
and especially Buddhism.

Invoking a Buddhist-like incantation, June writes, "I wish myself to a
place of Stillness and Tranquility of Mind." Indeed, one feels for her
predicament, which disrupts the tranquility of domestic life she so often
yearns for. On the other hand, both she and her husband have made deliberate choices to place themselves in highly contentious areas for what they
see as a higher purpose—to extend the present boundaries of the modern
state of Israel to its "biblically significant" areas, in disregard of Palestinian
claims. June, however, doesn't see her location on the frontline of the conflict as a deliberate choice because, for her, there is no longer any safe
haven. The same "terror" which abounds in Hebron also erupts within

Israel's borders, and even rears its head in international contexts. Clearly, for June, prevalent terror has defined the global condition. For this reason she imagines "terror" in Hebron, attacks in Tel Aviv, and those on the World Trade Center to be part of a single phenomenon. Of 9/11 she writes, "Our destinies are now intertwined. Global karma, I believe they call it."

June Leavitt's hodge-podge of doubt, spirituality, and motherhood speaks to some of the many ways her countercultural past is melded with an ultranationalist sensibility. From her point of view, these incongruities mark her as a proverbial outsider and witness; she claims to belong neither to the community she currently lives in nor to the (liberal) secular world that fails to appreciate the "immense spirituality" of the "Tomb of the Patriarchs" in Hebron. In short, June's marginality grants her the possibility of being versatile and fluid when it comes to forging a range of social ties and creating a broader consensus for the settlement project.

In keeping with these unconventional stances, her "location" on political issues often appears flexible as well. In fact, by her own accord, she is a staunch advocate of peace and "co-existence." Yet in her reframing of these terms, they take on a sense that is diametrically opposed to the way those in the Israeli peace camp use them. June, along with other settlers in Kiryat Arba, frequently takes settlement itself to be a form of "co-existence" (*dunkiyum*), while the Israeli left wing, not to mention Palestinians themselves, view settlements in Gaza and the West Bank as obstacles to peace. Her view of coexistence harkens back to an older Gush Emunim claim that Palestinians would be treated as respected residents (*ger toshav*) in a Jewish land according to the precepts of Jewish law, and that they should not be expelled. Nevertheless, June's version of coexistence does not mean that Palestinians themselves would be consulted on matters of governance, nor would they be extended the rights of citizenship. Instead, this idea of "co-existence" entails Jewish sovereignty and the acceptance by Palestinians of their subordinate status. Thus, under the banner of "co-existence," residents of Kiryat Arba opposed the system of West Bank bypass roads built in 1995, which served to strengthen settlement ties to urban centers within the Green Line but nevertheless "separated" settlers from Palestinian areas and limited their options for movement within them.

In short, the malleability of these referents and the ability of a religious right position to accommodate markers of a liberal sensibility in the Israeli context creates an opportunity to speak to the often sentimental and relatively moderate ethical sensibility of Jews living in the diaspora, as well as to a potentially sympathetic international audience. Yet in doing so, June Leavitt can reference and legitimate (within the parameters of an Israeli political landscape) some of the most volatile dimensions of settlement. Settlement operates on a variety of levels, and exclusivist claims to place are necessarily produced in relation to and fought out within a wider set of existing social relations. Ties to the Israeli government, Jewish diaspora, and an international public are regularly created through the media, computer technology, and transnational migration even though settlements present themselves as self-contained, authentic communities revitalizing a past ancestry. Because of June Leavitt's ability to engage multiple audiences, and her ability to tap into the dilemmas of Jewish identity in the United States, she has proven herself both an able spokesperson and an effective (albeit problematic) force in the battle to shape international public opinion.

A NOTE ON SOURCES

The biographical portion of this text is based on fieldwork conducted in Hebron and Jerusalem from 1994 to 1996 and in 2001, and on a field-based interpretation of June Leavitt's biographical writings. It is part of a larger ethnography (in progress) on space and place in settlement, entitled "Reinstating the Religious Nation." Names of Kiryat Arba residents who do not have a public profile have been changed to ensure anonymity. June Leavitt's first diary, *Im Labyrinth des Terrors: Tagebuch einer jüdischen Siedlerin,* was republished in 1996 by Ullstein press from the 1995 French edition published by Robert Laffont and entitled *Vivrè á Hebron.* Her second diary, published in the United States by Ivan R. Dee in 2002, is entitled *Storm of Terror: A Hebron Mother's Diary.* While the two diaries form a sequence, the first spanning 1992–95 and the second 2000–2002, they each contain recollections and accounts that overlap. Two other of June Leavitt's publications used in this biographical sketch include a diary excerpt published in 1994 in *US News & World Report* (April 18, 1994), and a *New York Times* op-ed piece published in 2002 and entitled "In Hebron, Death and Life."

SUGGESTIONS FOR FURTHER READING

For further reading on the dynamics of pre-state agricultural settlement in Palestine, see Gershon Shafir, *Land, Labor, and the Origins of the Israeli-Palestinian Conflict, 1882–1914* (Cambridge: Cambridge University Press, 1989). On Jewish fundamentalism and the Gush Emunim, see Aviezer Ravitzsky, *Messianism, Zionism, and Jewish Religious Radicalism* (Chicago: University of Chicago Press, 1996); Israel Shahak and Norton Mezvinsky, *Jewish Fundamentalism in Israel* (London: Pluto Press, 1999); Gideon Aran, "Jewish Zionist Fundamentalism: The Bloc of the Faithful in Israel (Gush Emunim), in *Fundamentalisms Observed,* ed. Martin Marty (Chicago: University of Chicago Press, 1991); and Tamar El-Or, *Next Year I Will Know More: Literacy and Identity among Young Orthodox Women in Israel* (Detroit: Wayne State University Press, 2002).

Two books by Ehud Sprinzak on the ascendance of the Israeli right wing can be recommended: see his *Brother against Brother: Violence and Extremism in Israeli Politics from Atalena to the Rabin Assassination* (New York: Free Press, 1999); and *The Ascendance of Israel's Radical Right* (New York: Oxford University Press, 1991). For a valuable analysis of Ariel Sharon's historical role vis-à-vis settlement and the impact of his policies on the most recent phase of the Israel-Palestine conflict, see Baruch Kimmerling, *Politicide: Ariel Sharon's War against the Palestinians* (London: Verso, 2003).

Chapter 25

Talal Rizk:
A Syrian Engineer in the Gulf

Michael Provence

During the late 1990s Syrian college graduates faced bleak prospects for employment. Despite modest efforts at economic reform and privatization since 1990, Syria's largely state-run economy has remained one of the region's most stagnant. With unemployment rates above 20 percent (higher than all neighboring states and nearly double that of Egypt or Turkey), millions of Syrian workers are forced to seek jobs abroad. By 2002, an estimated 1.4 million Syrians were working in Lebanon alone, much to the dismay of unemployed Lebanese. Another 300,000 Syrians work in the Persian Gulf states (170,000 in Saudi Arabia and 100,000 in Kuwait). Emerging from the American University in Beirut in 1998 with a degree in agricultural engineering and fluency in several languages, Talal Rizk soon discovered how limited his options were. Faced with the certainty of unemployment in Syria or a possibility of work abroad, Talal eventually chose the latter.

As told by Michael Provence, Rizk's story affords us a glimpse of the hopes and frustrations of a generation of educated Arabs and the limits of idealism in the face of political and economic realities. Raised in a middle-class Druze family in Damascus, Talal's parents were well educated and politicized, and they closely guided the education of their only son. Talal took naturally to school, especially history, literature, and languages. When it came time to choose a university in 1987, the family selected the American University at Beirut (AUB) in neighboring Lebanon. Despite the fact that Lebanon's civil war (1975–90) was still ongoing, AUB was considered a prestigious and a relatively safe school for Talal to attend. It was in his years at AUB that Talal came to understand firsthand both the Arab world's vast potentials and its dramatic failures. It was at this point that the obstacles and challenges he would encounter in his own life first became clear to him.

Talal Rizk derived abundant life lessons from his AUB years, not the least because of the timing of his studies there. In addition to his academic interests, the period coincided with the violent end of the civil war and the Syrian occupation in October 1990. Among students, for many (including Talal) this was a phase of political activism, the principle lesson of which was the peril of trying to navigate in the

volatile world of Syrian and Lebanese nationalism. As well, the period was marked
by harrowing and sometimes comical dorm exploits, which are evoked here.

Having overcome a major family crisis to complete his degree, Talal was confronted with the gritty political and economic realities of Syria in the early 1990s.
With some reluctance, he decided to seek work abroad, ultimately accepting a position unrelated to his degree, in Saudi Arabia. In Saudi Arabia Talal was quickly made
to understand where he fit into the local scene, including the migrant pecking
order, domestic Saudi social hierarchy, *kafil* (sponsorship), the government and
religious bureaucracy, and the Saudi culture of conspicuous consumption. His experiences and observations enable us to see why many educated Arabs of his generation find themselves caught between hope and despair.

Rizk's career path can be compared with profit to that of his contemporary, Nasir,
an Egyptian agriculture student whose story is told by Fanny Colonna. Rizk's experiences as a work migrant can also be juxtaposed to those of Haddou, the Moroccan
migrant laborer featured in part 3, and the family of Ghada, a contemporary Palestinian woman profiled by Celia Rothenberg in this section. —Eds.

Talal switched off his cell phone and gazed out the window at the traffic outside. He had just made a sale that would preserve his job for another month.
Since the beginning of the week, he had sold three gold kitchen fixture sets,
and he would finally make his monthly goal. Despite his new success, selling
such items bothered him. As a foreigner working in the Saudi Arabian port
city of Jeddah, he sometimes felt a creeping resentment toward his customers. They were able to purchase things far beyond his modest means.
Besides, the things he sold were not beautiful or durable. To Talal, they were
useless trinkets and would probably be replaced by something new next
year anyway. As Talal had presented the fixtures he'd just sold, the woman
had asked, "Don't you have something more expensive? I need something
that will take my breath away each time I gaze at it."

Still, Talal was grateful for the job. He was good at sales. He was well spoken and likable, but his academic training was in agricultural engineering
and he was passionately interested in history, politics, literature, and languages. He was fluent and cultured in five languages, and he felt starved for
intellectual stimulation. The job selling luxury bathroom fixtures had come
after years of unemployment and frustration in Syria, the country of his
birth. The work was sometimes hard since he was unfamiliar with the country and its business practices, but it was a start—and a huge improvement
over joblessness and relative destitution. His guest worker status placed him
in a state of limbo, but if he could find a more suitable job in line with his
university degree and training his future and livelihood would be secure.
He knew from experience that job security and a reasonable income were
something very few young men could be assured of in the early twenty-first
century. He also knew that as a Syrian Arab he occupied a relatively privi-

leged place in the pecking order of foreign workers in the Saudi Kingdom. It was a long road that had brought him to the Hamoud Brothers showroom in Jeddah.

Talal Rizk is a son of Damascus. The changes in the Arab Middle East since his birth in 1970 have been immense. His generation of young Arab men and women has known mostly disappointment and frustration. His grandparents' generation succeeded in the independence struggle against the French mandate in Syria. But his parents' generation mostly failed in their confrontations with Israel, and in building Arab unity, economic development, or a better society. For young people, the horizons are limited; the choices are quiet frustration, immigration, or religious extremism and refusal. The age of hope and idealism is over.

No one expected things to unfold this way, least of all young people like Talal from the rising middle class. His family is from the Druze religious minority, an offshoot of Shi'i Islam, and his grandparents were prominent in the rural Druze region of Jabal Hawran. His paternal grandfather was a cloth merchant near Damascus's Suq Hamidiyya, and his maternal grandfather was a landlord and farmer in the rural south. Both fought against the French during the mandate between 1920 and 1946, and both suffered for their involvement. His parents had been involved in early post-independence politics, and his father, who trained in Damascus and France as an orthopedic surgeon, had joined the Baath Party as a young man. Secular nationalist parties were very popular among students in the 1950s and 1960s, especially those from the sectarian minorities such as the Druze, 'Alawi, and Christians, and from the rural regions. Many students had joined the Baath, the Syrian Social Nationalist Party, or the Communist Party.

In the 1950s Talal's father had joined other idealistic young Baath Party activists in setting up health clinics in the countryside and lecturing villagers on hygiene, health care, education, and politics. Talal's mother had been active, too, and taught Arabic for a year in post-revolutionary Algeria in 1963. His parents were married in 1966, by which time his father had already grown disaffected with the Baath Party, after the 1963 coup and purge of many civilian activists. He resigned from the party to concentrate on his medical practice and his young family.

The early and mid-1960s were years of optimism in Syria. Egyptian President Gamal Abdel Nasser led the Arab world, and Syria's radical Baathist government advocated socialism and development, Arab unity, and Palestinian rights. Challenging Israel's regional hegemony was an important element in the radical program. But the challenge to Israel's dominance turned out to be largely rhetorical. Less than three years before Talal was born, Israeli forces had launched a war against Egypt, Jordan, and Syria. The June 1967 "Six Day War" discredited Nasser, the radical Syrian nationalists, and, in the eyes of many, the entire project of Arab unity and radical military government. Syria lost the Golan Heights to Israel, Jordan lost the West Bank, and Egypt lost all of the Sinai Peninsula. The defeat was devastating and the shock reverberated throughout the Arab world.

Talal's father had been recalled by the army to serve as a surgeon after the Israeli attack on Egypt that started the war. He ran a field hospital four kilometers from the Syrian border in the Golan Heights. When Israeli Phantom jet fighters bombed and destroyed the adjoining town and the hospital, his father and the one remaining doctor left the ruins and walked to the Syrian Army positions at the nearby front. They had waited in the hospital through air and artillery bombardments, thinking that the injured soldiers would need them, but as they walked, they found that the army command had ordered a general retreat toward Damascus. The army had abandoned the entire region and its inhabitants to the Israelis, and Talal's father and his friend were now deep inside the Israeli lines. They walked seventy kilometers between the advancing Israelis and the retreating Syrian army. When they arrived in the Syrian town of Qatana, they found a taxi and hired the driver to drive them to Damascus. The war was lost, and the entire Golan region had been overrun and occupied by the Israelis. Talal's father returned home, the shock of the defeat and the loss of the Golan perhaps more personal for him than for many.

Former Defense Minister Hafiz al-Asad took power in a coup in November 1970. Talal was eight months old. The new government blamed the previous government for the 1967 defeat and labeled the coup the "Corrective Movement." Asad was widely perceived to be less radical, more cautious, and more acceptable to the Damascus commercial middle class, which had vigorously opposed the socialist nationalization policy of the preceding Baathist government. Asad also undertook a massive military buildup and an alliance with the new Egyptian President, Anwar Sadat. Both Syria and Egypt received billions of dollars worth of Soviet military hardware in preparation for decisive action against Israel to break the stalemate and regain the lost territory.

The buildup led to the 1973 war. Talal's father was again recalled to serve and ran a hospital in the town of Qatana. The nights spent in the dark air-raid shelter with his mother and older sister are some of Talal's earliest memories. Feelings of helplessness, uncertainty, and fear led to his first stirrings of interest in politics and his efforts to understand the world. He remembers imagining that the terrifying Israelis must be somehow different from the people who populated the world of his direct experience. Years later, Talal would teach himself Hebrew by listening to Israeli Army radio. His curiosity undiminished, he studied Hebrew until he could read the Old Testament in its original language.

The 1973 war was a military disappointment but a political victory for both Asad and Sadat. Israel retained and even seized more Syrian and Egyptian land, but Syria and Egypt succeeded in regaining their dignity and capturing the interest of the United States for peace negotiations. The Egyptians eventually signed a separate peace treaty with Israel and regained the Sinai Peninsula. The U.N. brokered a disengagement agreement between Syria and Israel and Syria regained a little territory, but most of Golan has remained under Israeli occupation. In the absence of a peace agreement, Syria remains a front-line Arab country with Israel. As such, during the 1970s, it benefited from remittances and subsidies from wealthier Arab oil-exporting countries, as thousands of Syrians went to work in the oil-rich Arab Gulf states and sent their wages home.

The mid-1970s were good years for many in Syria. Talal's older sister was born in 1967, and in 1976 a second sister arrived. The family of five lived well and found a place among the new professional middle classes of Damascus. Talal's father built a thriving medical practice as a surgeon and bought an apartment in the Damascus neighborhood of Dawar Kafar Susa. He began to groom his only son to follow in his footsteps as a physician. Talal's parents persuaded him to think that this was the only career path for him. Upwardly mobile Syrian families hope ardently that their sons and daughters will score well on baccalaureate qualifying exams and be admitted to the national university departments of medicine, pharmacy, or engineering. The exams, taken after secondary school, are seen as determining the material and social status of young people, and their families as well. Other courses of study are neither as prestigious nor as remunerative, and are believed to lead to chronic unemployment or underemployment, to an inability to marry, and to an inability to leave the parents' home.

In Syria one is not always free to choose a career, a course of study, or even a spouse. General economic insecurity makes it necessary to deal with such issues differently, usually as family matters that are of collective concern. Like parents anywhere, Talal's mother and father had big dreams for his future. They sent him to study at the former French Missionary School in Damascus's Qasa' neighborhood. He learned French, and Arabic literature, and developed what would become a lifelong passion for languages and history. He tried unsuccessfully to convince his father that language and history should be his course of study. His father asked how he expected to feed himself in Syria with a degree in history. This was a fair question since his father was well aware that his professional historian friends, with doctorates from the Sorbonne, struggled ceaselessly to make a living and support their families.

Talal completed secondary school in 1987. As an only son, he was exempted from the mandatory two years of military service. His graduation exam scores were not high enough to be admitted to the Faculty of Medicine at Damascus University, and his father resolved to send him to the Université Saint Joseph in Beirut. Lebanon had been embroiled in a wrenching civil war since 1975, however, and among the bitterest rivals were the Druze and Maronite Christian political parties and militias. During the war, East Beirut, the location of the Université Saint Joseph, had become almost exclusively Maronite, and Talal's father realized that a Syrian Druze youth would not be safe in such an environment.

The family determined that the American University of Beirut, in the west of the city, would be safer. AUB had been founded by American missionaries in the mid-nineteenth century, and had long been the Arab world's most prestigious university. There were obstacles to admission for Talal. He was fluent in French, the language of instruction at Saint Joseph, but nearly illiterate in English, the language of instruction at AUB. Further, AUB had the stiffest admission requirements in the Middle East and at least a year of preparation would be necessary. He spent a year working on a family garden plot outside Damascus while his mother and father investigated possibilities for his education, and another year as a special preparatory student in Beirut.

Talal moved to Beirut in 1988. The civil war continued sporadically, and in the politicized atmosphere he was drawn to new friends and to political activism. He studied English by day and in the evenings began to attend meetings and lectures of the Syrian Social National Party (SSNP), also know as al-Hizb al-Suri al-Qawmi al-Ijtima'i. The party had been founded in the 1930s by a Greek Orthodox activist and political philosopher named Antun Sa'ada. He had lectured in the coffee houses surrounding AUB in the 1940s and attracted a large student following. The party appealed to many of the same secular and minority students as the Baath Party at the same time, but it emphasized a secular Greater Syria program rather than the mystical Pan-Arab program of the Baath. The two parties were rivals, and in 1949, after an attempted uprising, the new Syrian military government sent Antun Sa'ada to Lebanon to be executed, and banned the party in Syria. Sa'ada became a posthumous saint and near messiah to the party faithful. By the 1980s, party cells were scattered throughout Lebanon, more or less isolated from one another. Talal joined a close-knit group on campus and in West Beirut.

Talal was drawn to the spirit of vigorous intellectual debate and militant secularism that the party represented. He felt that the war in Lebanon, and many social problems in Syria, were based on the prevalence of sectarian identities, and he was repelled by the sectarian political parties. He rose rapidly in the student wing of the party because of his rhetorical skills and his ability to debate members of the Baath and Communist Parties on the AUB campus. Talal soon found, however, that there were limits to what could be discussed among party members. He pointed out that while the party founder, Antun Sa'ada, had been a brilliant editorialist and charismatic leader, his works of history and fiction were mediocre and his poetry was unsuccessful. Talal criticized Sa'ada's scholarship and compared it with the work of distinguished professional historians such as Philip K. Hitti and Kamal S. Salibi. Talal's criticism of the Leader, or al-Za'im, was considered treasonous by some of his comrades, but they tolerated his views because he was an effective speaker among the student parties. While Talal enjoyed the camaraderie of the party, he refused to abandon his other friends, continuing to maintain warm friendships among all the political groups on campus.

Shortly after Talal's arrival in Beirut, the Lebanese war entered its final, bloody phase. Since independence in 1943, the political system of Lebanon had been based on a sectarian division of power. The system had been designed under French colonial rule before independence. A Maronite Christian had always occupied the most powerful political office as president, a Sunni Muslim had always been prime minister, and a Shi'i Muslim had always been speaker of the parliament. Although Maronite Christians dominated politically, Muslims were more numerous in the general population. Members of the smaller sectarian groups, like the Druze and others, were also represented in parliament, but their members could not rise to the highest offices. Power was apportioned by sect and favored Christians. The political system failed to reflect the changing demographics of the country. In 1988 Amin Gemayal, the outgoing Maronite president, appointed the commander of the Maronite-dominated Lebanese Army, General Michel Aoun, as prime minister. The office of the prime minister had been the traditional preserve of the Sunni Muslims, and while Aoun resolved to establish his authority and expel the Syrian army from Lebanon, a parallel cabinet, led by former AUB economics professor Salim al-Hoss and supported by Syria, existed as well. As many noted at the time, Lebanon had two prime ministers, no president, and no effective government.

The Iraqi-supported forces of Michel Aoun in East Beirut declared war on the Syrian-supported government of Salim al-Hoss in West Beirut in early 1989. In March 1989 the American University of Beirut closed for the entire semester, the first time that had happened in more than a decade of war. The "Liberation War" of General Aoun led to the shelling of West Beirut, and hundreds of thousands of Beirutis, including university students and faculty, fled. Talal was forced to cut short his studies.

With no end to the conflict in sight, Talal waited in Damascus. His parents, meanwhile, discussed sending him to Canada to continue his education. He returned to Beirut four times during 1989. He visited the forlorn and abandoned campus and his damaged room during periods of ceasefire. In August 1989 he was trapped for days in Beirut because there were no taxis to Damascus. On 11 August, he spent a terrible sleepless night in the dormitory basement counting explosions while artillery shells passed between East and West Beirut. Talal lost count, but the newspapers reported that cross-town rivals had fired more than twenty thousand artillery shells that night.

The pre-war remnants of the Lebanese parliament signed the Ta'if agreement in September 1989. The agreement codified long-proposed changes to the Lebanese political system, to better reflect the demographic realities. It did not change the sectarian system. General Aoun rejected the agreement completely and refused to order his forces to stop fighting. The Ta'if agreement allowed for a limited Syrian army presence, but the Syrian government refrained from attacking Aoun's forces vigorously from fear of provoking intervention by Israel or the United States. Both Israel and the United States tacitly supported General Aoun and his regional sponsor, Saddam Hussein. Despite the optimism that greeted the Ta'if agreement and the support it received from most Lebanese, the militias kept fighting and the political situation continued to deteriorate.

AUB reopened in October, and Talal resumed his classes in November. Beirut was still in shock, and the future was uncertain for everyone. As he waited for friends and teachers to reappear on campus, Talal realized that some had been killed and that many others had left Beirut for good. Talal's parents wanted to direct their son's newly resumed studies. They expected him to take only scientific courses and to study agriculture, followed by medical school. Talal had other ideas, and he took advantage of the American college system to take history and Arabic literature classes and avoid declaring a major. He knew that if he declared history as a major, his parents would force him to withdraw from the university. This way, he managed to study what he wanted and still keep his family satisfied. Still, he felt anxious and torn between his own desires and the pressure of his family.

In August 1990, Iraq invaded Kuwait. General Aoun's forces remained in East Beirut, claiming that the Ta'if agreement and the Syrian presence in Lebanon were illegal. The removal of Iraqi support for General Aoun, Iraq's fall from U.S. favor, and the general climate of crisis and distraction over the crisis in Kuwait made it possible for the Syrian army to enter Lebanon in force. The Syrian army disarmed the militias and stopped the war. Thereafter, the Syrians remained in Lebanon and continued to dominate the Lebanese political scene, in violation of the Ta'if agreement. Opposition to the Syrian army's domination of Lebanon simmered under the surface. Beirut seemed to be full of Syrian soldiers.

One night, as Talal walked through the streets of West Beirut on the way to his dorm room, a Syrian soldier stopped him to ask him the time. Hearing his accent, the soldier realized that Talal was Syrian and invited himself and his comrade to accompany Talal to his room. Soldiers didn't usually come on campus, and particularly not in the dorms, and his unwelcome guests embarrassed Talal. Once he had entered the dorm, Kalashnikov-toting soldiers in tow, Talal realized that the situation was worse than he had imagined. The soldiers opened the door to his room, after which Talal's roommate, Elias Mufarrej, rushed in to tell Talal in a breathless whisper that he had heard that Talal had been arrested by Syrian security, or alternatively, that Talal was working for the Secret Police.

The two soldiers made themselves at home. One of them saw a big bottle of Dewar's White Label Scotch whisky hidden on the shelf. He asked Talal for a drink and then complained that Talal was too stingy with his whisky. The soldier took a big bowl, emptied the bottle into it, and began to trade determined slugs of whisky with his comrade. Talal realized a possible solution to his predicament. He passed a note to Elias. After an hour and a half, the soldiers were drunk and sprawled out on the floor. Talal and Elias carefully snatched their Kalashnikovs and nudged the soldiers, now laughing and singing, into the dormitory hall. They loudly insulted the soldiers in front of the frightened dorm residents. Then they took the guns and marched the soldiers to the Syrian Army checkpoint in a commandeered house just off the AUB campus near the university hospital. The drunken soldiers continued singing.

Two weeks later, Talal passed the checkpoint and saw the Sergeant standing guard. His head had been shaved completely smooth, and he now shouted, "Ya Talal!" Talal tried to ignore him, but he kept shouting. When Talal finally turned to face the soldier, he again shouted and waved, "Ya Talal . . . Ka'sak!" (Hey Talal . . . Cheers!). Apparently there were no hard feelings, though the Sergeant had obviously been punished. Talal's standing among the students in his dorm had risen, and no one accused him of cooperating with Syrian intelligence. Life at school seemed calm.

In September 1991, Talal's father died unexpectedly, and his carefree life at school came to an end. Talal was overwhelmed by the death of his father, and he now felt the crushing responsibility as the symbolic head of his family. He resolved to refocus his studies on the practical course his father had advocated. He began to take agriculture courses, but he was depressed and distracted and he frequently failed or withdrew without completing his classes. Without his father's income, money for his tuition became a serious burden. Since Syria had no private banks or a stock market, Talal's mother invested some of the family savings with merchants. Most of this money was lost when the merchants turned out to be swindlers. Talal, paralyzed by anxiety and uncertainty, withdrew from school. He stayed at home in Damascus for a year, submerged in reading history and politics and becoming ever more depressed. His father's estate was tied up in legal battles with other family members, and nothing could be sold to help support his mother and sisters, or to pay his tuition.

Talal finally was able to return to AUB, where his friend Ahmad 'Abdallah helped him to recover his focus. Ahmad had long been a hero to Talal;

they had been friends and sometime roommates since Talal had first entered AUB. Like Talal, Ahmad was a member of the militantly secular Syrian Social National Party, which he had joined in 1975 at the age of fourteen, after militia members executed his father in their village. In 1993, however, Ahmad was purged from the SSNP for publicly criticizing the infiltration of the party by Syrian military intelligence agents as well as the Syrian role in Lebanon. Post-war SSNP policy dictated blind obedience to Syria, and when Ahmad was expelled, Talal decided that friendship was far more important than political loyalty. As his father had resigned from the Baath thirty years before, Talal quietly resigned from the SSNP.

Talal and Ahmad became roommates in a small apartment off campus near the Corniche fronting on the Mediterranean. Talal admired Ahmad for his honesty and integrity. Ahmad's father had been murdered in front of him early in the war, and he had come to Beirut destitute and desperate. And yet he had rejected sectarianism or revenge and managed to support his extended family in his village and to pursue an education. Ahmad had started college at the age of twenty-eight and had earned a bachelor's and master's degree in clinical nursing. Through his example, and his encouragement, Talal was able to overcome his own depression and focus on his studies. He decided that his responsibilities and his duty to his father's memory and wishes had to prevail. In 1998, Talal earned a diploma in agricultural engineering and a bachelor's degree in agricultural sciences. It was time to return to Damascus and look for work.

The job situation in Syria was bad. Talal joined an army of unemployed graduates. Since there was a tremendous labor surplus, even poorly paid jobs ended up being filled based almost entirely on contacts and connections. Because his father was dead and he was estranged from paternal relatives, and because he had been away from Syria while at AUB, Talal had few connections. He was charming and well spoken, and got many interviews with influential people, but these came to nothing. His job search was punctuated by periods of unpaid exploitation when "potential employers" would promise him a job in return for translation work, or for work as an interpreter, or as a multilingual staffer of a trade show booth. In the meantime, he continued looking for a permanent job.

He also began to make new friends. Among them was a Chilean student of Arabic living in Damascus. Lily Marisol Delgado Cuzmar had traveled to Syria to continue her Arabic studies and to fulfill a dream to visit the land of her grandfather's birth. Lily and Talal fell in love, and while Lily learned Arabic, Talal learned Spanish. As he had learned other languages, he quickly became proficient in Spanish. After six months, Lily left the Catholic convent where she had been living and secretly moved into Talal's one-room apartment in a divided house in old Damascus. Soon, Gilberto and Clara Conde, Arabic students from Tijuana, Mexico, moved into the downstairs room. Talal found that he had a supportive and encouraging community of friends, and he redoubled his efforts to find some escape from unemployment. Meanwhile, his imagination was fueled by long evening discussions about international politics, history, and countries he hoped to visit.

In early summer 2000, Hafiz al-Asad, Syria's president for more than three decades, died unexpectedly. During that unsettled summer, Talal continued his job search outside of Syria. He returned to Lebanon, where he found that as a Syrian citizen he was ineligible to join the professional organization of engineers. He could not legally work in his second country. Over the course of more than two years, he had sought employment in the private sector, with state agencies and industries, and at embassies and international organizations. Once, he had come close to getting work with the U.N. World Food Program, helping Syrian bedouin survive the drought of 1999–2000, but that too came to nothing.

In Beirut, Talal ran into an old friend and schoolmate. His friend knew someone who could help in the job search, and eventually Talal was offered a job as a salesman of luxury construction materials in Saudi Arabia. He accepted the job and prepared to begin a sales career. By late summer 2000, Talal was back in Damascus frantically working to assemble the necessary papers to work in Saudi Arabia. He was required to produce documents from various Syrian ministries that would testify to his qualifications, his clean police record, the fact that he had been exempted from military service, and to provide proof of his good character.

The Syrian Foreign Ministry certified that Talal was a Sunni Muslim. The Syrian government extends this service to Syrian citizens of the non-Sunni Islamic sects, such as Druze, Ismailis, and Alawis. Syria is legally secular, so Talal's Syrian identity card indicated no religion. Saudi law, however, is based on a strict Sunni interpretation of Islam. Christian and Jewish guest workers are tolerated because Islamic law requires that they be considered protected monotheistic minorities, or "People of the Book." Members of the minority Islamic sects, by contrast, are considered heretics by the Saudi state. Many Syrian, Lebanese, Egyptian, and Palestinian Arabs are Christians, Druze, Shi'ia, Ismailis, or members of other minority religions. They manage to live and work in Saudi Arabia by concealing their true religious affiliations. Talal does not consider this much of an inconvenience, though he has never revealed his Druze religion to his Saudi friends.

In late summer 2000, Talal proposed marriage to Lily. Syrian commercial and criminal law is secular, but some aspects of the state's personal-status law correspond to the various religions in the country. Since Talal is Druze and Lily is Christian, it was difficult for them to marry, as it is difficult for people of different religions to marry in most Middle Eastern countries. Like thousands of Lebanese, Syrians, Israelis, and Egyptians before them, the couple made plans to marry in Cyprus, which has the most unrestricted marriage laws in the Middle East. Since Druze do not generally marry outside their faith, and since conversion is impossible, they decided not to share the news with Talal's mother. Lily's parents were thrilled and anxious to meet their new son-in-law, however. Talal was happy to have a family that loved and accepted him on the other side of the world, and he embraced Chilean culture with the same enthusiasm he had brought to his studies of Arabic, French, English, and Hebrew.

Talal moved to Saudi Arabia in December of 2000. Like all guest workers, he needed a Saudi *kafil*, or sponsor, to obtain his residency permit. The *kafil* approves applications for driver's licenses, renews work permits, approves changes of job or residence, and approves exit from the country. Even the opening of a bank account must be approved. Fortunately, Talal's *kafil* was the company he worked for. There are two sorts of *kafil*: institutional, or company *kafil*, and private, or Saudi, *kafil*. Sometimes workers whose *kafils* are individuals suffer mistreatment and extortion.

Talal was amazed by life in Saudi Arabia. When he arrived, he felt like Alice in Wonderland. Things were much different than in Syria or Lebanon. Women were barred from driving, and non-Muslim foreigners were barred from the holy cities. Some areas of the big cities were far more opulent than in Syria or Lebanon, and yet the economic gulf between rich and poor was wider. The social order in the Kingdom also appeared strange to him. Talal observed that Saudi Arabia was organized around two systems of social stratification—one system of wage and labor divisions, comprised of Saudi subjects and foreign workers, and one system of divisions among only Saudi subjects and based on family origin within the country. Talal found that as far as wages were concerned, he was near the top of a rough pyramid based not on qualifications or experience but on national origin. For a landscape architect with five years of experience, a Bangladeshi worker might earn as little as $320 per month. But Indian, Pakistani, or Filipino workers with similar qualifications generally earn more. Egyptians, Syrians, and Lebanese earn still more, up to around $1,800 monthly. Saudi subjects earn more again, and continental Europeans earn more than most Saudis of similar qualification but less than Anglos, who are generally at the top. A British or American landscape architect can be paid $8,000 a month for work roughly similar to that performed by others for far less. Talal was a highly educated and cultured member of one of the more-favored groups among Saudi guest workers, but he also felt great sympathy for the many guest workers who barely subsisted at the fringes of Saudi society, such as the Indian and Pakistani cleaners and janitors.

Talal observed a second hierarchy among Saudi subjects. The royal family and the members of the tribes that had early joined the Kingdom's modern founder, 'Abd al-'Aziz al-Sa'ud, are at the top of this hierarchy. Urban people from the dynasty's original heartland near Riyadh are in the second rank. The people of the Hijaz region of the Holy Cities of Mecca and Medina follow in status. Many of these people are descendants of Yemeni, Syrian, Indian, or Egyptian pilgrims and merchants who came to live in the homeland of the Prophet Muhammad. They dominate the Kingdom's commerce. Other Saudi groups follow in status. They include the various Shi'i minorities and followers of the Sufi orders.

Talal's job entailed selling high-end construction products and bath fixtures to wealthy people. While he was gregarious and charming, he had not been trained in such things and he often stumbled while describing the benefits of gold fixtures as opposed to chrome-plated ones. As an incisive observer of social life, he also felt strange selling fabulously expensive luxury goods to the most-favored among Saudi society. The ostentatious consumption of such things made him uncomfortable sometimes, particularly since he realized that some of the riches were based on the exploitation of foreign labor. His unfamiliarity with Saudi society and business practices often made it difficult for him to meet his sales targets. Still, he was grateful for the job and the opportunity.

Four months after he moved to the Saudi Kingdom, Talal found a new job as a project engineer for the largest landscaping company in the Gulf region. This was a big step up, and he began to feel more secure in his new home. Lily joined him after their marriage in Cyprus, and they moved to a larger apartment in Jeddah, a city on the Red Sea and the historical port for the Hijaz region's Holy Cities of Mecca and Medina. Talal also received a company car. While his career thrived, there was little for Lily to do and she spent most of her time at home waiting for Talal to return from long days at work.

Lily was frustrated by the limits on her life imposed in Saudi Arabia, and she grew unhappy with life there. Even at the convent in Damascus she had felt comparatively free and unrestrained. As a foreign woman in Saudi Arabia, she did not feel free, and she did not like spending her days and nights always at home. She wanted to find a job teaching Spanish, and while there was demand for teachers, the paperwork and the fact that Talal, a foreigner also, was Lily's legal *kafil,* or sponsor, made the job quest nearly impossible. Fortunately, Talal's salary was sufficient to allow Lily to return to Chile to visit her family. The lengthy visit rejuvenated her spirits and helped both her and Talal to appreciate one another better.

They both missed Damascus, however. Talal had had no desire to come to Saudi Arabia, but economic distress had forced his move. The financial insecurity he felt after his father's death had weighed heavily on him until his arrival in Jeddah. While his economic security is now assured, he does not feel socially secure in Saudi Arabia. He will always be an outsider in what he considers a tribal society. Still, he has never been mistreated in Saudi Arabia, and while he feels alienated by what he considers strange social practices, he is grateful for the opportunities he has found there. Law and order are more respected there than in Syria or Lebanon, and Talal believes the *kafil* law is entirely reasonable, since the vast petroleum resources of the Kingdom must be protected and preserved for the country's indigenous inhabitants.

Saudi society is undergoing tremendous changes, and the future of the Kingdom is unclear. The official Islamic character of Saudi life is becoming less strict. Saudi society had long been characterized by great religious conservatism and rigidity. Some of the conservatism was a response to the Cold War and the Third World colonial and postcolonial struggles of the 1950s and 1960s. In that period, the Saudi royal family forged an alliance with conservative religious authorities, who in turn lent the royal family powerful Islamic legitimacy. The combined efforts of the religious bureaucracy and the monarchy served to entrench royal and clerical power and undermine the political attraction of Communism and secular Arab nationalism. Tremendous oil wealth made it possible to provide generous financial incentives to all Saudi subjects, to compensate for the lack of political participation.

The Saudi state alliance between the government and the religious bureaucracy has long allowed the religious police, or *mutawwa'*, to patrol Saudi streets and enforce a rigid version of public morality. The religious police dress like traditional religious scholars and carry rough-hewn walking sticks. Since they meddle with others' business and are not armed, they are unpopular, and ordinary people sometimes retaliate against them. To impose order and uphold the prestige of the religious police, Saudi uniformed police officers often accompany them. The religious police typically try to herd men into the mosques at prayer times and force shop owners to close during prayers. They are sometimes known to strike women whose faced are uncovered faces in the marketplace with their sticks.

One day, a *mutawwa'* stopped Talal and Lily in their neighborhood. He examined their papers, seeing that Talal had the green residence card of a Muslim and that Lily had the red residence card of a non-Muslim. He asked why Lily had not yet converted to Islam. Talal answered noncommittally. The *mutawwa'* told Talal that his wife was a gift from Heaven and that Talal would reserve a place or himself in Heaven by converting Lily. Over the next weeks, the *mutawwa'* persisted, and Talal could not leave the apartment without being accosted by the man who continued to encourage him to convert Lily. After a few weeks, one day the *mutawwa'* saw Talal talking outside with a Lebanese friend; he approached and repeated his entreaty. Talal's Lebanese friend interrupted him, saying, "Well, sure, everybody should become a Muslim, but Talal has to convert himself to Islam before he can convert his wife!" The religious police are less respected in Saudi Arabia today than they once were.

The bargain between Saudi subjects, the monarchy, and the clerical establishment has become strained. In recent decades, the Saudi population has increased so rapidly that universal material prosperity can no longer be provided by the state. Radical clerics and their followers have used the official Islamic discourse to attack the monarchy for corruption and un-Islamic behavior. Ordinary people in Saudi Arabia fear for the future, and call the 2003 war in Iraq "The Third Nightmare." They speak of the "Khomeini Nightmare" of the 1980s, the "Saddam Nightmare" of the 1990s, and the "George Bush Nightmare" of the new century. The United States has criticized the Saudi ruling elite for its claimed ambivalence toward Islamist radicals. Unemployment and poverty among Saudi subjects has grown. Foreign workers like Talal supply most professional, skilled, and unskilled labor to the Saudi economy. Saudi youth are widely unemployed and underemployed, and employers prefer foreigners, who are believed to work harder for less money.

Most people believe there will be radical changes in the near future in Saudi Arabia. Modest changes have already taken place. The public religious discourse has become less radical, and the religious police have become a little less prevalent and much less powerful. The government has suppressed Islamist opposition groups more vigorously, and at the same time, and perhaps conversely, there have been a few hesitant steps toward greater democratization and transparency in government. Still, Talal does not want to build his career and future in the Kingdom. His life and work in Saudi Arabia is only a way station on his journey to something better with Lily. In any case, the changes in Saudi society may have come too late to prevent some kind of rupture or upheaval. Talal speaks from personal experience when he says that frustrated, unemployed people have nothing to lose.

In the 1960s, just before Talal was born, people in the Arab world dreamed of a rising tide of development and prosperity that would mobilize all of society for the greater good. Economic distress, war, and disappointment have led to a different kind of mobilization in the Arab world. While past generations dreamed of a single Arab nation undivided by borders, with freedom, prosperity, dignity, and justice for all its citizens, young people today dream of work and immigration visas so they can cross the still-rigid borders and find jobs and decent livelihoods.

Economic deprivation is widespread, and most people in the Arab world worry about the future. Still, those who loudly declare an end to Arab unity ignore the depth of feeling among ordinary people in all Arab countries. The oil-rich countries do not wish to share the ownership of their resources with their poor cousins, but sympathy for the Palestinians in their struggle with Israel, anger and confusion over the 2003 U.S. war on Iraq, and opposition to U.S. and Israeli policy in the Middle East unites people in the Arab world. People everywhere feel the injustice of the weak crushed by the strong in their region, and worry that they may be next. Every Saudi bank has a well-advertised charity fund for Palestinian and Iraqi windows and orphans. Many people contribute to these funds, and the oil-rich countries continue to provide jobs and opportunities to unemployed young people from poor Arab countries. Many young people still struggle against joblessness and frustration in their own countries.

In 2004, Talal counted himself among the fortunate rather than the frustrated and unemployed. He was grateful for his privileges and good luck, and he knew that many of his friends and contemporaries still faced an uphill climb. He and Lily had recently been accepted by the government of Canada for immigration and permanent residence. He resolved to save a year's salary before leaving, since the experience of unemployment and relative destitution had scarred him and made him cautious about his economic prospects. He was certain that he never again wanted to be without work and money. He had overcome much, and he looked forward to the future, hopeful his greatest struggles were behind him.

A NOTE ON SOURCES

As a Fulbright scholar in Syria, I met Talal Rizk in 1998. We became close friends and spent time together nearly every day for more than two years. The story is based on countless conversations between 1998 and 2004, and detailed written and telephone interviews in December 2003. His generous friendship and wisdom have enriched my life immeasurably.

SUGGESTIONS FOR FURTHER READING

For postcolonial Syrian history, see two books by Patrick Seale: *The Struggle for Syria: A Study in Post-war Arab Politics, 1945–1958* (New Haven, Conn.: Yale University Press, 1986); and *Asad of Syria: The Struggle for the Middle East,* with the assistance of Maureen McConville (Berkeley: University of California Press, 1995).

The late Hanna Batatu brought his customary thoroughness to Syrian politics in *Syria's Peasantry, the Descendents of its Lesser Rural Notables, and their Politics* (Princeton, N.J.: Princeton University Press, 1999). For a careful discussion of Syria's government and economy, see Volker Perthes, *The Political Economy of Syria under Asad* (London: I. B. Tauris, 1995).

For the Lebanese war from a political perspective, see Elizabeth Picard, *Lebanon, A Shattered Country: Myths and Realities of the Wars in Lebanon,* trans. Franklin Philip (New York: Holmes & Meier, 1996). For a more personal view, see Jean Said Makdisi, *Beirut Fragments: A War Memoir,* (New York: Persea Books, 1990).

An excellent discussion of Saudi history is Madawi al-Rasheed, *A History of Saudi Arabia* (Cambridge: Cambridge University Press, 2002).

GLOSSARY

alim (pl. *ulama*)	learned man, especially in law and other religious studies
amir (pl. *ashraf;* fem. *sharifa*)	title held by a politico-military commander or his companions
ayan	notables
ayatullah	highest rank in Shii hierarchy of scholars qualified to pronounce independent judgment in religious matters
baraka	blessing; holiness; spiritual power inherent in a saint
bey	Turkish title
bibi	daughter of an Iranian tribal leader, or *khan*
chador	a large cloth worn as a combination head covering, veil, and shawl usually by Muslim women, especially in Iran
dhikr	Sufi ritual
fakir	Sufi
fatwa	formal legal opinion issued by a *mufti*
fiqh	jurisprudence; the discipline of elucidating the Sharia
habous	see *waqf*
hadith	reported words and deeds of the Prophet Muhammad based on the authority of a chain of reliable transmitters
hajj	annual pilgrimage to Mecca

ilbeg	leader of an Iranian tribal confederacy
ilkhan	leader of an Iranian tribal confederacy
ilm	religious knowledge
imam	leader of prayer; in Shiite usage, the leader of the Muslim community
intifada	Palestinian uprising against Israeli occupation in West Bank and Gaza
jihad	war in accord with the Sharia against unbelievers; in Sufi usage, the moral struggle of the individual
kadkhoda	Iranian village headman
karamat	miracles
khalifa	successor; local official; a Sufi master
khan	caravansary; building given to diverse commercial and industrial purposes; Iranian tribal governor under *ilkhan* or *ilbeg*
kulughli	descendent of Ottoman military officer and local woman (*maghrib*); a family caste
madrasa	college of law and other religious studies
Mahdi	person who will appear at the end of days to establish Islam over all unrighteous forces
makhzan	the Moroccan government
mellah	Jewish quarter or ghetto (Morocco)
millet	in Ottoman Empire, non-Muslim communities benefiting from special administrative status
muezzin	individual who performs the call to prayer
mufti	Muslim jurisconsult
mujahid (pl. *mujahidin*)	warrior for the faith (in *jihad*)
mujtahid	scholar with authority to interpret Islamic law, especially in Shiite Islam
mullah	local Shiite teacher
muqaddam	head of a local Sufi *tariqa*
murabit (pl. *murabitin*)	Sufi teacher; head of a saintly lineage
pasha	Ottoman governmental official
qabaday	urban gang leader
qabila	tribe
qadi	judge according to Sharia law
qaid	local governor (Maghrib)
saddiqim	locally venerated Jewish saints (Morocco)

sayyid	descendent of Husayn, son of Fatima, the daughter of the Prophet
shabab	young men; retainers of a *shaykh* (Lebanon)
shahid	martyr
Sharia	Islamic law; more generally, Muslim belief and practice
sharif (pl. *ashraf*)	one who traces his descent to the Prophet
shaykh	elder; head of a Sufi order (Maghrib); landlord (Lebanon); head of an artisan guild
Shia	Muslims who hold to the right of Ali and his descendents to lead the Islamic community
sinf (pl. *asnaf*)	artisan guild
Sufi	follower of a mystic path, or *tariqa*
sultan	title of a ruler, head of state
Sunni	most Muslims, who accept the authority of the first generations of Muslims and the validity of the historic succession of caliphs, unlike the Shia and Kharijis
tariqa (pl. *turnq*)	Sufi way or brotherhood
ulama	scholars learned in the Sharia; see *alim*
waqf	pious foundation or endowment of properties to provide income for religious purposes
zawiya	Sufi *tariqa;* Sufi center for teaching and other activities

CONTRIBUTORS

Mehdi Abedi is Research Associate and Lecturer in Anthropology at Rice University.

Lila Abu-Lughod is Professor of Anthropology and Women's and Gender Studies at Columbia University.

Eqbal Ahmad (deceased 1999) was Professor Emeritus of International Relations and Middle Eastern Studies at Hampshire College.

Lois Beck is Professor of Anthropology at Washington University in St. Louis.

Edmund Burke, III is Professor of History at the University of California at Santa Cruz.

Julia Clancy-Smith is Associate Professor of History at the University of Arizona.

Fanny Colonna is Emerita Director of Research at the French National Center of Scientific Research (CNRS), and is attached to the Maison Méditerranéenne des Sciences de l'Homme at Aix en Provence (France).

Michael M. J. Fischer is Professor of Anthropology and Science and Technology Studies at the Massachusetts Institute of Technology.

Baya Gacemi is a journalist living in Algiers.

Ashraf Ghani is Afghanistan's Minister of Finance.

Joost Hiltermann is Middle East Project Director for the International Crisis Group.

Homa Hoodfar is Professor of anthropology at Concordia University (Montreal).

Nels Johnson is Senior Lecturer in Anthropology and Politics at Richmond College (London).

Akram F. Khater is Associate Professor of History and Director of International Programs at North Carolina State University

Antoine F. Khater is Professor of Physics at the Université de Maine, Le Mans (France).

Philip S. Khoury is Dean of Humanities and Social Science and Professor of History at the Massachusetts Institute of Technology.

David McMurray is Associate Professor of Anthropology at Oregon State University.

Tamara Neuman, an anthropologist who resides in Portland, Oregon, is currently writing an ethnography of settlement.

Julie Oehler is a writer who lives in Salinas, California.

Michael Provence is Assistant Professor of History at the University of California at San Diego.

Celia Rothenberg is Assistant Professor of Religious Studies and Health Studies at McMaster University.

Stuart Schaar is Professor of History at Brooklyn College, City University of New York.

Abdullah Schleifer is Director of Television Studies at the American University in Cairo.

Ehud R. Toledano is Professor of History at Tel Aviv University.

Sherry Vatter is Lecturer at California State University at Long Beach.

David N. Yaghoubian is Assistant Professor of History at California State University, San Bernardino.

Sami Zubaida is Reader in Politics and Sociology at Birkbeck College, the University of London.

Text: 10/12 Baskerville
Display: Baskerville